PERSONALITY

THEORY AND RESEARCH

Ninth Edition

Lawrence A. Pervin
Rutgers University

Daniel Cervone
University of Illinois at Chicago

Oliver P. John
University of California, Berkeley

John Wiley & Sons, Inc.

EXECUTIVE EDITOR	Ryan Flahive
ASSISTANT EDITOR	Lili DeGrasse
EDITORIAL ASSISTANT	Aliyah Vinikoor
MARKETING MANAGER	Kate Stewart
PRODUCTION MANAGER	Pamela Kennedy
PRODUCTION EDITOR	Sarah Wolfman-Robichaud
COVER DESIGN	Maddy Lesure
ILLLUSTRATION EDITOR	Sandra Rigby
PHOTO EDITOR	Jennifer MacMillan
PHOTO RESEARCHER	Lisa Passmore
COVER IMAGE	Chuck Close, *Maggie*, 1996, Oil on canvas, 30 x 24" (76.2 x 61 cm), Photograph by Ellen Page Wilson, reproduced courtesy of the artist and Pace Wildenstein, New York. © Chuck Close

This book was set in New Aster by LCI Design and printed and bound by
R.R.Donnelley/Willard. The cover was printed by Lehigh Press.

This book is printed on acid free paper.

To order books or for customer service please call 1-800-CALL WILEY (225-5945).

ISBN: 0-471-14994-2

Printed in the United States of America

10   9   8   7   6   5   4   3   2   1

PREFACE

This text introduces students to the two interlocking sides of personality psychology. One is the field's research side. Research on personality and individual differences is a vibrant, multinational enterprise. We have significantly updated this book since its previous edition to present the latest research methods and findings. These span an amazingly wide range. Molecular genetic techniques and brain imaging methods shed light on the biological bases of personality. Studies of personality and culture reveal connections between individual development and sociocultural settings.

The other side involves theory. In any science, a field's greatest intellectual achievements are its comprehensive theories; we remember Newton, Darwin, and Einstein not because of any particular experiment or scientific observation of theirs, but because they provided theoretical frameworks of breadth and power. This book presents students with the major theoretical frameworks that have guided the contemporary science of personality.

Throughout the text, coverage of theory and research is intertwined. We emphasize how classic and contemporary theories can be evaluated in light of current research evidence. However, in addition to chapters that combine theory and research, two of our chapters are specifically devoted to research advances in key areas of study. Chapter 9 reviews research on biological foundations of personality. Students learn about advances in the study of temperament, genetics, neuroscience, and evolutionary psychology. Chapter 14, entirely new since the last edition, covers research on personality in context. We review work on interpersonal relationships, cultural and socioeconomic factors, personality development across the life span, and the application of personality theory to questions of social change.

We, the three authors of this text, come to the field from different theoretical orientations: psychodynamic, social-cognitive, and trait-theoretic. This diversity, we feel, is an advantage. It has enabled us to achieve our goal of presenting each of the field's various theoretical perspectives in its very best light. Although we analyze each theory critically, our overarching aim is to present students with the fundamental insights and scientific strengths of each approach.

Many students who use this book may have little formal background in scientific psychology. Most, of course, will not go on to a career in the field. We have taken account of these facts in this revision. Much of the book has been rewritten to be more easily accessible to the student. This has been done, however, without sacrificing any of the intellectual strength that has long been the "backbone" of this text.

This ninth edition of *Personality: Theory and Research*, then, aims to:

1. *Present the major theoretical perspectives on personality.* We cover the field's major theoretical perspectives in depth. This, we feel, is vastly better than alternative strategies. Some textbooks cover a very large number of theories, including minor perspectives that have little relevance to

the contemporary scientific field. Such coverage may provide students with only superficial knowledge of important theories that should be understood deeply. Other textbooks organize themselves around research topics, and present little coverage of the field's major theoretical perspectives. For the student being introduced to the field, this approach is costly; the student fails to appreciate the ways in which theories have shaped the research enterprise throughout the field's history. Understanding personality psychology's major theories also is an important part of a broad liberal arts education; a number of the theories we discuss have influenced other fields of study and society at large.

We focus somewhat more on theoretical *perspectives* than on particular grand theories and theorists. We do present the student with much information about major theorists (e.g., Freud, Rogers) and their contributions. However, the contemporary science of personality is guided primarily by broad perspectives to which multiple theorists and researchers contribute. Our coverage reflects this fact.

2. *Integrate theory and research.* Our aim here is to show the student how theory and research inform one another. Theoretical developments spur research, and research contributes to the development, modification, and evaluation of personality theories.

3. *Integrate case material with theory.* By necessity, theory and research deal with abstractions and generalizations, rather than with specific and unique individuals. To bridge the gap between the general and the specific, we present case study material that illustrates how each theory assesses and interprets the individual. We follow one case throughout the book to show how the various theories relate to the same person. Thus, the student can ask: Are the pictures of a person gained through the lens of each theory completely different from each other, or do they represent complementary perspectives? Our inclusion of case material also enables the student who is interested in clinical psychology to see connections between personality psychology and clinical practice.

4. *Treat each theoretical approach objectively and even-handedly.* We present each theory on its own terms and only then evaluate it in relation to standard criteria. An analysis of strengths and limits of each theory thus follows the presentation of the given theory and its research basis. Our goal in these analyses is not to persuade the student of the merits of a particular approach, but to broaden students' understanding of the theories and to enhance and encourage their own critical thinking skills.

5. *Present the complex scientific field in an accessible manner.* There actually are two goals here. They differ, but they do not necessarily conflict. One is to teach students about the field of personality psychology as it really exists—including some of its nuances and complexities. Even the introductory student deserves to have more than a "watered-down" approach that, for example, merely presents one or two key ideas from each theory. The other goal is to make the material easily accessible. We relate scientific theories and research findings to students' own interests and concerns. We avoid jargon as much as possible. We have aimed for a straightforward writing style. One can provide an accessible text without underestimating students' intellectual potential.

We hope that this edition of *Personality: Theory and Research* will give students an appreciation of the complexity of personality, of the capacity of case studies and empirical research to shed light on this complexity, and of the scientific and practical value of systematic theorizing about the individual. We also hope that students may discover a particular theory of personality that makes personal sense to them and is useful in their own lives.

From DC: One of us (DC) is new to this project, having joined the author team for the 9th edition. Although I'm new to the text, it is not new to me. Eighteen years ago I filed the final copy of my dissertation at Stanford University, hopped in a car, drove to Chicago, and within a matter of days faced the daunting task of teaching my first class: a "Theories of Personality" course at the University of Illinois at Chicago. Fortunately I had the wisdom to choose as my text *Personality: Theory and Research* by Pervin, then in its 4th edition. The book proved to be an invaluable education resource - and not only for my students, but for me! Thus, I am particularly honored to have the opportunity to contribute to this volume, which has long been an integral part of my own learning and teaching experiences.

ACKNOWLEDGEMENTS

Our efforts to continue to improve the volume from one edition to the next have benefited greatly from the input of many individuals. Students in our classes have been a continuous source of stimulation and useful feedback. Melissa Camilleri of UIC made many contributions to the revision. For their helpful reviews we thank the following professors: Barbara A. Boccacio, Tunxis Community College; Eugenia Cox-Fuenzalida, University of Oklahoma; James Epps, University of South Florida; William G. Graziano, Purdue University; Thomas Holtgraves, Ball State University; Cathy Lawrenz, Johnson County Community College; Wade C. Rowatt, Baylor University; and Mia Weinberger-Biran, Miami University.

We are grateful also to the professionals at Wiley who have contributed their considerable skills to the production of the text, particularly Anne Smith, Lili DeGrasse, and Sarah Wolfman-Robichaud.

LAWRENCE A. PERVIN
Rutgers, the State University

DANIEL CERVONE
University of Illinois at Chicago

OLIVER P. JOHN
University of California, Berkeley

NOTE ON THE COVER IMAGE

The cover image is by the artist Chuck Close. The work consists of a grid of diamond-shaped images. Each diamond contains an individual, unique mini-painting. No individual diamond-shaped mini-painting looks anything like a person or even a part of a person; viewed "at close range," the diamonds merely "appear to be a cacophony of colors and shapes creating the visual equivalent of noise" (Taylor, 2001, p. 134). Yet, when one steps back and views the image holistically, things change. A coherent person emerges from the complex arrangement of the individual elements.

Close's work visually symbolizes the challenge faced by a personality psychologist. People do not possess "a personality" in the way they possess "a stomach" or "a nervous system" or even "an ability to do calculus." The term "personality," in other words, does not refer to a single, isolated biological or psychological part of a person. We don't just have a "lump of personality" sitting around somewhere in our brains. Instead, people possess a large number of psychological elements: emotional tendencies, mental abilities, memories, goals, beliefs about the world, beliefs about themselves, etc. Many branches of psychology view these individual qualities "at close range," one at a time. In so doing, they may appreciate the distinct parts but fail to see the whole person. In contrast, the personality psychologist must—like the viewer of Chuck Close's work—understand how the coherent individual person emerges from the complex arrangement of elements. The personality psychologist must not only appreciate the parts, but must step back to see the whole.

CONTENTS

CHAPTER 1

PERSONALITY THEORY: FROM EVERYDAY OBSERVATIONS TO SYSTEMATIC THEORIES, 1

WHY STUDY PERSONALITY?, 5

DEFINING PERSONALITY, 6

PERSONALITY THEORY AS AN ANSWER TO THE QUESTIONS OF WHAT, HOW, AND WHY, 7

Structure, 8
    Units of Analysis, 8
    Hierarchy, 10
Process, 11
Growth and Development, 13
    Genetic Determinants, 14
    Environmental Determinants, 15
    Psychopathology and Behavior Change, 19

IMPORTANT ISSUES IN PERSONALITY THEORY, 20

Philosophical View of the Person, 20
Internal and External Determinants of Behavior, 21
Consistency Across Situations and Over Time, 21
The Unity of Experience and Action and the Concept of Self, 23
Varying States of Awareness and the Concept of the Unconscious, 24
The Influence of the Past, Present, and Future on Behavior, 25
Can We Have a Science of Personality? What Kind of a Science Can It Be?, 26
Important Issues: Summary, 26

EVALUATION OF THEORIES, 27

The Function of a Personality Theory, 27
Comprehensiveness, Parsimony, and Research Relevance, 28
    Comprehensiveness, 28
Parsimony, 29
Research Relevance, 29
Evaluation of Theories: Summary, 30

THE PERSONALITY THEORIES: AN INTRODUCTION, 30

The Challenge of Constructing a Personality Theory, 30
The Personality Theories: A Preliminary Sketch, 31
    Differences among the Theories, 33

MAJOR CONCEPTS, 34

REVIEW, 34

CHAPTER 2

THE SCIENTIFIC STUDY OF PEOPLE, 35

THE DATA OF PERSONALITY PSYCHOLOGY, 37

LOTS of Data, 38

How Do Data from Different Sources Relate to One Another?, 39
Fixed versus Flexible Measures, 41
Personality Theory and Assessment, 42

GOALS OF RESEARCH: RELIABILITY, VALIDITY, ETHICAL BEHAVIOR, 42
Reliability, 43
Validity, 43
The Ethics of Research and Public Policy, 44

THREE GENERAL APPROACHES TO RESEARCH, 46
Case Studies and Clinical Research, 46
   Case Studies: An Example, 47
   Case Studies: Limitations, 48
Personality Questionnaires and Correlational Research, 50
   Correlational Research: An Example, 51
   Correlational Research: Limitations, 52
Laboratory Studies and Experimental Research, 53
   Experimental Research: An Example, 56
Evaluating Alternative Research Approaches, 58
   Case Studies and Clinical Research: Strengths and Limitations, 58
   Correlational Research: Strengths and Limitations, 59
   Laboratory, Experimental Research: Strengths and Limitations, 61
   Summary of Strengths and Limitations, 63
   The Use of Verbal Reports, 63

PERSONALITY THEORY AND PERSONALITY RESEARCH, 64

PERSONALITY ASSESSMENT AND THE CASE OF JIM, 65
Autobiographical Sketch of Jim, 66

MAJOR CONCEPTS, 67

REVIEW, 67

CHAPTER 3

A PSYCHODYNAMIC THEORY: FREUD'S PSYCHOANALYTIC THEORY OF PERSONALITY, 69

WHY STUDY FREUD?, 70

SIGMUND FREUD (1856–1939): A VIEW OF THE THEORIST, 71

FREUD'S VIEW OF THE PERSON AND SOCIETY, 74

FREUD'S VIEW OF THE SCIENCE OF PERSONALITY, 75

PSYCHOANALYSIS: A THEORY OF PERSONALITY, 76
Structure, 76
   The Concept of the Unconscious and Levels of Consciousness, 77
Process, 87
   Life and Death Instincts, 87
   The Dynamics of Functioning, 88
Anxiety, Mechanisms of Defense, and Contemporary Research on Defensive Processes, 89
Growth and Development, 99
   The Development of Thinking Processes, 99
   The Development of the Instincts, 102

MAJOR CONCEPTS, 110

REVIEW, 111

CHAPTER 4

A PSYCHODYNAMIC THEORY: APPLICATIONS AND EVALUATION OF FREUD'S THEORY, 113

CLINICAL APPLICATIONS, 114
Assessment: Projective Tests, 115
    The Rorschach Inkblot Test, 116
    The Thematic Apperception Test (TAT), 118
Illustrative Research Use and Evaluation, 119
    Projective Tests—Do They Work?, 120

PSYCHOPATHOLOGY, 122
Personality Types, 123
    The Oral Personality, 123
    The Anal Personality, 124
    The Phallic Character, 124
Conflict and Defense, 125

BEHAVIOR CHANGE, 126
Insights into the Unconscious: Free Association and Dream
      Interpretation, 126
The Therapeutic Process: Transference, 128

A CASE EXAMPLE: LITTLE HANS, 130
Description of the Problem, 130
Events Leading Up to Development of the Phobia, 131
Interpretation of the Symptom, 131
The Solution to the Oedipal Conflict, 133
Overall Evaluation, 133

THE CASE OF JIM, 134
Rorschach and TAT: Psychoanalytic Theory, 134
Comments on the Data, 137

RELATED POINTS OF VIEW, 137
Two Early Challenges to Freud, 138
    Alfred Adler (1870–1937), 138
    Carl G. Jung (1875–1961), 140
The Cultural and Interpersonal Emphasis, 143
    Karen Horney (1885–1952), 143
    Harry Stack Sullivan (1892–1949), 144

RECENT DEVELOPMENTS IN THE PSYCHODYNAMIC TRADITION, 145
Object Relations Theory, 146
    Narcissism and the Narcissistic Personality, 146
Attachment Theory and Adult Personal Relationships, 148
    Attachment Styles in Adulthood, 150
    Attachment Types or Dimensions?, 153

CRITICAL EVALUATION, 155
Major Contributions, 155
Limitations of the Theory, 155
    The Scientific Status of Psychoanalytic Theory, 156
    The Psychoanalytic View of the Person, 157
Summary Evaluation, 158

MAJOR CONCEPTS, 159

REVIEW, 159

CHAPTER 5

A PHENOMENOLOGICAL THEORY: CARL ROGERS'S PERSON-CENTERED THEORY OF PERSONALITY, 161

CARL R. ROGERS (1902–1987): A VIEW OF THE THEORIST, 163

ROGERS'S VIEW OF THE PERSON, 165

ROGERS'S VIEW OF SCIENCE, THEORY, AND RESEARCH, 166

THE PERSONALITY THEORY OF CARL ROGERS, 167

Structure, 167
  The Self, 167
  Measures of the Self-Concept, 168
Process, 173
  Self-Actualization, 173
  Self-Consistency and Congruence, 174
  The Need for Positive Regard, 179
Growth and Development, 180
  Self-Actualization and Healthy Psychological Development, 180
  Research on Parent-Child Relationships, 181
  Social Relations, Self-Actualization, and Well-Being
    Later in Life, 183
Conclusion, 185

MAJOR CONCEPTS, 185

REVIEW, 186

CHAPTER 6

A PHENOMENOLOGICAL THEORY: APPLICATIONS AND EVALUATION OF ROGERS'S THEORY, 187

CLINICAL APPLICATIONS, 188

Psychopathology, 189
  Self-Experience Discrepancy, 189
  Discrepancies among Parts of the Self, 191
Change, 192
  Therapeutic Conditions Necessary for Change, 192
  Outcomes of Client-Centered Therapy, 193

A CASE EXAMPLE: MRS. OAK, 195

Description of the Client and Problem, 195
Description of the Therapy, 195
Description of the Outcome, 197

THE CASE OF JIM, 197

Semantic Differential: Phenomenological Theory, 197
Comments on the Data, 198

RECENT DEVELOPMENTS IN THEORY AND RESEARCH, 199

Rogers's Shift in Emphasis: From Individuals to Groups
    and Society, 199
Fluctuations in Self-Esteem and Contingencies of Worth, 200
Internally Motivated Goals and Authenticity, 202

Cross-Cultural Research on the Self, 205
    Is Positive Self-Regard a Human Universal?, 206
    Regional Variations in Well-Being, 208
RELATED POINTS OF VIEW, 209
  The Human Potential Movement, 209
    Kurt Goldstein (1878–1965), 210
    Abraham H. Maslow (1908–1970), 210
  Existentialism, 212
CRITICAL EVALUATION, 214
  Phenomenology, 214
  The Concept of Self, 215
  Conflict, Anxiety, and Defense, 216
  Summary Evaluation, 217
MAJOR CONCEPTS, 219
REVIEW, 219

CHAPTER 7

TRAIT APPROACHES TO PERSONALITY: ALLPORT, EYSENCK, AND CATTELL, 221

THE TRAIT CONCEPT, 223
  What Is a Trait?, 223
  Basic Views Shared by Trait Theorists, 223
THE TRAIT THEORY OF GORDON W. ALLPORT (1897–1967), 225
  Traits and Distinctions among Kinds of Traits, 226
  Functional Autonomy, 227
  Idiographic Research, 228
  Comment on Allport, 228
THE THREE-FACTOR THEORY OF HANS J. EYSENCK (1916–1997), 229
  Trait Measurement: Factor Analysis, 230
    Factor Analysis and Identifying the Structure of Individual
      Differences, 230
  Basic Dimensions of Personality, 232
    Questionnaire Measures, 235
    Research Findings, 236
    Biological Bases of Personality Traits in Eysenckian Theory, 237
  Psychopathology and Behavior Change, 238
  Comment on Eysenck, 239
THE FACTOR-ANALYTIC TRAIT APPROACH OF RAYMOND B. CATTELL (1905–1998), 240
  Cattell's View of Personality Science, 241
    Kinds of Traits, 242
    Sources of Data: L-Data, Q-Data, OT-Data, 243
  Stability and Variability in Behavior, 246
  Comment on Cattell, 246
TRAIT THEORY: ALLPORT, EYSENCK, AND CATTELL, 248
MAJOR CONCEPTS, 249
REVIEW, 249

CHAPTER 8

TRAIT THEORY: THE FIVE-FACTOR MODEL; APPLICATIONS AND EVALUATION OF TRAIT APPROACHES TO PERSONALITY, 251

THE FIVE-FACTOR MODEL OF PERSONALITY: RESEARCH EVIDENCE, 254
Analysis of Trait Terms in Natural Language and in Questionnaires, 254
  The Fundamental Lexical Hypothesis, 257
Cross-Cultural Research: Are the Big Five Universal Dimensions?, 257
The Big Five in Personality Questionnaires, 260
  The NEO-PI-R and Its Hierarchical Structure: Facets, 260
Integration of Eysenck's and Cattell's Factors within the Big Five, 262

PROPOSED THEORETICAL MODEL FOR THE BIG FIVE, 263

GROWTH AND DEVELOPMENT, 267
Age Differences Throughout Adulthood, 267
Initial Findings from Childhood and Adolescence, 270
Stability and Change in Personality, 271

APPLICATIONS OF THE MODEL, 271
Vocational Interests, 271
Health and Longevity, 272
Clinical Psychology: Diagnosis and Treatment, 273

THE CASE OF JIM, 274
The 16 P.F. Questionnaire: Trait, Factor-Analytic Theory, 274
  Comments on the Data, 275
The Stability of Personality: Jim 5 and 20 Years Later, 276
Five-Factor Model: Self-ratings and Ratings by Wife on the NEO-PI, 279

EVALUATION: THE PERSON-SITUATION CONTROVERSY, 281
Longitudinal Stability, 282
Cross-Situational Stability, 282
Conclusion, 286

OVERALL EVALUATION OF TRAIT APPROACHES, 287
Strengths of the Approaches, 288
  Active Research Effort, 288
  Interesting Hypotheses, 288
  Potential Ties to Biology, 288
Limitations of the Approaches, 289
  Problems with the Method: Factor Analysis, 289
  Problems with the Trait Concept, 290
  What Is Left Out or Neglected?, 291

MAJOR CONCEPTS, 292

REVIEW, 292

CHAPTER 9

BIOLOGICAL FOUNDATIONS OF PERSONALITY, 293

TEMPERAMENT: VIEWS OF MIND-BODY RELATIONSHIPS FROM THE PAST TO THE PRESENT, 295
Constitution and Temperament: Early Views, 296
Constitution and Temperament: Longitudinal Studies, 298
Constitution and Temperament: Kagan's Research on Inhibited and
  Uninhibited Children, 300

EVOLUTIONARY THEORY AND PERSONALITY:
THE MODERN SYNTHESIS, PART I, 304
> Social Exchange and the Detection of Cheating, 306
> Sex Differences: Evolutionary Origins?, 308
>> Male-Female Mate Preferences, 308
>> Causes of Jealousy, 310
>> Evolutionary Origins of Sex Differences: How Strong Are the data?, 310
> Evolutionary Theory and the Big Five Personality Dimensions, 313
> Evolutionary Explanations: Comment, 315

GENES AND PERSONALITY:
THE MODERN SYNTHESIS, PART II, 317
> Behavioral Genetics, 318
>> Selective Breeding Studies, 318
>> Twin Studies, 318
>> Adoption Studies, 320
>> Heritability Coefficient, 320
>> Heritability of Personality: Findings, 322
>> Some Important Caveats, 322
>> Molecular Genetic Paradigms, 324
> Environments and Gene-Environment Interactions, 325
>> Shared and Nonshared Environment, 326
>> Understanding Nonshared Environment Effects, 328
>> Three Kinds of Nature-Nurture Interactions, 329
>> Summary and Caveats, 330

NEUROSCIENCE AND PERSONALITY, 331
> Localizing Brain Functions: Amygdala, 331
> Left and Right Hemispheric Dominance, 332
> Neurotransmitter Functioning: Dopamine and Serotonin, 333
> Neurobiology and the Three Major Temperament Dimensions, 333
>> Three Dimensions of Temperament: PE, NE, and DvC, 333
>> Emotional and Lifestyle Correlates of PE, NE, and DvC, 334
>> Biological Correlates of PE, NE, and DvC, 335
>> Biology and Personality Traits: Some Limitations, 336
> Plasticity: Biological Processes Are Both Cause and Effect, 336
> Summary, 337

NEUROSCIENTIFIC INVESTIGATIONS OF "HIGHER-LEVEL"
PSYCHOLOGICAL FUNCTIONS, 338
> Brain and Self, 338
> Brain and Moral Judgment, 339

BIOLOGY AND SOCIOPOLITICAL ISSUES, 340

MAJOR CONCEPTS, 341

REVIEW, 342

CHAPTER 10

BEHAVIORISM AND THE LEARNING APPROACHES TO PERSONALITY, 343

THE BEHAVIORISTIC VIEW OF THE SCIENCE OF
PERSONALITY, 345
> Environmental Determinism and Its Implications for the Concept of
>> Personality, 345
> Experimental Rigor, Observable Variables, and the Study of Simple Systems, 348

WATSON, PAVLOV, AND CLASSICAL CONDITIONING, 349
Watson's Behaviorism, 349
Pavlov's Theory of Classical Conditioning, 350
  Principles of Classical Conditioning, 351
Psychopathology and Change, 353
  Conditioned Emotional Reactions, 354
  The "Unconditioning" of Fear of a Rabbit, 355
  Additional Applications of Classical Conditioning, 356
  Systematic Desensitization, 357
A Reinterpretation of the Case of Little Hans, 359
Further Developments, 360

SKINNER'S THEORY OF OPERANT CONDITIONING, 362
A View of the Theorist, 362
Skinner's Theory of Personality, 364
  Structure, 365
  Process: Operant Conditioning, 365
  Growth and Development, 367
  Psychopathology, 368
  Behavioral Assessment, 369
  Behavior Change, 372
  Free Will?, 372

A COMPARISON OF LEARNING APPROACHES WITH EARLIER VIEWS, 374

CRITICAL EVALUATION, 375
Strengths of Learning Approaches, 375
Limitations of Learning Approaches, 376

MAJOR CONCEPTS, 378

REVIEW, 379

CHAPTER 11

A COGNITIVE THEORY OF PERSONALITY: GEORGE A. KELLY'S PERSONAL CONSTRUCT THEORY OF PERSONALITY, 381

GEORGE A. KELLY (1905–1966): A VIEW OF THE THEORIST, 384

KELLY'S VIEW OF THE SCIENCE OF PERSONALITY, 385

KELLY'S VIEW OF THE PERSON, 387

THE PERSONALITY THEORY OF GEORGE A. KELLY, 388
Structure, 388
  Constructs and Their Interpersonal Consequences, 389
  Types of Constructs and the Construct System, 389
  The Role Construct Repertory (Rep) Test, 392
  Unique Information Revealed by Personal Construct Testing, 393
  Cognitive Complexity/Simplicity, 395
Process, 398
  Anticipating Events, 398
  Anxiety, Fear, and Threat, 399

GROWTH AND DEVELOPMENT, 401

CLINICAL APPLICATIONS, 403
>   Psychopathology, 403
>   Change and Fixed-Role Therapy, 404

THE CASE OF JIM, 406
> Rep Test: Personal Construct Theory, 406
> Comments on the Data, 407

RELATED POINTS OF VIEW AND RECENT DEVELOPMENTS, 408
>   Contemporary Analyses of Person-Situation/Beliefs, 409

**CRITICAL EVALUATION:
STRENGTHS AND LIMITATIONS OF
PERSONAL CONSTRUCT THEORY, 411**

SUMMARY, 4112

MAJOR CONCEPTS, 413

REVIEW, 414

CHAPTER 12

SOCIAL-COGNITIVE THEORY: BANDURA AND MISCHEL, 415

**RELATING SOCIAL-COGNITIVE THEORY TO THE
PREVIOUS THEORIES, 416**

A VIEW OF THE THEORISTS, 418
>   Albert Bandura (1925–), 418
>   Walter Mischel (1930–), 419
>   Impact of the Theorists, 421

VIEW OF THE PERSON, 422

VIEW OF THE SCIENCE OF PERSONALITY, 423

**SOCIAL-COGNITIVE THEORY OF PERSONALITY:
STRUCTURE, 424**
>   Competencies and Skills, 424
>   Beliefs and Expectancies, 425
>   The Self and Self-Efficacy Beliefs, 426
>   Self-Efficacy and Performance, 428
>   Goals, 431
>   Evaluative Standards, 433
>   The Nature of Social-Cognitive Personality Structures, 434

SOCIAL-COGNITIVE THEORY OF PERSONALITY: PROCESS, 434
>   Reciprocal Determinism, 435
>   Personality as a Cognitive-Affective Processing System (CAPS), 436
>   Observational Learning, 439
>   Acquisition versus Performance, 441
>   Vicarious Conditioning, 444
>   Self-Regulation and Motivation, 445
>   Self-Efficacy, Goals, and Self-Evaluative Reaction, 446
>   Self-Control and Delay of Gratification, 449
>   Learning Delay of Gratification Skills, 449
>   Mischel's Delay of Gratification Paradigm, 450

MAJOR CONCEPTS, 455

REVIEW, 455

CHAPTER 13

SOCIAL-COGNITIVE THEORY: EXTENSIONS, APPLICATIONS, AND EVALUATION, 457

COGNITIVE COMPONENTS OF PERSONALITY: BELIEFS, GOALS, AND EVALUATIVE STANDARDS, 459
Beliefs about the Self and Self-Schemas, 459
Self-Schemas and Reaction-Time Methods, 461
Self-Based Motives and Motivated Information Processing, 463
Learning versus Performance Goals, 466
Causes of Learning versus Performance Goals: Implicit Theories, 468
Standards of Evaluation, 470
Self-Standards and Self-Discrepancies, 471
A "General Principles" Approach to Personality, 473

CAUSAL EXPLANATIONS AND ATTRIBUTIONS, 473
Consequences of Causal Attributions, 474

CLINICAL APPLICATIONS, 476
Stress and Coping, 477
Pathology and Change, 479
Ellis's Rational-Emotive Therapy, 479
Beck's Cognitive Therapy for Depression, 480
The Cognitive Triad of Depression, 480
Research on Faulty Cognitions,, 480
Cognitive Therapy, 481
Psychopathology: Modeling, Self-Conceptions, and Perceived Self-Efficacy, 482
Self-Efficacy, Anxiety, and Depression, 483
Self-Efficacy and Health, 484
Therapeutic Change: Modeling and Guided Mastery, 486

THE CASE OF JIM, 490
Social-Cognitive Theory: Goals, Reinforcers, and Self-Efficacy Beliefs, 490
Comment, 492
Additional Assessments, 492

COMPARATIVE ANALYSIS: RELATING SOCIAL-COGNITIVE THEORY TO THE PREVIOUS APPROACHES, 494

CRITICAL EVALUATION, 497
Strengths, 497
Systematic Research on Important Phenomena and Evidence, 497
A Theory Open to Change, 498
View of the Person and Social Concern, 498
Limitations, 499
Not Yet a Systematic, Unified Theory, 499
Relative Neglect of Important Areas, 499

MAJOR CONCEPTS, 501

REVIEW, 502

CHAPTER 14

PERSONALITY IN CONTEXT: INTERPERSONAL RELATIONS, CULTURE, AND DEVELOPMENT ACROSS THE COURSE OF LIFE, 503

INTERPERSONAL RELATIONSHIPS, 506

Rejection Sensitivity, 506
    "Hot" and "Cool" Focus, 509
  Transference in Interpersonal Relationships, 510

STRATEGIES FOR MEETING ACADEMIC AND SOCIAL CHALLENGES: OPTIMISTIC STRATEGIES AND DEFENSIVE PESSIMISM, 512

KNOWLEDGE, APPRAISAL, AND CROSS-SITUATIONAL COHERENCE, 515

PERSONALITY DEVELOPMENT IN SOCIOECONOMIC CONTEXT, 518
  Causes and Effects of Personality Attributes, 519
  Personality, Gender, and Historical Context, 521

PERSONALITY FUNCTIONING ACROSS THE LIFE SPAN, 522
  Psychological Resilience in the Later Years, 522
  Emotional Life in Older Adulthood: Socioemotional Selectivity, 523

PERSONS IN CULTURES, 525
  Two Strategies for Thinking about Personality and Culture, 525
    Strategy #1: Personality...and Culture?, 525
    Strategy #2: Culture and Personality, 527
  Personality and Self as Socially Constructed within Culture, 528
    Independent and Interdependent Views of Self, 529

PERSONALITY PROCESSES AND SOCIAL CHANGE, 532
  Media Modeling of Prosocial Behavior, 533
    Literacy, 534
    HIV/AIDS Prevention, 535

SUMMARY, 537

MAJOR CONCEPTS, 537

REVIEW, 538

CHAPTER 15

AN OVERVIEW OF PERSONALITY THEORY, ASSESSMENT, AND RESEARCH, 539

COMMON GROUND AND REMAINING CHALLENGES, 541
  Philosophical View of the Person, 541
  Internal and External Causes of Behavior, 544
  The Unity of Behavior and the Concept of the Self, 545
  Varying States of Awareness and the Concept of the
    Unconscious, 546
  Relationships among Cognition, Affect, and Overt Behavior, 547
  Influences of the Past, Present, and Future on Behavior, 548

PERSONALITY THEORY AS AN ANSWER TO THE QUESTIONS OF WHAT, HOW, AND WHY, 548
  Personality Structure, 548
  Process, 550
  Growth and Development, 551
  Psychopathology, 552
  Change, 553
  Biological Foundations and Levels of Explanation, 553
  Relationships among Theory, Assessment, and Research, 555

THE CASE OF JIM, 555
    Comparison of the Assessment Data on Different Theories, 555
    Stability and Change Over Time, 556
    Jim's Reflections on the Data, 556
OVERVIEW AND A FINAL SUMMING UP, 557
REVIEW, 558

GLOSSARY, 559

REFERENCES, 567

PHOTO CREDITS, 599

NAME INDEX, 601

SUBJECT INDEX, 609

PERSONALITY THEORY: FROM EVERYDAY OBSERVATIONS TO SYSTEMATIC THEORIES

WHY STUDY PERSONALITY?

DEFINING PERSONALITY

PERSONALITY THEORY AS AN ANSWER TO THE QUESTIONS OF WHAT, HOW, AND WHY
  Structure
    Units of Analysis
    Hierarchy
  Process
  Growth and Development
    Genetic Determinants
    Environmental Determinants
      Culture
      Social Class
      Family
      Peers
  Psychopathology and Behavior Change

IMPORTANT ISSUES IN PERSONALITY THEORY
  Philosophical View of the Person
  Internal and External Determinants of Behavior
  Consistency Across Situations and Over Time
  The Unity of Experience and Action and the Concept of Self

Varying States of Awareness and the
  Concept of the Unconscious
The Influence of the Past, Present, and
  Future on Behavior
Can We Have a Science of Personality?
  What Kind of a Science Can It Be?
Important Issues: Summary

EVALUATION OF THEORIES
  The Functions of a Personality Theory
  Comprehensiveness, Parsimony, and Research Relevance
    Comprehensiveness
    Parsimony
    Research Relevance
  Evaluation of Theories: Summary

THE PERSONALITY THEORIES: AN INTRODUCTION
  The Challenge of Constructing a Personality Theory
  The Personality Theories: A Preliminary Sketch
    Differences Among the Theories

MAJOR CONCEPTS

REVIEW

My friend is not very self-confident. She's my friend but she always tries to show that she's better by trying to take my boyfriends away from me. She's a fake friend, obviously. She could be fun to hang out with, until there is a guy on the way. She would try to do everything to show that she's better, because, really, she's got low self-esteem. She always has to have a guy by her side, to feel good. Otherwise she feels worthless.

This person I know is extremely insecure about himself. This insecurity has embodied itself in bizarre behavior patterns, which ultimately describe a sad, paranoid soul who has undergone many hardships, not necessarily digesting the origin of such mishaps. Instead of recognizing himself as the instigator he has chosen to blame others for his actions.

I can be selfish, but I believe it is because I try to be perfect. Perfect in the sense I want to be an "A" student, a good mother, a loving wife, an excellent employee, a nourishing friend. My significant other thinks I try too hard to be "Mother Theresa" at times—not that that is a bad thing. But I can drive myself insane at times. I have led a hard childhood and adulthood life, therefore I believe I am trying to make up for all the bad times. I want to be productive, good — make a difference in my world.

I'm a real jackass. I'm intelligent enough to do well in school and study genetics, but have no idea when to shut up. I often am very offensive and use quite abrasive language, although I'm shy most of the time and talk to few people. I'm sarcastic, cruel, and pompous at times. Yet I've been told that I'm kind and sweet; this may be true, but only to those I deem worthy of speaking to with some frequency. I'm very fond of arguing and pretty much argue for fun.

My friend is an outgoing, fun-to-be-with person. Although when he feels that something is not right, I mean according to his standards, he is a perfectionist in an obsessive manner. If he feels that someone is not capable of completing a job he takes over and does it himself. Behind closed doors his temper is unbelievable, loud, and never happy. In a social environment he is Mr. Happy-Go-Lucky.

This person is shy at times. They tend to open up to some people. You never know when they're happy or sad. They never show their real feelings and when they do it's so hard for them. They did have a trauma experience that closed them up—where they seem to be afraid to let their real self show. They are funny and do have a lot of fun and are fun to be around but at times it's hard to know if they're really having a good time. The person is loved by a lot of people, and is an extremely giving person, but they don't like "seriousness."

These sketches were not written by professional psychologists or by advanced students in the field. They were written by people just like you: students enrolled in a course on the psychology of personality, who were writing on the very first day of class. When we, the authors of this textbook, teach this course, we commonly begin by asking class members to describe their own personality, as well as that of a friend. Students' descriptions are insightful and richly detailed—so much so that one is forced to ask: Is the class filled with "personality theorists"?

In a sense, the answer to this question is "yes." We are all personality theorists. We all spend countless hours asking questions about ourselves ("Why am I depressed?" "Why do I become so anxious when I have to speak in public?") and other people ("Why are my parents so weird?" "If I introduce Maria to Mike, will they hit it off?"). In answering these question, we develop ideas—rich, complex, sophisticated ideas—about why people act the way they do. We develop our own theories about personality.

The fact that we think so much about people raises an important point for you to consider now, at the outset of your course in personality psychology. The point is the following: You already know a lot about the subject matter of this course. You probably know more about the subject matter of this class, at its very beginning, than you do about any other course you could possibly take in college. By comparison, imagine what would happen if a professor in a different course asked students to do what we ask: to write a description of the course's main subject matter on the first day of class. Consider a math, history, or chemistry course: "Please describe integral calculus." "Outline the causes of the Bolshevik Revolution." "Describe your favorite chemical bond." Such requests would be absurd. While these courses are designed to *introduce* you to the subject matter, this course is different. Personality "needs no introduction." You already know, and can describe in detail, a great many "personalities." You have ideas about what makes people tick and how people differ from one another. You use these ideas to understand events, to predict future events, and to help your friends handle the stresses, bumps, and bruises of life. You already possess, and use, your own theory of personality.

"But"—you may be asking yourself—"if I already know so much about personality, why should I take this class? What can I learn about personality from professional personality psychologists? What are the personality theorists who are discussed in this book accomplishing that I'm not?" This chapter addresses these questions. Specifically, it introduces the field of personality psychology by considering three questions:

QUESTIONS TO BE ADDRESSED IN THIS CHAPTER

1. How do the scientific theories of personality psychology differ from the ideas about persons developed by ordinary people in their daily life?

2. Are there basic areas of human functioning that we would expect a theory of personality to cover? Put differently, which questions concerning human functioning puzzle us and for which questions do we want a theory of personality to provide answers?

3. Since there exists more than one theory of personality, are there broad issues on which the theories differ (e.g., issues such as the fundamental nature of humans, the importance of genes versus experience, the importance of the unconscious)?

The phrasing of these questions provides a preview to their answers. On the one hand, there are similarities between our everyday thinking about people and the activities of the scientist who studies them for a living. Both the layperson and the scientist want to know why people do what they do, how people differ from one another, and how one can predict people's reactions to important life events. Phrased more formally, both the layperson and the scientist want to develop a model of human functioning, to use that model to describe individual differences, and to use the models of human functioning and individual differences to predict people's behavior.

On the other hand, there is a big difference between your intuitive theories about personality and the activities of the personality psychologist. The psychologist is charged with developing a *scientific* theory. This, in essence, means three things. The first involves scientific observation. Unlike you in your daily life, the psychologist cannot be content with learning about people merely by observing a small set of friends and acquaintances. Instead, the personality psychologist must develop formal, objective ways of learning about the psychological makeup of a diversity of people. These scientific observations may sometimes reveal surprising facts about human nature that violate your intuitions—and those of the psychologist! The other differences involve theory. The second difference, then, is that the psychologist's theory must be formulated in a very systematic manner. The assumptions of the theory must be articulated, its terminology must be defined clearly, and the relations among the different parts of the theory must be spelled out. Third, the psychologist's theory must be testable. If you tell a friend that "my parents are weird," your friend is not likely to say "Prove it!" But the scientific community says "Prove it!" any time a scientist says anything. The personality psychologist, then, must develop theoretical ideas that can be evaluated by objective scientific evidence. In personality psychology, this can be extremely difficult. This is because the field's subject matter includes features of mental life—goals, dreams, wishes, impulses, conflicts, emotions, unconscious mental defenses—that are enormously complex and difficult to study scientifically.

The fundamental challenge for the personality psychologist, then, is not only to say something interesting and insightful about people. It is to develop a theoretical framework for learning about people that is scientifically credible and testable. This is what distinguishes the ideas of the personality psychologist from those of the poet, the playwright, the pop psychologist—or the student writing personality sketches on the first day of class. All these people may provide insight into the human condition. But the personality psychologist is uniquely charged with the task of developing a comprehensive, scientifically testable theory of human nature and individual differences. Because this task is so difficult, much of our coverage is devoted to questions about how scientists develop theories of personality and how you can evaluate the theories they have developed. Specifically, this chapter focuses on what a personality theory is: what topics a theory of personality should include and what functions it should serve. At the end of the chapter, we preview the personality theories that we will discuss in detail in later chapters. The material in this chapter, as well as Chapter 2, provides intellectual tools that you can use to evaluate the personality theories you will learn about throughout your course.

WHY STUDY PERSONALITY?

Why should you take a course in personality? Why are some people so taken by the field that they decide to become personality psychologists? A basic attraction of the field is that it addresses the questions "Why are people the way they are? Why am I the way I am?" We are all fascinated by such questions, and personality psychology promises to answer them. Admittedly, this text and the scientific field it reviews may not definitively answer all of your questions. Yet much scientific progress has been made in understanding persons and the differences among them. This book will introduce you to some of the answers that contemporary scientific research can provide, while also introducing you to the best and most influential theoretical frameworks that have been developed for studying people.

Students taking an introductory course in psychology—the typical "Psych 101"—often are dismayed. In that course, the field of psychology does not seem to be about whole, intact people. Instead one learns about "parts of people" (the visual system, the autonomic nervous system, long-term memory, etc.) and some of the things people do (learning, problem solving, decision making, etc.). "But where in psychology", one reasonably might ask, "does one learn about the whole, intact person"? The answer is here, in the psychology of personality. Personality theorists address the total person, and try to understand how all the different aspects of an individual's functioning are intricately related to each other. For example, personality research is not the study of perception, but it does address how individuals differ in their perceptions and how these differences relate to those individuals' total functioning. The study of personality, then, focuses not only on psychological processes but on the relations among these processes. Understanding how these processes interact to form an integrated whole often involves more than understanding each of them separately. People function as organized wholes, and it is in the light of such organization that we must understand them (Magnusson, 1999). A key reason for studying personality psychology, then, is that it is the subfield of psychology that most directly addresses that most complex and interesting of topics: the whole, integrated, coherent, unique individual.

There is yet another reason for learning about the material in this course. The personality theories we will discuss have been influential not only within the confines of scientific psychology. They have influenced society at large. The ideas of the personality theorists have become part of the intellectual tradition of the past century. As such, these ideas *already* have influenced your own thinking, prior to your even taking this course. You already may say that someone has a big "ego," may call a friend an "introvert," or may believe that a seemingly innocuous slip of the tongue actually reveals something about the underlying motives of the speaker. If so, you already are using some of the language and ideas of the personality theorists. This course, then, provides insight into some of the foundations of your own ways of thinking about people—ways of thinking that you have acquired by living in a culture that, to at least a small degree, has been influenced by the work of the personality theorists.

To summarize, the scientific study of personality directly addresses the question of why we are the way we are. Like yourself, the personality theorist grapples with the potentially bewildering complexity of people and the differences among them. Unlike you, the personality theorist tries to create a systematic framework that can be tested scientifically. The scientific challenge is to sort through all the complexity and to identify meaningful relationships among psychological processes that can form the basis of a theory of personality that is scientifically sound and socially useful. The challenge and importance of this task attracts us—and, we hope, you too—to the study of personality.

| DEFINING PERSONALITY | The field of personality addresses three issues that sometimes are difficult to reconcile: (1) Human Universals, (2) Individual Differences, and (3) Individual Uniqueness. In studying universals, one asks: What is generally true of people? What are universal features of human nature and basic operating principles of personality? Regarding the second issue, individual differences, the questions are: How do people differ from one another? Are there basic categories or dimensions of individual differences? Finally, regarding uniqueness, the primary questions are: What makes people unique? How can one possibly explain the uniqueness of the individual person in a lawful scientific manner? Personality psychologists address dozens of more specific questions—Why do some achieve and others not? Why do some perceive things in one way and others in a different way? Why do some suffer from considerable stress and others not?—but all of these specific issues are addressed in terms of overarching questions about universal properties of personality, individual differences, and the uniqueness of the individual. |

Given this three-part focus, how are we to define "personality"? Many words have multiple meanings, and "personality" is certainly no exception. Different people use the word in different ways. In fact, there are so many different meanings that one of the first textbooks in the history of the field (Allport, 1937) devoted an entire chapter merely to the question of how the word "personality" can be defined!

Philosophers teach us that if one wants to know what a word means, one should see how the word is used (Wittgenstein, 1953). Different people use the word "personality" in different ways. The general public often uses the term to represent a value judgment: If you like someone, it is because he or she has a "good" personality or "lots of personality." A boring person has "no personality." Personality scientists, however, use the word differently. The scientist is not trying to provide subjective value judgments about people. He or she is trying to advance objective scientific inquiry into persons. A scientific definition of personality tells us what areas are to be studied and suggests how we might best study them.

For the present, let us use the following working definition of **personality**: *Personality refers to those characteristics of the person that account for consistent patterns of feeling, thinking, and behaving.* This is a very broad definition that allows us to focus on many different aspects of the person. At the same time, it suggests that we attend to consistent patterns of behavior and to qualities inside the person that account for these regularities, as opposed, for example, to looking exclusively at qualities in the environment that account for such regularities. The regularities of interest to us include the thoughts, feelings, and overt (observable) behaviors of people. Of particular interest to us is how these thoughts, feelings, and overt behaviors relate to one another, or cohere, to form the unique, distinctive individual.

Although one definition of personality has been suggested here, others are possible. Alternative definitions should not be construed as right or wrong; rather, they may be more or less useful in directing us to important areas of understanding. Thus, a definition of personality is useful to the extent that it helps advance the field as a science.

To summarize, the scientific exploration of personality involves systematic efforts to discover and explain regularities in the thoughts, feelings, and overt behaviors of people as they lead their daily lives. Personality scientists try to develop theories that enable one to understand these regularities. One hopes that these theories also can be used to benefit human welfare. It is to the nature of such theories of personality that we now turn.

PERSONALITY THEORY AS AN ANSWER TO THE QUESTIONS OF WHAT, HOW, AND WHY

Now that we have provided a definition of personality, we can consider some new questions. They concern the goals of theorizing. When developing a theory of personality, what goals is the theorist trying to achieve? What questions is the personality theorist trying to answer? What do we seek to explain with a theory of personality?

If we study individuals intensively, we want to know what they are like, how they became that way, and why they behave as they do. Thus, we want a theory to answer the questions of what, how, and why.

The "what" refers to the characteristics of the person and how these characteristics are organized in relation to one another. Is the person anxious, persistent, and high in need for achievement? If so, are they anxious and persistent because they are high in need for achievement? Or are they persistent and high in need for achievement because they are anxious?

The "how" refers to the determinants of a person's personality. How did genetic influences contribute to the individual's personality? How did environmental forces and social learning experiences contribute to the person's development? How did biology and environment interact with each other? How do people, through their own choices and efforts, contribute to their own personality development?

The "why" refers to the reasons for the individual's behavior. Answers refer to the motivational aspects of the individual—why he or she moves at all, and why in a specific direction. If an individual seeks to make a lot of money, why was this particular path chosen? If a child does well in school, is it to please parents, to use talents, to bolster self-esteem, or to compete with peers? Is a mother overprotective because she happens to be affectionate, because she seeks to give her children what she missed as a child, or because she seeks to avoid any expression of the resentment and hostility she feels toward the child? Is a person depressed as a result of humiliation, because of the loss of a loved one, or because of a feeling of guilt? A theory should help us understand to what extent depression is characteristic of a person, how this personality characteristic developed, why depression is experienced in specific circumstances, and why the person behaves in a certain manner when depressed. If two people tend to be depressed, why does one go out and buy things whereas the other withdraws into a shell?

In answering the questions of what, how, and why, there are four areas that a personality theory should cover. These are (1) Structure—the basic units or building blocks of personality; (2) Process—the dynamic aspects of personality, including motives; (3) Growth and Development—how we develop into the unique person each of us is; and (4) Psychopathology and Behavior Change—how people change and why they sometimes resist change or are unable to change. Consideration of each of these four areas is necessary to obtain comprehensive answers to questions about the what, how, and why of personality.

STRUCTURE

The concept of personality **structure** refers to stable or enduring aspects of personality. People possess psychological qualities that endure from day to day and from year to year. The enduring qualities that define the individual and distinguish individuals from one another are what the psychologist refers to as personality structures. In this sense, they are comparable to parts of the body, or to concepts such as atoms and molecules in physics. They represent the building blocks of personality theory.

Units of Analysis

Theories can be compared in terms of the structural concepts they use to address the what, how, and why of personality. As you will see throughout this text, different types of structural concepts have been developed by different personality theorists to conceptualize the enduring qualities of personality. Another way of saying this is that different theories of personality feature different kinds of basic variables, or different **units of analysis**. Different units of analysis may each be "correct," in their own way. Yet each may provide different types of information about an object. For example, you may now be sitting in a chair. The chair could be described as weighing X number of pounds, as costing Y number of dollars, or as being moderately "well made." Each of these units of analysis—pounds, dollars, degree of "well made"—tells us something about the chair. The things they tell us may be systematically related; poorly made chairs may weigh and cost less. Yet the units of analysis are conceptually distinct. Similarly, different theories of personality use conceptually distinct units of analysis to conceptualize the structure of personality.

One unit of analysis that has often been used to describe personality structure is that of a personality **trait**. A trait construct refers to the consistency of an individual's responses to a variety of situations. A person who consistently acts in a way that we call "conscientious" might be said to have the trait of "conscientiousness." Used in this way, trait constructs approximate the kind of concept the layperson uses to describe people. One way to think about traits is to consider how you would describe someone you have met recently. You might describe them with adjectives such as "outgoing," "honest," "disagreeable," or "open-minded." In using any of these adjectives, you implicitly would be saying that the individual is, relatively consistently, more "outgoing," "honest," "disagreeable," or "open-minded" than the average person. You would be using these trait terms in a manner that is very similar to that used by many personality trait theorists. Trait variables are almost always thought of as continuous dimensions; people have more or less of a given trait, with most people being in the middle and some people falling toward either extreme.

The concept of **type** refers to the clustering of many different traits. Compared to the trait concept, that of type implies a greater degree of regularity and generality to behavior. Although people can have many traits to varying degrees, they are generally described, by psychologists using type constructs, as belonging to a specific type. For example, individuals have been described as being introverts or extroverts, and in terms of whether they move toward, away from, or against others (Horney, 1945). More recently, some researchers have explored combinations of personality dimensions and suggested that there are three types of persons: people who respond in a resilient manner to psychological stress, people who respond in a manner that is socially inhibited or emotionally overcontrolled, and people who respond in an uninhibited or undercontrolled manner (Asendorpf, Caspi, & Hofstee, 2002). Psychologists interested in the development of personality in childhood have suggested that child-parent relations can be understood as consisting of three or four distinct types (Bakermans-Kranenburg & Van Ijzendoorn, 1993). The key notion associated with a type construct that makes it different than a trait construct is that alternative types are seen as qualitatively distinct categories. In other words, people of one versus another type do not simply have more or less of a given characteristic, but have categorically different characteristics. This is most easily explained with an analogy outside of psychology. Height clearly is not a type variable. Even though we call some people "tall" and others "short," we recognize these words do not identify distinct categories of people. Instead, height is a continuous dimension. In contrast, biological sex is categorical. Unlike "tall" and "short," "man" and "woman" identify qualitatively distinct categories of persons.

It is possible to use concepts other than trait or type to describe personality structure and the organization among structures of personality. Personality can be viewed as a **system**, that is, as a collection of highly interconnected parts that work together to produce the phenomenon we call "personality functioning." Some personality theorists posit a relatively simple system in which a small number of basic components have few connections to one another. Other theorists view personality as a highly complex system in which large numbers of psychological components are intricately linked to one another (Mischel & Shoda, 1998).

Theorists who view personality as a system recognize that people have distinctive characteristics that are well described by personality trait and type constructs. However, they tend not to use trait or type concepts as their basic units of analysis for explaining a person's behavior. In these approaches, a term such as "conscientiousness" does not correspond to a structure that a person has; instead, it functions merely as description of what a person does. An analogy may be helpful to understand this reasoning. You may know that the weather in the city of San Francisco is very "pleasant." But you would not say that "pleasantness" is a structural feature of San Francisco in the way that, for example, hills are a structural feature. San Francisco does not "have" hills in the same way that it "has" pleasantness of weather. If we were in the science of meteorology, we would not explain the weather in San Francisco by saying that the city "has pleasantness" that caused the pleasant weather. The term pleasantness is a *description* of qualities that are *explained* in terms of a

The four basic personality types

complex system of meteorological forces. Similarly, many personality psychologists would not explain a person's conscientiousness by saying that the person "has conscientiousness" but by exploring a system of emotional and thought processes that produce the behavior that we describe as conscientious. The units of analysis in the scientific explanation would be the emotional and thought processes and the interconnections among them.

Hierarchy

In addition to the issue of units of analysis, there is another consideration in the study of personality structure. It involves the notion of **hierarchy**. Some theories of personality view the structures of personality as being organized hierarchically. Some structural units are seen as higher in order, and therefore as controlling the function of other units. In general, two things are related hierarchically if one of them is an example of the other or serves the purpose of the other. The relation between "trees" and "plants" is hierarchical in that trees are an example of plants. "Jogging" and "getting in shape" are related hierarchically in that jogging serves the purpose of getting in shape (whereas getting in shape does not "serve the purpose of" jogging).

Interestingly, the notion of hierarchy can be applied to different types of units of analysis in the study of personality. For example, if one explains personality in terms of people's goals, then a hierarchical model would specify broad high-level goals (e.g., be successful, be a good person) that are associated with more specific, lower-level goals (e.g., get a promotion at work, be kind to strangers; Carver & Scheier, 1998). There is a hierarchy in that the lower-level goals are simply a way of accomplishing the higher-level aims (e.g., people may help a strager in order to accomplish the goal of being a good person). If one adopts personality trait units, then high-level traits (e.g., extraversion, conscientiousness) would organize narrower, lower-level tendencies (e.g., sociability, punctuality; John, Hampson, & Goldberg, 1991). There is a hierarchy here in that the lower-level traits are simply a way of exhibiting the higher-level characteristics (e.g., being punctual is a way of being conscientious). In contrast, some theorists do not explicitly posit a hierarchy of personality structures. Instead, they see different systems of personality as influencing each other in a mutual, back-and-forth manner that is not necessarily hierarchical (e.g., Bandura, 1999).

Personality theories, then, differ in their fundamental building blocks, that is, in the basic units of analysis that they use to describe and explain the enduring psychological attributes that comprise the structure of an individual's personality.

PROCESS

Just as theories can be compared in their structures, they can be compared in the dynamic motivational concepts they use to account for behavior. These concepts refer to the **process** aspects of human behavior. Three major categories of motivational concepts have been employed by personality psychologists: pleasure or hedonic motives, growth or self-actualization motives, and cognitive motives (Pervin, 2003). Pleasure or hedonic motivational concepts emphasize the pursuit of pleasure and the avoidance of pain. There are two major variants of such theories of motivation: tension reduction models and incentive models. One major personality theorist referred to these as "push" or "pitchfork theories" versus "pull" or "carrot theories" (Kelly, 1958). According to tension reduction "pitchfork" models of motivation, physiological needs create tensions that the individual seeks to reduce by satisfying those needs. For example, hunger or thirst creates tension that can be relieved by eating or drinking. The term *drive* typically has been used to refer to internal states of tension that activate and direct people toward tension reduction. In contrast with such tension reduction models, in "pull" or "carrot" models the emphasis is on endpoints, goals, or incentives that the person seeks to achieve. For example, the person may seek to achieve money, fame, social acceptance, or power. Although here it is the goal that is stressed rather than an internal state of tension, it should be clear that, nevertheless, the pursuit of pleasure is being emphasized, in this case the pleasure associated with achievement of the goal. It is for this reason that incentive theories of motivation as well as tension reduction theories are considered to be hedonic or pleasure-oriented theories of motivation.

In contrast with such pleasure-oriented theories, other motivational theories emphasize the efforts of the organism to achieve growth and self-fulfillment. According to this view, individuals seek to mature psychologically and realize their potential. The development of the self is paramount, even at the cost of increased tension in simple biological systems.

Motivation: *Personality theories emphasize different kinds of motivation (e.g., tension reduction, self-actualization, power, etc.).*

Example: Behaviorists

Finally, in cognitive theories of motivation, the emphasis is on the person's efforts to understand and predict events in the world. Rather than seeking pleasure or self-fulfillment, according to such theories the person has a need for consistency or a need to know. For example, the person may seek to maintain a consistent picture of the self and to have others behave in a predictable way. In this case, consistency and predictability are emphasized even at the price of pain or discomfort. Thus, it is suggested that people at times may prefer an unpleasant event to a pleasant one if the former makes the world seem more stable and predictable (Swann, 1992, 1997).

Personality psychologists have devoted their attention to different types of motivational processes at different points in the history of the field (Little, 1999; McAdams, 1999). In the first half of the 20th century, investigators primarily explored tension-reduction and incentive processes. In the middle of the 20th century, researchers began to note that organisms often engage in exploratory activities in which they learn about their environment, even if they are not explicitly rewarded for doing so. Such observations led the psychologist R. W. White (1959) to conceptualize a process in humans called *competence motivation*, in which people are motivated to deal competently or effectively with the environment. Indeed, as individuals mature, more of their behavior appears to be involved with developing skills for the sake of mastery or for dealing effectively with the environment, and less of their behavior appears to be exclusively in the service of tension reduction. Later in the century, the field of psychology increasingly explored thinking processes, or cognition, and this trend naturally directed the attention of personality psychologists to cognitive motives for consistency and predictability, as well as mental representations of goals that motivate behavior toward anticipated end-points.

Must one choose among the various theories of motivation: tension reduction, self-fulfillment, cognitive/goal? It may be that each of these perspectives captures an aspect of human motivation. People are biologically and psychologically complex. They may possess multiple motivational systems that come into play under different conditions. Sometimes people seek pleasure, sometimes personal growth, and sometimes cognitive consistency and predictability. Different motivational theories, then, may capture different aspects of human motivation. Contemporary psychologists recognize this, and often study the ways in which different types of motivational processes—some involving emotional impulses, others involving rational thought—combine to influence psychological outcomes (e.g., Lowenstein et al., 2001). Nonetheless, as you will see, different personality theories have tended to emphasize one model or another to account for motivational processes. As a result, the different theories of personality discussed in this book provide distinct portraits of human nature.

GROWTH AND DEVELOPMENT

One of the most profound challenges facing personality psychologists is to account for personality development, that is, the psychological development of individuals into mature adults who differ from one another psychologically. A primary scientific challenge is to understand the main causes of individual differences. The classic division of possible causes separates "nature" from "nurture." On the one hand, we may be who we are because of our biological nature, that is, because of biological features that we inherited. On the other hand, our personality may reflect our nurturing, that is, our experiences when we were being raised as children. In a joking manner, we might say: If you don't like your personality, who should you blame: Your parents, because of the way they nurtured you? Or your parents, because of the genes they passed on to you that shaped your biological nature?

Psychological research has tended to highlight either nature or nurture as a cause of personality at different points in the field's history. In the middle parts of the 20th century, theorists focused heavily on environmental causes of behavior and devoted relatively little attention to genetic influences. Starting in the 1970s (Loehlin & Nichols, 1976), investigators began systematic studies of similarity in the personalities of twins. As we will discuss in detail in a later chapter, these studies provided unambiguous evidence that inherited factors contribute to personality. In recent years, however, there has been a third trend. Researchers have begun to identify interactions between genetic and environmental factors. They have recognized that nature and nurture are not separate influences. Instead, they are influences that interact dynamically. For example, environmental experiences activate genetic mechanisms so that certain types of experiences can alter the biology of the organism (Gottlieb, 1998). Increasingly, then, both psychologists and biologists (Ehrlich, 2000; Grigorenko, 2002; Lewontin, 2000) recognize that the problem with the traditional "nature versus nurture" question was the word "versus." Biological and environmental factors are not competing forces, but factors that interact, often in complementary ways, in the development of the persons (Plomin, 1994; Plomin & Caspi, 1999; Plomin, Chipuer, & Loehlin, 1990; Ridley, 2003).

Given the established importance of both genetic and environmental factors, the question you might now be asking yourself is: What aspects of personality are affected by what types of biological and environmental influences? This is a big question whose answers are considered throughout this textbook. For now, though, we will provide a quick preview of some of the factors highlighted by contemporary findings in personality psychology.

Genetic Determinants

Genetic factors play a major role in determining personality and individual differences (Caspi, 2000; Plomin & Caspi, 1999; Rowe, 1999). Scientific advances are beginning to enable the personality psychologist to go beyond this rather general statement, and to pinpoint specific paths of influence. One way to accomplish this is to identify a specific quality of personality that is thought to have a biological basis. Such qualities are often referred to as aspects of **temperament**, a term that refers to biologically based emotional and behavioral tendencies that are evident in early childhood (Strelau, 1998). A temperament characteristic that has been studied in this manner is fearfulness and inhibited behavior in reaction to novel circumstances, such as circumstances involving strangers (Kagan, 1994, 1999). Findings suggest that people differ in the functioning of brain systems in the frontal cortex and limbic system that are involved in fear response, and that these biological differences contribute to psychological differences in people's tendencies to experience fearful, inhibited behavior (Schmidt & Fox, 2002). Since genetic factors contribute to the development of the brain, this type of analysis enables the personality psychologist to understand links from genes to biological systems to behavior in a relatively precise manner. An interesting feature of this work is that it also shows that there is a role for the environment in the development of shy versus non-shy behavior. There is some evidence that temperamentally shy children who experience day care, where they encounter large numbers of other children every day, are less likely to remain shy than are children who are raised entirely at home (Schmidt & Fox, 2002).

Another advance in the field integrates work in personality psychology with findings in the field of molecular genetics. Rather than referring merely to the influence of an organism's overall set of genetic material, or the genome, researchers are beginning to identify specific elements of the genome that are involved in the development of elements of the nervous systems that affect people's behavior (Plomin & Caspi, 1998). A major focus of investigation is the link from genes to neurotransmitter systems (Grigorenko, 2002), that is, chemicals in the brain through which neurons communicate with one another. The functioning of neurotransmitters influences brain activity that, in turn, affects people's moods and reactions to stimuli in the environment. By linking variations in the genome to variations in these biochemicals, researchers can then begin to specify exactly how genetic mechanisms influence specific aspects of personality.

Genetic bases of personality also are explored by evolutionary psychologists, that is, psychologists who study the evolutionary basis of psychological characteristics (Buss, 1991, 1995, 1999, 2000; Buss & Kenrick, 1998). According to such psychologists, many patterns of behavior reflect our evolutionary heritage. It is obvious that contemporary human beings possess biological mechanisms because those mechanisms proved successful over the course of evolution. According to evolutionary psychologists, contemporary humans also possess *psychological* mechanisms that are a product of our evolution. People are predisposed to engage in certain types of behavior because

Determinants of Personality: *Genetic differences and different life experiences, both within and outside the family, contribute to personality differences among siblings.*

those behaviors contributed to survival and reproductive success over the course of human evolution. The merits and limitations of this perspective are discussed in detail in Chapter 9. For now, however, note that an evolutionary analysis of genetic influences differs fundamentally from the analyses reviewed in the two preceding paragraphs. In an evolutionary analysis, investigators are not interested in genetic bases of individual *differences*. Instead, they are searching for the genetic basis of human *universals*, that is, psychological features that all people have in common. Most of our genes are shared. Even so-called "racial differences" involve merely superficial differences in features such as skin tone; the basic structure of the human brain is universal (Cavalli-Sforza & Cavalli-Sforza, 1995). The evolutionary psychologist suggests, then, that we all inherit psychological mechanisms that predispose us to respond to the environment in ways that proved successful over the course of evolution. Such responses might come into play when we attract members of the opposite sex, take care of children, act in an altruistic manner toward members of our social group, or respond emotionally to objects and events. Regarding the latter point, there is much evidence that a number of basic emotions (e.g., anger, sadness, joy, disgust, fear) are experienced in the same way across cultures (Ekman, 1992, 1993, 1994; Elfenbein & Ambady, 2002; Izard, 1991, 1994), as would be expected if these emotions were part of our evolutionary heritage. Cultural influences and social learning play an enormous role in determining exactly what type of events trigger a given emotion. But the emotion system itself may still have an evolutionary basis.

Environmental Determinants

Even the most biologically oriented of psychologists recognizes that the environment plays a critical role in the development of our personalities. If we did

THE EVOLUTION OF MIND AND PERSONALITY

Since the very beginning of scientific psychology, writers have recognized that the human brain, like the rest of human anatomy, is a product of evolution. The book generally recognized as the first great textbook in the field, William James's (1890) *Principles of Psychology*, concluded with a chapter that explained how Charles Darwin's theory of evolution was relevant to the understanding of mental structures. The central idea in relating biological principles of evolution to psychological analyses of mind and personality is that, at birth, the human mind is *not* a "blank slate." It is *not* the case that the mind, at birth, lacks any mental contents or inherent tendencies. Instead, thanks to processes of natural selection over the course of evolution, people are born with natural human tendencies and abilities. Neural mechanisms that produce psychological tendencies that proved adaptive over the course of evolution have become an inherent part of our mental makeup.

In the contemporary field, no personality scientist will doubt that our personalities are, in part, a product of evolution. Yet major questions remain. They include the question of "how big a part?" of mental life is explained by evolutionary ancestry (as opposed to social experiences that we have after we are born), as well as questions about the implications of the findings of evolutionary psychology for our understanding of human beings and for the design of social policies to improve human welfare.

In recent years, these issues have been of interest not only to psychologists and other scientists, but to the public at large. In part, this is due to the writings of Steven Pinker, a psychologist at the Massachusetts Institute of Technology. In his book, *The Blank Slate* (Pinker, 2002), Pinker suggests that society has been too slow to accept the notion that people are a product of their species' evolutionary past. People find it pleasant to think that psychological qualities can be changed through new experiences. We hope, for example, that improved parenting, better education, and more enlightened social policies can create a kinder and gentler world—a world with less prejudice and aggression and more tolerance and peace. But, Pinker points out, there might be features of human psychology that are enormously difficult to change because they are the products of evolution. Those psychological features that proved adaptive over the course of our evolutionary history may be fixed, "hardwired" features of the current human mind. Recognizing the influence of evolutionary factors on the shaping of the mind is, then, key to understanding the basic nature of human nature. Such an understanding, in turn, may be critical to devising humane, effective social policies, and to recognizing when social policies won't work.

Pinker's analyses currently are a point of controversy in the field of psychology and beyond. Some people outside of psychology feel that Pinker's evolutionary framework explains only very limited aspects of the human experience. For example, in reviewing Pinker's book in the *New Yorker* magazine, the scholar Louis Menand (2002) notes that much of human activity seems completely disconnected from the actions and events of the evolutionary past. Many people devote much of their time to creating works of art, playing or listening to music, or reading about and developing systems of religion or philosophical thought. It is difficult to see how people's propensity to create and appreciate these novel, imaginative, intellectual products can be explained in terms of evolutionary forces, since during the course of evolution people devoted most of their time to activities directly related to survival and reproduction. Of course, it might be possible for an evolutionary psychologist such as Pinker to explain, in retrospect, how evolutionary forces might have supported these complex, creative human capacities. But that brings one to a second concern. Biologists sometimes fault evolutionary psychology for being based on very little firm scientific evidence. Some judge that the evidence on which the arguments of evolutionary psychology are based are "surprisingly unrigorous. Too often, data are skimpy, alternative hypotheses are neglected, and the entire enterprise threatens to skip into undisciplined storytelling" (Orr, 2003, p. 18). Evolutionary psychologists may counter that they are still at an early stage of their work, and that future research may confirm their views of human nature.

SOURCES: James (1980); Menand (2002); Orr (2003); Pinker (2002); Smith (2002).

not grow up in a society with other people, we would not even be "persons" in the way in which that term commonly is understood. Our concept of self, our goals in life, and the values that guide us develop in a social world. Some environmental determinants make people similar to one another, whereas others contribute to individual differences and individual uniqueness. The environmental determinants that have proven to be important in the study of personality development include culture, social class, family, and peers.

Culture   Significant among the environmental determinants of personality are experiences individuals have as a result of membership in a particular culture. Each culture has its own institutionalized and sanctioned patterns of learned behaviors, rituals, and beliefs. These culture practices, which in turn often reflect long-standing religious and philosophical beliefs, provide people with answers to significant questions about the nature of the self, one's role in one's community, and the values and principles that are most important in life. As a result, most members of a culture will have certain personality characteristics in common. Interestingly, people often may be unaware of such cultural influences because they take them for granted. For example, people in North America and Western Europe may not appreciate the extent to which their conception of themselves and their goals in life are shaped by living in a culture that strongly values the rights of the individual, and that contains numerous social systems in which individuals compete with one another in an economic marketplace to improve their financial and social status. Since everyone in these regions of the world experiences these cultural features, we take them for granted and may assume that they are universal. Yet much evidence indicates that people in other regions of the world experience different cultural features. Asian cultures appear to place a greater value on a person's contribution to his or her community, rather than on individualism and personal gain (Nisbett et al., 2001). In fact, even in the Western world, cultural beliefs about the individual's role in society has changed from one historical period to another. The idea that individuals compete against one another in an economic marketplace in order to improve their position in life is a feature of contemporary Western societies, but it was not evident in these same societies in the Middle Ages (Heilbroner, 1986).

Culture, then, may exert an influence on personality that is subtle yet pervasive. The culture we live in defines our needs and our means of satisfying them; our experiences of different emotions and how we express what we are feeling; our relationships with others and with ourselves; what we think is funny or sad; how we cope with life and death; and what we view as healthy or sick (Cross & Markus, 1999; Fiske et al., 1998; Markus & Kitayama, 1991).

Social Class   Although certain patterns of behavior develop as a result of membership in a culture, others may develop as a result of membership in a particular social class within a given culture. Few aspects of an individual's personality can be understood without reference to the group to which that person belongs. One's social group—whether lower class or upper class, working class or professional—is of particular importance. Social class factors help determine the status of individuals, the roles they perform, the duties they are bound by, and the privileges they enjoy. These factors influence how individuals see themselves and how they perceive members of other social classes, as well as how they earn and spend money. Research indicates that socioeconomic status influences the cognitive and emotional development of the individual (Bradley & Corwyn, 2002). Like cultural factors, then, social class factors influence people's capacities and tendencies, and shape the ways people define situations and respond to them.

Family   Beyond the similarities determined by environmental factors such as membership in the same culture or social class, environmental factors lead to considerable variation in the personality functioning of members of a single culture or class. One of the most important environmental factors is the influence of the family (Collins et al., 2000; Halverson & Wampler, 1997; Maccoby, 2000). Parents may be warm and loving or hostile and rejecting, overprotective and possessive or aware of their children's need for freedom and autonomy. Each pattern of parental behavior affects the personality development of the child. Parents influence their children's behavior in at least three important ways:

1. Through their own behavior, they present situations that elicit certain behavior in children (e.g., frustration leads to aggression).
2. They serve as role models for identification.
3. They selectively reward behaviors.

At first, we may think of family practices as an influence that makes family members similar to one another. Yet family practices also can create differences within a family. Consider differences between male and female family members. Historically, in many societies, male children have received family privileges and opportunities that were unavailable to female children. These differences in how families have treated boys versus girls surely did not make boys and girls similar to one another; they contributed to differences in male and female development. In addition to gender, other family practices that may produce differences between family members involve birth order. Recent findings indicate that parents often express subtle preferences toward first-born children (Keller & Zach, 2002) and that first-born children are more achievement-oriented and conscientious than later-born siblings (Paulhus, Trapnel, & Chen, 1999).

Peers   What environmental features outside of family life are important to personality development? The child's experiences with members of his or her peer group are one feature. Indeed, peer influences are so strong that some psychologists view them as more important to personality development than family experiences; the psychologist Judith Rich Harris contends that "experiences in childhood and adolescent peer groups, not experiences at home, account for environmental influences on personality development. The answer to the question 'Why are children from the same family so different from one another?' (Plomin & Daniels, 1987) is, because they have different experiences outside the home and because their experiences inside the home do not make them more alike" (Harris, 1995, p. 481). Thus, within-family variations in genetic material plus outside-of-family social influences are seen as determining personality in this view.

What is suggested here is that children learn many things in the home, but these influences are specific to the home environment (Harris, 2000). In social settings outside the home, experiences with peers may be a greater influence on personality styles. The peer group serves to socialize the individual into acceptance of new rules of behavior and provides for experiences that will have long-lasting influences on personality development. Consistent with this view, research findings indicate that friendships have relatively specific effects on personality development. Children who experience high-quality friendships may not have a higher overall sense of self-esteem as a result, but they do have more positive social relationships with their peers; on the other hand, children who experience low-quality friendships that involve a lot of arguing and conflict seem to develop disagreeable, antagonistic styles of behavior (Berndt, 2002).

PSYCHOPATHOLOGY AND BEHAVIOR CHANGE

Constructing a personality theory may strike you as an "ivory tower" activity, that is, an abstract intellectual exercise that fails to relate to the important concerns of everyday life. Yet nothing could be farther from the truth. Personality theories are potentially of great practical importance. People often face complicated psychological problems: they are depressed and lonely; a close friend is addicted to drugs; they are anxious about sexual relations; frequent arguments threaten the stability of a romantic relationship. To solve such problems, one requires some sort of conceptual framework that specifies causes of the problem and factors that might bring about change. In other words, one needs a personality theory.

Historically, the practical problems that have been most important to the development of personality theories have involved psychopathology. Many of the theorists discussed in this book were also therapists. They began their careers by trying to solve practical problems they faced when trying to help their clients. Their theories were, in part, an attempt to systematize the lessons about human nature that they learned by working on practical problems in therapy.

Not all personality theories had clinical origins. Some theories began with other forms of data about personality, as we will discuss in Chapter 2. Nonetheless, the ability to benefit people experiencing psychological distress is a crucial "bottom line" that can be used to evaluate any and all personality theories. A complete theory of personality must include analyses of why some people are capable of coping with the stresses of daily life and generally experience psychological well-being, whereas others experience frequent psychological distress and poor patterns of coping. The theory should also suggest techniques for modifying pathological forms of behavior.

<table>
<tr><td>

IMPORTANT ISSUES IN PERSONALITY THEORY

</td><td>

We have just reviewed four topic areas that are addressed in the study of personality: (1) personality structure, (2) personality processes, (3) personality development, and (4) psychopathology and behavior change. Next, we will consider a series of conceptual issues that are central to the field. By "conceptual issues," we mean a set of questions about personality that are so fundamental that they may arise no matter what topic one is addressing. Throughout the relatively brief history of personality theory, a number of issues have confronted theorists repeatedly (Pervin, 2002). The ways in which they treat these issues do much to define the major characteristics of each theoretical position. Thus, in reviewing various personality theories we must consider how much attention each theorist gives to these issues and how that theorist resolves each issue.

</td></tr>
</table>

PHILOSOPHICAL VIEW OF THE PERSON

Personality theorists do not confine themselves to narrow questions about human behavior. Instead, they boldly tackle the big, broad question: What is the basic nature of human nature? Personality theorists, in other words, provide philosophical views about the basic nature of human beings. One critical thing to consider when evaluating a theory, then, is the overall view of the person that it provides.

Personality theories embrace strikingly different views of the essential qualities of human nature. Some incorporate a view in which people seem like "rational actors." People reason about the world, weigh the costs and benefits of alternative courses of action, and behave based on these rational calculations. In this view, individual differences primarily reflect differences in the thought processes that go into these calculations.

Other perspectives recognize that humans are animals. The human organism, in this view, is primarily driven by irrational, animalistic forces. Rational thought processes are seen as relatively weak components of personality, compared to powerful animalistic drives.

During the latter decades of the 20th century, a popular view of persons involved a computer metaphor. People were seen as information processors who stored and manipulated symbolic representations of the world. Since people move around in the world, some argued that robots, rather than computers, provide a closer analogy to human nature (Carver & Scheier, 1998).

One should recognize that different views of human nature have arisen in different sociohistorical circumstances. Proponents of different points of view have had different life experiences, and have been influenced by different historical traditions. Thus, beyond scientific evidence and fact, theories of personality are influenced by personal factors, by the spirit of the time, and by philosophical assumptions characteristic of members of a given culture (Pervin, 2002). Although based on observed data, theories selectively emphasize certain kinds of data and go beyond what is known, and therefore can be influenced by personal and cultural factors. To some extent, in developing psychological theories we talk about ourselves. In itself this is not a problem. Only when personal experiences become more important than other kinds of experience and ignore research evidence do personal determinants of a theory become a problem.

INTERNAL AND EXTERNAL DETERMINANTS OF BEHAVIOR

Is human behavior determined by processes inside the person or by external causes? The issues here concern the relationship between, and the relative importance of, internal and external determinants. All theories of personality recognize that factors inside the organism and events in the surrounding environment are important in determining behavior. However, the theories differ in the level of importance given to internal and external determinants. Consider the differences in view of two of the most influential psychologists of the 20th century: Sigmund Freud and B. F. Skinner. According to Freud, we are controlled by internal forces that reside primarily in our unconscious minds. According to Skinner, environmental forces are paramount: "A person does not act upon the world, the world acts upon him" (1971, p. 211). In the Freudian view, then, the internal dynamics of the mind are causally responsible for overt patterns of behavior. To Skinner, the person is a passive victim of events in the environment.

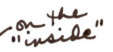

"on the 'inside'"

Freud and Skinner represent views that most psychologists now would see as extreme. Virtually all personality psychologists today acknowledge that it is necessary to consider both external and internal determinants of human action. Nonetheless, contemporary theories continue to differ markedly in the degree to which they emphasize one versus the other factor. These differences become apparent when one examines the basic variables—or, as we called them earlier, the basic units of analysis—of a given theory. Consider two perspectives you will read about in later chapters. In trait theories of personality, the basic units of analysis refer to structures in the person that purportedly are inherited and produce highly generalized patterns of behavior (McCrae & Costa, 1999). In social-cognitive theories of personality, the basic units of analysis are knowledge structures and thinking processes that are acquired through interaction with the social and cultural environment (Bandura, 1999; Mischel & Shoda, 1995). As you can infer from their basic units, these theories differentially emphasize internal and external determinants of personality.

CONSISTENCY ACROSS SITUATIONS AND OVER TIME

How consistent is personality from situation to situation? To what extent are you "the same person" when with friends as you are with your parents? Or when you are at a party versus a classroom discussion? And how consistent is personality across time? How similar is your personality now to what it was when you were a child? And, how similar will it be 20 years from now?

Answering these questions is more difficult than it may appear. In part, this is because one has to decide on what counts as an example of personality consistency versus inconsistency. One generally needs a theory of personality in order to make this decision. Consider a simple example. Suppose you have two supervisors at a job, one male and one female, and that you tend to act in an agreeable manner toward one supervisor and disagreeably toward the other. Are you being "inconsistent" in your personality? If one thinks that a basic feature of personality is "agreeableness," then the answer is yes. But suppose this situation were analyzed by a psychologist who adheres to psychoanalytic theory, which suggests that (a) people you encounter in your adult life may symbolically represent parental figures, and that (b) a basic personality dynamic involves attraction toward one's opposite-sex parent and rivalry toward the same-sex parent—something called an "Oedipal complex." From this view, you may be acting in a very consistent manner. The different job supervisors may symbolically represent different parental figures, and you may be consistently reenacting Oedipal motives that cause you to act in a different manner toward one versus the other person.

Even if people agree on what counts as consistency, they may disagree about the factors that cause personality to be consistent. Consider consistency over time. It unquestionably is the case that individual differences are stable, to a significant degree, over long periods of time (Fraley, 2002; Roberts & Del Vecchio, 2000). If you are more extraverted than your friends today, you are quite likely to be more extraverted than these same people 20 years from now. Yet questions may arise regarding why this is the case. One possibility is that the core structures of personality are basically inherited and that they change little across the course of life. Another possibility, however, is that the environment plays a critical role in fostering consistency. Exposure to the same family members, friends, educational systems, and social circumstances over long periods of time may cause consistency in personality (Lewis, 2002). A key implication is that even though personality may tend to be consistent over time, it is not *necessarily* consistent. Significant changes in life circumstances might bring about significant personality change.

No personality theorist thinks that you will fall asleep an introvert and wake up the next morning an extravert. Yet the field's theoretical frameworks do provide different views on the nature of personality consistency and change, and on people's capacity to vary their personality functioning across time and place. To some theorists, variation in behavior is a sign of inconsistency in personality. To others, it may reflect a consistent personal capacity to adapt one's behavior to the different requirements of different social situations (Mischel,

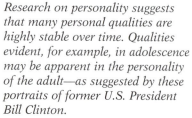

Research on personality suggests that many personal qualities are highly stable over time. Qualities evident, for example, in adolescence may be apparent in the personality of the adult—as suggested by these portraits of former U.S. President Bill Clinton.

1968). The question of consistency, then, is another important issue on which different theoretical positions can be found.

THE UNITY OF EXPERIENCE AND ACTION AND THE CONCEPT OF SELF

Our psychological experiences generally have an integrated, or coherent, quality to them (Cervone & Shoda, 1999b). Our actions are patterned and organized, rather than random and chaotic. As we move from place to place, we retain a stable sense of ourselves, our past, and our goals for the future. There is a unity to our experiences and action.

Although we take it for granted that our experiences are unified, in some sense this fact is quite surprising. The brain contains a large number of information-processing systems, many of which function at the same time, in partial isolation from one another (Pinker, 1997). If we examine the contents of our own conscious experiences, we will find that most of thoughts our fleeting. It is hard to keep any one idea in mind for long periods. Seemingly random ideas "pop into our heads." Nonetheless, we rarely experience the world as chaotic or our lives as disjointed. Why?

There are two types of answers to this question. One is that the multiple components of the mind function as a complex *system*. The parts are interconnected, and the patterns of interconnection enable the multi-part system to function in a smooth, coherent manner. Computer simulations of personality functioning (Nowak, Vallacher, & Zochowski, 2002), as well as neuroscientific investigations of the reciprocal links among brain regions (Tonini & Edelman, 1998), are beginning to shed light on how the mind manages to produce coherence in experience and action.

The second type of answer involves the concept of the *self*. Although we may experience a potentially bewildering diversity of life events, we do experience them from a consistent perspective, that of ourselves (Harré, 1998). We are able to construct coherent autobiographical memories, which contribute to coherence in our understanding of who we are (Conway & Pleydell-Pearce, 2000). The concept of the self, then, has proven valuable in accounting for the unity of experience (Baumeister, 1999; Robins, Norem, & Cheek, 1999).

Traditionally, the concept of the self has been emphasized for three reasons. First, our awareness of ourselves represents an important aspect of our phe-

The Concept of Self: *Personality psychologists are interested in how the concept of self develops and helps to organize experience.*

nomenological or subjective experience. Second, considerable research suggests that how we feel about ourselves is not a mere reflection of our life experiences; instead, self-referent thought causally influences our behavior (Bandura, 1997). Third, as noted, the concept of the self is used to express the organized, integrated aspects of human personality functioning. In asking whether the concept of the self is necessary, the noted theorist Gordon Allport (1958) suggested that many psychologists have tried in vain to account for the integration, organization, and unity of the human person without making use of the concept of the self.

Without a concept of self, the theorist is left with the task of developing an alternative concept to express the integrated aspects of human functioning. As you will see, some personality theorists have attempted to construct theoretical frameworks that contain few if any "self" concepts. On the other hand, reliance on the concept of the self leaves the theorist with the task of defining self in a way that makes it possible to be studied systematically, rather than leaving it vaguely defined as some strange inner being. Thus, how to account for the organized aspects of personality, and the use of the concept of the self in this regard, remains a major issue of concern for personality psychologists.

VARYING STATES OF AWARENESS AND THE CONCEPT OF THE UNCONSCIOUS

Are we aware of the contents of our mental life? Or do most mental activities occur outside of awareness, or unconsciously? On the one hand, a great deal of what the brain does unquestionably occurs without one's awareness. Consider what is happening as you read this book. Your brain is engaging in large numbers of activities ranging from the monitoring of your internal physiological states to the deciphering of the marks of ink that constitute the words on this page. All this occurs without your conscious attention. You do not consciously have to think to yourself "I wonder if these squiggles of ink form words?" or "maybe I should check to see if sufficient amounts of oxygen are getting to my bodily organs?" The brain does these things automatically. The questions for the personality psychologist, however, are the degree to which significant aspects of personality functioning occur outside of awareness and how to conceptualize the mental systems that give rise to conscious and unconscious processes (Kihlstrom, 1990, 1999; Pervin, 1999, 2003).

The first personality psychologist to provide comprehensive answers to these questions was Freud, whose work we will review beginning in Chapter 3. A great many contemporary psychologists acknowledge that Freud was correct in recognizing that much of mental life is unconscious (Westen, 1998). Yet many are uncomfortable with the details of Freud's account of the unconscious. Contemporary research has revealed that a much wider array of activities than Freud envisioned can occur without conscious awareness (Kihlstrom, 1999).

The fact that many mental activities can occur outside of awareness does not imply that the most significant of personality processes involve unconscious thought. People engage in much self-reflection. They are particularly likely to reflect on themselves when they face life circumstances of great importance, where the decisions that are made (e.g., whether and where to attend college, whether to marry a person, whether to have children, what profession to pursue) have major long-term consequences. In these critical circumstances, conscious processes are influential. Thus, many personality psychologists study conscious self-reflection, even while recognizing that many aspects of mental life occur outside of awareness.

THE INFLUENCE OF THE PAST, PRESENT, AND FUTURE ON BEHAVIOR

To what extent are we "prisoners of our past" as opposed, for example, to always being shaped by our view of the future? The issue is the importance of the past, present, and future in governing behavior. Theorists agree that behavior can be influenced only by factors operating in the present; a basic principle of causality is that presently active processes are the causes of events. In this sense, only the present is important in understanding behavior. But the present can be influenced by experiences in the remote past or in the recent past. Similarly, what one is thinking about in the present can be influenced by thoughts about the immediate future or the distant future. People vary in the extent to which they worry about the past and the future. And personality theorists differ in their concern with the past and the future as determinants of behavior in the present.

At one extreme lies psychoanalytic theory, which attaches importance to early learning experiences. At the other extreme lies social-cognitive theory, which takes a proactive, agentic view of personality functioning in which forethought is central to personality functioning, and in which people are seen to have a large capacity for change (Bandura, 2001). The issue is not whether events that happened in the past can have lasting effects or whether anticipations about the future can have effects in the present (theorists undoubtedly agree that both are possible and occur), but how to conceptualize the role of past experiences and future anticipations and connect their influence to what is occurring in the present.

The Effects of Early Experience: *Psychologists generally agree that early experiences can be important for personality development, but they disagree on whether these experiences lead to the development of relatively fixed personality characteristics.*

CAN WE HAVE A SCIENCE OF PERSONALITY? WHAT KIND OF A SCIENCE CAN IT BE?

A final issue of importance concerns the type of theory of personality that one reasonably can pursue. We have taken it for granted thus far that one can craft a *science* of personality, in other words, that it is possible to use the methods of science to understand the nature of persons. This assumption seems like a safe one. People are objects in a physical universe. They consist of biological systems comprised of physical and chemical parts. Science thus should be able to tell us something about them.

Nonetheless, one can reasonably ask about what type of scientific analysis could apply to the understanding of personality. Much of the progress of science has involved analyses that are reductionistic. A system is understood by reducing a complex whole to its simpler parts, and showing how the parts give rise to the functioning of the whole.

Such analyses work wonderfully when applied to physical systems. A biological system, for example, can be understood in terms of the biochemistry of its parts. The chemistry, in turn, can be understood in terms of the underlying physics of the chemical components. But personality is not merely a physical system. People construct, and respond to, *meaning*. We assign meaning to the events we experience. We strive to understand ourselves, not just as physical entities but as persons with an identity. There is no guarantee that the traditional scientific procedures of breaking a system into constituent parts will be sufficient to understand these processes of meaning construction. Indeed, numerous scholars have suggested that they may not, and have warned psychologists against importing the methods of the physical sciences into the study of human meaning systems (Geertz, 2000; Polkinghorne, 1988; Taylor, 1989).

To such commentators, the idea that people have "parts" is "at best a metaphor" (Harré, 1998, p. 15). The risk of adopting this metaphor is that, to use a cliché, "the whole may be greater than the sum of the parts." By analogy, consider an analysis of a great work of art, such as daVinci's *Mona Lisa*. In principle, one could analyze its parts: there's paint of one color over here, paint of some other color there, and so on. But this sort of analysis will not enable one to understand the greatness of the painting. This requires viewing the work as a whole and understanding the historical context in which it was made. By analogy, a listing of the psychological parts of an actual person may, in principle, leave one lacking a holistic understanding of the individual and the developmental processes that contributed to his or her uniqueness. A final important issue to bear in mind throughout this textbook, then, is whether the personality theorists are as successful as was daVinci at providing holistic psychological "portraits" of complex individuals.

IMPORTANT ISSUES: SUMMARY

In attempting to account for the what, how, and why of human functioning, personality theorists are confronted with many issues. Seven issues of particular importance have been mentioned here: (1) the philosophical view of the person; (2) the relation between internal (personal) and external (situational) influences in determining behavior; (3) the consistency of personality across situations and over time; (4) the coherence and unity of personality functioning; (5) the role of varying states of awareness and the concept of the unconscious; (6) the role of the past, present, and future in governing behavior; and

(7) the promise, and potential limits, of a scientific analysis of personality. Of course, many other issues concern personality theorists and account for differences among them, but the purpose here has been to point to the main ones. The importance of these and other issues will become increasingly clear as we consider the positions of the various theorists in the chapters that follow.

EVALUATION OF THEORIES

As we have noted, a unique feature of the scientific field of personality psychology is that it contains more than one guiding theory. Multiple theories of personality inform us about human nature and individual differences. A natural question, then, is how to evaluate the theories, one versus the other. How can one judge the strengths and limitations of the various theories? What are the criteria that should be used to evaluate them?

THE FUNCTIONS OF A PERSONALITY THEORY

To evaluate something, one generally asks what something is supposed to do. One then can judge how well it is doing it. A more formal way to say this is that one asks about the functions that the entity is supposed to serve. One then evaluate the degree to which it is carrying out those functions.

What, then, are the functions of a personality theory? What is a personality theory supposed to do? Like all scientific theories, theories of personality serve two key functions: (1) they organize existing information, and (2) they foster new knowledge, that is, they contribute to the acquisition of new information that is logically predictable from the theory.

The first of these functions is obvious. Scientific research provides an array of facts about personality, personality development, and individual differences. Rather than merely listing these facts in an unordered manner, it would be useful to organize them systematically. A logical, systematic ordering of facts would constitute a useful theory. It would enable one to keep track of what scientists know about personality and thereby to put that knowledge to use.

The second function is somewhat less obvious. A theory should have generative properties; that is, it should help to generate new knowledge. In biology, Darwin's theory of natural selection was useful not only because it organized known facts about the world's flora and fauna. Its additional value is that it opened new pathways of knowledge about biology. Similarly, in personality psychology, some theories have proven to be highly generative. They have prompted researchers who are familiar with the theory to use its ideas to generate new knowledge about personality. A particularly exciting feature of some personality theories is that they have highlighted entirely new areas of study that people might never have thought to investigate were it not for the theory. Psychodynamic theory opened the door to the possibility that many of our most important thoughts and emotions are unconscious. Evolutionary psychology suggests that contemporary patterns of social behavior are not learned in society, but inherited from our ancient ancestors. Behaviorism raises the possibility that actions that we attribute to our free choice, or "free will," are ultimately caused by the environment. These theories' fascinating and sometimes radical hypotheses about human nature have prompted much valuable new investigation into human nature.

COMPREHENSIVENESS, PARSIMONY, AND RESEARCH RELEVANCE

What enables a theory to fulfill these functions? What properties of a theory are most important to its ability to organize known facts and to generate new knowledge? Three criteria of particular importance are a theory's comprehensiveness, parsimony or simplicity, and research relevance (Hall & Lindzey, 1957). Theories of personality, then, can be evaluated according to these three criteria: is the theory comprehensive? Does it account for the facts of personality in a simple, parsimonious way? Does its theoretical structure facilitate scientific research on important aspects of personality functioning. The first two criteria, comprehensiveness and parsimony, relate particularly strongly to the first of the two functions of a theory, organizing known facts. The third criterion, research relevance, bears on the second function, the generation of new scientific knowledge.

Comprehensiveness

A good theory is comprehensive. That is, it encompasses and accounts for a wide variety of aspects of the psychological life of the individual. It addresses each of the questions outlined earlier: the what, how, and why of personality. It addresses the wide range of internal and external determinants of behavior reviewed previously. Although the field of psychological has a large number of theories about specific psychological phenomena, it has only a relatively few frameworks with enough comprehensiveness that they even can be called a "theory of personality."

No theory accounts for everything. It is important, then, to ask how many different kinds of phenomena the theory can account for, that is, to ask about the theory's comprehensiveness. The notion of comprehensiveness includes not only the number of issues that a theory addresses, but their significance. A theory that addressed a wide range of facts but that left out significant topics—e.g., how personality develops—would not be seen as comprehensive.

While asking about comprehensiveness, one also should consider the specificity with which a theory treats the topics of personality. We not only want a theory to cover many different phenomena in a general way, but to be very exact in its coverage. A good theory should specify processes that are involved in personality functioning, and do so in a manner than enables one to make specific predictions about behavior. The concepts of **bandwidth** and **fidelity** encompass the criteria under consideration. The concept of bandwidth relates to the range of phenomena covered by a theory, what might be called its range of convenience. The concept of fidelity relates to the phenomena to which it is particularly applicable, what can be called its focus of convenience. An analogy may be drawn here to a comparison of radios. A truly excellent radio picks up a wide variety of stations (bandwidth) and receives the signals of each with great clarity (fidelity). Similarly, an excellent theory of personality accounts for a large range of phenomena with great clarity and specificity. However, often we are forced to make a trade-off between bandwidth and fidelity. One radio brings in more signals but with lesser clarity; another radio has great clarity but brings in only a limited number of stations. Similarly, personality theories often are stronger in one characteristic than another, covering a broader range of phenomena at a lesser degree of specificity or a narrower range of phenomena at a greater degree of specificity. Thus, although recognizing that both comprehensiveness and specificity—bandwidth and fidelity—are desirable, we must at times be prepared to consider trade-offs between the two.

Parsimony

Along with being comprehensive, a theory should be simple and parsimonious. It should account for varied phenomena in an economical, internally consistent way. This is true of theories throughout the sciences. A remarkable feature of Newton's theorizing in physics, for example, is that it is relatively simple. Rather than providing a complex theoretical system in which different laws of motion were used to account for the behavior of different objects, Newton succeeded in providing universal laws that could describe the motion of everything ranging from small objects to large planets. Similarly, the personality psychologist seeks a simple theory, that is, a theory that can account for a wide range of psychological issues via a relatively small set of principles. As you will see, this goal was achieved admirably by many of the theorists you will learn about in this book.

The two goals of simplicity and comprehensiveness raise a question of the appropriate level of organization and abstraction of a personality theory. As theories become more comprehensive and parsimonious, they tend to become more abstract. Therefore it is important that, in becoming abstract, theories retain concepts that relate clearly to the behavior studied. In other words, fuzzy or unclear concepts should not be the price paid for a theory becoming more parsimonious.

Research Relevance

Finally, a theory is not true or false, but useful or not useful. A good theory has research relevance in that it leads to many new hypotheses, which can then be confirmed through systematic research. It has what Hall and Lindzey (1957) called empirical translation: It specifies variables and concepts in such a way that there is agreement about their meaning and about their potential for measurement. Empirical translation means that the concepts in a theory are clear, explicit, and lead to the expansion of knowledge; they must have predictive power. In other words, a theory must contain testable hypotheses about relationships among phenomena. To the degree that it does contain them, it is better able to perform the second function of a personality theory, namely, generating new knowledge about persons.

The quality of being testable may strike you as being so obvious that it perhaps need not be stated. Of course a theory should be testable; if it is not, it does not even qualify as a scientific theory. All the theories we will discuss are testable, and have been subjected to many tests. Yet the theories do differ in the degree to which they are open to *negative tests*, that is, procedures that potentially could show a feature of a theory to be inaccurate. Consider an idea of Sigmund Freud's, namely that the contents of dreams are fulfillments of unconscious wishes. It is clear what a positive test of the theory would be: One analyzes a dream until one discovers an unconscious wish. But it is difficult to specify a negative test. If one does not discover an unconscious wish that is being fulfilled, a Freudian might not agree that the theory has been disproven. Instead, he or she might contend that the wish is really there, but that it is so traumatic that it is buried deep in the unconscious. Once one allows for this reasoning, it is difficult to subject this aspect of psychoanalytic theory to a negative test.

EVALUATION OF THEORIES: SUMMARY

The criteria of comprehensiveness, parsimony, and research relevance provide the basis for a comparative evaluation of theories of personality. In comparing theories, however, we can ask two questions: Do they address themselves to the same phenomena? Are they at the same stage of development? Two theories that deal with different kinds of behavior may each be evaluated in relation to these three criteria. Nevertheless, we need not choose between the two theories; each can be allowed to lead to new insights, with the hope that at some point both can be integrated into a single, more comprehensive theory. Finally, a new and immature theory may be unable to account for many phenomena but may lead to a few important observations and show promise of becoming more comprehensive with time. Such a theory may be unable to explain phenomena considered to be understood by another established theory, but may represent a breakthrough in significant areas formerly left untouched. It is like having a new idea, one that needs to be tested further but which seems to explain phenomena formerly puzzling or unaccounted for. As you will see, some of the theories that we will discuss have been around for more than a century, whereas others are much newer and therefore still in a state of theoretical development. An exciting aspect of personality psychology is that, compared to a field such as physics, we are still in a relatively early stage of the discipline's history. One can observe important ideas currently taking shape. Those of you who choose to go into the field have the opportunity to contribute directly to the development of a science of personality.

THE PERSONALITY THEORIES: AN INTRODUCTION

We have now reviewed a series of points: topics that must be addressed by a personality theory; important issues that arise as one confronts these topics; and criteria that can be used to evaluate a theory of personality. Now, in the final section of this chapter, we turn to the theories themselves.

THE CHALLENGE OF CONSTRUCTING A PERSONALITY THEORY

Even a brief reflection on the issues we have reviewed thus far will make it clear that someone who wishes to construct a comprehensive theory of personality faces an extremely difficult task. The theory must address an exceptionally wide range of issues. It must incorporate a broad range of determinants of personality development and functioning. The theory must be consistent with evidence ranging from the study of individual differences in genetic mechanisms to cultural variations in social practices. The ideal personality theorist would be a master of all trades.

Do we have this ideal? Is there a single person who has managed to construct a theory that is so comprehensive in its scope, and so consistent with the entire range of scientific evidence, that it is accepted universally? The answer, quite simply, is no. There exist different theoretical frameworks. Each has its strengths, and each its limitations. More importantly, each has its unique virtues; in other words, each of a variety of theories provides some unique insights into human nature, where those insights also are supported by scientific evidence. It is for this reason that this textbook is organized around personality theories—plural.

At first, the fact that you will be learning about multiple theories in a course on the psychology of personality might seem odd. Most other scientific disciplines are not presented as a series of theories. If you are taking a course in chemistry or physics, your textbook for that class probably is not organized around distinct theoretical frameworks. Instead, there is a commonly accepted framework—or what is generally called a "paradigm"—that guides investigation in the area. In part, this reflects the maturity of these scientific disciplines, which have been around longer than the science of psychology. Yet even the "mature sciences" may feature different theoretical views of the same phenomenon. Suppose you were to ask a physicist about the nature of light. You might learn that physics has a theory that says that light is a wave. And you might learn that physics also has a theory that says that light is composed of individual particles. If you were to ask "Which theory is wrong?" you would be told "Neither." Light acts as a wave and a particle. Both a wave theory and a particle theory capture important information about the nature of light.

The same is true for the personality theories you will learn about. Whatever the limitations of each, it is undoubtedly the case that each theoretical perspective captures important information about human nature. As you read about them, you should not be asking yourself "Which theory was right, and which ones are wrong?" Instead, it is better to evaluate them according to how useful they are in advancing knowledge regarding issues of scientific and social importance. Even a theory that gets some things wrong may have practical value (Proctor & Capaldi, 2001). Despite its limitations, it may serve as a valuable guide to basic research as well as to applications.

THE PERSONALITY THEORIES: A PRELIMINARY SKETCH

What, then, are the personality theories? What theoretical frameworks have had the biggest impact on the field? This book will introduce you to six theoretical approaches to the study of personality. We will provide a very brief sketch of these approaches here, so that you can get a sense of the terrain ahead.

We begin with psychodynamic theory (Chapters 3 and 4), the approach pioneered by Freud. Psychodynamic theory views the mind as an energy system; the basic biological energies of the body reside, in part, in the mind. Mental energies, then, are directed to the service of basic bodily needs. However, people generally cannot gratify sexual and other bodily desires whenever they wish. Instead, the drive to gratify bodily needs often conflicts with the dictates of society. Behavior, then, reflects a conflict between biological desires, on the one hand, and social constraints, on the other. In psychoanalysis, the mind is said to contain different systems that serve different functions: satisfying bodily needs, representing social norms and rules; and striking a strategic balancing between biological drives and social constraints. An additional defining feature of psychodynamic theory is that much of this mental activity is said to occur outside of one's conscious awareness. We are not aware of the drives that underlie our emotions and behavior; they are unconscious.

Phenomenological theories, reviewed next (Chapters 5 and 6), contrast starkly with the psychodynamic view. Phenomenological theories are less concerned with unconscious process, and more concerned with people's conscious experience of the world around them—that is, their phenomenological experience. Phenomenological theorists recognize that people have biologically based motives, yet they believe that people also possess "higher" motives involving personal growth and self-fulfillment, and that these motives are more important to personal well-being than are the animalistic drives highlighted by Freud. Finally, compared to psychodynamic approaches, phenomenological theory places much greater emphasis on the self. The development of a stable and coherent understanding of oneself is seen as key to psychological health.

Trait approaches to personality, reviewed in Chapters 7 and 8, differ strikingly from both of the previous formulations. The differences reflect not only different views about the nature of personality, but different scientific beliefs about the best way of building a personality theory. Most trait theorists believe that, to construct a theory of personality, one must begin by solving two scientific problems: (1) developing a reliable measure of individual differences, and (2) determining which individual differences are most important to measure. Once these problems are solved, one would be able to measure the most important individual differences in personality, and these measurements could serve as a basis for constructing a comprehensive theory of persons. An exciting development in the late–20th-century history of the field is that many personality psychologists came to conclude that these problems had, in fact, been solved. Much consensus has been achieved on the question of what individual differences are most important and on how they can be measured.

Chapter 9 addresses one of the most exciting aspects of contemporary personality science, namely, research on the biological foundations of personality. This includes findings regarding the genetic bases of personality traits, as well as work revealing the brain systems that underlie individual differences. In this chapter, we devote coverage not only to trait theories but to evolutionary psychology. Evolutionary psychologists explain contemporary patterns of social behavior in terms of mental mechanisms that are a product of our evolutionary past.

Chapter 10 introduces the ideas of behaviorism, which represent a learning approach to personality. In behavioral theories, behavior is seen as an adaptation to rewards and punishments experienced in the environment. Since different people experience different patterns of reward in different settings, they naturally developed different styles of behavior. Basic learning processes, then, are said to account for the stylistic variations in behavior that we call "personality." Behaviorism presents a profound challenge to the theories presented previously. To the behaviorist, the units of analysis of the previous theories—the psychodynamics theorist's "unconscious forces," the "self" of phenomenological theories, personality "traits"—are not causes of behavior. They merely are descriptions of patterns of thinking, emotion, and behavior that ultimately are caused by the environment that, according to the behaviorist, shapes our behavior.

Chapter 11 introduces a very different theoretical approach, that of personality construct theory. Personal construct theory addresses people's capacity to interpret the world. Unlike the behaviorist, who is most concerned with how the environment determines our experiences, the personal construct theorist studies the subjective ideas, or constructs, that people use to interpret the environment. One person may view the college environment as "challenging," another as "boring;" one person may view dating circumstances as "romantic," another as "sexually threatening." Personal construct theorists explore the possibility that most individual differences in personality functioning stem from the different constructs that people use to interpret their world.

The final theoretical perspective is that of social-cognitive theory (Chapters 12 and 13). In some respect, social-cognitive theory is similar to the personal construct approach; social-cognitive theorists study personality by analyzing the thinking processes that come into play as people interpret their world. However, the social-cognitive perspective expands upon personal construct theory in at least two important ways. First, as suggested by its name, social-cognitive theory explores in detail the social settings in which people acquire knowledge, skills, and beliefs. Personality develops through back-and-forth influences, or *reciprocal interactions*, between people and the settings (i.e., the family, interpersonal, social, and cultural settings) of their lives. Second, social-cognitive theory devotes much attention to questions of *self-regulation*, which refers to the psychological processes through which people set goals for themselves, control their emotional impulses, and execute courses of action.

Chapter 14 considers personality in context. We explore contemporary research that illustrates the critical point that you often can learn much about people's personalities by studying the life contexts—the social situations, cultural settings, interpersonal relationships, etc.—that make up their life. This research heavily capitalizes on the social-cognitive perspective discussed in Chapters 12 and 13, while providing a broad portrait of contemporary psychological research on social settings and the individual. We end, in Chapter 15, with a brief summary of the terrain we have covered.

Differences among the Theories

When we started this preliminary sketch of the personality theories, you may have asked yourself "Do these theories really differ from one another in important ways?" By now, it should already be clear that the answer to this question is "yes." Not only do the theories differ, but theoretical perspectives often have developed in explicit opposition to one another. Theorists perceive problems in one theory, and embark on a new theoretical direction. The differences among the theories involve differences both in basic views of human nature and in views of how best to construct a scientific theory of persons.

The fact that there exist multiple theories does not mean that the psychology of personality consists merely of "warring camps" of investigators who spend their days arguing the merits of one versus another theoretical position. The field has seen much cumulative scientific progress. As the science has progressed, different theoretical perspectives have gained or lost influence, depending on whether their ideas proved able to fuel the progress of the discipline. Some theoretical positions have evolved over time, with modifications being made in light of scientific results. As a result of this evolution, some theoretical positions are closer to one another than they used to be. Indeed, it is possible to discern signs of an emerging consensus position that might guide the field in the future; we return to this possibility in our closing chapter.

Despite signs of convergence, at the present time personality psychology contains theoretical positions that differ markedly. And maybe this is not such a bad thing. The presence of different theories serves an important function. It forces investigators to consider not only research findings that derive from their own favorite theory, but results that come from other theories and that might challenge their own favorite view. Theoretical diversity thus can accelerate the overall progress of a discipline. It can cause theorists to refine to their positions in the face of a diverse range of research findings and theoretical challenges. As one wise observer has put it, in commenting on the progress of the social and psychological sciences, the "deployment of distinct inquiries…[that] force deep-going reconsiderations upon one another" is what "drive[s] the enterprise erratically onward" (Geertz, 2000, p. 199).

We hope you enjoy our review of personality psychology, and the theories and research that drive it along the bumpy road of scientific progress.

✱ Know

MAJOR CONCEPTS

Bandwidth   A concept referring to the range of phenomena covered by a theory.

Fidelity   A concept referring to the specificity or clarity with which a theory relates to phenomena.

Hierarchy   A relation between entities in which one of them is an example of, or serves the purpose of, the other. In any given personality theory, different variables often are related hierarchically.

✱Personality   Those characteristics of the person that account for consistent patterns of experience and action.

✱Process   In personality theory, the concept that refers to the motivational aspects of personality.

✱ Structure   In personality theory, the concept that refers to the more enduring and stable aspects of personality.

System   A collection of highly interconnected parts that function together; in the study of personality, dis-

tinct psychological mechanisms may function together as a system that produces the psychological phenomena of personality.

Temperament   Biologically based emotional and behavioral tendencies that are evident in early childhood.

Trait   An enduring psychological characteristic of an individual; or a type of psychological construct (a "trait construct") that refers to such characteristics.

Type   A cluster of personality traits that may constitute a qualitatively distinct category of persons (i.e., a personality type).

Units of analysis   A concept that refers to the basic variables of a theory; different personality theories invoke different types of variables, or different basic units of analysis, in conceptualizing personality structure.

✱Process — pg. 11

REVIEW

1. We all act as personality psychologists in our efforts to observe, explain, and predict human behavior.

2. Personality theories address the questions of what (structure), why (process), and how (growth and development) concerning human functioning. They also address questions concerning the nature of psychopathology and personality change.

3. A number of issues have confronted personality theorists throughout the relatively brief history of the field. Responses to these issues play a major role in defining the essential characteristics of the theory developed by each theorist.

4. Compared to the average person, scientific personality psychologists make more systematic observations, make their theories more explicit, and provide for more rigorous testing of specific predictions.

5. In evaluating theories, we are interested in the criteria of comprehensiveness, parsimony, and research relevance.

6. Theories organize what is known and suggest answers to questions about what is not yet known. Although the role of theory in the study of personality has been debated, it is suggested that theory is important to our goals of understanding and explaining human behavior.

THE SCIENTIFIC STUDY OF PEOPLE

List the 3 general approaches to research

THE DATA OF PERSONALITY PSYCHOLOGY
   LOTS of Data
   How Do Data from Different Sources Relate to One Another?
   Fixed versus Flexible Measures
   Personality Theory and Assessment

GOALS OF RESEARCH: RELIABILITY, VALIDITY, ETHICAL BEHAVIOR
   Reliability
   Validity
   The Ethics of Research and Public Policy

THREE GENERAL APPROACHES TO RESEARCH
   Case Studies and Clinical Research
      Case Studies: An Example
      Case Studies: Limitations
   Personality Questionnaires and Correlational Research
      Correlational Research: An Example
      Correlational Research: Limitations

Laboratory Studies and Experimental Research
   Experimental Research: An Example
Evaluating Alternative Research Approaches
   Case Studies and Clinical Research: Strengths and Limitations
   Correlational Research: Strengths and Limitations
   Laboratory, Experimental Research: Strengths and Limitations
Summary of Strengths and Limitations
The Use of Verbal Reports

PERSONALITY THEORY AND PERSONALITY RESEARCH

PERSONALITY ASSESSMENT AND THE CASE OF JIM
   Autobiographical Sketch of Jim

MAJOR CONCEPTS

REVIEW

Chapter Focus

Three students in a course on personality work together on a research project. They have been instructed to develop a research method for studying the effects of achievement motivation on academic performance. At their first meeting, they realize that they have drastically differing opinions about how to proceed. Alex is convinced that the best approach is to follow one student over the course of the semester, carefully recording all relevant information (grades, changes in motivation, feelings about courses, etc.) to obtain a complete and in-depth picture of a particular case. Sarah, however, thinks little of Alex's idea because his conclusions would apply only to that one person. She suggests that the group develop a set of motivation questions and give the questions to as many students as possible. She then would examine the correlation between questionnaire responses and performance in school. Yolanda thinks that neither of these approaches is good enough. She thinks that the best way to understand things scientifically is to run experiments. She suggests an experimental manipulation that causes some people to feel motivated and others to feel unmotivated, followed by a measure of test performance.

The students' views illustrate the three major methods in personality research: *case studies; correlational studies* using questionnaires; and *laboratory experiments*. This chapter introduces you to these three research methods. First, however, we review the different types of information, or data sources, that might go into any study, as well as the general goals that investigators have when they conduct research on personality.

QUESTIONS TO BE ADDRESSED IN THIS CHAPTER

1. What kind of information is it important to obtain when studying personality?

2. What does it mean to say that scientific observations must be "reliable" and "valid"? *understand*

3. How should we go about studying people? Should we conduct research in the laboratory or in the natural environment? Through the use of self-reports or reports of others? Through studying many subjects or a single individual?

4. How much difference does it make to study people with one or another type of data? Or through one versus another approach to research? In other words, to what extent will the person "look the same" when studied from different vantage points or perspectives?

In Chapter 1, we suggested that, at an intuitive level, all people are personality psychologists. Both you and the professional personality scientist develop complex and insightful thoughts about people. The job of the personality scientist, however, differs from yours. The personality scientist must formulate his or her ideas very explicitly, so that they can be tested by objective scientific evidence.

Just as we all are intuitive personality theorists, we are also intuitive personality researchers. We observe differences among people, as well as consistent patterns of behavior within individuals. However, the "research" of the ordinary person differs from that of the personality scientist. Scientists follow established procedures to ensure that they obtain information that is as objective and accurate as possible. They check these procedures to ensure that their observations are reliable and stable, rather than occurring by chance or error. They report the procedures in publications, so that other investigators can replicate their procedures and verify their findings. Rarely in our daily lives do we do any of this in a systematic way.

This chapter is devoted to the research procedures of the personality psychologist. Our subsequent chapters explore personality theories. You should bear in mind, however, that questions about theory and research are not as separate as this division of chapters might suggest. It might seem as if psychologists first should conduct a large amount of "theory-free" research, and then develop a theory to explain their findings. But this is impossible because there is no such thing as "theory-free" research. Research involves the systematic study of relationships among events. Generally, we need a theory to identify the events that are most important to study. We also need a theory to tell us how to study them. Suppose, for example, that you wanted to test the idea that people who are anxious about dating relationships do not perform as well as they should on exams in college courses because their anxiety interferes with their learning. To test this, you would have to begin by measuring people's level of anxiety. But how? It is impossible to proceed without making some theoretical assumptions. One option would be to ask people directly "Are you anxious about dating?" But this option makes two risky assumptions: (1) that people are aware of their level of anxiety, and thus are capable of reporting it, and (2) that people will tell you, honestly and accurately, about their anxiety if you ask. These assumptions could be wrong, and a personality theory might specify exactly how they are wrong. For example, psychodynamic theories suggest that some people are so anxious that they are not even aware of their anxiety. They repress it. This theory suggests that you need a different research method. Other potential research procedures, such as measuring physiological arousal or brain functioning to index levels of anxiety, similarly rest on theoretical ideas about what anxiety is, what its underlying causes are, and how it is expressed. Thus, theory and research are closely linked. Theory without research can be mere speculation. Research without theory is an impossibility.

There is more than one way to get scientific information, or data, about persons. Consider the options. You could ask a person to tell you what she is like. Alternatively, you could observe her in her day-to-day activities to see for yourself. Or, since this would be rather time-consuming, you could ask other people who know this person well to report on her personality. A fourth possibility would be one that does not rely on anyone's subjective observations or judgments, but instead looks at objective facts about the person's life (school records, job performance, etc.).

THE DATA OF PERSONALITY PSYCHOLOGY

LOTS OF DATA

Personality psychologists have recognized these options and have defined four categories of data that one might use in research (Block, 1993). They also have created a handy acronym to make it easy to remember them. The four types of data are: (1) life record data (L-data), (2) observer data (O-data), (3) test data (T-data), and (4) self-report data (S-data)—or, LOTS of data. Personality psychologists consider four data types because each one, individually, has unique strengths and limitations (Ozer, 1999).

L-data consist of information that can be obtained from a person's life history or life record. For example, if one is interested in the relation between intelligence and school performance, one can make use of official school records of intelligence test scores and grades. If interested in the relation between personality and criminality, one does not have to ask people "Have you committed any crimes?" and rely on the truthfulness of their answers. Instead, court records of arrests and convictions supply an objective measure of criminality. For many personality characteristics, however, such objective records are not available, so other data sources must be considered.

O-data consist of information provided by knowledgeable observers such as parents, friends, or teachers. Generally such persons are provided with a questionnaire or other rating form with which they rate the target individual's personality characteristics. For example, friends might complete a questionnaire in which they rate an individual's level of friendliness, extraversion, or conscientiousness. Sometimes observers are trained to observe individuals in their daily lives and to make personality ratings based on these observations. As one example, camp counselors have been trained to observe systematically the behavior of children at camp, in order to relate specific forms of behavior (e.g., verbal aggression, physical aggression, compliance) to features of the camp setting or to general personality characteristics (e.g., self-confidence, emotional health, social skills) (Shoda, Mischel, & Wright, 1994; Sroufe, Carlson, & Shulman, 1993). As is clear from these examples, O-data can consist of observations of very specific pieces of behavior or of more general ratings based on observations of behavior. In addition, data on any individual can be obtained from one observer or from multiple observers (e.g., one friend or many friends, one teacher or many teachers). In the latter case, one can check for agreement or reliability among observers.

T-data consist of information obtained from experimental procedures or standardized tests. For example, ability to tolerate delay of gratification might be measured by determining how long a child will work at a task to obtain a larger reward rather than a smaller reward that is immediately available (Mischel, 1990, 1999b). Performance on a standardized test such as an intelligence test would also be illustrative of T-data.

Finally, **S-data** consist of information provided by the subject himself or herself. Typically such data are in the form of responses to questionnaires. In these cases the person is taking the role of observer and making ratings relevant to the self (e.g., "I am a conscientious person"). Personality questionnaires can be relevant to single personality characteristics (e.g., optimism) or can attempt to cover the entire domain of personality. Self-reports clearly have limitations. People may be unaware of some of their own psychological characteristics. They may be motivated to present themselves in a positive manner to the psychologist administering the test. However, self-report measures are convenient, in that they are relatively easy to obtain. Also, they sometimes are the only valid way to assess a psychological characteristic of interest (e.g., subjective perceptions of oneself or a stimulus). Thus, self-reports are the most commonly used source of data in personality psychology.

The LOTS categories are a useful system for keeping track of the alternative sources of data the personality psychologist may employ. You will see many examples of these different types of evidence about personality throughout the chapters of this book. However, two points must be kept in mind. First, researchers do not need to choose only one source of data for their research. Quite commonly, they combine data sources. This combination can add to one's confidence in research findings. For example, researchers who try to identify the most important dimensions of individual differences find that analyses of different data sources (S and O data) yield the same dimensions; the same five personality factors are found whether one analyzes people's reports about themselves or other people's reports about them (McCrae & Costa, 1987). Such a finding bolsters confidence in the conclusion that these dimensions are, indeed, of basic importance.

The second point is that some forms of data do not easily fit into this four-category LOTS scheme. As the field of personality psychology has progressed, new types of measurement have been developed. Thus, additional categories may be necessary to capture the diversity of data that the contemporary psychologist uses to assess personality characteristics (Cervone & Caprara, 2001). For example, some researchers employ *implicit* individual-difference measures; that is, measures designed to tap beliefs or self-evaluations of which people may not be consciously (i.e., explicitly) aware (Fazio & Olson, 2003). One popular implicit measure involves reaction-time methodology, in which researchers measure how long it takes for people to answer a question. An implicit test of self-esteem, for example, might measure how long it takes people to respond to stimuli involving the self when those stimuli are associated with positive versus negative terms (Greenwald & Banaji, 1995; Greenwald et al., 2002). Other researchers employ diary methods, which are techniques in which people are asked to report about their psychological experiences soon after their occurrence, rather than completing a questionnaire that inquires about things that have happened in the distant past (Bolger, Davis, & Rafaeli, 2003). Diary methods have a major advantage. People may forget important details of experiences that they had a week, a month, or a year previously. By asking people to report on their current experiences one or more times every day, diary methods avoid the problem of forgetting, as well as eliminate biases that may occur when people try to remember emotionally significant events that occurred far in the past.

HOW DO DATA FROM DIFFERENT SOURCES RELATE TO ONE ANOTHER?

Having introduced four categories of data, a question to ask is whether measures obtained from the different types of data agree with one another (Pervin, 1999). If a person rates herself as high on conscientiousness, will others (e.g., friends, teachers) rate her similarly? If an individual scores high on a questionnaire measure of depression, will ratings given by a professional interviewer lead to a similar score? If an individual rates himself as high on extraversion, will he score high on that trait in a laboratory-designed situation to measure that trait (e.g., participation in a group discussion)?

The seemingly simple question of whether different data sources relate to one another is more complicated than it sounds. Numerous factors influence the degree to which data sources are related. One is the question of which data sources one is talking about. Personality psychologists frequently have found that self-reports (S-data) are often discrepant from scores obtained from laboratory procedures (T-data). Self-report questionnaires tend to involve broad judgments that relate to a wide variety of situations (e.g., "I generally am pretty even-tempered") whereas experimental procedures measure personality characteristics in a very specific context. This difference often is critical, resulting in discrepancies between the two types of data.

Self-reports (S-data) and observer reports (O-data) tend to be related more closely. Personality psychologists commonly find significant levels of agreement when comparing self-ratings to observer ratings (e.g., Funder, Kolar, & Blackman, 1995; McCrae & Costa, 1987). Yet here, too, different types of research procedures can lead to different conclusions (Coyne, 1994; John & Robins, 1994a; Kenny et al., 1994; McCrae & Costa, 1990; Pervin, 1996, 1999). When the personality characteristic being rated is highly evaluative (e.g., stupid, warmhearted), self-perception biases enter the rating process, lowering agreement between self and observer ratings (John & Robins, 1993, 1994a; Robins & John, 1997). Moreover, some personality characteristics are more observable and easier to judge than others (e.g., sociability versus neuroticism), leading to greater agreement between self and observer ratings as well as to greater agreement among ratings obtained from different observers of the same person (Funder, 1989, 1993, 1995; John & Robins, 1993). Furthermore, some individuals appear to be easier to read or more "judgable" than others (Colvin, 1993). In sum, a variety of factors—including the degree to which a personality characteristic is evaluative and observable, and the degree to which the person being rated is "judgable"—affect the correspondence between data sources.

In general, the different sources of data about personality should be recognized as having their own advantages and disadvantages. Self-report questionnaires have a clear advantage: People know a lot about themselves, so if a psychologist wants to know a person, maybe the best thing to do is to ask them about themselves (Allport, 1961; Kelly, 1955). Yet, self-report methods have limits. People's descriptions of themselves on questionnaires can be influenced by irrelevant factors such as the phrasing of test items and the order in which items appear on a test (Schwarz, 1999). People also may lie or may unconsciously distort their questionnaire responses (Paulhus, Fridhandler, & Hayes, 1997), perhaps in an attempt to present themselves in a positive light. For such reasons, some researchers feel that the best measure of an individual's personality is questionnaire ratings by *others* who know the person. Yet here, too, problems may arise; different raters may sometimes rate the same person in quite different ways (Hofstee, 1994; John & Robins, 1994a; Kenny et al., 1994). As a result, some psychologists contend that the field should not rely so heavily on questionnaires—whether those questionnaires are self-reports or are reports by other people who are familiar with a given individual. Instead, objective measures of behavior and of biological systems underlying that behavior may be a more reliable source of evidence for building a science of personality (Kagan, 2003). Yet the personality psychologist is often interested in aspects of personal experience that do not have any simple behavioral or biological markers. If one wants to know about people's conscious perceptions of themselves and their beliefs about the world around them, then we're back where we started: the best thing to do is to ask them.

FIXED VERSUS FLEXIBLE MEASURES

Another way in which sources of data about personality can differ involves the question of whether measures are fixed or flexible. By "fixed," we are referring to procedures in which exactly the same measures (e.g., exactly the same test items) are administered to all the people in a psychological study, and scores for all the people are computed in exactly the same way. Such "fixed" procedures are, by far, the most commonly employed method in personality psychology. If psychologists want to know about people's characteristics, they generally give large groups of people precisely the same test items, and compute scores for everyone in a common manner. Doing so has obvious advantages. It yields a testing procedure that is objective and simple.

There are, however, two potential limitations to this fixed method of assessment. One is that some of the test items that the psychologist asks may be irrelevant to some of the individuals who are taking the test. If you have ever taken a personality questionnaire, you may have felt that some of the questions were good ones, in that they tapped into an important feature of your personality, whereas others were not good ones, in that they asked about things that are irrelevant to you. A fixed testing procedure does not differentiate between the two types of items; it simply adds up all of your responses and computes for you a total score on a test. The second limitation is that there may be features of your personality that are not on the test. You may possess some idiosyncratic psychological quality—an important past experience, a unique skill, a guiding religious or moral value, a long-term goal in life—that is not mentioned anywhere on the psychologist's test.

These limitations can, in principle, be overcome by adopting testing procedures that are more flexible, in other words, procedures that do something other than merely give all people a common set of questions. Various options are available (Cervone, Shadel, & Jencius, 2001; Cervone & Shadel, 2003). For example, one option is to give people a fixed set of test items, but to allow them to indicate which items are more or less relevant to them (Markus, 1977). Another is to give people unstructured personality tests, that is, tests in which the items allow people to describe themselves in their own words, rather than forcing them to respond to descriptions worded entirely by the experimenter. A question such as "True or false: I like going to large parties" would be a structured item, whereas the question "What activities do you enjoy on the weekends?" would be unstructured. Unstructured methods have proven to be quite valuable in assessing self-concept. These methods include asking people to list words or phrases that describe important aspects of their personality (Higgins, King, & Mavin, 1982), or to tell stories that relate their memories of important life experiences that they have had (Woike & Polo, 2001).

Personality psychologists have a technical vocabulary to describe these fixed versus flexible measures. Fixed measures that are applied in the same manner to all persons are referred to as **nomothetic**. The term comes from the Greek for "law," nomos, and refers here to the search for scientific laws that apply, in a fixed manner, to everyone. Flexible assessment techniques that are tailored to the particular individual being studies are referred to as **idiographic**. This term comes from the Greek *idios*, referring to personal, private, and distinct characteristics (as in the word "idiosyncratic"). In general, then, nomothetic techniques are ones that describe a population of persons in terms of a fixed set of personality variables, using a fixed set of items to measure them. Idiographic techniques, in contrast, have the primary goal of obtaining a portrait of the potentially unique, idiosyncratic individual. As you will see in later chapters, the personality theories differ in the degree to which they rely on fixed versus flexible, and nomothetic versus idiographic testing procedures.

PERSONALITY THEORY AND ASSESSMENT

With the options of four different sources of data, and idiographic versus nomothetic testing procedures, how is one to choose? How does one select among the options available for getting information about persons? Inevitably, choices are shaped by theoretical considerations. One's theoretical views about personality determine what one thinks about different measurement procedures. Measuring personality is not like measuring the mass of a rock. Everyone agrees that the mass of a rock can be measured in terms of pounds (or something arithmetically equivalent, like kilograms). But since different personality theories use different units of analysis, as we discussed in Chapter 1, there is no uniform agreement among personality psychologists regarding exactly what personality variables should be measured and how to measure them.

To some personality psychologists, the important thing to measure is people's typical patterns of behavior. To others, who emphasize people's skills, capabilities, and plans for the future, it may be more important to measure people's life goals—which may or may not be reflected in a person's current behavior. (You may have the goal of becoming a parent, and this goal may be important in understanding your personality, but if you are not yet a parent then this feature of your personality may not be reflected in your current day-to-day behavior.) Many personality psychologists employ nomothetic assessment procedures, because they believe that there exists a small number of psychological characteristics that we each possess in greater or lesser amounts. Other theories try to capture the idiosyncrasy of the individual, and believe that nomothetic procedures provide only a superficial depiction of the depth of an individual's character.

The relations between theory and choice of measurement will be illustrated again and again as you read the subsequent chapters of this book. For now, note that the relation between theory and research procedures underscores a theme from our first chapter. It is impossible to study personality by first collecting a lot of data, and then creating a theory. This is because one needs a theory to decide what type of data it is most valuable to collect, and how to interpret the data that one gets.

GOALS OF RESEARCH: RELIABILITY, VALIDITY, ETHICAL BEHAVIOR

No matter what question one is studying, and no matter what method one chooses, a research project cannot succeed unless its procedures possess two qualities. One's observations of personality (1) must be replicable (if the study is run twice it should turn out the same way both times); and (2) the measure must relate to the theoretical concept of interest in a given study. In the language of research, measures must be reliable and valid (West & Finch, 1997).

RELIABILITY ✱ Know ✗ ✓

The concept of **reliability** refers to the extent to which observations can be replicated. The question is whether measures are dependable, or stable. If we give people a personality measure, and then give it to them again a short time later, we expect that the measure will reveal similar personality characteristics at the two time points. If it does not, it is said to be unreliable.

Various factors may affect the reliability of a psychological test. Some involve the psychological state of the people who are being observed. People's responses may be affected by transient factors such as what their mood happens to be at the time that they are observed. For example, if a person is taking the same personality test on two different days, and responses on one day are altered by a chance event that day that puts them in a good or bad mood, then scores on the two days will differ. This resulting lack of reliability is a problem if the test is assumed to measure stable personality characteristics that are relatively uninfluenced by temporary states or moods. Other factors involve the test itself. Variations in instructions to subjects, or ambiguities in test items, can lower reliability. Carelessness in scoring a test or ambiguous rules for interpreting scores can also lead to a lack of agreement, or lack of reliability, among testers.

The notion of reliability commonly is measured in two different ways, with the different techniques providing answers to different questions about a test (West & Finch, 1997). One reliability question involves internal consistency: Do the different items on the test correlate with one another, as one would expect if each item is a reflection of a common psychological construct. The second question is one previously noted, namely, test-retest reliability: If people take the test at two different points in time, do their scores correlate with one another. The differences between the types of reliability are made plain by a simple example. Suppose one added a few intelligence test items to a test of extraversion. The test-retest reliability of measure would remain high (since people would probably have similar performance on the intelligence test items at different points in time). But the internal consistency of the test would be lowered (since responses on extraversion and intelligence test items probably would not be correlated).

VALIDITY ✱ Know ✗

In addition to being reliable, observations must be valid. The concept of **validity** refers to the extent to which observations actually reflect the phenomena of interest in a given study. The concept of validity is best illustrated by an example in which a measure is not valid: One could assess people's intelligence by measuring the size of their head, and the measure could be perfectly reliable, but it would not be valid because head size is not actually an indicator of the mental capabilities that we call "intelligence" (Gould, 1981).

If there is no evidence that a given measure is valid, then it is of little use. Suppose, for example, that we have a reliable test for the personality traits of neuroticism or extraversion, but no evidence that the tests measure what they purport to measure. Of what use are they? To constitute a useful measure, we need evidence that the test is indicative of the psychological construct of interest. The test, in other words, must have **construct validity** (Cronbach & Meehl, 1955; Ozer, 1999).

To establish that a test possesses construct validity, personality psychologists generally try to show that the test relates systematically to some external criterion, that is, to some measure that is independent of (i.e., external to) the test itself. Theoretical considerations guide the choice of an external criterion. For example, if one were to develop a test of the tendency to experience anxiety, and wanted to establish its construct validity, one would use theoretical ideas about anxiety to choose external criteria (e.g., physiological indices of anxious arousal) that the test should predict. One generally would establish validity by showing that the test correlates with the external criterion. However, in addition to correlational data, tests of validity might involve comparisons of two groups of people who are theoretically relevant to the test. A group of people who have been diagnosed by clinical psychologists as suffering from an anxiety disorder, for example, should get higher scores on the purported anxiety test than people who have not been so diagnosed; otherwise one obviously would not have a valid test of anxiety.

There are other aspects to "validity," as the term commonly is used (Ozer, 1999; West & Finch, 1997). For example, if one is proposing a new personality test, then one should be able to demonstrate that the test has "discriminant validity": it should be distinct, empirically, from other tests that already exist. If, hypothetically, one proposes a new test of "worrying tendencies" and finds that it correlates with existing tests of neuroticism, then the new test is of little value because it lacks discriminant validity.

In sum, reliability concerns the questions of whether a test provides a stable, replicable measure, and validity concerns the questions of whether a measure actually taps into the psychological construct it is supposed to be measuring. Reliability is necessary for validity. If a test is unreliable, that means that test scores are being affected by extraneous factors, which in turn implies that the scores are reflecting something other than the psychological construct of interest.

Note that questions of reliability and validity involve not only statistical issues in the analysis of tests, but theoretical issues in the test's interpretation. For example, for some psychological constructs, one might not expect measures of the construct to have high degrees of test-retest reliability. Suppose one wants to measure people's current emotional state, or mood. Since people's moods may fluctuate from day to day, it is natural that a mood measure may show low test-retest reliability. Similarly, questions of validity strongly involve conceptual considerations. Validity concerns the interpretation of a test (West & Finch, 1997). Questions that ask people about their tendencies to enjoy contemporary art, listen to classical music, and read books of philosophy may be only moderately valid if interpreted as indicators of intelligence, but may have high validity if interpreted as measures of intellectual tendencies, or openness to experience (McCrae & Costa, 1999).

THE ETHICS OF RESEARCH AND PUBLIC POLICY

As a human enterprise, research involves ethical issues. Ethical questions arise in both the conduct of research and the reporting of research results. These questions are of enduring concern to psychology's scientific community (Smith, 2003). In part, this concern reflects the impact of a number of studies in past years that brought into sharp focus some of the issues involved. For example, in one research effort that won a prize from the American Association for the Advancement of Science, subjects were told to teach other subjects ("learners") a list of paired associate words and to punish them with an electric shock when an error was made (Milgram, 1965). The issue investigated was obedience to authority. Although actual shock was not used, the subjects believed that it was being used and often administered high levels despite pleas from the learners that it was painful. In another research effort in which a prison environment was simulated, subjects adopted the roles of guards and prisoners (Zimbardo, 1973). Subject "guards" were found to be verbally and physically aggressive to subject "prisoners," who allowed themselves to be treated in a dehumanized way.

Such programs are dramatic in terms of the issues they raise, but the underlying question concerning ethical principles of research is fundamental. Do experimenters have the right to require participation? To deceive subjects? What are the ethical responsibilities of researchers to subjects and to psychology as a science? The former has been an issue of concern to the American Psychological Association, which has adopted a list of relevant ethical principles (Ethical Principles of Psychologists, 1981). The essence of these principles is that "the psychologist carries out the investigation with respect and concern for the dignity and welfare of the people who participate." This includes evaluating the ethical acceptability of the research, determining whether subjects in the study will be at risk in any way, and establishing a clear and fair agreement with research participants concerning the obligations and responsibilities of each. Although the use of concealment or deception is recognized as necessary in some cases, strict guidelines are presented. It is the investigator's responsibility to protect participants from physical and mental discomfort, harm, and danger.

The ethical responsibility of psychologists includes the interpretation and presentation of results as well as the conduct of the research. Of late there has been serious concern in science generally with "the spreading stain of fraud" (APA Monitor, 1982). Some concern with this issue began many years ago with charges that Sir Cyril Burt, a once prominent British psychologist, intentionally misrepresented data in his research on the inheritance of intelligence. Unfortunately, this problem is not entirely a thing of the past; questions about the validity of data occasionally arise in the contemporary field (Ruggiero & Marx, 2001). The issue of fraud is one that scientists do not like to recognize or talk about because it goes against the essence of the scientific enterprise. Although fraudulent data and falsified conclusions are rare, psychologists are beginning to face up to their existence and to take constructive steps to solve the problem. Aside from professional integrity, the greatest safeguard against scientific fraud is the requirement that it be possible for other investigators to replicate all findings.

Much more subtle than fraud, and undoubtedly of much broader significance, is the issue of the effects of personal and social bias on the ways in which issues are developed and the kinds of data that are accepted as evidence in support for a given enterprise (Pervin, 2003). In considering sex differences, for example, to what extent are research projects developed in a way that is free from bias? To what extent is evidence for or against the existence of sex differences equally likely to be accepted? To what extent do our own social and political values influence not only what is studied but how it is studied and the kinds of conclusions we are prepared to reach (Bramel & Friend, 1981)? As noted, although scientists make every effort to be objective and remove all possible sources of error and bias from their research, this remains a human enterprise with the potential for personal, social, cultural, and political influence.

Finally, we may note the role of research in personnel decisions and the formulation of public policy. Though still in an early stage of development as a science, psychology does relate to fundamental human concerns, and psychologists often are called on to administer tests relevant to employment or admissions decisions and to suggest the relevance of research for public policy. Personality tests often are used as part of employment, promotion, or admission to graduate programs; research findings have influenced government policy in regard to immigration policy, early enrichment programs such as Head Start, and television violence. This being the case, psychologists have a responsibility to be careful in the presentation of their findings and to inform others of the limits of their findings in regard to personnel and policy decisions.

THREE GENERAL APPROACHES TO RESEARCH

Although all personality researchers hold the goals of reliability, validity, and theory development in common, they differ in strategy concerning the best routes to these goals. In some cases, the differences in research strategies are minor, limited to the choice of one experimental procedure or test over another. In other cases, however, the differences are major and express a more fundamental difference in approach. Research in personality has tended to follow one of three directions, and we now turn to a description of these approaches, including examples of each approach taken from the contemporary scientific literature in personality psychology.

CASE STUDIES AND CLINICAL RESEARCH

One way to learn about personality is to study individual persons in great detail. Many psychologist feel that in-depth analyses of individual cases, or **case studies**, are the only way to capture the complexities of human personality. In a case study, a psychologist has extensive contact with the individual who is the target of the study, and tries to develop an understanding of the psychological structures and processes that are most important to that individual's personality. Using a term introduced earlier, case studies inherently are *idiographic* methods, in that the goal is to obtain a psychological portrait of the particular individual under study.

Case studies may be conducted purely for purposes of research. Historically, however, case studies have commonly been conducted as part of clinical treatment. Clinical psychologists, of course, must gain an understanding of the unique qualities of their clients in order to craft an intervention, so the clinical setting inherently provides case studies of personality. Case studies by clinicians have played an important role in the development of some major theories of personality. In fact, many of the theorists we will discuss in this book were trained as clinical psychologists, counseling psychologists, or psychiatrists. They initially tried to solve the problems of their patients, and then used the insights obtained in this clinical setting to develop their theories of personality.

Tactics of Research: *Case studies represent one approach to personality research.*

Case Studies: An Example

To illustrate the insights that can be gained by a systematic case study, we will consider work by the Dutch personality psychologist Hubert Hermans (2001). Hermans is interested in the fact that people's thoughts about themselves—or their self-concept—is generally multifaceted. People think of themselves as having a variety of psychological characteristics. These concepts about the self develop as individuals interact with other people. Since we each have interactions with many different people, different aspects of our self-concept might often be relevant to different situations that feature different individuals. You might see yourself as being serious and articulate when interacting with professors, fun-loving and confident when hanging out with friends, and romantic yet anxious when on a date. To understand someone's personality, then, it might be necessary to study how different aspects of the self come into play as

The challenges of social life vary so greatly that we may adapt to them by being "different selves" in different settings.

people think about their life from different viewpoints that involve individuals who play different roles in their life. Hermans (2001) refers to these different viewpoints as different "positions" one can take in viewing oneself.

This view of the self-concept raises a major challenge for most forms of research. Correlational and experimental studies generally provide a small amount of information about each of a large number of people. But to understand the complexity of self-concept as Hermans describes it requires a large amount of information about a person and the individuals and social circumstances that make up that person's life. When this level of detail about the individual is required, personality psychologists turn to the technique of case studies.

Hermans (2001) reports a case study that reveals the complexity of personality in our modern day and age, in which people from different cultures come in contact with one another much more frequently than in the past, due to the migration of individuals from one part of the world to another for purposes of education or employment. The case he reports is that of a 45-year-old man from Algeria named Ali. Although this man grew up in northern Africa, for more than 20 years Ali had been living in northern Europe; he worked for a Dutch company and married a woman from the Netherlands.

As part of this case study, Hermans employed a systematic research method that can be used in the study of a single individual. The method is one in which an individual is asked to list characteristics that describe their own attributes, as well as listing people and situations that are important to them. The individual is then asked to indicate the degree to which each personal characteristic is important, or prominent, in each of the situations. Using these ratings, Hermans provides a graphic depiction of the organization of the individual's beliefs. In the graphs, an inner circle represents personal characteristics and an outer circle represents other people and situations.

Figure 2.1 represents these psychological characteristics in the case of Ali. The graph reveals an interesting fact about Ali. He views his life as having distinct components, and he exhibits different personality characteristics in these different life settings. One component of his self-concept involved family members, on both his own side of the family and his wife's. These people tended to be very accepting of him. When he was with these people, Ali was happy and outgoing, and was willing to make sacrifices for other individuals. Yet, Ali's view of himself and his social world contained a second component. As is readily understandable for someone who has moved to a new culture that may not always be accepting of immigrants, Ali recognized that some people discriminated against him or held political views with which he disagreed. With these people, he felt vulnerable and disillusioned. Interestingly, he also felt this way with his sister, who both he and his wife viewed as "the witch of the family" (Hermans, 2001, p. 359). The detailed information provided by this case study, then, provides insight into the textures of this individual's life that is generally unavailable through other research methods.

Case Studies: Limitations

The benefits of case studies such as this one are clear. They can capture much of the complexity in an individual's personality, as it manifests itself in the unique circumstances of the person's life. However, case studies have two significant drawbacks.

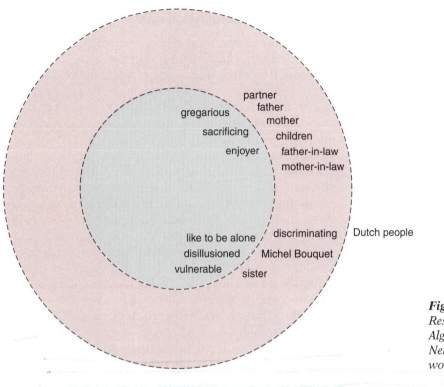

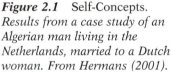

Figure 2.1 Self-Concepts.
Results from a case study of an Algerian man living in the Netherlands, married to a Dutch woman. From Hermans (2001).

The first is that, after one obtains a case study portrait of an individual, there is no way of knowing if the things one has learned about that individual apply to individuals in general. One cannot determine if the case study findings are representative of the population at large. For example, although Ali seemed to have different experiences with people who did accept him in the new culture versus those who did not, the findings of this case study do not enable one to determine how common such experiences are among people in general.

The second limitation involves the task of identifying causes. In personality science, as in any science, researchers hope to identify the causes of the phenomena they study. They wish not only to describe a person, but to explain how an individual's personality develops and how personality characteristics and life events causally influence one another. A case study may provide a wonderful description, but it generally cannot provide a definite causal explanation. For example, imagine a clinical case study that describes changes in an individual's psychological well-being that occur over the course of a year-long clinical treatment. The case study may describe the changes with great accuracy. But it cannot enable one to conclude, definitively, that the treatment caused the changes. Other events in the person's life may have had causal influence. The person may have improved simply as a result of personal maturity that was gained over the course of a year's time; the person may have improved, then, even if there had been no treatment.

The desire to study larger samples of persons and to establish the causal influence among variables motivate researchers to pursue the following two approaches to research: personality questionnaires and correlational research.

∠∙ PERSONALITY QUESTIONNAIRES AND CORRELATIONAL RESEARCH

Personality tests and questionnaires are used where the intensive study of individuals is not possible or desirable, and where it is not possible to conduct laboratory experiments. Beyond this, the advantage of personality questionnaires is that a great deal of information can be gathered on many people at one time. Although no one individual is studied as intensively as with the case study approach, the investigator can study many different personality characteristics in relation to many different research participants.

The use of personality tests and questionnaires has tended to be associated with an interest in the study of individual differences. Many personality psychologists believe that the critical first step in understanding human nature is to chart the differences among people. Personality questionnaires often are designed to measure these individual differences. For example, personality psychologists might have an interest in using questionnaires to measure individual differences in anxiety, self-consciousness, friendliness, the tendency to take risks, or other psychological qualities.

In addition to measuring these personality variables, the psychologist generally wishes to know how they go together. Are anxious people more friendly than less anxious people? Or less friendly? Do self-conscious people take fewer risks? Are risk-taking people friendlier? Such questions are addressed in **correlational research**. This term comes from the statistic used to gauge the degree to which two variables go together: the **correlation coefficient**. A correlation coefficient is a number that reflects the degree to which two measures are linearly related. If people who have higher scores on one variable tend also to have higher scores on the other one, then the variables are said to be *positively* correlated. (Anxiety and self-consciousness would tend to be correlated in this way.) If people who have higher scores on one variable tend to have *lower* scores on the other one, then the variables are said to be *negatively* correlated. (Anxiety and self-confidence might be correlated this way, since people who express low self-confidence are likely to report being relatively more

Tactics of Research: *Personality questionnaires are used to obtain a great deal of information about many subjects.*

anxious.) Finally, if two variables do not go together in any systematic linear manner, they are said to be uncorrelated. (Anxiety and friendliness may be uncorrelated, since both anxious and non-anxious people may be either friendly or unfriendly.) The correlation coefficient is computed in such a way that a perfect positive correlation—this is, a correlation in which the point falls exactly on a single line—is a correlation of 1.0. A perfect negative correlation is one of –1.0. A correlation of zero indicates that there is no linear relation between two measures.

Note that the term "correlational research" refers to a research *strategy*, not merely to a particular statistical measure (the correlation). The strategy is one in which researchers examine the relation among variables in a large population of people, where none of the variables is experimentally manipulated. In some circumstances, researchers may not compute a simple correlation coefficient to examine the relation between two variables; they may, for instance, use more complex statistical procedures that determine whether two variables are related, even after controlling for the influence of some other variables. (For example, one might ask whether intelligence test scores are related to personal income after controlling for other variables, such as the income level of one's parents.) Even if such alternative approaches to analyzing data are used, one would still have a correlational research strategy if one is looking at the relation among variables without manipulating these variables experimentally.

Correlational Research: An Example

A compelling example of the power of correlational research to answer questions that cannot be answered through any other technique is found in a study relating personality characteristics to longevity (Danner, Snowdon, & Friesen, 2001). The question being asked in this research is whether the tendency to experience positive emotions is related to how long people live. Prior work had established that people's emotional life can influence their physical well-being. For example, emotions are associated with activation of the autonomic nervous system (ANS); ANS activity, in turn, influences the cardiovascular system (Krantz & Manuck, 1984), which is critical to health. The implication of this prior work is that if one could identify people who differ in their tendencies to experience positive and negative emotions, and could follow these people for a long enough period of time, one might find that people who tended to experience high degrees of positive emotion will live longer. Note that this is a question that can *only* be answered through correlational research. A case study is not convincing because, even if one does identify a case in which someone experiences a lot of positive emotions and lives for many years, it is impossible to know if the single case is typical of people in general. An experimental study is impossible, both because one cannot easily manipulate people's general tendency to experience emotional states and because it would be unethical to manipulate a variable that might lower people's length of life.

Correlational research on this topic could be conducted thanks to a project known as the "nun study" (Danner et al., 2001). This is a study of a large number of Catholic nuns living in the United States. The nuns in the study were all born before the year 1917. In 1930, they had been asked by an administrative official of the Catholic church to write an autobiography. The researchers, with the permission of the nuns, read these autobiographies and coded them

Research indicates that individuals who experience a relatively high level of positive emotions tend to live longer.

according to the amount of positive emotions expressed in the writing. Some autobiographies contained relatively little positive emotional content (e.g., "I intend to do the best for our order, for the spread of religion and for my personal sanctification"), whereas others indicated that the writer experienced high degrees of positive emotion ("the past year . . . has been a very happy one. Now I look forward with eager joy . . ."; Danner et al., 2001, p. 806).

During the 1990s and the year 2000, approximately 40% of the nuns, who at the time ranged in age from 75 to 95 years, died. The researchers could relate the experience of positive emotions, as indicated in the biographies of 1930, to length of life at the end of the century.

This study revealed a strikingly large relation between emotional experience and length of life. Nuns who experienced more positive emotions in the 1930s lived longer. The relation between emotional experience and longevity can be represented by counting the number of positive emotion words that were used in the autobiographies and dividing the population into quartiles (i.e., four groupings, each representing approximately one-fourth of the population) ranging from low to high amounts of emotion words (Table 2.1). Of the nuns who had expressed a high amount of positive emotions, only about one-fifth died during the observation period. Of the nuns who expressed low amounts of positive emotion, more than half died! This is true even though the high and low groups were of the same age at the beginning of the observation period.

Correlational Research: Limitations

Correlational studies have been enormously popular among personality psychologists. Yet it is important to be aware of two limitations of this research strategy. The first limitation is one that differentiates correlational studies

Table 2.1   Relation between Expression of Positive Emotions in Writing as Measured Early in Life and Longevity

Positive Emotion Words	Age	Died (%)
Quartile I (low)	79.9	55
Quartile II	81.1	59
Quartile III	79.7	33
Quartile IV (high)	79.0	21

SOURCE: Danner, D. D., Snowdon, D. A., & Friesen, W. V. (2001). Positive emotions in early life and longevity: Findings from the nun study. *Journal of Personality & Social Psychology, 80,* 804–813.

from case studies. Case studies provide richly detailed information about an individual. In contrast, correlational studies provide relatively superficial information about individual persons. A correlational study will provide information about an individual's scores on the various personality tests that happen to have been used in the research. But if there are some other variables that are important to an individual person, a correlational study generally will not reveal them.

The second limitation is one that case studies and correlational studies share. As in a case study, in a correlational study is it difficult to draw firm conclusions about causality. The fact that two variables are correlated does not mean that one variable necessarily caused the other. There could be a "third variable" that influenced both of the variables in one's study and that caused those variables to be correlated. For example, in the nun study, it is possible that some psychological, biological, or environmental factor that was not measured in the study caused some nuns to experience fewer positive emotions *and* to live less long. As a hypothetical example, if one conducted a study akin to the nun study with college students, one might find that positive emotionality would predict longevity. But that would not necessarily mean that the tendency to experience positive emotions during college caused people to live longer. For example, levels of academic success could function as a third variable. Students who are doing extremely well in college might experience more positive emotions as a result of their academic success. They also might obtain more lucrative jobs after graduation, again as a result of their academic success. Their high-paying jobs might enable them to pay for superior health care, which in turn could lengthen their life whether or not they continue to experience frequent position emotions. In this hypothetical example, emotions and length of life would be correlated, but not because of any direct causal connection between the two. The difficulty of drawing conclusions about causality from either case studies or correlational studies leads investigators to pursue a third approach to research, namely, laboratory experiments.

3 LABORATORY STUDIES AND EXPERIMENTAL RESEARCH

One of the great achievements of science is not a research finding but a research method: the controlled experiment. The key feature of a controlled experiment is that participants are assigned at *random* to an experimental condition. The overall experiment contains a number of different conditions

CURRENT APPLICATIONS

PERSONALITY AND HEALTH

As is evident from the "nun study" reviewed in the text, a major area of application for contemporary personality psychology is that of health. Investigators try to discover individual differences in personality qualities that are systematically related to health outcomes.

A particularly informative example of this research trend comes from recent work by a research team from Finland and the United States (Räikkönon, Matthews, & Salomon, 2003). The health outcome of interest to them was cardiovascular disease. As these authors review, the biological factors that put people at risk for cardiovascular problems are already well known. A cluster of factors including obesity, high blood pressure, abnormal levels of lipids (blood fats) in the bloodstream, and insulin resistance (a reduced sensitivity to the action of insulin) puts people at risk for heart problems. Also, it is known that the presence of this cluster of health problems—referred to as "metabolic syndrome"—tends to persist from childhood to adulthood; people who suffer from obesity and insulin resistance as children are likely to suffer from these same problems when they are adults.

It is important, then, to determine the causes of metabolic syndrome. The question the researchers asked is whether personality factors in childhood might predict the development of these biological risk factors.

The personality factor that they chose to study was hostility. This decision was based on prior research. Earlier work had demonstrated a relation, among adults, between cardiovascular problems and tendencies to react to life events with hostility and anger. The authors thus predicted that individual differences in hostility in children would predict the development of aspects of metabolic syndrome.

Note that this is a difficult prediction to test. The idea is not merely that hostility and cardiovascular risk factors will go together, or be correlated. The specific hypothesis is that hostility will *predict* the development of risk factors. Children who experience high amounts of hostility at one point in time are predicted to experience relatively *higher* levels of hostility at a later point in time. Testing this idea requires a longitudinal research design, that is, a research project in which the relevant variables are assessed at different time points.

The authors executed such a research project. They studied a large group of African-American and European-American children and adolescents. Assessments were conducted twice, at time points separated by an average of more than three years. At both time points, the researchers examined children with high versus low amounts of the cardiovascular risk factors, and asked whether these children differed in their levels of hostility.

At time 1 (i.e., the first assessment session), children with high versus low cardiovascular risk factors did not yet differ in hostility. A different way of saying this is that, at time 1, there existed a group of children who varied from one another in their tendency to experience hostility, but who did not yet differ in cardiovascular risk factors. The question, then, is: What would happen three years? Over the subsequent three years of time, would children who were more hostile gradually develop the health problems that put people at risk for heart disease?

The researchers found that, as they had expected, hostility predicted the development of cardiovascular risk factors. The graph (Figure 2.2) displays the results for two factors: obesity (measured by body mass index) and insulin resistance. The vertical axis plots levels of hostility, which were assessed by means of an interview; a trained interviewer

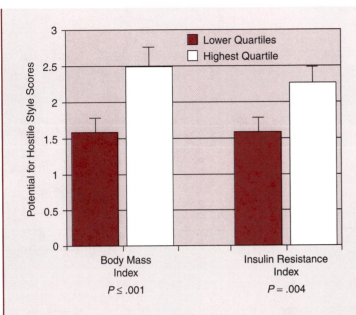

Figure 2.2　*The figure relates individual differences in hostility to the presence of biological factors that are known to put people at risk for cardiovascular problems. People with higher levels of two risk factors, involving body mass (left) and insulin resistance (right), were found to exhibit higher levels of hostility. From Räikkönon, Matthews, & Salomon (2003).*

asked the research participants a series of questions designed to reveal individual differences in their potential to react to situations with a hostile, competitive style of response. Children who developed the two features of the metabolic syndrome by time 2 were found to have differed in hostility at time 1. More hostile children, then, were more likely to develop the cardiovascular risk factors.

Further research is required to determine exactly what explains the link from hostility to health problems. As the authors explain, one possibility is that the development and maturation of biological systems (e.g., growth hormones) is responsible for both hostility and health problems. However,

another possibility is that more hostile children are more likely to engage in behaviors that, in turn, create health risks. Hostility may be related to unhealthy lifestyles (smoking, alcohol use, reduced physical activity), and these lifestyles may contribute to the development of health problems. This latter possibility is particularly interesting because it raises the possibility that psychological interventions might have long-term health benefits. Interventions that teach children to control their tendencies to react to the world in a hostile manner may promote better lifestyles and superior health.

SOURCE: Räikkönon, Matthews, & Salomon (2003).

that manipulate one or more variables of interest. If people in one condition respond differently than people in another, then one can conclude that the variable that was manipulated causally influenced their responses. This conclusion is valid precisely because people are assigned to conditions randomly. Random assignment assures that there is no systematic relationship between the experimental conditions and people's pre-experimental psychological tendencies. If people in different conditions act differently after the experimental manipulation, despite being the same before it occurred, then the manipulation was the cause of the differences in response. This research strategy, in which variables are manipulated through the random assignment of persons to different conditions, is the hallmark of **experimental research**.

One technique for learning about personality is laboratory research. Participants take part in activities in controlled laboratory settings that are designed to identify the ways that specific personality processes contribute to emotion, thinking processes, and performance.

Experimental Research: An Example

A powerful example of experimental research comes from work by Claude Steele (1997) and colleagues, who have investigated a phenomenon known as "stereotype threat." Work on stereotype threat explores circumstances in which people are trying to perform well in front of others (e.g., they are taking an exam and other people, such as the course instructor, will know how well they have performed). In such situations, there sometimes exist negative stereotypes concerning the performance of particular social groups. For example, according to some stereotypes, women may not be as good at math as men, or people of different ethnic backgrounds might be thought to be more or less intelligent. If an individual is a member of a group for which there is a stereotype, and if the individual thinks of the stereotype, then a psychological threat arises. There is a threat in the individual's mind that he or she might confirm the stereotype. In many circumstances, this stereotype threat may interfere with one's performance. For example, if you are taking a difficult exam and become distracted by thoughts that you might confirm a stereotype associated with a group of which you are a member, then this distraction might, like any distraction, cause you to perform less well.

In principle, one could study stereotype threat processes through case studies or correlational studies. However, as we have noted, these approaches would not provide convincing evidence that stereotype threat causally influences performance. To explore this potential causal influence, Steele and colleagues have studied stereotype threat experimentally (Steele, 1997). For example, they have examined the performance of African-American and European-American college students on verbal test items of the sort that might be included on an intelligence test; a negative stereotype about intelligence is one of various stereotypes about African Americans that persist in U.S. culture. The experiment featured two conditions. In one, all participants first completed a demographic questionnaire in which they were asked to indicate their race. In the other, the demographic questionnaire was omitted. Black and white students were assigned at random to one or the other condi-

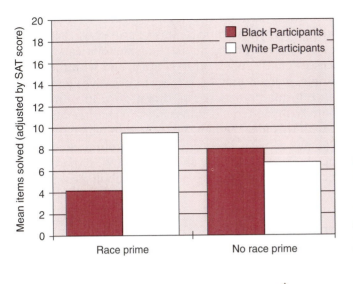

Figure 2.3 *Mean performance on a difficult verbal test, by Black and White research participants, in each of two experimental conditions. The condition varied in whether participants were (Race prime condition) or were not (No race prime condition) asked to indicate their race prior to taking the test. From Steele, 1997.*

tion. The results of the study revealed that completing the demographic questionnaire lowered the subsequent test performance of black students (Figure 2.3)—stereotype-threat processes caused them to perform less well than whites. Although we review this study for the purpose of illustrating the experimental method, one, of course, should also note its social implications. By asking about racial background on demographic questionnaires, one may inadvertently produce differences in intelligence test scores. Thus, if a group of black students were to obtain lower intelligence test scores than white stu-

Research indicates that if there exists a negative social stereotype about a group, then individual members of that group may perform less well on a test because of stereotype threat processes that interfere with their performance. This can occur even when the individuals are of high intelligence and ability.

dents, this would not necessarily mean that they possess less intelligence; instead, they could be suffering from stereotype-threat processes that cause the test scores to underestimate their actual intellectual capabilities.

Stereotype-threat processes can occur in other settings and with members of other groups. For example, women may be subject to negative stereotypes with regard to performance in mathematics. The threat of confirming these stereotypes may contribute to male-female differences in mathematics test performance. Consistent with this idea, gender differences in which men outperform women in mathematics have been shown to be eliminated when stereotype threat is reduced (Spencer, Steele, & Quinn, 1999). Experimental research on stereotype threat thus illuminates a general psychological process that contributes to important life outcomes.

EVALUATING ALTERNATIVE RESEARCH APPROACHES

Having now reviewed the three major research strategies, we are in a position to evaluate them in detail. As we already have noted, each has strengths and limitations (Table 2.2).

Case Studies and Clinical Research: Strengths and Limitations

A major advantage of case studies, particularly as they are conducted in clinical settings, is that they overcome the potential superficiality and artificiality of correlational and experimental methods. In a case study, the investigator learns about deeply important aspects of an individual's life, which may not occur in a brief experiment or a survey questionnaire. Clinicians conducting

Table 2.2   Summary of Potential Strengths and Limitations of Alternative Research Methods

Potential Strengths	*Potential Limitations*
CASE STUDIES AND CLINICAL RESEARCH	
1. Avoid the artificiality of laboratory.	1. Lead to unsystematic observation.
2. Study the full complexity of person–environment relationships.	2. Encourage subjective interpretation of data.
3. Lead to in-depth study of individuals.	3. Entangled relationships among variables.
LABORATORY STUDIES AND EXPERIMENTAL RESEARCH	
1. Manipulates specific variables.	1. Excludes phenomena that cannot be studied in the laboratory.
2. Records data objectively.	2. Creates an artificial setting that limits the generality of findings.
3. Establishes cause–effect relationships.	3. Fosters demand characteristics and experimenter expectancy effects.
QUESTIONNAIRES AND CORRELATION RESEARCH	
1. Study a wide range of variables.	1. Establish relationships that are associational rather than causal.
2. Study relationships among many variables.	2. Problems of reliability and validity of self-report questionnaires.
3. Large samples easily obtained.	3. Individuals not studied in depth.

case studies directly observe how the client thinks and feels about events. One examines the behavior of interest directly and does not have to extrapolate from a somewhat artificial setting to the real world.

A further advantage is that clinical research may be the only feasible way of studying some phenomena. When one needs to study the full complexity of personality processes, individual-environment relationships, and the within-person organization of personality, in-depth case studies may be the only option.

In-depth study of a few individuals has two main features that stand in contrast with research on groups (Pervin, 1983). First, relationships established for a group as a whole may not reflect the way any individual behaves or the way some subgroups of individuals behave. An average learning curve, for example, may not reflect the way any one individual learns. Second, by considering only group data, one may miss some valuable insights into processes going on in particular individuals. Some time ago, Henry Murray argued for the use of individual as well as group studies as follows: "In lay words, the subjects who gave the majority response may have done so for different reasons. Furthermore, a statistical answer leaves unexplained the uncommon (exhibited-by-the-minority) response. One can only ignore it as an unhappy exception to the rule. Averages obliterate the 'individual characters of individual organisms' and so fail to reveal the complex interaction of forces which determine each concrete event" (1938, p. viii). At the same time, such research may involve subjective impressions on the part of researchers, resulting in different observations by each investigator. Insofar as researchers make observations on a subjective basis, they accumulate data that decline considerably in reliability and validity.

Regarding limitations of the case study method, we already have noted two: findings of one case study may not generalize to other people, and the case study method does not provide firm evidence that one psychological process causally influences another. There is a third limitation. Case studies often rely on the subjective impressions of researchers. Rather than relying exclusively on objective measurement procedures, one often must rely on impressionistic reports—for example, impressions of a client's progress written by his or her clinician. The problem is that these reports may reflect not only the qualities of the person being studied, but the qualities of the person who prepares the report. In a typical case study, there is no guarantee that a different researcher examining the same case would come to the same conclusions. This subjective element can lower the reliability and validity of case-study evidence.

Correlational Research and Questionnaires: Strengths and Limitations

As previously noted, a main advantage of correlational studies using questionnaires is that it is possible to study large numbers of people. This has always been an advantage of the correlational strategy; however, in the era of the Internet, it is an even bigger advantage since psychologists can put questionnaires on the Internet and thereby gather information from populations that are dramatically larger and more diverse than was typically previously available.

Another advantage of the correlational approach concerns reliability. Many questionnaires provide extremely reliable indices of the psychological constructs they are designed to measure (Epstein, 1979). This is important in that the reliability of the tests is necessary to detect important features of personality that might be overlooked if one employed measures lacking reliability. For example, researchers find that individual differences in personality traits are highly stable over time; people who differ in extraversion or conscientiousness in young adulthood will probably differ in middle- and later-adulthood as well (e.g., Costa & McCrae, 2002). One could not detect this fact unless the measures of the personality traits were highly reliable.

Regarding limitations, we have noted that correlational studies provide weaker evidence of causal relationship than do experimental studies and that they provide more superficial information about individuals than one generally acquires from a case study. A third limitation concerns the widespread reliance on self-report questionnaires. When describing themselves on a questionnaire, people may be biased to answer items in a way that has nothing to do with the exact content of the items or the psychological construct that the psychologist is trying to assess. These biases are called **response styles**. Two illustrative response-style problems can be considered. The first is called acquiescence. It involves the tendency to agree consistently (or disagree consistently) with items regardless of their content. For example, a test taker may prefer to say "yes" or " I agree" when asked questions, rather than saying " no" or "I disagree." The second response style is called social desirability. Instead of responding to the intended psychological meaning of a test item, a subject may respond to the fact that different types of responses are more or less desirable. If, hypothetically, a test item asks "Have you ever stolen anything from a store?", the answer "no" is clearly a more socially desirable response than "yes. people are biased to answer questions in a socially desirable manner, then their test scores may not accurately reflect their true psychological characteristics.

A research report that highlights the problem of distortion of questionnaire responses, while also emphasizing the potential value of clinical judgment, is that of Shedler, Mayman, & Manis (1993). In this research, conducted by psychologists with a psychoanalytic orientation who were skeptical of accepting self-report data at face value, individuals who "looked good" on mental health questionnaire scales were evaluated by a psychodynamically oriented clinician. On the basis of his clinical judgments, two subgroups were distinguished: one defined as being genuinely psychologically healthy in agreement with the questionnaire scales and a second defined as consisting of individuals who were psychologically distressed but who maintained an illusion of mental health through defensive denial of their difficulties. Individuals in the two groups were found to differ significantly in their responses to stress. Subjects in the illusory mental health group were found to show much higher levels of coronary reactivity to stress than subjects in the genuinely healthy group. Indeed, the former subjects were found to show even greater levels of coronary reactivity to stress than subjects who reported their distress on the mental health questionnaire scales. The differences in reactivity to stress between the genuinely healthy subjects and the "illusory" healthy subjects were considered not only to be statistically significant but medically significant as well. Thus, it was concluded that "for some people, mental health scales appear to be legitimate measures of mental health. For other people, these scales appear to measure defensive denial. There seems to be no way to know from the test score alone what is being measured in any given respondent" (Shedler et al., 1993, p. 1128).

Those who defend the use of questionnaires note that such problems often can be eliminated through careful test construction and interpretation. Psychologists can reduce or eliminate the effects of acquiescence by varying the wording of items on a test so that consistent "yes" responses do not give one a higher overall test score. They can employ questionnaires that are specifically designed to measure the degree to which a given person tends to endorse socially desirable responses. Comprehensive personality questionnaires commonly include test items or scales to measure whether subjects are faking or trying to present themselves in a particularly favorable or socially desirable way. Including such scales in a research project, however, often is inconvenient or costly, and thus, they often are lacking in particular studies.

Laboratory, Experimental Research: Strengths and Limitations

In many ways, our ideal image of scientific investigation is laboratory research. Ask someone for their description of a scientist, and they are likely to conjure up an image of someone in a sterile lab. As we have already seen, this image is too limited; personality psychologists employ a range of scientific methods, and laboratory research is but one of them. Yet it is an important one. The experimental approach, as we have noted, has the unique ability to manipulate variables of interest and thereby to establish cause-effect relationships. In the experiment that is properly designed and carried out, every step is carefully planned to limit effects to the variables of interest. Few variables are studied, so that the problem of disentangling complex relationships does not exist. Systematic relationships between changes in some variables and consequences for other variables are established so that the experimenter can say: "If X, then Y." Full details of the experimental procedure are reported so that the results can be replicated by investigators in other laboratories.

Psychologists who are critical of laboratory research suggest that too often such research is artificial and limited in relevance to other contexts. The suggestion is that what works in the laboratory may not work elsewhere. Furthermore, although relationships between isolated variables may be established, such relationships may not hold when the complexity of actual human behavior is considered. Also, since laboratory research tends to involve relatively brief exposures to stimuli, such research may miss important processes that occur over time. As you read about personality research in the subsequent chapters of this book, a question to ask yourself is how successful the different theories are in establishing experimental findings that generalize to real-world situations.

As a human enterprise, experimental research with humans lends itself to influences that are part of everyday interpersonal behavior. The investigation of such influences might be called the social psychology of research. Let us consider two important illustrations. First, there may be factors influencing the behavior of human subjects that are not part of the experimental design. Among such factors may be cues implicit in the experimental setting that suggest to the subject that the experimenter has a certain hypothesis and, "in the interest of science," the subject behaves in a way that will confirm it. Such effects are known as **demand characteristics** and suggest that the psychological experiment is a form of social interaction in which subjects give purpose and meaning to things (Orne, 1962; Weber & Cook, 1972). The purpose and meaning given to the research may vary from subject to subject in ways that are not part of the experimental design and thereby serve to reduce both reliability and validity.

Complementing these sources of error or bias in the subject are unintended sources of influence or error in the experimenter. Without realizing it, experimenters may either make errors in recording and analyzing data or emit cues to the subjects and thus influence their behavior in a particular way. Such unintended **experimenter expectancy effects** may lead subjects to behave in accordance with the hypothesis (Rosenthal, 1994; Rosenthal & Rubin, 1978). For example, consider the classic case of Clever Hans (Pfungst, 1911). Hans was a horse that by tapping his foot could add, subtract, multiply, and divide. A mathematical problem would be presented to the horse and, incredibly, he was able to come up with the answer. In attempting to discover the secret of Hans's talents, a variety of situational factors were manipulated. If Hans could not see the questioner or if the questioner did not know the answer, Hans was unable to provide the correct answer. On the other hand, if the questioner knew the answer and was visible, Hans could tap out the answer with his foot. Apparently the questioner unknowingly signaled Hans when to start and stop tapping his hoof: The tapping would start when the questioner inclined his head forward, increase in speed when the questioner bent forward more, and stop when the questioner straightened up. As can be seen, experimenter expectancy effects can be quite subtle and neither the researcher nor subject may be aware of their existence.

It should be noted that demand characteristics and expectancy effects can occur as sources of error in all three forms of research. However, they have been considered and studied most often in relation to experimental research. In addition, as noted, experimental research often is seen as most closely approximating the scientific ideal. Therefore, such sources of error are all the more noteworthy in relation to this form of research.

Many of the criticisms of experimental research have been attacked by experimental psychologists. In defending laboratory experiments, the following statements are made: (1) Such research is the proper basis for testing causal hypotheses. The generality of the established relationship is then a subject for further investigation. (2) Some phenomena would never be discovered outside of the laboratory. (3) Some phenomena can be studied in the laboratory that would be difficult to study elsewhere (e.g., subjects are given permission to be aggressive in contrast with the often quite strong restraints in natural social settings). (4) There is little empirical support for the contention that subjects typically try to confirm the experimenter's hypothesis or for the significance of experimental artifacts more generally. Indeed, many subjects are more negativistic than conforming (Berkowitz & Donnerstein, 1982).

Even if one accepts these four points, there remains one criticism of laboratory research that is difficult, if not impossible, to overcome. It is that some phenomena simply cannot be produced in the laboratory. A personality theory may make predictions about people's emotional reactions to extreme levels of stress or their thoughts about highly personal matters. For such questions, laboratory methods may not work. It would be unethical to create extremely high levels of stress in the lab. In a brief laboratory encounter, people are unlikely to reveal any thoughts about matters that are highly personal. The personality scientist sometimes is not afforded the luxury of the simple laboratory study.

SUMMARY OF STRENGTHS AND LIMITATIONS

In assessing these alternative approaches to research we must recognize that we are considering potential, rather than necessary, strengths and limitations (Table 2.2). In fact, findings from one approach generally coincide with those from another approach (Anderson, Lindsay, & Bushman, 1999). What it comes down to is that each research effort must be evaluated on its own merits and for its own potential in advancing understanding rather than on some preconceived basis. Alternative research procedures can be used in conjunction with one another in any research enterprise. In addition, data from alternative research procedures can be integrated in the pursuit of a more comprehensive theory.

THE USE OF VERBAL REPORTS

All three forms of research—case studies, correlational studies, and laboratory experiments—commonly make use of verbal reports, that is, things people say about their psychological states. Research does not necessarily have to use verbal reports. For example, if one wants to know people's emotional reactions, one could code their facial expressions or physiological responses rather than asking them to report, verbally, the emotions they are feeling. Nonetheless, a very large percentage of research on personality relies on verbal report data.

In making use of verbal reports, we are confronted with special problems associated with such data. Treating what people say as accurate reflections of what has actually occurred or is actually going on has come under attack from two very different groups. First, psychoanalysts and dynamically oriented psychologists (Chapters 3 and 4) argue that people often distort things for unconscious reasons: "Children perceive inaccurately, are very little conscious of their inner states and retain fallacious recollections of occurrences. Many adults are hardly better" (Murray, 1938, p. 15). Second, many experimental psychologists argue that people do not have access to their internal processes and respond to interviewer questions in terms of some inferences they make about what must have been going on rather than accurately reporting what actually occurred (Nisbett & Wilson, 1977; Wilson, Hull, & Johnson, 1981). For example, despite experimenter evidence that subjects make decisions in accord with certain experimental manipulations, the subjects themselves may report having behaved in a particular way for very different reasons. Or, to take another example, when consumers are asked about why they purchased a product in a supermarket they may give a reason that is very different from what can experimentally be demonstrated to have been the case. In a sense, people give subjective reasons for behaving as they do, but may not give the actual causes. In sum, the argument is that whether for defensive reasons or because of "normal" problems people have in keeping track of their internal processes, verbal self-reports are questionable sources of reliable and valid data (West & Finch, 1997; Wilson, 1994).

Other psychologists argue that verbal reports should be accepted for what they are—data (Ericsson & Simon, 1993). The argument is made that there is no intrinsic reason to treat verbal reports as any less useful data than an overt motor response such as pressing a lever. Indeed, it is possible to analyze the verbal responses of people in as objective, systematic, and quantitative fashion as their other behavioral responses. If verbal responses are not automatically discounted, then the question becomes: Which kinds of verbal responses are most useful and trustworthy? Here the argument is made that subjects can only report about things they are attending to or have attended to. If the experimenter asks the subject to remember or explain things that were never attended to in the first place, the subject will either make an inference or state a hypothesis about what occurred (White, 1980). Thus, if you later ask persons why they purchased one product over another in the supermarket when they were not attending to this decision at the time, they will give you an inference or a hypothesis rather than an account of what occurred.

Those who argue in favor of the use of verbal reports suggest that when they are elicited with care and the circumstances involved are appreciated, they can be a useful source of information. Although the term *introspection* (i.e., verbal descriptions of a process going on inside a person) was discredited long ago by experimental psychologists, there is now increased interest in the potential use of such data. In accepting the potential use of verbal reports, we may expand the universe of potential data for rich and meaningful observation. At the same time, we must keep in mind the goals and requirements of reliability and validity. Thus, we must insist on evidence that the same observations and interpretations can be made by other investigators and that the data do reflect the concepts they are presumed to measure. In appreciating the merits and vast potential of verbal reports, we must also be aware of the potential for misuse and naive interpretation. In sum, verbal reports as data should receive the same scrutiny as other research observations.

PERSONALITY THEORY AND PERSONALITY RESEARCH

In Chapter 1, we considered the nature of personality theory: psychologists' efforts to systematize what is known about personality and to point research in directions that yield new knowledge. In this chapter, we have considered the nature of personality research: psychologists' efforts to bring objective scientific evidence to bear on their theories. We reviewed the kinds of data obtained by personality psychologists, and then the strengths and limits of three traditional types of personality research (case studies, correlational research, and laboratory experiments).

As we already have noted, personality theory and personality research are not two separate, unrelated enterprises. They are inherently intertwined. Theory and research are related for two reasons, one of which we already have noted: Theoretical conceptions suggest avenues for exploration and specify the types of data that qualify as "evidence" about personality. Personality researchers are interested in a person's physiological reactions and are uninterested in their astrological signs because personality theories contain ideas that relate physiology to psychological functioning, while leaving no room for the influence of astrological forces.

Theory and research tend to be related in another way. Theorists have preferences and biases concerning how research should be conducted. The father of American behaviorism, John B. Watson, emphasized the use of animals in research in part because of his discomfort in working with humans. Sigmund Freud, founder of psychoanalytic theory, was a therapist who did not believe that important psychoanalytic phenomena could be studied in any manner other than in therapy. Hans Eysenck and Raymond Cattell, two trait theorists of historic importance, were trained, early in their careers, in sophisticated statistical methods involving correlation, and these methods fundamentally shaped their theoretical ideas. Historically, personality researchers have tended to fall on one or the other side of three issues associated with the three approaches to research: (1) "making things happen" in research (experimental) versus "studying what has occurred" (correlational); (2) all persons (experimental) versus the single individual (clinical); and (3) one aspect or few aspects of the person versus the total individual. In other words, there are preferences or biases toward clinical, experimental, and correlational research. Despite the objectivity of science, research is a human enterprise and such preferences are part of research as a human enterprise. All researchers attempt to be as objective as possible in the conduct of their research and generally they give "objective" reasons for following a particular approach to research. That is, the particular strengths of the research approach followed are emphasized relative to the strengths and limitations of alternative approaches. Beyond this, however, a personal element enters in. Just as psychologists feel more comfortable with one or another kind of data, they feel more comfortable with one or another approach to research.

Further, different theories of personality are linked with different research strategies and thereby with different kinds of data. In other words, the links among theory, data, and research are such that the observations associated with one theory of personality often are of a fundamentally different type than those associated with another theory. The phenomena of interest to one theory of personality are not as easily studied by the research procedures useful in the study of phenomena emphasized by another theory of personality. One personality theory leads us to obtain one kind of data and follow one approach to research whereas another theory leads us to collect different kinds of data and follow another approach to research. It is not that one or another is better but rather that they are different, and these differences must be appreciated in considering each approach to theory and research. This has been true historically, and remains true in the current scientific discipline (Cervone, 1991). Since the remaining chapters in this text are organized around the major theoretical approaches to personality, it is important to keep such linkages and differences in mind in comparing one theory with another.

As we have seen, personality research involves the effort to measure individuals on a personality characteristic assumed to be of theoretical importance. The term *assessment* generally is used to refer to efforts to measure personality aspects of individuals in order to make an applied or practical decision: Will this person be a good candidate for this job? Will this person profit from one or another kind of treatment? Is this person a good candidate for this training program? In addition, the term assessment often is used to refer to

PERSONALITY ASSESSMENT AND THE CASE OF JIM

the effort to arrive at a comprehensive understanding of individuals by obtaining a wide variety of information about them. In this sense, assessment of a person involves administering a variety of personality tests or measures in the pursuit of a comprehensive understanding of their personality. As noted, such an effort also provides for a comparison of results from different sources of information. This book assumes that each technique of assessment gives a glimpse of human behavior, and that no one test gives, or can hope to give, a picture of the total personality of an individual. People are complex, and our efforts to assess personality must reflect this complexity. In the chapters that follow, we will consider a number of theories of personality and approaches to personality assessment. In addition, we will consider the assessment of an individual, Jim, from the standpoint of each theory and approach to assessment. Through this approach we will be able to see the relation between theory and assessment, and also to consider the extent to which different approaches result in similar pictures of the person.

Before we describe Jim, some details concerning the assessment project will be presented. Jim was a college student when, in the late 1960s, he volunteered to serve as a subject for a project involving the intensive study of college students. He participated in the project mainly because of his interest in psychology, but also because he hoped to gain a better understanding of himself. At the time, a variety of tests were administered to him. These tests represented a sampling of the tests then available. Obviously, theories of personality and associated tests that had not been developed at the time could not be administered. However, Jim agreed to report on his life experiences and to take some additional tests 5, 20, and 25 years later. At those times, an effort was made to administer tests developed in association with emerging theories of personality.

Thus, we do not have the opportunity to consider all the tests at the same point in time. However, we are able to consider the personality of an individual over an extended period of time, and thereby examine how the theories—and the tests—relate to what occurred earlier in life and what followed later. Let us begin with a brief sketch derived from Jim's autobiography and follow him throughout the text as we consider the various approaches to personality.

AUTOBIOGRAPHICAL SKETCH OF JIM

In his autobiography Jim reported that he was born in New York City after the end of World War II and received considerable attention and affection as a child. His father is a college graduate who owns an automobile sales business; his mother is a housewife who also does volunteer reading for the blind. Jim described himself as having a good relationship with his father and described his mother as having "great feelings for other people—she is a totally 'loving' woman." He is the oldest of four children, with a sister four years younger and two brothers, one five years younger and one seven years younger. The main themes in his autobiography concern his inability to become involved with women in a satisfying way, his need for success and his relative failure since high school, and his uncertainty about whether to go on to graduate school in business administration or in clinical psychology. Overall he felt that people had a high estimate of him because they used superficial criteria, but that inwardly he was troubled.

We have here the bare outline of a person. Hopefully, the details will be filled in as he is considered from the standpoint of different personality theories. Hopefully, by the end of the book, a complete picture of Jim will emerge.

learned helpness

MAJOR CONCEPTS

L-data   Life record data or information concerning the person that can be obtained from their life history or life record.

O-data   Observer data or information provided by knowledgeable observers such as parents, friends, or teachers.

T-data   Test data or information obtained from experimental procedures or standardized tests.

S-data   Self-report data or information provided by the subject.

Case studies   An approach to research in which one studies an individual person in great detail. This strategy commonly is associated with clinical research, that is, research conducted by a therapist in the course of in-depth experiences with a client.

Correlational coefficient   A numerical index that summarizes the degree to which two variables are related linearly.

Correlational research   An approach to research in which existing individual differences are measured and related to one another, rather than being manipulated as in experimental research.

Demand characteristics   Cues that are implicit (hidden) in the experimental setting and influence the subject's behavior.

Experimenter expectancy effects   Unintended experimenter effects involving behaviors that lead subjects to respond in accordance with the experimenter's hypothesis.

Experimental research   An approach to research in which the experimenter manipulates a variable of interest, usually by assigning different research participants, at random, to different experimental conditions.

Idiographic (strategies)   Strategies of assessment and research in which the primary goal is to obtain a portrait of the potentially unique, idiosyncratic individual.

Nomothetic (strategies)   Strategies of assessment and research in which the primary goal is to identify a common set of principles or laws that apply to all members of a population of persons.

Reliability   The extent to which observations are stable, dependable, and can be replicated.

Response style   The tendency of some subjects to respond to test items in a consistent, patterned way that has to do with the form of the questions or answers rather than with their content.

Validity   The extent to which observations reflect the phenomena or constructs of interest to us (also "construct validity").

① *Locus of Control- Rotter's concept expressing a generalized expectancy or belief concerning the determinants of rewards + punishments — internal or external — i.e. scale*

REVIEW

1. Research involves the systematic study of relationships among phenomena or events. Four types of data are obtained in personality research: L-data, O-data, T-data, and S-data (LOTS). Three approaches to personality research are clinical research, laboratory experimentation, and correlational research using questionnaires.

2. All research shares the goals of reliability and validity—of obtaining observations that can be replicated and for which there is evidence of a relation to the concepts of interest. As a human enterprise, research involves ethical questions concerning the treatment of subjects and the reporting of data.

3. Clinical research involves the intensive study of individuals. This research method was illustrated by a case study involving the self-concept of an individual as he confronted the different social situations of his life.

4. In correlational research the investigator measures two or more variables and determines the degree to which they are associated with each other. Questionnaire measures are particularly important in correlational research. This research method was illustrated with research in which personality factors were found to predict longevity.

5. Experimental research involves the manipulation of one or more variables, to determine their causal

impact on outcomes of interest. This approach to research was illustrated by the manipulation of variables related to the phenomenon of stereotype threat.

6. Theories of personality differ in their preferences for types of data and approaches to research. In other words, there tend to be linkages among the-ory, type of data, and method of research. It is important to keep such linkages in mind as the major theories of personality are considered in the chapters that follow. A single case studied from the standpoint of each theoretical perspective also will be presented for illustrative and comparative purposes.

3

A PSYCHODYNAMIC THEORY: FREUD'S PSYCHOANALYTIC THEORY OF PERSONALITY

WHY STUDY FREUD?

SIGMUND FREUD (1856–1939): A VIEW OF THE THEORIST

FREUD'S VIEW OF THE PERSON AND SOCIETY

FREUD'S VIEW OF THE SCIENCE OF PERSONALITY

PSYCHOANALYSIS: A THEORY OF PERSONALITY
  Structure
    The Concept of the Unconscious and Levels of Consciousness
    Levels of Consciousness
    The Motivated Unconscious
    Relevant Psychoanalytic Research
    Current Status of the Concept of the Unconscious
    The Psychoanalytic Unconscious and the Cognitive Unconscious
    Id, Ego, and Superego

Process
  Life and Death Instincts
  The Dynamics of Functioning
  Anxiety, Mechanisms of Defense, and Contemporary Research on Defensive Processes
  Denial
  Projection
  Isolation, Reaction Formation, and Sublimation
  Repression
Growth and Development
  The Development of Thinking Processes
  The Development of the Instincts
  Stages of Development
  Erikson's Psychosocial Stages of Development
  The Importance of Early Experience

MAJOR CONCEPTS

REVIEW

Chapter Focus

The number one player on the tennis team is getting ready to play for the state title. She has never met her opponent before, so she decides to introduce herself before the match. She strolls out onto the court where her opponent is warming up and says, "Hi, I'm Amy. Glad to beat you." You can imagine how embarrassed Amy was! Flustered, she corrected her innocent mistake and walked over to her side of the court to warm up. "Wow," Amy thought, "where did that come from?"

Was Amy's verbal slip so innocent? Freud wouldn't have thought so. In his view, Amy's silly mistake was actually a very revealing display of unconscious aggressive drives. Freud's psychoanalytic theory is illustrative of a psychodynamic and clinical approach to personality. Behavior is interpreted as a result of the dynamic interplay among motives, drives, needs, and conflicts. The research consists mainly of clinical investigations as shown in an emphasis on the individual, in the attention given to individual differences, and in attempts to assess and understand the total individual. Contemporary researchers, however, devote much attention to the challenge of studying psychodynamic processes in the experimental laboratory.

QUESTIONS TO BE ADDRESSED IN THIS CHAPTER

1. How did Freud develop his theory and how did historical and personal events shape this development?

2. What scientific evidence is there for the existence of unconscious influences on our lives?

3. Anxiety often is a very painful emotion. What are the means people use to protect themselves from too much anxiety?

4. Can people repress memories of childhood trauma and then recover these memories as adults?

5. How important is early experience for later personality development?

WHY STUDY FREUD?

Before addressing these questions, we will consider another question you may be asking yourself: Why study Freud? Why, in the beginning of the 21st century, are we beginning our coverage of personality theories with the work of someone who first developed his theory in the late 1800s? You may already know that many contemporary scientists reject significant aspects of psychoanalytic theory. This only underscores the question: Why study Freud?

There are three answers. The first is that Freud's work has had an enormous impact on the intellectual life of our culture. Psychoanalysis has influenced Western thought to a degree that probably exceeds that of all the other personality theories combined. Scholarship not only in the social sciences, but in the arts and the humanities, has been influenced by psychoanalytic thinking. Products of popular culture—movies, music, art—commonly contain Freudian themes. Freud's impact has been large primarily because his ideas were startling. They disrupted commonly accepted views of human nature and society. "It is a shattering experience for anyone seriously committed to the Western tradition of morality and rationality to take a steadfast, unflinching look at what Freud has to say. It is humiliating to be compelled to admit the grossly seamy side of so many grand ideals. To experience Freud is to partake a second time of the forbidden fruit" (Brown, 1959, p. xi).

The second reason for studying Freud is that is it difficult to appreciate fully any of the other personality theories without first considering the strengths and limits of psychoanalysis. This is because most of the other theories were developed, at least in part, as a reaction against psychoanalytic theory. The theorists discussed in subsequent chapters were all quite familiar with Freud's theory. They perceived limitations in his work, and this inspired them to develop novel theories of their own.

The third reason is that there are some topics that are central to human experience, that were addressed directly by Freud, but that receive relatively little coverage in frameworks other than psychodynamic theory. Freud proposed a theory of extraordinary breadth and boldness. He tackled phenomena that are extremely difficult to study: dreams, sexual desires, internal mental conflicts, and the psychological life of the infant. If one asks what personality theory has to say about these critical topics, a complete answer absolutely must include the contributions of Freud.

Regarding the development of the theory itself, psychoanalytic theory developed from therapeutic work. Freud was a physician. At first, he was not trying to develop a personality theory. He merely wanted to alleviate the physical and psychological distress of his patients. However, Freud concluded that his patient's problems had complex psychological causes that involved conflicts among mental forces. From this basic insight, Freud developed an overall view of personality in which behavior is a result of struggles among drives and needs that inevitably conflict. Because of these conflicts, overt behavior may be more complicated than it appears. An action may express a motive either directly or in a subtle, disguised way. The same behavior can satisfy different motives in different people or a variety of motives in one person. For example, eating can satisfy a hunger need but it also can symbolically satisfy a need for love; being a doctor can satisfy a need to help others, as well as serve as a way of overcoming anxieties about illness and bodily harm. These psychological functions occur at different levels of awareness, with individuals often being unaware of the forces underlying their actions.

In sum, in this chapter we will review a theory grand in scope, encompassing phenomena as simple as an everyday slip of the tongue and as complex as the development of human culture. Whatever its limits, it is a theory that demands our attention because it has profoundly shaped scientific progress in psychology and society's view of human nature.

Sigmund Freud was born in Austria in 1856. He was the first child of his parents, although his father, 20 years older than his mother, had two sons by a previous marriage. Although his birth was followed by that of seven more children, the intellectually precocious Freud remained his mother's favorite—and

SIGMUND FREUD (1856–1939): A VIEW OF THE THEORIST

Sigmund Freud

he knew it. Later in life, Freud famously commented that a man who has been the indisputable favorite of his mother "keeps for life the feeling of a conqueror, that confidence of success that often induces real success" (Freud, 1900, p. 26). As a boy he dreamed of becoming a great general or government official. But concern about anti-Semitism in these fields led Freud, who was Jewish, to consider a career in medicine.

In medical school, Freud received training that profoundly shaped the personality theory he developed later in life. A particular influence was Ernst Brücke, a noted physiologist who was a leader in an intellectual movement of the time that was known as **mechanism**. The mechanist movement argued that the principles of natural science could explain not only the behavior of physical objects, but human thought and behavior as well (Gay, 1998). People could be understood in terms of physical and chemical mechanisms that are the causes of experience and behavior. One could, then, have a complete natural science of persons. Nowadays we generally take this idea for granted. But in Freud's time, it was a point of debate. Brücke viewed humans as dynamic physiological systems whose functioning adheres to the physical principle of conservation of energy. This view laid the foundation for the dynamic view of personality that Freud later developed (Sulloway, 1979).

After earning his medical degree, Freud worked in the field of neurology. Some of his early research involved a comparison of adult and fetal brains. He concluded that the earliest structures persist and are never buried, a view that was a precursor to his later views of personality development. For financial reasons, Freud eventually abandoned a research career and turned toward medical practice. Personally, Freud experienced periodic depressions and attacks of anxiety, occasionally using cocaine to calm the agitation and dispel the depression. During these years he married and had three daughters and three sons.

A critical event during these years for Freud was learning about a technique called **catharsis**, which was taught to him by a long-time professional associate, the Viennese physician Joseph Breuer. Catharsis refers to a release and freeing of emotions by talking about one's problems. In the cathartic technique that Breuer developed in work with a patient known as Anna O, the person being analyzed is encouraged to relive traumatic psychological events that are the original source of their emotional distress. By reliving them, the pent-up emotions associated with the events could be released; in common colloquial terms, we might say that the person experiences relief from traumatic emotions by getting the experience "off their chest" or getting it "out of their system." A key point is that, before the catharsis, the person is not consciously aware of the source of their emotional distress; the idea that had caused distress had been unconscious. Breuer and Freud collaborated on a book, *Studies in Hysteria*, that presented these ideas. However, at this point, Freud had developed little of the rest of the theoretical structure that was later to become known as psychoanalysis.

In 1897, the year following his father's death, Freud was plagued by periods of depression. Intellectual pursuits provided some distraction from his pain, yet Freud sought more relief by understanding his own unconscious: "My recovery can only come through work in the unconscious; I cannot manage with conscious efforts alone." To understand his unconscious mental life, Freud began an activity that proved utterly fundamental to the development of psychoanalysis: a self-analysis. Freud analyzed the contents of his own experiences, concentrating in particular on the meaning of his dreams, which he thought would be revealing of unconscious thoughts and desires. For the rest of his life he continued self-analysis, devoting the last half-hour of his workday to it.

Freud at first tried a variety of techniques in his therapeutic work, including hypnosis, which he had learned about from the renowned French psychiatrist Jean Charcot. Finding that not all patients could be hypnotized, he explored other methods, eventually hitting upon one that became crucial to his efforts: **free association**. In the free-association technique, the person being analyzed allows all of his or her thoughts to come forth without inhibition or falsification of any kind. The idea is to let one's thoughts flow freely, to discover potentially hidden associations among ideas. For Freud, the free-association technique was not only a treatment method but a scientific method. It provided the primary evidence for his theory of personality.

In 1900, Freud published his most significant work, *The Interpretation of Dreams*. In this book, Freud no longer was concerned merely with the treatment of patients. Instead, he began to develop a theory of the mind, that is, a theory of the basic structures and working principles of the human psyche. Only 600 copies of the book were sold in its first eight years of publication. Yet Freud began to develop a professional following. In 1902, the Psychoanalytic Society was formed, and was joined by a number of people who went on to become outstanding psychoanalysts. Freud's writing and development of theory progressed, but with increased public attention came increased public abuse. In 1904, Freud wrote on the *Psychopathology of Everyday Life*, and in 1905 he published *Three Essays on the Theory of Sexuality*. The latter presented Freud's views on infantile sexuality and its relation to perversions and neuroses. This resulted in ridicule of Freud, who was seen as an evil and wicked man with an obscene mind. Medical institutions were boycotted for tolerating Freud's view; an early follower, Ernest Jones, was forced to resign his neurological appointment for inquiring into the sexual life of his patients.

Despite these obstacles, Freud's international stature grew. Lectures in the United States in 1909 greatly enhanced Freud's profile outside of Europe. He had, by now, achieved sufficient fame and acceptance and had a waiting list of patients.

But Freud had problems, too. By 1919 he had lost all his savings in World War I. In 1920, a daughter, age 26, died. Perhaps most significant was Freud's fear for the lives of two sons who were in the war. Out of this historical context Freud, age 64, in 1920 developed his theory of the death instinct—a wish to die, which is in opposition to the life instinct or a wish for survival. The subsequent spread of anti-Semitism and growing power of the Nazis in the 1930s only compounded Freud's distress. Yet, he continued to develop his theorizing throughout this period. Many of the most significant aspects of psychoanalytic theory were developed during these last 20 years. Freud died on September 23, 1939, at the age of 83.

Freud, the man, has been glorified by many as a compassionate, courageous genius. Others, noting his many battles and breaks with colleagues, see him as rigid, authoritarian, and intolerant of the opinions of others (Fromm, 1959). Whatever the interpretation of Freud's personality, he unquestionably pursued his work with great courage. He bravely presented personal details of his own life as revealed in self-analysis. He courageously withstood the criticism of colleagues and the scorn of society at large. He did this, as he wrote to an associate, "in the service" of "a dominating passion…a tyrant [that] has come my way…it is psychology" (Gay, 1998, p. 74).

FREUD'S VIEW OF THE PERSON AND SOCIETY

Psychoanalysis contains views of the person and of society, and even a total philosophy of life. These views must be understood in historical context. Although Freud struggled to develop a theory free of personal and sociohistorical biases, psychoanalytic theory reflects themes that were current in late 19th- and early 20th-century Europe. It was inherently impossible for Freud to overcome this historical limitation to his theorizing. On the one hand, one might expect that a person could overcome such limits through objective scientific observation. But Freud's scientific observations were of middle- and upper-class patients who themselves were part of the culture of the time.

At the heart of the psychoanalytic view of the person is that the human is an **energy system**. Freud postulated a system in which energy flows, gets sidetracked, or becomes dammed up. There is a limited amount of energy, and if it is used in one way, there is much less of it to be used in another way. The energy that is used for cultural purposes is no longer available for sexual purposes, and vice versa. If the energy is blocked from one channel of expression, it finds another, generally along the path of least resistance. The goal of all behavior is pleasure, that is, the reduction of tension or the release of energy.

Why the assumption that the mind is an energy system? The assumption is traceable to the excitement scientists were then experiencing in physics. According to the 19th-century physicist Helmholtz's principle of the conservation of energy, matter and energy can be transformed but not destroyed. Not only physicists but also members of other disciplines were studying the laws of energy changes in a system. As already noted, in medical school Freud came under the influence of the physiologist Brücke, who viewed humans as moved by forces according to the principle of the conservation of energy, a view apparently translated by Freud into the psychological realm of behavior. The age of energy and dynamics provided scientists with a new conception of humans, "the view that man is an energy system and that he obeys the same physical laws which regulate the soap bubble and the movement of the planets" (Hall, 1954, pp. 12–13).

A second feature of Freud's view of persons, beyond the idea of persons as energy systems, is the notion that humans are driven by sexual and aggressive drives, or instincts. To Freud, sexual and aggressive drives are not learned from society. They are an instinctual feature of human nature. Freud (1930) writes: "The bit of truth behind all this—one so eagerly denied—is that men are not gentle, friendly creatures wishing for love, who simply defend themselves if they are attacked, but that a powerful measure of desire for aggression has to be reckoned as a part of their instinctual endowment" (p. 85). This instinct of aggression lies "at the bottom of all relations of affection and love between human beings—possibly with the single exception of that of a mother to her male child" (p. 89).

Along with the aggressive drive, Freud placed great emphasis on the sexual drive and the conflict between the expression of sexuality and social prohibitions. The emphasis on sexual inhibition reflects the Victorian period of which Freud and his patients were a part. For Freud, the person in pursuit of pleasure is in conflict with society and civilization. People function according to a *pleasure principle*; they seek "unbridled gratification" of all desires. This conflicts with the demands of society, which of course prohibit people from freely expressing sexual desires whenever and however they wish. When sexual energy cannot be released, is does not merely disappear. It is conserved (as suggested by the physics principle of conservation of energy). Energy that would otherwise be released in the pursuit of sexual pleasure, but that is inhibited due to social constraints, may be channeled to conform to the aims of society. A wide range of activities—indeed, Freud believed the whole range of cultural productivity—were expressions of sexual and aggressive energy that were prevented from expression in a more direct way.

Regarding society, one possible view of society is that it corrupts the individual. Children may be seen as "innocent" beings who learn about the darker side of life from the social world. Such a view is suggested by the biblical narrative in which Adam and Eve are corrupted by the temptations of Satan and fall from grace. Freud presented a view of society that is the very *opposite* of this. In Freud's view, society does not teach the innocent child about sexuality and aggression. Instead, the child is born with sexual and aggressive drives. Society curbs those drives, teaching the child to inhibit them. One outgrowth of the conflict between the individual drives and social demands is misery and neurosis. To Freud, the price of progress in civilization is personal misery, the forfeiting of happiness, and a heightened sense of guilt.

We can see, then, that beyond the formal conceptualization of a theory of personality, there is a view of the person implicit in psychoanalysis. According to this view, humans—like other animals—are driven by instincts or drives and operate in the pursuit of pleasure. People operate as energy systems, building, storing, and releasing, in one form or another, basically the same energy. All behavior is determined, much of it by forces outside of awareness. In the end, psychoanalysis sides with the instincts and seeks a reduction in the extent to which the instincts are frustrated.

Freud's training in medical sciences cultivated in him a deep appreciation of the relationship between theory and research and the need for sharp definitions of theoretical concepts. Yet he also recognized that, in the early stages of a science, speculative theorizing might be necessary. Thus, he boldly plunged ahead in theorizing in a manner that is uncommon among contemporary psychologists.

FREUD'S VIEW OF THE SCIENCE OF PERSONALITY

Apart from the details of his theory, a major contribution of Freud's is the nature of the scientific observation he made. Freud's observations were based on the analysis of patients. He relied on clinical case study evidence (as we discussed in Chapter 2). Freud cared little about efforts to verify psychoanalytic principles in the laboratory. When a psychologist wrote to tell Freud of his experimental studies of one psychoanalytic concept, Freud responded that psychoanalytic concepts were based on a wealth of reliable observations and thus, did not need independent experimental verification. He was satisfied with using the intensive clinical study of the individual patient as his major research method. This research method allows the accumulation of considerable data about an individual. Probably no other method in psychology even approximates the wealth of material gathered about a single person by the psychoanalyst.

CURRENT QUESTIONS

WHAT PRICE THE SUPPRESSION OF EXCITING THOUGHTS?

Freud suggested that the price of progress in civilization is increased inhibition of the pleasure principle and a heightened sense of guilt. Does civilization require such an inhibition? What are the costs to the individual of efforts to suppress wishes and inhibit "unbridled gratification" of desires?

Recent research by Daniel Wegner and his associates suggests that the suppression of exciting thoughts may be involved in the production of negative emotional responses and the development of psychological symptoms such as phobias (irrational fears) and obsessions (preoccupation with uncontrollable thoughts). In this research, subjects were told not to think about sex. Trying not to think about sex produced emotional arousal, just as it did in subjects given permission to think about sex. Although arousal decreased after a few minutes in both groups, what followed differed for subjects in the two groups. In the first group, the effort to suppress exciting thoughts led to the intrusion of these thoughts into consciousness and the reintroduction of surges of emotion. This was not found when subjects were given the opportunity to think about sex.

The researchers suggest that the suppression of exciting thoughts can promote excitement; that is, the very act of suppression may make these thoughts even more stimulating than when we purposefully dwell on them. In sum, such efforts at suppression may not serve us well either emotionally or psychologically.

SOURCE: Petrie, Booth, & Pennebaker, 1998; Wegner, 1992; 1994; Wegner et al., 1990.

Although Freud viewed psychoanalysis as part of the science of psychology, most of the early research was conducted by medical professionals in a therapeutic setting. Only much later did psychologists apply the field's traditional scientific techniques to the concepts of psychoanalysis. As we consider psychoanalytic concepts, we shall continue to see this struggle between the complex, uncontrolled observations of the clinical setting and the systematic, controlled study of phenomena in the laboratory. Indeed, of late, there has been considerable criticism of the uncontrolled nature of Freud's observations and the way he reported them: "Instead of training scientists, Freud ended up training practitioners in a relatively fixed system of ideas" (Sulloway, 1991, p. 275).

PSYCHOANALYSIS: A THEORY OF PERSONALITY

We now consider the details of psychoanalytic theory, keeping in mind its emphasis on clinical investigations and a view of human functioning as the result of an interplay among forces.

STRUCTURE

What structural units does psychoanalytic theory use to account for human behavior? Freud provided not one, but two models of the structure of mind. The models are closely related. One concerns the question of levels of consciousness: Are the contents of mind something that we are aware of (conscious) or not (unconscious)? The other concerns functional systems in the mind; this is Freud's famous three-part model of id, ego, and superego. We first review levels of consciousness and the concept of the unconscious, and then turn to Freud's model of functional systems of personality.

The Concept of the Unconscious and Levels of Consciousness

It is hard to overestimate the importance of the concept of the unconscious to psychoanalytic theory. To Freud, "Psychoanalysis aims at and achieves nothing more than the discovery of the unconscious in mental life" (1924, p. 397). The concept of the unconscious suggests that there are aspects of our functioning of which we are not fully aware. The psychoanalytic theory of personality suggests that much of our behavior, perhaps the majority of it, is determined by unconscious forces, and that much of our psychic energy is devoted either to finding acceptable expression of unconscious ideas or to keeping them unconscious.

Levels of Consciousness According to psychoanalytic theory, psychic life can be described in terms of the degree to which we are aware of mental phenomena. There are three levels of awareness. The **conscious** level involves phenomena of which we are aware at any given moment; the contents of this information about Freud that you currently are reading is part of your consciousness. The **preconscious** refers to mental contents of which we *could* become aware if we attended to them. For example, before reading the present sentence, you probably have not been thinking about your phone number; it was not part of your consciousness. But you easily could think of your phone number (indeed, you may be doing so right now!); it is a simple matter to attend to this information and bring it to consciousness. Prior to bringing it to consciousness, your phone number, and an unaccountably large number of additional mental contents, are preconscious. The third level is the **unconscious**. Unconscious mental contents are parts of the mind that we are unaware of and cannot become aware of except under special circumstances. Psychoanalytic theory is particularly interested in contents that are unconscious because of their anxiety-provoking content. A fundamental idea of psychoanalytic theory is that we have the goal of protecting ourselves against the anxiety associated with some of our thoughts and desires, and that we accomplish this goal by keeping these ideas outside of consciousness, storing them instead in the unconscious.

Freud was not the first person to recognize that parts of mental life are unconscious. He was, however, the first to explore qualities of unconscious life in detail and to attribute major importance to them in our daily lives. Through the analysis of dreams, slips of the tongue, neuroses, psychoses, works of art, and rituals, Freud attempted to understand the properties of the unconscious. What he found was a quality of psychic life in which nothing was impossible. The unconscious is alogical (opposites can stand for the same thing), disregards time (events of different periods may coexist), and disregards space (size and distance relationships are neglected so that large things fit into small things and distant places are brought together).

It is in the dream that the workings of the unconscious become most apparent. Here we are exposed to the world of symbols, where many ideas may be telescoped into a single word, where a part of any object may stand for many things. Through processes of symbolization, a penis can be represented by a snake or nose, a woman by a church, chapel, or boat, and an octopus engulfing a mother. It is through this process that we are allowed to think of writing as a sexual act—the pen is the male organ and the paper is the woman who receives the ink (the semen) that flows out in the quick up-and-down movements of the pen (Groddeck, 1923). In *The Book of the It*, Groddeck gives many fascinating examples of the workings of the unconscious and offers the following as an example of the functioning of the unconscious in his own life.

> I cannot recall her [my nurse's] appearance. I know nothing more than her name, Bertha, the shining one. But I have a clear recollection of the day she went away. As a parting present she gave me a copper three-pfennig piece. A Dreier... Since that day I have been pursued by the number three. Words like trinity, triangle, triple alliance, convey something disreputable to me, and not merely the words but the ideas attached to them, yes, and the whole complex of ideas built up around them by the capricious brain of a child. For this reason, the Holy Ghost, as the Third Person of the Trinity, was already suspect to me in early childhood; trigonometry was a plague in my school days... Yes, three is a sort of fatal number for me.
>
> SOURCE: *Groddeck, 1923, p. 9.*

The Motivated Unconscious   At its roots, psychoanalytic theory is a motivational theory of human behavior. As noted, the theory suggests that much of our behavior is motivated by unconscious influences. As will be discussed in greater detail later in the chapter, the suggestion is that some thoughts, feelings, and motives exist in the unconscious—rather than being part of conscious awareness—for motivated reasons. If these ideas were to enter conscious awareness, they would cause discomfort or psychological pain. Thus, in keeping with our basic desire to pursue pleasure and avoid pain, we seek to banish such thoughts from awareness. A wide variety of thoughts may cause pain and thus, be kept out of consciousness; this might include, for example, traumatic memories; feelings of envy, hostility, or sexual desire directed toward a forbidden person; or a desire to harm a loved one.

A critical feature of psychoanalytic theory is that unconscious thoughts influence conscious experience. Unconscious material expresses itself in our daily behavior. This occurs in a wide variety of ways: slips of the tongue, misperceptions, accidents, "out of character" or seemingly irrational behavior, emotions that we cannot explain, and feelings of anxiety, depression, or guilt. In other words, our underlying "true" feelings and motives can express themselves despite our efforts to bury them in the unconscious. It is not just that there are parts of ourselves that we are unaware of but that these parts influence our daily behavior, often in ways that are perplexing to us and others.

Relevant Psychoanalytic Research   The unconscious is never observed directly. What evidence, then, support the belief that there is an unconscious part of mind? Let us review the range of evidence that might be considered supportive of the concept of the unconscious, beginning with Freud's clinical observations. Freud realized the importance of the unconscious after observing hypnotic phenomena. As is well known, people under hypnosis can recall things they

While some slips of the tongue may represent merely a confusion among choice of words, others seem to illustrate Freud's suggestion that slips express hidden wishes. (Illustration by Patrick McDonnell, 1987 Psychology Today Magazine, Sussex Publishers, Inc.)

previously could not. Furthermore, they perform things under posthypnotic suggestion without consciously "knowing" that they are behaving in accordance with that suggestion; that is, they fully believe that what they are doing is voluntary and independent of any suggestion by another person. When Freud discarded the technique of hypnosis and continued with his therapeutic work, he found that often patients became aware of memories and wishes previously buried. Frequently, such discoveries were associated with painful emotion. It is indeed a powerful clinical observation to see a patient suddenly experience tremendous anxiety, sob hysterically, or break into a rage as he or she recalls a forgotten event or gets in touch with a forbidden feeling. Thus, it was clinical observations such as these that suggested to Freud that the unconscious includes memories and wishes that not only are not currently part of our consciousness but are "deliberately buried" in our unconscious.

What of experimental evidence? In the 1960s and 1970s experimental research focused on unconscious perception or what was called **perception without awareness**. Can the person "know" something without knowing that he or she knows it? For example, can the person hear or perceive stimuli, and be influenced by these perceptions, without being aware of these perceptions? Currently this is known as *subliminal perception*, or the registration of stimuli at a level below that required for awareness. For example, in some early relevant research one group of subjects was shown a picture with a duck image shaped by the branches of a tree. Another group was shown a similar picture but without the duck image. For both groups the picture was presented at a rapid speed so that it was barely visible. This was done using a tachistoscope, an apparatus that allows the experimenter to show stimuli to subjects at very

CURRENT APPLICATIONS

FAILURE, UNHAPPINESS, AND UNCONSCIOUS MOTIVATION

In his study of "Those Wrecked by Success," Freud described individuals who, because of feelings of guilt, fell ill once they had achieved some long-cherished wish. More recently, psychoanalyst Roy Schafer has described the unconscious meanings that success, failure, happiness, and unhappiness can have for people. He suggests that repetitive failure and chronic unhappiness typically are self-inflicted rather than expressions of inescapable events. For example, in one case a man underachieved to ward off the envy of others, and in another case a young man pursued failure to protect the self-esteem of his unsuccessful father: "Thus, for this young man, failure was also a success of a kind, while being a success was also a failure." In a third case, a woman was extremely self-sacrificing to retain the love of others. Although the "pursuit of failure" and the "idealization of unhappiness" are seen as being found in members of both sexes, Schafer suggests that the former is more prevalent in men and the latter in women. This is not to say, however, that all cases of failure or unhappiness are motivated by the result of unconscious conflicts.

SOURCE: Schafer, 1984.

"*He's mad as hell. He has this need to fail and he keeps getting promoted.*"

Drawing by Stan Hunt; © 1980 The New Yorker Magazine, Inc.

fast speeds, so that they cannot be consciously perceived. The subjects then were asked to close their eyes, imagine a nature scene, draw the scene, and label the parts. Would the two groups differ, that is, would subjects in the group "seeing" the picture with the duck image draw different pictures than subjects in the other group? And, if so, would such a difference be associated with differential recall as to what was perceived? What was found was that more of the subjects viewing the "duck" picture had significantly more duck-related images (e.g., "duck," "water," "birds," "feathers") in their drawings than did subjects in the other group. However, these subjects did not report seeing the duck during the experiment and the majority even had trouble finding it when they were asked to look for it. In other words, the stimuli that were not consciously perceived still influenced the imagery and thoughts of the subjects (Eagle, Wolitzky, & Klein, 1966).

The mere fact that people can perceive and be influenced by stimuli of which they are unaware does not suggest that psychodynamic or motivational forces are involved. Is there evidence that such is or can be the case? Two relevant lines of research can be noted. The first, called **perceptual defense**, involves a process by which the individual defends against the anxiety that accompanies actual recognition of a threatening stimulus. In a relevant early experiment, subjects were shown two types of words in a tachistoscope: neutral words such as apple, dance, and child and emotionally toned words such as rape, whore, and penis. The words were shown first at very fast speeds and then at progressively slower speeds. A record was made of the point at which the subjects were able to identify each of the words and their sweat gland activity (a measure of tension) in response to each word. These records indicated that subjects took longer to recognize the emotionally toned words than the neutral words and showed signs of emotional response to the emotionally toned words before they were verbally identified (McGinnies, 1949). Despite criticism of such research (e.g., did subjects identify the emotionally toned words earlier but were reluctant to verbalize them to the experimenter?), there appears to be considerable evidence that people can, outside of awareness, selectively respond to and reject specific emotional stimuli (Erdelyi, 1984).

Another line of research has examined a phenomenon called **subliminal psychodynamic activation** (Silverman, 1976; 1982; Weinberger, 1992). In this work, researchers attempt to stimulate unconscious wishes without making them conscious. This generally is done by presenting material that is related to either threatening or anxiety-alleviating unconscious wishes and then observing participants' subsequent reactions. The material is shown for extremely brief periods of time, in theory, long enough to activate the unconscious wish but short enough so that it is not recognized consciously. In the case of threatening wishes, the material is expected to stir up unconscious conflict and thus, to increase psychological disturbance. In the case of an anxiety-alleviating wish, the material is expected to diminish unconscious conflict and thus, to decrease psychological disturbance. For example, the content "I Am Losing Mommy" might be upsetting to some subjects, whereas the content "Mommy and I Are One" might be reassuring.

In a series of studies, Silverman and colleagues produced such subliminal psychodynamic activation effects. In one study this method was used to present conflict-intensifying material ("Loving Daddy Is Wrong") and conflict-reducing material ("Loving Daddy Is OK") to female undergraduates. For subjects prone to conflict over sexual urges, the conflict-intensifying material, presented outside of awareness, was found to disrupt memory for passages presented after the subliminal activation of the conflict. This was not true for the conflict-reducing material or for subjects not prone to conflict over sexual urges (Geisler, 1986). What is key here is that the content that is upsetting or relieving to various groups of subjects is predicted beforehand on the basis of psychoanalytic theory and that the effects occur only when the stimuli are perceived subliminally or unconsciously.

Another interesting use of the subliminal psychodynamic activation model involves the study of eating disorders. In the first study in this area, healthy college-age women and women with signs of eating disorders were compared in terms of how many crackers they would eat following subliminal presentation of three messages: Mama Is Leaving Me, Mama Is Loaning It, Mona Is Loaning It (Patton, 1992). Based on psychoanalytic theory, the hypothesis tested was that subjects with an eating disorder struggle with feelings of loss and abandonment in relation to nurturance and therefore would seek substitute gratification in the form of eating the crackers once the conflict was activated subliminally through the message "Mama Is Leaving Me." Indeed, the eating disorder subjects who received the abandonment stimulus (Mama Is Leaving Me) below threshold showed significantly more cracker eating than subjects without an eating disorder or subjects with an eating disorder exposed to the abandonment stimulus above threshold. This study was replicated with the additional use of pictorial stimuli—a picture of a sobbing baby and a woman walking away along with the "Mommy Is Leaving Me" message and a picture of a woman walking along with the neutral stimulus, in this case "Mommy Is Walking." Once more, significantly more crackers were eaten by the women with eating disorders subliminally exposed to the abandonment phrase and picture than by the women with eating disorders exposed to these stimuli above threshold or by the women without an eating disorder exposed to the stimuli above or below threshold (Gerard, Kupper, & Nguyen, 1993). Once more it was suggested that only when the stimuli were presented subliminally were they able to activate unconscious wishes and conflicts.

Some view the research on perceptual defense and subliminal psychodynamic activation as conclusive experimental evidence of the importance of psychodynamic, motivational factors in determining what is "deposited into" and "kept in" the unconscious (Weinberger, 1992). However, the experiments have frequently been criticized on methodological grounds, and at times some of the effects have been difficult to replicate or reproduce in other laboratories (Balay & Shevrin, 1988, 1989; Holender, 1986).

Current Status of the Concept of the Unconscious   The concept of a motivated unconscious continues to lie at the heart of psychoanalytic theory. How is the concept viewed more generally by psychologists in the field? At this point almost all psychologists, whether psychoanalytic or otherwise, would agree that many mental events occur outside of conscious awareness and that unconscious processes influence what we attend to and how we feel. For example, consider the view of a leading contemporary researcher who is now a follower of psychoanalytic theory: "Our conclusion, perhaps discomforting for the layperson, is that unconscious influences are ubiquitous. It is clear that people sometimes consciously plan and act. More often than not, however, behavior is influenced by unconscious processes; that is, we act and then, if questioned, make our excuses" (Jacoby et al., 1992, p. 82).

Striking contemporary evidence of unconscious influences on everyday behavior comes from work by the social psychologist John Bargh and his colleagues (Bargh, 1997). For example, in one experiment research participants worked on a task with another individual. Unbeknownst to the participant, the other individual was part of the study—an experimental "confederate." This confederate exhibited very poor abilities on the task. In this setting, then, the participant faced two conflicting goals. On the one hand, there is the goal of achieving: One is supposed to perform as well as possible. On the other hand, there is a personal or affiliation goal: Performing well might make the other person, who is doing poorly, feel bad, so one might achieve the goal of affiliating with the individual by lowering one's own performance. Bargh and colleagues (Bargh & Barndollar, 1996) manipulated the goals in a manner that did not call participants' conscious attention to them. Prior to the study, participants were asked to complete a word puzzle. In different experimental conditions, the words in the puzzle were related either to achievement or to affiliation. The idea is that the words would activate one versus the other goal, even if participants were unaware that this activation of goal contents was occurring. As predicted, compared to affiliation goals, activating achievement goals in the word puzzle caused participants to solve more problems when working on the task with the other individual. Importantly, participants in the study did not report being aware of the influence of the word puzzle task. Thus, their actions were caused by a goal of which they were not consciously aware.

The Psychoanalytic Unconscious and the Cognitive Unconscious   There is an important point to consider about this study (Bargh & Barndollar, 1996) and many others like it. On the one hand, the study demonstrates nonconscious influences on behavior, as Freud would have predicted. On the other hand, the content of the unconscious material in the study had little, if anything, to do with the material studied by Freud. Bargh and colleagues did not manipulate thoughts of sex or aggression. They did not study people's emotional reactions to material of deep psychological significance. Instead, they manipulated everyday social goals on a mundane laboratory task. Their findings, then, indicate the existence of unconscious influences, but these are unconscious influences that may have little to do with the psychological experiences discussed by Freud. This distinction—between the traumatic sexual and aggressive unconscious content of interest to Freud, and the relatively mundane unconscious content studied by many contemporary researchers in personality and social psychology—suggests that one should distinguish between the psychoanalytic unconscious and what has been called the cognitive unconscious (Kihlstrom, 1990, 1999; Pervin, 2003).

As we have seen, the psychoanalytic view of the unconscious emphasizes the irrational, illogical nature of unconscious functioning. In addition, the contents of the unconscious are presumed by analysts mainly to involve sexual and aggressive thoughts, feelings, and motives. Finally, analysts emphasize that what is in the unconscious is there for motivated reasons and these contents exert a motivational influence on daily behavior. In contrast to this, according to the cognitive view of the unconscious there is no fundamental difference in quality between unconscious and conscious processes. According to this view, unconscious processes can be as intelligent, logical, and rational as conscious

Table 3.1   Comparison of Two Views of the Unconscious: Psychoanalytic and Cognitive

Psychoanalytic View	Cognitive View
1. Emphasis on illogical, irrational unconscious processes.	1. Absence of fundamental difference between conscious and unconscious processes.
2. Content emphasis on motives and wishes.	2. Content emphasis on thoughts.
3. Emphasis on motivated aspects of unconscious functioning.	3. Focus on nonmotivated aspects of unconscious functioning.

processes. Second, the cognitive view of the unconscious emphasizes the variety of contents that may be unconscious, with no special significance associated with sexual and aggressive contents. Third, related to this, the cognitive view of the unconscious does not emphasize motivational factors. According to the cognitive view, cognitions are unconscious because they cannot be processed at the conscious level, because they never reached consciousness, or because they have become overly routinized and automatic. For example, tying one's shoe is so automatic that we no longer are aware of just how we do it. We act similarly with typing and where letters are on the keyboard. Many of our cultural beliefs were learned in such subtle ways that we cannot even spell them out as beliefs. As noted in Chapter 1, we are not even aware of them until we meet members of a different culture. However, such unconscious contents are not kept there for motivated reasons. Nor do they necessarily exert a motivational influence on our behavior. Finally, there is evidence that subliminal stimuli can affect our thoughts and feelings but these stimuli need not be of special psychodynamic significance such as a threatening wish (Klinger & Greenwald, 1995; Nash, 1999) (Table 3.1).

Many of these contrasting views are captured in the following statement by Kihlstrom, a leading proponent of the cognitive view of the unconscious:

> The psychological unconscious documented by latter-day psychology is quite different from what Sigmund Freud and his psychoanalytic colleagues had in mind in Vienna. Their unconscious was hot and wet; it seethed with lust and anger; it was hallucinatory, primitive, and irrational. The unconscious of contemporary psychology is kinder and gentler than that and more readily bound and rational, even if it is not entirely cold and dry.
>
> SOURCE: Kihlstrom, Barnhardt, & Tataryn, 1992, p. 788.

Although efforts are being made to integrate the psychoanalytic and cognitive views of the unconscious (Bornstein & Masling, 1998; Epstein, 1994; Westen & Gabbard, 1999), generally these differing points of view remain. In sum, although the importance of unconscious phenomena is recognized, and the investigation of such phenomena has become a major area of research, the uniquely psychoanalytic view of the unconscious remains questionable for many, perhaps most, nonpsychoanalytic investigators.

Id, Ego, and Superego   In 1923 Freud developed a more formal structural model for psychoanalysis. It featured three personality structures: the id, the ego, and the superego. Each refers to a different aspects of people's functioning.

The **id** represents the source of all drive energy. The energy for a person's functioning originally resides in the life and death, or sexual and aggressive instincts, which are part of the id. In its functioning, the id seeks the release of excitation, tension, and energy. It operates according to the **pleasure principle**, which is particularly simple to define: the id pursues pleasure and avoids pain. The point is that the id does not do anything else. In does not devise plans and strategies for obtaining pleasure, or wait patiently for a particularly pleasing object to appear. Instead, it seeks immediate tension release. It has qualities of a spoiled child: It wants what it wants when it wants it. The id cannot tolerate frustration and is free of inhibitions. It shows no regard for reality and can seek satisfaction through action or through imagining that it has gotten what it wants; the fantasy of gratification is as good as the actual gratification. It is without reason, logic, values, morals, or ethics. In sum, the id is demanding, impulsive, blind, irrational, asocial, selfish, and finally, pleasure-loving.

In marked contrast to the id is the **superego**, which represents the moral branch of our functioning. The superego contains ideals for which we strive, as well as punishments (guilt) we expect if we violate ethical codes. The superego, then, is an internal representation of the moral rules of the external, social world. It functions to control behavior in accord with these rules, offering rewards (pride, self-love) for "good" behavior and punishments (guilt, feelings of inferiority) for "bad" behavior. The superego may function on a very primitive level, being relatively incapable of reality testing—that is, of modifying its action depending on circumstances. In such cases, the person is unable to distinguish between thought and action, feeling guilty for thinking something even if it did not lead to action. Furthermore, the individual is bound by black-white, all-none judgments and by the pursuit of perfection. Excessive use of words such as good, bad, judgment, and trial express a strict superego. But the superego can also be understanding and flexible. For example, people may be able to forgive themselves or someone else if it is clear that something was an accident or done under severe stress. In the course of development, children learn to make such important distinctions and to see things not only in all-or-none, right-or-wrong, black-or-white terms.

The third psychoanalytic structure is the **ego**. Whereas the id seeks pleasure and the superego seeks perfection, the ego seeks reality. The ego's function is to express and satisfy the desires of the id in accordance with two things: opportunities and constraints that exist in the real world, and the demands of the superego. Whereas the id operates according to the pleasure principle, the ego operates according to the **reality principle**: gratification of the instincts is delayed until a time at which something in reality enables one to obtain maximum pleasure with the least pain or negative consequences. As a simple example, sexual drives in the id may impel you to make a sexual advance toward someone you find attractive. But the ego may stop you from acting impulsively; it would monitor reality, judging whether there is any chance that you might actually succeed and delaying action until it develops a strategy that might bring success. According to the reality principle, the energy of the id may be blocked, diverted, or released gradually, all in accordance with the demands of reality and the superego. Such an operation does not contradict the pleasure principle, but rather represents a temporary suspension of it. It functions, in George Bernard Shaw's words, so as "to be able to choose the line

"Double Scotches for me and my super-ego, and a glass of water for my id, which is driving."

Psychoanalytic Theory: *Freud emphasized the concepts of id, ego, and superego as structures of personality. (Drawing by Handelsman; © 1972 The New Yorker Magazine, Inc.)*

of greatest advantage instead of yielding in the direction of least resistance." The ego is able to separate wish from fantasy, can tolerate tension and compromise, and changes over time. Accordingly, it expresses the development of perceptual and cognitive skills, the ability to perceive more and think in more complex terms. For example, a person can begin to think in terms of the future and what is best in the long run. All these qualities are in contrast with the unrealistic, unchanging, demanding qualities of the id.

Although the ego may sound like the decision-maker, or the "executive," of personality, Freud thought that the ego was weaker than the metaphor of executive implies. Instead, a central metaphor of psychoanalysis is that the ego is like a rider on a wild horse (the id). The horse provides all the energy. The rider tries to direct it. But, ultimately, the more powerful beast may end up going wherever it wants. Freud himself spent relatively little time investigating the ego, instead thinking that is was more valuable to investigate in detail the influence of the powerful forces of the id; as we will see in our next chapter, this differentiates Freud's work from that of subsequent psychodynamic theorists, who were more concerned with ego functioning.

In sum, Freud's ego is logical, rational, and tolerant of tension. In its actions, it is subject to control by three masters: the id, the superego, and the world of reality.

The concepts of conscious, unconscious, id, ego, and superego are highly abstract and are not always defined with great precision. Furthermore, there is some lack of clarity because the meaning of some concepts changed as the theory developed, but the exact nature of the change in meaning was never spelled out (Madison, 1961). Finally, it should be clear that these are *conceptualizations* of phenomena. Freud provided psychology with a picturesque, concrete language for conceptualizing mental functioning. But the concreteness of the language should not mislead one into simply assuming that there exists an entity in your mind, and everyone else's, that exactly corresponds to the Freudian terminology. There is no energy plant inside us with a little person controlling its power. We do not "have" an id, ego, and superego in the way that we have a head, torso, and heart. Instead, according to the theory there are qualities of human behavior that are usefully conceptualized in these structural terms. The structures achieve greater definition in relation to the processes implied in them, and it is to these processes that we now turn.

PROCESS

In Chapter 1, we explained that personality theories contain two parts: analyses of personality structures and of personality processes. The id, ego, and superego are personality structures; they are conceptualizations of enduring mental systems. We now consider the process aspects of psychoanalytic theory, that is, its conceptualization of motivational dynamics.

As noted, Freud viewed the person as an energy system that obeyed the same laws as other energy systems. Energy may be altered and transformed, but it never "just disappears." Even in transformation, it essentially remains the same energy. According to the theory, the source of all psychic energy lies in states of excitation within the body that seek expression and tension reduction. These states are called instincts, or drives. They represent constant, inescapable mental forces.

Within this framework, two questions naturally arise: (1) How many types of energy are there? If energy is conceived of as an instinct or drive, this question is, how many basic human instincts are there, and what are they? (2) What happens to this energy? In other words, how is it expressed in everyday experience and action?

Life and Death Instincts

In your daily life, you engage in a wide variety of activities involving friends, family, romantic partners, education, work, sports, arts, music, and so forth. Since these different activities seem basic to human functioning, you might be tempted to imagine that each activity is associated with a "basic instinct" (an instinct to have friends, to bond with family, etc.). But this sort of "multi-instinct model" is not the sort of theory that Freud pursued. Instead, throughout his career, Freud tried to explain the diversity of human activity in terms of a very small number of instincts. He worked toward exactly the sort of theory we previewed in Chapter 1, in which the complexities of human behavior are understood through a theory that is relatively simple.

Although Freud always tried to explain behavior in terms of a small number of basic instincts or drives, his thoughts about the exact nature of these drives changed during his career. In an earlier view, he proposed ego instincts, relating to tendencies toward self-preservation, and sexual instincts, relating to tendencies toward preservation of the species. In a later view—which stands as the final, classic psychoanalytic model—there were still two instincts, but they were the **life** and **death instincts**. The life instinct included drives associated previously with both the earlier ego and sexual instincts; in other words, the life instincts impel people toward the preservation and reproduction of the organism. Freud gave a name to the energy of the life instinct; **libido**.

The death instinct is the very opposite of the life instinct. In involves the aim of the organism to die or return to an inorganic state. (No name has come to be commonly associated with the energy of the death instinct.) At an intuitive level, it may immediately strike you that the notion of a "death instinct" is unusual if not implausible. Why would people have an instinct to die? Such intuitions would match those of many psychologists, including many psychoanalysts; the death instinct remains one of the most controversial and least accepted parts of psychoanalytic theory. Yet the idea of a death instinct was consistent with some ideas of 19th-century biology with which Freud was familiar (Sulloway, 1979) and also, Freud felt, was consistent with observations of the human condition. Sadly, many people escape psychological problems through suicide, which can be understood as a manifestation of a drive to die. Furthermore, Freud felt that the death instinct was often turned away from oneself and directed toward others in acts of aggression. This occurs so commonly that some analysts refer to the instinct as an aggressive instinct.

This model of motivation processes is highly integrated with Freud's model of psychoanalytic structures. The sexual and death/aggressive drives are parts of one of the psychoanalytic structures, namely, the id. The id, as you will recall, is the first of the personality structures, that is, the one with which we are born. An implication, then, is that sexual and aggressive drives are part of the basic human nature that we are born with. We do not have to learn to have sexual and death/aggressive drives. We are born with them. To Freud, our psychological lives are essentially powered by these two basic drives.

The Dynamics of Functioning

If one posits only two instinctual drives, one faces an intellectual puzzle: How can one account for the diversity of motivated human activities, many of which do not seem obviously related to sex or aggression. Freud solved this puzzle with a creative and often highly insightful model of the dynamics of psychological functioning. Freud's analysis of dynamics addresses the question of what happens to instinctual energy, that is, how the energy can be modified prior to its expression in observable behavior.

In psychoanalytic theory, the instincts are characterized as aiming at the immediate reduction of tension, at achieving satisfaction and pleasure. In this way, the instincts have an "animalistic" quality to them. However, unlike animals, people are capable of delaying and modifying instincts before they are expressed. Different people also may differ, one from another, in their characteristic ways of modifying instinctual energy, and these differences underlie much of the uniqueness of personal functioning, according to Freud.

In the dynamics of functioning, what exactly can happen to one's instincts? They can, at least temporarily, be blocked from expression, expressed in a modified way, or expressed without modification. For example, affection may be a modified expression of the sexual instinct, and sarcasm a modified expression of the aggressive instinct. It is also possible for the object of gratification of the instinct to be changed or displaced from the original object to another object. Thus, the love of one's mother may be displaced to the wife, children, or dog. Each instinct may be transformed or modified, and the instincts can combine with one another. Football, for example, can gratify both sexual and aggressive instincts; in surgery there can be the fusion of love and destruction. It should already be clear how psychoanalytic theory is able to account for so much behavior on the basis of only two instincts. It is the fluid, mobile, changing qualities of the instincts and their many alternative kinds of gratification that allow such variability in behavior. In essence, the same instinct can be gratified in a number of ways and the same behavior can have different causes in different people.

Virtually every process in psychoanalytic theory can be described in terms of the expenditure of energy in an object or in terms of a force inhibiting the expenditure of energy, that is, inhibiting gratification of an instinct. Because it involves an expenditure of energy, people who direct much of their efforts toward inhibition end up feeling tired and bored. The interplay between expression and inhibition of instincts forms the foundation of the dynamic aspects of psychoanalytic theory. The key to this is the concept of anxiety. In psychoanalytic theory, anxiety is a painful emotional experience representing a threat or danger to the person. In a state of "free-floating" anxiety, individuals are unable to relate their state of tension to an external object; in contrast, in a state of fear, the source of tension is known. Freud had two theories of anxiety. In the first theory, anxiety was viewed as a result of undischarged sexual impulses—dammed-up libido. In the later theory, anxiety represented a painful emotion that acted as a signal of impending danger to the ego. Here, anxiety, an ego function, alerts the ego to danger so that it can act.

The psychoanalytic theory of anxiety states that at some point the person experiences a trauma, an incident of harm or injury. Anxiety represents a repetition of the earlier traumatic experience, but in miniature form. Anxiety in the present, then, is related to an earlier danger. For example, the child may be severely punished for some sexual or aggressive act. Later in life, the person may experience anxiety in association with the inclination to perform the same sexual or aggressive act. The earlier punishment (trauma) may or may not be remembered. In structural terms, what is suggested is that anxiety develops out of a conflict between the push of the id instincts and the threat of punishment by the superego. That is, it is as if the id says "I want it," the superego says "How terrible," and the ego says "I'm afraid."

Anxiety, Mechanisms of Defense, and Contemporary Research on Defensive Processes

Anxiety is such a painful state that we are incapable of tolerating it for very long. How are we to deal with such a state? If, as Freud suggests, our minds harbor sexual and aggressive instincts that are socially unacceptable, then how do we manage not to be anxious all the time? Freud's answer to this question constitutes one of the most enduring aspects of his theory of personality. He proposed that we mentally "defend" ourselves against anxiety-provoking thoughts. People develop **defense mechanisms** against anxiety. We develop ways to distort reality and exclude feelings from awareness so that we do not feel anxious. These defense mechanisms are functions carried out by the ego; they are a strategic effort by the ego to cope with the socially unacceptable impulses of the id.

Denial

Some things are too terrible to be true.

Bob Dylan [1]

Freud distinguished among a number of distinct defense mechanisms. Some of them are relatively simple, or psychologically primitive, whereas others are more complex. A particularly simple defense mechanism is **denial**. People may, in their conscious thoughts, deny the existence of a traumatic or otherwise socially unacceptable fact; the fact is so "terrible" that they deny that it is "true," as Dylan's lyric above suggests. People may begin using the defense mechanism of denial in childhood. There may be denial of reality, as in a girl who denies she lacks a penis or in the boy, who, in fantasy, denies a lack of power, or denial of an internal impulse, as when an irate person protests "I do not feel angry." The saying that someone "doth protest too much" gives specific reference to this defense. Denial of reality is commonly seen where people attempt to avoid recognizing the extent of a threat. The expression "Oh, no!" upon hearing of the death of a close friend represents the reflex action of denial. Children have been known to deny the death of a loved animal and long afterward to behave as if it were still alive. When Edwin Meese, former attorney general in the Reagan administration, was asked how much he owed in legal bills, he replied, "I really don't know. It scares me to look at it, so I haven't looked at it." The mother of former U.S. President Bill Clinton was quoted as saying "When bad things happen, I brainwash myself to put them out of my mind. Inside my head, I construct an airtight box. I keep inside it what I want to think about and everything else stays behind the walls. Inside is white, outside is black. The only gray I trust is the streak in my hair." A friend of the author's organizes her mail into three "in boxes" on her desk that are labeled "Unimportant Stuff," "Important Stuff," and "Stuff I'm Afraid to Look At."

Denial. *(CALVIN AND HOBBES © Watterson. Dist. by UNIVERSAL PRESS SYNDICATE. Reprinted with permission. All rights reserved.)*

Initially, such avoidance may be conscious, but later it becomes automatic and unconscious, so that the person is not even aware of "not looking."

Denial of reality is also seen when people say or assume that "It can't happen to me" in spite of clear evidence of impending doom. This defense was seen in Jews who were victims of the Nazis. Steiner (1966), in his book on the Nazi concentration camp Treblinka, describes how the population acted as if death did not exist, in spite of clear evidence to the contrary. He notes that the extermination of a whole people was so unimaginable that the people could not accept it. They preferred to accept lies rather than to bear the terrible trauma of the truth.

Another illustration of denial of reality has to do with how people cope with unpredictable disasters such as earthquakes. For some time, a major earthquake has been predicted for southern California. In 1983, the University of California at Los Angeles commissioned a panel to study the vulnerability of campus buildings to such an event. The results of the panel's findings were widely distributed in a report to the university community. A study of individuals who were aware of the report and the danger found that respondents in the very poor structures were significantly more likely to deny the seriousness of the situation and to doubt the experts' predictions than were respondents in the better structures. In addition, both groups showed ignorance of basic earthquake safety information and had taken no measures to prepare for an earthquake. It was concluded, "The results of this study suggest that individuals at risk for a catastrophic event whose occurrence is highly likely, but whose timing is unknown, may cope with that threat by ignoring or denying the seriousness of the situation." That respondents were typically aware of the threat and that residents of very poor seismic structures showed more questioning and denial than individuals in good seismic structures suggest that these perceptions are efforts to cope with the event, rather than a result of simple ignorance or misinformation" (Lehman & Taylor, 1987, pp. 551, 553).

Is denial necessarily a bad thing? Should we always avoid self-deception? Psychoanalysts generally assume that although the mechanisms of defense can be useful in reducing anxiety, they also are maladaptive in turning the person away from reality. Recall that in Chapter 2 there was discussion of defensive subjects with an illusion of mental health who showed signs of greater stress than either healthy subjects or nondefensive psychologically unhealthy subjects (Shedler, Mayman, & Manis, 1993). Thus, psychoanalysts view "reality orientation" as fundamental to emotional health and they doubt that distortions about oneself and others can have value for adaptive functions (Colvin & Block, 1994; Robins & John, 1996).

Yet, some psychologists suggest that positive illusions and self-deceptions, often based on denial or similar distortions of reality, can be constructive and adaptive. For example, it is suggested that positive illusions about one's self, about one's ability to control events, and about the future can be good, perhaps essential, for mental health (Taylor & Armor, 1996; Taylor & Brown, 1988, 1994; Taylor et al., 2000). The answer to these differing views appears to depend on the extent of distortion, how pervasive it is, and the circumstances under which it occurs. For example, it may be helpful to have positive illusions about oneself as long as they are not too extreme. And, denial and self-deception may provide temporary relief from emotional trauma and help the person avoid becoming overwhelmed by anxiety or depression. Denial may be adaptive where action is impossible, as when a person is in a situation that cannot

Denial and Addiction: *One of the most frequently cited characteristics of alcoholics and drug addicts is denial. Former Brooklyn Dodger pitcher Johnny Podres describes how he'd come home drunk, his mother would say he was an alcoholic, and he'd say "Not me." Another former Dodger pitcher, Don Newcombe, also a reformed alcoholic, describes how he and his drinking buddies would all deny their problem: "That's part of the syndrome— the denial syndrome." And in seeking to understand why N.Y. Mets pitcher Dwight Gooden would agree to be tested for cocaine use when he was using cocaine, one expert suggested that "massive denial is the hallmark of cocaine addiction. There is some denial in all addictions, but it is probably greatest in cocaine abuse."* (The New York Times, *July 30, 1983, and April 4, 1987)*

be altered (e.g., a fatal illness). On the other hand, denial certainly is maladaptive when it prevents one from taking constructive action, as when denial prevents one from taking signs of illness seriously and obtaining proper treatment.

Projection   Another relatively primitive defense mechanism is **projection**. In projection, what is internal and unacceptable is projected out and seen as external. People defend against the recognition of their own negative qualities by projecting them on to others. For example, rather than recognize hostility in the self, an individual sees others as being hostile. Much laboratory research has been devoted to the study of projection. At first, researchers found it difficult to demonstrate the phenomenon in the lab (Halpern, 1977; Holmes, 1981). However, in more recent years investigators have documented that, in fact, people tend to project their undesired psychological qualities onto others.

Newman and colleagues have studied projection by analyzing specific thinking processes that might lead people to project their undesired qualities onto others (Newman, Duff, & Baumeister, 1997). The basic idea is that people tend to dwell on those features of themselves that they do not like. Whenever one dwells on a topic, the topic comes to mind easily—in the language of this research, the topic becomes "chronically accessible" (Higgins & King, 1981). So if you think that you are "lazy," and you dwell on this feature of self, then the concept of "laziness" might come to mind relatively quickly and frequently for you. This reasoning puts one just one step away from the phenomenon of projection. This final step is that, whenever one interprets the actions of other people, one does so by using concepts in one's own mind. If one interprets other's actions using ideas that also are negative features of one's own self-concept, then one ends up "projecting" these negative features onto others. To return to our example, if "laziness" comes to mind quickly for you, and you see a person sitting on a beach in the middle of a workday, you might conclude that they are a "lazy" person. Someone else, in contrast, might merely conclude that the person is relaxing, rather than being lazy.

Experimental findings support this interpretation of projection (Newman et al., 1997). In this research, participants were exposed to bogus negative feedback on two personality attributes. They then were asked to try to suppress thoughts about one of the two attributes while they discussed the other one; such thought-suppression instructions often "backfire," causing people subsequently to think about the personal quality that they were trying to suppress. Later in the experimental session, participants viewed a videotape that depicted a somewhat anxious-looking individual. Participants were asked to rate this person on a series of personality trait dimensions. Findings revealed that participants projected their suppressed negative quality onto others. In other words, they judged that the *other* person possessed the negative personality attribute that they themselves had been trying not to think about earlier in the experiment.

The work of Newman et al. (1997) highlights a theme that we have seen earlier in this chapter. On the one hand, their findings confirm an intuition of Freud's: People sometimes defend against their own negative qualities by projecting these qualities onto others. On the other hand, their work does not directly confirm the exact account of defensive processing provided by Freud. Unlike expectations based on Freudian theory, the findings of Newman et al. (1997) indicate that projection occurs with respect to relatively mundane psychological qualities (e.g., "lazy") that are not in any obvious way connected to the psychosexual instincts of the id. Furthermore, in explaining their findings, Newman et al. (1997) rely on explanatory principles that are based on principles of social cognitive psychology (discussed in Chapters 12 and 13) rather than on principles of psychoanalysis.

Isolation, Reaction Formation, and Sublimation In addition to denial and projection, another way to deal with anxiety and threat is to isolate events in memory or to isolate emotion from the content of a memory or impulse. In **isolation**, the impulse, thought, or act is not denied access to consciousness, but it is denied the normal accompanying emotion. For example, a woman may experience the thought or fantasy of strangling her child without any associated feelings of anger. The result of using the mechanism of isolation is intellectualization, an emphasis on thought over emotion and feeling, and the development of logic-tight compartments. In such cases, the feelings that do exist may be split, as in the case where a man separates women into two categories, one with whom there is love but no sex and the other with whom there is sex but no love (Madonna-whore complex).

CURRENT APPLICATIONS

DENIAL: HEALTHY OR SICK? ADAPTIVE OR MALADAPTIVE?

Should we avoid self-deception? Is knowing all there is to know a sign of health? Psychoanalysts generally assume that although the mechanisms of defense are useful in reducing anxiety, they also are maladaptive in turning a person away from reality. For example, consider the potentially damaging effects of denial. A person who denies threatening signs may not be in a position to respond adaptively. Thus, women who discover a lump in their breast and delay going to a doctor because of denial of the possible seriousness of the lump may seriously reduce the chances of surgical success. Or men who deny the symptoms of a heart attack and continue to exercise or climb stairs may turn out to have made a fatal mistake.

However, there is evidence that denial and self-deception can also be constructive and adaptive. For example, take the person who has had a severe, incapacitating illness such as polio or cancer. Denial and self-deception can provide temporary relief from the emotional trauma and help the person to avoid being overwhelmed by anxiety, depression, or anger. Defensive processes can then facilitate optimism, and thereby allow constructive participation in rehabilitative efforts. In this case, denial as a coping process can be adaptive. It can be good for your health!

What sense can one make out of this conflicting evidence? It has been suggested that denial generally is maladaptive where it interferes with action that might otherwise improve the person's condition. However, denial generally is adaptive where action is impossible or irrelevant and where excessive emotion may interfere with recuperative efforts. Should the doctor tell all to the patient? Evidently this depends not only on the above factors, but also on the patient's personality. Some people seek out information and function best when they are fully informed. Other people avoid information and function best when they know only what is essential. In other words, denial may or may not be adaptive, depending on the circumstances, and information may or may not be helpful, depending on the person's coping style.

SOURCE: Lazarus, 1993; Miller & Mangan, 1983; Robins & John, 1996; Taylor, 1989; Taylor & Armor, 1996.

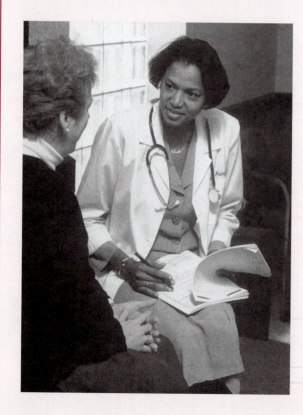

Denial: *How much information is useful to the patient?*

People who use the defense mechanism of isolation also often use the mechanism of **undoing**. Here the individual magically undoes one act or wish with another. "It is a kind of negative magic in which the individual's second act abrogates or nullifies the first, in such a manner that it is as though neither had taken place, whereas in reality both have done so" (A. Freud, 1936, p. 33). This mechanism is seen in compulsions in which the person has an irresistible impulse to perform some act (e.g., the person undoes a suicide or homicide fantasy by compulsively turning off the gas jets at home), in religious rituals, and in children's sayings such as "Don't step on the crack or you'll break your mother's back."

In **reaction formation**, the individual defends against expression of an unacceptable impulse by only recognizing and expressing its opposite. This defense is evident in socially desirable behavior that is rigid, exaggerated, and inappropriate. The person who uses reaction formation cannot admit to other feelings, such as overprotective mothers who cannot allow any conscious hostility toward their children. Reaction formation is most clearly observable when the defense breaks down, as when the model boy shoots his parents or when the man who "wouldn't hurt a fly" goes on a killing rampage. Of similar interest here are the occasional reports of judges who commit crimes or of pious religious figures who engage in inappropriate sexual conduct.

A defense mechanism that you may recognize in yourself is **rationalization**. Rationalization is a more complex, "mature" defense mechanism than is a process such as denial in that, in rationalization, people do not simply deny that a thought or action occurred. In rationalization people recognize the existence of an action, but distort its underlying motive. Behavior is reinterpreted so that it appears reasonable and acceptable; the ego, in other words, constructs a rational motive to explain an unacceptable action that is actually caused by the irrational impulses of the id. Particularly interesting is that with rationalization the individual can express the dangerous impulse, seemingly without disapproval by the superego. Some of the greatest atrocities of humankind have been committed in the name of love. Through the defense of rationalization, we can be hostile while professing love, immoral in the pursuit of morality.

Another device used to express an impulse of the id in a manner that is free of anxiety is **sublimation**. In this relatively complex defense mechanism, the original object of gratification is replaced by a higher cultural goal that is far removed from a direct expression of the instinct. Whereas the other defense mechanisms meet the instincts head on and, by and large, prevent discharge, in sublimation the instinct is turned into a new and useful channel. In contrast to the other defense mechanisms, here the ego does not have to maintain a constant energy output to prevent discharge. Freud interpreted daVinci's Madonna as a sublimation of his longing for his mother. Becoming a surgeon, butcher, or boxer can represent sublimations, to a greater or lesser degree, of aggressive impulses. Being a psychiatrist can represent a sublimation of "Peeping Tom" tendencies. In all, as noted, Freud felt that the essence of civilization is contained in a person's ability to sublimate sexual and aggressive energies.

Repression

Every man has reminiscences which he would not tell to everyone but only to his friends. He has other matters in his mind which he would not reveal even to his friend, but only to himself, and that in secret. But there

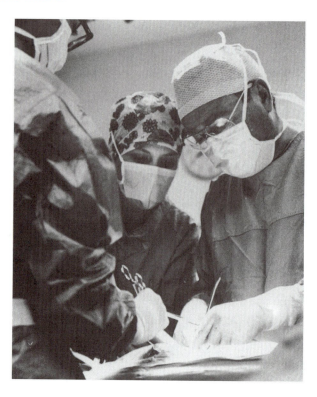

Sublimation: *In performing surgery, aggressive impulses can be turned toward useful, constructive ends.*

are other things which a man is afraid to tell even to himself, and every decent man has a number of such things stored away in his mind.

Dostoyevsky's *Notes from the Underground*

Finally, we come to the major defense mechanism of psychoanalytic theory: **repression**. In repression, a thought, idea, or wish is dismissed from consciousness. It is so traumatic and threatening to the self that it is buried in the unconscious, "stored away" in the depths of the mind. Repression is viewed as playing a part in all the other defense mechanisms and, like these other defenses, requires a constant expenditure of energy to keep that which is dangerous outside of consciousness.

Freud first recognized the defense mechanism of repression in his therapeutic work. After many weeks or months of therapy, patients would remember traumatic events from their past (and experience a catharsis, as we discussed earlier). Prior to recalling the event, the idea of the event, of course, was in the person's mind. But it was outside of the person's conscious awareness. Freud reasoned that the person first experienced the event consciously, but that the experience was so traumatic that the individual repressed it.

To Freud, these therapeutic experiences were sufficient evidence to establish the reality of repression. However, reflecting its importance to psychoanalytic theory, many other investigators over the years have studied repression experimentally, in the lab. An early study was done by Rosenzweig (1941). He varied the level of personal involvement in a task, and then studied research participants' (in this case, college undergraduates) recall of their success or failure on the activity. Rosenzweig found that when participants were personally involved with the experiment, they recalled a larger proportion of tasks that they had been able to complete successfully than tasks they had been unable to complete; they presumably repressed the experiences of failure. When the students did not feel threatened, they remembered more of the uncompleted tasks. In research conducted more recently, women high in sex guilt and women low in sex guilt were exposed to an erotic videotape and asked to report their level of sexual arousal. At the same time, their level of physiological response was recorded. Women high in sex guilt were found to report less arousal than those low in sex guilt but to show greater physiological arousal. Presumably the guilt associated with sexual arousal led to repression or blocking of awareness of the physiological arousal (Morokoff, 1985).

Particularly compelling evidence of the fact that people sometimes repress psychological experiences comes from extensive research on *repressive coping style*. The idea behind this line of research is that some people are particularly prone to repress unacceptable experiences. You may know such people. If you ask them how they are doing, they say "fine, I'm OK," even if it is obvious to you that they are experiencing a lot of stress and anxiety. Weinberger, Schwartz, and Davidson (1979) conducted a seminal study in this area. These investigators solved two problems confronted by anyone who wishes to do research on this topic: (1) How does one identify people who are particularly likely to repress events (i.e., "repressors"). The challenge, of course, is that people who repress their own negative qualities are not likely to tell you that they do so; they may not be consciously aware that they are repressors. (2) How does one demonstrate that the repressors actually are experiencing stressful emotions that they do not admit having? Weinberger and colleagues solved the first problem by using a technique we discussed in Chapter 2, namely, a social desirability scale. They administered a social desirability scale plus a self-report measure of anxiety to a large group of undergraduates, and reasoned that people who (a) report extremely low levels of anxiety, but also (b) score high on social desirability (i.e., they give a wide variety of responses that seem designed to hide undesirable personal qualities) are not actually people with low levels of anxiety but, rather, highly anxious people who are repressing their anxieties. Those with low anxiety levels, high anxiety levels, and repressors were then invited to participate in a laboratory study in which they were asked to complete word phrases, some of which contained material with sexual or aggressive content. Physiological measures of anxious arousal were taken while participants performed this task. The findings (Figure 3.1) revealed that the repressors—who had described themselves, in their conscious self-reports, as low in anxiety—were actually high in anxiety. The physiological measures indicated that they experienced a level of anxious arousal that exceeded not only the low anxious persons, but even the people who had described themselves as high in anxiety.

In another fascinating study of repression, subjects were asked to think back to their childhood and recall any experience or situation that came to mind. They also were asked to recall childhood experiences associated with each of five emotions (happiness, sadness, anger, fear, and wonder) and to indicate the earliest experience recalled for each emotion. Subjects were divided into repressors and two types of nonrepressors (high anxious and low anxious nonrepressors) on the basis of their response to questionnaires. Did the subjects differ in recall, as would be suggested by the psychoanalytic theory of

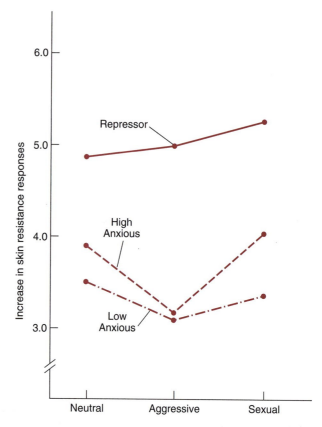

Figure 3.1 *Spontaneous skin resistence (a physiological index of anxiety) among three types of research participants (repressors, high anxious, and low anxious persons) as they responded to phrases containing neutral, aggressive, and sexual content. From Weinberger et al. (1979).*

repression? It was found that repressors recalled fewer negative emotions and were significantly older at the time of the earliest negative memory recalled (Figure 3.2). The authors concluded: "The pattern of findings is consistent with the hypothesis that repression involves an inaccessibility to negative emotional memories and indicates further that repression is associated in some way with the suppression or inhibition of emotional experiences in general. The concept of repression as a process involving limited access to negative affective memories appears to be valid" (Davis & Schwartz, 1987, p. 155).

Research along these lines supports the view that some individuals may be characterized as having a repressive style (Weinberger, 1990). Such individuals report little tendency to experience negative affect and have relatively stereotyped emotional responses. They have rather consistent self-images, report little inclination to change, and resist information that might produce such change. Although they are relatively calm, such calmness appears to be bought at a price. Thus, for example, they appear to be physiologically more reactive to stress than are nonrepressors and more prone to develop a variety of illnesses (Contrada, Czarnecki, & Pan, 1997; Derakshan & Eysenck, 1997; Weinberger & Davidson, 1994). Reporting on related research, Schwartz indicated that the cheerfulness of repressors masks high blood pressure and high pulse rates, putting them at risk for illnesses such as heart disease and cancer (APA Monitor, 1990, p. 14). This view fits with other evidence suggesting that a lack of emotional expressiveness is associated with increased risk of illness (Cox & MacKay, 1982; Levy, 1991; Temoshok, 1985, 1991).

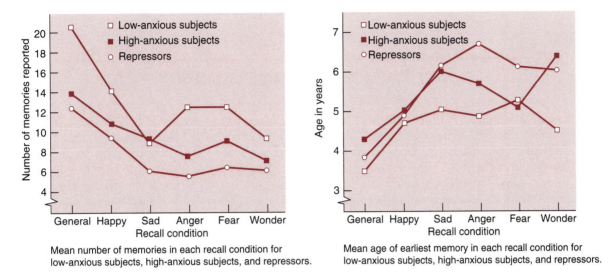

Mean number of memories in each recall condition for low-anxious subjects, high-anxious subjects, and repressors.

Mean age of earliest memory in each recall condition for low-anxious subjects, high-anxious subjects, and repressors.

Figure 3.2 *Repression and Affective Memories. (Davis & Schwartz, 1987) (Copyright © 1987 by the American Psychological Association. Reprinted by permission.)*

In considering the status of the concept of repression, we return to issues considered in relation to the concept of the unconscious, which is not surprising since the two are linked so closely. On the one hand, contemporary research has firmly established that people are sometimes motivated to banish from their conscious experience thoughts that are threatening or painful. As Freud would have expected, some people who consciously report that they are free from psychological distress in reality harbor anxiety-related thought and emotions of which they appear not to be aware. On the other hand, it is not clear that contemporary experimental research supports precisely the conception of repression put forth by Freud. Consider the research on repressive coping style. It documents repression among a select subset of people (repressors), whereas Freud's theory postulated that all persons repress emotionally traumatic material. Furthermore, this research documents repression using relatively simple laboratory stimuli that surely do not evoke the deep-seated and utterly traumatic experiences that Freud studied in his patients.

GROWTH AND DEVELOPMENT

The psychoanalytic theory of personality development takes into consideration all aspects of the development of character (personality). There are two major aspects to the theory of development. The first is that the individual progresses through stages of development. The second emphasizes the importance of early events for all later behavior. An extreme psychoanalytic position would go so far as to say that the most significant aspects of later personality have been formed by the end of the first five years of life.

The Development of Thinking Processes

The psychoanalytic theory of the development of thinking processes focuses on the change from **primary process** thinking to **secondary process** thinking.

CURRENT QUESTIONS

RECOVERED MEMORIES OR FALSE MEMORIES?

Psychoanalysts suggest that through the defense mechanism of repression people bury memories of traumatic experiences of childhood in the unconscious. They also suggest that under some conditions, such as psychotherapy, individuals can recall their forgotten experiences. On the other hand, others question the accuracy of adult recall of childhood experiences. The issue has reached headline proportions as individuals report recalling experiences of childhood sexual abuse and initiate lawsuits against individuals now recalled to be the perpetrators of the abuse. Although some professionals are convinced of the authenticity of these memories of sexual abuse, and suggest that a disservice is done to the person when we do not treat them as real, others question their authenticity and refer to them as part of a "false memory syndrome." While some view the recovery of these memories as beneficial to those who previously repressed the trauma of abuse, others suggest that the "memories" are induced by the probing questions of therapists convinced that such abuse has taken place.

An article in a professional psychological journal asks: "What scientific basis is there for the authenticity of memories of sexual abuse that were 'repressed' but then "remembered" with the help of a therapist? How are scientists, jurists, and distressed individuals themselves to distinguish true memories from false ones?" Answering these questions is difficult. On the one hand, we know that people can forget events that subsequently are remembered. This is obvious from one's own experiences in remembering events from one's past. Yet there is an alternative possibility that is intriguing—indeed, somewhat disturbing. It is that we might sometimes "recall" events that never occurred in the first place. We might sometimes have "false memories."

Research documents that it is possible for people to experience false memories, that is, recollections of events that did not, in fact, occur. For example, Mazzoni and Memon (2003) conducted a study involving three experimental sessions that each were separated in time by one week. In the first session, adult research participants completed a survey in which they reported the likelihood that they had experienced each of a large series of life events in their childhood. In session two, the experimenters conducted an experimental manipulation involving two of the events from the survey. The two events were minor medical procedures: a tooth extraction and the removal of a skin sample from one's small finger. For one of the events, participants merely were exposed to a paragraph of information about the type of event. For the other event, participants were asked to imagine the event occurring. In the third session, participants completed the survey again and reported any memories they had of the two target events. The hypothesis was that imagining the events—i.e., forming a mental imagine of the event occurring in one's life years earlier—could cause people to believe that the event, in fact, had occurred. This is what happened (see Figure 3.3). Whether they had imagined the tooth extraction or the removal of a skin sample, participants were more likely to believe that the event had occurred and to imagine some aspects of the event if they merely had been asked to imagine it a week earlier. A critical aspect of this particular study is that one of the events, the skin sample removal, surely had never occurred to the participants; medical records in the area that the study was conducted indicated that physicians never employed the procedure. Thus, the findings showed that participants ended up remembering information (e.g., aspects of the physical setting, the medical personnel involved) about an event that never had occurred.

This sort of study does not resolve the question of whether the memories of a particular client in therapy are accurate or false. In individual cases, this issue surely will remain controversial. Psychologists have no reliable method of distinguishing between "recovered memories" and "false memories" in each individual case. However, the research does demonstrate that it is at least possible for people to "remember" events that demonstrably had not occurred.

SOURCES: American Psychological Society Observer, 1992; Loftus, 1993, *New York Times*, April 8, 1994, p. A1; Mazzoni & Memon, 2003; Williams, 1994.

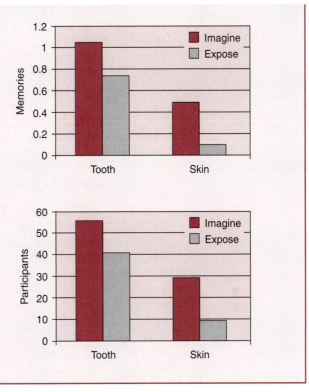

Figure 3.3 *The graphs display amount of memories recalled (top) and percentage of participants who experienced significant memory of events (bottom) as a result of either imagining the event occurring or merely being exposed to information about the event.*

Primary process thinking is the language of the unconscious in which reality and fantasy are indistinguishable. Aspects of primary process thinking are seen in dreams. Here events occur in more than one place at the same time, characteristics of different people and objects are combined, events shift rapidly back and forth in time, and what in waking life is impossible occurs with ease. Secondary process thinking is the language of consciousness and reality testing. Parallel to this is the development of the ego and superego. With the development of the ego, the individual becomes more differentiated, as a self, from the rest of the world and there is a decrease in self-preoccupation.

Epstein (1994) has made a related distinction in types of thinking, that between experiential thinking and rational thinking. These are viewed as two fundamentally different ways of knowing, one associated with feelings and experience and the other with intellect. Experiential thinking, analogous to primary process thinking, is viewed as earlier in evolutionary development and characterized by being holistic, concrete, and heavily influenced by emotion. Often it is used in interpersonal situations to be empathic or intuitive. Rational thinking, analogous to secondary process thinking, is viewed as later in evolutionary development and characterized by being more abstract, analytical, and following the rules of logic and evidence. For example, rational thinking would be used in solving mathematical problems. The potential conflict between the two systems of thought can be seen in an experiment in which subjects were asked to choose between drawing a winning red jelly bean from a bowl that contained 1 out of 10 red jelly beans, and a bowl that contained 8 out of 100 red jelly beans (Denes-Raj & Epstein, 1994). Having been told the proportion of red jelly beans in the two bowls, subjects knew that the rational thing to do was to select the bowl with the higher proportion—1 out of 10. Yet, despite this, many subjects felt that their chances were better with the bowl that contained more red jelly beans, despite the poorer odds. This conflict between what they felt and what they knew expressed the conflict between the experiential and rational thought systems. According to Epstein (1994), the two systems are parallel and can act in conjunction with one another as well as in conflict with one another. This is likely the case in most creative activities. Also, there are individual differences in the extent to which each system is developed and available for use in specific enterprises.

The Development of the Instincts

The most significant part of the psychoanalytic theory of development concerns the development of the instincts. The source of the instincts is states of bodily tension, which tend to focus on certain regions of the body, called **erogenous zones**. According to the theory, there is a biologically determined development of, and change in, the major erogenous zones of the body. At any one time the major source of excitation and energy tends to focus on a particular zone, with the location of that zone changing during the early developmental years. The first erogenous zone is the mouth, the second the anus, and the third the genitals. The mental and emotional growth of the child are dependent on the social interactions, anxieties, and gratifications that occur in relation to these zones.

Stages of Development   The first major area of excitation, sensitivity, and energy is the mouth. It is the locus of excitation that leads to the name **oral stage**. Early oral gratification occurs in feeding, thumb sucking, and other mouth movements characteristic of infants. In adult life, traces of orality are seen in chewing gum, eating, smoking, and kissing. In the early oral stage the child is passive and receptive. In the late oral stage, with the development of teeth, there can be a fusion of sexual and aggressive pleasures. In children, such a fusion of instinctual gratification is seen in the eating of animal crackers. In later life, we see traces of orality in various spheres. For example, academic pursuits can have oral associations within the unconscious: one is given "food for thought," asked to "incorporate" material in reading, and told to "regurgitate" what has been learned on exams.

In the second stage of development, the **anal stage** (ages two and three), there is excitation in the anus and in the movement of feces through the anal passageway. The expulsion of the feces is believed to bring relief from tension and pleasure in the stimulation of the mucous membranes in that region. The pleasure related to this erogenous zone involves the organism in conflict. There is conflict between elimination and retention, between the pleasure in release and the pleasure in retention, and between the wish for pleasure in evacuation and the demands of the external world for delay. This latter conflict represents the first crucial conflict between the individual and society. Here the environment requires the child to violate the pleasure principle or be punished. The child may retaliate against such demands by intentional soiling (diarrhea); associate having bowel movements with losing something important, which leads to depression; or associate having bowel movements with giving a prize or gift to others, which may be associated with feelings of power and control.

In the **phallic stage** (ages four and five), excitation and tension come to focus in the genitals. The biological differentiation between the sexes leads to psychological differentiation. The male child develops erections, and the new excitations in this area lead to increased interest in the genitals and the realization that the female lacks the penis. This leads to the fear that he may lose his penis—**castration anxiety**. The father becomes a rival for the affections of the mother, as suggested in the song "I Want a Girl Just Like the Girl That Married Dear Old Dad." The boy's hostility toward the father is projected onto the father, with the consequent fear of retaliation. This leads to what is known as the **Oedipus complex**. According to the Oedipus complex, every boy is fated to kill his father in fantasy and marry his mother. The complex can be heightened by actual seductiveness on the part of the mother. Castration anxiety can be heightened by actual threats from the father to cut off the penis. These threats occur in a surprising number of cases.

For an interesting illustration of an effort to test the concept of the Oedipus complex, we can return to the subliminal psychodynamic activation studies of the unconscious. As previously described, in this research stimuli are presented to subjects subliminally in a tachistoscope. When certain stimuli register subliminally, they presumably activate unconscious conflicts and either intensify or alleviate these conflicts, depending on the nature of the conflict and the stimulus presented. The point of the current experiment was to manipulate the degree of Oedipal conflict in males and to observe the effects of their performance in a competitive situation (Silverman et al., 1978). The stimuli chosen to intensify or alleviate Oedipal conflict were "Beating Dad Is Wrong" and "Beating Dad Is OK." In addition, a number of other stimuli were presented, including the neutral stimulus "People Are Walking." These stimuli were presented tachistoscopically to male college students after they engaged in a dart-throwing competition. The subjects were tested again for dart-throwing performance following subliminal exposure to each of the stimuli. As expected, the two Oedipal stimuli had clear-cut effects in different directions. The "Beating Dad Is OK" stimulus was followed by significantly higher scores than those following the neutral stimulus, whereas the "Beating Dad Is Wrong" stimulus was followed by significantly lower scores than those following the neutral stimulus (Table 3.2).

What is interesting about this research is that whereas the theoretical formulation was derived from clinical material with patients, the experimental testing involved normal college males. The assumption of the experimenters was that "since most persons are vulnerable to some degree of neurotic behav-

Table 3.2 Oedipal Conflict and Competitive Performance

Dart Score	"Beating Dad Is Wrong"	"Beating Dad Is OK"	"People Are Walking"
TACHISTOSCOPIC PRESENTATION OF THREE STIMULI			
Mean, Prestimulus	443.7	444.3	439.0
Mean, Poststimulus	349.0	533.3	442.3
Difference	-94.7	+90.0	+3.3

Partial results adapted from Silverman et al., 1978, p. 346. Copyright by the American Psychological Association. Reprinted by permission.

ior and since, according to psychoanalytic understanding, Oedipal conflict often plays a central pathogenic role, we anticipated that the clinically based relationship might apply to a 'normal' college population" (p. 342). Two additional points are worthy of note since there have been difficulties in replicating this type of research. First, the results were not obtained when the stimuli were presented above threshold. The psychodynamic activation effects appear to operate at the unconscious rather than at the conscious level. Second, the authors emphasize that the experimental stimuli must relate to the motivational state of the subjects and the response measured must be sensitive to changes in this motivational state. Thus, in the experiment aforementioned, subjects were first "primed" with picture and story material containing Oedipal content and then the task was presented as one involving competition.

The developmental processes during this stage are somewhat different for the female. She realizes the lack of a penis and blames the mother, the original love object. In developing **penis envy**, the female child chooses the father as the love object and imagines that the lost organ will be restored by having a child by the father.[1] Whereas the Oedipus complex is abandoned in the boy because of castration anxiety, in the female it is started because of penis envy. As with the male, conflict during this period is in some cases accentuated by seductiveness on the part of the father toward the female child. And, as with the male, the female child resolves the conflict by keeping the father as a love object but gaining him through identification with the mother.

Do children actually display Oedipal behaviors or are these all distorted memories of adults, in particular patients in psychoanalytic treatment? A study investigated this question through the use of parents' reports of parent-child interactions, as well as through the analysis of children's responses to stories involving parent-child interaction. It was found that at around age four, children show increased preference for the parent of the opposite sex and an increased antagonism toward the parent of the same sex. These behaviors diminish at around the age of five or six. What is interesting in this study is that although the researchers came from a differing theoretical orientation, they concluded that the reported Oedipal behaviors coincided with the psychoanalytic view of Oedipal relations between mothers and sons and between fathers and daughters (Watson & Getz, 1990).

As part of the resolution of the Oedipus complex, the child identifies with the parent of the same sex. The child now gains the parent of the opposite sex through **identification** with, rather than defeat of, the parent of the same sex. The development of an identification with the parent of the same sex is a critical issue during the phallic stage and, more generally, is a critical concept in developmental psychology. In identification, individuals take on themselves the qualities of another person and integrate them into their functioning. In identifying with their parents, children assume many of the same values and morals. It is in this sense that the superego has been called the heir to the resolution of the Oedipus complex.

According to Freud, all major aspects of our personality character develop during the oral, anal, and phallic stages of development. Although Freud gave

---

[1] Psychoanalytic theory has been criticized by feminists on a variety of grounds. Perhaps more than any other concept, the concept of penis envy is seen as expressing a chauvinistic, hostile view toward women. This issue will be addressed in Chapter 4 in the "Critical Evaluation" section.

Oedipus Complex, Competition, and Identification: *For the male child to become competitive, there must not be too much anxiety about rivalry with the father. Jim Burt, of the N.Y. Giants football team, carried his son around the field after winning the 1987 Super Bowl. He describes his son, Jim Jr., age 4 1/2, as "So much like me it's frightening. He's got the same fire in his eyes. And like when we wrestle together on the rug, he always wants to win."*

relatively little attention to developmental factors after the resolution of the Oedipus complex, he did recognize their existence. After the phallic stage, the child enters latency. The meaning of the **latency stage** has never been clear in psychoanalytic theory. An assumption of a decrease in sexual urges and interest during the ages of 6 through 13 might have fit observations of Victorian children, but it does not fit observations of children in other cultures. A more plausible assumption, and one more difficult to test, is that there are no new developments during this stage in terms of the ways in which children gratify their instincts.

The onset of puberty, with the reawakening of the sexual urges and Oedipal feelings, marks the beginning of the **genital stage**. The significance of this period for individuals and for their functioning in society is demonstrated in the initiation rites of many cultures (e.g., the Jewish bar mitzvah). Dependency feelings and Oedipal strivings that were not fully resolved during the pregenital stages of development now come back to rear their ugly heads. The turmoil of adolescence is partly attributable to these factors. According to Freud, successful progression through the stages of development leads to the psychologically healthy person—one who can love and work.

Erikson's Psychosocial Stages of Development   It is clear that in the psychoanalytic theory of development, major attention is given to the first five years and to the development of the instincts. Ego psychologists have tried, within this framework, to give greater attention to other developments during the early years and to significant developments that take place during the latency and genital stages. Erik Erikson (1902–1994), one of the leading ego psychoanalysts, describes development in psychosocial terms rather than merely in sexual terms (Table 3.3). Thus, the first stage is significant not just because of the localization of pleasure in the mouth, but because in the feeding situation a

Erik H. Erikson

Table 3.3   Erikson's Eight Psychosocial Stages of Development and Their Implications for Personality

Psychosocial Stage	Age	Positive Outcomes	Negative Outcomes
Basic Trust vs. Mistrust	1 year	Feelings of inner goodness, trust in oneself and others, optimism	Sense of badness, mistrust of self and others, pessimism
Autonomy vs. Shame and Doubt	2–3 years	Exercise of will, self-control, able to make choices	Rigid, excessive conscience, doubtful, self-conscious shame
Intitiative vs. Guilt	4–5 years	Pleasure in accomplishments, activity, direction and purpose	Guilt over goals contemplated and achievements initiated
Industry vs. Inferiority	Latency	Able to be absorbed in productive work, pride in completed product	Sense of inadequacy and inferiority, unable to complete work
Identity vs. Role Diffusion	Adolescence	Confidence of inner sameness and continuity, promise of a career	Ill at ease in roles, no set standards, sense of artificiality
Intimacy vs. Isolation	Early Adulthood	Mutuality, sharing of thoughts, work, feelings	Avoidance of intimacy, superficial relations
Generativity vs. Stagnation	Adulthood	Ability to lose oneself in work and relationships	Loss of interest in work, impoverished relations
Integrity vs. Despair	Later Years	Sense of order and meaning, content with self and one's accomplishments	Fear of death, bitter about life and what one got from it or what did not happen

relationship of trust or mistrust is developed between the infant and the mother. Similarly, the anal stage is significant not only for the change in the nature of the major erogenous zone, but also because toilet training is a significant social situation in which the child may develop a sense of autonomy or succumb to shame and self-doubt. In the phallic stage the child must struggle with the issue of taking pleasure in, as opposed to feeling guilty about being assertive, competitive, and successful.

For Erikson (1950), the latency and genital stages are periods when the individual develops a sense of industry and success or a sense of inferiority, and perhaps most important of all, a sense of identity or a sense of role diffusion. The crucial task of adolescence, according to Erickson, is the establishment of a sense of ego identity, an accrued confidence that the way one views oneself has a continuity with one's past and is matched by the perceptions of others. In contrast to people who develop a sense of identity, people with role diffusion experience the feeling of not really knowing who they are, of not knowing whether what they think they are matches what others think of them, and of not knowing how they have developed in this way or where they are heading in the future. During late adolescence and the college years, this struggle with a sense of identity may lead to joining a variety of groups and to considerable anguish about the choice of a career. If these issues are not resolved during this time, the individual is, in later life, filled with a sense of despair; life is too short, and it is too late to start all over again.

In his research on the process of identity formation, Marcia (1994) has identified four statuses individuals can have in relation to this process. In Identity Achievement, the individual has established a sense of identity following exploration. Such individuals function at a high psychological level, being capable of independent thought, intimacy in interpersonal relations, complex moral reasoning, and resistance to group demands for conformity or group manipulation of their sense of self-esteem. In Identity Moratorium, the individual is in the midst of an identity crisis. Such individuals are capable of high levels of psychological functioning, as indicated in complex thought and moral reasoning, and also value intimacy. However, they are still struggling with just who they are and what they are about, and are less prepared than the identity achievers to make commitments. In Identity Foreclosure, the individual is committed to an identity without having gone through a process of exploration. Such individuals tend to be rigid, highly responsive to group demands for conformity, and sensitive to manipulation of their self-esteem. They tend to be highly conventional and rejecting of deviation from perceived standards of right and wrong. Finally, in Identity Diffusion, the individual lacks any strong sense of identity or commitment. Such individuals are very vulnerable to blows to their self-esteem, often are disorganized in their thinking, and have problems with intimacy. In sum, Marcia suggests that individuals differ in how they go about handling the process of identity formation, with such differences being reflected in their sense of self, thought processes, and interpersonal relations. Although not necessarily establishing fixed patterns for later life, how the process of identity formation is handled is seen as having important implications for later personality development.

Continuing with his description of the later stages of life and the accompanying psychological issues, Erikson suggests that some people develop a sense of intimacy, an acceptance of life's successes and disappointments, and a sense of continuity throughout the life cycle, whereas other people remain isolated from family and friends, appear to survive on a fixed daily routine, and focus on both past disappointments and future death. Although the ways in which people do and do not resolve these critical issues of adulthood may have their roots in childhood conflict, Erikson suggests that this is not always the case

Identity vs. Role Diffusion: *In adolescence, a sense of ego identity is developed partly by having one's sense of self confirmed by the perceptions of friends.*

and that they have a significance of their own (Erikson, 1982). In sum, Erikson's contributions are noteworthy in three ways: (1) he has emphasized the psychosocial as well as the instinctual basis for personality development; (2) he has extended the stages of development to include the entire life cycle and has articulated the major psychological issues to be faced in these later stages; and (3) he has recognized that people look to the future as well as to the past, and how they construe their future may be as significant a part of their personality as how they construe their past.

The Importance of Early Experience   Psychoanalytic theory places enormous emphasis on the role of early life events for later personality development. Much of adult life is a repetition of themes established during the early developmental stages. Many contemporary researchers, however, suggest a much greater potential for development and change in personality across the entire life span. Although the issue is complex, with no uniform consensus (Caspi & Bem, 1990), many scholars highlight the fact that, to a degree not fully appreciated by Freud, changes in an individual's environment that occur later in life can bring about changes in personality (Kagan, 1998; Lewis, 2002). Indeed, in contrast to the themes established by Freud, a major trend in contemporary psychology is the study of personality dynamics across the entire course of life, from childhood to older adulthood (Baltes, Staudinger, & Lindenberger, 1999).

The complexities of the issue can be illustrated with two studies. The first, conducted by a psychoanalyst (Gaensbauer, 1982), involved the study of affect development in infancy. The infant, Jenny, was first studied systematically when she was almost four months old. Prior to this time, at the age of three months, she had been physically abused by her father. At that time she was brought to the hospital with a broken arm and a skull fracture. She was described by hospital personnel as being a "lovable baby"—happy, cute, sociable, but also as not cuddling when held and as being "jittery" when approached by a male. Following this history of abuse, Jenny was placed in a foster home, where she received adequate physical care but minimal social interaction. This was very much in contrast with her earlier experience with her natural mother, who spent considerable time with her and breast-fed her "at the drop of a hat." The first systematic observation occurred almost a month after placement in the foster home. At this time Jenny's behavior was judged to be completely consistent with a diagnosis of depression—lethargic, apathetic, disinterested, collapsed posture. A systematic analysis of her facial expressions indicated five discrete affects, each meaningfully related to her unique history. Sadness was noted when she was with her natural mother. Fearfulness and anger were noted when she was approached by a male stranger but not when approached by a female stranger. Joy was noted as a transient affect during brief play sequences. Finally, interest-curiosity was noted when she interacted with female strangers.

After she was visited in her foster home, Jenny was placed in a different foster home where she received warm attention. Following two weeks in this environment, she was again brought to the hospital for further evaluation, this time by her second foster mother. This time she generally appeared to be a normally responsive infant. She showed no evidence of distress and even smiled at a male stranger. After an additional month at this foster home, she was brought to the hospital by her natural mother for a third evaluation. Generally, she was animated and happy. However, when the mother left the room, she cried intensely. This continued following the mother's return despite repeated attempts to soothe her. Apparently separation from her natural mother continued to lead to a serious distress response. In addition, sadness and anger were frequently noted. At eight months old, Jenny was returned to her natural mother, who left her husband and received counseling. At the age of 20 months, she was described as appearing to be normal and having an excellent relationship with her mother. However, there continued to be the problem of anger and distress associated with separation from her mother.

From these observations, we can conclude that there was evidence of both continuity and discontinuity between Jenny's early emotional experiences and her later emotional reactions. In general, she was doing well and her emotional responses were within the normal range for infants of her age. At the same time, the anger reactions in response to separations and frustration appeared to be a link to the past. The psychoanalyst conducting the study suggested that perhaps isolated traumatic events are less important than the repeated experiences of a less dramatic but more persistent nature. In other words, the early years are important, but more in terms of patterns of interpersonal relationships than in terms of isolated events.

The second study, conducted by a group of developmental psychologists, assessed the relationship between early emotional relationships with the mother and later psychopathology (Lewis, et al., 1984). In this study, the attachment behavior toward their mother of boys and girls one year of age was observed. The observation involved a standardized procedure consisting of a period of play with the mother in an unstructured situation, followed by the departure of the mother and a period when the child was alone in the playroom, and then by the return of the mother and a second free play period. The behavior of the children was scored systematically and assigned to one of three attachment categories: avoidant, secure, or ambivalent. The avoidant and ambivalent categories suggested difficulties in this area. Then at six years of age, the competence of these children was assessed through the completion by the mothers of a Child Behavior Profile. The ratings of the mothers were also checked against teacher ratings. On the basis of the Child Behavior Profile the children were classified into a normal group, an at-risk group, and a clinically disturbed group.

What was the relationship between early attachment behavior and later pathology? Two aspects of the results are particularly noteworthy. First, the relationships were quite different for boys than for girls. For boys, attachment classification at one year of age was significantly related to later pathology. Insecurely attached boys showed more pathology at age six than did securely attached boys. On the other hand, no relationship between attachment and later pathology was observed for girls. Second, the authors noted a difference between trying to predict pathology from the early data (prospective) as opposed to trying to understand later pathology in terms of earlier attachment difficulties (retrospective). If one starts with the boys who at age six were identified as being at risk or clinically disturbed, 80 percent would be found to have been assigned to the avoidant- or ambivalent-attachment category at age one. In other words, a very strong statistical relationship exists. On the other hand, if one took all boys classified as insecurely attached (avoidant or ambivalent) at age one and predicted them to be at risk or clinically disturbed at age six, one would be right in only 40 percent of the cases. The reason for this is that far more of the boys were classified as insecurely attached than were later diagnosed as at risk or disturbed. Thus, the clinician viewing later pathology would have a clear basis for suggesting a strong relationship between pathology and early attachment difficulties. On the other hand, focusing on the data in terms of prediction would suggest a much more tenuous relationship and the importance of other variables. As Freud himself recognized, when we observe later pathology, it is all too easy to understand how it developed. On the other hand, when we look at these phenomena prospectively, we are made aware of the varied paths that development can follow.

As previously noted, the issues relevant to the importance of early experience for later personality development are complex. Perhaps we must seek a more differentiated approach to the question rather than a black-or-white answer. For example, the importance of early experience for later personality development might depend on the characteristic being studied. Perhaps some personality characteristics, once formed, are more resistant to change than are others. The role of early experience might also depend on the intensity of particular experiences, their duration, and the extent to which differing experiences occurred earlier and later. Thus, for example, the effects of maternal deprivation may depend on how serious and long-lasting the deprivation is, as well as on the role of positive experiences both before and following deprivation. Finally, we may note the distinction between what may occur and what must inevitably occur. Psychoanalytic theory can be accurate in portraying the possible effects of early experience, particularly as seen in various forms of psychological disturbance where a pattern of relationships is established early and maintained over time, without postulating that such effects are inevitable.

MAJOR CONCEPTS

Anal stage   Freud's concept for that period of life during which the major center of bodily excitation or tension is the anus.

Anxiety   In psychoanalytic theory, a painful emotional experience that signals or alerts the ego to danger.

Catharsis   The release and freeing of emotion through talking about one's problems.

Castration anxiety   Freud's concept of the boy's fear, experienced during the phallic stage, that the father will cut off the son's penis because of their sexual rivalry for the mother.

Conscious   Those thoughts, experiences, and feelings of which we are aware.

Death instinct   Freud's concept for drives or sources of energy directed toward death or a return to an inorganic state.

Defense mechanisms   Freud's concept for those mental strategies used by the person to reduce anxiety. They function to exclude from awareness of some thought, wish, or feeling.

Denial   The defense mechanism in which a painful internal or external reality is denied.

Ego   Freud's structural concept for the part of personality that attempts to satisfy drives (instincts) in accordance with reality and the person's moral values.

Energy system   Freud's view of personality as involving the interplay among various forces (e.g., drives, instincts) or sources of energy.

Erogenous zones   According to Freud, those parts of the body that are the sources of tension or excitation.

Free association   In psychoanalysis, the patient's reporting to the analyst of every thought that comes to mind.

Genital stage   In psychoanalytic theory, the stage of development associated with the onset of puberty.

Id   Freud's structural concept for the source of the instincts or all of the drive energy in people.

Identification   The acquisition, as characteristics of the self, of personality characteristics perceived to be part of others (e.g., parents).

Isolation   The defense mechanism in which emotion is isolated from the content of a painful impulse or memory.

Latency stage   In psychoanalytic theory, the stage following the phallic stage in which there is a decrease in sexual urges and interest.

Libido   The psychoanalytic term for the energy associated first with the sexual instincts and later with the life instincts.

Life instinct   Freud's concept for drives or sources of energy (libido) directed toward the preservation of life and sexual gratification.

Mechanism   An intellectual movement of the 19th century which argued that basic principles of natural science could explain not only the behavior of physical objects, but human thought and action.

Oedipus complex   Freud's concept expressing the boy's sexual attraction to the mother and fear of castration by the father, who is seen as a rival.

Oral stage   Freud's concept for that period of life during which the major center of bodily excitation or tension is the mouth.

Penis envy   In psychoanalytic theory, the female's envy of the male's possession of a penis.

Perception without awareness   Unconscious perception or perception of a stimulus without conscious awareness of such perception.

Perceptual defense   The process by which an individual defends (unconsciously) against awareness of a threatening stimulus.

Phallic stage   Freud's concept for that period of life during which excitation or tension begins to be centered in the genitals and during which there is an attraction to the parent of the opposite sex.

Pleasure principle   According to Freud, psychological functioning based on the pursuit of pleasure and the avoidance of pain.

Preconscious   Freud's concept for those thoughts, experiences, and feelings of which we are momentarily unaware but can readily bring into awareness.

Primary process   In psychoanalytic theory, a form of thinking that is not governed by logic or reality testing and that is seen in dreams and other expressions of the unconscious.

Projection   The defense mechanism in which one attributes to (projects onto) others one's own unacceptable instincts or wishes.

Rationalization   The defense mechanism in which an acceptable reason is given for an unacceptable motive or act.

Reaction formation   The defense mechanism in which the opposite of an unacceptable impulse is expressed.

Reality principle   According to Freud, psychological functioning based on reality in which pleasure is delayed until an optimum time.

Repression   The primary defense mechanism in which a thought, idea, or wish is dismissed from consciousness.

Secondary process   In psychoanalytic theory, a form of thinking that is governed by reality and associated with the development of the ego.

Subliminal psychodynamic activation   The research procedure associated with psychoanalytic theory in which stimuli are presented below the perceptual threshold (subliminally) to stimulate unconscious wishes and fears.

Sublimation   The defense mechanism in which the original expression of the instinct is replaced by a higher cultural goal.

Superego   Freud's structural concept for the part of personality that expresses our ideals and moral values.

Unconscious   Those thoughts, experiences, and feelings of which we are unaware. According to Freud, this unawareness is the result of repression.

Undoing   The defense mechanism in which one magically undoes an act or wish associated with anxiety.

REVIEW

1. Psychoanalytic theory illustrates a psychodynamic, clinical approach to personality. The psychodynamic emphasis is expressed in the interpretation of behavior as a result of the interplay among motives or drives. The clinical approach is expressed in the emphasis on material observed during intensive treatment of individuals.

2. Events in Freud's life played a role in the development of his theory and influenced his approach toward science. Illustrative here are the emphasis on the death instincts in relation to World War I, his emphasis on sex in relation to inhibitions concerning sexuality found in Victorian society, and the energy model then popular in other branches of science.

3. Two sets of structural concepts are key to psychoanalytic theory. The first relates to levels of consciousness-conscious, preconscious, and uncon-

scious. The second relates to different aspects of people's functioning as expressed in the concepts of id, ego, and superego, roughly corresponding to drives (instincts), an orientation toward reality, and morals.

4. Experimental research on the unconscious is illustrated by the study of perception without awareness and subliminal psychodynamic activation. Although there remains dispute concerning the importance of unconscious phenomena, almost all psychologists agree that we can be influenced by stimuli that are outside of conscious awareness.

5. In psychoanalytic theory the person is viewed as an energy system, and the source of energy lies in the life and death instincts or the sexual and aggressive instincts.

6. Crucial to the dynamics of psychological functioning are the concepts of anxiety and the defense mechanisms. Anxiety is a painful emotion that acts as a signal of impending danger. The defense mechanisms represent ways of distorting reality and excluding feelings from awareness so that we do not feel anxious. Repression, in which a thought or wish is dismissed from consciousness, is particularly important in this regard.

7. According to psychoanalytic theory, the individual progresses through stages of development. The development of the instincts is related to changes in the sensitivity of different parts of the body (erogenous zones) and is expressed in the concepts of oral, anal, and phallic stages. The Oedipus complex, which develops during the phallic stage, is seen as a particularly important psychological development and has been the subject of considerable research.

8. Psychoanalyst Erik Erikson attempted to broaden and extend psychoanalytic theory through an emphasis on the psychosocial stages of development.

9. Psychoanalytic theory emphasizes the importance of early experience, particularly during the first five years of life, for later personality development. Research on the relationship between early experiences and later psychopathology illustrates an effort to study the importance of early experience for later personality development. The importance of early events probably is influenced by the intensity of these events and whether subsequent events further strengthen what has been formed or turn personality development in new directions.

4

A PSYCHODYNAMIC THEORY: APPLICATIONS AND EVALUATION OF FREUD'S THEORY

CLINICAL APPLICATIONS
Assessment: Projective Tests
The Rorschach Inkblot Test
The Thematic Apperception Test (TAT)
Illustrative Research Use and Evaluation
Projective Tests—Do They Work?

PSYCHOPATHOLOGY
Personality Types
The Oral Personality
The Anal Personality
The Phallic Character
Conflict and Defense

BEHAVIOR CHANGE
Insights into the Unconscious: Free Association and Dream Interpretation
The Therapeutic Process: Transference

A CASE EXAMPLE: LITTLE HANS
Description of the Problem
Events Leading Up to Development of the Phobia
Interpretation of the Symptom
The Solution to the Oedipal Conflict
Overall Evaluation

THE CASE OF JIM
Rorschach and TAT: Psychoanalytic Theory
Comments on the Data

RELATED POINTS OF VIEW
Two Early Challenges to Freud
Alfred Adler (1870–1937)
Carl G. Jung (1875–1961)
The Cultural and Interpersonal Emphasis
Karen Horney (1885–1952)
Harry Stack Sullivan (1892–1949)

RECENT DEVELOPMENTS IN THE PSYCHODYNAMIC TRADITION
Object Relations Theory
Narcissism and the Narcissistic Personality
Attachment Theory and Adult Personal Relationships
Attachment Styles in Adulthood
Attachment Types or Dimensions?

CRITICAL EVALUATION
Major Contributions
Limitations of the Theory
The Scientific Status of Psychoanalytic Theory
The Psychoanalytic View of the Person
Summary Evaluation

MAJOR CONCEPTS

REVIEW

Chapter Focus

When you were a kid, did you ever play the cloud game? It had to be a day when there were big white fluffy clouds against the blue background of the sky. You would lie on your back in the grass with a friend and stare at the clouds until you "saw" something. If you tried long and hard enough you could find all kinds of interesting things: animals, dragons, the face of an old man. Quite often, pointing out your discoveries to your friend was impossible. Exactly what you saw could only be seen by you. Why did you see the things you saw? It must have been something about you that you "projected" onto the cloud in the sky.

This is the basic idea behind projective tests such as the Rorschach Inkblot Test and the Thematic Apperception Test (TAT). In this chapter, we focus on these tests because they are techniques of personality assessment associated with psychodynamic theory. Projective tests use ambiguous stimuli to elicit highly individualistic responses which can then be interpreted by the clinician. This chapter also considers Freud's attempts to understand and explain the symptoms presented by his patients and his efforts to develop a systematic method of treatment. After considering more recent developments in psychoanalytic theory, including challenges to Freud's ideas from other psychodynamic theorists, we turn to a critical evaluation and summary.

QUESTIONS TO BE ADDRESSED IN THIS CHAPTER

1. Which personality tests are best suited to assess an individual's personality from a psychoanalytic standpoint?
2. How can we understand the diverse forms of psychopathology from a psychoanalytic perspective?
3. How does psychoanalytic therapy attempt to facilitate psychological growth and improved psychological functioning?
4. Why did various early followers of Freud reject psychoanalysis in favor of an alternative theory?
5. How can we evaluate psychoanalysis as a theory of personality?

CLINICAL APPLICATIONS

Psychoanalysis is a clinical theory of personality, focusing on the intensive study of the person. The theory emphasizes unconscious processes and the interplay among motives. These theoretical ideas, however, cannot merely stand by themselves as an abstract intellectual structure. To obtain a theory that is useful, one must relate the abstract ideas to concrete procedures for assessing personality and for treating psychopathology. This chapter considers the ways in which psychoanalytic thinkers have addressed this challenge.

We begin with the problem of assessment, and with the attempted solution provided by projective tests.

ASSESSMENT: PROJECTIVE TESTS

Although many different personality tests can be used with psychoanalytic theory, the ones most closely linked to the theory are **projective tests**. The defining feature of projective tests is that the test items are ambiguous. The test contains stimuli whose meaning is unclear. Test takers are asked to interpret the stimuli, in other words, to say what they think the test items mean. The idea is that their interpretations will reveal aspects of the test taker's personality. Note that this is utterly unlike a standard questionnaire or survey. Usually people writing items for a questionnaire strive for clarity. For a typical questionnaire, an item such as "Do you like things?" would be a terrible test item because it is so ambiguous. "What things are you talking about?", the test taker would ask. But on a projective test, this ambiguity is the very point of the test. The psychologist is interested in how the test taker constructs meaning out of the vague stimulus. The assumption is that the test taker's responses will be indicative of emotional themes and thinking styles that come into play in the person's day-to-day thoughts about the events of their life.

The term *projection* in relation to assessment techniques was first used in 1938 by Henry A. Murray, but the importance of projective tests was first emphasized most clearly by L. K. Frank in 1939. Frank argued against the use of standardized tests, which he felt classified people but told little about them as individuals. He argued for the use of tests that would offer insight into individuals' private worlds of meanings and feelings. Such tests would allow individuals to impose their own structure and organization on stimuli and would thereby express a dynamic conception of personality.

In this section we consider two projective tests, the Rorschach Inkblot Test and the Thematic Apperception Test (TAT). Both are unstructured—meaning that they allow subjects to respond in their own unique ways. Both are also disguised tests, in that generally subjects are not aware of their purpose or of how particular responses will be interpreted. Psychoanalytic theory is related to projective tests as follows:

1. Psychoanalytic theory emphasizes individual differences and the complex organization of personality functioning. Personality is viewed as a process through which the individual organizes and structures external stimuli in the environment. Projective tests allow subjects to respond with complete freedom in terms of both content and organization.

2. Psychoanalytic theory emphasizes the importance of the unconscious and defense mechanisms. In projective tests, the directions and stimuli provide few guidelines for responding, and the purposes of the test and interpretations of responses are hidden from the subject.

3. Psychoanalytic theory emphasizes a holistic understanding of personality in terms of relationships among parts, rather than the interpretation of behavior as expressive of single parts or personality characteristics. Projective tests generally lead to holistic interpretations based on the patterning and organization of test responses rather than on the interpretation of a single response reflecting a particular characteristic.

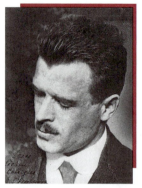

Hermann Rorschach

The Rorschach Inkblot Test

Although inkblots had been used earlier, Hermann Rorschach, a Swiss psychiatrist, first fully grasped the potential use of these stimuli for personality assessment. Rorschach put ink on paper and folded the paper so that symmetrical but ill-defined forms were produced. These inkblots were then shown to hospitalized patients. Through a process of trial and error, the inkblots that elicited different responses from different psychiatric groups were kept, while those that did not were discarded. He experimented with thousands of inkblots and finally settled on 10; the test, then, consists of 10 cards containing these inkblots.

Rorschach was well acquainted with the work of Freud, the concept of the unconscious, and the dynamic view of personality. The development of his test certainly seems to have been influenced by this view. Rorschach felt that the data from the inkblot test would increase understanding of the unconscious and have relevance for psychoanalytic theory. He used psychoanalytic theory in his own interpretations of subjects' responses.

When conducting the test, the experimenter tries to make the subjects relaxed and comfortable while providing them with sufficient information to complete the task. The test is presented as "just one of many ways used nowadays to try to understand people," and the experimenter volunteers as little information as possible; "It is best not to know much about the procedure until you have gone through it." Subjects are asked to look at each card and tell the examiner what they see—anything that might be represented on the card. Individuals are free to focus on the whole image or any aspect of the

Rorschach Inkblot Test: *The Rorschach interpreter assumes that the subject's personality is projected onto unstructured stimuli such as inkblots. (Drawing by Ross; © 1974 The New Yorker Magazine, Inc.)*

inkblot that they wish, and to provide any interpretation that comes to mind. All responses are recorded on the test record.

In interpreting the Rorschach, one is interested in how the response, or percept, is formed, the reasons for the response, and its content. The basic assumption, as noted earlier, is that the way individuals form their perceptions is related to the way they generally organize and structure stimuli in their environments. Perceptions that match the structure of the inkblot suggest a good level of psychological functioning that is well oriented toward reality. On the other hand, poorly formed responses that do not fit the structure of the inkblot suggest unrealistic fantasies or bizarre behavior. The content of subjects' responses (whether they see mostly animate or inanimate objects, humans or animals, and content expressing affection or hostility) makes a great deal of difference in the interpretation of the subjects' personalities. For example, compare the interpretations we might make of two sets of responses, one where animals are seen repeatedly as fighting and a second where humans are seen as sharing and involved in cooperative efforts.

Beyond this, content may be interpreted symbolically. An explosion may symbolize intense hostility; a pig, gluttonous tendencies; a fox, a tendency toward being crafty and aggressive; spiders, witches, and octopuses, negative images of a dominating mother; gorillas and giants, negative attitudes toward a dominating father; and an ostrich, an attempt to hide from conflicts (Schafer, 1954). Two illustrative stimuli and responses are presented in Figure 4.1.

Response: *"Two bears with their paws touching one another playing pattycake or could be they are fighting and the red is the blood from the fighting."*

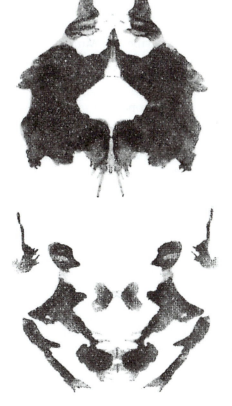

Response: *"Two cannibals. Supposed to see something in this? African natives bending over a pot. Possibly cooking something—hope they're not man-eaters. I shouldn't make jokes—always liking humor. (Are they male or female?) Could be male or female. More female because of breasts here. But didn't impress me at first glance as being of either sex."*

Figure 4.1 Examples from the Rorschach Inkblot Test. *The inkblot illustrations reproduced here are from the Rorschach location chart. The actual inkblot cards contain color. (Reprinted by permission of Hans Huber, Publishers.)*

It is important to recognize that the Rorschach test is not interpreted on the basis of one response alone, but in relation to the total sum of responses. However, each response is used to suggest hypotheses or possible interpretations about the individual's personality. Such hypotheses are checked against interpretations based on other responses, on the total response pattern, and on the subject's behavior while responding to the Rorschach. In relation to the subject's behavior, the examiner notes all unusual behavior and uses this as a source of data for further interpretation. For example, a subject who constantly asks for guidance may be interpreted as dependent. A subject who seems tense, asks questions in a subtle way, and looks at the back of the cards may be interpreted as suspicious and possibly paranoid.

The Thematic Apperception Test (TAT)

Another widely used projective test is the Thematic Apperception Test (TAT), developed by Henry Murray and Christina Morgan. The TAT consists of cards with scenes on them. Most depict one or two people in some important life situation, though some cards are more abstract. The subject is asked to make up a story based on the scene on the card, including what is going on, the thoughts and feelings of the participants, what led up to the scene, and the outcome. Since the scenes often are ambiguous, they leave considerable room for individuality in the content of subjects' stories: "The test is based on the well-recognized fact that when a person interprets an ambiguous social situation he is apt to expose his own personality as much as the phenomenon to which he is attending" (Murray, 1938, p. 530).

Some TAT cards are shown to both male and female subjects; others are shown to members of one sex only. An illustrative card and responses given to it by two different individuals are shown in Figure 4.2. The card, given to female subjects, is described by Murray as "The portrait of a young woman. A weird old woman with a shawl over her head is grimacing in the background." Common themes given in response to this card are stories of disappointment with a parent, of parental pressure, and of sad thoughts about the past. In addition, some women appear to see the younger woman as having a vision of her evil self or of herself in old age (Holt, 1978).

The thinking behind the TAT is clearly related to the psychodynamic view. According to Murray (1938), the TAT is used to discover unconscious and inhibited tendencies. The assumption is that subjects are not aware they are talking about themselves and thus, their defenses can be bypassed: "If the procedure had merely exposed conscious fantasies and remembered events it would have been useful enough, but it did more than this. It gave the experimenter excellent clues for the divination of unconscious thematic formations!" (p. 534).

TAT responses of subjects can be scored systematically according to a scheme developed by Murray, or on a more impressionistic basis (Cramer, 1996; Cramer & Block, 1998). The test is used both in clinical work and in experimental studies of human motivation. The TAT assumes a close relationship between the expressed fantasy (story about the TAT card) and underlying motivation, as well as a relationship between such fantasy and behavior. Efforts to test these assumptions have met with mixed results. Fantasy can be associated with the expression of motives in behavior and can also substitute

Henry Murray

Illustration 1: *This is the picture of a woman who all of her life has been a very suspicious, conniving person. She's looking in the mirror and she sees reflected behind her an image of what she will be as an old woman—still a suspicious, conniving sort of person. She can't stand the thought that that's what her life will eventually lead her to and she smashes the mirror and runs out of the house screamimg and goes out of her mind and lives in an institution for the rest of her life.*

Illustration 2: *This woman has always emphasized beauty in her life. As a little girl she was praised for being pretty and as a young woman was able to attract lots of men with her beauty. While secretly feeling anxious and unworthy much of the time, her outer beauty helped to disguise these feelings from the world and, sometimes, from herself. Now that she is getting on in years and her children are leaving home, she is worried about the future. She looks in the mirror and imagines herself as an old hag—the worst possible person she could become, ugly and nasty—and wonders what the future holds for her. It is a difficult and depressing time for her.*

Sample Card from the Thematic Apperception Test.

Figure 4.2   Illustrative TAT Card and Responses to It.

for the expression of motives in behavior. Thus, for example, a person with a strong motive to be aggressive with others may express this motive in both fantasy (TAT) and behavior, but the person may also express it in fantasy and block it from expression in overt behavior.

ILLUSTRATIVE RESEARCH USE

Projective tests have been used in many types of research, both in relation to psychoanalytic theory and apart from it. A study of comedians, clowns, and actors illustrates the use of projective tests and the psychodynamic approach (Fisher & Fisher, 1981). The study attempted to understand the origins, motivations, and personalities of those who make people laugh as opposed to those who entertain through acting. Professional clowns, comedians, and actors were interviewed and given projective tests such as the Rorschach and TAT.

What can such research contribute to our understanding of comedians and clowns? First, they were found to be funny early in life, particularly in school, despite little support from their parents for their comic endeavors. Second, a number of motivations seemed to contribute to their decision to be comedians. Among the motivations suggested by the data are the following:

1. **Power.** The ability to control an audience and make people laugh.
2. **Preoccupation with good versus evil and positive presentation of self.** "We would propose that a major motive of comedians in conjuring up funniness is to prove that they are not bad or repugnant. They are obsessed with defending their basic goodness" (p. 69).
3. **Concealment and Denial.** Humor is used to escape from difficulty and as a screen to hide behind when feeling embarrassed or inferior.
4. **Anarchy.** Comedians belittle accepted norms, leave nothing sacred, and make everything laughable.

Let us consider illustrative Rorschach evidence for two of these motivations. First is the concern with good/bad or virtue/evil. A scoring system was devised to consider how frequently such themes appeared in the Rorschach records. Illustrative responses were those referring directly to good and bad (e.g., bad person, virtuous look), those referring to religious matters (e.g., church, angel, devil, heaven, purgatory), and those referring to persons often linked with good/bad (e.g., police officer, criminal, judge, sinner). The Rorschach records of 35 comedians and clowns were found to have significantly more such good/bad references than did the records of 35 actors who were not comedians. Second is the concern with concealment and denial. Many of the Rorschach responses seemed to express denial that things are as bad or threatening as they seem. For example, consider the following responses: "Faces. Evil looking. The evil not very evil. A put on." "Mephisto...charming character." "Tiger. Lovable tiger." "Monster...He's nice." "Wolfman... He's misunderstood...People are afraid. If you walk up and talk to him, he's a decent thing." "Two devils. Funny devils. Not to be taken seriously." In analyzing the Rorschach records of comics, it was found that they contained significantly more of these "not bad" images than did the records of actors. In addition, the records of comics were found to have significantly more concealment themes (e.g., hiding, mask, disguise, magic, tricks) than did the records of actors.

Projective Tests—Do They work?

Projective tests have been widely used by personality and clinical psychologists during the past half-century. The tests have been administered to literally millions of persons (Lilienfeld, Wood, & Garb, 2000). Given their widespread use over the years, the natural question to ask is "Do they work?" By "work," in the context of psychological testing, one generally means "Do they predict important life outcomes?" In the terminology we introduced in Chapter 2, the question is whether the tests are *valid*.

This question is more complicated than it sounds. There are at least two complications. The first is the possibility that projective tests predict some types of outcomes but not others. It might be impossible to give a simple "yes/no" answer to the question "Do projective tests work?" because they might work, or be valid, for predicting only some types of outcomes. A second complication is that there are different ways of scoring projective tests. Over the years, different psychologists have developed different schemes for interpreting and classifying people's responses to projective test items (e.g., Cramer, 1991; Exner, 1986; Westen, 1990). It is possible, then, that some scoring systems might work well, whereas others might not.

These complications suggest that one cannot answer the question of whether projective tests work by considering only one or two isolated studies. Instead, what is required are comprehensive reviews of the various scoring schemes and the range of outcomes that the psychologist might wish to predict. A particularly extensive review of this sort was completed by Lilienfeld and colleagues (2000). These authors were attentive to the complexities involved in assessing the validity of projective tests. They reviewed research on a variety of projective methods, including the Rorschach and TAT, and on a variety of methods for scoring responses on these tests.

What did they find? On the one hand, their review indicated that some scoring methods are valid for some purposes. For example, when TAT stories are scored for the presence of themes related to achievement motivation, as suggested by psychologists such as David McClelland (McClelland, Koestner, & Weinberger, 1989), there is evidence that the TAT responses are correlated with measures of motivated behavior. TAT motive measures also predict the degree to which people remember daily events, with individuals showing greater memory for events that are linked to their motives (Woike, 1995; Woike, Gershkovich, Piorkowski, & Polo, 1999). However, such positive results proved to be exceptions. Lilienfeld and colleagues (2000) review indicated that projective tests commonly do *not* work. For example, although there may be a variety of ways to score Rorschach responses, the choice of scoring scheme seems not to make much difference; "the overwhelming majority of Rorschach indexes" (Lilienfeld et al., 2000, p. 54) were not consistently related to outcomes of interest. And although there may be some validity to methods for scoring achievement themes in TAT responses, "most TAT scoring systems" (p. 54), like the Rorschach systems, also lack validity.

These negative conclusions about the validity of projective tests are congruent with those of many other scholars (e.g., Dawes, 1994, Rorer, 1990) who have taken an objective look at research on projective tests and have found that they simply do not work well enough to be used in clinical practice. Indeed, the Lilienfeld group (2000) recommend that students of psychology no longer should obtain extensive training in the use of these tests, and note that a committee of the American Psychological Association has concurred that projective tests should not be a component of 21st-century training in psychology.

Why don't projective tests work very well, that is, why is it that they rarely enable psychologists to predict life outcomes with high levels of accuracy? There are many possible reasons, but two stand out as particularly important. The first concerns the question of inter-judge reliability: If two psychologists (two "judges") score a person's responses to a projective test, will they agree with one another (will the judgments be reliable)? When using standard questionnaires, the reliability of scoring can be taken for granted; for example, if you take a multiple-choice test, a person or a machine-scoring system can score the test with perfect accuracy. But with projective tests, psychologists are not dealing with simple multiple-choice responses but, rather, with complex verbal statements that must be interpreted. The psychologist's interpretations may reflect not only the thoughts of the person taking the test, but those of the psychologist who does the scoring. The thoughts, feelings, and interpretive biases of the psychologist may influence the scoring of the test. If different psychologists have different interpretive biases, then inter-judge reliability will be low. Research indicates that projective tests often do suffer from this problem. The inter-judge reliability of scoring is not sufficiently high. Even when using the most well-developed of the Rorschach scoring systems, "only about half" of the Rorschach variables reach a "minimum acceptable threshold" of reliability (Lilienfeld et al., 2000, p. 33). If different psychologists do not even agree on how to score a person's test responses, then the scores that they compute are, of course, unlikely to yield accurate predictions of the person's behavior.

A second limitation is that the content of the projective test items commonly has nothing to do with the content of the test taker's day-to-day life. It might be that an individual exhibits a distinctive style of thinking when contemplating, for example, relations with members of the opposite sex to which he or she is attracted. A psychological test that contained stimuli representing members of the opposite sex might pick up on this thinking style. But there is no guarantee that the person's thinking style will manifest itself when he or she is confronted with abstract blotches of ink. The few projective tests that are successful tend to be useful "stimuli that are especially relevant to the construct being assessed" (Lilienfeld et al., 2000, p. 55); for example, researchers interested in people's thoughts about interpersonal relations might use TAT cards that feature interpersonal themes (Westen, 1991). But this commonly is not done; instead, context commonly has been disregarded, and a generic set of stimulus materials (e.g., the set of Rorschach cards) is used to predict an individual's thoughts and feelings in a wide variety of contexts. And here the predictions commonly fail. As you will see in subsequent chapters, other personality theories employ psychological testing procedures that are much more sensitive to these issues of social context than are the projective tests of psychodynamic theory.

What do the limitations of projective testing say about Freud's psychoanalytic theory of personality? On the one hand, some might argue that they say very little. In evaluating Freud, it is important to recall that he himself did not develop or use projective tests. He relied entirely on the free association method in clinical interviews. So Freud's theory might be fine, even if the testing procedures developed by followers of Freud are flawed. On the other hand, one potential achievement of a personality theory is that its theoretical ideas might inspire the construction of psychological testing procedures with high levels of reliability and validity. Whatever its other strengths, psychoanalysis generally has failed to achieve this goal. Although future developments may well improve the validity of testing methods, and thus respond to the criticisms that have been raised (Lilienfeld et al., 2000), psychological testing and prediction unquestionably is not a strength of the psychodynamic tradition.

PSYCHOPATHOLOGY

It can be difficult to appreciate psychoanalytic theory without first understanding the nature of the often strange and puzzling behaviors that were brought to Freud's attention. Freud spent most of his professional time working with patients with neurotic disorders. In fact, the most critical elements in his theory are based on the observations that came from this work. In the course of these investigations, Freud decided that the psychological processes of his patients were not peculiar to those with neurotic disturbances, but could be found to one degree or another, and in one form or another, in all people. Thus, though originally based on observations with patients, his theory is a general theory of personality functioning rather than only a theory of abnormal behavior.

PERSONALITY TYPES

As noted, Freud thought that the first five years of life were critical in the individual's development. During these years, it is possible for a number of failures to occur in the development of the instincts. Such failures in the development are called **fixations**. If individuals receive so little gratification during a stage of development that they are afraid to go to the next stage, or if they receive so much gratification that there is no motivation to move on, a fixation will occur. If a fixation occurs, the individual will try to obtain the same type of satisfaction that was appropriate for an earlier stage of development during later stages. For example, the individual fixated at the oral stage may continue to seek oral gratification in eating, smoking, or drinking. A developmental phenomenon related to that of fixation is **regression**. In regression, the individual seeks to return to an earlier mode of satisfaction, an earlier point of fixation. Regression often occurs under conditions of stress, so that many people overeat, smoke, or drink too much alcohol only during periods of frustration and anxiety.

The Oral Personality

The concepts of the stages of development, fixation, and regression are of tremendous importance to the psychoanalytic theory of development. One of its most fascinating aspects is the way in which personality characteristics are developed in early life and maintained thereafter. For each of the early stages of development, there is a corresponding character type that is developed because of partial fixations at that stage (Table 4.1). The characteristics of the **oral personality**, for example, relate to processes going on during the oral stage of development that the individual maintains in later life. Oral personalities are narcissistic in that they are only interested in themselves and do not have a clear recognition of others as separate entities. Other people are seen

Table 4.1   Personality Characteristics Associated with Psychoanalytic Personality Types

Personality Type	Personality Characteristics
Oral	Demanding, impatient, envious, covetous, jealous, rageful, depressed (feels empty), mistrustful, pessimistic
Anal	Rigid, striving for power and control, concerned with shoulds and oughts, pleasure and possessions, anxiety over waste and loss of control, concern with whether to submit or rebel
Phallic	*Male:* exhibitionistic, competitive, striving for success, emphasis on being masculine—macho—potent *Female:* naive, seductive, exhibitionistic, flirtatious

only in terms of what they can give (feed). Oral personalities are always asking for something, either in terms of a modest, pleading request or an aggressive demand.

The Anal Personality

The **anal personality** stems from the anal stage of development. In contrast to gratification associated with the mouth and oral activity, which can be expressed in adulthood in a relatively unrepressed form, the gratifications of anal impulses must undergo considerable transformation. In general, the traits of the anal character are related to processes going on at the anal stage of development that have not been completely relinquished. The important processes are the bodily processes (accumulation and release of fecal material) and interpersonal relations (the struggle of wills over toilet training). Tying the two together, the anal person sees excretion as symbolic of enormous power. That such a view persists is shown in many everyday expressions such as the reference to the toilet as "the throne." The change from the oral to the anal character is one from "give me" to "do what I tell you," or from "I have to give you" to "I must obey you."

The anal character is known by a triad of traits, called the anal triad: orderliness and cleanliness, parsimony and stinginess, and obstinacy. The emphasis on cleanliness is expressed in the saying "Cleanliness is next to godliness." The anal-compulsive personality has a need to keep everything clean and in order, representing a reaction formation against an interest in things that are disorderly and unclean. The second trait of the triad, parsimony/stinginess, relates to the anal-compulsive's interest in holding on to things, an interest dating back to a wish to retain the powerful and important feces. The third trait in the triad, obstinacy, relates to the anal character's infantile defiance against parting with stools, particularly on command by others. Dating back to toilet training and the struggle of wills, anal personalities often seek to be in control of things and have power or dominance over others.

The Phallic Character

Just as the oral and anal character types reflect partial fixations at the first two stages of development, the **phallic** character represents the result of a partial fixation at the stage of the Oedipus complex. Fixation here has different implications for men and women, and particular attention has been given to the results of partial fixation for males. Whereas success for the oral person means "I get," and success for the anal person means "I control," success for the phallic male means "I am a man." The phallic male must deny all possible suggestions that he has been castrated. For him, success means that he is "big" in the eyes of others. He must at all times assert his masculinity and potency, an attitude exemplified by Theodore Roosevelt's saying, "Speak softly but carry a big stick." The excessive, exhibitionistic quality to the behavior of these people is expressive of the underlying anxiety concerning castration.

The female counterpart of the male phallic character is known as the hysterical personality. As a defense against Oedipal wishes, the little girl identifies to an excessive extent with her mother and femininity. She uses seductive and flirtatious behavior to maintain the interest of her father but denies its sexual intent. The pattern of behavior then is carried over into adulthood, where she may attract men with flirtatious behavior but deny sexual intent and generally appear to be somewhat naive. Hysterical women idealize life, their partners, and romantic love, often finding themselves surprised by life's uglier moments.

CONFLICT AND DEFENSE

According to Freud, all psychopathology relates to an effort to gratify instincts that have been fixated at an earlier stage of development. Thus, in psychopathology the individual still seeks sexual and aggressive gratification in infantile forms. However, because of its association with past trauma, expression of this wish may signal danger to the ego and lead to the experience of anxiety. As a result, there is a conflict situation in which the same behaviors are associated with both pleasure and pain. For example, a person may seek to be dependent on others but fear that if this is done he or she will be vulnerable to frustration and loss (pain). Another example is a wish to indulge in sexual behavior that is blocked by feelings of guilt and fear of punishment or injury. A third example is the conflict between a wish to retaliate against powerful others—representing the parents—and a fear that these figures will themselves retaliate with force and destruction. In each case there is a conflict between a wish and anxiety. In such a situation the result is often that the individual can't "say no," can't be assertive, or otherwise feels blocked and unhappy (Table 4.2).

As noted in the preceding discussion, a critical part of the conflict is anxiety. To reduce the painful experience of anxiety, defense mechanisms, as outlined in Chapter 3, are brought into play. Thus, for example, the person may deny his or her aggressive feelings or project them onto others. In either case, the person no longer has to be afraid of the aggressive feelings. In sum, in psychopathology there is a conflict between a drive or wish (instinct) and the ego's sense (anxiety) that danger will ensue if the wish is expressed (discharged). To guard against this and to ward off anxiety, defense mechanisms are used. In structural terms, a neurosis is a result of conflict between the id

Table 4.2   Psychoanalytic Theory of Psychopathology

Illustrative Conflicts		*Behavior Consequences of Defense Mechanisms*
WISH	ANXIETY	DEFENSE
I would like to have sex with that person.	Such feelings are bad and will be punished.	Denial of all sexual behavior, obsessive preoccupation with the sexual behavior of others.
I would like to strike out at all those people who make me feel inferior.	If I am hostile they will retaliate and really hurt me.	Denial of wish or fear: "I never feel angry," "I'm never afraid of anyone or anything."
I would like to get close to people and have them feed me or take care of me.	If I do they will smother me or leave me.	Excessive independence and avoidance of getting close to people or fluctuations between approaching people and moving away from them; excessive need to take care of others.

and the ego. In process terms, an instinct striving for discharge triggers anxiety, leading to a defense mechanism.

In many cases the conflict between the id and ego, between instinct and defense, leads to the development of a **symptom**. A symptom, such as a tic, psychological paralysis, or compulsion, represents a disguised expression of a repressed impulse. The meaning of the symptom, the nature of the dangerous instinct, and the nature of the defense all remain unconscious. For example, a mother may be painfully obsessed with the fear that something will happen to her child. Underlying the obsession may be rage at her child and anxiety about the harm she may do to the child. The symptom of the obsession expresses both the mother's feelings that she may harm or injure the child and her defense against it in terms of excessive preoccupation with the child's welfare. To take another example, in a hand-washing compulsion—in which a person feels compelled to wash his or her hands continuously—the symptom may express both the wish to be dirty or do "dirty" things and the defense against the wish in terms of excessive cleanliness. In both of these cases the person is unaware of the wish or the defense and is troubled only by the symptom. Many people do not suffer from such specific problems or symptoms, but analysts suggest that all psychological problems can still be understood in these terms.

To summarize the psychoanalytic theory of psychopathology, there is an arrest in the development of the person that is associated with conflicts between wishes and fears. The wishes and fears that were part of a specific time period in childhood are now carried over into adolescence and adulthood. The person attempts to handle the anxiety that is a painful part of this conflict by using defense mechanisms. However, if the conflict becomes too great, the use of defense mechanisms can lead to neurotic symptoms or psychotic withdrawal from reality. Symptoms express the unconscious conflict between the wish or drive and anxiety. In each case of abnormal behavior there is an unconscious conflict between a wish and a fear that dates back to an earlier period in childhood. So as adults, there continue to be childlike parts of us that, under stress and some other conditions, may become more active and troublesome.

BEHAVIOR CHANGE

How does behavior change come about? Once a person has established a behavioral pattern, a way of thinking about and responding to situations, through what process does a change in personality take place? The psychoanalytic theory of growth suggests that there is a normal course of human personality development, one that occurs because of an optimum degree of frustration. Where there has been too little or too much frustration at a particular stage of growth, personality does not develop normally and a fixation takes place. When this occurs, the individual repeats patterns of behavior regardless of other changes in situations. Given the development of such a neurotic pattern, how is it possible to break the cycle and move forward?

INSIGHTS INTO THE UNCONSCIOUS: FREE ASSOCIATION AND DREAM INTERPRETATION

In his early efforts to change behavior, Freud used a method called cathartic hypnosis. The view then held was that neurotic symptoms would be relieved by the discharge of blocked emotions. Freud did not like using hypnosis; since

CURRENT APPLICATIONS

EMOTIONAL SUPPRESSION AND HEALTH

More than 50 years ago, psychoanalysts suggested a relation between personality dynamics and health, in particular a relation between specific conflicts and specific somatic difficulties. In developing the area of psychosomatic medicine, each disorder was thought to result from a specific emotional constellation. For example, peptic ulcers, described as the "Wall Street stomach," were thought to result from an unconscious craving for love and dependence, which was defended against by an active, productive, aggressive lifestyle. Hypertension was thought to be associated with individuals who were gentle in outward manner but boiling with rage inside.

This line of psychology fell into disfavor because the relation between psychological factors and bodily illness seemed more complex than was originally suggested. Although different in form, currently there is a return to interest in some of these early psychoanalytic views. In particular, there is evidence that the continued suppression of emotion can be detrimental to one's health. For example, it may play a negative role in the course of cancer, ulcers, and heart disease. Alternatively, the expression, or nonsuppression, of emotion may represent an active, adaptive style of coping that reduces the risk of illness and bodes well for the course of an illness.

SOURCES: Jensen, 1987; Levy, 1984; Pennebaker, 1985, 1990; Petrie, Booth & Pennebaker, 1998; Temoshok, 1985, 1991.

I happen to believe a nasty disposition is good for your health.

not all patients could be hypnotized, the results were often transient, and he did not feel that he was learning much about mental functioning. The second development in technique was that of "waking suggestion". Here Freud put his hand on the patient's head and assured the patient that he or she could recall and face repressed past emotional experiences. With the increased interest in the interpretation of dreams, Freud focused on the **free association** method as basic to psychoanalysis. In free association the patient is asked to report to the analyst every thought that comes to mind, to delay reporting nothing, to withhold nothing, to bar nothing from coming to consciousness.

Dreams are the "royal road" to the unconscious. Through the free association method the analyst and patient are able to go beyond the manifest (obvious) content of the dream to the latent content, to the hidden meaning that expresses the unconscious wish. Dreams, like symptoms, are disguises and partial wish fulfillments. In the dream, the person can satisfy a hostile or sexual wish in a disguised and thereby safe way. For example, rather than dreaming of killing someone, one may dream of a battle in which a particular figure is killed. In such a case the wish may remain at least somewhat obvious, but in other cases the wish may be much more disguised. Free association allows the disguise to be uncovered.

At first, Freud thought that making the unconscious conscious was sufficient to effect change and cure. This was in keeping with an early emphasis on repressed memories as the basis for pathology. Freud then realized that more than the recovery of memories was involved. Rather, emotional insight into the wishes and conflicts that had remained hidden was necessary.

The process of therapeutic change in psychoanalysis involves coming to grips with emotions and wishes that were previously unconscious and struggling with these painful experiences in a relatively safe environment. If psychopathology involves fixation at an early stage of development, then in psychoanalysis individuals become free to resume their normal psychological development. If psychopathology involves damming up the instincts and using energy for defensive purposes, then psychoanalysis involves a redistribution of energy so that more energy is available for mature, guiltless, less rigid, and more gratifying activities. If psychopathology involves conflict and defense mechanisms, then psychoanalysis involves reducing conflict and freeing the patient from the limitations of the defensive processes. If psychopathology involves an individual dominated by the unconscious and the tyranny of the id, then psychoanalysis involves making conscious what was unconscious and putting under control of the ego what was formerly under the domination of the id or superego.

THE THERAPEUTIC PROCESS: TRANSFERENCE

In sum, then, psychoanalysis is viewed as a learning process in which the individual resumes and completes the growth process that was interrupted when the neurosis began. The principle involved is the reexposure of a patient, under more favorable circumstances, to the emotional situations that could not be handled in the past. Such reexposure is affected by the transference relationship and the development of a transference neurosis. The term **transference** refers to a patient's development of attitudes toward the analyst based on attitudes held by that patient toward earlier parental figures. In the sense that transference relates to distortions of reality based on past experiences, transference occurs in everyone's daily life and in all forms of psychotherapy. For example, there is research evidence that individuals have mental images associated with emotion that are based on early interpersonal relationships. These emotionally laden mental representations influence the ways in which we view and respond to other individuals as well as feelings about ourselves. Often this occurs in an automatic, unconscious way (Andersen & Chen, 2002).

In expressing transference attitudes toward the analyst, patients duplicate in therapy their interactions with people in their lives and their past interactions with significant figures. For example, if patients feel that the analyst's taking notes may lead to exploitation by the analyst, they are expressing attitudes they hold toward people they meet in their daily existence and earlier figures in their lives. In free associating, oral characters may be concerned about whether they are "feeding" the analyst and whether the analyst gives them enough in return; anal characters may be concerned about who is controlling the sessions; phallic characters may be concerned about who will win in competitive struggles. Such attitudes, often part of the unconscious daily existence of the patient, come to light in the course of analysis.

Although transference is a part of all relationships and of all forms of therapy, psychoanalysis is distinctive in using it as a dynamic force in behavior change. Many formal qualities of the analytic situation are structured to enhance the development of transference. The patient lying on the couch supports the development of a dependent relationship. The scheduling of frequent meetings (up to five or six times a week) strengthens the emotional importance of the analytic relationship to the patient's daily existence. Finally, the fact that patients become so tied to their analysts, while knowing so little about them as people, means that their responses are almost completely determined by their neurotic conflicts. The analyst remains a mirror or blank screen on which the individual projects wishes and anxieties.

Freud's consulting room.

Encouraging transference, or providing the circumstances that allow it to develop, leads to the development of the transference neurosis. It is here that patients play out, full-blown, their old conflicts. Patients now invest the major aspects of their relationship with the analyst with the wishes and anxieties of the past. The goal is no longer to get well, but to gain from the analyst what they had to do without in childhood. Rather than seeking a way out of competitive relationships, they may only seek to castrate the analyst; rather than seeking to become less dependent on others, they may seek to have the analyst gratify all their dependency needs. The fact that these attitudes have developed within the analysis allows patients and their analysts to look at and understand the instinctual and defensive components of the original infantile conflict. Because the patient invests considerable emotion in the situation, the increased understanding is emotionally meaningful. Change occurs when insight has been gained, when patients realize, on both an intellectual and an emotional level, the nature of their conflicts and feel free, in terms of their new perceptions of themselves and the world, to gratify their instincts in a mature, conflict-free way.

Whereas guilt and anxiety prevented growth in the past, the analytic situation allows the individual to deal anew with the old conflicts. Why should the response be any different at this time? Basically, change occurs in analysis because of the three therapeutic factors. First, in analysis the conflict is less intense than it was in the original situation. Second, the analyst assumes an attitude that is different from that of the parents. Finally, patients in analysis are older and more mature, that is, they are able to use parts of their ego that have developed to deal with the parts of their functioning that have not developed. These three factors, creating as they do the opportunity for relearning, provide the basis for what Alexander and French (1946) call the "corrective emotional experience." Psychoanalytic theory suggests that through insight into old conflicts, through an understanding of the needs for infantile gratifications and recognition of the potential for mature gratification, and through an understanding of old anxieties and a recognition of their lack of relevance to current realities, patients may progress toward maximum instinctual gratification within the limits set by reality and their own moral convictions.

A Case Example: Little Hans

Although many psychiatrists and psychologists have spent considerable time treating patients, Freud is one of the very few who have reported cases in detail. Most of Freud's cases come from early in his career. Although these case presentations are useful in understanding many aspects of psychoanalytic theory, it is important to remember that they occurred prior to Freud's development of his theory of the sexual and aggressive instincts, prior to the development of the structural model, and prior to the development of the theory of anxiety and defense mechanisms.

Description of the Problem

The case of Little Hans, published in 1909, deals with the analysis of a phobia in a five-year-old boy. It involves the treatment of the boy by his father and does not represent Freud's direct participation in the therapeutic process. The boy was bothered by a fear that a horse would bite him, and therefore refused to leave the house. The boy's father kept detailed notes on his treatment and frequently discussed his progress with Freud. Although the "patient" was not treated by Freud, the case of Little Hans is important because it illustrates the theory of infantile sexuality, the functioning of the Oedipus complex and castration anxiety, the dynamics of symptom formation, and the process of behavior change.

Events Leading Up to Development of the Phobia

Our account of events in the life of Little Hans begins at age three. At this point he had a lively interest in his penis, which he called his "widdler." What was striking about Hans during this period was his pleasure in touching his own penis and his preoccupation with penises—or "widdlers"—in others. For example, he wanted to know if his mother had a widdler and was fascinated with the process by which cows are milked. The interest in touching his penis, however, led to threats by his mother. "If you do that, I shall send you to Dr. A. to cut off your widdler. And then what will you widdle with?" Thus, there was a direct castration threat on the part of a parent, in this case the mother. Freud pinpointed this as the beginning of Hans's castration complex.

Hans's interest in widdlers extended to noting the size of the lion's widdler at the zoo and analyzing the differences between animate and inanimate objects—dogs and horses have widdlers, tables and chairs do not. Hans was curious about many things, but Freud related his general thirst for knowledge to sexual curiosity. Hans continued to be interested in whether his mother had a widdler and said to her, "I thought you were so big you'd have a widdler like a horse." When he was three and a half, a sister was born, who also became a focus for his widdler concerns. "But her widdler's still quite small. When she grows up, it'll get bigger all right." According to Freud, Hans could not admit what he really saw, namely, that there was no widdler there. To do so would mean that he

would have to face his own castration anxieties. These anxieties occurred at a time when he was experiencing pleasure in the organ, as witnessed in his comments to his mother while she dried and powdered him after his bath.

HANS: Why don't you put your finger there?

MOTHER: Because that'd be piggish.

HANS: What's that? Piggish? Why? *(laughing)* But it's great fun.

Thus Hans, now more than four years old, was preoccupied with his penis, experienced pleasure in it and concern about the loss of it, and began some seduction of his mother. It was at this point that his nervous disorders became apparent. The father, attributing the difficulties to sexual overexcitation due to his mother's tenderness, wrote Freud that Hans was "afraid that a horse will bite him in the street" and that this fear seemed somehow to be connected with his having been frightened by seeing a large penis. As you remember, he had noticed at a very early age what large penises horses have, and at that time he inferred that, as his mother was so large, she must "have a widdler like a horse." " Hans was afraid of going into the street and was depressed in the evenings. He had bad dreams and was frequently taken into his mother's bed. While walking in the street with his nurse, he became extremely frightened and sought to return home to be with his mother. The fear that a horse would bite him became a fear that the horse would come into his room. He had developed a full-blown phobia, an irrational dread or fear of an object. What more can we learn about this phobia? How are we to account for its development? As Freud notes, we must do more than simply call this a small boy's foolish fears.

Interpretation of the Symptom

The father attempted to deal with his son's fear of horses by offering him an interpretation. Hans was told that the fear of horses was nonsense, that the truth was that he (Hans) was fond of his mother and that the fear of horses had to do with an interest in their widdlers. On Freud's suggestion, the father explained to Hans that women do not have widdlers. Apparently this provided some relief, but Hans continued to be bothered by an obsessive wish to look at horses, though he was then frightened by them. At this point, his tonsils were taken out and his phobia worsened. He was afraid that a white horse would bite him. He continued to be interested in widdlers in females. At the zoo, he was afraid of all the large animals and was entertained by the smaller ones. Among the birds, he was afraid of the pelican. In spite of his father's truthful explanation, Hans sought to reassure himself. "And everyone has a widdler. And my widdler will get bigger as I get bigger, because it does grow on me." " According to Freud, Hans had been making comparisons among the sizes of widdlers and was dissatisfied with his own. Big animals reminded him of this defect and were disagreeable to him. The father's explanation heightened his castration anxiety, as expressed in the words "it does grow on me, as if it could be cut off. For this reason he resisted the information, and thus it had no therapeutic results. "Could it be that living beings really did exist which did not possess widdlers? If so, it would no longer be so incredible that they could take his own widdler away, and, as it were, make him into a woman."

At around this time, Hans reported the following dream. "In the night there was a big giraffe in the room and a crumpled one; and the big one called out because I took the crumpled one away from it. Then it stopped calling out; and then I sat down on top of the crumpled one." The father's interpretation was that he, the father, was the big giraffe, with the big penis, and the mother was the crumpled giraffe, missing the genital organ. The dream was a reproduction of a morning scene in which the mother took Hans into bed with her. The father warned her against this practice ("The big one called out because I'd taken the crumpled one away from it"), but the mother continued to encourage it. The mother encouraged and reinforced the Oedipal wishes. Hans stayed with her and, in

the wish fulfillment of the dream, he took possession of her ("Then the big giraffe stopped calling out; and then I sat down on top of the crumpled one").

Freud's strategy in understanding Hans's phobia was to suspend judgment and to give his impartial attention to everything there was to observe. He learned that prior to the development of the phobia, Hans had been alone with his mother at a summer place. There, two significant events occurred. First, he heard the father of one of his friends tell her that a white horse there bit people and that she was not to hold her finger up to its mouth. Second, while pretending to be horses, a friend who rivaled Hans for the affection of the little girls fell down, hit his foot, and bled. In an interview with Hans, Freud learned that Hans was bothered by the blinders on horses and the black band around their mouths. The phobia became extended to include a fear that horses dragging a heavy van would fall down and kick their feet. It was then discovered that the exciting cause of his phobia—the event that capitalized on a psychological readiness for the formation of a phobia—was that Hans had witnessed a horse falling down. While walking outside with his mother one day, Hans had seen a horse pulling a van fall down and begin to kick its feet.

The central feature in this case was the phobia about the horse. What is fascinating in this regard is how often associations concerning a horse came up in relation to the father, the mother, and Hans himself. We have already noticed Hans's interest in his mother's widdler in relation to that of a horse. To his father, he said at one point: "Daddy, don't trot away from me." Could the father, who wore a mustache and eyeglasses, be the horse that Hans was afraid of, the horse that would come into his room at night and bite him? Or could Hans himself be the horse? Hans was known to play horse in his room, to trot about, fall down, kick about with his feet, and neigh. He repeatedly ran up to his father and bit him, just as he feared the horse would do to him. Hans was overfed. Could this relate to his concerns about large, fat horses? Finally, Hans was known to have called himself a young horse and to have a tendency to stamp his feet on the ground when angry, similar to what the horse did when it fell down. To return to the mother, could the heavily laden carts symbolize the pregnant mother and the horse falling down the birth or delivery of a child? Are such associations coincidental or can they play a significant role in our understanding of the phobia?

According to Freud, the major cause of Hans's phobia was his Oedipus conflict. Hans felt considerable affection for his mother, more than he could handle during the phallic stage of his development. Although he had deep affection for his father, he also considered him a rival for his mother's affections. When he and his mother stayed at the summer cottage and his father was away, he was able to get into bed with his mother and keep her for himself. This heightened his attraction for his mother and his hostility toward his father. For Freud, "Hans was really a little Oedipus who wanted to have his father 'out of the way,' to get rid of him, so that he might be alone with his handsome mother and sleep with her. This wish had originated during his summer holidays, when the alternating presence and absence of his father had drawn Hans's attention to the condition upon which depended the intimacy with his mother which he longed for." The fall and injury to his friend and rival during one of those holidays was significant in symbolizing the defeat for Hans of his rival.

The Solution to the Oedipal Conflict

When he returned home from the summer holidays, Hans's resentment toward his father increased. He tried to suppress the resentment with exaggerated affection. He arrived at an ingenious solution to the Oedipal conflict. He and his mother would be parents to children and the father could be the granddaddy. Thus, as Freud notes, "The little Oedipus had found a happier solution than that prescribed by destiny. Instead of putting his father out of the way, he had granted him the same happiness that he desired himself: he made him a grandfather and let him too

marry his own mother." But such a fantasy could not be a satisfactory solution, and Hans was left with considerable hostility toward his father. The exciting cause of the phobia was the horse falling down. At that moment, Hans perceived a wish that his father might similarly fall down and die. The hostility toward his father was projected onto the father and was symbolized in the horse, because he himself nourished jealous and hostile wishes against him. He feared the horse would bite him because of his wish that his father would fall down, and fears that the horse would come into his room occurred at night when he was most tempted by Oedipal fantasies. In his own play as a horse and in his biting of his father, he expressed an identification with his father. The phobia expressed the wish and the anxiety and, in a secondary way, accomplished the objective of leaving Hans home to be with his mother.

In sum, both his fear that a horse would bite him and his fear that horses would fall down represented the father who was going to punish Hans for the evil wishes he was harboring against him. Hans was able to get over the phobia and, according to a later report by Freud, he appeared to be functioning well. What factors allowed the change? First, there was the sexual enlightenment by the father. Although Hans was reluctant to accept this and it at first heightened his castration anxiety, it did serve as a useful piece of reality to hold onto. Second, the analysis provided by his father and by Freud was useful in making conscious for Hans what had formerly been unconscious. Finally, the father's interest in and permissive attitude toward Hans's expression of his feelings allowed a resolution of the Oedipus conflict in favor of an identification with the father, diminishing both the wish to rival the father and the castration anxiety, and thereby decreasing the potential for symptom development.

Overall Evaluation

The case of Little Hans has many problems as a piece of scientific investigation. The interviewing was done by the father in an unsystematic way. The father himself was a close adherent of Freud's and therefore was possibly biased somewhat in his observations and interpretations. Freud himself was dependent on secondhand reports. He was aware of the limitations of the data, but he was also impressed with them. Whereas before he had based his theory on the childhood memories of adult patients, now, in the case of Little Hans, he began to observe the sexual life of children.

It is hard to draw conclusions about the theory in terms of this one case. The presentation does not contain all of Freud's observations on Hans. Furthermore, it is but a single case, and it is taken from an early point (1909) in Freud's work. On the other hand, we do get an appreciation of the wealth of information available to the analyst and, moreover, of the problems inherent in evaluating and interpreting such data. We must necessarily get a feeling for Freud's ability to observe and describe phenomena and his efforts to come to terms with the complexity of human behavior. In this one case alone we have descriptions of phenomena relevant to the following: infantile sexuality, fantasies of children, functioning of the unconscious, the process of conflict development and conflict resolution, the process of symptom formation, symbolization, and the dream process. In reading such a case, we cannot fail to be impressed by Freud's courageous efforts to discover the secrets of human functioning and by his willingness to do the job that needed to be done, in spite of limitations in his observations and in full recognition of the complexity of the phenomena he was trying to understand.

THE CASE OF JIM

Rorschach and Thematic Apperception Test (TAT): Psychoanalytic Theory

The Rorschach Inkblot Test and the thematic apperception test (TAT), both projective, were administered to Jim by a professional clinical psychologist. On the Rorschach, Jim gave relatively few responses—22 in all. This is surprising in view of other evidence of his intelligence and creative potential. It may be interesting to follow his responses to the first two cards and to consider the interpretations formulated by the psychologist, who also is a practicing psychoanalyst.

CARD 1

JIM:	The first thing that comes to mind is a butterfly.
INTERPRETATION:	Initially cautious and acts conventionally in a novel situation.
JIM:	This reminds me of a frog. Not a whole frog, like a frog's eyes. Really just reminds me of a frog.
INTERPRETATION:	He becomes more circumspect, almost picky, and yet tends to overgeneralize while feeling inadequate about it.
JIM:	Could be a bat. More spooky than the butterfly because there is no color. Dark and ominous.
INTERPRETATION:	Phobic, worried, depressed, and pessimistic.

CARD 2

JIM: Could be two headless people with their arms touching. Looks like they are wearing heavy dresses. Could be one touching her hand against a mirror. If they're women, their figures are not good. Look heavy.

INTERPRETATION: Alert to people. Concern or confusion about sexual role. Anal-compulsive features. Disparaging of women and hostile to them—headless and figures not good. Narcissism expressed in mirror image.

JIM: This looks like two faces facing each other. Masks, profiles—more masks than faces—not full, more of a façade, like one with a smile and one with a frown.

INTERPRETATION: He presents a façade, can smile or frown, but doesn't feel genuine. Despite façade of poise, feels tense with people. Repeated several times that he was not imaginative. Is he worried about his productivity and importance?

A number of interesting responses occurred on other cards. On the third card Jim perceived women trying to lift weights. Here again was a suggestion of conflict about his sexual role and about a passive—as opposed to an active—orientation. On the following card he commented that "somehow they all have an Alfred Hitchcock look of spooky animals," again suggesting a possible phobic quality to his behavior and a tendency to project dangers into the environment. His occasional references to symmetry and details suggested the use of compulsive defenses and intellectualization while experiencing threat. Disturbed and conflicted references to women come up in a number of places. On Card 7, he perceived two women from mythology who would be good if they were mythological but bad if they were fat. On the next to last card he perceived "some sort of a Count, Count Dracula. Eyes, ears, cape. Ready to grab, suck blood. Ready to go out and strangle some woman." The reference to sucking blood suggested tendencies toward oral sadism, something that also appeared in another percept of vampires that suck blood. Jim followed the percept of Count Dracula with one of pink cotton candy. The tester interpreted this response as suggesting a yearning for nurturance and contact behind the oral sadism; that is, the subject uses oral aggressive tendencies (e.g., sarcasm, verbal attacks) to defend against more passive oral wishes (e.g., to be fed, to be taken care of, and to be dependent).

The examiner concluded that the Rorschach suggested a neurotic structure in which intellectualization, compulsivity, and hysterical operations (irrational fears, preoccupation with his body) are used to defend against anxiety. However, it was suggested that Jim continues to feel anxious and uncomfortable with others, particularly authority figures. The report from the Rorschach concluded: "He is conflicted about his sexual role. While he yearns for nurturance and contact from the motherly female, he feels very guilty about the cravings and his intense hostility toward women. He assumes a passive orientation, a continual role playing and, behind a façade of tact, he continues his rage, sorrow, and ambition."

What kinds of stories did Jim tell on the TAT? Most striking about these stories were the sadness and hostility involved in all interpersonal relationships. In one story a boy is dominated by his mother, in another an insensitive gangster is capable of gross inhumanity, and in a third a husband is upset to learn that his wife is not a virgin. In particular, the relationships between men and women constantly involve one putting down the other. Consider this story.

> Looks like two older people. The woman is sincere, sensitive, and dependent on the man. There is something about the man's expression that bespeaks of insensitivity—the way he looks at her, as if he conquered her. There is not the same compassion and security in her presence that she feels in his. In the end, the woman gets very hurt and is left to fend for herself. Normally I would think that they were married but in this case I don't because two older people who are married would be happy with one another.

In this story we have a man being sadistic to a woman. We also see the use of the defensive mechanism of denial in Jim's suggestion that these two people cannot be married since older married people are always happy with one another. In the story that followed the aforementioned one, there is again the theme of hostile mistreatment of a woman. In this story there is a more open expression of the sexual theme, along with evidence of some sexual role confusion.

> This picture brings up a gross thought. I think of Candy. The same guy who took advantage of Candy. He's praying over her. Not the last rites, but he has convinced her that he is some powerful person and she's looking for him to bestow his good graces upon her. His knee is on the bed, he's unsuccessful, she's naive. He goes to bed with her for mystical purposes. [Blushes] She goes on being naive and continues to be susceptible to that kind of thing. She has a very, very sweet compassionate look. Could it possibly be that this is supposed to be a guy wearing a tie? I'll stick with the former.

The psychologist interpreting these stories observed that Jim appeared to be immature, naive, and characterized by a gross denial of all that is unpleasant or dirty, the latter for him including both sexuality and marital strife. The report continued: "He is vacillating between expressing sadistic urges and experiencing a sense of victimization. Probably he combines both, often in indirect expressions of hostility while feeling unjustly treated or accused. He is confused about what meaningful relationships two people can have. He is ambivalently idealistic and pessimistic about his own chances for a stable relationship. Since he sees sex as dirty and as a mode for using or being used by his partner, he fears involvement. At the same time he craves attention, needs to be recognized, and is often preoccupied with sexual urges."

Between the Rorschach and the TAT, a number of important themes emerge. One theme involves a general lack of warmth in interpersonal relationships, in particular a disparaging—and at times sadistic— orientation toward women. In relation to women, Jim has a conflict between sexual preoccupation and the feeling that sex is dirty and involves hostility. The second theme involves experiencing tension and anxiety behind a façade of poise. A third theme involves conflict and confusion about his sexual identity. Although there is evidence of intelligence and creative potential, there also is evidence of rigidity and inhibition in relation to the unstructured nature of the projective tests. Compulsive defenses, intellectualization, and denial are only partially successful in helping him deal with his anxieties.

Comments on the Data

This data about Jim highlights the most attractive feature of projective tests. Their disguise enables one to penetrate the façade of someone's personality (in psychoanalytic terms, his defenses) to view the person's underlying needs, motives, or drives. The picture of Jim revealed in the Rorschach and TAT differs from that presented in his autobiography (Chapter 2), which provided some evidence of conflicted relationships with women yet did not uncover the psychological themes evident in Jim's projective test responses.

As we not only examine psychoanalytic theory but also look forward to other theories to come, an interesting point arises. It is difficult to see how other theories of personality could make as much use of this data about Jim as psychoanalytic theory can. The assessment practices associated with other theories are unlikely to reveal this sort of information. It is only on the Rorschach that we obtain content such as "women trying to lift weights," "Count Dracula... ready to grab, suck blood. Ready to go out and strangle some woman," and "pink cotton candy." The TAT is unique in revealing references to themes of sadness and hostility in interpersonal relationships. These responses allow for the psychodynamic interpretations. An important part of Jim's personality functioning appears to involve a defense against sadistic urges. The references to sucking blood and to cotton candy, together with the rest of his responses, allow for the interpretation that he is partially fixated at the oral stage. In relation to this, it is interesting to observe that Jim has an ulcer, which involves the digestive tract, and that he must drink milk to manage this condition.

The history of psychoanalytic theory includes the development of schools or groups with different, often antagonistic, points of view. Freud changed many aspects of psychoanalytic theory during the course of his professional career. However, he and his followers clashed on many issues. To a certain extent

RELATED POINTS OF VIEW AND RECENT DEVELOPMENTS

there was what has been described as a religious or political quality (Fromm, 1959) to psychoanalysis, with the traditional followers being considered among the faithful and those who deviated from the fundamental principles being cast out from the movement. This pattern started during Freud's life and continued afterward. A theorist such as Erik Erikson is still highly regarded by most traditional psychoanalysts, whereas the theorists considered below often are not. Frequently it is hard to determine the basis for the response to one or another theorist. However, as a general rule, a theorist must retain a commitment to the following concepts to be considered a part of Freudian psychoanalysis: the sexual and aggressive instincts, the unconscious, and the stages of development. As we shall see, the theorists considered questioned one or another on these concepts and thereby approached the understanding of humans somewhat differently.

TWO EARLY CHALLENGES TO FREUD

Among the many early analysts who broke with Freud and developed their own schools of thought were Alfred Adler and Carl G. Jung. Both were early and important followers of Freud, Adler having been president of the Vienna Psychoanalytic Society and Jung president of the International Psychoanalytic Society. Both split with Freud over what they felt was an excessive emphasis on the sexual instincts. The split with Jung was particularly painful for Freud since Jung was to be his "crown prince" and chosen successor. While other individuals also split with Freud and developed their own schools of thought, Adler and Jung were among the earliest, and remain the best known.

Alfred Adler (1870–1937)

For approximately a decade, Alfred Adler was an active member of the Vienna Psychoanalytic Society. However, in 1911, when he presented his views to the other members of this group, the response was so hostile that he left it to form his own school of Individual Psychology. What ideas could have been considered so unacceptable to psychoanalysts? We cannot consider all of Adler's theory, but we can consider some of his early and later views to get a feeling for the important differences between those views and psychoanalysis.

Perhaps most significant in Adler's split from Freud was his greater emphasis on social urges and conscious thoughts than on instinctual sexual urges and unconscious processes. Early in his career Adler became interested in organ inferiorities and how people compensate for them. A person with a weak organ may attempt to compensate for this weakness by making special efforts to strengthen that organ or to develop other organs. For example, someone who stutters as a child may attempt to become a great speaker, or someone with a defect in vision may attempt to develop special listening sensitivities. Whereas initially Adler was interested in bodily organ weaknesses, gradually he became interested in psychological feelings of inferiority and compensatory strivings to mask or reduce these painful feelings. Thus, whereas Freudians might see Theodore Roosevelt's emphasis on toughness and carrying a "big stick" as a defense against castration anxiety, Adlerians might see him as expressing compensatory strivings against feelings of inferiority associated with boyhood weaknesses. Whereas Freudians might see an extremely

Alfred Adler

Birth Order: *Alfred Adler emphasized the importance of birth order in personality development. Twenty-one of the first 23 U.S. astronauts were first-born or only sons.*

aggressive woman as expressing penis envy, Adlerians might see her as expressing a masculine protest or rejection of the stereotyped feminine role of weakness and inferiority. According to Adler, how a person attempts to cope with such feelings becomes a part of his or her style of life—a distinctive aspect of his or her personality functioning.

These concepts already suggest a much more social rather than biological emphasis. This social emphasis increasingly became an important part of Adler's thinking. At first Adler spoke of a will to power as an expression of the person's efforts to cope with feelings of helplessness dating from infancy. This emphasis gradually shifted to an emphasis on striving for superiority. In its neurotic form this striving could be expressed in wishes for power and control over others; in its healthier form it could be expressed as a "great upward drive" toward unity and perfection. In the healthy person the striving for superiority is expressed in social feeling and cooperation as well as in assertiveness and competition. From the beginning people have a social interest, that is, an innate interest in relating to people and an innate potential for cooperation.

Adler's theory is also noteworthy for its emphasis on how people respond to feelings about the self, how people respond to goals that direct their behavior toward the future, and how the order of birth among siblings can influence their psychological development. In relation to birth order, many psychologists have noted the tendency for only sons or first-born sons to achieve more than later sons in a family. For example, 21 of the first 23 U.S. astronauts were first-born or only sons. Sulloway (1996) has placed the issue of birth order in an evolutionary context, suggesting that first-borns tend to be conscientious and conservative, preserving their first-place status in the family, whereas later-borns, seeking to establish alternative routes to status and success, are "born to rebel." Although this view remains controversial, support for Sulloway's account of "conservative first-borns" and "rebellious later-borns" comes from both his own research and that of others (Paulhus, Trapnell, & Chen, 1999). Many of Adler's ideas have found their way into the general public's thinking and are related to views later expressed by other theorists. Contemporary researchers, like Adler, have become interested in power as a fundamental determinant of human behavior (Keltner, Gruenfeld, & Anderson, 2003). However, Adler's school of individual psychology itself has not had a major impact on personality theory and research.

Carl G. Jung (1875–1961)

Jung split with Freud in 1914—a few years after Adler—and developed his own school of thought called Analytical Psychology. This was a particularly profound event for Freud and the psychoanalytic movement. As noted previously, Freud had viewed Jung as an intellectual leader and his natural successor who could ensure the progress of psychoanalysis after Freud's death. The two men also had developed an extremely close relationship, with their written correspondence suggesting that they related as much in the style of father and son as professional colleagues. However, this relationship began to deteriorate beginning in 1909, due to a mixture of professional and personal conflicts (Gay, 1998). In 1914, Jung resigned his position as president of the International Psychoanalytic Association.

Carl Jung

Like Adler, Jung was distressed with what he felt was an excessive emphasis on sexuality. Jung viewed the libido not as a sexual instinct, but as a generalized life energy. Although sexuality is a part of this basic energy, the libido also includes strivings for pleasure and creativity. To Jung, this reinterpretation of the libido was the primary reason for his break with Freud.

Jung's analytic psychology features additional themes that differentiate it from Freud's psychoanalysis. Jung felt that Freud overemphasized the idea that our current behavior is a repetition of our past, with the instinctual urges and psychological repressions of childhood being repeated in adult life. Instead, Jung believed that personality developed also is marked by a forward-moving directional tendency. People try to acquire a meaningful personal identity and a sense of meaning in self. Indeed, people are so forward-looking that they commonly devote efforts to religious practices that prepare them for a life after death.

A particularly distinguishing feature of Jung's psychology is his emphasis on the evolutionary foundations of the human mind. Jung accepted Freud's emphasis on the unconscious as a storehouse of repressed experiences from one's life. But he added to this idea the concept of the **collective unconscious**. According to Jung, people have stored within their collective unconscious the cumulative experiences of past generations. The collective unconscious, as opposed to the personal unconscious, is universal. It is shared by all humans as a result of their common ancestry. It is part of our human as well as our animal heritage, and thus is our link with the collective wisdom of millions of years of past experience: "This psychic life is the mind of our ancient ancestors, the way in which they thought and felt, the way in which they conceived of life and the world, of gods and human beings. The existence of these historical layers is presumably the source of belief in reincarnation and in memories of past lives" (Jung, 1939, p. 24).

The collective unconscious contains universal images or symbols, known as archetypes. Archetypes, such as the Mother archetype, are seen in fairy tales, dreams, myths, and some psychotic thoughts. Jung was struck with similar images that keep appearing, in slightly different forms, in different cultures that are distant from one another. For example, the Mother archetype might be expressed in different cultures in a variety of positive or negative forms: as life giver, as all giving and nurturant, as the witch or threatening punisher ("Don't fool with Mother Nature"), and as the seductive female. Archetypes may be represented in our images of persons, demons, animals, natural forces, or objects. The evidence in all cases for their being a part of our collective unconscious is their universality among members of different cultures from past and current time periods.

Another important aspect of Jung's theory was his emphasis on how people struggle with opposing forces within them. For example, there is the struggle between the face or mask we present to others, represented in the archetype of the *persona*, and the private or personal self. If people emphasize the persona too much, there may be a loss of sense of self and a doubting about who they are. On the other hand, the persona, as expressed in social roles and customs, is a necessary part of living in society. Similarly, there is the struggle between the masculine and feminine parts of ourselves. Every male has a feminine part (the archetype of the *anima*) and every female has a masculine part (the archetype of the *animus*) to their personality. If a man rejects his feminine part he may emphasize mastery and strength to an excessive degree, appearing cold and insensitive to the feelings of others. If a woman rejects her masculine part she may be excessively absorbed in motherhood. Psychologists currently interested in stereotyped sex roles would probably applaud Jung's emphasis on these dual aspects in everyone's personality, although they might question his characterizing some as specifically masculine and others as feminine. An interesting yet controversial feature of Jung's analysis is the contention that gender-role stereotypes are not a product of an individual's social experience, but of the experiences of one's ancestors over the course of evolution. A similar idea is found in contemporary evolutionary psychology (Chapter 9).

Jung emphasizes that all individuals face a fundamental personal task: finding unity in the self. The task is to bringing into harmony, or integrate, the various opposing forces of the psyche. The person is motivated and guided along the path to personal knowledge and integration by the most important of all Jungian archetypes: the self. In Jungian psychology "the self" does not refer to one's conscious beliefs about one's personal qualities. Instead, the self is an unconscious force, specifically, an aspect of the collective unconscious that functions as an "organizing center" (Jung and collaborators, 1964, p. 161) of the person's entire psychological system. Jung believed that the self often is represented symbolically in circular figures—the circle representing a sense of wholeness that can be achieved through self-knowledge. Mandalas, which are circular symbols that contain pathways toward a centerpoint, serve as vivid symbols of the struggle for knowledge of our true selves. Since the self is an archetype of the collective unconscious, and the collective unconscious is a universal aspect of human personality, according to Jungian theory one should expect to find similar symbolic representations of the self across

The psychologist Carl Jung hypothesized that mandalas symbolize people's universal striving for a whole, complete sense of self. Since the archetype of the self is a universal feature of the human mind according to Jung, similar mandala symbols should be found across diverse cultures. And they are. These two mandalas, similar though they may be in overall design, come from very widely separated cultures; Tibet in central Asia (left) and a Native American society in the southwestern United States (right).

diverse human cultures. And one does. Symbols found in human cultures separated widely in time and place often contain remarkably similar imagery that, according to Jung, represents the universal unconscious motive to grow in self-knowledge.

To Jung, the search for the self is a never-ending quest. "Personality as a complete realization of the fullness of our being is an unattainable ideal. But unattainability is no counter argument against an ideal, for ideals are only signposts, never goals" (Jung, 1939, p. 287). The struggle described here can become a particularly important aspect of life once people have passed the age of 40 and defined themselves to the outside world in a variety of ways.

Another contrast in Jung's theory is that between introversion and extraversion. Everyone relates to the world primarily in one of two directions, though the other direction always remains a part of the person. In the case of introversion, the person's basic orientation is inward, toward the self. The introverted type is hesitant, reflective, and cautious. In the case of extraversion the person's basic orientation is outward, toward the outside world. The extraverted type is socially engaging, active, and adventuresome.

As with Adler, we have considered only some of the highlights of Jung's theory. Jung is considered by many to be one of the great creative thinkers of the 20th century. His theory has influenced intellectual trends in many fields outside of psychology. Jungian centers for clinical training continue to exist in many countries. Yet Jung's work has had little impact within scientific psychology. To a large degree, this reflects the fact Jung often did not state his ideas in a manner that could be tested according to standard scientific methods. His imaginative theorizing commonly was more speculative than that of other personality theorists—so speculative that elements of this theorizing are difficult, if not impossible, to support or to disprove through objective scientific methods.

THE CULTURAL AND INTERPERSONAL EMPHASIS

With the later shift in psychodynamic thinking from Europe to the United States, one finds theorists emphasizing social rather than biological forces in behavior. Collectively, these theorists are called neo-Freudians, recognizing both their theoretical debt to Freud and their development of new theoretical positions. Some of these theorists, such as Karen Horney, emigrated to the United States prior to World War II. Other theorists, notably Harry Stack Sullivan, were born and trained in this country.

Karen Horney (1885–1952)

Karen Horney was trained as a traditional analyst in Germany and came to the United States in 1932. Shortly thereafter she split with traditional psychoanalytic thought and developed her own theoretical orientation and psychoanalytic training program. In contrast to Adler and Jung, Horney felt that her views were built on the tremendous contributions of Freud and were not replacements of them. Perhaps the major difference between her and Freud centers on the question of universal biological influences as opposed to cultural influences: "When we realize the great import of cultural conditions on neuroses, the biological and physiological conditions, which are considered by Freud to be their root, recede into the background" (1937, p. viii). She was led to this emphasis by three major considerations. First, Freud's statements concerning women made Horney think about cultural influences: "Their influence on our ideas of what constitutes masculinity or femininity was obvious, and it became just as obvious to me that Freud had arrived at certain conclusions because he failed to take them into account" (1945, p. 11). Second, she was associated with another psychoanalyst, Erich Fromm, who increased her awareness of the importance of social and cultural influences. Third, Horney's observations of differences in personality structure between patients seen in Europe and the United States confirmed the importance of cultural influences. Beyond this, these observations led her to conclude that interpersonal relationships are at the core of all healthy and disturbed personality functioning.

Horney's emphasis in neurotic functioning is on how individuals attempt to cope with basic anxiety—the feeling a child has of being isolated and helpless in a potentially hostile world. According to her theory of neurosis, in the neurotic person there is conflict among three ways of responding to this basic anxiety. These three patterns, or neurotic trends, are known as moving toward, moving against, and moving away. All three are characterized by rigidity and the lack of fulfillment of individual potential, the essence of any neurosis. In moving toward, a person attempts to deal with anxiety by an excessive interest in being accepted, needed, and approved of. Such a person accepts a dependent role in relation to others and, except for the unlimited desire for affection, becomes unselfish, undemanding, and self-sacrificing. In moving against, a person assumes that everyone is hostile and that life is a struggle

Karen Horney

against all. All functioning is directed toward denying a need for others and toward appearing tough. In moving away, the third component of the conflict, the person shrinks away from others into neurotic detachment. Such people often look at themselves and others with emotional detachment, as a way of not getting emotionally involved with others. Although each neurotic person shows one or another trend as a special aspect of their personality, the problem is really that there is conflict among the three trends in the effort to deal with basic anxiety.

Before leaving Horney, we should consider her views concerning women. These views date back to her early work within traditional psychoanalytic thought and are reflected in a series of papers collected in *Feminine Psychology* (1973). As noted from the start, Horney had trouble accepting Freud's views of women. She felt that the concept of penis envy might be the result of a male bias in psychoanalysts who treat neurotic women in a particular social context: "Unfortunately, little or nothing is known of psychologically healthy women, or of women under different cultural conditions" (1973, p. 216). She suggested that women are not biologically disposed toward masochistic attitudes of being weak, dependent, submissive, and self-sacrificing. Instead, these attitudes indicated the powerful influence of social forces.

In sum, both in her views of women and in her general theoretical orientation, Horney rejected Freud's biological emphasis in favor of a social, interpersonal approach. Partly as a result of this difference, she held a much more optimistic view concerning people's capacity for change and self-fulfillment.

Harry Stack Sullivan (1892–1949)

Of the theorists considered in this section, Sullivan is the only one born and trained in the United States, the only one who never had direct contact with Freud, and the one who most emphasized the role of social, interpersonal forces in human development. In fact, his theory has been known as the Interpersonal Theory of Psychiatry (1953), and his followers consider themselves part of the Sullivan school of interpersonal relations.

Sullivan placed great importance on the early relationship between the infant and the mother in the development of anxiety and in the development of a sense of self. Anxiety may be communicated by the mother in her earliest interaction with the infant. Thus, from the start, anxiety is interpersonal in character. The self, a critical concept in Sullivan's thinking, similarly is social in origin. The self develops out of feelings experienced while in contact with others and from reflected appraisals or perceptions by a child as to how he or she is valued or appraised by others. Important parts of the self, particularly in relation to the experience of anxiety as opposed to security, are the "good me" associated with pleasurable experiences, the "bad me" associated with pain and threats to security, and the "not me", or the part of the self that is rejected because it is associated with intolerable anxiety.

Sullivan's emphasis on social influences is seen in his views on the development of the person. These views are somewhat similar to Erikson's in their emphasis on interpersonal influences and in their emphasis on important stages beyond the Oedipus complex. Particularly noteworthy is Sullivan's emphasis on the juvenile era and preadolescence. During the juvenile stage— roughly the grammar school years—a child's experiences with friends and

Harry Stack Sullivan

Peers: *Harry Stack Sullivan emphasized the importance of peers and a close friend of the same sex during preadolescence.*

teachers begin to rival the influence of his or her parents. Social acceptance becomes important, and the child's reputation with others becomes an important source of self-esteem or anxiety. During preadolescence, a relationship to a close friend of the same sex becomes particularly important. This relationship of close friendship, of love, forms the basis for the development of a love relationship with a person of the opposite sex during adolescence. Today, many child psychologists suggest that early relationships with peers may be equal in importance to the early relationship with the mother (Lewis et al., 1975).

As with the other theorists in this section, we have considered only a few of the major concepts of Sullivan's interpersonal theory. Sullivan's work is noteworthy in its social emphasis, in its emphasis on the development of the self, and in the outstanding contributions that he made to the treatment of schizophrenic patients.

RECENT DEVELOPMENTS IN THE PSYCHODYNAMIC TRADITION

Within the psychodynamic theory, let us consider the progress associated with clinical investigations and with systematic research. From its inception with Freud and continuing to the present, developments within psychoanalytic theory generally have been based on clinical investigation—that is, on analysis of individual cases. One important development has been the extension of psychoanalytic investigation to age groups and forms of psychopathology rarely treated by Freud and his followers. As noted, Little Hans was treated by his father. Most psychoanalytic material on childhood and adolescence was based on memories reported by adult patients. The situation changed considerably with the efforts of individuals such as Anna Freud and Melanie Klein, who used psychoanalytic concepts in the treatment of children; now much of the psychotherapy of children and adolescents in Great Britain and the United States is based on psychoanalytic theory. The treatment procedure is modified according to the age group being treated (e.g., with children, play therapy is used as a substitute for dream analysis as a route to the unconscious), but the essential theoretical concepts remain the same.

In addition to expanding their clinical efforts to the treatment of children, psychoanalysts increasingly have been concerned with different types of patient problems than those generally faced by Freud. In the words of one analyst, today's patients come from a different social and cultural context than did Freud's, and they bring with them different problems. Rather than presenting with "typical neuroses," they seek help for depression, for feelings of emptiness, and for lives "lacking zest and joy" (Wolf, 1977). Such changes in the major problems coming to the attention of analysts have led to new theoretical advances, not from a dissatisfaction with Freudian theory per se, but from the need to understand and solve different clinical problems.

OBJECT RELATIONS THEORY

Clinical concern with problems of self-definition and with an excessively vulnerable sense of self-esteem have led analysts to become increasingly interested in how, during the earliest years, a person develops a sense of self and then attempts to protect its integrity. As a group, the individuals concerned with such questions are known as object relations theorists (Greenberg & Mitchell, 1983; Westen & Gabbard, 1999). The word *object* here refers to people rather than to physical objects. Thus, the interest is in how experiences with important people in the past are represented as parts or aspects of the self and then affect one's relationships with others in the present. Although there are differences among object relations theorists, and although some depart from traditional psychoanalytic theory more than others, generally there is a greater emphasis on people as relationship seeking rather than as focused on the expression of sexual and aggressive instincts. For example, an important relationship with a nurturant grandmother can be represented as a nurturant part of the self. On the other hand, an important relationship with a grandmother perceived to be selfish can lead to a selfish self-representation.

Narcissism and the Narcissistic Personality

In relation to this interest in the disturbances in the sense of self, psychoanalytic attention has focused particularly on the concept of narcissism and the narcissistic personality. The two figures most important in this area are Heinz Kohut and Otto Kernberg. In the development of a healthy sense of self and a healthy narcissism, an individual has a clear sense of self, has a satisfactory and reasonably stable level of self-esteem, takes pride in accomplishments, and is aware of and responsive to the needs of others while responding to his or her own needs. In the narcissistic personality, there is a disturbance in an individual's sense of self, a vulnerability to blows to self-esteem, a need for the admiration of others, and a lack of empathy with the feelings and needs of others. While being vulnerable to intense feelings of worthlessness and powerlessness (shame and humiliation), a narcissistic individual has a grandiose sense of self-importance and is preoccupied with fantasies of unlimited success and power. Such individuals tend to have an exaggerated feeling of being entitled to things from others, of deserving the admiration and love of others, and of being special or unique. They are capable of being very giving to others, though generally not on an emotional or empathic level, but also of being very demanding. They at times idealize others around them—as well as themselves—but at other times may completely devalue others. In therapy it is not unusual for the narcissistic individual to idealize the therapist as extremely insightful at one moment, and to berate the same therapist as stupid and incompetent in the next moment.

Henry Murray, who developed the TAT, also developed a questionnaire to measure narcissism (Figure 4.3). More recently, a Narcissistic Personality Inventory (NPI) (Raskin & Hall, 1979, 1981) has been developed (Emmons, 1987) (Figure 4.3). Individuals scoring high on the NPI have been found to use many more self-references (e.g., I, me, mine) than those scoring low (Raskin & Shaw, 1987). In another study a relationship was found between high scores on the NPI and being described by others as exhibitionistic, assertive, controlling, and critical-evaluative (Raskin & Terry, 1987). Individuals scoring high on narcissism have been found to evaluate their performance more positively than it is evaluated by peers or staff, demonstrating a significant self-enhancement bias relative to individuals scoring low on narcissism (John & Robins, 1994a; Robins & John, 1997). Moreover, whereas most people feel uncomfortable and self-conscious when they see themselves in a mirror or on videotape, this was not the case for narcissistic individuals. Just like the mythical Narcissus who admired his own reflection in a pond, narcissistic individuals spent more time looking at themselves in mirrors, preferred to watch themselves rather than another person on videotape, and indeed received an "ego boost" from watching themselves on videotape (Robins & John, 1997).

Recently, researchers have focused on the thinking processes and interpersonal tendencies of narcissistic individuals (Morf & Rhodewalt, 2001; Rhodewalt & Sorrow, 2002). Narcissistic persons are found to have not only a self-aggrandizing attributional style but also fairly simple self-concepts and a cynical mistrust of others (Rhodewalt & Morf, 1995). These findings are con-

---

Murray's Narcissism Scale (1938, p. 181)

I often think about how I look and what impression I am making upon others.

My feelings are easily hurt by ridicule or by the slighting remarks of others.

I talk a good deal about myself, my experiences, my feelings, and my ideas.

Narcissism Personality Inventory (Raskin & Hall, 1979)

I really like to be the center of attention.

I think I am a special person.

I expect a great deal from other people.

I am envious of other people's good fortune.

I will never be satisfied until I get all that I deserve.

Figure 4.3 Illustrative Items from Questionnaire Measures of Narcissism.

sistent with the picture of the narcissist as a person preoccupied with the maintenance of their exaggerated self-esteem. In relation to this, it is not surprising that narcissistic individuals seek romantic partners who will be admiring of them, in contrast with nonnarcissistic individuals who seek caring partners (Campbell, 1999).

Much of the research on narcissism has been correlational, relating scores on the NPI to scores on other questionnaires or to observations of behavior (e.g., self-references, looking at self in the mirror). However, investigators increasingly have employed experimental methods. For example, building on clinical observations that narcissists respond to criticism or threat to self-esteem with feelings of rage, shame, or humiliation, Rhodewalt & Morf (1998) exposed individuals high and low on narcissism (NPI) to experiences of success and failure on two tests described as a measures of intelligence. Since the items on the measure were moderately difficult, subjects would be uncertain about the accuracy of their responses and feedback concerning accuracy could be manipulated by the experimenters. To observe the effects of failure following success as opposed to preceding success, half the subjects received success feedback for the first test and failure feedback for the second test, and the other half the reverse order of feedback. Following each test, subjects were asked to respond to questions concerning their emotions and to indicate their attributions for their performance. As predicted, individuals high on narcissism (NPI) reacted to failure with greater anger than did individuals scoring low on narcissism, particularly when the failure followed success (Table 4.3). This result was consistent with the view that narcissistic anger is a response to perceived threats to the narcissist's grandiose self-image. In addition, individuals scoring high on narcissism were found to be particularly vulnerable to swings in self-esteem as a consequence of receiving positive and negative feedback about the self. Feelings of happiness were similarly greatly affected by such feedback (Table 4.3). Finally, narcissists were found to be more self-aggrandizing in attributing success to their own ability, and more blaming of others in accounting for failure, than were less narcissistic subjects. In sum, the experimental findings supported the clinical observations concerning the vulnerability of narcissists to blows to their self-esteem and their response to such blows with anger.

ATTACHMENT THEORY AND ADULT PERSONAL RELATIONSHIPS

This theory deals with the effect of early experiences on personality development, and their relationship to later personality functioning. Although not specifically a part of psychoanalytic theory or object relations theory, attachment theory has many points in common with both.

Current attachment theory is largely based on the early theoretical work of the British psychoanalyst John Bowlby and the empirical work of the developmental psychologist Mary Ainsworth (Ainsworth & Bowlby, 1991; Bretherton, 1992; Rothbard & Shaver, 1994). Bowlby was trained as a psychoanalyst and was interested in the effects of early separation from parents on personality development. This was a major problem in England during World War II when many children were sent to the countryside, far from their parents, to be safe from enemy bombing of the cities. In his conceptual work, Bowlby was largely influenced by developments in ethology, a part of the field

Table 4.3   Self-Esteem, Anger, and Happiness Ratings of Subjects High and Low on Narcissism Following Success and then Failure (Left) and Following Failure and then Success (Right)

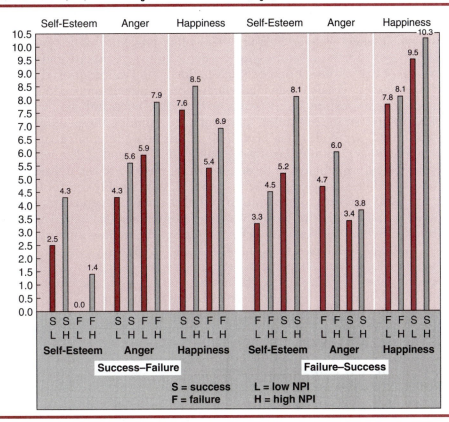

SOURCE: Adapted from Rhodewalt & Morf, 1998.

of biology that focuses on the study of animals in their natural environment, and by developments in general systems theory, a part of the field of biology that focuses on general principles of operation of all biological systems. His clinical observations and reading of the literature led Bowlby to formulate a theory of the development of the **attachment behavioral system** (ABS). According to this theory, a developing infant goes through a series of phases in the development of an attachment to a major caregiver (generally the mother) and of the use of this attachment as a "secure base" for exploration and separations. The ABS is viewed as something programmed within infants, a part of our evolutionary heritage that has adaptive value. It provides for both the maintenance of close contact with the mother and exploration of the environment from that secure base of contact.

As a further part of the development of the ABS, the infant develops **internal working models** or mental representations (images) of itself and its primary caregivers. These working models are associated with emotion. Based on interactional experience during infancy, they provide the basis for the development of expectations about future relationships. In the emphasis on the importance of early emotional relationships for personality development and future relationships, attachment theory is similar to psychoanalytic theory and object relations theory.

A major advance in attachment theory was based on a research methodology: the Strange Situation procedure developed by Mary Ainsworth (Ainsworth, Bleher, Waters, & Wall, 1978). This procedure is a systematic observation of infants' responses to the departure (separation) and return (reuniting) of the mother or other caregiver. Such observations proved important because they revealed individual differences in attachment style. Not all parent-child relationships are the same, and key differences among them were revealed in the strange-situation paradigm. To capture these differences, Ainsworth and her colleagues classified infants into different attachment types. About 70 percent of infants were classified as being of a Secure attachment type; secure infants were those who were sensitive to the departure of the mother but greeted her upon being reunited, were readily comforted, and were then able to return to exploration and play. About 20 percent of infants displayed an attachment style that was labeled Anxious-Avoidant. This style was marked by little protest over separation from the mother and, upon her return, avoidance in terms of turning, looking, or moving away from the mother. Finally, about 10 percent of infants were classified as Anxious-Ambivalent; these infants had difficulty separating from the mother and reuniting with her upon her return. Their behavior mixed pleas to be picked up with squirming and insistence on being let down.

Attachment Styles in Adulthood

In more recent years, psychologists have used the attachment framework to understand not only parent-child relationships, but romantic relationships in adulthood. Individual differences in emotional bonds in infancy may be related to individual differences in the way emotional bonds are established later in life. To study this possibility, Hazan & Shaver (1987) had research participants complete a newspaper survey or "love quiz." As a measure of attachment style, the newspaper readers described themselves as fitting one of three categories in terms of their relationships with others. These three categories were descriptive of the three attachment styles (Figure 4.4). As a measure of their current style of romantic love, subjects were asked to respond to questions listed under a banner headline in the newspaper: "Tell Us About the Love of Your Life." Responses to the questions concerning the most important love relationship they ever had formed the basis for scores on 12 love experience scales (Figure 4.4). Additional questions were asked concerning each person's view of romantic love over time and recollections of childhood relationships with parents and between parents.

Did the different types of respondents (secure, avoidant, anxious-ambivalent) also differ in the way they experienced their most important love relationships? As the means for the three groups on the love scales indicate, this appears to be the case. Secure attachment styles were associated with experiences of happiness, friendship, and trust; avoidant styles with fears of closeness, emotional highs and lows, and jealousy; and anxious-ambivalent styles with obsessive preoccupation with the loved person, a desire for union, extreme sexual attraction, emotional extremes, and jealousy. In addition, the three groups differed in their views or mental models of romantic relationships: secure lovers viewed romantic feelings as being somewhat stable but

Adult Attachment Types
Which of the following best describes your feelings?

Secure (*N = 319, 56%*): I find it relatively easy to get close to others and am comfortable depending on them and having them depend on me. I don't often worry about being abandoned or about someone getting too close to me.

Avoidant (*N = 145, 25%*): I am somewhat uncomfortable being close to others; I find it difficult to trust them completely, difficult to allow myself to depend on them. I am nervous when anyone gets too close, and often love partners want me to be more intimate than I feel comfortable being.

Anxious/Ambivalent (*N = 110, 19%*): I find that others are reluctant to get as close as I would like. I often worry that my partner doesn't really love me or won't want to stay with me. I want to merge completely with another person, and this desire sometimes scares people away.

Scale Name	Sample Item	Attachment Type Means		
		Avoidant	Anxious/ ambivalent	Secure
Happiness	My relationship with _____ (made/makes) me very happy.	3.19	3.31	3.51
Friendship	I (considered/consider) _____ one of my best friends.	3.18	3.19	3.50
Trust	I (felt/feel) complete trust in _____.	3.11	3.13	3.43
Fear of closeness	I sometimes (felt/feel) that getting too close to _____ could mean trouble.	2.30	2.15	1.88
Acceptance	I (was/am) well aware of _____'s imperfections but it (did/does) not lessen my love.	2.86	3.03	3.01
Emotional extremes	I (felt/feel) almost as much pain as joy in my relationship with _____.	2.75	3.05	2.36
Jealousy	I (loved/love) _____ so much that I often (felt/feel) jealous.	2.57	2.88	2.17
Obsessive preoccupation	Sometimes my thoughts (were/are) uncontrollably on _____.	3.01	3.29	3.01
Sexual attraction	I (was/am) very physically attracted to _____.	3.27	3.43	3.27
Desire for union	Sometimes I (wished/wish) that _____ and I were a single unit, a "we" without clear boundaries.	2.81	3.25	2.69
Desire for reciprocation	More than anything, I (wanted/want) _____ to return my feelings	3.24	3.55	3.22
Love at first sight	Once I noticed _____, I was hooked.	2.91	3.17	2.97

Figure 4.4 Illustrative Items and Means for Three Attachment Types for 12 Love Experience Scales. *(Hazan & Shaver, 1987. Copyright © 1987 by the American Psychological Association. Reprinted by permission.)*

also waxing and waning, and discounted the kind of head-over-heels romantic love often depicted in novels and movies; avoidant lovers were skeptical of the lasting quality of romantic love and felt that it was rare to find a person one can really fall in love with; anxious-ambivalent lovers felt that it was easy to fall in love but rare to find true love. Finally, secure subjects, in comparison with subjects in the other two groups, reported warmer relationships with both parents, as well as between their two parents.

Subsequent research has extended these findings in two ways. First, it has been suggested that attachment style exerts a pervasive influence on people's relationships with others and on their self-esteem (Feeney & Noller, 1990). Second, attachment style appears to be related to orientation toward work: Secure subjects approach their work with confidence, are relatively unburdened by fears of failure, and do not allow work to interfere with personal relationships; anxious-ambivalent subjects are very much influenced by praise and fear of rejection at work and allow love concerns to interfere with work performance; avoidant subjects use work to avoid social interaction and, although they do well financially, are less satisfied with their jobs than secure subjects (Hazan & Shaver, 1990).

Although many of these studies of attachment style have relied on self-report measures, a clever study by Fraley and Shaver (1998) made use of naturalistic observation to examine the relation between attachment style and separation behavior in couples. In this study the behavior of couples temporarily separating from each other was observed in an airport. The research proceeded as follows: First a member of the research team approached couples waiting in the airport lobby and asked if they would be willing to fill out a questionnaire on "The Effects of Modern Travel on Close Relationships" that was to be used in a class project. Most (95 percent) couples agreed to participate. Each member of the couple filled out the questionnaire independently. Included in the questionnaire was a measure of attachment style. While the questionnaires were being completed, another member of the research team took a seat within viewing distance of the couple and then took notes on their interactions while they awaited flight departure. These behaviors were coded into attachment behavior categories such as Contact Seeking (e.g., kissing, watching from window after partner has boarded), Contact Maintenance (e.g., hugging, unwillingness to let go), Avoidance (e.g., looking elsewhere, breaking off contact), and Resistance (e.g., wanting to be held but also resisting contact, signs of anger or annoyance). The question addressed was whether individuals differing in attachment style would differ in their separation behavior. Such a relationship was found for women, although not for men. Compared to nonavoidant women, highly avoidant women were less likely to seek and maintain contact with their partners and to provide care and support to their partners, and were more likely to show withdrawal behavior such as pulling away and not making eye contact. Interestingly, the behavior of avoidant women was quite different when they were accompanying their partner in travel as opposed to separating from them. Whereas the above behaviors were true of avoidant women during separation, when they were to be flying with their partner (a setting that poses no threat of abandonment), they were more likely to seek care from and contact with their partners. In sum, at least for women, the attachment dynamics originally found in studies of children also applied in the context of adult romantic relationships.

Attachment Types or Dimensions?

As we noted, Ainsworth suggested that individual differences in attachment style could be understood in terms of three attachment types. In other words, she proposed what we called (back in Chapter 1) units of analysis involving type variables. The idea was that different attachment types are qualitatively distinct.

Although the idea that infants differ in attachment style makes sense, the specific notion that these differences involve qualitatively distinct categories of persons in less intuitive. It is rare that individual differences in observable psychological qualities differ categorically. Usually the psychological tendencies we observe—individual differences in anxiety, friendliness, etc.—are each affected by a large number of factors. When any given outcome is affected by a large number of causes, the outcome usually varies dimensionally, not categorically. For example, a large number of factors affects people's scores on IQ tests: educational experiences, genetics, familiarity with the language and cultural assumptions of the test. As a result, IQ scores are distributed as a continuous dimension, not as distinct categories. A question for contemporary research on attachment styles, then, is: Do these styles really differ categorically?

Recent evidence suggests that the answer to this question is "no." Fraley and Spieker (2003) examined data from a very large number of 15-month-old children who had participated in the strange-situation paradigm. Rather than merely asking how many children fell into one versus another attachment category, they asked a logically prior question: Are there attachment *categories* in the first place? Or might the differences among children actually involve simple dimensions? This question can be addressed through somewhat complex, yet highly informative, statistical procedures that ask whether different psychological characteristics go together so consistently that they form distinct categories (Meehl, 1992). The results indicated that, for attachment styles, this was *not* the case. Instead, variations in attachment involved continuous dimensions.

These findings raise the question of exactly what dimensions might best capture individual differences in attachment style. One possibility involves a theoretical model of individual differences in internal working models of the self and others (Bartholomew & Horowitz, 1991; Griffin & Bartholomew, 1994). Following Bowlby, according to this model attachment patterns can be defined in terms of two dimensions, reflecting the internal working model of the self and the internal working model of others (Figure 4.5). Each dimension involves a positive end and a negative end. Illustrative of the positive self end would be a sense of self-worth and expectations that others will respond positively. Illustrative of the positive other end would be expectations that others will be available and supportive, lending themselves to closeness. As can be seen in Figure 4.5, this model leads to the addition of a fourth attachment style, that of Dismissing. Individuals with this attachment pattern are not comfortable with close relationships and prefer not to depend on others, but still retain a positive self-image. Current research suggests some use for this four-pattern model, relative to the three-pattern model, but it is still an open question as to how many attachment patterns it is best to identify.

The research presented here just scratches the surface of what has become an important area of investigation. Attachment styles have been associated

Positive Other

Secure
(Comfortable with
intimacy and autonomy)

Preoccupied
(Preoccupied with
relationships)

Positive Self   **Negative Self**

Dismissing
(Dismissing of intimacy;
counter-dependent)

Fearful
(Fearful of intimacy;
socially avoidant)

Negative Other

Figure 4.5   Bartholomew's Dimensions of Self and Other Internal Working Models
and Associated Attachment Patterns. *(Bartholomew & Horowitz, 1991; Griffin &
Bartholomew, 1994. Copyright © 1994 by the American Psychological Association.
Reprinted by permission.)*

with partner selection and stability of love relationships (Kirkpatrick & Davis,
1994), with the development of adult depression and difficulties in interpersonal relationships (Bartholomew & Horowitz, 1991; Carnelley, Pietromonaco,
& Jaffe, 1994; Roberts, Gotlib, & Kassel, 1996), with movement toward becoming more religious (Kirkpatrick, 1998), and with how individuals cope with
crises (Mikulciner, Florian, & Weller, 1993). In addition, one study suggests that
attachment style develops out of family experiences shared by siblings, rather
than being strongly determined by genetic factors (Waller & Shaver, 1994).
Thus, an impressive research record is beginning to develop (Cassidy & Shaver,
1999; Simpson & Rholes, 1998).

At the same time, it is important to keep a number of points in mind. First,
despite suggestive evidence of continuity of attachment style, there also is evidence that these styles are not fixed in stone. At this point the amount of continuity over time of attachment style, and the reasons for greater or lesser continuity, remain issues of considerable debate (Fraley, 1999; Thompson, 1998).
Second, these studies tend to look at attachment patterns as if each person
had just one attachment style. Yet, there is evidence that the same individual
can have multiple attachment patterns, perhaps one in relationships with
males and another with females, or one for some contexts and another for different contexts (Baldwin, 1999; Sperling & Berman, 1994). Finally, it is important to recognize that much of this research involves the use of self-reports
and the recall of experiences in childhood. In other words, we need more evidence about the actual behavior of individuals with different adult attachment
patterns and research that follows individuals from infancy through adulthood. Some efforts, known as longitudinal research, currently are underway
(Sroufe, Carlson, & Shulman, 1993). In sum, research to date supports
Bowlby's view of the importance of early experience for the development of
internal working models that have powerful effects on personal relationships.
At the same time, further research is needed to define the experiences in child-

hood that determine these models, the relative stability of such models, and the limits of their influence in adulthood.

CRITICAL EVALUATION

In evaluating psychoanalysis as a theory of personality, we must keep in mind that it is a complex theory with many components, with some concepts being more fundamental to the theory than others. Thus, for example, the concept of the latency stage of development is less fundamental than the emphasis on the importance of early experience in shaping personality development. Also, in considering psychoanalysis as a theory, it is important to keep it distinct from psychoanalysis as a method of therapy. The issue of therapeutic success with psychoanalysis has not been dealt with here because it is not essential to an understanding of the theory or our evaluation of it. The effectiveness of therapy is a very complex matter, still little understood, and it is hard to extrapolate from this area of research to an evaluation of the theory of personality.

MAJOR CONTRIBUTIONS

How good a theory of personality is psychoanalysis? Clearly, Freud made major contributions to psychology. Psychoanalysis has led to the use of new techniques, such as free association and dream interpretation, and has been a significant force in the development and use of special tests in the assessment of personality. In addition, two outstanding contributions are noteworthy. First, psychoanalysis made a major contribution to the discovery and investigation of phenomena. As we go beyond some of the superficialities of human behavior, we are impressed with Freud's observations, which become particularly apparent in clinical work with patients. Whether we choose to interpret these phenomena as characteristic of all human functioning, as Freud did, or merely as idiosyncratic to neurotics, we are forced to take account of these observations as data concerning human behavior.

The first major contribution by Freud, then, was the richness of his observations and the attention he paid to all details of human behavior. The second was the attention he gave to the complexity of human behavior at the same time that he developed an extremely encompassing theory. Psychoanalytic theory emphasizes that seemingly similar behaviors can have very different antecedents and that very similar motives can lead to quite different behavior. Generosity can express genuine affection or an effort to deal with feelings of hostility; the lawyer and the criminal whom he or she defends or prosecutes may, in some cases, be closer to one another psychologically than most of us care to realize. Out of this recognition of complexity comes a theory that accounts for almost all aspects of human behavior. No other theory of personality comes close to psychoanalytic theory in accounting for such a broad range of behavior. Few others give comparable attention to the functioning of the individual as a whole.

LIMITATIONS OF THE THEORY

In making these contributions, Freud stands as a genius and an investigator of tremendous courage. What, then, are the limitations of psychoanalysis as a theory? Two major criticisms are worthy of note. The first involves the scientific status of psychoanalysis, the second the psychoanalytic view of the person.

The Scientific Status of Psychoanalytic Theory

One can raise a variety of questions about the adequacy of psychoanalysis as a theory of personality. These questions can be raised in relation to specific components of the theory as well as in relation to the total enterprise. For example, in terms of the former, consider the problems associated with the energy model found in psychoanalytic theory. We have already noted that this model was based on other scientific models present at the time of Freud's emerging theory. However, such a model now is out of date and research clearly indicates the inadequacy of it. People do not always seek tension reduction; in fact, often stimulation and tension are desired. Thus, the entire model of motivation as based on physiological drives has been found to be wanting in the field. The energy model is perhaps useful as a metaphor for personality functioning but it hardly does justice to the complexity of human functioning.

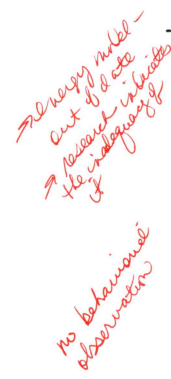

Of even greater consequence, however, is what are perhaps fundamental scientific flaws in the entire psychoanalytic enterprise. The terms of psychoanalysis are ambiguous. There are many metaphors and analogies that can, but need not, be taken literally. Examples are latency, death instinct, Oedipus complex, and castration anxiety. Does castration anxiety refer to the fear of loss of the penis, or does it refer to the child's fear of injury to his body at a time when his body image is becoming more important to his self-esteem? The language of the theory is so vague that investigators often are hard pressed to agree on precise meanings of the terms. How are we to define libido? Even where the constructs are well defined, often they are too removed from observable and measurable behavior to be of much empirical use. Concepts such as id, ego, and superego have considerable descriptive power, but it is often hard to translate them into relevant behavioral observations.

And what of the scientific use of clinical data? Many critics suggest that psychoanalysts use observations influenced by the theory to support the theory, while glossing over the problem that committed observers (analysts) may bias the response of their subjects and bias their own perceptions of the data. Whereas some suggest that observations drawn from patients in analysis are adequate grounds for testing psychoanalytic concepts (Edelson, 1984), others suggest that clinical data remain suspect and are an inadequate basis for testing the theory (Grunbaum, 1984, 1993). Rather than constituting unbiased observations of experiences and recollections by patients, many critics suggest that Freud often biased his observations through the use of suggestive procedures and by inferring that memories existed at the unconscious level (Crews, 1993; Esterson, 1993; Powell & Boer, 1994). Eysenck, a frequent and passionate critic of psychoanalysis, whose views we will consider later in this textbook, suggests that "we can no more test Freudian hypotheses on the couch than we can adjudicate between the rival hypotheses of Newton and Einstein by going to sleep under the apple tree" (1953, p. 229).

What we have, then, is a theory that is at times confusing and often difficult to test. This problem is complicated further by the way in which psychoanalysts can account for almost any outcome, even opposite outcomes. If one behavior appears, it is an expression of the instinct; if the opposite appears, it is an expression of a defense; if another form of behavior appears, it is a compromise between the instinct and the defense. The problem with the theory is not that it leaves room for such complexity, but that it fails to state which behavior will occur, given a specific set of circumstances. In not providing such statements, psychoanalytic theory does not leave itself open to disproof or to the negative test.

Finally, there is a problem in the way in which psychoanalysts often defend the theory. Analysts often respond to criticism of the theory by suggesting that the critics are being defensive in not recognizing and accepting the importance of phenomena such as infantile sexuality. Psychoanalysts who advance such arguments in a routine way perpetuate some of the early developments of psychoanalysis as a religious movement rather than as a scientific theory. Kohut, whose influential work on narcissism has been noted, has described the dilemma he faced when he no longer believed in certain traditional aspects of psychoanalysis. Not only did he face difficulties in giving up views formerly dear to him, but he also had to face the condemnation of traditional analysts (Kohut, 1984).

In noting these criticisms of the status of psychoanalysis as a scientific theory, it is important to recognize that Freud was aware of most of these objections. He was not a naive scientist; his position, rather, was that the beginning of scientific activity consists of the description of phenomena, and that at the early stages some imprecision is inevitable. Also, Freud was acutely aware of the difficulties in using psychoanalytic insights for predictive purposes. He noted that the analyst was on safe ground in tracing the development of behavior from its final stage backward, but that if he proceeded in the reverse direction, an inevitable sequence of events no longer seemed to be apparent. His conclusion was that psychoanalysis does a better job of explaining than of predicting. When he developed his theory, Freud did not have the benefit of a discipline in psychology that supported his efforts to develop a scientific theory. Unfortunately, Freud was excessively dependent on a medical, therapeutic environment when he was committed to developing a system with broader relevance.

The Psychoanalytic View of the Person

In addition to these questions raised by scientific critics, psychoanalysis has been criticized by humanists and proponents of the existential point of view in psychology and psychiatry. According to this view, a theory of the person as an energy system oriented toward tension reduction hardly does justice to the creative, self-actualizing efforts of individuals. It is also suggested that psychoanalysis emphasizes the forces within the individual while generally neglecting the forces within the family and the broader society. Relevant here is the criticism that psychoanalytic theory has received from feminists. Although Freud often is misinterpreted, he did see certain traits, such as receptivity, dependence on others, sensitivity, vanity, and submissiveness, as part of the feminine orientation. These characteristics were seen as part of women because of biological influences and because of psychological reactions to their awareness of the lack of a penis—Freud's concept of penis envy. The concept of penis envy symbolizes for many women a "biology is destiny" view on the part of Freud and an inadequate appreciation of cultural factors. Karen Horney, among others, questioned many of Freud's views concerning women and female sexuality—and, as noted earlier, proposed instead a view of feminine development that emphasized cultural influences. Interestingly, although psychoanalysis has come under attack by feminists, perhaps more

FREUD AT A GLANCE

	Structure	Process	Growth and Development
	Id, ego, superego; unconscious, preconscious, conscious	Sexual and aggressive instincts; anxiety and the mechanisms of defense	Erogenous zones; oral, anal, phallic stages of development; Oedipus complex

than any other theory, it has almost always had major female figures within its ranks (e.g., Anna Freud, Helene Deutsch, Greta Bibring, Margaret Mahler, Clara Thompson, and Frieda Fromm-Reichman).

SUMMARY EVALUATION

Today, views concerning Freud's works and contributions range from the judgment that it is literature and not psychology to the view that "although commentators periodically declare that Freud is dead, his repeated burials lie on shaky grounds" (Westen, 1998). While some are critical of psychoanalytic errors made in the treatment of certain disorders (e.g., schizophrenia) (Dolnick, 1998) and of limited evidence supportive of psychoanalysis's major hypotheses, others are more supportive of its treatment methods and cite its enduring contributions to empirical research (Westen & Gabbard, 1999). How, then, are we to summarize our evaluation of Freud and psychoanalytic theory (Table 4.4)? As an observer of human behavior and as a person with a creative imagination, Freud was indeed a genius with few, if any, equals. The theory he developed certainly has the virtue of being comprehensive. No other personality theory approximates psychoanalysis in the range of behavior considered and the interpretations offered. Given such scope, the theory is economical. The structural and process concepts it uses are relatively few. Furthermore, the theory has suggested many areas for investigation and has led to much research. Although relevant to the theory, however, much of this research does not offer an explicit test of a theory-derived hypothesis, and little of it has been

Table 4.4   Summary of Strengths and Limitations of Psychoanalytic Theory

Strengths	*Limitations*
1. Provides for the discovery and investigation of many interesting phenomena.	1. Fails to define all its concepts clearly and distinctly.
2. Develops techniques for research and therapy (free association, dream interpretation, transference analysis).	2. Makes empirical testing difficult, at times impossible.
3. Recognizes the complexity of human behavior.	3. Endorses the questionable view of the person as an energy system.
4. Encompasses a broad range of phenomena.	4. Tolerates resistance by parts of the profession to empirical research and change in the theory.

Pathology	Change	Illustrative Case
Infantile sexuality; fixation and regression; conflict; symptoms	Transference; conflict resolution; "Where id was, ego shall be"	Little Hans

used to extend and develop the theory. The major problem with psychoanalytic theory is the way in which the concepts are formulated; that is, ambiguity in the concepts and in the suggested relationships among concepts has made it very difficult to test the theory. The question for psychoanalytic theory is whether it can be developed to provide for specific tests, or whether it will be replaced in the future by another theory that is equally comprehensive and economical but more open to systematic empirical investigation.

MAJOR CONCEPTS

Anal personality   Freud's concept of a personality type that expresses a fixation at the anal stage of development and relates to the world in terms of the wish for control or power.

Attachment behavioral system (ABS)   Bowlby's concept emphasizing the early formation of a bond between infant and caregiver, generally the mother.

Collective unconscious   Carl Jung's term for inherited, universal, unconscious features of mental life that reflect the evolutionary experience of the human species.

Fixation   Freud's concept expressing a developmental arrest or stoppage at some point in the person's psychosexual development.

Internal working model   Bowlby's concept for the mental representations (images) of the self and others that develop during the early years of development, in particular in interaction with the primary caretaker.

Free association   In psychoanalysis, the patient's reporting to the analyst of every thought that comes to mind.

Oral personality   Freud's concept of a personality type that expresses a fixation at the oral stage of development and relates to the world in terms of the wish to be fed or to swallow.

Phallic character   Freud's concept of a personality type that expresses a fixation at the phallic stage of development and strives for success in competition with others.

Projective test   A test that generally involves vague, ambiguous stimuli and allows subjects to reveal their personalities in terms of their distinctive responses (e.g., Rorschach Inkblot Test, Thematic Apperception Test).

Regression   Freud's concept expressing a person's return to ways of relating to the world and the self that were part of an earlier stage of development.

Symptom   In psychopathology, the expression of psychological conflict or disordered psychological functioning. For Freud, a disguised expression of a repressed impulse.

Transference   In psychoanalysis, the patient's development toward the analyst of attitudes and feelings rooted in past experiences with parental figures.

REVIEW

1. Projective tests, such as the Rorschach Inkblot Test and Thematic Apperception Test (TAT), are linked with psychoanalytic theory. Such tests are unstructured and disguised, leaving room for individuals to respond in unique ways and for the interpretation of responses to be hidden from the subject.

2. Projective tests offer an opportunity to study fantasy and the complexity of organization of individual perceptions. However, they also present problems of reliability and validity of interpretation.

3. The psychoanalytic theory of psychopathology emphasizes the importance of fixations, or failures in development, and regression, or the return to earlier modes of satisfaction. The oral, anal, and phallic character types express personality patterns resulting from partial fixations at earlier stages of development.

4. The psychoanalytic theory of psychopathology emphasizes the conflict between instinctual wishes for gratification and the anxiety associated with these wishes. Defense mechanisms represent ways to reduce anxiety but can result in the development of symptoms.

5. Psychoanalysis is a therapeutic process in which the individual gains insight into and resolves conflicts dating back to childhood. The methods of free association and dream interpretation are used to gain insight into unconscious conflicts. Therapeutic use is also made of the transference situation, in which patients develop attitudes and feelings toward their therapist that relate to experiences with earlier parental figures.

6. The case of Little Hans illustrates how a symptom, such as a phobia, can result from conflicts associated with the Oedipus complex.

7. A number of early analysts broke with Freud and developed their own schools of thought. Alfred Adler emphasized social concepts more than biological concepts, and Carl Jung emphasized a generalized life energy more than a specific sexual energy.

8. Analysts such as Karen Horney and Harry Stack Sullivan emphasize the importance of cultural factors and interpersonal relations, and are part of the group known as neo-Freudians.

9. Recent clinical developments in psychoanalysis have focused on problems in self-definition and self-esteem. Psychoanalysts in this group, known as object relations theorists, emphasize the importance of relationship seeking as opposed to the expression of sexual and aggressive instincts. The concepts of narcissism and the narcissistic personality have gained particular attention. Bowlby's attachment model and related research illustrate the importance of early experiences for later personal relationships, as well as other aspects of personality functioning.

10. An evaluation of psychoanalysis suggests its tremendous contribution in calling attention to many important phenomena and developing techniques for research and therapy. At the same time, the theory suffers from ambiguous, poorly defined concepts and problems in testing specific hypotheses.

5

A PHENOMENOLOGICAL THEORY: CARL ROGERS'S PERSON-CENTERED THEORY OF PERSONALITY

CARL R. ROGERS (1902–1987): A VIEW OF THE THEORIST

ROGERS'S VIEW OF THE PERSON

ROGERS'S VIEW OF SCIENCE, THEORY, AND RESEARCH

THE PERSONALITY THEORY OF CARL ROGERS

Structure
   The Self
   Measures of the Self-Concept
      The Q-Sort Technique
      Adjective Checklist and Semantic Differential

Process
   Self-Actualization

Self-Consistency and Congruence
   States of Incongruence and Defensive Processes
   Research on Self-Consistency and Congruence
The Need for Positive Regard
Growth and Development
Self-Actualization and Healthy Psychological Development
Research on Parent-Child Relationships
Social Relations, Self-Actualization, and Well-Being Later in Life
Conclusion
MAJOR CONCEPTS
REVIEW

Chapter Focus

You are really nervous before a first date, so your mother gives you some advice: "Just be yourself. Your true self." But that advice doesn't seem too helpful. Well-intentioned though she may be, Mom raises two problems. First, you want to impress your date and get him or her to like you. What if your date does not like your "true self"? Even if you do like Mom's plan, there is a second problem: What exactly is your "true" self?

The nature of the self, and the tension between being yourself versus wanting to be liked by other people, are central concerns in the personality theory developed by Carl Rogers. Rogers first addressed these concerns in his work as a clinical psychologist. He combined his clinical insights with systematic empirical research to develop a theory of the totality of the individual that highlighted the person's efforts to develop a meaningful sense of self.

In addition to being a self theory, Rogers's work also can be categorized as a *phenomenological* theory. A phenomenological theory is one that emphasizes the individual's subjective experience of his or her world, in other words, his or her phenomenological experience. As a therapist, Rogers's overarching goal was to understand the client's phenomenological experience of the self and the world in order to assist the client in personal growth. As a theorist, his overarching goal was to develop a framework to explain the nature and development of the self as the core element of personality.

Rogers's phenomenological self theory can also be described by another term: *humanistic*. Rogers's work is part of a humanistic movement in psychology whose core feature was to emphasize people's inherent potential for growth.

This chapter, then, introduces you to the theory—the phenomenological, humanistic, self theory—that is the enduring legacy of one of the great American psychologists of the 20th century, Carl Rogers.

QUESTIONS TO BE ADDRESSED IN THIS CHAPTER

1. How important a part of personality is a person's self-concept? How can the self-concept be assessed?

2. Freud emphasized the tension-reducing, pleasure-seeking aspects of human motivation. Is it possible to view human motivation in other terms, for example, in terms of seeking growth, self-enhancement, and self-actualization?

3. How important is it for us to have a stable self-concept? How important is it for our internal feelings to match our self-concept? What do we do when feelings are in conflict with our self-beliefs?

4. What are the childhood conditions that produce a positive sense of self-worth?

In the previous chapters, you learned about Freud's psychoanalytic theory. In this second introduction of a specific theoretical position, you will see a theory that strikingly differs from Freud's. Carl Rogers does not deny that Freud had important insights into human nature. But he does disagree with many of the emphases of Freudian theory: its depiction of humans as controlled by unconscious forces; its assertion that personality is determined, in a fixed manner, by experiences early in life; its associated belief that adult psychological experience is a repeating of the repressed conflicts of the past. Rogers places dramatically greater emphasis on people's conscious perceptions of the present, on the role of interpersonal experiences across the course of life, and on people's capacity to grow toward psychological maturity.

In some ways, Rogers's work was similar to Freud's. Like Freud, Rogers's theory originally was a theory of psychotherapeutic change. Both Freud and Rogers developed their beliefs about psychotherapy into general theories of personality. However, as you will see, Rogers was more successful than Freud at combining clinical intuitions with objective research.

"I speak as a person, from a context of personal experience and personal learning." This is the way Rogers introduces his chapter "This Is Me" in his 1961 book *On Becoming a Person*. The chapter is a personal, very moving account by Rogers of the development of his professional thinking and personal philosophy. Rogers states what he does and how he feels about it.

CARL R. ROGERS (1902–1987): A VIEW OF THE THEORIST

> This book is about the suffering and the hope, the anxiety and the satisfaction, with which each therapist's counseling room is filled. It is about the uniqueness of the relationship each therapist forms with each client, and equally about the common elements which we discover in all these relationships. This book is about the highly personal experiences of each one of us. It is about a client in my office who sits there by the corner of the desk, struggling to be himself, yet deathly afraid of being himself.... It is about me as I try to perceive his experience, and the meaning and the feeling and the taste and the flavor that it has for him.... It is about me as I rejoice at the privilege of being a midwife to a new personality—as I stand by with awe at the emergence of a self, a person, as I see a birth process in which I have had an important and facilitating part.... The book is, I believe, about life, as life vividly reveals itself in the therapeutic process—with its blind power and its tremendous capacity for destruction, but with its overbalancing thrust toward growth, if the opportunity for growth is provided.
>
> Source: Rogers, 1961a, pp. 4–5.

Carl R. Rogers was born on January 8, 1902, in Oak Park, Illinois. He was reared in a strict and uncompromising religious and ethical atmosphere. His parents had the welfare of their children constantly in mind and inculcated in them a worship of hard work. Rogers's description of his early life reveals two main trends that are reflected in his later work. The first is the concern with moral and ethical matters. The second is the respect for the methods of science. The latter appears to have developed out of exposure to his father's efforts to operate their farm on a scientific basis and Rogers's own reading of books on scientific agriculture.

Rogers started his college education at the University of Wisconsin, majoring in agriculture, but after two years he changed his professional goals and

Carl R. Rogers

decided to enter the ministry. During a trip to Asia in 1922, he had a chance to observe commitments to other religious doctrines as well as the bitter mutual hatreds of French and German people, who otherwise seemed to be likable individuals. Experiences like these influenced his decision to go to a liberal theological seminary, the Union Theological Seminary in New York. Although he was concerned about questions regarding the meaning of life for individuals, Rogers had doubts about specific religious doctrines. Therefore, he chose to leave the seminary, to work in the field of child guidance, and to think of himself as a clinical psychologist.

Rogers obtained his graduate training at Teachers College, Columbia University, receiving his Ph.D. in 1931. He described his experience as leading to a "soaking up" of both the dynamic views of Freud and the "rigorous, scientific, coldly objective, statistical" views then prevalent at Teachers College. Again, there were the pulls in different directions, the development of two somewhat divergent trends. In his later life Rogers attempted to bring these trends into harmony. Indeed, these later years represent an effort to integrate the religious with the scientific, the intuitive with the objective, and the clinical with the statistical. Throughout his career, Rogers tried continually to apply the objective methods of science to what is most basically human.

> Therapy is the experience in which I can let myself go subjectively. Research is the experience in which I can stand off and try to view this rich subjective experience with objectivity, applying all the elegant methods of science to determine whether I have been deceiving myself. The conviction grows in me that we shall discover laws of personality and behavior which are as significant for human progress or human relationship as the law of gravity or the laws of thermodynamics.
>
> SOURCE: Rogers, 1961a, p. 14.

In 1968, Rogers and his more humanistically oriented colleagues formed the Center for the Studies of the Person. The development of the Center expressed a number of shifts in emphasis in the work of Rogers—from work within a formal academic structure to work with a collection of individuals who shared a perspective, from work with disturbed individuals to work with normal individuals, from individual therapy to intensive group workshops, and from conventional empirical research to the phenomenological study of people. Rogers believed that most of psychology was sterile and generally felt alienated from the field. Yet the field continued to value his contributions. He was president of the American Psychological Association in 1946–1947, was one of the first three psychologists to receive the Distinguished Scientific Contribution Award (1956) from the profession, and in 1972 was the recipient of the Distinguished Professional Contribution Award.

With Rogers, the theory, the man, and the life are interwoven. In his chapter "This Is Me," Rogers lists 14 principles that he learned from thousands of hours of therapy and research. Here are some illustrations:

1. In my relationships with persons I have found that it does not help, in the long run, to act as though I were something that I am not.

2. I have found it of enormous value when I can permit myself to understand another person.

3. Experience is, for me, the highest authority…it is to experience that I must return again and again, to discover a closer approximation to truth as it is in the process of becoming in me.

4. What is most personal and unique in each one of us is probably the very element which would, if it were shared or expressed, speak most deeply to others.

5. It has been my experience that persons have a basically positive direction.

6. Life, at its best, is a flowing, changing process in which nothing is fixed.

SOURCE: Rogers, 1961a, pp. 16–17.

ROGERS'S VIEW OF THE PERSON

Rogers's clinical experiences convinced him of a central tenet of his personality theory: that the core of our nature is essentially positive. The direction of our movement is toward self-actualization. It is Rogers's contention that religion, particularly the Christian religion, has taught us to believe that we are basically sinful. Furthermore, Rogers contends that Freud and his followers have presented us with a picture of the person with an id and an unconscious that would, if permitted expression, manifest itself in incest, murder, and other crimes. According to this view, we are at heart irrational, unsocialized, and destructive of self and others. For Rogers, we may at times function in this way, but at such times we are neurotic and not functioning as fully developed human beings. When we are functioning freely, we are free to experience and to fulfill our basic nature as positive and social animals.

Aware that others may seek to draw parallels between the behaviors of other animals and the behavior of humans, Rogers draws his own parallels. For example, he observes that, although lions are often seen as ravening beasts, actually they have many desirable qualities: they kill only when hungry and not for the sake of destroying, they grow from helplessness and dependence to independence, and they move from being self-centered in infancy to being cooperative and protective in adulthood.

To those who may call him a naive optimist, Rogers is quick to point out that his conclusions are based on more than 25 years of experience in psychotherapy:

> I do not have a Pollyanna view of human nature. I am quite aware that out of defensiveness and inner fear individuals can and do behave in ways which are incredibly cruel, horribly destructive, immature, regressive, antisocial, hurtful. Yet one of the most refreshing and invigorating parts of my experience is to work with such individuals and to discover the strongly positive directional tendencies which exist in them, as in all of us, at the deepest levels.
>
> SOURCE: Rogers, 1961a, p. 27.

Here is a profound respect for people, a respect that is reflected in Rogers's theory of personality and his person-centered approach to psychotherapy.

ROGERS'S VIEW OF SCIENCE, THEORY, AND RESEARCH

Through his career, Rogers promoted a **phenomenological** approach to personality. According to his phenomenological position (1951), each individual perceives the world in a unique way. These perceptions make up an individual's **phenomenal field**. The phenomenal field of the individual includes both conscious and unconscious perceptions, including those of which an individual is aware and is not aware. But the most important determinants of behavior, particularly in healthy people, are the ones that are conscious or capable of becoming conscious. Thus, Rogers's approach differs from the psychoanalytic emphasis on the unconscious. Although the phenomenal field is essentially a private world of the individual, we can attempt to perceive the world as it appears to individuals, to see behavior through their eyes and with the psychological meaning it has for them.

Rogers was committed to **phenomenology** as a basis for the science of the person. According to Rogers, research in psychology must involve a persistent, disciplined effort to understand the phenomena of subjective experience. In following the path of science, these efforts need not start in the laboratory or at the computer. Rogers believed that clinical material, obtained during psychotherapy, offered a valuable source of phenomenological data.

In attempting to understand human behavior, Rogers always started with clinical observations and then used these observations to formulate hypotheses that could be tested in a rigorous way. He viewed therapy as a subjective "letting go" experience, and research as an objective effort with its own kind of elegance; he was as committed to one as a source for hypotheses as he was to the other as a tool for their confirmation.

Throughout his career, Rogers attempted to bridge the gap between the subjective and the objective, just as in his youth he felt a need to bridge the gap between religion and science. Within this context, Rogers was concerned with the development of psychology as a science and with the preservation of people as individuals who are not simply the pawns of science.

Rogers's main focus was on the process of psychotherapy, and his theory of personality is an outgrowth of his theory of therapy. His work contrasts with psychoanalysis in terms of both theory and research methods. Regarding theory, psychoanalytic theory emphasizes biological drives, the unconscious, tension reduction, and early character development. In contrast, Rogers's phenomenological approach emphasizes conscious perceptions, feelings regarding social interactions, self-actualization motives, and processes of change. Regarding research methods, psychoanalysts believed that clinical interviews or projective tests must be used to circumvent the action of defense mechanisms. In contrast, Rogers's believed that people had the capacity to report, in a highly meaningful manner, on the nature of their own psychological experience; research thus could employ relatively simple self-report methods.

THE PERSONALITY THEORY OF CARL ROGERS

STRUCTURE

The Self

The distinction we introduced in Chapter 1 between structure and process aspects of personality theories is particularly helpful in understanding the theory of Carl Rogers. The key structural concept in the Rogerian theory of personality is the **self**. According to Rogers, the individual perceives external objects and experiences, and attaches meanings to them. The total system of perceptions and meanings make up the individual's phenomenal field. Those parts of the phenomenal field seen by the individual as "self," "me," or "I" make up the self. The self, or **self-concept**, represents an organized and consistent pattern of perceptions. Although the self changes, it always retains this patterned, integrated, organized quality. Because the organized quality endures over time and characterizes the individual, the self is a personality structure.

Two additional points are noteworthy in relation to Rogers's concept of the self. First, the self is not a little person inside of us. The self does not "do" anything. The individual does not have a self that controls behavior. Rather, the self represents an organized set of perceptions. Second, the pattern of experiences and perceptions known as the self is, in general, available to awareness—that is, it can be made conscious. Although individuals do have experiences of which they are unaware, the self-concept is primarily conscious. Rogers believes that such a definition of the self is accurate and is a necessary one for research. A definition of the self that included unconscious material, according to Rogers, could not be studied objectively. (Note that Rogers's use of the term "self" differs from that of Carl Jung, whose views were discussed in the previous chapter. Jung thought of the self as an unconscious archetypal force, whereas Rogers uses the term "self" to refer to our conscious self-concept.)

A related structural concept is the **ideal self**. The ideal self is the self-concept that an individual would most like to possess. It includes the perceptions and meanings that potentially are relevant to the self and that are valued highly by the individual. Rogers thus recognizes that our views of ourselves contain two distinct components: the self that we believe we are now, and the self that we ideally see ourselves becoming in the future.

IS THE SENSE OF SELF UNIQUELY HUMAN?

Most dog owners have at some time experimented with placing a mirror in front of their dog. Is there self-recognition? Animal research suggests that species lower than primates do not recognize themselves in mirrors. Chimpanzees are able to do so, provided that they have some exposure to mirrors. Given such experience, chimps will use the mirror to examine and groom themselves (self-directed behavior) rather than ignore the image or react to it as it if it is another member of the species (e.g., fish showing aggressive displays toward a mirror image).

Self-Recognition: *Whereas almost all other species are indifferent to their images in a mirror, or react to them as another animal, humans begin to be fascinated with their self-reflection at an early age.*

Research on the development of self-directed mirror behavior in infants suggests that the development of self-recognition is a continuous process, starting as early as four months of age. At this point infants show some response to relationships between self-movements and changes in mirror images. And what of recognition of specific features of the self? If an infant looks at itself in the mirror, has rouge placed on its nose, and then looks in the mirror again, will the infant respond to the rouge mark in a way expressive of self-recognition? Such specific feature recognition, in terms of self-directed mirror behavior, appears to begin at about the age of one year.

The recognition of self, whether expressed through self-directed mirror behavior or otherwise, can be related to the development of consciousness and mind. Clearly it is a matter of considerable psychological significance. Not only does it mean that we can be aware of ourselves and have feelings about ourselves, but also that we can have knowledge of and empathy for the feelings of others. It would indeed be ironic if the very processes that allow us to feel worst about ourselves also provided us with the opportunity to feel most empathetic with others.

Mirror mirror on the wall, is that me after all? This appears to be a question that only members of a few species can address. In humans some maturation is required, but self-recognition begins to develop fairly early and remains a significant part of life thereafter.

SOURCE: Lewis & Brooks-Gunn, 1979; Robins, Norem, & Check, 1999.

Measures of the Self-Concept

Rogers maintained that he did not begin his work with the concept of the self. In fact, in his first work he thought that self was a vague, scientifically meaningless term. However, as he listened to clients expressing their problems and attitudes,

(Reprinted with special permission of King Features Syndicate.)

he found that they tended to talk in terms of the self; clients would report that they "did not feel like themselves," "were disappointed in themselves," and so forth. It became clear to Rogers, then, that the self was a psychological structure through which people were interpreting their world. Although impressed with the self-statements of clients, Rogers felt that he needed an objective definition of the concept, a way to measure it, and a research tool.

The Q-Sort Technique Rogers began his research by recording therapy interview sessions and then categorizing all words that referred to the self. After the early research with recorded interviews, he used the Q-sort developed by Stephenson (1953). The **Q-sort** technique has been used frequently to measure the self-concept. In this approach the experimenter gives the subject a group of cards, each containing a statement concerning some personality characteristic. One card might say "Makes friends easily," another might say "Has trouble expressing anger," and so on for each of the cards. Subjects are asked to read these statements (generally about 100) and then sort the cards according to which statements they feel are most descriptive of them and which are least descriptive. The subjects are asked to arrange the cards into a certain distribution, of which one end represents "Most characteristic of me" and the other "Least characteristic of me." Subjects are told how many piles of cards are to be used and how many cards are to go into each pile. For example, with 100 cards the subject might be asked to sort the cards into 11 piles as follows: 2-4-8-11-16-18-16-11-8-4-2. The distribution is a statistically normal one and expresses the subjects' comparative estimates of how descriptive each characteristic is.

Thus, the Q-sort involves a task in which the subject sorts a number of statements, in this case about the self, into categories ranging from most characteristic to least characteristic. In addition, the identical terms can be sorted into the same number of categories in terms of the ideal self—from "most like my ideal self" to "least like my ideal self." This provides for a quantitative measure of the difference or discrepancy between self and ideal self. As we shall see (in Chapter 6), such concepts and measures are important in relation to psychopathology and therapeutic change. The Q-sort leads to data that represent a systematic expression of subjects' perceptions of parts of their phenomenal fields. However, it does not represent a completely phenomenological report, since subjects must use statements provided by the experimenter, instead of their own, and must sort the statements into prescribed piles, rep-

CURRENT QUESTIONS

SELF-IDEAL CONGRUENCE: SEX DIFFERENCES OVER TIME?

Rogers's notion of the ideal self, and the Q-sort method he espoused, still influence contemporary research on the self-concept. One example is the work by Block and Robins (1993) who examined change in self-esteem from adolescence into young adulthood. Has your self-esteem changed from your early teens to your early twenties? According to Block and Robins, the answer to this question may depend on your gender: on average, self-esteem increases for males and decreases for females over these formative years of life.

Level of self-esteem was defined as the degree of similarity between the perceived self and the ideal self. Both of these constructs were measured by an adjective Q-sort, which includes such self-descriptive items as "competitive," "affectionate," "responsible," and "creative." Subjects whose perceived self was highly similar to their ideal self were high in self-esteem. In contrast, subjects whose perceived self was highly dissimilar to their ideal self were low in self-esteem.

Between the ages of 14 and 23 males became more self-confident and females became less self-confident. Whereas at age 14 they scored similar in self-esteem, by age 23 males were much higher. Apparently, males and females differ in how they experience the adolescent years and how they negotiate the transition into adulthood. For men, the news is good: this phase of life is associated with coming closer to one's ideal. Unfortunately, the opposite is true for women: they move further away from their ideal as they enter adulthood.

What are the personality attributes that characterize men and women with high self-esteem? Block and Robins used extensive interview data collected at age 23 and found that the high self-esteem women valued close relationships with others. High self-esteem men, in contrast, were more emotionally distant and controlled in their relationships with others. These sex differences in relationships reflect the very different expectations society holds for what it means to be a man or a woman. Not surprisingly, those young adults whose personalities fit these cultural expectations well are more likely to feel good about themselves and have a self-concept that is close to their ideal self.

Left unanswered by this study is a phenomenological question that would have been of interest to Rogers: What is the content of the ideal self? Do males and females differ in their perceptions of what constitutes the ideal? The ideal self seems particularly susceptible to external influence—what we perceive as valued in society. The content of the ideal self tells us something about the attributes a person values and thus uses to derive self-esteem. An interesting question for future research is how the content of the ideal self influences psychological adjustment. Does the person's ideal self capture characteristics of a self-actualized human being or society's definition of what constitutes the ideal man or woman?

resenting a normal distribution, rather than according to a distribution that makes the most sense to them.

Adjective Checklist and Semantic Differential   Other efforts to obtain subjective reports about the self have made use of the adjective checklist, in which subjects check adjectives that they feel are applicable to them, and the semantic differential (Osgood, Suci, & Tannenbaum, 1957). Developed as a measure of attitudes and the meanings of concepts, rather than as a specific test of personality, the semantic differential has potential as a useful technique for personality assessment. In filling out the semantic differential, the individual rates a concept on a number of seven-point scales defined by polar adjectives such as good-bad, strong-weak, or active-passive. Thus, a subject would rate a concept such as "My Self" or "My Ideal Self" on each of the polar adjective scales. A rating on any one scale would indicate whether the subject felt that one of the adjectives was very descriptive of the concept or somewhat descriptive, or whether neither adjective was applicable to the concept. The ratings are made in terms of the meaning of the concept for the individual.

Like the Q-sort, the semantic differential is a structured technique in that the subject must rate certain concepts and use the polar adjective scales provided by the experimenter. This structure provides for the gathering of data suitable for statistical analysis but, also like the Q-sort, it does not preclude flexibility as to the concepts and scales to be used. There is no single standardized semantic differential. A variety of scales can be used in relation to concepts such as father, mother, and doctor to determine the meanings of phenomena for the individual. For example, consider rating the concepts "My Self" and "My College" on scales such as liberal-conservative, scholarly–fun-loving, and formal-informal. To what extent do you see yourself and your college as similar? How does this relate to your satisfaction as a student at this college? In some research very similar to this, it was found that the more students viewed themselves as dissimilar to their college environment, the more dissatisfied they were and the more likely they were to drop out (Pervin, 1967a,b).

An illustration of the way in which the semantic differential can be used to assess personality is in a case of multiple personality. In the 1950s two psychiatrists, Corbett Thigpen and Harvey Cleckley, made famous the case of "the three faces of Eve." This was the case of a woman who possessed three personalities, each of which predominated for a period of time, with frequent shifts back and forth. The three personalities were called Eve White, Eve Black, and Jane. As part of a research endeavor, the psychiatrists were able to have each of the three personalities rate a variety of concepts on the semantic differential. The ratings were then analyzed both quantitatively and qualitatively by two psychologists (C. Osgood and Z. Luria) who did not know the subject. Their analysis included both descriptive comments and interpretations of the personalities that went beyond the objective data. For example, Eve White was described as being in contact with social reality but under great emotional stress; Eve Black was described as out of contact with social reality but quite self-assured; and Jane was described as superficially very healthy but quite restricted and undiversified. A more detailed, although still incomplete description of the three personalities based on the semantic differential ratings is presented in Figure 5.1. The analysis on the basis of these ratings turned out to fit quite well with the descriptions offered by the two psychiatrists (Osgood & Luria, 1954).

The Q-sort, adjective checklist, and semantic differential all approach the Rogerian ideal of phenomenological self-report; they provide data that are statistically reliable and theoretically relevant. It can be argued that people have many self-concepts rather than a single self-concept, that these tests do not get at unconscious factors, and that the tests are subject to defensive distortion. Rogers felt, however, that these tests provide useful measures for the concepts of self and ideal self.

CURRENT QUESTIONS

ONE SELF OR MANY SELVES?

Rogers emphasized the self-concept as expressing the organizing pattern of perceptions associated with the self. The self represented a patterned whole that could be measured by instruments such as the Q-sort and the semantic differential. However, today many psychologists suggest that the individual may have many selves—some good and some bad, some actualized in the present and some potential selves for the future.

Consider, for example, the following two individuals. Ivan Boesky was a Wall Street superstar who made a fortune and then brought shame to himself and scandal to the industry because of his illegal activities. While on Wall Street he showed a ferocious desire to accumulate wealth, while at the same time contributing to charities, colleges, or public institutions—apparently without much fanfare or wish for special treatment. In 1984 he said of himself: "I'm a person composed of a bunch of sides. There is self-interest, but there is also a second side of me, that affects a hundred things I do. Public service. Philanthropy."

Hector "Macho" Camacho was a boxing champion who had two sides to himself that were "as different as Clark Kent is from Superman." Hector was a rather subdued person, with his own share of doubts and fears. Macho Man liked to drive deluxe autos at fast speeds, posed for *Playgirl* magazine, told others he was handsome and one awesome fighter. In his own words: "Hector is not as bad as Macho Man. Macho Man is the performer, the boxer. Hector is the humble nice guy who lends money out on the street of Spanish Harlem."

In addition, according to a story in the *APA Monitor* (April, 2000), many people use the Internet to explore different selves. Psychologist John Suler is quoted as follows: "The Web is a safe place to try out different roles, voices, and identities. It's sort of like training wheels for the self you want to bring out in real life" (p. 17).

Can one speak of a self-concept or must psychologists be concerned with relations among multiple selves?

SOURCES: *New York Times*, June 13, 1986, and December 22, 1986.

Eve White	Perceives the world in an essentially normal fashion, is well socialized, but has an unsatisfactory attitude toward herself. The chief evidence of disturbance in the personality is the fact that ME (the self-concept) is considered a little bad, a little passive, and definitely weak.
Eve Black	Eve Black has achieved a violent kind of adjustment in which she perceives herself as literally perfect, but, to accomplish this break, her way of perceiving the world becomes completely disoriented from the norm. If Eve Black perceives herself as good, then she also has to accept HATRED and FRAUD as positive values.
Jane	Jane displays the most "healthy" meaning pattern, in which she accepts the usual evaluations of concepts by her society yet still maintains a satisfactory evaluation of herself. The self concept, ME, while not strong (but not weak, either) is nearer the good and active directions of the semantic space.

Figure 5.1 Brief Personality Descriptions, Based on Semantic Differential Ratings, in a Case of Multiple Personality. *(Osgood & Luria, 1954.)*

PROCESS

Self-Actualization

Freud viewed the essential components of personality as relatively fixed and stable, and he developed an elaborate theory of the structure of personality. Rogers's view of personality emphasized change, and he used few concepts of structure in his theory. Freud considered the person as an energy system. Thus, he developed a theory of dynamics to account for how this energy is discharged, transformed, or dammed up. Rogers thought of people as forward moving. Therefore, he tended to deemphasize the tension-reducing aspects of behavior in favor of an emphasis on **self-actualization**, that is, the fulfillment of one's inherent potentialities. Whereas Freud placed great emphasis on drives, for Rogers there was no motivation in the sense of drives per se. Instead, people's basic tendency is toward self-actualization: "The organism has one basic tendency and striving—to actualize, maintain, and enhance the experiencing organism" (Rogers, 1951, p. 487).

Rogers chose to postulate a single motivation to life and to stay close to that idea rather than to be tied to abstract conceptualizations of many motives. In a poetic passage, he described life as an active process, comparing it to the trunk of a tree on the shore of the ocean as it remains erect, tough, and resilient, maintaining and enhancing itself in the growth process: "Here in this palm-like seaweed was the tenacity of life, the forward thrust of life, the ability to push into an incredibly hostile environment and not only to hold its own, but to adapt, develop, become itself" (Rogers, 1963, p. 2).

The concept of actualization involves the tendency of an organism to grow from a simple entity to a complex one, to move from dependence toward independence, from fixity and rigidity to a process of change and freedom of expression. The concept includes the tendency of each person to reduce needs or tension, but it emphasizes the pleasures and satisfactions that are derived from activities that enhance the organism.

Although Rogers was generally concerned with measures for his concepts, he never did develop a measure of the self-actualizing motive. Over the years a number of scales have been developed to measure self-actualization. One such effort involves a 15-item scale that measures the ability to act independently, self-acceptance or self-esteem, acceptance of one's emotional life, and trust in interpersonal relations (Figure 5.2). Scores on this questionnaire measure of self-actualization have been found to be related to other questionnaire measures of self-esteem and health, as well as to independent ratings of individuals as self-actualizing persons (Jones & Crandall, 1986).

> It is always necessary that others approve of what I do. (F)
>
> I am bothered by fears of being inadequate. (F)
>
> I do not feel ashamed of any of my emotions. (T)
>
> I believe that people are essentially good and can be trusted. (T)

Figure 5.2 Illustrative Items from an Index of Self-Actualization. *(Jones and Crandall, 1986.)*

Self-Actualization: *Rogers emphasizes the basic tendency of the organism toward self-actualization.*

More recently, Ryff (1995; Ryff & Singer, 1998, 2000) has postulated a multifaceted conception of positive mental health, which includes self-acceptance, positive relations with others, autonomy, environmental mastery, purpose in life, and personal growth. The personal growth component is conceptually close to Rogers's view of the growth process and self-actualization. Her questionnaire, the Personal Growth Scale, defines someone high on personal growth as someone who has a feeling of continued development, a sense of realizing their potential, being open to new experiences, and is changing in ways that reflect more self-knowledge and effectiveness. Additionally, there is evidence that people are happiest when pursuing goals congruent with the self (Little, 1999; McGregor & Little, 1998).

Self-Consistency and Congruence

The concept of an organism moving toward actualization has not been the subject of empirical investigation. Much more critical to the process aspects of the theory and to research has been Rogers's emphasis on self-consistency and congruence between self and experience. According to Rogers, the organism functions to maintain consistency (an absence of conflict) among self-perceptions and congruence between perceptions of the self and experiences: "Most of the ways of behaving which are adopted by the organism are those which are consistent with the concept of the self" (Rogers, 1951, p. 507).

The concept of **self-consistency** was developed by Lecky (1945). According to Lecky, the organism does not seek to gain pleasure and to avoid pain but, instead, seeks to maintain its own self-structure. The individual develops a value system, the center of which is the individual's valuation of the self. Individuals organize their values and functions to preserve the self-system. Individuals behave in ways that are consistent with their self-concept, even if this behavior is otherwise unrewarding to them. Thus, if you define yourself as a poor speller, you will try to behave in a manner consistent with this self-perception.

In addition to self-consistency, Rogers emphasized the importance of **congruence** between the self and experience. This suggests that people will try to bring together, or make congruent, what they feel with how they view themselves. For example, to view oneself as a kind person and feel warm and empathic toward others would represent such congruence. On the other hand, to view oneself as a kind person and experience feelings of cruelty toward others would represent a state of **incongruence**.

States of Incongruence and Defensive Processes   Do individuals ever experience inconsistencies in the self or a lack of congruence between self and experience? If so, how do they function to maintain consistency and congruence? According to Rogers, we experience a state of incongruence when there is a discrepancy between the perceived self and actual experience. For example, if you view yourself as a person without hate and you experience hate, you are in a state of incongruence. The state of incongruence is one of tension and internal confusion. When it exists and the individual is unaware of it, he or she is potentially vulnerable to anxiety. Anxiety is the result of a discrepancy between experience and the perception of the self. Again, the person whose self-concept is that he or she never hates anyone will experience anxiety whenever hateful feelings are experienced to any degree at all.

For the most part, we are aware of our experiences and allow them into consciousness. However, we also may perceive an experience as threatening, as being in conflict with the self-concept, and may not allow it to become conscious. Through a process called **subception**, we can be aware of an experience that is discrepant with the self-concept before it reaches consciousness. The response to the threat presented by recognition of experiences that are in conflict with the self is that of defense. Thus, we react defensively and attempt to deny awareness to experiences that are dimly perceived to be incongruent with the self-structure.

Two defensive processes are distortion of the meaning of experience and denial of the existence of the experience. **Denial** serves to preserve the self-structure from threat by denying it conscious expression. **Distortion**, a more common phenomenon, allows the experience into awareness but in a form that makes it consistent with the self: "Thus, if the concept of self includes the characteristic 'I am a poor student,' the experience of receiving a high grade can be easily distorted to make it congruent with the self by perceiving in it such meanings as, 'That professor is a fool'; 'It was just luck'" (Rogers, 1956, p. 205). What is striking about this last example is the emphasis it places on self-consistency. What is otherwise likely to be a positive experience, receiving a high grade, now becomes a source of anxiety and a stimulus for defensive processes to be set in operation. In other words, it is the relation of the experience to the self-concept that is key.

CURRENT QUESTIONS

CONSISTENT OR VARIABLE VIEW OF THE SELF: WHICH IS BETTER?

In everyday life, people play many different social roles. We are children, friends, lovers, students, workers, sometimes all of these within the same day. For each significant role that we play in life, we develop an image of ourselves within that role. How do you see yourself across the social roles that are important in your life? The following exercise is designed to let you explore this question for yourself.

Think about yourself in the roles of student, friend, and son or daughter. Then describe how you see yourself in that role by rating yourself on the five descriptive statements listed below using the following scale:

DISAGREE			AGREE	
Strongly	A little	Neither/nor	A little	Strongly
1	2	3	4	5

How I see myself in each role:

	Son or Daughter	Friend	Student	Maximum discrepancy
Is assertive.	5	5	4	1
Tries to be helpful.	5	5	4	1
Is punctual.	5	5	5	0
Worries a lot.	4	4	5	1
Is clever, sharp-witted.	4	4	3	1

Once you have made your ratings, you are able to explore how consistent or variable your self-concept is across these roles. For each of the five statements, subtract the lowest from the highest of the three role ratings. Consider the first statement "Is assertive" as an example.

If you rated yourself a 5 in the Son/Daughter role, a 3 in the Friend role, and a 1 in the student role, then your maximum discrepancy score would be 5 minus 1 = 4. You might want to ask yourself what such a discrepancy means and how it may have developed. You can also calculate all five discrepancy scores and then add them together to create a total self-concept variability score. Your score should fall within the range of 0 to 20, with 0 representing a highly consistent view of self across these roles and 20 representing a highly variable self view. How variable is your self-concept in general?

As Donahue, Robins, Roberts, and John (1993) showed in two studies, some individuals see themselves as essentially the same person across their various social roles, whereas others see themselves quite differently. For example, one woman saw herself as fun-loving and easygoing across all her roles. In contrast, another woman saw herself as fun-loving and easygoing with her friends but as quite serious with her parents. Which of these two individuals is likely to be better adjusted—the first who has a more consistent self-concept across her roles or the second who has a more variable self-concept?

What would Rogers predict? Recall that Rogers theorized that the psychologically adjusted individual has a coherent and integrated self. Thus, Rogers's theory predicts that very high variability in the self-concept can be bad for mental health because it is indicative of fragmentation and a lack of an integrated "core" self. An alternative prediction is that variability is good because it provides specialized role identities that enable the individual to respond flexibly and adaptively to various role requirements (e.g., Gergen, 1971).

The results reported by Donahue and her colleagues clearly favored Rogers's position. Individuals with highly variable role identities were more likely to be anxious, depressed, and low in self-esteem. Their relationships with parents had been unusually difficult while growing up, and in early adulthood they were less satisfied with how they were doing in their relationships and in their careers. Not surprisingly, they also changed jobs and relationship partners more frequently than did individuals who had more coherent self-concepts.

These findings suggest that various forms of psychological problems and instability are related to inconsistencies in the self-concept across roles. In other words, the inconsistent self is fragmented, rather than specialized. When thinking about your own level of self-concept variability, however, do not assume that a high score is necessarily indicative of psychological problems. What is most important is that you feel comfortable with your particular style of negotiating your own self-image within your various social roles. If you don't feel comfortable, then you may want to consider ways in which you might strive for a more unified self-image across the social roles you act out in your daily life. A recent book by Harary and Donahue (1994) provides many useful exercises and detailed information about these issues.

Sources: Donahue, Robins, Roberts, & John, 1993; Harary & Donahue, 1994.

Research on Self-Consistency and Congruence An early study in this area was performed by Chodorkoff (1954), who found that subjects were slower to perceive words that were personally threatening than they were to perceive neutral words. This tendency was particularly characteristic of defensive, poorly adjusted individuals. Poorly adjusted individuals, in particular, attempt to deny awareness to threatening stimuli.

Additional research by Cartwright (1956) involved the study of self-consistency as a factor affecting immediate recall. Following Rogers's theory,

"Hi, there, the me nobody knows!"

Incongruence: *A discrepancy between the perceived self and actual experience is experienced as a state of incongruence. (Drawing by H. Martin; © 1971 The New Yorker Magazine, Inc.)*

Cartwright hypothesized that individuals would show better recall for stimuli that are consistent with the self than for stimuli that are inconsistent. He hypothesized further that this tendency would be greater for maladjusted subjects than for adjusted subjects. In general, subjects were able to recall adjectives they felt were descriptive of themselves better than they were able to recall adjectives they felt were most unlike themselves. Also, there was considerable distortion in recall for the latter, inconsistent adjectives. For example, a subject who viewed himself as hopeful misrecalled the word "hopeless" as being "hopeful," and a subject who viewed himself as friendly misrecalled the word "hostile" as being "hospitable." As predicted, poorly adjusted subjects (those applying for therapy and those for whom psychotherapy had been judged to be unsuccessful) showed a greater difference in recall than did adjusted subjects (those who did not plan on treatment and those for whom psychotherapy had been judged to be successful). This difference in recall scores was due particularly to the poorer recall of the maladjusted subjects for inconsistent stimuli.

In a related study, an effort was made to determine the ability of subjects to recall adjectives used by others to describe them (Suinn, Osborne, & Winfree, 1962). Accuracy of recall was best for adjectives used by others that were consistent with the self-concept of subjects and was poorest for adjectives used by others that were inconsistent with the self-concept. In sum, the accuracy of recall of self-related stimuli appears to be a function of the degree to which the stimuli are consistent with the self-concept.

The studies just discussed relate to perception and recall. What of overt behavior? Aronson and Mettee (1968) found results that were consistent with Rogers's view that individuals behave in ways that are congruent with their self-concepts. In a study of dishonest behavior, they reasoned that if people are tempted to cheat, they will be more likely to do so if their self-esteem is low than if it is high; that is, whereas cheating is not inconsistent with generally low self-esteem, it is inconsistent with generally high self-esteem. The data gathered indeed suggested that whether or not an individual cheats is influenced by the nature of the self-concept. People who have a high opinion of themselves are likely to behave in ways they can respect, whereas people with a low opinion of themselves are likely to behave in ways that are consistent with that self-image.

More recent research supports the view that the self-concept influences behavior in varied ways (Markus, 1983). What is particularly noteworthy here is the suggestion that people often behave in ways that will lead others to confirm the perception they have of themselves—a self-fulfilling prophecy (Darley & Fazio, 1980; Swann, 1992). For example, people who believe they are likable may behave in ways that lead others to like them, whereas others who believe themselves to be unlikable may behave in ways that lead others to dislike them (Curtis & Miller, 1986). For better or for worse, your self-concept may be maintained by behaviors of others that were influenced in the first place by your own self-concept!

Another recent finding is that people with low self-esteem are so prone to maintain a consistent self-concept that they sometimes fail to take even simple actions that might put them in a better mood. They seem resigned to maintaining a poor self-image and the experience of negative emotions. Heimpel, Wood, Marshall, & Brown (2002) conducted a series of studies designed to test the hypothesis that people who report having low self-esteem are less motivated to change their negative moods, as compared to people with high self-esteem. In one study, people were put into a sad mood through a mood induction, that is, an experimental manipulation designed to create temporary positive or negative feelings. Research participants were then given the opportunity to select a videotape to watch. One of the videos from which people could select was a video of comedy routines—a topic that everyone thought would put them in a good mood. The selection of the comedy video when in a negative mood, then, would be a choice for inconsistency, specifically, a choice to take action to change one's mood from negative to positive, rather than maintaining a consistent negative mood. It might seem to you as if everyone would choose to put themselves in a better mood. But this is not what happened. Although the large majority of high self-esteem persons chose to watch the comedy video when in a negative mood, only a minority of low self-esteem persons chose to watch it (Heimpel et al., 2002). Most of the low self-esteem persons, in other words, failed to make a choice that would change their negative mood. Their choice produced consistency—a consistent negative mood—even when they could have made themselves feel better. The tendency to maintain consistency in psychological experience, then, may sometimes override a simple hedonistic tendency to have emotionally positive experiences.

pursuit of pleasure

The Need for Positive Regard

We have, then, a number of studies supporting the view that the individual attempts to behave in accordance with the self-concept and that experiences inconsistent with the self-concept are often ignored or denied. In Rogers's earlier writing, no mention was made of the reasons for the development of a rift between experience and self and, therefore, the need for defense. In 1959 Rogers presented the concept of the **need for positive regard**. The need for positive regard includes seeking warmth, liking, respect, sympathy, and acceptance and is seen in the infant's need for love and affection. If the parents give the child unconditional positive regard, if the child feels "prized" by the parents, there will be no need to deny experiences. However, if the parents make positive regard conditional, the child will be forced to disregard its own experiencing process whenever it conflicts with the self-concept. For example, if a child feels that he or she will only receive love (positive regard) for always being loving, he or she will deny all feelings of hate and struggle to preserve a picture of the self as loving. In this case the feeling of hate not only is incongruent with the self-concept but also threatens a child with the loss of positive regard. Thus, the imposition of conditions of worth on a child leads to the denial of experiences—the rift between organism and self. The origins of inaccuracies in the self-concept, the origins of conflict between an individual's experience and the self-concept, lie in that individual's attempt to retain love.

To summarize, Rogers did not feel a need to use the concepts of motives and drives to account for the activity and goal-directedness of the organism. For him, the person is basically active and self-actualizing. As part of the self-actualizing process, we seek to maintain a congruence between self and experience. However, because of past experiences with conditional positive regard, we may deny or distort experiences that threaten the self-system.

Positive Regard: *Healthy personality development is fostered through the communication of unconditional positive regard to the child.*

GROWTH AND DEVELOPMENT

Rogers did not really have a theory of growth and development and did not do research in the area in terms of long-term studies or studies of parent-child interaction. Basically, Rogers believed that growth forces exist in all individuals. The natural growth process of the organism involves greater complexity, expansion, increasing autonomy, greater socialization—in sum, self-actualization. The self becomes a separate part of the phenomenal field and grows increasingly complex. As the self emerges, an individual develops a need for positive regard. If the need for positive regard by others becomes more important than being in touch with one's own feelings, individuals will screen various experiences out of awareness and will be left in a state of incongruence.

Self-Actualization and Healthy Psychological Development

Essentially, then, the major developmental concern for Rogers is whether the child is free to grow within a state of congruence, to be self-actualizing, or whether the child will become defensive and operate out of a state of incongruence. Healthy development of the self takes place in a climate in which the child can experience fully, can accept him- or herself, and can be accepted by the parents, even if they disapprove of particular types of behavior. This point is emphasized by most child psychiatrists and psychologists. It is the difference between a parent saying to a child, "I don't like what you are doing" and saying, "I don't like you." In saying "I don't like what you are doing," the parent is accepting the child while not approving of the behavior. This contrasts with situations in which a parent tells a child, verbally or in more subtle ways, that his or her behavior is bad and that he or she is bad. The child then feels that recognition of certain feelings would be inconsistent with the picture of him- or herself as loved or lovable, leading to denial and distortion of these feelings.

Research on Parent-Child Relationships

A variety of studies suggest that acceptant, democratic parental attitudes facilitate the most growth. Whereas children of parents with these attitudes show accelerated intellectual development, originality, emotional security, and control, the children of rejecting, authoritarian parents are unstable, rebellious, aggressive, and quarrelsome (Baldwin, 1949). What is most critical is children's perceptions of their parents' appraisals. If they feel that these appraisals are positive, they will find pleasure in their bodies and in their selves. If they feel that these appraisals are negative, they will develop insecurity and negative appraisals of their bodies (Jourard & Remy, 1955). Apparently, the kinds of appraisals that parents make of their children largely reflect the parents' own degree of self-acceptance. Mothers who are self-accepting also tend to accept their children (Medinnus & Curtis, 1963).

An extensive study of the origins of self-esteem gives further support to the importance of the dimensions suggested by Rogers. Coopersmith (1967) conducted a study of self-esteem, which he defined as the evaluation an individual makes and customarily maintains with regard to the self. Self-esteem, then, is a personal judgment of worthiness. It is a general personality characteristic, not a momentary attitude or an attitude specific to individual situations. Self-esteem was measured by a 50-item Self Esteem Inventory, with most of the items coming from scales previously used by Rogers. Children filled out the inventory and their scores were used to define groups with high, medium, and low self-esteem. Compared to children low in self-esteem, those high in self-esteem were found to be more assertive, independent, and cre-

Fostering Creative Potential:
Psychological conditions of safety and freedom help develop the creative potential of children.

ative. The high self-esteem subjects were also less likely to accept social definitions of reality unless they were in accord with their own observations, were more flexible and imaginative, and were capable of finding more original solutions to problems. In other words, the subjective estimates of self-esteem had a variety of behaviors attached to them.

What are the origins of self-esteem? Coopersmith obtained data on the children's perceptions of their parents, ratings from staff members who interviewed the mothers, and responses from the mothers to a questionnaire relating to child-rearing attitudes and practices. The results indicated that external indicators of prestige such as wealth, degree of education, and job title did not have as overwhelmingly significant an effect on self-esteem as is often assumed. Instead, the conditions in the home and the immediate interpersonal environment had the major effect on judgments of self-worth. Apparently children are influenced in their self-judgments through a process of reflected appraisal in which they take the opinions of them expressed by others who are important to them and then use these opinions in their own self-judgments.

What kinds of parental attitudes and behaviors appeared to be important in the formation of self-esteem? Three areas of parent-child interaction seemed to be particularly important. The first area concerned the degree of acceptance, interest, affection, and warmth expressed toward the child. The data revealed that the mothers of children with high self-esteem were more loving and had closer relationships with their children than did the mothers of children with low self-esteem. The interest on the part of the mother appeared to be interpreted by children as an indication of their significance, that they were worthy of the concern, attention, and time of those who were important.

The second critical area of parent-child interaction related to permissiveness and punishment. The data revealed that the parents of children with high self-esteem made clear demands that were firmly enforced. Reward generally was the preferred mode of affecting behavior. In contrast to this pattern, the parents of children with low self-esteem gave little guidance and were harsh and disrespectful in their treatment. These parents did not establish and enforce guidelines for their children, were apt to use punishment rather than reward, and tended to stress force and loss of love.

Finally, differences were found in parent-child interactions in relation to democratic practices. Parents of children with high self-esteem established an extensive set of rules and were zealous in enforcing them, but treatment within the defined limits was noncoercive and recognized the rights and opinions of the child. Parents of children low in self-esteem set few and poorly defined limits, and were autocratic, dictatorial, rejecting, and uncompromising in their methods of control. Coopersmith summarized his findings as follows: "The most general statement about the origins of self-esteem can be given in terms of three conditions: total or nearly total acceptance of the children by their parents, clearly defined and enforced limits, and the respect and latitude for individual actions that exist within the defined limits" (1967, p. 236). Coopersmith further suggested that it is the perception of the parents by the child, and not necessarily the specific actions they express, that is important. Further, the total climate in the family influences the child's perception of the parents and their motives.

Another study further supports the relevance of such child-rearing conditions for the development of creative potential. According to Rogers, children raised by parents who provide conditions of psychological safety and psycho-

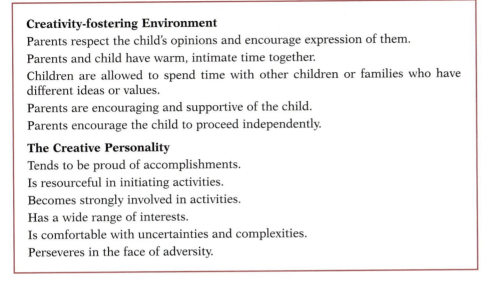

Creativity-fostering Environment

Parents respect the child's opinions and encourage expression of them.

Parents and child have warm, intimate time together.

Children are allowed to spend time with other children or families who have different ideas or values.

Parents are encouraging and supportive of the child.

Parents encourage the child to proceed independently.

The Creative Personality

Tends to be proud of accomplishments.

Is resourceful in initiating activities.

Becomes strongly involved in activities.

Has a wide range of interests.

Is comfortable with uncertainties and complexities.

Perseveres in the face of adversity.

Figure 5.3 Illustrative Characteristics of Creativity-fostering Environments and the Creative Personality. *(Adapted from Harrington, Block, & Block, 1987.)*

logical freedom are more likely to develop creative potential than children raised by parents who do not provide these conditions. Conditions of psychological safety are provided by parental expressions of unconditional positive regard for the child and empathic understanding, and conditions of psychological freedom are expressed in permission to engage in unrestrained expression of ideas. In a test of this view, child-rearing practices and parent-child interaction patterns were measured for children between the ages of three and five years (Figure 5.3). Independent measures of creative potential in the children were obtained prior to their admission to school and in adolescence. In support of Rogers's theory, measures of childhood (preschool) environmental conditions of psychological safety and freedom were significantly associated with creative potential—both in preschool and in adolescence (Harrington, Block, & Block, 1987).

Some psychologists have argued that the concept of self-esteem is too global, that is, that people have self-esteem levels in specific areas rather than a global self-esteem. Thus, for example, one may have high self-esteem socially but not academically, or high self-esteem as a worker but not as a parent. Although such variations in self-esteem undoubtedly exist, others note that there is evidence that the concept of global self-esteem has merit and how people feel about themselves generally has implications for many aspects of psychological functioning (Dutton & Brown, 1997). In our next chapter, which explores applications and evaluations of Rogers's theorizing, we consider in more detail the relation between self-esteem and performance.

Social Relations, Self-Actualization, and Well-Being Later in Life

We noted earlier that Rogers emphasized the human capacity for change across the course of life. Although we have just reviewed research on childhood antecedents of self-esteem, Rogers theoretical position suggests that,

+ Extrinsic Motivation

**CURRENT
QUESTIONS**

INTRINSIC MOTIVATION:
GET PAID MORE AND BE LESS INTERESTED IN YOUR WORK?

Would you expect children reinforced for drawing to be more or less interested in drawing than children not reinforced? Would you expect college students rewarded for playing with a puzzle to be more or less interested in continuing to play with puzzles than students not rewarded? In perhaps surprising findings that are consistent with Rogers's emphasis on self-actualization, and in conflict with reinforcement theory, in both of these cases intrinsic interest in and motivation to perform the activity were lessened by rewards for performance!

Apparently rewards and other forms of control can interfere with the development of intrinsic motivation or involvement in an activity because of interest in it rather than because of rewards associated with performance. Circumstances that provide for feelings of challenge, competence, and self-determination appear to provide for the development of intrinsic motivation. Thus, parenting styles that are autonomy-oriented rather than control-oriented foster the development of intrinsic motivation.

People oriented toward intrinsic motivation have been found to prefer challenging tasks, to respond with effort and persistence after failure, to be creative and expressive, and to be high in self-esteem. Athletes, employees, and students have all been found to perform better under conditions encouraging intrinsic motivation as opposed to conditions emphasizing extrinsic rewards or external control.

Recent studies show, however, that the detrimental effects of reward may occur only under certain conditions. Thus, the research suggests getting paid more may not result in enjoying one's work less, but it does suggest that money isn't everything.

SOURCES: Deci & Ryan, 1985, 1991; Deci, Koestner, & Ryan, 1999; Eisenberger, Pierce, & Cameron, 1999; Kasser & Ryan, 1996; Koestner & McClelland, 1990; Lepper, Greene, & Nisbett, 1973.

---

later in life, people's psychological well-being should be affected by the degree of acceptance and positive regard they received in their daily social interactions. Recent research bears on this hypothesis.

Roberts and Chapman (2000) analyzed data from a long-term longitudinal study of the psychological development of adult women. In this dataset, women were studied over a 30-year period extending from young adulthood into midlife. Although the study was not organized according to the personality theory of Carl Rogers, it did contain two key measures that can be seen as highly relevant to Rogerian hypotheses. One measure was an index of psychological well-being; participants indicated their sense of well-being, including feelings of self-esteem, at four time points across the 30-year time period of the study. The second measure was an index of role quality, that is, whether people experienced supportive social relations in life roles including both marriage and work. Rogerian theory of course would predict that positive, supportive social relations would increase psychological well-being. The supportive relations should provide people with a sense of positive regard and make them less likely to engage in defensive processing that might contribute to psychological distress and a lower sense of self.

A key feature of this longitudinal research is that, by studying people at different points in their lives, the researchers could examine the impact of role quality on *changes* in well-being. These analyses generally were in accord with predictions that one would make from Rogerian theory. People who experienced a high degree of distress in their marriage and work roles experienced lower levels of well-being, whereas people who experienced more satisfying social roles showed positive changes in their well-being and personal maturity (Roberts & Chapman, 2000). Although it is difficult to establish causality in this type of research (that is, to determine whether social relations actually exerted a causal influence on well-being), the results are consistent with the Rogerian hypothesis that views of self and psychological well-being can change across the course of life and that the degree of positive regard one received from significant individuals in one's life can contribute directly to these changes.

CONCLUSION

Rogers's views on parents' characteristics and practices that influence the development of self-esteem have influenced the thinking of researchers and childcare experts. Although they do not always refer to Rogers, in many cases their emphasis on respect for children and protection of children's self-esteem speaks to the influence of Rogers and other members of the human potential movement. His emphasis on the conditions that promote or block self-actualization receives further attention in the next chapter, where we consider the clinical applications of the theory.

MAJOR CONCEPTS

Congruence   Rogers's concept expressing an absence of conflict between the perceived self and experience. Also one of three conditions suggested as essential for growth and therapeutic progress.

Denial   A defense mechanism, emphasized by both Freud and Rogers, in which threatening feelings are not allowed into awareness.

Distortion   According to Rogers, a defensive process in which experience is changed so as to be brought into awareness in a form that is consistent with the self.

Ideal self   The self-concept the individual would most like to possess. A key concept in Rogers's theory.

Incongruence   Rogers's concept of the existence of a discrepancy or conflict between the perceived self and experience.

Phenomenal field   The individual's way of perceiving and experiencing his or her world.

Phenomenology   The study of human experience; in personality psychology, an approach to personality theory that focuses on how the person perceives and experiences the self and the world.

Positive regard, need for   Rogers's concept expressing the need for warmth, liking, respect, and acceptance from others.

Q-sort   An assessment device in which the subject sorts statements into categories following a normal distribution. Used by Rogers as a measure of statements regarding the self and the ideal self.

Self-actualization   The fundamental tendency of the organism to actualize, maintain, enhance itself, and fulfill its potential. A concept emphasized by Rogers and other members of the human potential movement.

Self-concept (or the "Self")   The perceptions and meaning associated with the self, me, or I.

Self-consistency   Rogers's concept expressing an absence of conflict among perceptions of the self.

Subception   A process emphasized by Rogers in which a stimulus is experienced without being brought into awareness.

REVIEW

1. The phenomenological approach emphasizes an understanding of how people experience themselves and the world around them. The person-centered theory of Carl Rogers is illustrative of this approach.

2. Throughout his life Rogers attempted to integrate the intuitive with the objective, combining a sensitivity to the nuances of experience with an appreciation for the rigors of science.

3. Rogers emphasized the positive, self-actualizing qualities of the person. In his research he emphasized a disciplined effort to understand subjective experience or the phenomenal field of the person.

4. The key structural concept for Rogers was the self—the organization of perceptions and experiences associated with the "self," "me," or "I." Also important is the concept of the ideal self, or the self-concept the person would most like to possess. The Q-sort is one method used to study these concepts and the relation between them.

5. Rogers deemphasized the tension-reducing aspects of behavior and, instead, emphasized self-actualization as the central human motive. Self-actualization involves continuous openness to experience and the ability to integrate experiences into an expanded, more differentiated sense of self.

6. Rogers also suggested that people function to perceive self-consistency and to maintain congruence between perceptions of the self and experience. However, experiences perceived as threatening to the self-concept may, through defensive processes such as distortion and denial, be prevented from reaching consciousness. A variety of studies support the view that people will behave in ways to maintain and confirm the perception they have of themselves.

7. People have a need for positive regard. Under conditions of unconditional positive regard, children and adults are able to grow within a state of congruence and be self-actualizing. On the other hand, where positive regard is conditional, people may screen experiences out of awareness and limit their potential for self-actualization.

8. Children are influenced in their self-judgments through the process of reflected appraisal. Parents of children with high self-esteem are warm and accepting but also are clear and consistent in their enforcement of demands and standards.

9. Children develop beliefs concerning the malleability of psychological characteristics, contrasted in terms of an entity theory or an incremental theory. Of particular significance in this regard is the evaluation they make concerning the goodness-badness of the self.

6

A PHENOMENOLOGICAL THEORY: APPLICATIONS AND EVALUATION OF ROGERS'S THEORY

CLINICAL APPLICATIONS
  Psychopathology
    Self-Experience Discrepancy
    Discrepancies among Parts of the Self
  Change
    Therapeutic Conditions Necessary for
      Change
    Outcomes of Client-Centered Therapy

A CASE EXAMPLE: MRS. OAK
  Description of the Client and Problem
  Description of the Therapy
  Description of the Outcome

THE CASE OF JIM
  **Semantic Differential: Phenomenological
    Theory**
  Comments on the Data

**RECENT DEVELOPMENTS IN
THEORY AND RESEARCH**
  **Rogers's Shift in Emphasis: From
    Individuals to Groups and Society**

**Fluctuations in Self-Esteem and
  Contingencies of Worth**
**Internally Motivated Goals and
  Authenticity**
Cross-Cultural Research on the Self
  Is Positive Self-Regard a Human Universal?
  Regional Variations in Well-Being

RELATED POINTS OF VIEW
  The Human Potential Movement
    Kurt Goldstein (1878–1965)
    Abraham H. Maslow (1908–1970)
  Existentialism

CRITICAL EVALUATION
  Phenomenology
  The Concept of Self
  Conflict, Anxiety, and Defense
  Summary Evaluation

MAJOR CONCEPTS

REVIEW

Chapter Focus

Do you have a friend you talk to when you are feeling sad, or upset, or angry? During difficult times, this friend might seem like the only person in the world who can make you feel better. And what does your friend make you feel better about? School? Relationships? Maybe. But if you're lucky, your friend makes you feel better about that most important of things: yourself. By letting you explore and express your feelings, a talk with your friend somehow improves your sense of self. You end up being more accepting of your limitations and more appreciative of your virtues.

Providing this type of relationship, and accomplishing this sort of change in self-concept, was Carl Rogers's goal in his client-centered therapy. This therapeutic approach, which was a foundation on which he built his theory of personality (Chapter 5), is one focus of this chapter. As you will learn, in therapy Rogers tried to discover how his clients denied and distorted aspects of their everyday experience. He then created a therapy setting that enabled them to abandon these distortions, explore their true self, and thus experience personal growth.

A second focus of this chapter is contemporary research on the self. Much current research in personality science bears on Rogers's ideas about self and personality. As you learn about these research findings, you will see that some of them confirm Rogers's original ideas, others extend them in novel directions, and yet others challenge aspects of Rogers's thinking. This second focus speaks to a primary goal of this book: enabling you, the student, to use contemporary research findings to evaluate classic theoretical conceptions of human nature.

Finally, we present case studies that concretely illustrate Rogers's theoretical ideas, consider other significant figures in the human potential movement (Kurt Goldstein, Abraham H. Maslow), and provide an overall evaluation of Rogerian theory.

QUESTIONS TO BE ADDRESSED IN THIS CHAPTER

1. How does a lack of congruence between self and experience contribute to psychological distress?

2. What therapeutic conditions are necessary to bring about psychological change?

3. What are the implications of contemporary research—including cross-cultural research on self-concept, motivation, and personality—for Rogers's phenomenological theory?

4. How do Rogers's ideas relate to existentialism and to theoretical conceptions in the human potential movement?

CLINICAL APPLICATIONS

In this chapter we will consider Rogers's views on psychopathology, psychotherapy, and personality change. These views are an important part of the theory; in fact, the major part of Rogers's professional life involved these clinical applications. The person-centered approach developed first in counseling, where it was known as client-centered therapy, "meaning that a person seeking help was not treated as a dependent patient but rather as a responsible client" (Rogers, 1977, p. 5). Rather than focusing on an illness model of abnormal behavior and a medical model of a doctor treating a patient, Rogers emphasized the individual's drive toward health, the conditions that may interfere with such growth, and the therapeutic conditions that help to remove obstacles to self-actualization. We will also consider recent developments that bear on Rogerian theory, including cross-cultural studies of self-concept that raise questions about whether or not the exact psychological dynamics studied by Rogers in the United States are a universal feature of human psychological experience.

PSYCHOPATHOLOGY

Self-Experience Discrepancy

The essential elements of Rogers's view of psychopathology were given in the last chapter. For Rogers, the healthy person can assimilate experiences into the self-structure. Such a person experiences a **congruence** between self and experience. They are open to experiences rather than interpreting events in a defensive manner. In contrast, the neurotic person's self-concept has become structured in ways that do not fit organismic experience. Such a person denies awareness to significant sensory and emotional experiences. Experiences that are incongruent with the self-structure are subceived as threatening and are either denied or distorted. This condition is known as **self-experience discrepancy**. It results in a rigid, defensive maintenance of the self against experiences that threaten the wholeness of the self and frustrate the need for positive self-regard.

Rogers did not differentiate among types of pathology; he did not want to develop a diagnostic scheme in which individual persons were treated merely as examples of one versus another category of psychological disorder. He did, however, differentiate among forms of defensive behaviors. For example, one such defensive behavior is rationalization. In rationalization, a person distorts behavior in such a way as to make it consistent with the self. If you view yourself as a person who never makes mistakes and then a mistake seems to occur, you may rationalize it by blaming the error on another person. Another defensive behavior is fantasy. A man who defensively believes himself to be an adequate person may fantasize that he is a prince and that all women adore him, and he may deny any experiences that are inconsistent with this image. A third example of defense behavior is projection. Here an individual expresses a need, but in such a form that the need is denied to awareness and the behavior is viewed as consistent with the self. People whose self-concept involves no "bad" sexual thoughts may feel that others are making them have these thoughts.

The descriptions of these defensive behaviors are quite similar to the ones given by Freud. For Rogers, however, the important aspect of these behaviors is their handling of an incongruence between self and experience by denial in awareness or distortion of perception: "It should be noted that perceptions are excluded because they are contradictory, not because they are derogatory" (Rogers, 1951, p. 506). Furthermore, the classification of the defenses is not as critical to Rogerian theory as it is to Freudian theory.

CURRENT QUESTIONS

IDEAL SELF AND FEARED SELF— MOTIVATING FACETS OF THE SELF?

The day before a big test you find yourself visualizing what it would feel like to get an A. Then you imagine what it would be like to get an F. Both possibilities can feel very real. The A may seem so ideal, and the F so frightening, that you decide to study an extra hour.

What are your ideal and feared selves? Some research has emphasized the ideal self and the feared self and compared them with the current self as the individual perceives it (e.g., Harary & Donahue, 1994). Here is an exercise that you may find useful for thinking about your ideals and fears in relation to your current self-concept.

First think about how you see yourself in general and rate your current self-concept as you perceive it right now using the five descriptive statements listed below. Next, consider your ideal self—the way you wish your personality would be—and rate it using the same five statements. Finally, consider your feared self—the way you are afraid your personality might become—and rate it accordingly. For all three types of ratings, use the following scale and enter your ratings in the appropriate column:

Once you have completed your ratings, you can compute two discrepancy scores, one for the discrepancy between current and ideal self and another between current and feared self. For example, consider a person who is quite a partier (a current self rating of 5 on "outgoing") but feels that ideally she should be more reserved and spend more time on schoolwork (an ideal self rating of 3); the resulting current-ideal discrepancy (−2) indicates that she needs to cut back on social activities to get closer to the ideal self. Another person might feel he has overcome his shyness (a current self rating of 3 on "outgoing") but fears that he might drift back into his lonely old self (a feared self-rating of 1). The resulting current-feared discrepancy (+2) is positive and indicates that for now he is successfully avoiding this feared self.

You might find it interesting to calculate the two discrepancy scores for each of the five rating dimensions and consider where your current self stands in relation to your ideal self and feared selves. Your current self might be further from your ideal self (and closer to your feared self!) on some dimensions more than others. Are these discrepant aspects of your personality ones that you would like to change? The key is to know what you want for yourself (your ideals),

DISAGREE			AGREE	
Strongly	A little	Neither/nor	A little	Strongly
1	2	3	4	5

How I see my various selves:

	Current Self	Ideal Self	Feared Self	Current minus Ideal	Current minus Feared
Outgoing, not reserved.	___	___	___	___	___
Forgiving, doesn't hold grudges.	___	___	___	___	___
Is lazy.	___	___	___	___	___
Is tense, easily stressed out.	___	___	___	___	___
Sophisticated in art, music, or literature.	___	___	___	___	___

what you don't want (your fears), and what motivates you. Some people are inspired by visualizing their ideal self and others are jump-started into action by the image of their feared self. Which one sounds more like you? If you want to change, a good way to start is to visualize the vast array of possibilities in your life.

Discrepancies among Parts of the Self

Acording to Rogers, then, psychological pathology results from discrepancies between self-concept and actual experience. Much contemporary research similarly focuses on the role of discrepancies in psychological distress. However, this work differs somewhat from that of Rogers. It tends to focus less on discrepancies between self and experience, and more on an internal psychological discrepancy: discrepancies between different parts of self—in particular, between the actual self and ideal self.

In this research, people are asked to describe how they actually are (their actual self) and how they ideally would like to be (their ideal self). Researchers determine the degree to which these different descriptions are discrepant. (For example, if you say "I actually am lazy" and "ideally, I would be hard-working," that is coded as a self-discrepancy.) The discrepancy between actual-self and ideal-self ratings is often used as a measure of adjustment—the smaller the discrepancy between self and ideal self, the more well-adjusted. Many studies have been conducted in support of the view that health and self-esteem are associated with the relation between the self and ideal self. For example, Higgins, Bond, Klein, and Strauman (1986) found that people with large discrepancies between self and ideal self are more likely to be depressed. Other research suggests that how close one feels to the feared (or undesired) self may be even more critical to adjustment (Ogilvie, 1987). In other words, self-esteem and life satisfaction may depend more on not being like one's feared self than on being like one's ideal self.

The psychologist Tory Higgins (1987, 1999) has proposed a general theory relating self and affect. His work constitutes an intriguing contemporary elaboration of Rogers's notion that self-inconsistencies produce emotional difficulties. It valuably extends Rogers's thinking by differentiating between two aspects of one's future self: an ideal self and an "ought self." Whereas the ideal self-concept captures the individual's hopes, ambitions, and desires, the ought self-concept consists of the individual's beliefs about duties, responsibilities, and obligations.

According to Higgins's theory, discrepancies between actual self and ideal self lead to dejection-related emotions. For example, if someone has an ideal self of being an A student but receives a C in a class, he or she would likely feel disappointed, sad, or even depressed. In contrast, discrepancies between self and ought self should lead to agitation-related emotions. For example, if someone has an ought self of being an A student but receives a C, he or she would likely feel fearful, threatened, or anxious. Thus, the distinction between ideal self and ought self is important because it helps separate two kinds of self-relevant emotions: those related to dejection (e.g., disappointment, sadness, depression) and those related to agitation (e.g., fear, threat, anxiety).

Higgins argues that ideal and ought selves serve as self-guides to direct and organize social behavior. However, while they sometimes work together, these self-guides may also come into conflict. What we idealize for ourselves and what we feel obligated to do are not always the same. For example, some women feel conflict between their own wish to be successful professionals (an ideal self) and societal expectations that they ought to be mothers (an ought self). It is these kinds of conflicts that Rogers felt clients need to become aware of and work through in order to change in therapy.

It should also be noted that Higgins' work, while being highly relevant to that of Rogers, was not developed within a Rogerian theoretical framework. Instead, Higgins (1999) draws on principles of social cognition that were not part of Rogerian theory, but that are central to the social-cognitive perspective on personality that we will cover later in the text (Chapters 12 and 13). Thus, we will return to Higgins' analyses of self-concept later in our text.

CHANGE

In our previous chapter, you learned about Rogers's theory of personality. Those ideas constitute Rogers's most important contributions to personality science. However, developing those ideas was not Rogers's own highest priority. His main professional focus was the process of psychotherapy. Rogers committed himself to understanding how personality *change* can come about. The process of change, or of becoming, was his greatest concern. His most enduring contribution to understanding change was work in which he outlined necessary conditions of therapy; he described, in other words, types of circumstances and events that need to occur in the relationship between client and therapist in order for personality change to come about. We now consider these conditions.

Therapeutic Conditions Necessary for Change

In his early work, Rogers emphasized the therapist's use of the technique of reflection of feeling. In this nondirective approach, therapists do not guide the flow of events in therapy, but merely summarize or "reflect" back to the client an understanding of what the client says; such a technique can proide to the client a sense of feeling thoroughly and deeply understood by the therapist. Because some nondirective counselors were perceived as passive and uninterested, Rogers changed his focus to an emphasis on counselors being client-centered. In this **client-centered therapy**, the therapist not only uses the technique of reflection, but plays a more active role in understanding the experiences of the client.

Ultimately, Rogers believed that the critical variable in client-centered therapy is the therapeutic climate (Rogers, 1966). If therapists can provide three conditions in their relationships with their clients, in a way that is phenomenologically meaningful to the clients, then therapeutic change will occur. The three conditions hypothesized by Rogers to be critical to therapeutic movement are congruence or genuineness, unconditional positive regard, and empathic understanding.

Genuine therapists are themselves. They do not present a scientific or medical façade. Instead, the therapist is interpersonally open and transparent. The therapist experiences events in the therapeutic encounter in a natural manner and shares with the client their genuine feelings—even when feelings toward the client are negative. "Even with such negative attitudes, which seem so potentially damaging but which all therapists have from time to time, I am suggesting that it is preferable for the therapist to be real than to put on a false posture of interest, concern, and liking that the client is likely to sense as false" (Rogers, 1966, p. 188). The client thus experiences a real interpersonal relationship with the therapist, rather than the stilted, formal relationship that one might usually experience with a health- or mental-health-care provider.

The second condition essential for therapeutic movement is **unconditional positive regard**. This means that the therapist communicates a deep and genuine caring for the client as a person. The client is prized in a total, unconditional way. The experience of respect and unconditional positive regard enables the client to explore their inner self with confidence.

Finally, the condition of **empathic understanding** involves the therapist's ability to perceive experiences and their meaning to the client during the moment-to-moment encounter of psychotherapy. The therapist does not provide a technical "diagnosis" of the client's problems. The client is not presented with reformulation of his or her life in technical psychological jargon. Instead, through active listening, the therapist strives to understand the meaning and subjective feeling of the events experienced by the client, and to make it clear to clients that they are being understood empathically.

In Rogers's view, these three therapeutic conditions are of fundamental importance, independent of the theoretical orientation of the therapist. Classic research on the psychotherapeutic process supports this contention. Fiedler (1950) had research participants listen to the recorded interviews of experts and nonexperts of the psychoanalytic, nondirective (Rogerian), and Adlerian schools. The judges then sorted a number of descriptive items according to the extent to which they were characteristic of the interview. Compared to nonexperts, experts were found to be more successful in creating an ideal therapeutic relationship. Independent of orientation, expert therapists were able to understand, communicate with, and maintain rapport with the client. Rogers's identification of conditions that foster success in psychotherapy stands as one of his most enduring contributions to psychology.

Outcomes of Client-Centered Therapy

One of Rogers's landmark contributions was his opening up the field of psychotherapy for systematic investigation. During the 1940s and 1950s, Rogers and colleagues began to determine systematically the changes associated with client-centered therapy. Rogers did not want to rely merely on the case study reports of therapists; as Rogers recognized, those reports are not a scientific, objective record of the success of therapy since the therapist may be biased to conclude that his or her own therapy strategy was a success. Rogers thus employed objective measures of psychological change.

These measures revealed systematic change resulting from client-centered therapy. Changes included a decrease in defensiveness and an increase in openness to experience among clients; the development of a more positive and more congruent self; development of more positive feelings toward others; and a shift away from using the values of others to asserting their own evalu-

CURRENT APPLICATIONS

DRINKING, SELF-AWARENESS, AND PAINFUL FEELINGS

Why do people abuse alcohol and drugs? Why, after treatment, do so many relapse? In Chapter 3 it was suggested that many alcoholics and drug addicts use the defense mechanism of denial to cope with painful feelings. However, evidence of this relationship was not presented, nor was there analysis of how the self is experienced by substance abusers. This would appear to be important since substance abusers commonly report that they use drugs to handle painful feelings, with alcoholics often reporting that they drink to create a blur that blots out the painful aspects of life. Though not conducted within the Rogerian framework, some recent research in this area is relevant to Rogers's views. The basic hypothesis of this research is that alcohol reduces self-consciousness and that alcoholics high in self-consciousness drink to reduce their awareness of negative life experiences. Individuals high in self-consciousness of inner experiences are those who would describe themselves in terms of statements such as the following: "I reflect about myself a lot;" "I'm generally attentive to my inner feelings;" "I'm alert to changes in my mood."

In laboratory research with social drinkers, it has been found that individuals high in self-consciousness consume more alcohol following failure experiences than do members of three other groups—individuals high in self-consciousness following success experiences and individuals low in self-consciousness regardless of whether they experience success or failure. Further, in a study of alcohol use in adolescents, it was found that increased alcohol use was associated with poor academic experience for students high in self-consciousness but not for those low in self-consciousness.

But what of alcoholics? And what about relapse? The latter would appear to be particularly significant since one-half to three-quarters of all treated alcoholics relapse within six months of the end of treatment. In a study of relapse in alcohol abuse following treatment, results comparable to the above were found; relapse appeared to be a joint function of negative events and high self-consciousness. In many different populations and kinds of studies, a consistent relationship has been found between drinking, high self-consciousness, and experiences of personal failure. The research suggests that many individuals drink to reduce their level of awareness of painful negative experiences.

SOURCES: Baumeister, 1991; Hull, Young, & Jouriles, 1986; Pervin, 1988.

Defensive Behaviors: *Alcohol can be used to reduce awareness of painful feelings.*

ations. This work was done not only with neurotic clients, but eventually with schizophrenic patients (Rogers, 1967). Rogers found that the three conditions of psychotherapy were critical in improving the lives of these patients as well. However, the therapeutic climate was found to depend on a complex dynamic interaction between patient and therapist, rather than on patient or therapist factors alone. Further, there was evidence that patients of therapists who were generally competent and conscientious, yet were unable to establish positive therapeutic conditions, sometimes got worse.

In summary, athough the details and applications of client-centered therapy changed somewhat over the years, it retained core features that are tied closely to Rogers's overall conception of personality (Rogers, 1942, 1977). Rogers believed strongly in the capacity of the client to change and grow—to be motivated toward self-actualization. As a result of this belief, he concluded that the main goal of the therapist was to provide a relationship in which the client could experience his or her natural growth toward maturity, productivity, and independence. The theory behind client-centered has an "if-then" quality: If certain therapeutic conditions exist, then processes inherently will occur that lead to personality change.

A Case Example: Mrs. Oak

As noted, one of Rogers's outstanding contributions to the field of psychotherapy was his leadership in opening it up as an area for investigation. He made available verbatim transcripts of therapy, films of client-centered therapy sessions, and a file of recorded therapy sessions that could be used for research purposes. In his 1954 book on psychotherapy and personality change, Rogers presented an extensive analysis of a single case, the case of Mrs. Oak. As Rogers observed, it is the individual case that makes a total research investigation come to life, that brings diverse facts together in the interrelated way in which they exist in life. The case of Mrs. Oak is presented here to illustrate the Rogerian approach to an understanding of personality.

Description of the Client and Problem

Mrs. Oak was a housewife in her late 30s when she came to the University of Chicago Counseling Center for treatment. At that time, she was having great difficulty in her relationships with her husband and with her adolescent daughter. Mrs. Oak blamed herself for her daughter's psychosomatic illness. Mrs. Oak was described by her therapist as a sensitive person who was eager to be honest with herself and deal with her problems. She had little formal education but was intelligent and had read widely. Mrs. Oak was interviewed 40 times over a period of five-and-one-half months, at which point she terminated treatment.

Description of the Therapy

In the early interviews, Mrs. Oak spent much of her time talking about specific problems with her daughter and her husband. Gradually, there was a shift from these reality problems to descriptions of feelings:

> And secondly, the realization that last time I was here I experienced a—an emotion I had never felt before—which surprised me and sort of shocked me a bit. And yet I thought, I think it has a sort of a—the only word I can find to describe it, the only verbalization is a kind of cleansing. I—I really felt terribly sorry for something, a kind of grief.
>
> p. 311

At first the therapist thought Mrs. Oak was a shy, almost nondescript person who was neutral toward her. He quickly sensed, however, that she was a sensitive and interesting person. His respect for her grew, and he described himself as experiencing a sense of respect for—and awe of—her capacity to struggle ahead through turmoil and pain. He did not try to direct or guide her; instead, he found satisfaction in trying to understand her, in trying to appreciate her world, in expressing the acceptance he felt toward her.

MRS. OAK: And yet the—the fact that I—I really like this, I don't know, call it a poignant feeling. I mean…I felt things that I've never felt before. I like that, too. Uh-uh…maybe that's the way to do it. I—I just don't know today.

THERAPIST: M-hm. Don't feel at all sure, but you know that you somehow have a real, a real fondness for this poem that is yourself. Whether it's the way to go about this or not, you don't know.

p. 314

Given this supportive therapeutic climate, Mrs. Oak began to become aware of feelings she had previously denied to awareness. In the 24th interview, she became aware of conflicts with her daughter that related to her own adolescent development. She felt a sense of shock at becoming aware of her own competitiveness. In a later interview, she became aware of the deep sense of hurt inside of her.

MRS. OAK: And then of course, I've come to…to see and to feel that over this…see, I've covered it up. (Weeps) But…and…I've covered it up with so much bitterness, which in turn I had to cover up. (Weeps) That's what I want to get rid of! I almost don't care if I hurt.

THERAPIST: (Gently) You feel that here at the basis of it, as you experienced it, is a feeling of real tears for yourself. But that you can't show, mustn't show, so that's been covered by bitterness that you don't like, that

you'd like to be rid of. You almost feel you'd rather absorb the hurt than to…than to feel bitterness. (Pause) And what you seem to be saying quite strongly is, "I do hurt, and I've tried to cover it up."

MRS. OAK: I didn't know it.

THERAPIST: M-hm. Like a new discovery really.

MRS. OAK: (Speaking at the same time) I never really did know. But it's…you know, it's almost a physical thing. It's…sort of as though I—I—I were looking within myself at all kinds of…nerve endings and—and bits of—of…things that have been sort of mashed. (Weeping)

p. 326

At first, this increased awareness led to a sense of disorganization. Mrs. Oak began to feel more troubled and neurotic, as if she were going to pieces. She said she felt as though she were a piece of structure or a piece of architecture that had parts removed from it. In struggling with these feelings, Mrs. Oak began to recognize the dynamics of anxiety that had operated in her and to discover how, in an attempt to cope with anxiety, she had deserted her self. She described her previous inability to recognize and "sort of simply embrace" fear. She described her feeling that the problem for her and for many others is that they get away from the self.

Intermittently, Mrs. Oak expressed her feelings toward the therapist. At first she felt resentful that the therapist was not being very helpful and would not take responsibility for the sessions. During the course of therapy, she felt very strongly at times that the therapist didn't "add a damn thing." But, also in the course of therapy, she developed a sense of relationship with the therapist and how this relationship compared with the descriptions her friends had given of their relationships in psychoanalysis. She concluded that her relationship with the therapist was different, something she would never be casual about, and was the basis of therapy.

I'm convinced [Rogers wrote], and again I may sound textbookish, that therapy is only as deep as this combination, this relationship, as the need in the client is as deep as the need, and as deep as the willingness for the relationship to grow on the part of the therapist.

p. 399

Description of the Outcome

Progress did not occur in all areas. By the end of therapy, Mrs. Oak still had sexual conflicts. However, significant gains had been made in a number of areas. She began to feel free to be herself, to listen to herself, and to make independent evaluations. Mrs. Oak began to stop rejecting the feminine role and, more generally, began to accept herself as a worthwhile human being. She decided that she could not continue in her marriage, and she arrived at a mutually agreeable divorce with her husband. Finally, she obtained and held a challenging job. Through the conditions created within the therapeutic environment, Mrs. Oak was able to break down defenses that had been maintaining a marked incongruence between her self and her experience. With this increase in self-awareness, she was able to make positive changes in her life and become a more self-actualized human being.

Semantic Differential: Phenomenological Theory

THE CASE OF JIM

Jim filled out the semantic differential, rating the concepts self, ideal self, father, and mother on 104 scales. Typical scales were authoritarian-democratic, conservative-liberal, affectionate-reserved, warm-cold, and strong-weak. Each of the four concepts was rated on the same scales so that comparisons could be made of the meaning of these concepts for Jim. The test is clearly different from the Rorschach in being undisguised rather than disguised. The semantic differential test does not immediately follow from Rogerian theory. However, we can interpret data from the test in relation to Rogerian theory, since there is a phenomenological quality to the data and since we are assessing the individual's perception of his self and his ideal self.

First, we look at the ways in which Jim perceives his self. Jim sees himself as intelligent, friendly, sincere, kind, and basically good—as a wise person who is humane and interested in people. At the same time, other ratings suggest that he does not feel free to be expressive and uninhibited. Thus, he rates himself as reserved, introverted, inhibited, tense, moral, and conforming. There is a curious mixture of perceptions: being involved, deep, sensitive, and kind while also being competitive, selfish, and disapproving. There is also the interesting combination of perceiving himself as being good and masculine but simultaneously weak and insecure. One gets the impression of an individual who would like to believe that he is basically good and capable of genuine interpersonal relationships at the same time that he is bothered by serious inhibitions and high standards for himself and others.

This impression comes into sharper focus when we consider the self-ratings in relation to those for the ideal self. In general, Jim did not see an extremely large gap between his self and his ideal self. However, large gaps did occur on a number of important scales. In an arbitrary way, we can define a gap of three or more positions on a 7-point scale as considerable and important. Thus, for example, Jim rated his self as 2 on the weak-strong scale and his ideal self as 7 on the same scale—a difference of five positions. In other words, Jim would like to be much stronger than he feels he is. Assessing his ratings on the other scales in a similar way, we find that Jim would like to be more of each of the following than he currently perceives himself to be: warm, active, equalitarian, flexible, lustful, approving, industrious, relaxed, friendly, and bold. Basically two themes appear. One has to do with warmth. Jim is not as warm, relaxed, and friendly as he would like to be. The other theme has to do with strength. Jim is not as strong, active, and industrious as he would like to be.

Jim's ratings of his parents give some indication of where he sees them in relation to himself in general and to these qualities in particular. First, if we compare the way Jim perceives his self with his perception of his mother and father, he clearly perceives himself to be much more like his father than his mother. Also, he perceives his father to be closer to his ideal self than his mother, although he perceives himself to be closer to his ideal self than either his mother or his father. However, in the critical areas of warmth and strength, the parents tend to be closer to the ideal self than Jim is. Thus, his mother is perceived to be more warm, approving, relaxed, and friendly than Jim, while his father is perceived to be stronger, more industrious, and more active than Jim. The mother is perceived as having an interesting combination of personality characteristics. On the one hand, she is perceived as affectionate, friendly, spontaneous, sensitive, and good. On the other, she is perceived as authoritarian, superficial, selfish, unintelligent, intolerant, and uncreative.

Comments on the Data

With the autobiography and the semantic differential we begin to get another picture of Jim. We learn of his popularity and success through high school and of his good relationship with his father. We find support for the suggestions from the projective tests of anxiety and difficulties with women. Indeed, we learn of Jim's fears of ejaculating too quickly and not being able to satisfy women. However, we also find an individual who believes himself to be basically good and interested in doing humane things. We become aware of an individual who has a view of his self and a view of his ideal self, and of an individual who is frustrated because of the feelings that leave a gap between the two.

Given the opportunity to talk about himself and what he would like to be, Jim talks about his desire to be warmer, more relaxed, and stronger. We feel no need here to disguise our purposes, for we are interested in Jim's perceptions, meanings, and experiences as he reports them. We are interested in what is real for Jim—in how he interprets phenomena within his own frame of reference. We want to know all about Jim, but all about Jim as he perceives himself and the world about him.

When using the data from the semantic differential, we are not tempted to focus on drives, and we do not need to come to grips with the world of the irrational. In Rogers's terms, we see an individual who is struggling to move toward self-actualization, from dependence toward independence, from fixity and rigidity to freedom and spontaneity. We find an individual who has a gap between his intellectual and emotional estimates of himself. As Rogers would put it, we observe an individual who is without self-consistency, who lacks a sense of congruence between self and experience.

Having now learned about the basics of Rogers's personality theory and therapy approach, and having seen it "in action" in the case studies of Mrs. Oak and Jim, we can move ahead to consider developments in phenomenological studies of the self. Some of these developments were started years ago by Rogers himself. Others involve contemporary research conducted by people who may or may not call themselves "Rogerians," yet who explore topics that are at the heart of Rogers's conception of human nature.

RECENT DEVELOPMENTS IN THEORY AND RESEARCH

ROGERS'S SHIFT IN EMPHASIS: FROM INDIVIDUALS TO GROUPS AND SOCIETY

Throughout his career, Rogers's emphasis on phenomenology, the self, and the change process was consistent. Yet he did display a shift in his feelings about research. Early in his career he endeavored to combine clinical sensitivity with scientific rigor. Later, Rogers appeared to move increasingly toward sole reliance on personal, phenomenological studies: "To my way of thinking, this personal, phenomenological type of study—especially when one reads all of the responses—is far more valuable than the traditional 'hard-headed' empirical approach. This kind of study, often scorned by psychologists as being 'merely self-reports,' actually gives the deepest insight into what the experience has meant" (Rogers, 1970, p. 133). Rogers felt that the yield of orthodox scientific studies was minute compared to the insights obtained from clinical work.

Another shift in emphasis for Rogers was from one-to-one therapy relationships to groups. In his book *On Encounter Groups* (Rogers, 1970), Rogers stated that changes occur more rapidly and clearly in small, intensive groups. Of particular interest to Rogers was the marital partnership group and alternatives to marriage (Rogers, 1972), where Rogers highlighted questions of openness, honesty, sharing, and movement toward awareness of inner feelings in relationships. Finally, Rogers extended his person-centered approach to administration, minority groups, interracial, intercultural, and international relationships. Rogers expressed a revolutionary spirit in his belief that the person-centered approach could produce a change in the concepts, values, and procedures of our culture: "It is the evidence of the effectiveness of a person-centered approach that may turn a very small and quiet revolution into a far more significant change in the way humankind perceives the possible. I am much too close to the situation to know whether this will be a minor or a major event, but I believe it represents a radical change" (p. 286).

In the later years of his career, then, Rogers moved away from an exclusive focus on personality dynamics and self-concept. However, among researchers in personality, questions of the self and feelings of self-worth increasingly attracted attention. We turn now to some of these contemporary research findings and their implications for Rogers's theorizing.

FLUCTUATIONS IN SELF-ESTEEM AND CONTINGENCIES OF WORTH

Rogers's ideas about the self implied that people possess a relatively stable sense of self-worth, or self-esteem. To bring about changes in people's sense of self, it appeared that systematic efforts, such as client-centered therapy, were required. In contrast to this view, some contemporary research suggests that self-esteem may fluctuate to a greater extent than Rogers had anticipated. Particularly informative work on this topic comes from the psychologists Jennifer Crocker and Connie Wolfe (2001).

Crocker and Wolfe (2001) are interested in "contingencies of self-worth." Their idea is that a person's self-esteem depends on—or is "contingent on" — positive and negative events. Self-esteem rises when we get an A+ in a class and falls when we get an F–. We feel better about ourselves when someone asks us out on a date, and worse when we ask someone out and they laugh at us and hang up the phone. It is these successes and failures that are the **contingencies of self-worth** on which self-esteem depends. Although a person's typical, average level of self-esteem may be relatively stable, their day-to-day sense of self-worth may fluctuate considerably as they experience these positive and negative contingent events.

In addition to the possibility of fluctuations in self-esteem, Crocker and Wolfe's theoretical framework highlights another point. People may differ in the degree to which any given event is, for them, a contingency of self-worth. One person might not care much about their grades in classes because they're basically interested in getting dates. Another might not be concerned with acceptance/rejection by dating partners, because their only big concern is academic grades. Such people should experience fluctuating self-esteem in different situations. "The impact of events" on one's self-esteem should depend "on the perceived relevance of those events to one's contingencies of self-worth" (Crocker & Wolfe, 2001, p. 594).

Crocker and colleagues have applied their theoretical ideas to a topic of particular relevance to those readers of this book who might be considering going to graduate school: fluctuations in self-esteem among college students as they receive acceptances and rejections from graduate programs (Crocker, Sommers, & Luhtanen, 2002). Participants in this study completed a measure of self-esteem, as well as measures of positive and negative affect, twice a week on a regular schedule, as well as on any days on which they received a notification of admission (or not) from a graduate program. This enabled the investigators to study fluctuations in self-esteem. At the outset of the study, the degree to which each participant's self-worth was contingent on academic success was measured; this was done by asking people to report the degree to which they get a self-esteem boost from events such as getting good grades. This procedure enabled the investigators to test the hypothesis that self-esteem would fluctuate as a result of acceptances/rejections, but only for students for whom academic success was an important contingency of self-

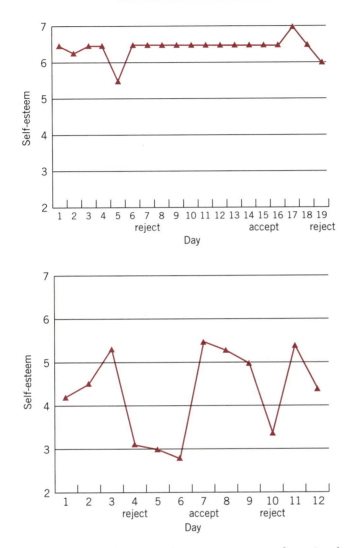

Figure 6.1 Daily reports of self-esteem for two participants from Crocker, Sommers, and Luhtanen (2002). *Participants in the top (bottom) panel did not (did) base their self-esteem on academic performance. For the student who did base self-esteem on academic performance, self-esteem varied as a result of graduate school acceptances and rejections.*

worth. This hypothesis was confirmed (Figure 6.1). Among students who based their self-esteem on academic performance, self-esteem went up and down as a result of acceptances and rejections (respectively). However, among students for whom academic success was not a central element of self-worth, the same objective events—graduate school acceptances and rejections—had little impact on self-esteem.

The analyses of Crocker and colleagues are a valuable extension of Rogers's analyses of self-concept. They extend the work by identifying particular social contexts that contribute not only to typical, average levels of self-esteem, but to those day-to-day fluctuations in people's sense of self that are so much a part of everyday life.

INTERNALLY MOTIVATED GOALS AND AUTHENTICITY

In the middle of the 20th century, psychology experienced a decline of interest in the concept of the self. Many psychologists felt that it was difficult, if not impossible, to formulate a theory of self-concept that was scientifically sound. However, in the past 25 years, things have changed dramatically. Advances in psychological theory as well as in research methods ushered in what might be seen as an "era of self-concept." Research on the self probably became the most frequently researched topic in personality and social psychology (Pervin, 1999, 2003; Robins, Norem, & Cheek, 1999; Leary & Tangney, 2002). However, relatively little of this research cites the work of Rogers. Much current interest in the self comes out of a cognitive orientation that differs from Rogers's theorizing. As we will discuss in more detail in Chapters 12 and 13, this cognitive orientation is more sensitive than was Rogers to the possibility that people possess multiple views of self that vary from one context to another, rather than a global sense of self as Rogers discussed. Personality psychologists following this newer view would suggest that individuals may have multiple sources of self-esteem rather than a global self-esteem. For example, one recent study compared the specific view of self-esteem with the global view in terms of their ability to predict people's reactions to success and failure. What was found was that global self-esteem better predicted emotional reactions to performance outcomes than did specific self-esteem, suggesting that the effects of global self-esteem are not reducible to the way people think about their specific qualities. In agreement with Rogers, the investigators suggested that "high self-esteem is an unconditional feeling of affection for oneself that does not depend on the perception that one has any particular positive quality or qualities" (Dutton & Brown, 1997, p.146).

Another research trend that is in accord with Rogers's views is recent work on the concept of **authenticity**, defined as the extent to which a person behaves in accord with their self as opposed to behaving in terms of roles that foster false self-presentations (Ryan, 1993; Sheldon, Ryan, Rawsthorne, & Ilardi, 1997). According to this humanistic point of view, consistency of behavior across situations may or may not reflect authenticity. Rather, authenticity is defined in terms of experiencing behavior as authored by the self—one feels that one is being true to oneself rather than phony or expressing a false self. Certainly, we all are aware of times when we have felt we were being more "authentic" and other times when we felt we were being "inauthentic" or "phony." Is the degree to which an individual feels authentic in situations in daily life related to measures of satisfaction and well-being? Indeed, this has been found to be the case. That is, in accord with the prior theorizing of humanistic and phenomenologically oriented psychologists, authenticity was found to be associated with being a more fully functioning person. In addition to this overall relationship with psychological being, it was found that the more genuine and self-expressive people feel they are in a specific situation, the more extraverted, agreeable, conscientious, and open to experience they are likely to be in that situation (Sheldon et al., 1997). In other words, individuals may vary in their behavior from situation to situation, but the critical question is whether they feel they are being authentic and true to their self overall as well as in specific situations.

Related to the concept of authenticity is the question of the kinds of goals that individuals pursue. Is the individual pursuing goals that fit his or her enduring personal interests and values? Or are the individual's daily goals dictated by external sources or internal feelings of conflict, guilt, and anxiety (Deci and Ryan, 1991; Sheldon & Elliot, 1999)? Recall that in Chapter 5 there was discussion of intrinsic motivation, the motivation to engage in an activity because of interest in it rather than because of rewards associated with performance (i.e., extrinsic motivation). According to Deci and Ryan's (1985, 1991; Ryan & Deci, 2000) self-determination theory, people have an inherent psychological need to act in autonomous, self-determined ways and to engage in tasks that are intrinsically meaningful as opposed to action that is coerced, forced, or compelled, whether by internal forces or external forces. There are at least two critical elements to this difference. First, there is the question of whether action is autonomous, or self-initiated as opposed to controlled by others, or externally regulated. In addition, there is the question of whether action is freely chosen as opposed to compelled. Action conducted out of feelings of guilt and anxiety would emanate from within the person but would have a compelled as opposed to freely chosen quality, and would not qualify as self-determined action. In sum, self-determined action is action that takes place because of its intrinsic interest to the person and its quality of being freely chosen.

Does it make a difference whether action is reflective of self-determined motivation? Recent research indeed suggests that people show greater effort and persistence in relation to autonomous goals than in relation to goals that are pursued only because of external pushes or internal sanctions such as anxiety or guilt (Koestner, Lekes, Powers, & Chicoine, 2002; Sheldon & Elliot, 1999). In addition, there is evidence that the pursuit of self-determined, intrinsic, approach goals is associated with physical health and psychological well-being in contrast with the deleterious effects of the pursuit of forced, extrinsic, avoidance goals (Dykman, 1998; Elliot & Sheldon, 1998; Elliot, Sheldon, & Church, 1997; Kasser & Ryan, 1996). Thus, it is suggested that "to the extent that goal self-concepts do not represent or are not concordant with the true self, people may not be able to meet their psychological needs" (Sheldon & Elliot, 1999, p. 485). This conclusion is supported not only by individual experiments but by "meta-analyses," that is, analyses of the results of *multiple* experiments in which one computes an overall index of the degree to which variables are related across a number of individual studies. Meta-analyses confirm the hypothesis that people make particularly good progress on personal goals when the goals are "self-concordant," that is, consistent with one's own personal values rather than being imposed by someone else (Koestner et al., 2002).

From a humanistic standpoint, these results make perfectly good sense. Yet, two caveats are worthy of note. First, it is important to keep in mind that it is not the goal per se that is important but why the goal is being pursued. For example, some research has argued that a goal such as financial success represents an extrinsic goal, implying external control, whereas a goal such as community involvement (e.g., making the world a better place) represents an intrinsic goal, implying autonomy, self-determination, and self-actualiza-

CURRENT APPLICATIONS

DOES HIGH SELF-ESTEEM IMPROVE ONE'S LIFE?

Sometimes the ideas of personality theorists contribute to the ideas of a culture. Such is the case for Carl Rogers. As we have seen, his theory emphasizes the idea that people strive to maintain a positive sense of self. The influence of Rogers's thinking is one of a number of factors that has contributed to a widespread interest—among both psychologists and the public at large—in self-esteem. Everybody seems to know what self-esteem is, to view self-esteem as a good thing, and to want more of it. Educators commonly try to boost self-esteem in their students. People who craft social policy often try to enhance the esteem of members of society. The idea that high self-esteem is good and low self-esteem is bad is accepted so commonly that it seems nearly impossible that the idea might be limited—if not, in many applications, wrong. Yet that is the conclusion suggested by a recent scientific review.

Baumeister, Campbell, Krueger, & Vohs (2003) recently took on a large task: systematically reviewing the extensive scientific literature relating self-esteem to valued life outcomes such as higher levels of performance, interpersonal success, and health. If you subscribe to the belief that "self-esteem is good," their review might cause you to cancel your subscription. In one area of life after another, scientific results were found to yield little evidence that self-esteem contributes to positive life outcomes.

An important aspect of this review was that the authors focused on the relation between self-esteem and objective outcomes. Merely determining whether people who report having high self-esteem also say that "their life is great!" is not too valuable scientifically for an obvious reason: People who say that they have high self-esteem may be

biased to report that their life "is great" even when things are not going well at all. The key question for the review, then, was whether self-reported self-esteem was related to important life outcomes measured through objective procedures—that is, procedures other than people's self-reports.

It is here that the scientific evidence was weak. The authors found that the existing scientific results "do not support the view that self-esteem has a strong effect on school achievement" (p. 13); "fail to confirm" the possibility that "people with high self-esteem [are]...more popular and socially skilled than others" (p. 20); and yield "no strong evidence [that]...high self-esteem leads to improved performance on the job" (p. 15). Data linking low " self-esteem to violence, aggression, and antisocial tendencies" was found to be "mixed at best" (p. 24).

Why are the links between self-esteem and positive life outcomes so weak? Baumeister and colleagues suggest that, in part, it is because high self-esteem may sometimes have negative effects. For example, people with highly inflated self-views may be narcissistic, acting in a self-centered way that alienates others (e.g., Colvin, Block, & Funder, 1995).

The authors suggest that these scientific findings have significant implications for social policy. Since the links between self-esteem and positive life outcomes often are surprisingly weak, it may make little sense for society to invest in educational programs and related initiatives that are designed merely to enhance people's views of themselves. With regard to the construct of self-esteem itself, they suggest the potential value of "splitting" the construct into "subcategories" (p. 38); the notion of self-esteem, in other words, may incorporate a number of personality processes that actually are distinct (narcissism, confidence in performance, beliefs about one's personality attributes, emotional tendencies). Some aspects of self-esteem may enhance performance even if others do not.

SOURCE: Baumeister et al., 2003.

tion (Kasser & Ryan, 1996). However, other research indicates that the same goal can be pursued for intrinsic or extrinsic reasons, suggesting that goals such as financial success and community involvement can express either motivation. On the basis of such reasoning, Carver & Baird (1998) predicted and found that endorsement of intrinsic reasons for a goal, whether financial success or community involvement, were associated with self-actualization in contrast with endorsement of extrinsic reasons for the same goals. In other words, in accord with self-determination theory, it was the motivation for the goal that was key. This is important in reminding us that we cannot assume that we know the motivation for a goal just from awareness of the content of the goal.

The second caveat is the following. It is easy to assume that these principles of motivation apply to all people. However, recent research suggests that they may be culturally specific rather than "universal" features of human psychology. In this work, Anglo-American and Asian-American children were compared in terms of their relative intrinsic motivation when choices were (a) made for them, versus (b) made by authority figures or peers. Anglo-American children showed more intrinsic motivation when they made their own choices. However, Asian-American children showed greater intrinsic motivation when their choices were made *for them* by trusted authority figures or peers (Iyengar & Lepper, 1999). Thus, the extent to which self-determination reflects a universal human need requires careful consideration and more research. More generally, the Rogerian emphasis on self-actualization may be most appropriate to understanding people who live in a Western culture in which Rogers formulated his theory.

CROSS-CULTURAL RESEARCH ON THE SELF

The research on intrinsic motivation among Asian-American and Anglo-American children that we have just reviewed raises a general question. Carl Rogers was an American psychologist. He developed his theory on the basis of clinical experiences with Americans. Most of the psychological research on self-processes conducted during Rogers's lifetime was conducted with citizens of the United States, Canada, or Western Europe. The question that arises, then, is as follows: Does Rogers's work provide us with a general view of human nature, or with a view that pertains primarily to people in the industrialized Western world? This is a deep and important question that has relevance far beyond the personality theory of Carl Rogers. All theoretical conceptions of human nature inevitably are constructed by people who live in a certain geographical location, in a certain culture, at a certain point in history. The question, then, is whether the theorist possibly can circumvent the lim-

Research suggests that people in Western and Eastern cultures differ, with Western cultures promoting the enhancement of self-esteem and Eastern cultures supporting psychological tendencies that involve a striving for self-improvement.

its of his or her circumstances to provide a theoretical framework that applies to all persons, in all cultures and all historical contexts.

In other sciences, theorists commonly do achieve this goal. The biologist who discovers the basic functioning of, for example, the immune system is safe in the assumption that the discovery applies to all people, across time and place. The difficult question is whether this sort of assumption holds with regard to the psychological systems that we call "personality." We will take up this question with respect to a particular feature of the theory of Carl Rogers, namely, his belief in a universal need for positive self-regard.

Is Positive Self-Regard a Human Universal?

As we have reviewed, Rogers believed that all people have a need for positive self-regard. To Rogers, unconditional acceptance of the individual, whatever his or her faults may be, is the pathway to psychological health. Such unconditional regard builds the individual's sense that he or she is a valued, "prized" person. In the absence of such unconditional regard, the individual's need for a positive self-view may be unfulfilled, leading to psychological distress.

But is this how things work for all persons the world over? If psychological processes regarding the self are akin to biological processes, then the answer is yes. But psychological processes involving the self may not be like this. The very notion of "self" —of one's identity, one's role in family and society, one's goals, one's purpose in life—is acquired socially. People acquire a sense of self from interaction with the individuals who make up their family, community, and wider culture. It is possible, then, that some cultures in essence *teach* people to have a need for positive regard; a culture that values the individual and individual achievements may foster the belief that individuals should enhance their own well-being. In principle, other cultures may teach people a different way of life that does not involve a striving for positive self-regard.

Compelling evidence that there are, in fact, variations from culture to culture in the nature and functioning of self-esteem are found in the study of differences between Japanese and American culture. Heine, Lehman, Markus, & Kitayama (1999) review evidence that the basic patterns and functions of self-

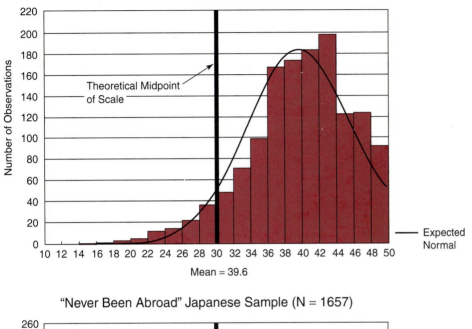

European Canadian Sample (N = 1402)

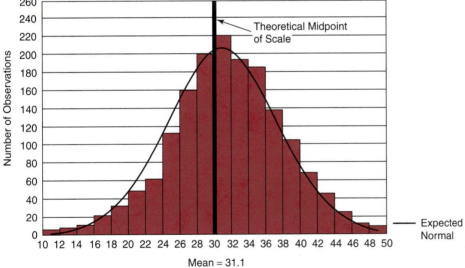

"Never Been Abroad" Japanese Sample (N = 1657)

Figure 6.2 Graphs display distributions of self-esteem scores among European Canadians and citizens of Japan. *From Heine et al., 1999.*

esteem seem to vary from one culture to another. In the United States, most people report having relatively high self-esteem; as Rogers might have predicted, people seem biased to maintain positive self-views. But in Japan there is no sign whatsoever of this bias (Figure 6.2); as many people report low self-esteem as high self-esteem. In psychological studies conducted in the U.S., people seem inevitably to engage in psychological strategies to maintain high self-esteem; for example, they compare themselves to others who are not doing well, they blame others for personal failure, and they lower the perceived importance of activities on which they cannot perform competently (reviewed in Brown, 1998). But Heine and colleagues (1999, p. 780) "are unable to find clear and consistent evidence of any self-esteem maintenance strategies within the Japanese psychological literature."

Rather than being prone to an enhancement of self-esteem, Heine and colleagues (1999; also see Kitayama & Markus, 1999; Kitayama, Markus, Matsumoto, & Norasakkunkit, 1997) contend that Japanese culture makes one prone to self-criticism. In Japan, this self-criticism serves a valuable personal and social function. It motivates people toward self-improvement that can benefit the individual and his or her society. In Japan, then, self-criticism is not "bad." It is not a sign of being depressed or "down on oneself." Instead, it is "good" —that is, it is a functional, valuable way for individuals to mesh with their surrounding culture. Consistent with this view, tendencies toward self-criticism and the experience of discrepancies between the actual and ideal self are predictive of depression in North America, but are less strongly related to depression in Japan (Heine et al., 1999).

In summary, it appears that the cultures of the U.S. and of Japan teach people different ways of evaluating the self. If you, the reader, are a citizen of North America, then you may be particularly prone to engage in psychological strategies that maintain a positive view of self. If your professor gives you a bad grade on a paper, you may conclude that there is something wrong with the professor. If a romantic partner dumps you, you may conclude that the relationship wasn't all that important anyway. If you didn't get into the college of your choice, you may conclude that it was because you didn't take your application seriously enough. These conclusions are functional in the cultural system of the United States; they enable you to maintain a high sense of self-esteem in a culture that values high self-esteem. But if you are a citizen of Japan, you may be much more likely to draw other conclusions that are more self-critical; in so doing, you would be fitting in with a culture that values continual personal improvement. These variations in the nature and functioning of self-evaluation and self-esteem are understandable in light of contemporary research on culture and personality; however, these variations were not well anticipated by Carl Rogers when he formulated his theory of personality and self.

Regional Variations in Well-Being

Recent research suggests that the psychological dynamics of interest to Carl Rogers not only vary from one culture to another (e.g., American versus Japanese culture, as reviewed above). The research indicates that they also vary within-culture from one region to another. Evidence comes from research conducted within the United States. Plaut, Markus, & Lachman (2002) analyzed data from a national survey of psychological well-being of Americans at midlife (the average participant was in his or her mid-40s). Plaut and associates reasoned that different geographic regions within the U.S. have societal patterns that are distinct enough, and relevant enough to psychological well-being, that they may produce different patterns of psychological experience. For example, the Rocky Mountain regions of the American West are typified by a particularly strong spirit of rugged individualism and of potentialities for growth—a spirit prevalent since the time that rugged, individualistic pioneers first moved into the area. In contrast, regions of the southeast-

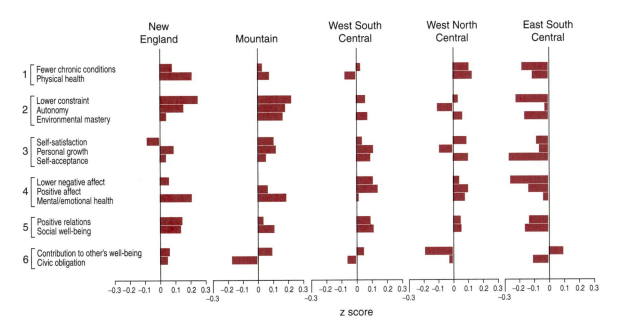

Figure 6.3 Figure displays reports of psychological well-being among research participants living in different regions of the United Stated. *From Plaut et al., 2002.*

ern United States (the "Deep South") are typified by Southern grace and hospitality and a respect for the traditions of the past; the Plaut group (2002, p. 173) quote William Faulkner as writing that "the past is alive in the South, in fact, it's not even past." Such sociocultural conditions, which look back to the past rather than ahead to the future, would not be expected to foster strong feelings of personal growth; combined with the fact that the most salient feature of the region's past is the South's defeat in the Civil War, these conditions might also foster a lower sense of self-acceptance.

As anticipated, these different social settings were associated with different patterns of psychological well-being (Figure 6.3). Americans in the southeastern U.S. reported experiencing relatively low levels of personal growth and self-acceptance as compared to Americans in other regions. Americans in the Mountain region, as well as those in the New England states (which are known for an individualism that dates back to the time of Puritan settlers) reported high levels of autonomy and a sense of personal growth.

To some degree, these results are consistent with the basic outlines of Rogerian theory. Patterns of social interaction predicted self-reported patterns of well-being, as Rogers would have expected. On the other hand, the analyses of Plaut and colleagues (2002) highlight the influence of broad sociocultural factors that received lesser attention from Rogers.

THE HUMAN POTENTIAL MOVEMENT

RELATED POINTS OF VIEW

It was noted in the previous chapter that the tone and spirit of the Rogerian position are apparent in other theories of personality, particularly in the emphasis on the continuous striving of the organism to realize its inherent

Kurt Goldstein

potential. Together with similar emphases by others, Rogers's position is part of the human potential movement that has been called the "third force" in psychology (e.g., Goble, 1970), offering an alternative to psychoanalysis and to behaviorism. Although there are theoretical differences among them, many humanist theories of personality are joined in the **human potential movement**. These theories respond to current concerns (e.g., anxiety, boredom, and lack of meaning) with an emphasis on self-actualization, fulfillment of potential, and openness to experience. Two major figures in this tradition are Kurt Goldstein and Abraham H. Maslow.

Kurt Goldstein (1878–1965)

Kurt Goldstein came to the United States in 1935, at age 57, after achieving considerable status as a neurologist and psychiatrist in Germany. During World War I he had extensive experience working with brain-injured soldiers, and this work formed the foundation for his later views. He was impressed with the separation of functions that often occurs in brain-injured patients in contrast with the smooth, coordinated brain functioning of normal individuals. What he observed as differences in brain functioning and disturbances due to brain injury he extended to other aspects of personality functioning. Thus, for example, a healthy person is characterized by flexible functioning, whereas a disturbed person is characterized by rigid functioning. A healthy person is characterized by planned and organized functioning, whereas a disturbed person is characterized by mechanical functioning. A healthy person can delay and anticipate the future, whereas a disturbed person is bound by the past and the immediacy of the present. Yet, at the same time, Goldstein was impressed with the tremendous adaptive powers of his brain-injured patients, the same powers he felt were basic to all human functioning.

Like Freud, Goldstein (1939) had an energy view of the organism. However, his views concerning the movement and direction of energy flow differed considerably from that of Freud: "Freud fails to do justice to the positive aspect of life. He fails to recognize that the basic phenomenon of life is an incessant process of coming to terms with the environment; he only sees escape and craving for release. He only knows the lust of release, not the pleasure of tension" (1939, p. 333). Rather than seeking tension reduction, Goldstein feels the main motive for people is self-actualization. All aspects of human functioning are basically expressions of this one motive—to actualize the self. It can be expressed in such simple ways as eating or in such lofty ways as our highest creative productions, but in the final analysis it is this motive that guides our behavior. Each person has inner potentials that are there to be fulfilled in the growth process. It is the recognition of this that ties Goldstein to others in the human potential movement.

Goldstein's work with brain-injured patients was important for workers in that area. In addition, his views on the general nature of human functioning have had a significant influence on humanist thinkers in the field of psychology.

Abraham H. Maslow (1908–1970)

Abraham Maslow (1968, 1971) was a major theorist in the human potential movement. He described this psychology as the "third force" in American psychology, contrasting it with the other forces—psychoanalysis and behavior-

Abraham H. Maslow

ism—which provided more pessimistic conceptions of human nature. Maslow proposed that people are basically good or neutral rather than evil, that there is in everyone an impulse toward growth or the fulfillment of potentials, and that psychopathology is the result of twisting and frustration of the essential nature of the human organism. Society often causes such twisting and frustration, and there is a problem when we assume that the result of this twisting and frustration is the essential nature of the organism. Rather, we should recognize what could occur were these obstacles to be removed. Here we see one of the reasons for the popularity of the human potential movement among those who feel excessively restricted and inhibited by their environment. Maslow speaks to these concerns and encourages the belief that things can be better if people are free to express themselves and be themselves.

In addition to this overall spirit, Maslow's views have been important in two ways. First, he suggested a view of human motivation that distinguishes between such biological needs as hunger, sleep, and thirst and such psychological needs as self-esteem, affection, and belonging. One cannot survive as a biological organism without food and water; likewise, one cannot develop fully as a psychological organism without the satisfaction of other needs as well. Thus, these needs can be arranged in a hierarchy from basic physiological needs to important psychological needs (Figure 6.4). Maslow suggested that, in their research and theorizing, psychologists have been overly concerned with basic biological needs, especially the organism's response to tension caused by biological deficits. While accepting that such motivation exists, Maslow highlighted higher-level motivational processes of the sort that are expressed when people are creative and are fulfilling their potential.

A second major contribution by Maslow (1954) was his intensive study of healthy, self-fulfilling, self-actualizing individuals. These were figures from the past as well as some who were living at the time. From this research Maslow concluded that self-actualizing people have the following characteristics: they accept themselves and others for what they are; they can be concerned with themselves but also are free to recognize the needs and desires of others; they are capable of responding to the uniqueness of people and situations rather

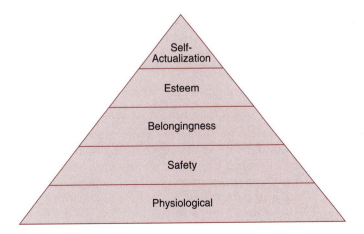

Figure 6.4   Illustrative Questionnaire Items Measuring Maslow's Hierachy of Needs *(arranged from low to high in the hierarchy). (Lester et al., 1983)*

than responding in mechanical or stereotyped ways; they can form intimate relationships with at least a few special people; they can be spontaneous and creative; and they can resist conformity and assert themselves while responding to the demands of reality. Who are such people? Illustrative figures are Lincoln, Thoreau, Einstein, and Eleanor Roosevelt. Clearly these are very special individuals, and few people have all or even most of these characteristics to any substantial degree. What is suggested, however, is that all of us have the potential to move increasingly in the direction of these qualities. In this focus on the positive aspects of life and human potentials, Maslow's work anticipated a "positive psychology" or "human strengths" movement that has developed in recent years in the field (Aspinwall & Staudinger, 2002).

At times, the views of Maslow and other leaders of the human potential movement sound almost religious and messianic. At the same time, they speak to the concerns of many people and serve as a corrective influence on other views that represent the human organism as passive, fragmented, and completely governed by tension-reducing motives from within or rewards from the environment. More recently the spirit of the human potential movement has been captured by Csikszentmihalyi in his concept of optimal experience or flow. The flow concept relates to positive states of consciousness which have the following characteristics: a perceived match between personal skills and environmental challenge; a high level of focused attention; involvement in an activity such that time seems to fly by and irrelevant thoughts and distractions do not enter into consciousness; a sense of intrinsic enjoyment in the activity; a temporary loss of self-consciousness such that the self is not aware of functioning or regulating activity. The flow experience can take place in activities as diverse as work, hobbies, sports, dancing, and social interactions. It is expressed in statements such as " When I am involved, everything just seems to come to me. I just float along, feeling both excited and calm, and want it to continue endlessly. It's not possible rewards that count but just the pleasure in the activity itself." Csikszentmihalyi's interest in the positive aspects of human functioning began with his observation during World War II that, although many people lost their decency, others expressed the best of what people can be. Subsequently he was influenced by the work of Carl Rogers and Abraham Maslow, leading to an emphasis on the study of strength and virtue as opposed to weakness and pathology. Today his work is part of a growing emphasis in the field on positive subjective experience and healthy, adaptive functioning (Seligman & Csikszentmihalyi, 2000).

EXISTENTIALISM

The approach known as existentialism is well-established in the intellectual world, yet it does not have a particularly secure place in mainstream academic psychology. Existentialism has its roots in the writings of the 19th-century Danish philosopher Søren Kierkegaard. In contrast to prior philosophical systems that emphasized human rationality and the importance of broad, abstract social and cultural systems, Kierkegaard provided a philosophy that highlighted the importance of the individual—his or her emotions, passions, and capacity of free will. These qualities of human existence were so central to Kierkegaard that his work was seen as a philosophy of existence, or an **existentialism** (Solomon & Higgins, 1996). In the 20th century, existentialism was advanced most prominently by the French philosopher Jean-Paul Sartre, who emphasized the human capacity and responsibility to imagine alternative possibilities for oneself and thus to overcome whatever constraints in life that one may face.

In general, there are two defining elements to existentialist views. One is a concern with existence—the person in the human condition. The existentialist is concerned with phenomena that are inherent in the nature of being alive, human, and existing. What constitutes the essence of existence varies for different existentialists; however, all agree that certain concerns are fundamental to the very nature of our being and cannot be ignored, dismissed, explained away, or trivialized. Perhaps most of all, for the existentialist, people and experience are to be taken seriously (Pervin, 1960b). The second defining existentialist view is a focus on the significance of the individual. The existentialist sees the person as singular, unique, and irreplaceable. For Kierkegaard, the only existential problem is to exist as an individual. A number of additional emphases are related to this valuing of the individual. First, there is an emphasis on freedom. In the existentialist view freedom, consciousness, and self-reflection are what distinguish humans from other animals. Second, freedom involves responsibility. Each person is responsible for choices, for action, for being authentic, or for acting in "bad faith." Ultimately, each person is responsible for his or her own existence. Third, there is the existential concern with death, for it is here as nowhere else that the individual is alone and completely irreplaceable. Finally, there is an emphasis on phenomenology and an understanding of the unique experience of each person. Events are looked at in terms of their meaning for the individual rather than in terms of some standardized definition or the confirmation of some hypothesis. Thus, there is an interest in how any intrinsically human phenomenon can be experienced and given meaning—time, space, life, death, the self, or whatever.

We can perhaps better appreciate this approach by considering a few illustrations. For one, we can consider Rogers's (1980) discussion of loneliness. What is it that constitutes the existential experience of loneliness? Rogers suggested a number of contributing factors: the impersonality of our culture, its transient quality and anomie, the fear of a close relationship. However, what most defines loneliness is the effort to share something very personal with someone and to find that it is not received or is rejected: "A person is most lonely when he has dropped something of his outer shell or façade—the face with which he has been meeting the world—and feels sure that no one can understand, accept, or care for the part of his inner self that lies revealed" (quoted in Kirschenbaum, 1979, p. 351). On the other hand, there may also be the feeling of being understood (Van Kaam, 1966). Here the person has the sense that another individual can empathize in an understanding, accepting way. The feeling of being understood is associated with safety and relief from existential loneliness.

Another illustration involves the search for meaning in human existence (Frankl, 1955, 1958). The existential psychiatrist Viktor Frankl struggled to find meaning while in a concentration camp during World War II. He suggests that the will to meaning is the most human phenomenon of all, since other animals never worry about the meaning of their existence. Existential frustration and existential neurosis involve frustration and lack of fulfillment of the will to meaning. Such a "neurosis" does not involve the instincts or biological drives but rather is spiritually rooted in the person's escape from freedom and responsibility. In such cases the person blames destiny, childhood, the environment, or fate for what is. The treatment for such a condition, logotherapy, involves helping patients to become what they are capable of being, helping them to realize and accept the challenges of the opportunities that are open to them.

These are brief vignettes of representative existential concerns. Can they help us understand why existentialism is such a powerful force among some and so dismissed by others? For many people, existentialism speaks in a profound, humane way to issues that are of concern to them. On the other hand, other psychologists are critical of existentialism. In particular, there is criticism of an approach that abandons hope of predicting behavior in a lawful way and that has yet to establish its use as a therapy.

CRITICAL EVALUATION

We conclude our coverage of Rogers's theory by evaluating it critically. Such an evaluation includes questions such as: To what extent does Rogers's view of the person omit or underestimate some critical causes of behavior? Might his emphasis on conscious, phenomenal experiences have some drawbacks? To what extent does Rogers's theory, including his views of anxiety and defense, represent a departure from Freud?

PHENOMENOLOGY

The phenomenological approach represents psychologists' effort to come to terms with human experience as it occurs. The approach addresses life as it is experienced by the person, without splintering this experience into parts or reducing it to physiological principles that fail to relate to the human experience. What are the limits to such an approach?

One key limit is that it may exclude from investigation critical variables that are outside of human conscious experience. If we restrict ourselves to that which people report, we may ignore important aspects of human functioning. A complete science of psychology must include, yet must go beyond the phenomenal world to develop concepts that are related to objective measures and that include aspects of thought and emotional life of which people may be unaware. The study of the phenomenal self is a legitimate part of psychology as long as it is studied empirically, with a boundless curiosity that is tempered by discipline and not with carefree speculation. Empathy is a legitimate mode of observation, but we must make sure that the observations made are reliable and that they can be checked against data from other modes of observation. Rogers was aware of these challenges to the phenomenological approach. His response was that the phenomenological approach is a valuable, perhaps necessary, one for psychology, but not the only one to be used (Rogers, 1964).

To turn to our second question, to what extent is the theory based on unbiased phenomenological investigation? The question was well put by MacLeod (1964, p. 138) in response to a presentation by Rogers: "On what basis are you so convinced that you have understood your client better than Mr. Freud has understood his patient?" Rogers's response was that the client-centered therapist brings fewer biases and preconceptions to therapy because of a lighter "baggage of preconceptions." The client-centered therapist is more likely to arrive at an understanding of the phenomenal world of an individual than is the Freudian analyst. In an early paper, Rogers (1947) stated that if one read the transcripts of a client-centered therapist, one would find it impossible to form an estimate of the therapist's views about personality dynamics. But we do not know that this is actually the case. Furthermore, that statement was made at a time when the theory was not well developed and therapists were being nondirective. With the development of the theory and the increased emphasis on client-centered but active involvement by the therapist, is this still true? We know that minor behaviors of the interviewer, including expressions such as "m-hm," may exert a profound effect on the verbalizations and behavior of the person being interviewed (Greenspoon, 1962). As one reads the transcripts of the therapy sessions, the comments of the counselor do not appear to be random or inconsequential as far as content is concerned. Counselors appear to be particularly responsive about the self and about feelings, and appear to formulate some of their statements in theory-related terms:

THERAPIST OF MRS.OAK: I'd like to see if I can capture a little of what that means to you. It is as if you've gotten very deeply acquainted with yourself on a kind of a brick-to-brick experiencing basis, and in that sense you have become more self-ish...in the discovering of what is the core of you as separate from all the other aspects, you come across the realization, which is a very deep and pretty thrilling realization, that the core of the self is not only without hate but is really something more resembling a saint, something really very pure, is the word I would use.

SOURCE: Rogers, 1954, p. 239

This point (of influence of the interviewer on the client) is critical, since so much of Rogers's data comes from clinical interviews.

In summary, the phenomenological approach has distinct merits and potential dangers. Rogers recognized that it is not the only approach to psychology and that it must be associated with empirical investigation. However, he did not consider adequately the role of unconscious forces in behavior. Furthermore, we are still unclear about the extent to which the behavior of the client in client-centered therapy is, in fact, free of the biases and preconceptions of the counselor

THE CONCEPT OF SELF

In evaluating Rogers' conception of the self, a number of considerations are important. Rogers assumed that the self was rather constant across time and situations; that is, the way people view themselves at one point in time and in one situation is related to their views of themselves at other points in time and in other situations. Furthermore, the Rogerian concept of self assumes a total whole instead of a composite of unrelated parts.

Is there evidence to support these assumptions? Research supports the view that the self-concept is fairly stable across situations and over time

(Coopersmith, 1967; Robins, Norem, & Cheek, 1999). Donahue, Robins, Roberts, and John's (1993) findings (see the box on Current Questions in Chapter 5, pp. 176–177) support Rogers's views; having a self-concept that is consistent rather than variable across social roles is associated with good psychological adjustment. Similarly, high self-esteem has been related to both the temporal stability and internal consistency of the self-concept (Campbell & Lavallee, 1993). Other studies suggest, however, that individuals may have multifaceted views of self (Markus & Nurius, 1986). Does this multifaceted perspective on the self contradict Rogers's conception of a unified core self? Not necessarily. Rogers's conception emphasized coherence, not simplicity; having a self with the multiple components that are integrated with one another is consistent with Rogers's view of the self.

Finally, as reviewed here, the basic structure of the self, as well as the extent of the need for positive regard, may vary from culture to culture (Heine et al., 1999). For example, one of the distinctive differences between Eastern and Western cultures is the degree to which the self is viewed as connected to others (Markus & Cross, 1990). In Eastern cultures, the self-concept consists of connection with others, and individuals are parts that cannot be understood when separated from the greater, collective whole. This cultural understanding of self stands in contrast to the dominant view of the self in Western civilization, which views the self as unique and separate from others. The question, then, is whether Rogers's notions of the self, ideal self, self-consistency and self-actualization are applicable outside the Western cultures with which he was most familiar, and within which he developed his theory.

In accepting the concept of the self as important for us as personality psychologists, we must be concerned with assessment hazards. One problem with many of the tests used to assess the self is that the items are not relevant to certain populations or miss important aspects of particular individuals. Our concepts of self are so varied that it is hard to develop a standard test that will tap the uniqueness of each individual. A second problem concerns the extent to which subjects are willing to give, or are capable of giving, honest self-reports. There is considerable evidence that self-reports can be influenced by conscious efforts to present oneself in socially desirable ways as well as by unconscious defensive processes (John & Robins, 1994a; Paulhus, 1990). It is assessment problems such as these that have frustrated so many investigators and left so many questions unanswered (Wylie, 1974). An interesting contemporary development is that researchers are attempting to develop "implicit" measures of self-concept; rather than relying on people's explicit, conscious self-reports about themselves, these implicit techniques involve subtle, indirect measures, such as measures of the speed with which people respond to certain words or ideas related to the self-concept (Asendorpf, Banse, & Mücke, 2002; Greenwald et al., 2002). In principle, these implicit measures may circumvent reluctance people may experience in explicitly describing features of their personality.

CONFLICT, ANXIETY, AND DEFENSE

As we have seen, Rogers provided a view of anxiety and defense that in some ways was similar to Freud's. Both recognized that people may psychologically defend against threatening events, and that such defensive processes may signal, and contribute to, anxiety and other forms of psychological distress. Their theories differed in what they said about the underlying causes of these psychological processes. Freud emphasized unconscious instincts, drive reduction, and the influence of early childhood development. Rogers stressed here-and-now experiences and their perceptual inconsistency with the self-concept. The ultimate goal for Freud was the proper channeling of the drives. The ultimate goal for Rogers was a state of congruence between organism and self. Rogers's analyses are fairly clear until he attempts to account for the development of a rift between organismic experience and self. Here, as you have seen, he introduces the concept of the need for positive regard. People may falsify their values and experiences to gain the positive regard of others (Rogers, 1959). This statement complicates Rogers's overall position. People seem fundamentally motivated to avoid the pain associated with loss of love from others. This is not an unreasonable view of humans. But, in terms of Rogers's theorizing, it is hard to reconcile this position—that people are fundamentally motivated to avoid the pain of loss of love—with another of Rogers's contentions, namely, that people are fundamentally motivated to attain self-actualization. Self-actualization is clearly a different type of motive than pain avoidance. It also is hard to put together these two motives with yet another one discussed by Rogers: the motive to maintain congruence between self and experience. In discussing anxiety, defense, and human motivation, Rogers did insightfully identify fundamentally human tendencies. Yet he did not create a theoretical structure in which the different parts coherently fit together. His thinking lacks the overall theoretical coherence and elegance of Freud's. This reflects the fact that Rogers developed more of his professional efforts to therapy processes than to theory construction.

SUMMARY EVALUATION

How, then, may Rogers's theory be evaluated? Is it comprehensive, parsimonious, and relevant to research? The theory would appear to be reasonably comprehensive, though many areas of neglect remain. The theory says relatively little about the course of growth and development or about the specific factors that determine one or another pattern. In contrast with Freud, one finds strikingly little mention of sex and aggression or of feelings such as guilt and depression, yet much of our lives seem to be concerned with these feelings. The theory appears to be economical, particularly in relation to the process of change. Out of all the complexities of psychotherapy, Rogers attempted to define the few necessary and sufficient conditions for positive personality change.

In terms of research relevance, much of the theory expresses a philosophical, perhaps religious, view of the person. Assumptions most related to this view, such as the drive toward actualization, have remained assumptions and, until recently, have not provided the basis for research. Also, the system is still without a measure of self-experience congruence. However, it is clear that the theory has provided extremely fertile ground for research. Rogers always kept clinical work, theory, and research in close touch with one another. Most of his work reflected a reluctance to sacrifice the rigors of science for the intuitive aspects of clinical work, and all of his work reflected an unwillingness to sacrifice the rich complexities of behavior for the empirical demands of science. As is properly the case, the development of his system was the result of a con-

ROGERS AT A GLANCE

Structure	Process	Growth and Development
Self; ideal self	Self-actualization; congruence of self and experience; incongruence and defensive distortion and denial	Congruence and self-actualization versus incongruence and defensiveness

stant interplay among gross observations, theoretical formulations, and systematic research efforts.

This chapter on Rogers concludes by stating four major contributions (Table 6.1). Going beyond the discipline of psychology, Rogers developed a point of view and an approach toward counseling that have influenced teachers, members of the clergy, and people in business. Within psychology, Rogers opened up the area of psychotherapy for research. By recording interviews, by making interviews and transcripts available to others, by developing clinically relevant measures of personality, and by demonstrating the potential value of research in the area, Rogers led the way in the legitimization of research on psychotherapy.

Finally, more than any other personality theorist, Rogers focused both theoretical and empirical attention on the nature of the self. The study of the self has always been a part of psychology, but it has, at times, been in danger of being dismissed as "mere philosophy." As MacLeod (1964) notes, you may not find many papers on the self at meetings of experimental psychologists, but clinicians find the problem staring them in the face. More than any other personality theorist, Rogers attempted to be objective about what is otherwise left to the artists:

> Slowly the thinker went on his way and asked himself: What is it that you wanted to learn from teachings and teachers, and although they taught you much, what was it they could not teach you? And he thought: It was the Self, the character and nature of which I wished to learn. I wanted to rid myself of the Self, to conquer it, but I could not

Table 6.1   Summary of Strengths and Limitations of Rogers's Theory and Phenomenology

Strengths	Limitations
1. Focuses on important aspects of human existence.	1. May exclude certain phenomena (unconscious processes, defenses, etc.) from research and clinical concern.
2. Attempts to recognize the holistic, integrated aspects of personality.	2. Lacks objective measures of behavior beyond self-report.
3. Tries to integrate humanism and empiricism.	3. Ignores the impossibility of being totally phenomenological—that is, making observations that are totally free of bias and preconception.
4. Aims at systematic inquiry into the necessary and sufficient conditions for therapeutic change.	

Pathology	Change	Illustrative Case
Defensive maintenance of self; incongruence	Therapeutic atmosphere: congruence, unconditional positive regard, empathic understanding	Mrs. Oak

conquer it, I could only deceive it, could only fly from it, could only hide from it. Truly, nothing in the world has occupied my thoughts as much as the Self, this riddle, that I live, that I am one and am separate and different from everybody else, that I am Siddhartha; and about nothing in the world do I know less than about myself, about Siddhartha.

Source: Hesse, 1951, p. 40.

MAJOR CONCEPTS

Authenticity The extent to which the person behaves in accord with their self as opposed to behaving in terms of roles that foster false self-presentations.

Congruence Rogers's concept expressing an absence of conflict between the perceived self and experience. Also one of three therapist conditions suggested as essential for growth and therapeutic progress.

Contingencies of self-worth The positive and negative events on which one's feelings of self-esteem depend.

Client-centered therapy Rogers's term for his earlier approach to therapy in which the counselor's attitude is one of interest in the ways in which the client experiences the self and the world.

Empathic understanding Rogers's term for the ability to perceive experiences and feelings and their meanings from the standpoint of another person. One of three therapist conditions essential for therapeutic progress.

Existentialism An approach to understanding people and conducting therapy, associated with the human potential movement, that emphasizes phenomenology and concerns inherent in existing as a person. Derived from a more general movement in philosophy.

Human potential movement A group of psychologists, represented by Rogers and Maslow, who emphasize the actualization or fulfillment of individual potential, including an openness to experience.

Self-experience discrepancy Rogers's emphasis on the potential for conflict between the concept of self and experience—the basis for psychopathology.

Unconditional positive regard Rogers's term for the acceptance of a person in a total, unconditional way. One of three therapist conditions suggested as essential for growth and therapeutic progress.

REVIEW

1. For Rogers, the neurotic person is one who is in a state of incongruence between self and experience. Experiences that are incongruent with the self-structure are subceived as threatening and may be either denied or distorted.

2. Research in the area of psychopathology has focused on the discrepancy between the self and ideal self, and the extent to which individuals disown or are vague about their feelings.

3. Rogers's focus was on the therapeutic process. The critical variable in therapy was seen as the therapeutic climate. Conditions of congruence (genuineness), unconditional positive regard, and empathic understanding were seen as essential to therapeutic change.

4. The case of Mrs. Oak, an early case published by Rogers, illustrates his publication of recorded therapy sessions for research purposes.

5. Rogers's views are part of the human potential movement, which emphasizes self-actualization and the fulfillment of each individual's potential. Kurt Goldstein, Abraham H. Maslow, and existentialists like Viktor Frankl are also representatives of this movement.

6. Although there are major differences in the theoretical formulations of Freud and Rogers, in both of their formulations the concepts of conflict, anxiety, and defense played a major role in the dynamics of behavior.

7. Rogers made an important contribution in focusing attention on the self as an important area for psychological investigation and in opening up the area of psychotherapy for research. His work focused on important aspects of human experience, emphasized the positive strivings of people, and suggested that basic conditions are necessary for therapeutic change. At the same time, questions can be raised about the phenomenological approach as a method of research and about the lack of adequate measures for concepts such as the self-actualization motive.

Every child should be treated w/ respect + disciplined (teach w/ love + respect)

2 Personality type

1) Fully functioning - Rogerian

2) ※ mal-adjusted - reared w/ conditional positive regard - developed conditions of worth, have defenses + incongruent between yourself + self-concept has

has rec'd u/c positive regard, no defensiveness, no conditions of worth, have self-concept

→ Have these features:
1) openness to experience - try new things, be receptive; eager, curious, excited

2) Existential living - living in the moment, flexibles, spontaneous

3) Organismic trusting - intuition, know's what's best for them

4) Experiential freedom - subjective sense of free will can make up your own mind

5) creativity - ability to produce new, exciting, effective ideas

7

TRAIT APPROACHES TO PERSONALITY: ALLPORT, EYSENCK, AND CATTELL

[handwritten notes:] 2)* Conformity" feel Manipulated defenses live according to a pre-conceived plan — restrictive not very creative

THE TRAIT CONCEPT
  What Is a Trait?
  Basic Views Shared by Trait Theorists
THE TRAIT THEORY OF
GORDON W. ALLPORT (1897–1967)
  Traits and Distinctions among Kinds of Traits
  Functional Autonomy
  Idiographic Research
  Comment on Allport
THE THREE-FACTOR THEORY OF
HANS J. EYSENCK (1916–1997)
  Trait Measurement: Factor Analysis
    Factor Analysis and Identifying the Structure of Individual Differences
  Basic Dimensions of Personality
    Questionnaire Measures
    Research Findings

Biological Bases of Personality Traits in Eysenckian Theory
  Psychopathology and Behavior Change
  Comment on Eysenck
THE FACTOR-ANALYTIC TRAIT APPROACH OF RAYMOND B. CATTELL (1905–1998)
  Cattell's View of Personality Science
    Kinds of Traits
    Sources of Data: L-Data, Q-Data, OT-Data
  Stability and Variability in Behavior
  Comment on Cattell
TRAIT THEORY: ALLPORT, EYSENCK, AND CATTELL
MAJOR CONCEPTS
REVIEW

Chapter Focus

Chris has just graduated from college and started a job in a new city. He feels lonely and wants to meet some new people. After some hesitation, he decides to place a personals ad. He stares at his blank computer screen—what should he write? What kinds of personality characteristics would you choose to describe yourself? He chooses "Unconventional, sensitive, fun-loving, happy, humorous, kind, slender graduate, 22, seeks similar qualities in sane soulmate." Somebody who can be described this way may indeed be a desirable date!

The personality characteristics that Chris has described are what are known as personality *traits*. Personality traits are psychological characteristics that are stable over time and across situations; it's a good bet that somebody who is sensitive and kind today will also be sensitive and kind a month from now. This chapter is about traits, defined as broad dispositions to behave in particular ways.

Specifically, in this chapter you will learn about three personality trait theories and their associated research programs. Two of these theories—those of Hans Eysenck and of Raymond Cattell—attempt to identify the basic *dimensions* of personality traits, that is, basic characteristics that everyone shares to a greater or lesser degree. The two associated research programs rely on a particular statistical procedure, *factor analysis*; this statistical procedure is used to identify the most basic individual differences in personality traits.

Historically, the trait approach has been popular in American and British psychology and, in the field's recent era, in personality psychology in Europe as well. Part of this popularity reflects the methodological sophistication of factor-analytic research methods and the relatively consistent research results that they yield. Part of this popularity also is rooted in the common-sense nature of trait theory; the scientific theories of personality traits have an intuitive appeal because their basic units of analysis, personality traits, are similar to simple nonscientific, "folk" understandings of personality.

QUESTIONS TO BE ADDRESSED IN THIS CHAPTER

1. How can we characterize the consistent ways in which individuals differ in their feelings, thoughts, and behavior? How many different traits are needed to adequately describe these personality differences?

2. To what extent do individual differences have a genetic, inherited basis?

3. If individuals can be described in terms of their characteristic traits, how are we to explain variability in behavior across time and situations?

In the preceding chapters, we emphasized one major representative of each theoretical point of view. In this chapter on trait theory, we consider the views of a number of theorists. In the earlier chapters it was easy to pinpoint a major figure to represent that school of thought. This is not nearly as easy with trait theory.

People love to talk about personality. We can spend hours discussing people's char- **THE TRAIT CONCEPT**
acteristics: our boss is grumpy; our roommate, sloppy; our professor, quick-wit-
ted. (Well, we hope your professor is quick-witted rather than sloppy and grumpy.)
We even discuss the loyalty of our dog and laziness of our cat. When talking about
people we commonly use personality **trait** terms—words that describe people's
typical styles of experience and action. For example, when asked to write a personality description of a friend, many students produce a list of personality trait
descriptors such as friendly, kind, happy, lazy, moody, and shy (John, 1990).
Apparently, people think that traits are central to personality. Likewise, personality researchers associated with the trait approach consider traits as the major units
of personality. Obviously there is more to personality than traits, but traits have
clearly loomed large throughout the history of personality psychology.

WHAT IS A TRAIT?

Broadly speaking, personality traits refer to consistent patterns in the way
individuals behave, feel, and think. When we describe an individual with the
trait term "kind," we mean that this individual tends to act kindly over time
(both last week and this week) and across situations (both with the elderly
neighbor and with the lame dog). This broad definition implies that traits may
serve three major functions: They may be used to summarize, to predict, and
to explain a person's conduct. Thus, one of the reasons for the popularity of
trait concepts is that they provide an economical way to summarize how one
person differs from another; attributing the trait "kind" to a person summarizes a history of many different acts of kindness. Traits have the promise that
they allow us to make predictions about the person's future behavior; the bride
expects the kind bridegroom to become a kind husband. Finally, traits suggest
that the explanation for the person's behavior will be found in the individual
rather than in the situation; a kind person will act kindly even when there is
no situational pressure or external reward for doing so, thus suggesting some
kind of internal process or mechanism that is producing the behavior.

This broad characterization captures how traits generally are conceptualized in the scientific literature. However, in its generality it glosses over some
difficult issues on which trait theorists differ. In other words, although trait theorists are part of a family of theorists who share certain views, there also are
differences among members of the family. Beyond the definition given above,
it is difficult, if not impossible, to generate one generally accepted definition of
the trait concept: "Traits are many things to many theorists" (Wiggins, 1997, p.
98). The exact nature and function, strengths and limits of trait concepts have
long been, and continue to be, a subject of debate (Pervin, 1994a).

BASIC VIEWS SHARED BY TRAIT THEORISTS

Although trait theories differ from one another in important respects, they
nonetheless share some fundamental assumptions. As you begin your study of
the trait approach, it is important to understand these shared assumptions,
which together define the trait approach.

The most basic assumption of the trait point of view is that people possess
broad predispositions, called traits, to respond in particular ways. In other

words, it is assumed that personality can be useful characterized in terms of an individual's consistent likelihood of behaving, feeling, or thinking in a particular way (e.g., their likelihood of acting in an outgoing and friendly manner, or of feeling nervous and worried, or of being reliable and conscientious). People who have a strong tendency to behave in these ways are described as being high on these traits, whereas people with a lesser tendency to behave in these ways are described as low on the traits. The person who frequently is outgoing would be called "high on extraversion," whereas the unreliable, forgetful individual might be "low on conscientiousness." All trait theorists agree that these generalized tendencies to act in one versus another manner are the fundamental building blocks of personality.

A related assumption is that there is a direct correspondence between the person's performance of trait-related actions and their possession of the corresponding trait. People who act (or report that they act) in a more extraverted or conscientious manner than others are thought, by the trait theorist, to possess more of (to be "higher on") the corresponding traits of extraversion and conscientiousness. This point may seem so obvious that it isn't even worth stating. You may be thinking that "of course people who display more of the trait-related behavior have more of the trait." But note how this thinking contrasts with an earlier theory we covered, namely, psychoanalysis. To the psychoanalyst, someone who reports being more "calm and at ease" than other people may not, in reality, possess more of the psychological characteristic of "calmness." Instead, the person may be so anxious that they are repressing their anxieties and merely saying that they are calm. Psychoanalysis, as well as other personality theories we will cover later in the text, recognize that there may be highly indirect relations between overt behavior and underlying personality characteristics. In contrast, the research procedures of trait theory assume that overt behavior and underlying traits are linked in a more direct, one-to-one manner. If someone reports a low amount of trait-related behavior on a test of personality traits, then they are said to possess low amounts of the given trait.

Another shared assumption is that human behavior and personality can be organized into a hierarchy. An illustration of this hierarchical point of view comes from the work of Eysenck (Figure 7.1). Eysenck suggests that, at its simplest level, behavior can be considered in terms of specific responses. However, some of these responses are linked together and form more general habits. Again, we generally find that groups of habits tend to occur together to form traits. For example, people who prefer meeting people to reading also generally enjoy themselves at a lively party, suggesting that these two habits can be grouped together under the trait of sociability. To take another example, people who act without thinking first also tend to shout back at others, suggesting that these two habits can be grouped together under the trait of impulsiveness. At an even higher level of organization, various traits may be linked together to form what Eysenck has called secondary, higher-order factors or superfactors. How we find such traits and determine the hierarchical organization of personality will be discussed shortly. What is important to recognize here is the conceptualization of personality as organized at various levels.

In sum, trait theories suggest that people display broad predispositions to respond in certain ways; that these dispositions are organized in a hierarchical manner; and that the trait concept can be a foundation for a scientific theory of personality.

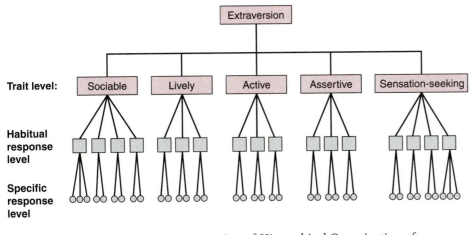

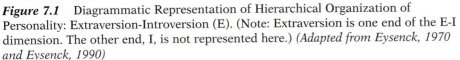

Figure 7.1 Diagrammatic Representation of Hierarchical Organization of Personality: Extraversion-Introversion (E). (Note: Extraversion is one end of the E-I dimension. The other end, I, is not represented here.) *(Adapted from Eysenck, 1970 and Eysenck, 1990)*

THE TRAIT THEORY OF GORDON W. ALLPORT (1897–1967)

A figure of great historical importance to the development of trait theory, and of personality psychology in general, was the Harvard University psychologist Gordon W. Allport. History remembers Allport as much for the issues he raised and the principles he emphasized than for a particular theory he created. Throughout his long and influential career, Allport highlighted the healthy and organized aspects of human behavior. This emphasis contrasted with other views of the time that emphasized the animalistic, neurotic, tension-reducing, and mechanistic aspects of behavior. Allport criticized psychoanalysis in this regard; he was particularly fond of telling the following story. While traveling through Europe at age 22, Allport decided it would be interesting to visit Freud. When he entered Freud's office, he was met with expectant silence as Freud waited to learn of Allport's mission. Finding himself unprepared for silence, Allport decided to start an informal conversation with the description of a four-year-old boy with a dirt phobia, whom he had met on the train. After he completed his description of the boy and his compulsive mother, Freud asked, "And was that little boy you?" Allport describes his response as follows:

> Flabbergasted and feeling a bit guilty, I contrived to change the subject. While Freud's misunderstanding of my motivation was amusing, it also started a deep train of thought. I realized that he was accustomed to neurotic defenses and that my manifest motivation (a sort of rude curiosity and youthful ambition) escaped him. For therapeutic progress he would have to cut through my defenses, but it so happened that therapeutic progress was not here an issue. This experience taught me that depth psychology, for all its merits, may plunge too deep, and that psychologists would do well to give full recognition to manifest motives before probing the unconscious.

SOURCE: Allport, 1967, p. 8.

Gordon W. Allport

A particularly amusing aspect of this episode is that Allport personally was very meticulous, punctual, neat, and orderly—possessing many of the characteristics associated by Freud with the compulsive personality. Freud's question may not have been as far off as Allport suggested!

Allport's first publication, written with his older brother Floyd, centered on traits as an important aspect of personality theory (Allport & Allport, 1921). Allport believed that traits are the basic units of personality. According to him, traits actually exist and are based in the nervous system. They represent generalized personality dispositions that account for regularities in the functioning of a person across situations and over time. Traits can be defined by three properties—frequency, intensity, and range of situations. For example, a very submissive person would frequently be very submissive over a wide range of situations.

TRAITS AND DISTINCTIONS AMONG KINDS OF TRAITS

In a now classic analysis of personality descriptors, Allport and Odbert (1936) differentiated personality traits from other important units of analysis in personality research. Allport and Odbert defined traits as "generalized and personalized determining tendencies—consistent and stable modes of an individual's adjustment to his environment" (1936, p. 26). Traits are thus different from states and activities which describe those aspects of personality that are temporary, brief, and caused by external circumstances. Chaplin, John, and Goldberg (1988) replicated Allport and Odbert's classifications of personality descriptors into three categories: traits, states, and activities. Table 7.1 lists examples of each of the three categories. For example, whereas a person may well be gentle throughout his or her lifetime, an infatuation (an internal state) typically does not last and even the most enjoyable carousing must come to an end.

Having distinguished traits from states and activities, the next question is whether there might exist different kinds of trait. Allport addressed this question by distinguishing among cardinal traits, central traits, and secondary dispositions. A cardinal trait expresses a disposition that is so pervasive and outstanding in a person's life that virtually every act is traceable to its influence. For example, we speak of the Machiavellian person, named after Niccolò Machiavelli's portrayal of the successful Renaissance ruler; of the sadistic person named after the Marquis de Sade; and of the authoritarian personality who sees virtually everything in black and white, stereotyped ways. Generally people have few, if any, such cardinal traits. **Central traits** (e.g., honesty, kindness, assertiveness) express dispositions that cover a more limited range of sit-

Table 7.1   Prototypical Examples of Traits, States, and Activities

Traits	States	Activities
Gentle	Infatuated	Carousing
Domineering	Pleased	Ranting
Trustful	Angry	Snooping
Timid	Invigorated	Leering
Cunning	Aroused	Reveling

SOURCE: Chaplin et al., 1988.

uations than is true for cardinal traits. **Secondary dispositions** are traits that are the least conspicuous, generalized, and consistent. In other words, people possess traits with varying degrees of significance and generality.

It is important to recognize that Allport did not say that a trait is expressed in all situations independent of the characteristics of the situation. Indeed, Allport recognized the importance of the situation in explaining why a person does not behave the same way all the time. He wrote: "traits are often aroused in one situation and not in another" (Allport, 1937, p. 331). For example, even the most aggressive people can be expected to modify their behavior if the situation calls for nonaggressive behavior, and even the most introverted person may behave in an extraverted fashion in certain situations. A trait expresses what a person generally does over many situations, not what will be done in any one situation. According to Allport, both trait and situation concepts are necessary to understand behavior. The trait concept is necessary to explain the consistency of behavior, whereas recognition of the importance of the situation is necessary to explain the variability of behavior.

FUNCTIONAL AUTONOMY

Allport is known not only for his emphasis on traits but for his concept of the **functional autonomy** of human motives. His idea is that the motives of an adult may have their roots in the tension-reducing motives of the child; however, the adult grows out of the early motives, becoming independent of (or "autonomous from") these earlier tension-reducing efforts. What originally began as an effort to reduce hunger or anxiety can become a source of pleasure and motivation in its own right. What began as an activity designed to earn a living can become pleasurable and an end in itself. Although hard work and the pursuit of excellence can be motivated originally by a desire for

Functional Autonomy: *Sometimes a person may select an occupation for one reason, such as job security, and then remain in it for other motives, such as pleasure in the activity itself.*

approval from parents and other adults, they can become valued ends in them-selves—pursued independently of whether they are emphasized by others. Thus, "what was once extrinsic and instrumental becomes intrinsic and impelling. The activity once served a drive or some simple need; it now serves itself, or in a larger sense, serves the self-image (self-ideal) of the person. Childhood is no longer in the saddle; maturity is" (Allport, 1961, p. 229). This of course sets Allport's work apart from Freud's, since Freud explained adult behaviors in terms of early childhood drives whose basic motivational force endured throughout adulthood.

IDIOGRAPHIC RESEARCH

Finally, a distinguishing feature of Allport is that he emphasized the uniqueness of the individual. Unlike the other trait theorists we will discuss, Allport pri-marily endorsed an idiographic approach to research. As we explained in Chapter 2, an idiographic strategy is an approach to research that focuses on the potentially unique individual. In-depth studies of individual persons are viewed as a path for learning about people generally. This approach contrasts with that of other trait theorists who have adopted nomothetic research proce-dures or procedures in which large numbers of individuals are studied and the researcher tries to describe variations in personality in the population at large.

One part of Allport's idiographic research procedures was his use of materi-als unique to the individual case. For example, Allport published 172 letters from a particular woman. These letters provided the basis for clinical charac-terization of her personality as well as for quantitative analysis. Another part of idiographic research involves using the same measures for all people but com-paring an individual's scores on one scale with his or her scores on other scales, rather than with the scores of other people on each scale. For example, one may want to know if a given person values being with people more than he or she values acquiring possessions. This question calls for a comparison within the individual. For some purposes, this may be more important than knowing whether that individual values being with people more or less than does anoth-er person, or values acquiring possessions more or less than another person, both being across-persons comparisons. This idiographic research emphasis highlights the pattern and organization of traits within a person rather than a person's standing, relative to others, on isolated trait variables. Finally, Allport's emphasis on the uniqueness of the individual led him to suggest that there are unique traits for each person that cannot be captured by science.

COMMENT ON ALLPORT

As we noted, Allport holds a cherished place in the field's history. In 1924, he offered the first course on personality ever taught in the United States. His 1937 text, *Personality: A Psychological Interpretation*, was a basic text in the field for 25 years. He raised many critical issues and discussed the trait con-cept with such balance and wisdom that this book can still be read with prof-it today (e.g., John & Robins, 1993). For example, Allport (1961) valuably sug-gested that behavior generally expresses the action of many traits, that con-flicting dispositions can exist within the person, and that traits are expressed in part by the person's selection of situations as opposed to his or her response to situations. A recent biography of Allport (Nicholson, 2002) highlights his contributions not only to trait psychology, but to the overall emergence of the psychology of personality as a unique scientific discipline.

Despite these virtues, there are limitations to Allport's contributions. Although he clarified the concept of trait, he did little research to establish the existence and utility of specific trait concepts. He believed that many traits were hereditary, but did no research to substantiate this. He convincingly documented that people display unique and consistent patterns of trait-related behavior, but he did not provide a detailed processing model to explain that behavior, in other words, a model of the exact psychological processes that motivate and guide the trait-related actions.

His emphasis of idiographic methods also had some negative effects. Some people interpreted his focus on the idiosyncratic individual to mean that it was impossible to create a science of personality that yielded general, lawful psychological principles. In retrospect, this was a poor reading of Allport's efforts. Individual people have much more complexity than do the physical and chemical entities that are the subjects of study in the physical sciences. To build an adequate science of human beings, it may be utterly necessary to study individual persons in detail. Idiographic strategies may be necessary to general understanding, rather than being an impediment to them. In principle, detailed case studies may yield insight into general principles that are found across individual cases. This is the strategy used by Freud, who obtained a relatively simple, general personality based on idiographic studies (his case studies of his patients). It is a strategy followed successfully in some other human sciences; for example, a famed anthropologist who studies, in detail, the meaning systems of particular cultures concludes that, as a general principle of scientific understanding, "the road to the general, to the revelatory simplicities of science, lies through a concern with the particular, the circumstantial, the concrete" (Geertz, 1973, p. 53). However, this idiographic approach is not the one pursued by trait theorists other than Allport. Subsequent trait theorists put little stock in idiographic studies. Instead, they studied populations of individuals and tried to identify the most important individual differences in the population at large. We now consider two such theories, which were constructed by the two most influential trait theorists of the 20th century, Hans J. Eysenck and Raymond B. Cattell.

THE THREE-FACTOR THEORY OF HANS J. EYSENCK (1916–1997)

Hans J. Eysenck was born in Germany in 1916 and later fled to England to escape Nazi persecution. His work was influenced by methodological advances in the statistical technique of factor analysis; by the thinking of European psychologists who studied personality types (especially Jung and Kretschmer); by research on the heredity of psychological characteristics; and by the experimental work on classical conditioning by the Russian physiologist Pavlov (see Chapter 10). His work included a broad sampling of both normal and pathological populations.

Eysenck led a life characterized by enormous energy and productivity. He is one of the most influential and cited psychologists of the 20th century (Haggbloom et al., 2002). He continued to publish and speak at conferences even after his retirement. In the 1980s, he founded and edited the journal

Hans J. Eysenck

Personality and Individual Differences, an international journal devoted primarily to research on personality traits, temperament, and the biological foundations of personality—all issues Eysenck cared deeply about. Eysenck died in 1997, after seeing through the re-publication of three of his early books and shortly after finishing his last book, *Intelligence: A New Look* (Eysenck, 1998).

TRAIT MEASUREMENT: FACTOR ANALYSIS

Eysenck was strict in his standards for scientific pursuits. He greatly emphasized conceptual clarity and precise measurement. Much of his efforts were devoted to developing reliable measures of personality traits.

Eysenck's belief in the need for precise measure made him a harsh critic of psychoanalytic theory. As you will recall, psychoanalysts did not provide precise, reliable measures of their psychological constructs. This, Eysenck believed, was a serious shortcoming. In constructing a trait theory, Eysenck sought to avoid this problem through the use of reliable measures of individual differences. In pursuing trait theory, he emphasized the need to develop adequate measures of personality traits. He felt that such measures were absolutely necessary to obtain a theory that could be tested and, if faulty, disproved. He felt that such measures also were necessary for science to identify the presumed biological foundations of each trait.

Eysenck's emphasis on biological foundations of personality traits is particularly noteworthy. He recognized that, without understanding the biology of traits, trait explanations could be "circular"—where "circular explanations" are those that go around in a conceptual circle, with a trait concept being used to explain the very behavior that served as the basis for inferring the existence of the trait in the first place. For example, think of a friend of yours who frequently talks in a friendly and outgoing manner to other people. How would you describe her behavior? You might say that she is "sociable." Now consider another question: How would you *explain* her behavior? You might say that she is acting sociable because she has the trait of sociability. But if you said this, you wouldn't be providing a very good explanation; indeed, your explanation would violate basic principles of scientific explanation (e.g., Nozick, 1981). The problem is that the only reason you know that your friend "has the trait of sociability" is because you saw her act in a sociable manner. Your explanation thus goes around in logical circles: it uses a word ("sociable") to describe a pattern of behavior, and then uses that same word to explain the existence of the pattern of behavior that was described. Eysenck recognized that trait theory can break out of such conceptual circles by going beyond the mere use of words, and identifying biological systems that correspond to trait. We consider his degree of success in identifying such systems below.

Factor Analysis and Identifying the Structure of Individual Differences

The basis for Eysenck's emphasis on measurement and the development of a classification of traits is the statistical technique of **factor analysis**. Eysenck and other trait theorists (Cattell; the five-factor approaches discussed in the next chapter) use factor analysis to answer one of the most important questions in trait theory: What are the basic traits, that is, the most fundamental dimensions of individual differences?

In a factor-analytic study, a large number of test items are administered to many subjects. Inevitably, some of these items are positively correlated with one another. In other words, people who answer a question (e.g., "Do you often go to loud and noisy parties?") in one way answer other questions (e.g., "Do you enjoy spending time with large groups of people?") in the same manner. Also, some items are negatively correlated (e.g., responses to "Do you prefer to stay home at night rather than going out?" might be negatively correlated with answers to the two previous questions above). In principle, large clusters of items might be correlated in this manner. These cluster correlations might reflect the influence of an underlying "factor," that is, something that is responsible for the correlations among the items. Factor analysis, then, is a statistical technique for identifying patterns, or clusters, among a large set of correlated items. Using the questions above, a factor analysis would identify the fact that the three items are intercorrelated and would report that they are part of a single mathematical factor. The psychologist, by looking at the content of the test items, might then give the factor a name such as "sociability."

According to most trait theorists, the factors that are identified in factor-analytic studies correspond to structures of personality. Factor analysis, then, is how trait theorists identify personality structures; the factors are the basic structures of personality in trait theory. The use of factor analysis to identify personality structures has some significant advantages as compared to the procedures used by previous theorists. Previously (e.g., in the work of Freud, Jung, or Rogers), theorists relied heavily on their intuition. They observed clinical cases and intuited that certain personality structures were responsible for their clients' behavior. But human intuition can be faulty (Nisbett & Ross, 1980). Rather than relying on intuition to identify personality structures, the trait theorist relies on an objective statistical procedure, factor analysis. Factor analysis provides an objective way of identifying the degree to which things (variables, test responses) covary, that is, appear and disappear together.

Yet the use of factor analysis is not entirely objective. For example, although the statistical procedure identifies patterns of covariation in test responses, it does not answer the question of why the responses covary. It is the researcher, using his or her knowledge of psychology and relying on his or her theoretical beliefs, who infers the existence of some common entity (the factor) and comes up with a label to describe the factor. The final results of a factor-analytic study, then, partly hinge on decisions and interpretations made by the researcher. Different investigators, using similar correlational and factor-analytic methods, may reach different conclusions. For example, consider the most frequently studied personality trait, extraversion. A central question in its study is "What are its core features?" In the contemporary field, some researchers conclude that the core of extraversion is reward sensitivity, that is, that extraverts are highly motivated to attain positive, goal-related rewards (Lucas et al., 2000). Others, using similar correlational and factor-analytic methods, disagree, concluding instead that the core of extraversion is social attention; extraverts appear to enjoy being the object of attention (Ashton, Lee, & Paunonen, 2002).

Returning specifically to the work of Eysenck, to construct a personality theory Eysenck conducted factor analyses of participants' responses and then further "secondary" factor analyses. Secondary factor analyses are conducted when an initial set of factors are correlated with one another and an investigator seeks a small set of factors that are uncorrelated. Eysenck wanted to identify such a simple set of uncorrelated factors, which he saw as basic dimensions that underlie the trait factors found in the initial round of analysis. These dimensions represent secondary factors or **superfactors**. Thus, for example, the traits of sociability, activity, liveliness, and excitability can be grouped together under the superordinate concept of extraversion (see Figure 7.1). The term *superfactor* makes clear it defines a dimension with a low end (introversion) and a high end (extraversion), such that people may fall along various points between the two extremes. Eysenck, and almost all other investigators who work toward a nomothetic trait model of personality, assume that variations in personality consist of continuous dimensions rather than discrete categories.

BASIC DIMENSIONS OF PERSONALITY

In his early research, Eysenck used the factor-analytic methods described earlier and succeeded in identifying two basic dimensions of personality. In other words, his secondary factor analyses yielded two independent dimensions of individual differences, which he interpreted as the two central structures of human personality. Eysenck labeled these dimensions as: (1) **introversion-extraversion** and (2) **neuroticism** (alternatively called emotional stability versus instability). These factors were usually uncorrelated with each other (in other words, there are about as many extraverted neurotics as introverted neurotics, about as many emotionally stable extraverts as emotionally unstable extraverts, etc.). The fact that they are uncorrelated means that Eysenck's two-dimensional system can be represented as two perpendicular lines that together define a psychological space of personality traits (Figure 7.2). In principle, any individual can be located within this two-dimensional space; in the Eysenck theoretical system, everyone has a greater or lesser amount of extraversion and neuroticism.

An interesting feature of Eysenck's system (also represented in Figure 7.2) is that is relates to a very ancient description of individual differences. The Greek physicians Hippocrates (around 400 B.C.) and Galen (around 200 A.D.) proposed the existence of four basic personality types: melancholics, phlegmatics, cholerics, and sanguine. The details of ancient Greek theorizing about the causes of personality types have since been repudiated. However, Eysenck recognized that these ancient thinkers did validly recognize important variations among people. To Eysenck, people who were seen by the Greeks as being of a particular personality type (e.g., choleric) actually had a high amount of two associated personality traits (in the case of the choleric type, extraversion and emotional instability; see Figure 7.2). The fact that these variations in personality were evident in both the ancient world and contemporary society suggests that they might be fundamental features of human nature with a biological basis that transcends time and place.

The hierarchical organization of characteristics associated with extraversion was presented in Figure 7.1. The neuroticism dimension is defined by traits such as tense, moody, and low self-esteem. The hierarchical organization of characteristics associated with this factor are presented in Figure 7.3.

Following the initial emphasis on only two dimensions, Eysenck added a third dimension, which he called **psychoticism**. People high on this dimen-

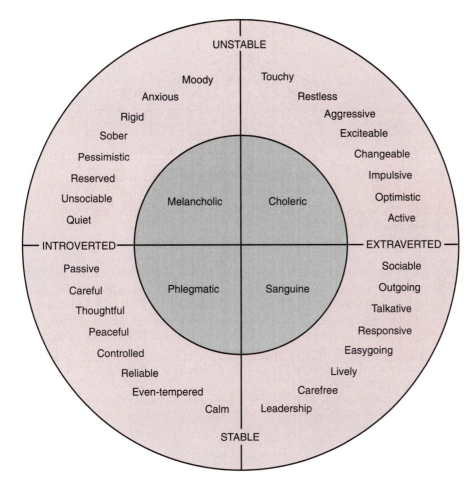

Figure 7.2· The Relationship of Two Dimensions of Personality Derived from Factor Analysis to Four Greek Temperamental Types. *(Eysenck, 1970). Reprinted by permission, Routledge & Kegan Paul Ltd., publishers.*

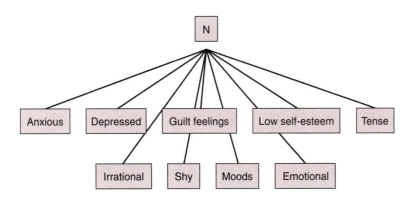

Figure 7.3 The Hierarchical Structure of Neuroticism (N). *(Eysenck, 1990). Reprinted by permission, Guilford Press.*

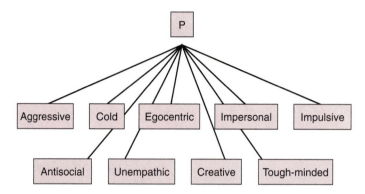

Figure 7.4 The Hierarchical Structure of Psychoticism (P). *(Eysenck, 1990).* *Reprinted by permission, Guilford Press.*

sion tend to be solitary, insensitive, uncaring about others, and opposed to accepted social custom. The hierarchical organization of characteristics associated with the psychoticism factor are presented in Figure 7.4. These three factors make up Eysenck's Psychoticism Extraversion Neuroticism (PEN) three-factor theory of personality. Eysenck and Long (1986) noted that there is considerable support for the existence of these three dimensions—they have been found in studies of different cultures, and there is evidence of an inherited component to each.

A further appreciation of Eysenck's theoretical system can be gained from a more detailed consideration of one of these three dimensions, that of intro-

Introversion-Extraversion: *Hans Eysenck suggests that a basic dimension of personality involves whether people tend to be unsociable, quiet, and passive (introverts) or sociable, outgoing, and active (extraverts).*

version-extraversion. According to Eysenck, the typical extravert is sociable, likes parties, has many friends, craves excitement, acts on the spur of the moment, and is spontaneous. In contrast to these characteristics, the introverted person tends to be quiet, introspective, reserved, reflective, distrustful of impulsive decisions, and prefers a well-ordered life to one filled with chance and risk.

Questionnaire Measures

Eysenck developed numerous questionnaires to measure people along the dimension of introversion-extraversion—the Maudsley Personality Inventory, the Eysenck Personality Inventory, and the Eysenck Personality Questionnaire. The typical extravert will answer yes to questions such as: Do other people think of you as very lively? Would you be unhappy if you could not see lots of people most of the time? Do you often long for excitement? In contrast, the typical introvert will answer yes to these questions: Generally, do you prefer reading to meeting people? Are you mostly quiet when you are with people? Do you stop and think things over before doing anything? Other illustrative items from the Maudsley and Eysenck personality inventories are presented in Figure 7.5. These include items relevant to neuroticism and a lie scale to detect individuals who are faking responses to look good, as well as items relevant to extraversion-introversion. Although the content and direction of scored responses may be obvious in some cases, in other cases this is not true. In addition to such questionnaires, other, more objective measures have been devised. For example, there is some suggestion that the "lemon drop test" may be used to distinguish between introverts and extraverts. In this test a standard amount of lemon juice is placed on the subject's tongue. Introverts and extraverts differ in the amount of saliva produced when this is done.

	Yes	No
1. Do you usually take the initiative in making new friends?	___	___
2. Do ideas run through your head so that you cannot sleep?	___	___
3. Are you inclined to keep in the background on social occasions?	___	___
4. Do you sometimes laugh at a dirty joke?	___	___
5. Are you inclined to be moody?	___	___
6. Do you very much like good food?	___	___
7. When you get annoyed, do you need someone friendly to talk about it?	___	___
8. As a child did you always do as you were told immediately and without grumbling?	___	___
9. Do you usually keep "yourself to yourself" except with very close friends?	___	___
10. Do you often make up your mind too late?	___	___

Note: The above items would be scored in the following way:
   Extraversion: 1 Yes, 3 No, 6 Yes, 9 No; *Neuroticism:* 2 Yes, 5 Yes, 7 Yes, 10 Yes; *Lie Scale:* 4 No, 8 Yes.

Figure 7.5   Illustrative Items for Extraversion, Neuroticism, and Lie Scale from the Maudsley Personality Inventory and Eysenck Personality Inventory.

Research Findings

Are there other significant and theoretically meaningful differences in behavior associated with varying scores on the extraversion-introversion dimension? Extraversion is probably the most extensively studied of all traits, in part because relevant behaviors are relatively easy to observe (Gosling et al., 1998). A review of the dimension presents an impressive array of findings (Watson & Clark, 1997). For example, introverts are more sensitive to pain than extraverts, they become fatigued more easily than extraverts, excitement interferes with their performance whereas it enhances performance for extraverts, and they tend to be more careful but less fast than extraverts. The following additional differences have been found:

1. Introverts do better in school than extraverts, particularly in more advanced subjects. Also, students withdrawing from college for academic reasons tend to be extraverts, whereas those who withdraw for psychiatric reasons tend to be introverts.

2. Extraverts prefer vocations involving interactions with other people, whereas introverts tend to prefer more solitary vocations. Extraverts seek diversion from job routine, whereas introverts have less need for novelty.

3. Extraverts enjoy explicit sexual and aggressive humor, whereas introverts prefer more intellectual forms of humor such as puns and subtle jokes.

4. Extraverts are more active sexually, in terms of frequency and different partners, than introverts.

5. Extraverts are more suggestible than introverts.

This last finding is illustrated in a study of a hyperventilating epidemic in England (Moss & McEvedy, 1966). An initial report by some girls of fainting and dizziness was followed by an outbreak of similar complaints, with 85 girls needing to be taken to the hospital by ambulance—"they were going down like ninepins." A comparison of the girls who were affected with those who were not demonstrated that, as expected, the affected girls were higher in both neuroticism and extraversion. In other words, those individuals whose personalities were most predisposed to suggestion proved most susceptible to influence by suggestions of a real epidemic.

Finally, the results of an investigation of study habits among introverts and extraverts may be of particular interest to college students. The research examined whether such personality differences are associated with differing preferences for where to study and how to study, as would be predicted by Eysenck's theory. In accord with Eysenck's theory of individual differences, the following was found: (1) extraverts more often chose to study in library locations that provided external stimulation than did introverts; (2) extraverts took more study breaks than did introverts; (3) extraverts reported a preference for a higher level of noise and for more socializing opportunities while studying than did introverts (Campbell & Hawley, 1982). Extraverts and introverts differ in their physiological responses to the same noise level (introverts show a greater level of response), and each functions best at his or her preferred noise level (Geen, 1984). An important implication of such research is that different

Table 7.2 Empirical Differences among College Students Linked to Extraversion–Introversion

Compared to Introverts, Extraverts...

Experience more daily positive emotions, like joy, excitement, and amusement
Experience more amusement when watching the same funny film
Express more positive emotions and have greater expressive confidence
Report greater happiness, well-being, and meaning in life
Interpret stressful events as challenges
Participate more in seminars
Take more study breaks
Study in library locations that provide more external stimulation
Are less disturbed by music when studying
Show less physiological responses to the same noise level
Have a greater number of leadership roles
Prefer jobs involving interactions with people
Seek diversion from job routine and prefer novelty
Have a larger number of friends
Are better at interpreting facial expressions and body language
Report less speech anxiety
Party more frequently
Enjoy explicit sexual and aggressive humor
Have more dating partners
Spend fewer weekend nights alone
Are more active sexually, both in frequency and number of partners
Consume more alcohol
Smoke more and find it harder to quit (maybe because nicotine is a stimulant)

SOURCES: Watson & Clark, 1997; Gross, 1999.

environmental designs for libraries and residence units might best fit the needs of introverts and extraverts. Other characteristics associated with extraverted college students are presented in Table 7.2.

Biological Bases of Personality Traits in Eysenckian Theory

What is the theoretical underpinning of the trait dimensions introversion-extraversion and emotional stability-instability? Eysenck was one of the first personality psychologists to explore in detail the biological basis of personality traits, a topic we cover in more detail in Chapter 9.

Regarding extraversion (i.e., the dimension introversion-extraversion), Eysenck suggested that individual variations in introversion-extraversion reflect differences in the neurophysiological functioning of the brain's cortex. The idea is that introverts are more arousable; they experience more cortical arousal from events in the world. As a result, highly intense social stimuli (e.g., a loud party) make them *over*aroused–an aversive state that they avoid. Introverts, then, are more restrained and inhibited. Conversely, extraverts experience less cortical arousal than introverts from a given stimulus, and therefore the extraverted person tends to seek out more intense social experiences. Research that directly measures the brain activity of introverts and extraverts provides some support for Eysenck's theorizing (Geen, 1997), as we review in Chapter 9. Eysenck himself generated much relevant evidence on the biology of this dimension, including evidence that introverts are more influenced by punishments in learning, whereas extraverts are more influenced by rewards.

Eysenck hypothesized that individual differences in introversion-extraversion along this dimension have both hereditary and environmental origins. Indeed, several studies of identical and fraternal twins suggest that heredity plays a major part in accounting for differences between individuals in their scores on this dimension (Loehlin, 1992; Plomin, 1994; Plomin & Caspi, 1999). Evidence that the dimension of introversion-extraversion consistently shows up in cross-cultural studies, that individual differences are stable over time, and that genetic factors make a strong contribution to such individual differences all argue for a strong biological basis for the dimensions. Indeed, many studies of various indices of biological functioning (e.g., brain activity, heart rate, hormone level, sweat gland activity) can be cited in support of this conclusion (Eysenck, 1990).

In sum, the introversion-extraversion dimension represents an important organization of individual differences in behavioral functioning that is rooted in inherited differences in biological functioning. These differences can be discovered through the use of factor analysis and measured through the use of questionnaires as well as laboratory procedures.

Let us now turn to the other two dimensions and briefly consider how the theory is extended into other realms. According to Eysenck, people high on neuroticism tend to be emotionally labile and frequently complain of worry and anxiety, as well as of bodily aches (e.g., headaches, stomach difficulties, dizzy spells). Here, too, an inherited biological difference in biological functioning is suggested. But, for neuroticism, Eysenck proposed that the relevant biological system is not the brain's cortex (as in extraversion) but instead the autonomic nervous system. Individuals high on neuroticism were said to possess an autonomic nervous system that responds quickly to stress and is slow to decrease this activity once danger disappears. The neurotic person thus seems "jumpy" and "stressed out." Unfortunately for Eysenckian theory, research has not consistently supported this physiological theory of neuroticism, as Eysenck himself fully recognized (Eysenck, 1990). Less is known about the biological basis for the psychoticism (P) dimension. However, here a genetic association is suggested, in particular an association linked with maleness; aggressiveness, a component of (P), is higher in men and may be affected by levels of testosterone (Eysenck, 1990).

PSYCHOPATHOLOGY AND BEHAVIOR CHANGE

Eysenck's theory of personality is closely linked to his theory of abnormal psychology and behavior change. The kind of symptoms or psychological difficulties one is likely to develop are related to basic personality characteristics and principles of nervous system functioning. According to Eysenck, a person develops neurotic symptoms because of the joint action of a biological system and experiences that contribute to the learning of strong emotional reactions to fear-producing stimuli. Thus, the vast majority of neurotic patients tend to have high neuroticism and low extraversion scores (Eysenck, 1982, p. 25). In contrast, criminals and antisocial persons tend to have high neuroticism, high extraversion, and high psychoticism scores. Such individuals show weak learning of societal norms.

Despite the strong genetic component in the development and maintenance of such disorders, Eysenck claimed that one need not be pessimistic concerning the potential for treatment: "The fact that genetic factors play a large part in the initiation and maintenance of neurotic disorders and also of criminal activities, is very unwelcome to many people who believe that such a state of affairs must lead to therapeutic nihilism. If heredity is so important, they say, then clearly behavior modification of any kind must be impossible. This is a completely erroneous interpretation of the facts. What is genetically determined are predispositions for a person to act and behave in a certain manner, when put in certain situations" (1982, p. 29). Accordingly, it is possible for a person to avoid certain potentially traumatic situations, to unlearn certain learned fear responses, or to learn (acquire) certain codes of social conduct. Thus, while emphasizing the importance of genetic factors, Eysenck was a major proponent of behavior therapy, or the systematic treatment of abnormal behavior according to the principles of learning theory. We will not extend Eysenck's discussion of behavior therapy here since the basic principles will be covered in the chapter on learning foundations of personality (Chapter 10).

We conclude our review of Eysenck's contributions by noting one other point. Eysenck was an outspoken critic of psychoanalysis. He contended that: (1) psychoanalysis is not a scientific theory since it is not falsifiable; (2) neurotic and psychotic disorders constitute separate dimensions rather than points on a continuum of regression; (3) abnormal behavior represents learned maladaptive responses rather than disguised expressions of underlying, unconscious conflicts; (4) all therapy involves the application, intended or otherwise, of learning principles. In particular, therapy with neurotic behaviors involves the unlearning or extinction of learned responses (Eysenck, 1979). According to Eysenck, psychoanalysis is not generally an effective method of treatment and succeeds only to the extent that the principles of behavior therapy are unwittingly or accidentally brought into play by the analyst.

COMMENT ON EYSENCK

Befitting a trait theorist, Eysenck's scientific record has been consistent in a number of ways. Noteworthy among the positive aspects of this record are the following: (1) Eysenck has been a prolific contributor to diverse areas. In addition to his continuing focus on individual differences and principles of behavior change, he contributed to the study of criminology, education, aesthetics, creativity, genetics, psychopathology, and political ideology. His personality tests have been translated into many foreign languages and are used in research around the world. (2) Eysenck consistently emphasized the value of both questionnaire and experimental research. Referring to Cronbach's discussion of the two disciplines of scientific psychology (Chapter 2), Eysenck suggests that he has "always looked upon these two disciplines not as in any sense rivals, but as complementary to each other, and indeed each one essential for the success of the other" (1982, p. 4). (3) Eysenck tied his personality variables to methods of measurement, a theory of nervous system functioning and learning, and an associated theory of psychopathology and behavior change. His theory goes beyond description and can be tested. (4) Historically, Eysenck was always prepared to swim against the tide and argue in favor of unpopular views: "I have usually been against the establishment and in favor of the rebels. Readers who wish to interpret this in terms of some inherited oppositional tendency, some acquired Freudian hatred of father substitutes, or in any other way are of course welcome. I prefer to think that on these issues the majority were wrong, and I was right. But then of course I would think that; only the future will tell" (1982, p. 298). Of course, this is Eysenck's own view of his own work. Many contemporary scholars would contend that the Eysenckian strategy of describing individual persons in terms of scores on a small number of universal personality dimensions is itself an "establishment" procedure against which the humanist might rebel.

Given his many contributions, one might ask why Eysenck has not been "universally celebrated by psychologists everywhere" (Loehlin, 1982, p. 623). Prominent among the reasons for this is Eysenck's tendency to dismiss the contributions of others and exaggerate the empirical support for his own point of view (Buss, 1982; Loehlin, 1982). Some psychologists familiar with Eysenck's work feel that it is significant, but that frequently he ignores contradictory findings and overstates the strength of positive results. In relation to this, two additional points can be made. First, alternative models have been proposed that better fit the available data. In one such model, it is suggested that individual differences on the dimensions of impulsivity and anxiety are critical (Gray, 1990). Here there is acceptance of the data emphasized by Eysenck and of the import of tying personality variables to biological functions, but different personality dimensions are emphasized. Second, many psychologists feel that it is impossible to account for individual differences with only two or three dimensions. As we shall see in the next section, the trait theorist Raymond Cattell suggested that we consider a larger number of traits and stay at that level of traits, rather than move to the superfactor level of personality description. Finally, there are psychologists who do not share the trait point of view at all, an issue that we will address in some detail in the next chapter. Finally, as Eysenck (1990) recognizes, a shortcoming of his work was that his theories of the biological bases of personality traits —particularly of neuroticism and psychoticism—lack consistent support.

THE FACTOR-ANALYTIC TRAIT APPROACH OF RAYMOND B. CATTELL (1905–1998)

Raymond B. Cattell was born in 1905 in Devonshire, England. He obtained a B.Sc. degree in chemistry from the University of London in 1924. Cattell then turned to psychology and obtained a Ph.D. degree at the same university in 1929. Before coming to the United States in 1937, Cattell did a number of studies in personality, and acquired clinical experience while directing a child guidance clinic. He held positions at Columbia, Harvard, Clark, and Duke universities. For 20 years he was a research professor of psychology and the director of the Laboratory of Personality Assessment at the University of Illinois. During his professional career, he published more than 200 articles and 15 books. Like Eysenck, Cattell stands as one of the most influential psychological scientists of the 20th century (Haggbloom et al., 2002).

Although relatively little is known of the experiences that shaped Cattell's life and work, a number of influences seem apparent. First, Cattell's interest in the use of factor-analytic methods in personality research and his attempt to develop a hierarchical theory of personality organization can be related to his associations with two of the same British psychologists who influenced

Eysenck: Spearman and Burt. Thus, although Cattell developed a theory that differed in some respects from Eysenck's, you should recognize that the theories are deeply similar; both Eysenck's and Cattell's personality trait theories share basic assumptions about the nature of personality traits and the usefullness of factor analysis in identifying a person's traits. A second influence is that Cattell's views on motivation were influenced by another British psychologist, William McDougall.

Raymond B. Cattell

Cattell's years spent jointly in personality research and clinical experience were a third influence on him. These years sensitized him to the assets and limitations of clinical and experimental research. Finally, Cattell's earlier experience in chemistry influenced much of his later thinking in psychology. In chemistry, the development of the periodic table by Dmitry Mendeleyev in 1869 led to renewed experimental activity. Just as Mendeleyev developed a classification of the elements in chemistry, much of Cattell's work can be viewed as an attempt to develop a classification of variables for experimental research in personality. Cattell hoped that factor analysis would lead psychology to its own periodic table of the elements.

CATTELL'S VIEW OF PERSONALITY SCIENCE

A key feature of Cattell's views on how to conduct a science of personality is a distinction he drew among three types of research methods. Cattell distinguished among three methods in the study of personality: **bivariate, multivariate**, and **clinical**. The typical bivariate experiment follows the classic experimental design of the physical sciences. In bivariate research, there are variables—an independent variable that is manipulated by the experimenter and a dependent variable that is measured to observe the effects of the experimental manipulations.

In contrast to bivariate research, in a multivariate method one studies interrelationships among many variables at once. Furthermore, in the multivariate experiment the investigator does not manipulate the variables. Instead, the experimenter allows life to make the experiments and then uses statistical methods to extract meaningful dimensions and causal connections. The method of factor analysis illustrates the multivariate method. Both the bivariate method and the multivariate method express a concern for scientific rigor. The difference between them is that, in the bivariate method, experimenters limit their attention to a few variables that they can manipulate in some way, whereas in the multivariate methods, experimenters consider many variables as they exist in a natural situation.

Cattell was quite critical of the bivariate method. Many of his criticisms are similar to those discussed in Chapter 2 in relation to laboratory research. First, he argues that attention to the relationship between two variables represents a simplistic and piecemeal approach to personality. Human behavior is complex and expresses the interactions among many variables. Having understood the relationship between two variables, one is left with the problem of understanding how these relate to the many other variables that are important in determining behavior. Second, the fact that bivariate experimenters attempt to manipulate the independent variable means that they must neglect many matters that are of real importance in psychology. Since the more important emotional situations cannot be manipulated and there-

Table 7.3   Cattell's Description of Bivariate, Clinical, and Multivariate Research Methods

Bivariate	Clinical	Multivariate
Scientific rigor, controlled experiments	Intuition	Scientific rigor, objective and quantitative analysis
Attention to few variables	Consideration of many variables	Consideration of many variables
Neglect of important phenomena	Study of important phenomena	Study of important phenomena
Simplistic, piecemeal	Interest in global events and complex patterns of behavior (total personality)	Interest in global events and complex patterns of behavior (total personality)

fore cannot be used in controlled experiments in humans, the bivariate researcher has been forced to attend to trivia, to look for answers in the behavior of rats, or to look for answers in physiology.

The third method, clinical, contrasts with the bivariate method in that clinical researchers can study important behaviors as they occur and look for lawfulness in the functioning of the total organism. Thus, in scientific aims and in philosophical assumptions, the clinical and multivariate methods are close to one another and separate from the bivariate method. Both the clinician and the multivariate researcher explore complex patterns of behavior as they naturally occur, allow life itself to be the source of psychologically significant manipulations, and address the total personality rather than isolated processes or fragmented pieces of knowledge. The clinician and the multivariate researcher do differ. The clinician uses intuition to understand clients, whereas the multivariate researcher uses formal measurements and statistical analyses. To Cattell, "the clinician has his heart in the right place, but perhaps we may say that he remains a little fuzzy in the head" (1959c, p. 45). In light of these similarities and differences, Cattell concluded that the clinical method is the multivariate method but without the latter's concern for scientific rigor.

In sum, Cattell felt that multivariate methods combine the desirable qualities of the bivariate and clinical methods (Table 7.3). He judged that the most important statistical technique in multivariate research was factor analysis (described earlier in the section on Hans Eysenck). The major difference between the two theorists is that Cattell preferred to work with a larger number of factors at the trait level. These factors have a more narrow definition but tend to correlate with each other. In contrast, Eysenck used secondary factor analysis to combine traits into a smaller number of uncorrelated superfactors, each of which covers a broader range of behavior. This difference between Eysenck and Cattell in their preferred level in the trait hierarchy is easily apparent in Figure 7.1.

CATTELL'S THEORY OF PERSONALITY

Kinds of Traits

The basic structural element for Cattell is the trait, which was defined earlier as a predisposition. The concept of trait assumes that behavior follows some pattern and regularity over time and across situations. Among the many possible distinctions between traits, two are of particular importance. The first is that among **ability** traits, **temperament** traits, and **dynamic** traits, and the second is that between surface traits and source traits.

Ability traits relate to skills and abilities that allow the individual to function effectively. Intelligence is an example of an ability trait. Temperament traits relate to the emotional life of the person and the stylistic quality of behavior. Whether one tends to work quickly or slowly, be generally calm or emotional, or act after deliberation or impulsively, all have to do with qualities of temperament that vary from individual to individual. Dynamic traits relate to the striving, motivational life of the individual, the kinds of goals that are important to the person. Ability, temperament, and dynamic traits are seen as capturing the major stable elements of personality.

The distinction between surface traits and source traits relates to the level at which we observe behavior. Surface traits express behaviors that on a superficial level may appear to go together but in fact do not always move up and down (vary) together and do not necessarily have a common cause. A source trait, on the other hand, expresses an association among behaviors that do vary together to form a unitary, independent dimension of personality. Whereas surface traits can be discovered through subjective methods such as asking people which personality characteristics they think go together, the refined statistical procedures of factor analysis are necessary to discover source traits. These source traits represent the building blocks of personality.

Sources of Data: L-Data, Q-Data, and OT-Data

How do we discover source traits that cover a variety of responses across many situations? Where do we find our building blocks? Cattell distinguished three sources of data that are similar to the LOTS classification of data sources we discussed in the beginning of Chapter 2: life record data (**L-data**), which include both objective life-event data and ratings by observers and peers; questionnaire data (**Q-data**), which are based on self-reports; and objective-test data (**OT-data**). The first, L-data, relates to behavior in actual, everyday situations such as school performance or interactions with peers. These may be actual counts of behaviors or ratings made on the basis of such observations. The second, Q-data, involves self-report data or responses to questionnaires, such as the Maudsley and Eysenck personality inventories discussed earlier in the chapter. The third, OT-data, involves behavioral miniature situations in which the subject is unaware of the relationship between the response and the personality characteristic being measured. According to Cattell, if multivariate, factor-analytic research is indeed able to determine the basic structures of personality, then the same factors or traits should be obtained from the three kinds of data. This is an important, logical, and challenging commitment.

Originally Cattell began with the factor analyses of L-data and found 15 factors that appeared to account for most of an individual's personality. He then set out to determine whether comparable factors could be found in Q-data. Thousands of questionnaire items were written and administered to large numbers of normal people. Factor analyses were run to see which items went together. The main result of this research is a questionnaire known as the Sixteen Personality Factor (16 P.F.) Questionnaire. Initially, Cattell made up neologisms, such as "surgency," to name his personality trait factors, hoping

Table 7.4   Cattell's 16 Personality Factors Derived from
Questionnaire Data

Reserved	Outgoing
Less intelligent	More intelligent
Stable, ego strength	Emotionality/neuroticism
Humble	Assertive
Sober	Happy-go-lucky
Expedient	Conscientious
Shy	Venturesome
Tough-minded	Tender-minded
Trusting	Suspicious
Practical	Imaginative
Forthright	Shrewd
Placid	Apprehensive
Conservative	Experimenting
Group-dependent	Self-sufficient
Undisciplined	Controlled
Relaxed	Tense

to avoid misinterpretations of them. Nonetheless, the terms given in Table 7.4 roughly capture the meanings of these trait factors. As can be seen, they cover a wide variety of aspects of personality, particularly in terms of temperament (e.g., emotionality) and attitudes (e.g., conservative). In general, the factors found with Q-data appeared to be similar to those found with L-data, but some were unique to each kind of data. Illustrative L-data ratings and Q-data items for one trait are presented in Figure 7.6.

Cattell was committed to the use of questionnaires, in particular, those derived from a factor-analytical perspective, such as the 16 P.F. On the other hand, he also expressed concern about the problems of motivated distortion and self-deception in relation to questionnaire responses. He also felt that the questionnaire is of particularly questionable utility with mental patients. Because of problems with L-data and Q-data, and because the original research strategy itself called for investigations with OT-data, Cattell's later efforts were concerned more with personality structure as derived from OT-data. It is the source traits as expressed in objective tests that are the "real coin" for personality research.

The results from L-data and Q-data research were important in guiding the development of miniature test situations; that is, the purpose was to develop objective tests that would measure the source traits already discovered. Thus, for example, a tendency to be assertive might be expressed in behaviors such as long exploratory distance on a finger maze test, fast tempo in arm-shoulder movement, and fast speed of letter comparisons. More than 500 tests were constructed to cover the hypothesized personality dimensions. These tests were administered to large groups of subjects, and repeated factoring of data from different research situations eventually led to the designation of 21 OT-data source traits.

As mentioned before, the source traits or factors found in L-data and Q-data could, for the most part, be matched to one another. How, then, do the OT-data factors match those derived from L-data and Q-data? Despite the years of research effort, the results were disappointing; although some rela-

---

SOURCE TRAIT EGO STRENGTH VS. EMOTIONALITY/NEUROTICISM (L-DATA AND Q-DATA)

Behavior Ratings by Observer

Ego Strength		*Emotionality/Neuroticism*
Mature	vs.	Unable to tolerate frustration
Steady, persistent	vs.	Changeable
Emotionally calm	vs.	Impulsively emotional
Realistic about problems	vs.	Evasive, avoids necessary decisions
Absence of neurotic fatigue	vs.	Neurotically fatigued (with no real effort)

Questionnaire Responses*

Do you find it difficult to take no for an answer even when what you want to do is obviously impossible?
   (a) yes   (b) *no*

If you had your life to live over again, would you:
   (a) *want it to be essentially the same?*   (b) plan it very differently?

Do you often have really disturbing dreams?
   (a) yes   (b) *no*

Do your moods sometimes make you seem unreasonable even to yourself?
   (a) yes   (b) *no*

Do you feel tired when you've done nothing to justify it?
   (a) *rarely*   (b) often

Can you change old habits, without relapse, when you decide to?
   (a) *yes*   (b) no

*answer in italic type indicates high ego strength.

Figure 7.6 Correspondence Between Data from Two Different Test Domains: L-data Ratings and Q-data Responses. *(Cattell, 1965.)*

tions were found across all three data sources, no direct one-to-one mapping of factors was possible.

In summary, we have described four steps in Cattell's research. (1) He set out to define the structure of personality in three areas of observation, called L-data, Q-data, and OT-data. (2) He started his research with L-data and through the factor analysis of ratings came up with 15 source traits. (3) Based on research findings, he developed the 16 P.F. Questionnaire, which contains 12 traits that match traits found in the L-data research and four traits that appear to be unique to questionnaire methods. (4) Using these results to guide his research in the development of objective tests, Cattell found 21 source traits in OT-data that appear to have a complex and low-level relation to the traits found in the other data.

The source traits found in the three types of observation do not complete Cattell's formulation of the structure of personality. However, the traits presented in this section do describe the general nature of the structure of personality as formulated by Cattell. In other words, here we have the foundation for psychology's table of the elements—its classification scheme. But what is the evidence for the existence of these traits? Cattell (1979) cited the following: (1) the results of factor analyses of different kinds of data; (2) similar results across cultures; (3) similar results across age groups; (4) utility in the prediction of behavior in the natural environment; and (5) evidence of significant genetic contributions to many traits.

STABILITY AND VARIABILITY IN BEHAVIOR

Cattell did not view persons as static entities who behaved the same way in all situations. How a person behaves at any one time depends not only on traits, but other considerations as well. Cattell noted two other concepts that are vital in explaining behavior: states and roles. Cattell used the concept of state to refer to emotional and mood changes that are partly determined by the provocative power of specific situations. Illustrative states are anxiety, depression, fatigue, arousal, and curiosity. Whereas traits describe stable and general action patterns, Cattell emphasized that the exact description of an individual at a given moment requires measurement of both traits and states: "Every practicing psychologist—indeed every intelligent observer of human nature and human history—realizes that the state of a person at a given moment determines his or her behavior as much as do his or her traits" (1979, p. 169). In other words, behavior in a particular situation cannot be predicted from traits alone without regard for whether the person is angry, tired, fearful, and so on.

Regarding the concept of **role**, Cattell noted that certain behaviors are more closely linked to social roles one must play than to personality traits one possesses. Social roles, not personality traits, explain why people shout at football games and not in churches (Cattell, 1979). Two people may act differently toward one another in different settings in which they play different roles. For example, a teacher may respond differently to a child's behavior in the classroom than when outside the classroom and no longer in the role of teacher.

In sum, although Cattell believed that personality factors lead to a certain degree of stability in behavior across situations, he also recognized that a person's mood (state) and the way he is presenting himself in a given situation (role) will influence his behavior: "How vigorously Smith attacks his meal depends not only on how hungry he happens to be, but also on his temperament and whether he is having dinner with his employer or is eating alone at home" (Nesselroade & Delhees, 1966, p. 583).

COMMENT ON CATTELL

One cannot help but be impressed with the scope of Cattell's efforts. His research touched on almost every dimension we have outlined as relevant to personality theory. Cattell was a major force in the development of new multivariate techniques, as well as techniques for determining the genetic contribution to personality. To further multivariate research, Cattell founded the Society for Multivariate Experimental Research (SMEP) in the 1960s. Most factor-analytic personality researchers in the United States became members of this prestigious society. Furthermore, Cattell endeavored to put his work in a cross-cultural perspective. In the words of one admirer: "Cattell's theory turns out to be a much more impressive achievement than has been generally recognized.... It seems fair to say that Cattell's original blueprint for personality study has resulted in an extraordinarily rich theoretical structure that has

"THE RIGHT STUFF": CHARACTERISTICS OF SUCCESSFUL BUSINESS EXECUTIVES

Some time ago Tom Wolfe wrote a book about the first U.S. team of astronauts. An all-male group, these were men who felt that they had the "right stuff"—the manly courage it took to make it as a test pilot and astronaut. Others had the necessary skill, but if they didn't have the right stuff they just didn't make it.

Most demanding occupations have their own kind of right stuff—the personality characteristics or traits that, in addition to skill, make for success. For example, what makes for a top business executive? According to some recent research, the difference between senior executives who make it to chief executive officer and those who do not often is subtle. Members of both groups show considerable talent and have remarkable strengths, as well as a few significant weaknesses. Although no one trait discriminates between the two groups, those who fall short of their ultimate goal frequently are found to have the following characteristics: they are insensitive to others, untrustworthy, cold—aloof—arrogant, overly ambitious, moody, volatile under pressure, and defensive. In contrast, those who make it to the top are most characterized by the traits of integrity and understanding others.

Actually, there is a long history of efforts to define the abilities and personal qualities of leaders. At one point, researchers began to give up on the hope of finding general leadership qualities. Leadership was seen as entirely situational in origin, with different skills and personal qualities being required in different situations. However, a recent review of the literature suggests that sounding the death knell of a trait approach to leadership probably was premature. Certain general qualities such as courage, fortitude, and conviction do stand out. In addition, the following traits seem to be generally characteristic of leaders: energetic, decisive, adaptive, assertive, sociable, achieving, and tolerant of stress.

Trait researchers, particularly those in industrial psychology, continue to try to define those personality characteristics that are essential for success in various fields. Thus, a variety of personality tests, including the 16 P.F., are used in many important aspects of personnel selection.

SOURCES: *Psychology Today*, February 1983; Holland, 1985.

"The Right Stuff": *Success in different occupations requires possessing certain traits. Sally Ride is America's first female astronaut to be a crew member aboard the space shuttle.*

generated more empirical research than any other theory of personality" (Wiggins, 1984, pp. 177, 190).

At the same time, many personality psychologists ignore the work of Cattell, in part because they question the validity of the tests Cattell used, his heavy reliance on factor analysis, and his theoretical speculation far beyond the data. Also, as was true for Eysenck, Cattell often overstated his data. Unfortunately, in being so committed to his point of view, he was at times unduly accepting of his own efforts and disparaging of the works of others. For example, the gains of clinical and bivariate approaches were minimized and those of the multivariate approach overstated.

TRAIT THEORY: ALLPORT, EYSENCK, AND CATTELL

When we began this chapter, we explained that there is no singular leading trait theorist. A lot of people have contributed to the development of the trait perspective. Their work shares common features that define a general trait approach. The main feature is the assumption that the core of personality consists of broad dispositions to respond in particular ways. Associated features, particularly in work of Eysenck and Cattell, are that personality traits can be identified by analyzing individual differences in the population; that these differences consist of continuous dimensions (rather than categories); that a person's expression of trait-related behavior is directly related to his or her possession of the corresponding personality trait; and that factor analyses of correlations among test responses in the population at large are the best method for identifying the structure of personality.

Within this general framework, Allport, Eysenck, and Cattell are three theorists of great historical importance. Although they are all "trait theorists," there are important differences among them. Perhaps the biggest difference concerns the use of factor analysis to determine the number and nature of personality traits. Allport was critical of the method because it provided information about differences *between* people rather than providing an analysis of the topic of central interest to the personality psychologist: the dynamics and (*within*-person) organization of the personality of the individual. Eysenck and Cattell, in contrast, were major proponents of this statistical technique. Another difference, among the factor analysts, is that Cattell emphasized as many as 20 distinct traits whereas Eysenck emphasized only three. Allport, of course, went even further than Cattell in suggesting that there are unique traits for each person, opening the door to investigation of an endless number of traits.

In addition to the issues of methodology and number of traits, these three trait theorists differ in their approach to the study of motivation. Whereas Eysenck did not use the concept of motive, both Allport and Cattell left room in their theories for this concept and suggested that research could explore the relation between traits and motives. Finally, whereas both Allport and Eysenck were very critical of psychoanalytic theory, Cattell was less rejecting.

Within a common point of view, then, major differences among the three theorists are found. As we will see in the following chapter, in recent decades greater consensus among trait researchers has been achieved. The historic contributions of Allport, Cattell, and Eysenck, as well as this newer consensus (Chapter 8), make trait theory a remarkably powerful force in the contemporary field of personality psychology.

MAJOR CONCEPTS

Ability, temperament, and dynamic traits   In Cattell's trait theory, these categories of traits capture the major aspects of personality.

Bivariate method   Cattell's description of the method of personality study that follows the classic experimental design of manipulating an independent variable and observing the effects on a dependent variable.

Cardinal trait   Allport's concept for a disposition that is so pervasive and outstanding in a person's life that virtually every act is traceable to its influence.

Central trait   Allport's concept for a disposition to behave in a particular way in a range of situations.

Clinical methods   Cattell's description of the method of personality study in which there is an interest in complex patterns of behavior as they occur in life but variables are not assessed in a systematic way.

Extraversion   In Eysenck's theory, one end of the introversion-extraversion dimension of personality characterized by a disposition to be sociable, friendly, impulsive, and risk taking.

Factor analysis   A statistical method for analyzing correlations among a set of personality tests or test items in order to determine those variables or test responses that increase or decrease together. Used in the development of personality tests and of some trait theories (e.g., Cattell, Eysenck).

Functional autonomy   Allport's concept that a motive may become independent of its origins; in particular, motives in adults may become independent of their earlier basis in tension reduction.

Introversion   In Eysenck's theory, one end of the introversion-extraversion dimension of personality characterized by a disposition to be quiet, reserved, reflective, and risk avoiding.

L-data   In Cattell's theory, life-record data relating to behavior in everyday life situations or to ratings of such behavior.

Multivariate method   Cattell's description of the method of personality study, favored by him, in which there is study of interrelationships among many variables at once.

Neuroticism   In Eysenck's theory, a dimension of personality defined by stability and low anxiety at one end and by instability and high anxiety at the other end.

OT-data   In Cattell's theory, objective test data or information about personality obtained from observing behavior in miniature situations.

Psychoticism   In Eysenck's theory, a dimension of personality defined by a tendency to be solitary and insensitive at one end and to accept social custom and care about others at the other end.

Q-data   In Cattell's theory, personality data obtained from questionnaires.

Role   Behavior considered to be appropriate for a person's place or status in society. Emphasized by Cattell as one of a number of variables that limit the influence of personality variables on behavior relative to situational variables.

Secondary disposition   Allport's concept for a disposition to behave in a particular way that is relevant to few situations.

Source trait   In Cattell's theory, behaviors that vary together to form an independent dimension of personality, which is discovered through the use of factor analysis.

State   Emotional and mood changes (e.g., anxiety, depression, fatigue) that Cattell suggested may influence the behavior of a person at a given time. The assessment of both traits and states is suggested to predict behavior.

Superfactor   A higher-order or secondary factor representing a higher level of organization of traits than the initial factors derived from factor analysis.

Surface trait   In Cattell's theory, behaviors that appear to be linked to one another but do not in fact increase and decrease together.

Trait   A disposition to behave in a particular way, as expressed in a person's behavior over a range of situations.

REVIEW

1. The trait concept represents a broad disposition to behave in a particular way. Traits are viewed as being organized in a hierarchy from specific responses to general styles of psychological functioning.

2. Allport differentiated the importance of traits for a person's personality with the concepts of cardinal traits, central traits, and specific dispositions. Allport also is known for the concept of functional autonomy, suggesting that adult motives may

become independent of earlier roots, and for his emphasis on the use of in-depth study of individuals (idiographic research).

3. Many trait theorists use the statistical technique of factor analysis to develop a classification of traits. Through this technique a group of items or responses (factors) are formed, the items in one group (factor) being closely related to one another and distinct from those in another group (factor).

4. According to Eysenck, the basic dimensions of personality are introversion-extraversion, neuroticism, and psychoticism. Questionnaires have been developed to assess people along these trait dimensions. Research has focused particularly on the introversion-extraversion trait dimension, where differences in activity level and activity preferences have been found. Eysenck suggests that individual differences in traits have a biological and genetic (inherited) basis. However, he also suggests that through behavior therapy important changes in personality functioning can occur.

5. Cattell distinguished among bivariate, multivariate, and clinical approaches to research in personality, favoring the multivariate study of interrelationships among many variables. Cattell also distinguished among ability, temperament, and dynamic traits, as well as between surface and source traits. Source traits represent an association of behaviors discovered through the use of factor analysis and are the building blocks of personality. Although his main research efforts have involved the use of questionnaires (16 Personality Factor Questionnaire), he has attempted to demonstrate that the same factors show up with the use of ratings and objective tests. Finally, Cattell suggested that behavior in a specific situation reflects additional influences, such as states and roles.

6. Trait theorists such as Allport, Eysenck, and Cattell share an emphasis on broad dispositions to respond as central to personality. However, their approaches differ in many ways, most importantly concerning the use of factor analysis to discover traits and the number of traits to be used in the description of personality.

8

TRAIT THEORY:
THE FIVE-FACTOR MODEL;
APPLICATIONS AND EVALUATION
OF TRAIT APPROACHES
TO PERSONALITY

THE FIVE-FACTOR MODEL
OF PERSONALITY:
RESEARCH EVIDENCE
  Analysis of Trait Terms in Natural
    Language and in Questionnaires
    The Fundamental Lexical Hypothesis
  Cross-Cultural Research: Are the Big Five
    Universal Dimensions?
  The Big Five in Personality Questionnaires
    The NEO-PI-R and Its Hierarchical
      Structure: Facets
  Integration of Eysenck's and Cattell's
    Factors within the Big Five

PROPOSED THEORETICAL MODEL
FOR THE BIG FIVE

GROWTH AND DEVELOPMENT
  Age Differences Throughout Adulthood
  Initial Findings from Childhood and
    Adolescence
  Stability and Change in Personality

APPLICATIONS OF THE MODEL
  Vocational Interests
  Health and Longevity
  Clinical Psychology: Diagnosis and
    Treatment

THE CASE OF JIM
  The 16 P.F. Questionnaire: Trait, Factor-
    Analytic Theory
    Comments on the Data
  The Stability of Personality: Jim 5 and 20
    Years Later
  Five-Factor Model: Self-ratings and Rating
    by Wife on the NEO-PI

EVALUATION: THE PERSON-SITUATION
CONTROVERSY
  Longitudinal Stability
  Cross-Situational Stability
  Conclusion

OVERALL EVALUATION OF TRAIT
APPROACHES
  Strengths of the Approaches
    Active Research Effort
    Interesting Hypotheses
    Potential Ties to Biology
  Limitations of the Approaches
    Problems with the Method: Factor Analysis
    Problems with the Trait Concept
    What Is Left Out or Neglected?

MAJOR CONCEPTS

REVIEW

Chapter Focus

You are applying to graduate school and Allport, Eysenck, and Cattell are writing you letters of recommendation. What would their three letters look like? Certainly they would differ. Eysenck would discuss your behavior and accomplishments in terms of his three broad superfactors, Cattell would consider twenty-some more specific traits, and Allport might weave a richly detailed idiographic portrayal, including many entirely unique trait configurations. While there might be some common themes in the letters, none of the theorists would ever give up his preferred theoretical position. That leads us to the question: How can we ever reach agreement about the basic traits if we cannot break this stalemate?

Suppose we proceed as follows. We ask a thousand people to write personality descriptions of a thousand others. Then we collect together all the trait-descriptive adjectives used in these descriptions. The result would be a list of personality descriptors that is not biased by any theoretical preconceptions. Certainly, with a thousand words, there would be considerable redundancy (e.g., perfect and flawless mean pretty much the same thing), permitting us to reduce the size of the list. If we then factor-analyze personality ratings on these traits, we should end up with the major dimensions of personality trait descriptions. The result may be a compromise that does not please everybody but at least it is arrived at through a fair set of procedures, and its practicality and usefulness will determine whether it is generally accepted in the field.

In this chapter we continue our discussion of trait theory and consider the efforts of trait researchers to reach a consensus using the procedures outlined above. We focus on the emerging consensus on the importance of five basic trait dimensions, and consider the evidence supporting this five-factor model, as well as its application to the individual. The chapter concludes with an overall evaluation of the trait approach to personality.

QUESTIONS TO BE ADDRESSED IN THIS CHAPTER

1. Is it possible for trait researchers to reach a consensus on one model of the organization of personality traits?

2. How many—and which—trait dimensions are necessary for a basic description of personality?

3. Can a trait model derived from factor analysis be connected to the personality terms we use in everyday language? Would we expect such a model to be universal across cultures? Would we expect it to make sense in terms of our evolutionary heritage?

4. What are the implications of individual differences in traits for career choice, physical health, and psychological well-being?

FoxTrot   by Bill Amend

Drawing by Bill Amend; © 1993 Universal Press Syndicate.

5. How stable or variable are traits over time and across situations? That is, how much does one's personality change over time and from situation to situation?

In the last chapter we considered the trait approaches of Allport, Eysenck, and Cattell. As indicated, these theorists share the view that traits are the fundamental units of personality, representing broad dispositions to respond in particular ways. At the same time, the three theorists have substantially different views about the use of factor analysis and about the number and nature of the trait dimensions that are needed for an adequate description of personality.

Like any field of scientific study, research on personality traits needs a generally agreed-upon model of its subject matter. Then researchers can study specified domains of traits, rather than examining separately the thousands of particular traits that make human beings individual and unique. Over the past 40 years, the number of personality concepts, and the number of questionnaire scales designed to measure them, has escalated without an end in sight. Researchers as well as applied personality assessors are faced with a bewildering array of trait measures from which to choose. In the English language alone, there are more than 5000 words describing personality traits. As Cattell put it, "the trouble with measuring traits is that there are too many of them!" (1965, p. 55). Organizing these different traits into a coherent structure was a major concern of trait researchers during the 1980s and 1990s.

For years, trait researchers, including Eysenck, Cattell, and others, vigorously debated the number and nature of the basic dimensions of personality traits. Because this issue was unresolved, the field remained fragmented and in disarray. Since the 1980s, a gradual improvement in the quality and sophistication of methods, especially factor analysis, has led to the beginnings of a consensus. Many researchers now agree that individual differences can be usefully organized in terms of five broad, bipolar dimensions (John & Srivastava, 1999; McCrae & Costa, 2003). These are widely known as the "Big Five" trait dimensions—not because they are so great but because of their extraordinary breadth and level of abstraction.

THE FIVE-FACTOR MODEL OF PERSONALITY: RESEARCH EVIDENCE

The past decade has witnessed an electrifying burst of interest in the most fundamental problem of the field—the search for a scientifically compelling taxonomy of personality traits. More importantly, the beginning of a consensus is emerging about the general framework of such a taxonomic representation.

SOURCE: Goldberg, 1993, p. 26.

Today we believe it is more fruitful to adopt the working hypothesis that the five-factor model of personality is essentially correct in its representation of the structure of traits.... If this hypothesis is correct—if we have truly discovered the basic dimensions of personality—it marks a turning point for personality psychology.

SOURCE: McCrae & John, 1992, p. 176.

What was the cause of these writers' unusually strong expressions of enthusiasm for their scientific model, the **Big Five** model of personality traits? Support for the model came from three main areas: factor analyses of large sets of trait terms in the language; cross-cultural research testing the universality of trait dimensions; and the relation of trait questionnaires to other questionnaires and ratings. In this chapter, we consider each of these areas, as well as various applications of the model.

ANALYSIS OF TRAIT TERMS IN NATURAL LANGUAGE AND IN QUESTIONNAIRES

As you have learned from previous chapters, psychologists build personality theories on different types of variables—different "units of analysis" (Chapter 1). How does one arrive at a set of basic units of analysis. Theorists such as Freud and Rogers relied on a combination of in-depth analysis of individuals (especially in therapy) and rational theory construction; that is, they combined their personal observations of people with their analytic skills as scientific theoreticians to construct a model of personality.

The **five-factor model** is built on a much simpler approach. Here, investigators try to find basic units of personality by analyzing the words that people—i.e., not just psychologists, but everyday, ordinary people—use to describe people's personalities. The basic procedure followed in this research is to have individuals rate themselves or others on a wide variety of traits carefully sampled from the dictionary (John, Angleitner, & Ostendorf, 1988). The ratings are then factor-analyzed (see Chapter 7 for a discussion of factor analysis) to see which traits go together. The questions to be answered are: How many different factors are needed to understanding the patterns of correlation in the data?, and What specifically are the factors?

Early work by Norman (1963), who drew upon research by Allport, Cattell, and others, indicated that five factors are necessary. Similar five-factor solutions were found repeatedly in numerous subsequent studies conducted by many different researchers in a wide range of data sources, samples, and assessment instruments (John, 1990). All five factors were shown to possess considerable reliability and validity and to remain relatively stable throughout adulthood (McCrae & Costa, 1990, 1994, 2003).

In 1981, Lewis Goldberg reviewed the existing research and, impressed with the consistency of its results, suggested that "it should be possible to

Lewis R. Goldberg

argue the case that any model for structuring individual differences will have to encompass—at some level—something like these 'Big Five' dimensions" (p. 159). Thus, the designation of the "Big Five" factors came into existence factors. Big was meant to refer to the finding that each factor subsumes a large number of more specific traits; the factors are almost as broad and abstract in the personality hierarchy as Eysenck's "superfactors."

And what, exactly, are these factors? Although slightly different terms have been used to label the Big Five factors, we shall use the terms Neuroticism (N), Extraversion (E), Openness (O), Agreeableness (A), and Conscientiousness (C) (Table 8.1). Note that the first letters of the Big Five dimensions spell out the word **OCEAN** (John, 1990, p. 96)—an easy way to remember all five dimensions.

To illustrate the meaning of the factors, Table 8.1 lists a number of trait adjectives that describe individuals scoring high and low on each. Neuroticism contrasts emotional stability with a broad range of negative feelings, including anxiety, sadness, irritability, and nervous tension. Openness to Experience describes the breadth, depth, and complexity of an individual's mental and experiential life. Extraversion and Agreeableness both summarize traits that are interpersonal, that is, they capture what people do with each other and to each other. Finally, Conscientiousness primarily describes task- and goal-directed behavior and socially required impulse control.

The factor definitions in Table 8.1 are based on the work by Costa and McCrae (1985; 1992). The definitions suggested by other researchers are quite

Table 8.1   The Big Five Trait Factors and Illustrative Scales

Characteristics of the High Scorer	Trait Scales	Characteristics of the Low Scorer
	NEUROTICISM (N)	
Worrying, nervous, emotional, insecure, inadequate, hypochodriacal	Assesses adjustment vs. emotional instability. Identifies individuals prone to psychological distress, unrealistic ideas, excessive cravings or urges, and maladaptive coping responses.	Calm, relaxed, unemotional, hardy, secure, self-satisfied
	EXTRAVERSION (E)	
Sociable, active, talkative, person-oriented, optimistic, fun-loving, affectionate	Assesses quantity and intensity of interpersonal interaction; activity level; need for stimulation; and capacity for joy.	Reserved, sober, unexuberant, aloof, task-oriented, retiring, quiet
	OPENNESS (O)	
Curious, broad interests, creative, original, imaginative, untraditional	Assesses proactive seeking and appreciation of experience for its own sake; toleration for and exploration of the unfamiliar.	Conventional, down-to-earth, narrow interests, unartistic, unanalytical
	AGREEABLENESS (A)	
Soft-hearted, good-, natured, trusting, helpful, forgiving, gullible, straightforward	Assesses the quality of one's interpersonal orientation along a continuum from compassion to antagonism in thoughts, feelings, and actions.	Cynical, rude, suspicious, uncooperative, vengeful, ruthless, irritable, manipulative
	CONSCIENTIOUSNESS (C)	
Organized, reliable, hard-working, self-disciplined, punctual, scrupulous, neat, ambitious, persevering	Assesses the individual's degree of organization, persistence, and motivation in goal-directed behavior. Contrasts dependable, fastidious people with those who are lackadaisical and sloppy.	Aimless, unreliable, lazy, careless, lax, negligent, weak-willed, hedonistic

SOURCE: Costa & McCrae, 1992, p. 2.

similar. For example, Goldberg (1992) has suggested an inventory of bipolar traits (e.g., silent-talkative) that individuals can use to rate their own standing on the Big Five dimensions. An abbreviated version of this inventory follows. Please consider the following instructions as you complete this inventory:

> Try to describe yourself as accurately as possible. Describe yourself as you see yourself at the present time, not as you wish to be in the future. Describe yourself as you are generally or typically, as compared with other persons you know of the same sex and of roughly your same age. For each of the trait scales listed, circle a number that best describes you on this dimension.

INTROVERSION VERSUS EXTRAVERSION

	Very		Moderately		Neither		Moderately		Very	
silent	1	2	3	4	5	6	7	8	9	talkative
unassertive	1	2	3	4	5	6	7	8	9	assertive
unadventurous	1	2	3	4	5	6	7	8	9	adventurous
unenergetic	1	2	3	4	5	6	7	8	9	energetic
timid	1	2	3	4	5	6	7	8	9	bold

ANTAGONISM VERSUS AGREEABLENESS

unkind	1	2	3	4	5	6	7	8	9	kind
uncooperative	1	2	3	4	5	6	7	8	9	cooperative
selfish	1	2	3	4	5	6	7	8	9	unselfish
distrustful	1	2	3	4	5	6	7	8	9	trustful
stingy	1	2	3	4	5	6	7	8	9	generous

LACK OF DIRECTION VERSUS CONSCIENTIOUSNESS

disorganized	1	2	3	4	5	6	7	8	9	organized
irresponsible	1	2	3	4	5	6	7	8	9	responsible
impractical	1	2	3	4	5	6	7	8	9	practical
careless	1	2	3	4	5	6	7	8	9	thorough
lazy	1	2	3	4	5	6	7	8	9	hardworking

EMOTIONAL STABILITY VERSUS NEUROTICISM

relaxed	1	2	3	4	5	6	7	8	9	tense
at ease	1	2	3	4	5	6	7	8	9	nervous
stable	1	2	3	4	5	6	7	8	9	unstable
contented	1	2	3	4	5	6	7	8	9	discontented
unemotional	1	2	3	4	5	6	7	8	9	emotional

CLOSEDNESS VERSUS OPENNESS TO NEW EXPERIENCE

unimaginative	1	2	3	4	5	6	7	8	9	imaginative
uncreative	1	2	3	4	5	6	7	8	9	creative
uninquisitive	1	2	3	4	5	6	7	8	9	curious
unreflective	1	2	3	4	5	6	7	8	9	reflective
unsophisticated	1	2	3	4	5	6	7	8	9	sophisticated

Very   Moderately   Neither   Moderately   Very

How did you score? How well do you think that your score captures your true personality? Keep in mind that this inventory is not a formal test but rather a useful exercise to familiarize yourself with the Big Five dimensions and how they might apply to yourself. Nonetheless, if you are interested in your overall Big Five scores, you may want to total up your responses for each factor. Simply add together all the five number you circled for E and divide that sum by 5. Then do the same for each of the other factors. On which factor did you have your highest score? On which did you score lowest? Do the five scores correspond to what you would have expected? Or were there some surprising discrepancies with the way you see yourself in general?

The Fundamental Lexical Hypothesis

The Big Five were designed to capture those personality traits that people consider most important in their lives. Goldberg has spelled out the rationale for this approach in terms of the **fundamental lexical** (language) **hypothesis**: "the most important individual differences in human transactions will come to be encoded as single terms in some or all of the world's languages" (Goldberg, 1990, p. 1216). The hypothesis, then, is that over time humans have found some individual differences particularly important in their interactions and have developed terms for easy reference to them. These trait terms communicate information about individual differences that are important to our own well-being or that of our group or clan. Thus, they are socially useful because they serve the purpose of prediction and control—they help us predict what others will do and thus control our life outcomes (Chaplin et al., 1988). They help answer questions about how an individual is likely to behave across a wide range of relevant situations.

There are some counter-examples to the lexical hypothesis. For example, some writers note that individuals differ in the degree to which they need variety in their lives, or the degree to which they can tolerate ambiguity when making decisions; contrary to the lexical hypothesis, there is no single term in the English language that corresponds to these qualities (McCrae & Costa, 1997). Nonetheless, the lexical hypothesis has been an important stimulant to research, and continues to guide much thinking in the field.

CROSS-CULTURAL RESEARCH: ARE THE BIG FIVE DIMENSIONS UNIVERSAL?

If there are universal questions concerning individual differences and human interaction, then one might expect the same basic trait dimensions to appear in many different languages—in other words, one might expect the Big Five factor structure to be universal. Is there evidence that this is the case? The amount of cross-cultural research on personality traits has increased dramatically in the past decade, primarily due to international research teams that have conducted multinational studies. Thus, it is possible to begin to provide an answer to this question.

Before considering the results of these studies, one must first consider their research methods. In the study of the universality of the Big Five, methodological issues can make a big difference. One issue involves translation. Many researchers studying the universality of personality traits do so by taking a personality questionnaire written in one language (e.g., English) and translating it into others (German, Japanese, etc.). Such translations can be tricky. Languages may lack one-to-one translations and even words that translate the same (e.g., English "aggressive" and the German word meaning "aggressive") do not necessarily mean the same (the German word for "aggressive" means hostile, rather than forceful-assertive). Thus, a word like "outgoing" (an extraversion trait) mistranslated from Japanese into English as "affectionate" (an agreeableness trait) might lead researchers to question whether they have found the same factor in the two languages. To illustrate such problems, Hofstee and colleagues (1997) identified 126 words that they could translate fairly directly across previous lexical studies in English, Dutch, and German and used them to compare the meanings of the factors in the three languages. Their findings showed considerable congruence across these three related languages, with one important exception: the Openness factor. The German and English were very similar but the Dutch factor included not only the expected traits related to intellect and imagination (e.g., inventive, original, imaginative) but also emphasized traits related to unconventionality and rebelliousness. A similar variant of Openness was found in Italian and Hungarian trait studies (Caprara & Perugini, 1994).

A recent quantitative review (De Raad et al., 1998) compared many of the European studies, and concluded that factors similar to the Big Five have been found in most of the languages but the evidence is least compelling for the Openness factor, which appears in various guises. Only a few studies of non-Western languages and cultures (Chinese, Japanese, Filipino) have been completed, and Openness again shows the weakest replicability.

It is important not to overstate evidence for universality. McCrae and Costa (1997) have taken a very strong position, suggesting that the Big Five personality structure is a human universal. The evidence for their conclusion involves translations of their Big Five instrument (the NEO-PI-R, to be considered shortly) into many languages. When researchers work with such translations, the same five factors result with great regularity. But you should note the potential limitation here. It is possible that the process of translating English-language questionnaires into another language forces the issue. The translation process may inadvertently impose certain psychological factors onto respondents in another culture—a culture where the factor may not arise spontaneously. For example, it might be that people in a given culture give relatively little thought to individual differences in Openness—unless a psychologist asks them to think about this feature of personality.

This consideration highlights the importance of an alternative research strategy. Rather than imposing an English-language scale onto members of a different language group, one could study each language group's indigenous personality terms, that is, personality descriptors taken from the native language being studied. When this happens, findings become more complex (Saucier & Goldberg, 1996). Results often differ depending on whether the trait terms are "imposed" on members of a culture as opposed to being drawn from the language of that culture itself. As an example, consider research conducted by Di Blas & Forzi (1999), who explored the structure of personality terms in Italian. They did *not* do this by translating a scale from English into Italian; instead, they selected items directly from the indigenous language. They then asked people to rate themselves on these terms and used factor analysis to see if the Big Five structure, common in English, would replicate in Italian. It didn't—that is, not all five factors replicated consistently. Instead, Di Blas and Forzi (1999, p.

476) "found consistently that a three-factor solution was more stable across participants and observers"; extraversion, agreeableness, and conscientiousness, which generally are more replicable than the other two components of the Big Five model (Saucier, 1997), were the factors found consistently in Italian. The traditional trait factor of neuroticism was not found in the Italian language (Di Blas & Forzi, 1999), a null result similar to that of other investigators (Caprara & Perugini, 1994). The authors suggest that cultural variations in the perceptions of negative emotions in different interpersonal settings may explain the difference between Italian and English-language results (Di Blas & Forzi, 1999).

Yet, sometimes seemingly large cultural variations seem not to make a big difference in the study of personality trait structures. For example, investigators have searched for the Big Five dimensions in the Turkish language and have found them, even when working with indigenous linguistic terms (Somer & Goldberg, 1999).

When scientific results vary from study to study, systematic reviews of the entire literature are of particular value. A recent review of attempts to recover the factor structure across multiple language groups concluded that the three factors identified in Italian— extraversion, agreeableness, and conscientiousness, could be found in most language groups; the other two factors (Neuroticism and Openness to Experience), then, are less cross-culturally reliable (Saucier, Hampson, & Goldberg, 2000).

The existence of variations in results from one country and language to another leads some to suggest that personality factors may exist that are unique to particular cultures. A potential example is a "Chinese tradition" factor (Cheung et al., 1996) which seems to capture values and attitudes considered important in traditional Chinese society. Such culture-specific factors are certainly possible, though further confirmation and replication is needed before we accept these factors as empirical fact. For example, it is possible that such factors do not reflect personality traits proper but other individual differences, such as attitudes and beliefs (e.g., conservative versus liberal).

In sum, there is growing (but still limited) evidence that people in diverse cultures, using very different languages, view individual differences in personality traits in ways similar to the Big Five (De Raad et al., 1998). At least three of the factors—and sometimes all five—are frequently found across cultures and language groups.

There is one caveat. Even if particular trait dimensions are identified cross-culturally, this does not necessarily mean that the various cultures all think about human nature in the same way. The results of trait-theoretical studies tell us what happens if researchers ask people within a culture to rate individual's personality traits. But it is possible that, in some cultures, people do not typically think of others primarily in terms of personality traits, that is, in terms of a person's typical behavioral tendencies. Work in anthropology (Geertz, 1973) and cultural psychology (Heine et al., 1999; Markus & Kitayama, 1991) suggests that, in Asian cultures, people are relatively more attuned to an individual's relation to their family and social group, rather than to an individual's isolated psychological traits. For example, a detailed analysis of person categories in Bali (Geertz, 1973) suggests that people commonly think of others in terms of their social status, public job title, and position within their family. These aspects of personhood are essential to defining the individual in that culture, even though they may be less central to selfhood in Western culture: although

"We [focus] upon psychological traits as the heart of personal identity...they [the Balinese], focusing on social position, say that their role is of the essence of their true selves" (Geertz, 1973, p. 386; also see Chapter 14). Studies of the cross-cultural replicability of the Big Five, then, inform us as to whether a given factor structure is replicated when people are asked to rate individuals' personality traits, but these findings do not inform us as to whether ideas other than personality traits are central to defining the individual in other cultures.

THE BIG FIVE IN PERSONALITY QUESTIONNAIRES

By now it probably is clear to the student of personality that the field does not suffer from a shortage of questionnaires. A questionnaire has been developed for almost every concept and in association with almost every theory of personality. A variety of questionnaire measures are available for assessing the Big Five as well. These include the abbreviated version of Goldberg's (1992) bipolar inventory measuring the Big Five with trait adjectives described earlier in this chapter. In addition, a very elaborate and widely used questionnaire is also available to measure the five factors; it is called the **NEO-PI-R**.

The NEO-PI-R and Its Hierarchical Structure: Facets

In three stages of test construction and revision, Costa and McCrae (1985, 1989, 1992) have developed a questionnaire, the NEO-Personality Inventory Revised (NEO-PI-R), to measure the Big Five personality factors. Originally they had focused only on the three factors of Neuroticism, Extraversion, and Openness, thus the title NEO-Personality Inventory. Subsequently they added the factors of agreeableness and conscientiousness to conform to the five-factor model. Moreover, they differentiated each of the Big Five factors (or domains) into six more specific facets; **facets** are the more specific traits or components that make up each of the broad Big Five factors.

The six facets defining each Big Five factor are listed in Table 8.2, along with a famous individual or fictional character who exemplifies a prototypical high scorer for each factor. For example, in Costa and McCrae's NEO-PI-R, Extraversion is defined by these six facets: Activity Level, Assertiveness, Excitement Seeking, Positive Emotions, Gregariousness, and Warmth. Don't these six facets capture traits that would describe former president Bill Clinton? Each facet is measured by 8 items, so that the most recent NEO-PI-R consists of a total of 240 items (i.e., 5 factors × 6 facets × 8 items). For example, two items from the Activity facet scale are "My life is fast-paced" and "When I do things, I do them vigorously" (Costa & McCrae, 1992, p. 70). Indeed, most observers would agree that Clinton thrived on his fast-paced life in the White House, and he certainly did things vigorously, as the following newspaper report suggests:

> CLINTON PARTIES HEARTY. Between parties, golf and reading, he has little time to rest:
>
> Less than a week into the vacation on Martha's Vineyard, he's stayed out past 11 each night, played saxophone with a jazz band, briefly debated a bicycle courier and attended at least four fundraisers and several parties. That doesn't count his two rounds of golf and the dozen hefty books he brought along.

Presidential vacations may say more about a chief executive's personality and inclinations than will a host of policy speeches. Ronald Reagan rode horses, cut brush, and made little fuss about summer reading lists. George Bush piloted loud powerboats. Richard Nixon walked the beach in black wing tips. Bill Clinton, renowned for his appetite for food, conversation, ideas and—well, let's leave it at that—apparently thinks vacations shouldn't be wasted on frivolities such as sleep but instead should be crammed with as much socializing, golfing, and reading as possible.

SOURCE: *San Francisco Chronicle*, August 25, 1999, p. A4.

When the NEO-PI-R is administered in research and clinical contexts, subjects indicate for each item the extent to which they agree or disagree, using a five-point rating scale. The resulting scales all have good reliability and show validity across different data sources, such as ratings by peers or spouses. McCrae

Table 8.2 Each Big Five Factor Consists of Six Facets and Is Illustrated by an Individual or Fictional Character Who Exemplifies a Prototypical High Scorer

Extraversion	Gregariousness Activity Level Assertiveness Excitement Seeking Positive Emotions Warmth	Bill Clinton U.S. President 1993–2001
Agreeableness	Straightforwardness Trust Altruism Modesty Tendermindedness Compliance	Radar, character from *M*A*S*H*
Conscientiousness	Self-discipline Dutifulness Competence Order Deliberation Achievement striving	Spock, character from *Star Trek*
Neuroticism	Anxiety Self-consciousness Depression Vulnerability Impulsiveness Angry hostility	Woody Allen, Movie Director
Openness to new experience	Fantasy Aesthetics Feelings Ideas Actions Values	Lewis Carroll, Author of *Alice in Wonderland*

and Costa (1990, 2003) argue strongly for the use of structured questionnaires to assess personality and are critical of projective tests and clinical interviews, which they consider unsystematic and prone to biases. Evidence shows that their NEO-PI-R scales also agree well with other Big Five instruments, such as Goldberg's (1992) adjective inventories (John & Srivastava, 1999; Benet-Martinez & John, 1998). Nonetheless, it is important to point out that there are also some differences in which facets are emphasized on each instrument. For example, Costa and McCrae place the warmth facet on Extraversion whereas other Big Five researchers find that warmth is more closely related to Agreeableness (John & Srivastava, 1999). Particular disagreement is found in the conceptualization of the fifth factor, Openness. Goldberg emphasizes intellectual and creative cognition in his measure of this factor, and thus calls it Intellect or Imagination; McCrae (1996) criticizes that view as a too narrow definition of the Openness factor (see Table 8.2). Thus, there are still some inconsistencies among the various researchers that eventually need to be worked out.

INTEGRATION OF EYSENCK'S AND CATTELL'S FACTORS WITHIN THE BIG FIVE

Assuming that the NEO-PI-R is an adequate measure of the five-factor model of personality, to what extent does it correlate with other measures, established by previous investigators? Costa and McCrae accepted this as a challenge to the validity of the test, as well as to the utility of the five-factor model, and offer considerable evidence suggesting that scores on the NEO-PI-R correlate as predicted with scores on other personality questionnaires. In particular, this is true for scores from other questionnaires based on factor analysis (see Chapter 7) such as Eysenck's inventories and Cattell's 16 personality factors (Costa & McCrae, 1992, 1994b).

These findings are important because they finally offer an integration of the older factor-analytic models with the Big Five and thus with each other. In particular, Eysenck's superfactors of Extraversion and Neuroticism were found to be virtually identical to the same-named dimensions in the Big Five, and Eysenck's Psychoticism superfactor was found to correspond to the combination of low Agreeableness and low Conscientiousness—people high in Psychoticism, such as criminals, are both disagreeable and irresponsible (Clark & Watson, 1999; Costa & McCrae, 1995; Goldberg & Rosolack, 1994).

Similarly, Cattell's 16 personality factor scales (Table 7.4 in the preceding chapter) map onto the broader Big Five dimensions in theoretically coherent ways (McCrae & Costa, 2003). For example, his scales Outgoing, Assertive, and Venturesome link with NEO-PI-R Extraversion; Trusting and Tender-minded link with Agreeableness; Conscientious, Controlled, and Sober with (no surprise here) Conscientiousness; Emotional, Tense, and Apprehensive with Neuroticism; and Imaginative and Experimenting with Openness. Referring back to Chapter 7, Figure 7.1, this analysis makes clear that Eysenck's three factors are as broad as the Big Five and even broader for Psychoticism, whereas Cattell's 16 factors are at roughly the same hierarchical level as the facet level in the Big Five. Based on results of this sort, proponents of the Big Five model suggest that it provides a comprehensive framework within Eysenckian and Cattellian constructs can be integrated.

Moreover, the NEO-PI-R shows theoretically coherent relations with personality measures obtained through other means (e.g., Q-sort ratings) and with questionnaires derived from rather different theoretical orientations (e.g., Murray's motivational model of personality). The latter is particularly important because it provides the possibility of establishing a link between traits and motives (Pervin, 1999). On the basis of these kinds of studies, McCrae and Costa argue that the five factors, as assessed by the NEO-PI, are both necessary and sufficient for describing the basic dimensions of personality. Indeed, they go beyond this to suggest that "no other system is as complete and yet as parsimonious" (1990, p. 51).

Another interesting aspect of the NEO-PI-R is that forms are available for both self-report and ratings by others. In several studies, subjects' self-ratings have been compared with ratings by their peers and spouses. McCrae and Costa (1990) report substantial agreement of self-ratings with ratings by peers and with ratings by spouses on all five factors. Agreement between self and spouse is greater than that between self and peer, perhaps because spouses generally know each other better than do friends or because spouses talk a lot about each others' personalities (see Kenny, 1994). Two major findings have emerged from this research: (1) following the distinction between S-data and O-data sources we made in Chapter 2, the same five factors are found in both self-reports and observer ratings, and (2) observers agree reasonably well with each other about the standing of individuals on each Big Five dimension. These findings provide further evidence for the use of self-report measures and the five-factor model of personality.

Thus far, we have said little about a critical conceptual point. It is the question of the conceptual status of the trait constructs. In this regard, note that constructs for characterizing people come in different types. Some terms are merely descriptive labels. They label the way a person tends to act. Other terms refer to psychological properties that a person is said to possess; they refer to mental structures or processes that are causes of the person's behavior. An analogy outside of psychological characteristics makes the distinction between descriptive and causal constructs obvious. Consider physical characteristics and the term "attractive." We often say that someone "is attractive" or is "more attractive than someone else." In doing so, we use the term "attractive" merely as a description. It describes, in a summary form, characteristics that are appealing—characteristics involving physique, facial features, a cute smile, "good hair," and so forth. Although a person really may have those individual physical characteristics, they do not also *have* attractiveness; in other words, we do not use the term attractiveness to refer to a separate biological system that causes the person to have an attractive physique, a cute smile, and so forth. The term "attractive" is a descriptive label, not a single thing that causally influences biological development.

PROPOSED THEORETICAL MODEL FOR THE BIG FIVE

What about trait terms such as the Big Five constructs? Are they merely descriptions of psychological characteristics? Or might the terms also correspond to real psychological entities that individuals possess, and thus, that causally explain the individual's behavior?

Many trait psychologists view the Big Five factors merely as descriptive, or believe that each factor corresponds to some undetermined complex combination of underlying psychological systems. However, in recent years a simpler and bolder theoretical view has been developed by McCrae & Costa (1996, 1999,

Paul T. Costa, Jr.

Robert R. McCrae

2003). They call their ideas the five-factor theory (Figure 8.1). Five-factor theory claims that the five primary traits are more than mere descriptions of ways that people differ. In five-factory theory, the traits are treated as things that really exist; each is seen as a psychological structure that each and every person has in varying amounts (in the way that everyone has, for example, a certain degree of height in varying amounts). The traits are said to causally influence each individual's psychological development. Phrased more technically, in five-factor theory the idea is that the five factors are basic dispositional tendencies that are possessed universally, that is, by all individuals.

McCrae and Costa propose that the factors have a biological basis. Behavioral differences linked to the Big Five are said to be determined by genetic influences on neural structures, brain chemistry, and so on. Indeed, in proposing this model, McCrae and Costa felt that the biological basis of the factors was so strong that the basic five dispositional tendencies are not influenced directly by the environment; their contention was that "Personality traits, like temperaments, are endogenous dispositions that follow intrinsic paths of development essentially independent of environmental influences" (McCrae et al., 2000, p. 173).

Two features of McCrae and Costa's five-factor theory distinguish their approach from that of many other trait theorists. One concerns a classic question for the field of psychology, that of "nature versus nurture" (see Chapter 1). McCrae and Costa's theory is perhaps the strongest "nature" position possible—that is, the strongest possible claim that inherited biology (nature) determines personality and social experience (nurture) has little effect. McCrae and Costa suggest that there is an intrinsic maturation to personality. As is evident from Figure 8.1, in five factor theory traits are expressions of human biology. They are said to be uninfluenced by the environment. The environment is seen to have some influence on features of the person other than their basic traits; for example, self-concept and attitudes are affected,

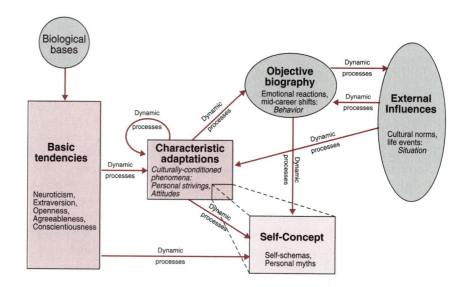

Figure 8.1   A Representation of the Five-Factor Theory Personality System. (Core components are in rectangles; interfacing components are in ellipses.) *(Costa & McCrae, 1999) Reprinted by permission, Guilford Press.*

according to five-factor theory by both basic traits and social experiences. But the traits themselves are inherited biological features in this theoretical view.

The second feature is that McCrae and Costa (1996, 2003) claim that the traits are not merely descriptions of individual differences (akin to "attractiveness" in the earlier example). In their five-factor theory, traits also are treated as causal factors that influence the life course of each and every individual. Each and every person is said to possess a certain level of each of the five factors. This trait level then causally influences the person's life experiences and ultimate psychological development. In five-factor theory, then, a trait construct such as "agreeableness" serves two functions. It not only is (1) a "dimension of individual differences…that applies to populations rather than people" but also is (2) "the underlying causal basis [of]…consistent patterns of thoughts, feelings" where this causal analysis "applies directly to people" (McCrae & Costa, 2003).

Overall, this model has considerable integrative potential, connecting a biological view of traits and environmental influences with the observable personality variables that are of such great concern to the other theoretical orientations represented in this book. At the same time, the model leaves open more questions than it answers. Three issues seem particularly problematic for five-factor theory. Since these three issues are of broad, general importance to personality theory, we will consider them in some detail. The first problem is how to link personality structures to personality processes. Note the arrows specifying "dynamic processes" in Figure 8.1. Trait theory has little to say about these processes; in McCrae and Costa's (1999) view, these are details to be filled in by other theoretical approaches to personality. This unquestionably is a significant theoretical limitation. A particular limitation is not merely that these dynamic processes are not filled in yet, but that it is not at all clear how, even in principle, they could be filled in. In general, personality theorists connect structures to processes by specifying the psychological mechanisms that make up the personality structure and then explaining how those mechanisms guide dynamic personality processing. For example, psychoanalysts posit that the basic mechanisms of the id involve unconscious, biologically based drives, and then explain how these unconscious forces influence observable behavior. But in five-factor theory, the biological and psychological mechanisms associated with the trait structures are unspecified. The traits are thought of merely as "tendencies." Since the causal mechanisms associated with the traits are unknown, it is difficult even to begin building a model that links them to dynamic processes.

The other two problems concern the two unique features of five-factor theory noted earlier. One is the idea that traits are not affected by social factors. The problem is that research findings contradict this theoretical idea. Particularly interesting data claim comes from analyses of changes in personality trait scores that are observed across historical periods. Twenge (2002) reasoned that cultural changes across periods of the 20th century might have caused changes in personality. Consider changes in the United States in the middle versus latter decades of the century. Compared to the 1950s, in the 1990s people experienced a culture with higher divorce rates, higher crime rates, smaller family size, and lesser contact with one's extended family (due to greater job and educational mobility of the population). These sociocultural changes, Twenge finds, were associated with higher levels of anxiety. By examining mean-level scores on anxiety and neuroticism scales in research reports published in the 1950s through 1990s, Twenge was able to demonstrate that anxiety increased significantly during this period. She also found significant increases in extraversion across decades of the 20th century, perhaps reflecting American society's increasing concern with individualism and personal assertiveness (Twenge, 2002). As Twenge notes, these historical changes, which were found to be rather large in size, directly contradict the hypothesis that personality traits are unaffected by social factors.

The third concern regarding five-factor theory is conceptually subtle, yet deeply important. Five-factor theory claims that the five factors are possessed by all individuals. The claim, in other words, is that all individuals possess psychological structures corresponding to each of the factors, with individuals varying in their level on each trait. To five-factor theorists, the factors are analogous to bodily organs (Costa & McCrae, 1998), which might vary in size from one person to another. The problem is that this theoretical claim does not follow, in any direct or logically necessary way, from the available research evidence. The evidence that supports the five-factor model involves statistical analyses of *populations* of persons. When one examines populations, one finds that the five factors do a good job of summarizing individual differences in the population at large. But this finding does not demonstrate that each and every individual in the population possesses each of the five factors. Questions about populations and about individual persons involve different levels of analysis. A statement that may be true about a population of persons (e.g., "the native American population in the United States is shrinking") may not necessarily be true of any individual persons (no individual Native American "is shrinking"; cf. Rorer, 1990).

The question, then, is whether the factors identified when studying populations enable one to make any claims about psychological structures possessed by individual persons. Recently, this question has been taken up in detail by Borsboom, Mellenbergh, and van Heerden (2003). These writers emphasize that the analysis of populations and of individuals are entirely different things. The only way to claim validly that the five factors explain the personality functioning of individuals would be to conduct factor analyses of individuals *one at a time* and to find that, for each individual person, the five-factor model is recovered. As they write, "if one wants to know what happens in a person, one must study that person. This requires representing individual processes where they belong, namely at the level of the individual...one cannot expect between-subjects analyses to miraculously yield information at this level" (Borsboom et al., 2003, p. 216).

At present, relatively few have even tried to find the five-factor structure at the level of the individual. Data that do exist suggest that the behavioral tendencies of individuals commonly differ from the tendencies described by the five-factor model (Borkenau & Ostendorf, 1998). To get an intuitive sense of how an individual's behavioral tendencies may differ from those described by the Big Five traits, think back to what you learned about psychoanalysis. According to the psychoanalytic notion of an Oedipal conflict, a person may display hostile behavior toward a same-sex parent and affectionate behavior toward an opposite-sex parent. In psychoanalysis, this varying, conflicting style of behavior is a basic behavioral tendency of the individual person. Yet nothing resembling Oedipal conflict is found as a single Big Five dimension. A factor analysis of between-person differences does not reveal this within-person style of behavior.

Theorists who are concerned with the difference between within-person and between-person analyses, then, argue that personality trait constructs identified in the study of differences among individuals in the population "abstract from the level of the individual [and] should, for this reason, not be conceptualized as explaining behavior at the level of the individual" (Boorsboom et al., 2003, p. 215). In this view, the big five factors still provide enormously important information. They valuably describe dimensions of variation among individuals in the population at large. The point is that these factors cannot be used also to explain the behavior of individual persons. We return to this issue in the evaluation of trait theory at the end of this chapter.

In general, Big Five researchers have focused their work on personality in adulthood, studying personality stability and change during adulthood and old age but leaving to developmental psychologists the question of how personality develops from infancy into the Big Five structure we know in adulthood. Although there is some difference in views among trait researchers concerning trait stability during childhood, most agree that trait stability is quite high throughout adulthood (Caspi & Roberts, 1999; McCrae & Costa, 1997; Roberts & Del Vecchio, 2000).

GROWTH AND DEVELOPMENT

AGE DIFFERENCES THROUGHOUT ADULTHOOD

Are general levels on the Big Five stable throughout adulthood or are there general changes associated with age? Initial studies in the United States suggested small, though significant, age effects. In particular, older adults score significantly lower in neuroticism, extraversion, and openness, and higher in agreeableness and conscientiousness than adolescents and young adults in their early 20s (e.g., college age) (Costa & McCrae, 1994b). In a way, some of these findings are encouraging, showing that growing older has some desirable effects. These findings make good sense when one compares high school and college students with their (older-adult) parents. On average, teenagers seem to be beset by more anxieties and concerns with acceptance and self-esteem (higher N), spend more time on the phone and in social activities with their friends (higher E), are more open to all kinds of experience and experimentation (higher O), but also are more critical and demanding of specific others and society in general (lower A), and less conscientious and responsible than others (parents, teachers, police) expect them to be (lower C).

Not surprisingly, we speak of "angry young men," not of "angry middle-aged men" or "angry grandfathers." Indeed, the teenage years and early 20s are the times of greatest discontent, turbulence, and revolt. The decrease in A and C also fits with findings from the literature on juvenile delinquency (related to low A and low C and Eysenck's Psychoticism), which decreases markedly after adolescence. More generally, the findings of changes on the Big Five during the 20s have been interpreted as indicating growth toward greater maturity by age 30; the assumption of adult roles in career and parenting brings about greater confidence and emotional balance as well as increased socialization and competence.

However, these findings are ambiguous because, as noted above, the observed differences may reflect not age changes but cohort differences, that is, differences due to generation effects associated with growing up during different time periods. In other words, differences might be due to historical factors (e.g., growing up during the Depression as opposed to during World War II or during the tumultuous 1960s) rather than age factors. For example, today's college students might be less conscientious than their parents' generation when they were in college. Subsequent research by McCrae, Costa, and their collaborators (McCrae et al., 2000; McCrae & Costa, 2003) addressed this limitation by studying age differences in a wide range of cultures. To illustrate, Figure 8.2 shows the findings for Conscientiousness for five cultures. The means are shown for five age groups: 14–17; 18–21; 22–29; 30–49; and 50 and older; when Figure 8.2 shows no entry, then there were not enough subjects for that particular age group. Age trends were generally similar for men and women, and the predicted increase was observed in each culture: people became increasingly conscientious with age.

More generally, McCrae and colleagues (2000) were able to replicate the findings obtained earlier in the United States although they had to modify somewhat their strong earlier stance that there is no personality change after age 30—the new cross-cultural data suggest that some of these age trends continue after age 30, though at a diminished rate. Note that the overall finding is quite astounding: the same pattern of personality trait change was observed across numerous diverse cultures, which differed considerably in their political, cultural, and economic conditions. These findings led McCrae and colleagues to argue that changes in personality trait levels are not closely linked to differential experiences across the life span; instead, as previously noted, they propose that these age differences reflect intrinsic maturation, just like other biologically based systems (e.g., McCrae, 2002).

Yet other researchers provide evidence that suggests somewhat greater degrees of change in personality traits in adulthood and a more significant role for social factors. Ravenna Helson and colleagues (e.g., Helson & Kwan,

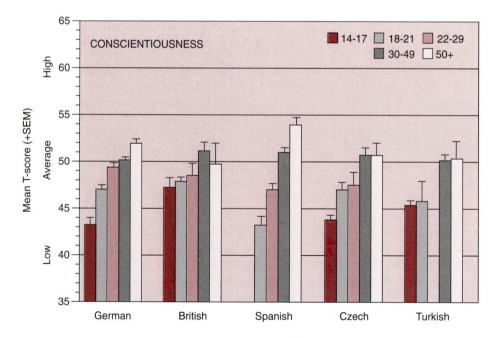

Figure 8.2   Mean Levels of Conscientiousness in Five Cultures. T scores are based on the mean and standard deviation of all respondents over age 21 within each culture. Error bars represent standard errors of the means. *(McCrae et al., 2000)* *Copyright © 2000 American Psychological Association. Reprinted by permission.*

CURRENT APPLICATIONS

AGREEABLENESS INCREASES WITH AGE

At thirty-five, Cage is quick to point out that he has responsibilities. "I have people I have to take care of," Cage says. "Back then, I was living out my fantasies...I wanted to be unpredictable and frightening, and I guess I was. I can't really imagine myself getting that angry now. I haven't punched a wall in years."

SOURCE: *Rolling Stone*, 1999.

Nicolas Cage at age 35: *No longer an angry man.*

2000; Helson, Kwan, John, & Jones, 2002) have studied a group of women residing in northern California over a particularly long period of time. The women were first studied around 1960, when they were seniors in college. Subsequent measures were taken as late as 40 years later, when the women were 61 years old. Clear evidence of changes in personality across adulthood were found. For example, women changed in self-reports of norm orientation (the degree to which one controls emotional impulses in accord with social norms, a quality that correlated with Big Five Agreeableness and Conscientiousness, Helson & Kwan, 2000). On most norm-orientation measures, women's scores consistently increased with increasing age. Conversely, on measures of social vitality (a measure that correlates with extraversion), consistent changes were found in the opposite direction; women scored lower in social vitality with increasing age. A particularly interesting aspect of this study is evidence that changes in women's personality were related to a sociocultural factor, namely, the women's movement, which began to usher in new ideas about gender and women's place in society during the 1960s and 1970s. Findings suggest that "women for whom the [women's] movement was important increased on...Self-acceptance, Dominance, and Empathy scales, that is, they became more 'empowered'—more confident, assertive, and involved in the affective understanding of others" (Helson & Kwan, 2000, p. 96). A recent review (Helson et al., 2002) indicates that such changes are found consistently across different studies and samples of research participants.

Further evidence of changes in personality trait scores during adulthood comes from work by Srivastava, John, Gosling, and Potter (2003). These researchers conducted an Internet survey. In the survey, a large sample of adults of varying ages from the United States and Canada completed a five-factor inventory. The analysis of survey responses revealed significant age-linked changes in most of the Big Five traits for both men and women. For example, self-ratings on the factor of Agreeableness increased significantly for both men and women between the ages of 31 and 50; as the authors note, these are years during which many adults are raising children and these nurturing experiences may alter agreeableness tendencies. The authors emphasize that these results "contradict the five-factor theory's brand of biologism" (Srivastava et al., 2003, p. 1051). In other words, they contradict the notion that personality trait levels are entirely inherited and are unaffected by social experiences (see Figure 8.1). Even though trait theories of personality devote less attention to social influences than do most of the other theoretical frameworks in the field, trait research increasingly provides evidence that personality develops across the course of life as a result of individuals' interactions with the social environment.

Other recent evidence of personality change comes from work that interestingly combines two theoretical approaches. Cramer (2003) explored the possibility that individual differences in the tendency to use alternative defense mechanisms (see Chapter 3) would predict changes in scores on Big Five traits. Her results indicated that the use of defense mechanisms in early adulthood predicted personality trait change in later adulthood; for example, people who tended to employ the relatively immature defense of denial and projection experienced higher levels of neuroticism in later years (Cramer, 2003). In summary, although trait scores are quite stable over time, there also is much indication that they can change in a meaningful, systematic manner.

INITIAL FINDINGS FROM CHILDHOOD AND ADOLESCENCE

The studies we just reviewed concern personality in adulthood. What about earlier periods of development? Much research has explored connections between infant temperament, childhood personality, and the Big Five in adulthood during the past decade (Halverson, Kohnstamm, & Martin, 1994). It is safe to suggest that earlier temperamental characteristics, such as sociability, activity, and emotionality (A. H. Buss & Plomin, 1984), develop and mature into dimensions we know as extraversion and neuroticism in adulthood. However, the exact linkages, and the processes by which this development takes place, have not yet been extensively studied.

One intriguing finding is that personality structure appears to be more complex and less integrated in childhood than in adulthood. Rather than the usual number of five factors, seven child factors were found in the United States (John, Caspi, Robins, Moffitt, & Stouthamer-Loeber, 1994). This finding was replicated in the Netherlands (van Lieshout & Haselager, 1994). Essentially, instead of one broad extraversion factor, the researchers found separate sociability and activity factors, and instead of one broad neuroticism factor, they found separate fearfulness and irritability factors. These findings suggest that the expression of personality may change over the course of development—during the course of adolescence, initially separate dimensions merge together to form the broader, more fully integrated personality dimensions we know in adulthood. The idea that the adult extraversion factor is foreshadowed by separate sociability and activity factors in childhood is consistent with the view that these two attributes are distinct, early emerging, and largely inherited temperament traits (A. H. Buss & Plomin, 1984) (see Chapter 9 for a discussion of temperament and heritability). Thus, John and colleagues suggest:

In early adolescence, when physical activity and athletics play a central role in peer relations and carry social status implications, Extraversion may manifest itself in part through social contact and in part through physical and social vigor. In adulthood, when most social contexts become the arena in which most individuals vie for social status and acceptance, Extraversion may be expressed primarily through social activity, assertiveness, and gregariousness.

SOURCE: John et al., 1994, p. 174.

STABILITY AND CHANGE IN PERSONALITY

How stable are individuals in regard to their basic tendencies during the life course? To the extent that personality traits are like temperament, do they follow the biologically determined path of stable development suggested by Costa and McCrae? Is the rank ordering of individuals on the Big Five stable throughout life even if average levels change somewhat? We will have more to say about this issue in the next chapter but here we may note that differing points of view exist. For example, one view suggests that personality development is largely biologically determined and continuous, that "the child is father of the man" (Caspi, 2000, p. 158). Another view is that although there is evidence of trait consistency across the life course, it is not so high as to warrant the conclusion that change does not occur (Roberts & Del Vecchio, 2000). And, a third view is that although general trait structure and levels remain fairly stable, there is evidence of change in individual trait levels (Asendorpf & van Aken, 1999). Of particular note here is evidence that parenting practices can impact on personality development and that work experiences can impact on personality development during young adulthood (Roberts, 1997; Suomi, 1999). At this point in time the data would appear to suggest the following: (1) Personality is more stable over short periods of time than over long periods of time. (2) Personality is more stable in adulthood than in childhood. (3) Although there is evidence of general trait stability, there are individual differences in stability during development. (4) Although there is evidence of general trait stability, the limits of environmental influence on change, during childhood and adulthood, remain to be determined.

APPLICATIONS OF THE MODEL

As has been indicated, the five-factor model is viewed by many current trait theorists as the basis for an adequate representation of the structure of personality traits. In addition, the NEO-PI-R is viewed as an adequate measure of these traits. An advantage of such consensus is that it enables a large number of researchers to use a common set of ideas and techniques in applications. We now review some of these applications of the five-factor model of personality traits, including areas of career choice, diagnosis of personality and psychopathology, and decisions concerning psychological treatment.

VOCATIONAL INTERESTS

Psychologists interested in the area of vocational (career) behavior suggest that personality is associated with the kinds of careers people choose and how they function in these occupations (De Fruyt & Salgado, 2003; Hogan & Ones, 1997; Roberts & Hogan, 2001). The idea is that people with certain characteristics will select certain occupations and will function better in some occupations than in others. For example, according to the five-factor model, individuals high in Extraversion should prefer and do better in social and enterprising occupations relative to individuals high in introversion. To take another example, people high on Openness to Experience should prefer and do better in artistic and investigative occupations (e.g., journalist, freelance writer) than individuals low on this trait. Since artistic and investigative occupations require curiosity, creativity, and independent thinking, they will be more suitable for individuals high on the Openness to Experience factor.

Although some psychologists suggest that the five-factor model is useful in predicting job performance (Hogan & Ones, 1997), others are more cautious in their evaluation and suggest that several important personality characteristics not within the model are useful in making such predictions (Hough & Oswald, 2000; Matthews, 1997). There is little question that assessments of Big Five traits have some predictive value in the workplace. Yet it is not entirely clear whether results are strong and consistent enough to be of significant practical value to employers. For example, a recent study of personality inventories used in the workplace, including measures of the Big Five factors, reported surprisingly weak results that the authors themselves labeled as "disconcerting" (Anderson & Ones, 2003, p. S60). A particularly discouraging result with regard to practical applications is that different measures of the same personality trait as it is expressed in the workplace failed to converge; this finding sounds "an important note of caution" in that the applied psychologist who wishes to select a certain type of individual in personnel selection would end up selecting different people depending on "which personality inventory is used" (Anderson & Ones, 2003, p. S62).

HEALTH AND LONGEVITY

The idea that personality is related to health dates back at least to the ancient Greeks, who believed there to be a link between disease and temperament. Recent research suggests there may be some truth to this belief. A long-term study points to the importance of conscientiousness in predicting who lives longer (Friedman et al., 1995a, 1995b). In this study, a large sample of children was followed for 70 years by several generations of researchers who kept track of which participants died and the causes of death. Adults who were conscientious as children (according to parent and teacher ratings at age 11) lived significantly longer and were about 30 percent less likely to die in any given year.

Why do conscientious individuals live longer? That is, what are the causal mechanisms that lead to these differences in longevity? First, the researchers ruled out the possibility that environmental variables, such as parental divorce, explain the conscientiousness effects. Second, throughout their lives, conscientious individuals were less likely to die from violent deaths, whereas less conscientious individuals took risks that led to accidents and fights. Third, conscientious people were less likely to smoke and drink heavily. The researchers suggest that conscientiousness is likely to influence a whole pattern of health-relevant behaviors. Thus, in addition to less likelihood of smoking and drinking heavily, they were more likely to do the following: engage in

Personality trait research indicates that people who are high on the trait of conscientiousness take better care of themselves and live longer.

regular exercise, eat a balanced diet, have regular physicals and observe medication regimens, and avoid environmental toxins.

In sum, the effects of being careless or carefree add up throughout one's life and can be quite harmful in the end. More generally, the effects of conscientiousness illustrate that individuals play an important role in making healthy or unhealthy environments for themselves. Friedman and colleagues (1995a) conclude that "Although common wisdom might argue that a self-indulgent boor may prosper by stepping on others, this does not seem to be the case. Nor do we find a triumph of the lazy, pampered drop-out. In terms of the rush toward death, the encouraging news may be that good guys finish last" (p. 76).

CLINICAL PSYCHOLOGY: DIAGNOSIS AND TREATMENT

The Big Five model and the NEO-PI-R are assumed to measure basic emotional, interpersonal, and motivational styles. A number of Big Five researchers have argued recently that many kinds of abnormal behavior may be considered exaggerated versions of normal personality traits (Costa & Widiger, 2001; Widiger, Verhuel, & van den Brink, 1999). In other words, many forms of psychopathology are seen as falling on a continuum with normal personality rather than as representing a distinct departure from the normal (Widiger, 1993). For example, the compulsive personality might be seen as someone extremely high on both Conscientiousness and Neuroticism, and the antisocial personality as someone extremely low on both Agreeableness and Conscientiousness. Thus, it may be the pattern of scores on the five factors that may be most important. This suggests that the five-factor framework would prove valuable not only as a taxonomy of individual differences in everyday personality functioning, but also as a tool for clinical diagnosis.

There also has been interest in using the Big Five model in choosing and planning psychological treatments (Harkness & Lilienfeld, 1997). With an understanding of the individual's personality, the therapist may be in a better position to anticipate problems and plan the course of treatment (MacKenzie, 1994; Sanderson & Clarkin, 1994). Another potentially important contribution may be the guidance that can be given in selecting the optimal form of therapy (Costa & Widiger, 1994; Costa & McCrae, 1992; T. R. Miller, 1991). The principle here is that just as individuals with different personalities function better or worse in different vocations, so too they may profit more or less from different forms of psychological treatment. For example, individuals high in Openness may profit more from therapies that encourage exploration and fantasy than would individuals low on this factor. The latter may prefer and profit better from more directive forms of treatment, including the use of medication. One clinician writing about this notes that he has often heard a patient low on Openness say something like, "Some people need to lie on a couch and talk about their mother. My 'therapy' is working out at the gym" (T. R. Miller, 1991, p. 426). In contrast, the person high on Openness may prefer the exploration of dreams found in psychoanalysis or the emphasis on self-actualization found in the humanistic-existential approach.

In summary, proponents of the five-factor model suggest that as a full portrait of the individual, the model will likely have many valuable applications to the areas of clinical psychology, as well as vocational guidance, health psychology, and other areas of importance. Such applications surely will continue into the future. While recognizing their value, some words of caution also are worth noting. Since many of the applications are recent and ongoing, the degree to which the five factors will prove useful in distinguishing among the many different types of personalities that can succeed in most occupations is not yet clear. Similarly, the model's ability to differentiate among different forms of psychopathology of interest to clinicians is not fully established. A further limitation from the perspective of the clinician is that the model shows more promise as a way of describing various forms of psychopathology than of explaining disorders (T. R. Miller, 1991); unlike some other theoretical approaches, the five-factor model offers little insight into the causal dynamics underlying specific pathologies. Finally, the model offers no therapeutic approach. In contrast to the other theories covered in this book, each of which is associated with a model for the treatment of individuals facing psychological difficulties, the five-factor model is silent in regard to how people can change. Indeed, since the theory suggests that a person's traits cannot change as a function of social experience, it inherently provides no direct insight into change mechanisms.

THE CASE OF JIM

The 16 Personality Favor (P.F.) Questionnaire: Trait, Factor-Analytic Theory

Let us now return to the case of Jim and consider how his personality is depicted by personality trait questionnaires. We begin with the 16 P.F. Questionnaire developed by Cattell. The following brief description of Jim's personality was written by a psychologist who assessed the results of Jim's 16 P.F. but was unaware of any of the other data on him.

> Jim presents himself as a very bright and outgoing young man although he is insecure, easily upset, and somewhat dependent.

Less assertive, conscientious, and venturesome than he may initially appear, Jim is confused and conflicted about who he is and where he is going, tends toward introspection, and is quite anxious. His profile suggests that he may experience periodic mood swings and may also have a history of psychosomatic complaints. Since the 16 P.F. has been administered to college students throughout the country, we can also compare Jim with the average college student. Compared to other students, Jim is more outgoing, intelligent, and affected by feelings—easily upset, hypersensitive, and often depressed and anxious.

Recall that the factor-analytic method allows us to reduce the number of specific traits necessary to describe Jim's personality. Four second-order factors have been derived from Cattell's 16 first-order trait factors: Low Anxiety-High Anxiety, Introversion-Extraversion, Tenderminded Emotionality-Alert Poise, and Subduedness (group-dependent, passive)-Independence. Jim's scores are extreme on two of these factors. First, as expected, Jim is extremely high on anxiety. This suggests that he is dissatisfied with his ability to meet the demands of life and to achieve what he desires. The high level of anxiety also suggests the possibility of physical disturbances and bodily symptoms. Second, Jim is very low on alert poise or, conversely, he is high on tenderminded emotionality. This suggests that rather than being an enterprising and decisive personality, Jim is troubled by emotionality and often becomes discouraged and frustrated. Although sensitive to the subtleties of life, this sensitivity sometimes leads to preoccupation and to too much thought before he takes action. Jim's other two scores indicate that he is neither particularly introverted nor extraverted, and neither excessively dependent nor independent. In summary, his outstanding characteristics are anxiety, sensitivity, and emotionality.

Comments on the Data

Before we leave the 16 P.F., it should be noted that two important features came out in sharper focus on this test than on any of the other assessment devices. The first is the frequency of Jim's mood swings. In reading the results on the 16 P.F., Jim stated that he has frequent and extreme mood swings, ranging from extreme happiness to extreme depression. During the latter periods, he tends to take his feelings out on others and becomes hostile to them in a sarcastic, "biting," or "cutting" way. The second feature of importance concerns psychosomatic complaints. Jim has had considerable difficulty with an ulcer and frequently must drink milk for the condition. Notice that although this is a serious condition that gives him considerable trouble, Jim did not mention it at all in his autobiography.

From the data on the 16 P.F. we can discern many important parts of Jim's personality. The concept of trait, expressing a broad reaction tendency and relatively permanent features of behavior, appears to be useful for the description of his personality. We learn from the 16 P.F. that although Jim is outgoing, he is basically shy and inhibited. Again the characteristics of being anxious, frustrated, and conflicted come through. But one is left wondering whether 16 dimensions are adequate for the description of personality, particularly when they are reduced to four broad dimensions. One also wonders whether a score in the middle of the scale means that the trait is not important for understanding Jim or simply that he is not extreme on that characteristic. The latter appears to be the case. Yet, when one writes up a personality description based on the results of the 16 P.F., the major emphasis tends to fall on scales with extreme scores.

Perhaps most serious, however, is that the results of the 16 P.F. are descriptive, but not interpretive or dynamic. The test yields only a pattern of scores—not a whole individual. Although the Cattelian theory takes into consideration the dynamic interplay among motives, the results of the 16 P.F. appear unrelated to this portion of the theory. Jim is described as being anxious and frustrated, but anxious about what and frustrated for what reason? Why is Jim outgoing and shy? Why does he find it so hard to be decisive and enterprising? The theory recognizes the importance of conflict in the functioning of the individual, but the results of the 16 P.F. tell us nothing about the nature of Jim's conflicts and how he tries to handle them. The factor traits appear to have some degree of validity, but they also tend to be abstract and leave out the richness of personality found in data from other assessment devices. Note that the same problem would have arisen if Jim had been assessed in terms of five-factor scores; one still would have obtained a collection of test scores, but little understanding of how and why one score might, for example, relate to another.

The Stability of Personality: Jim 5 and 20 Years Later

The material on Jim presented so far was written at approximately the time of his graduation from college in the late 1960s. Since then, sufficient time has elapsed to consider changes in his life and possible changes in his personality. This is particularly important in relation to trait theory since, as we have seen, considerable stability is suggested.

Five years after graduation Jim was contacted and asked (1) to indicate whether there had been significant life experiences for him since graduation and, if so, to describe how they had affected him and (2) to give a brief description of his personality and to describe the ways, if any, in which he had changed since graduation. His response follows.

> "After leaving college, I entered business school. I only got into one graduate school in psychology; it was not particularly prestigious, whereas I got into a number of excellent business schools, and so on that basis I chose to go to business school. I did not really enjoy business school, though it was not terribly noxious either, but it was clear to me that my interest really was in the field of psychology, so I applied to a couple of schools during the academic year but did not get in. I had a job in a New York import-export firm over the summer, and disliked it intensely enough to once more write to graduate schools over the summer. I was accepted at two, and then went into a very difficult decision-making process. My parents explicitly wanted me to return to business school, but I eventually decided to try

graduate school. My ability to make that decision in the face of parental opposition was very significant for me; it asserted my strength and independence as nothing else in my life ever had.

"Going through graduate school in the Midwest in clinical psychology was extremely significant for me. I have a keen professional identification as a clinician which is quite central to my self-concept. I have a system of thinking which is well-grounded and very central to the way I deal with my environment. I am entirely pleased with the decision I made, even though I still toy with the idea of returning to business school. Even if I do it, it would be to attain an adjunct degree; it would not change the fact that my primary identification is with psychology. I also fell in love during my first year in graduate school, for the first and only time in my life. The relationship did not work out, which was devastating to me, and I've not gotten completely over it yet. Despite the pain, however, it was a life-infusing experience.

"Last year I lived in a communal setting and it was a watershed experience for me. We worked a lot on ourselves and each other during the year, in our formal once-a-week groups and informally at any time, and it was a frequently painful, frequently joyful, and always a growth-producing experience. I am convinced that I would like to live communally as my basic style of life, though I need a very special group of people to do it with and would rather live alone or with one or two other people than with just any group. Our group is thinking about getting together again in a more permanent arrangement, and I may very well decide to live with them again beginning next year. Whether or not this happens, last year's experience was very significant for me, and therapeutic in every respect.

"Toward the end of last year, I began a relationship which has now become primary for me. I am living with a woman, Kathy, who is in a master's program in social work. She has been married twice. It is a sober relationship with problems involved; basically, there are some things about her that I am not comfortable with. I do not feel 'in love' at this point, but there are a great many things about her that I like and appreciate, and so I am remaining in the relationship to see what develops, and how I feel about continuing to be with her. I have no plans to get married, nor much immediate interest in doing so. The relationship does not have the passionate feeling that my other significant relationship had, and I am presently trying to work through how much of my feeling at that time was idealization and how much real, and whether my more sober feelings for Kathy indicate that she's not the right woman for me or whether I need to come to grips with the fact that no woman is going to be 'perfect' for me. In any event, my relationship with Kathy also feels like a wonderful growth-producing experience, and is the most significant life experience I am currently involved in.

"I think these constitute my significant life experiences since leaving college.

"I do not think I've changed in very basic ways since leaving college. As a result of going into psychology, I think of myself as somewhat more self-aware these days, which I think is helpful. As I remember your interpretation of the tests I took back then, you saw me as primarily depressive. At this point, however, I think of myself as being primarily obsessive. I think I am prone to depression, but on balance see myself as happier these days—less frequently depressed. I see my obsessiveness as a deeply ingrained characterological pattern, and have been thinking for some time now about going into analysis to work on it (amongst other things, of course). Though I consider my thinking about this serious, I am not yet very close to actually doing it. This is at least in part because I expect to be leaving Michigan at the end of this academic year, and so entering analysis at this point obviously makes no sense. On the other hand, it's a frightening proposition requiring a serious commitment, so there is some resistance to overcome over and above the geographic issue. Nevertheless, I see it as a definite possibility for myself in the next couple of years.

"Let me say a word about my history with psychotherapy as a patient. I have made a number of abortive efforts to become involved, only one of which was even moderately successful. I saw someone at college a handful of times, but as I remember it, it was very superficial in every sense. I did nothing my year at business school. During my first year in graduate school, I saw an analytically oriented psychiatrist for three 'evaluative sessions,' after which he recommended: (1) analysis; (2) group therapy; (3) analytically oriented individual therapy. I was not ready to enter either analysis or a group, and did not want to continue with what he considered a third alternative, so I stopped. My second year in graduate school, I saw an analytically oriented psychiatrist for between six and eight sessions, but became very frustrated with his giving me so little, so that when he recommended increasing the frequency of visits from once to twice a week, I terminated. A big issue for me was how good a therapist he was: I saw him as pretty average, and felt I wanted someone special. This is clearly a form of resistance, I know, though I still feel there was some reality to my impressions of him. During my third year in graduate school, I saw a nontraditional psychiatrist about ten times. He used a mixed bag of techniques: cathartic, Gestalt, behavioral, and generally folksy and friendly (very anti-analytic). At the end of our relationship, which I thought was somewhat useful at the time, we both felt I'd had enough therapy, and that what I needed were "therapeutic" life experiences: e.g., a relationship with a woman, some time to play, etc. Since then I have had some important therapeutic life experiences, the most significant of which was living in the house I lived in last year. As a result, I feel less immediate pressure to get help, and think of going into analysis to work through basis characterological issues (like my obsessiveness). In other words, I feel in less acute pain these days.

"As I said previously, I see myself as more similar to, than different from, the way I was five years ago. I think of myself as a witty, aware, interesting and fun-loving person. I continue to be quite moody, so sometimes none of these characteristics is in evidence at all. My sexual relationship with my girlfriend has put to rest my concern about my sexual adequacy (especially about premature ejaculation).

"I still see myself as having an 'authority' issue—i.e., being quite sensitive and vulnerable to the way in which those who have authority over me treat me. However, I see myself as having a number of important professional skills, and as being in the field I want to be in. I still have money issues—i.e., I am concerned about being paid fairly for what I do, I resent psychiatrists making more than me, I am vigilant around making sure I am not 'ripped off,' etc. I still have not fully come to grips with my father having money, and the fact that I will be getting some of that, but on the other hand I'm not terribly concerned about it, and it feels more like an intellectualized concern about the future than an emotional concern in the present. I am extremely compulsive, I very efficiently get done what needs to be done, and experience considerable anxiety when I am not on top of things. My life must be very well ordered for it to be possible for me to relax and enjoy myself. Unfortunately, the compulsiveness spills over into my personal life, so that my room must be orderly, my books stacked appropriately, etc., or else I experience anxiety. Again, this feels like a deeply ingrained pattern which would not be easy to overcome."

Jim, now in his 40s, is practicing as a consulting psychologist in a medium-sized city on the West Coast. The most important events over the past years for him have been his marriage, the birth of a child, and the stabilization of a professional identity.

Prior to his marriage he was involved in lengthy relationships with two women. Though they were very different from one another, he found himself critical and discontented with each. He met his current wife about four years ago. He describes her as calm and peaceful, with a good sense of perspective on life. Although she is somewhat like one of the earlier women, he feels that he has changed in a way that makes a lasting relationship more possible: "I have a greater capacity for acceptance of the other and a clearer sense of boundaries between me and others—she is she and I am I. And, she accepts me, foibles and all."

Jim feels that he has made progress in what he calls "getting out of myself," but feels that his narcissism remains an important issue: "I'm selectively perfectionistic with myself, unforgiving of myself. If I lose money I punish myself. As a teenager I lost twenty dollars and went without lunches all summer long. I didn't need the money. My family has plenty of it. But what I did was unforgiveable. Is it perfectionistic or compulsive? I push myself all the time. I must read the newspaper thoroughly seven days a week. I feel imprisoned by it a lot of the time. Can I give up these rituals and self-indulgences with the birth of a child? I must."

Five-Factor Model:
Self-ratings and Ratings by Wife on the NEO-PI

The NEO-PI as a measure of the five-factor model of personality was not available at the time of the original testing. Therefore, it seemed like a good idea to have Jim take the test at this time. In addition to the self-ratings, it was possible to obtain ratings of Jim by his wife. This offers an interesting opportunity to examine the degree of self-observer agreement, which the authors of the NEO-PI report to be generally high.

In terms of self-ratings, the most distinctive feature of Jim's personality is his very low standing on Agreeableness. The testing report based on his responses indicates that people with his score are antagonistic and tend to be brusque or even rude in dealing with others. In addition, they prefer competition to cooperation and express hostile feelings directly, with little hesitation. They are described by people as relatively stubborn, critical, manipulative, or selfish.

Two other significant features of Jim's responses were his very high ratings on Extraversion and Neuroticism. In terms of the former, the report indicates that such people greatly enjoy the company of others and often are described by others as sociable, fun-loving, and talkative. The more specific subscale scores indicate that he sees himself as forceful and dominant, and prefers to be a group leader rather than a follower. In terms of Neuroticism, Jim's score is characteristic of individuals prone to have a high level of negative emotion and frequent episodes of psychological distress. According to his interpretive report, such individuals tend to be moody, overly sensitive, low in self-esteem, dissatisfied, worriers, and described by friends as nervous, self-conscious, and high-strung.

In terms of the two remaining factors, Jim scored high on Conscientiousness, indicating a high need for achievement and ability to work in an organized way toward goals, and average on Openness, indicating he values the new and the familiar about equally. Additional personality correlates suggested in the report were that he likely uses ineffective coping responses in dealing with the stresses of everyday life and that he is overly sensitive to signs of physical problems and illnesses.

How similar a picture of Jim is given by his wife? On three of the five factors there is very close agreement. Both Jim and his wife saw him as very high on Extraversion, average on Openness, and very low on Agreeableness. There was a small difference in relation to Conscientiousness, with Jim rating himself slightly higher than his wife rated him. The big difference in ratings occurred in relation to Neuroticism, where Jim rated himself as very high and his wife rated him as low. The more specific subscales indicated that Jim saw himself as much more anxious, hostile, and depressed than his wife rated him to be. In addition, he viewed himself as somewhat more self-conscious and vulnerable than his wife rated him, although both agreed that he is average or below average in regard to these traits. Whereas Jim's self-ratings suggests a person who is anxious and prone to worry, his wife's ratings suggest an individual who is calm and generally free of worry. In addition, whereas his responses suggest a person with ineffective devices for coping with stress and oversensitivity to physical problems, his wife's ratings portray an individual with effective coping devices and a tendency to discount physical and medical complaints.

How are we to evaluate such a level of agreement? In some ways, this is like asking whether a glass is half-filled or half-empty. The generally high level of agreement supports the suggestion that self-ratings tend to be accurate. On the other hand, in one area the disagreement is dramatic. Perhaps Jim's wife generally sees him in a more positive way, perhaps even in a more accurate way, since Jim can be very self-critical. Another possibility is that, as indicated in his Rorschach report some 20 years earlier, Jim hides some of these negative emotions behind a façade of poise and does not share with his wife the negative emotions he actually feels. Of course, what we do not know is just how these differences in ratings influence their marriage, that is, whether the differences in perception represent areas of difficulty between them or instead are acceptable, perhaps even desirable, in terms of their marital relationship.

EVALUATION: THE PERSON-SITUATION CONTROVERSY

When we began our coverage of the trait approach in Chapter 7, we explained that "traits refer to consistent patterns in the way individuals behave, feel, and think." At the time (as you may have noticed) we skipped over a question: Exactly how consistent are an individual's patterns of behavior, feeling, and thought?" Consider your own experiences. Are you consistently extraverted? Or conscientious? Or agreeable? Or are you sometimes extraverted and, at other times, shy and inhibited? In some situations conscientious, but in others unreliable? Often agreeable, but sometimes in a disagreeable mood?

Since the 1960s, trait theory has often been criticized for overemphasizing the consistency of social behavior. Although various writers raised this criticism at the time, by far the most influential critique was that of Walter Mischel, whose book *Personality and Assessment* (1968) profoundly affected the field. Mischel's review of research evidence led him to conclude that people's behavior often varies—that is, is "inconsistent"—from one situation to another. This inconsistency, he reasoned, reflects a basic human capability, namely, the capability to discriminate between different situations and to vary one's actions in accord with the different rewards and punishments present in different circumstances. Mischel, of course, was not alone in his criticism; others have noted that trait constructs often are not very effective in predicting behavior (Bandura, 1999; Pervin, 1994), and have extended the argument that situational factors are of much greater importance in the determination of human behavior than trait theorists suggest. In the 1970s and early 1980s, debate over these questions—what came to be known as the **"person-situation controversy"**—dominated much of the professional field.

In considering whether people are "consistent" in their personality traits, one must distinguish between two aspects of such consistency: longitudinal stability and cross-situational consistency. The first, longitudinal stability, asks whether people high on a trait at one point in time are also high on that trait at another point in time. The second, cross-situational, asks whether people high on that trait in some situations are also high on that trait in other situations. Trait theorists suggest that both are true, that is, that people are stable over time and across situations in their trait personality characteristics. Of course, it is this view, particularly the aspect of cross-situational stability, that is attacked by proponents of a more situationist position.

LONGITUDINAL STABILITY

There is good evidence of the longitudinal stability of traits, even over extended periods of time (Block, 1971; Caspi, 2000; Conley, 1985). Longitudinal consistency exists in at least three forms. First, if one compares age groups, asking if 30-year-olds versus 50-year-olds differ on Big Five dimensions, one commonly finds rather small differences, a point that has been particularly emphasized by the five-factor theorists McCrae and Costa (1997, 2002).

Second, if one asks about person-to-person longitudinal stability—i.e., if Person X is more extraverted than Person Y when they are both 30 years old, will Person X still be more extraverted than Person Y when they are 40 years old?—one again finds evidence of significant stability. Interestingly, these forms of stability are evident not only when people rate their own personality, but when other people rate their personality. "Husbands' and wives' views of their spouses' personalities confirm the essential stability of personality" (McCrae & Costa, 1990, p. 95).

Thirdly, there is evidence of longitudinal stability of specific trait-related behaviors. Suppose one picked a particular behavior that is an example of a broader trait. For example, if one is interested in the trait of honesty, one might study whether people cheat on tests (Hartshorne & May, 1929). If one is interested in conscientiousness, one might record whether students show up on time for a class or take clear lecture notes (Mischel & Peake, 1983). When researchers have studied such behaviors at different points in time—for example, examining whether students who show up for class and take good notes at the beginning of an academic semester continue to do so in the middle of the semester—they generally have found strong evidence of longitudinal stability (Hartshorne & May, 1928; Mischel & Peake, 1983).

Why might there be considerable longitudinal stability to personality traits? One obvious possibility is that genetically determined biological factors influence personality traits; since biological structures are relatively stable across time, the traits are too. But theorists of personality and development also have emphasized that environmental factors contribute to longitudinal stability (Lewis, 2002). People select and shape their environments so as to reinforce their traits. An extravert does not just wait for situations to happen but seeks out others and often encourages others to be extraverted as well. Finally, once perceived in a certain way, others behave toward a person in a way that perpetuates already existing characteristics. Thus, although personality can change, there are powerful forces operating to maintain stability over time.

CROSS-SITUATIONAL STABILITY

The issue of cross-situational consistency is more complex than that of longitudinal consistency. One must consider a range of conceptual and methodological issues before one can make any sense of empirical results. One issue is how to decide that a person has acted, across situations, in a manner that we should call "consistent" or "inconsistent." It would not make sense for a person to behave the same way in all situations, nor would trait theorists expect this to happen. One would hardly expect evidence of aggressiveness in a religious ceremony or of agreeableness in a football game. The trait position that needs to be evaluated empirically is whether there is consistency across a range of situations where different behaviors are considered expressive of the same trait.

Another issue concerns research methodology. It is difficult to find consistency in specific behaviors performed in specific situations because single measures of behavior contain substantial *error of measurement*. To understand the notion of error of measurement, consider two different multiple-choice tests that you might take in the personality course in which you are enrolled. One test contains 50 questions written by your wise and thoughtful professor, who tries to ensure that all questions fairly represent the material in the course. The other test is written by the same wise and thoughtful professor, who continues to ensure that the questions are all fair, but on this second test there are only five questions instead of 50. The test with only five questions obviously is not as good of a test. It does not yield as accurate an estimate of your knowledge of the course material. To see why, suppose that you knew 100% of the answers to the questions but happened to make one stupid mistake in which you indicated "b" on a multiple-choice test item when you wanted to indicate "a." On the 50-item exam, you would still do great on the test: you'd have a 49/50, or 98%. But if the same thing happened on the shorter test, your one mistake would give you a 4/5, or only 80%. Psychologists use the notion of "error of measurement" to describe the fact that, as illustrated, shorter tests are more strongly affected by random factors that have nothing to do with one's true trait score.

Error of measurement is important in evaluating trait theory because, when asking about the consistency of personality traits, one must ensure that measures of the traits contain minimal error of measurement. As the psychologist Seymour Epstein (1983) has noted, research in personality psychology commonly has suffered from too much error of measurement. For example, a psychologist might construct a 50-item questionnaire to measure Conscientiousness, and then measure a single behavioral act of conscientious behavior to see if the trait predicts the behavior. But, in so doing, the psychologist may forget that the measure of behavior is, in essence, a one-item test. The research participant's conscientious behavior is only measured once. Since one-item tests have a high degree of error, the behavior measure may be so error-filled that it is impossible to predict. The solution to this problem is to sample a large number of behaviors and to average together, or aggregate, across multiple measures (Epstein, 1983). One reason trait psychologists like to use questionnaires is that they provide for the assessment of behavior in a wide range of situations that might be impossible to measure by other means.

So what happens if one takes these considerations into account and actually measures the consistency of trait-related behavior? One answer to this question comes from a study of the consistency of behaviors related to conscientiousness among college students, conducted by Mischel and Peake (1983; also see Current Applications box on page 284–285). These investigators solved the problem of determining what "counts" as conscientiousness by asking students to nominate behaviors that represent the trait in a college environment (e.g., taking clear class notes). They solved the problem of error of measurement by measuring behaviors on multiple occasions and aggregating the measures together (Epstein, 1983). Their results yielded impressive evidence of *longitudinal* stability of trait-related behaviors (Table 8.3); people who were relatively high on conscientiousness at one point of the semester continued to act conscientiously later in the semester. However, levels of *cross-situational* consistency were relatively low (Table 8.3). It was commonly the case that students were conscientious in some settings (e.g., they took good lecture notes) but not conscientious in other settings (e.g., their dorm room was a mess). It

CROSS-SITUATIONAL CONSISTENCY IN PUNCTUALITY: ARE SOME PEOPLE NOTORIOUSLY LATE?

"Five people showed up late to class the other night. This would be no big deal, except that the class they were late for was a class on how not to be late. The class, called 'Never Be Late Again,' is given once a month in a downtown San Francisco hotel by the Learning Annex...Della, a truck driver, said she has been late to work all her life. If she is late one more time, even by a single minute, she stands to lose her job. 'I need help,' she said."

SOURCE: John Carroll,
San Francisco Chronicle,
May 3, 1991, p. e10

Is it true that there is considerable cross-situational consistency in how late people are? Dudycha (1936) was the first psychologist to study punctuality empirically. He recorded children's arrival times to various school and social activities and found a modest degree of consistency. More recently, Mischel and Peake (1982) assessed various behavioral manifestations of conscientiousness, including several measures of subjects' arrival times. Their research findings indicated that behavioral consistency across situations was low at best. For example, people commonly might display signs of conscientiousness in classroom settings (e.g., taking clear lecture notes) but not display conscientiousness in other aspects of their life (e.g., the person might have a messy dorm room, despite having clear lecture notes).

Ware and John (1995) asked a slightly different question: Do self-reports on the broad Conscientiousness factor from the five-factor model help us predict individual differences in punctuality? The subjects were Berkeley students in the Masters of Business Administration Program whose arrival times at a managerial assessment program were recorded on several

days. Conscientiousness was measured with the NEO-PI self-report scale two weeks prior to the experiment, thus allowing the researchers to divide up the sample beforehand into high and low Conscientiousness groups. Individual differences in lateness were substantial; subjects' arrival times ranged from 30 minutes early (a score of –30) to 46 minutes late (a score of +46 on lateness).

There were two kinds of situations: one was an easy appointment time (5 p.m.) and the other a more difficult one (8 a.m.). The findings are illustrated in the figure below. Students high in Conscientiousness consistently arrived earlier than the students low in Conscientiousness, by about 5 minutes, and this effect held in both situations. Generally students were consistent in their relative promptness across the situations and their conscientiousness scores predicted lateness to a statistically significant degree (see accompanying figure).

How large is this conscientiousness effect? Five minutes late on one day may not seem that much. But consider that 50 percent of the students were classified as relatively low on Conscientiousness and they arrived an average of 5 minutes later for each of their

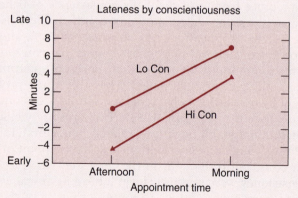

Lateness by conscientiousness

GEECH reprinted by permission of United Feature Syndicate, Inc.

appointments. That adds up to an hour late in 12 appointments. At a job, it would translate into almost a half hour of work missed per week, 2 hours per month, and 24 hours (that is, 3 whole work days) per year. Thus, what seems like a small effect can quickly snowball. No wonder that Della, the truck driver, is in trouble at her job! These findings illustrate, then, that people's self-reports of their tendencies to be conscientious can predict individual differences in an important life outcome.

SOURCES: Dudycha, 1936; Mischel & Peake, 1982; Ware & John, 1995.

is important to note that levels of cross-situational consistency were not zero; people did display some consistency in their trait-related behaviors. Furthermore, levels of cross-situational consistency are higher if one focuses on a subset of the conscientious behaviors; for example, high consistency is found across a set of acts that relate specifically to classroom-related consistency (Jackson & Paunonen, 1985). Nonetheless, Mischel and Peake (1983) emphasize that a basic fact of social life is that people may vary their behavior from one situation to another. In so doing, they commonly may display behaviors that are inconsistent with respect to a broad personality trait. This

Table 8.3 Cross-situational Consistency and Temporal Stability of Conscientious Behavior

	Self-Perceived Consistency	
	High	Low
Cross-situational consistency	.15	.13
Temporal stability	.71	.47

NOTE: Cross-situational consistency and temporal stability examined among people who saw themselves as relatively consistent and inconsistent (High and Low Self-Perceived Consistency). Data are from behaviors judged as highly representative of the trait under study, conscientiousness.

SOURCE: Mischel & Peake, 1983)

result was consistent with findings from much earlier in the field's history; a classic study by Hartshorn and May (1928) similarly indicated that levels of longitudinal stability could be quite high, whereas the cross-situational consistency of behaviors related to a broad trait might be low. More recent analyses (Fleeson, 2001) indicate that most people display a wide range of trait-relevant behavior, that is, most people are extraverted sometimes and introverted at other times, displaying a wide range of trait-relevant behavior across the different situations of their daily life.

There are other considerations to bear in mind when posing questions about cross-situational consistency. For example, behaviors that appear to be different may in fact be expressive of the same trait; being talkative, having many friends, and seeking strong stimulation all may be seen as indications of extraversion. One would expect this trait to be reflected in different behaviors in different situations. If room is left for such observations and measurements, consistency is observed (Buss & Craik, 1983; Loevinger & Knoll, 1983). A further consideration is that evidence of consistency is better when self-report data and observations in the natural environment are used as opposed to laboratory test data (Block, 1977). Laboratory situations may restrict the opportunities for individual differences to emerge (Monson et al., 1982). Most students who have been subjects in laboratory experiments will be aware that relatively little room is given for a wide range of responses. This is consistent with the effort of the experimenter to gain control over the variables and establish cause-effect relations. In addition, unlike the real world, laboratory tests do not provide the opportunity to seek, select, and shape the situation. In the real world, people behave consistently in part because they select and shape the very situations that influence their behavior (Caspi & Bem, 1990; Scarr, 1992). This is why naturalistic studies of consistency (e.g., Hartshorn & May, 1929; Mischel & Peake, 1983) are of such importance.

CONCLUSION

Where does this leave us in terms of the person-situation controversy? Like other questions in this field, answering this question is a bit like answering the question of whether a 10-ounce glass with 5 ounces of water is half empty or half full. The answer one reaches depends on the perspective one takes.

On the one hand, there unquestionably is positive evidence of consistency in trait-related behaviors. Consistency appears to a greater degree within delimited domains of situations (e.g., home, school, work, friends, recreation) than across domains of situations. An interesting implication is that since people tend to observe one another across limited ranges of situations, there may appear to be greater consistency than actually exists. But even looking across diverse settings, consistency correlations are greater than zero. The glass surely is not empty.

The other perspective is one emphasized by Mischel (1968, 1999b) and others (Cervone & Shoda, 1999a). Their argument essentially contains two parts. First, they note that all psychologists, trait theorists or not, would agree that the cross-situational consistency of behaviors that are recognized as related to broad traits, such as the Big Five, is not particularly large. Whether one thinks that typical correlations are .2, .3, or .4, it remains that the majority of variation is not predictable from global trait measures. The argument, then, is this: In building a theory of personality, why adopt constructs that one knows, for sure, only predict a minority of the variance in behavior? By analogy, if Isaac Newton had found that constructs such as "gravity" or "mass" enabled him to predict only a minority of variance in the behavior of physical objects (e.g., if his predictions correlated only .3 with observations of the physical world), would he have shouted "Eureka!"? Or wouldn't he have sought better constructs that might yield better predictions? The second part of the argument involves a basic fact of social life: People strategically vary their behavior to meet their needs and goals. For example, even if you're low on conscientiousness, you might act conscientiously in class when there's a really important exam coming up, or you might be interpersonally conscientious when trying to make a good impression on a date. If you're usually an agreeable person, you still might act in a disagreeable manner toward people you don't like or people who you think have something against you. Such variability in action is a natural part of life. Since people commonly vary their behavior in this manner as they adapt to different situations, many would argue that a science of personality should try to explain this variability. This requires additional types of personality variables, specifically, personality variables that speak not only to consistency in behavior but to strategic variability in action. Trait constructs, whatever their merits, do not explain variations in action; they correspond to average behavioral consistencies (e.g., your typical level of conscientiousness) not to behavioral variability (the fact that you sometimes are and sometimes are not conscientious).

To many psychologists, these arguments imply that some other types of psychological constructs—something beyond merely personality trait variables (Cervone & Shoda, 1999a)—are required for a psychology of personality. All personality psychologists—including trait theorists—recognize that people's behavior changes as they confront different situations. But something that differentiates the theories we will discuss in subsequent chapters from the efforts of trait theorists is that subsequent theories do not merely recognize situation-to-situation variability in behavior. They also try explicitly to incorporate, into their theories, personality variables that explain this variability (as well as explaining consistencies in behavior). This perspective suggests a way of resolving the "person versus situation" debate. It can be resolved by dropping the word "versus" and recognizing that one may learn more about persons by examining systematically the ways in which they react and adapt to different situations.

OVERALL EVALUATION OF TRAIT THEORY

Having reviewed various trait theories and some of the relevant evidence, it is time to evaluate the trait position. Although differences exist among trait theorists, they share an emphasis on individual differences in broad dispositions to behave in particular ways. During the 1970s and 1980s, it seemed as if the trait position might be buried by situationist criticism and the cognitive revolution. Today, trait research is flourishing again, so much so that one reviewer suggests that "after decades of doubt and discrimination, traits are back on top" (McAdams, 1992, p. 329).

Although it is true that reports of the death of trait theory were unfounded, it is equally the case that proclamations of discovery of the basic structure of personality seem premature. Let us try to provide a balanced assessment of the strengths and limitations of this important and controversial part of the field. We will begin by considering three important contributions of trait psychologists: the development of an active research effort, of interesting hypotheses, and of potential ties to the field of biology. This will be followed by consideration of three problem areas: problems with the method of factor analysis, problems with the trait concept, and the neglect of important aspects of personality.

STRENGTHS OF THE APPROACHES

Active Research Effort

As a group, trait psychologists have been very active in research. If the person-situation controversy has not been settled, at least there is considerable evidence of stability in personality functioning (Kenrick & Funder, 1988). Recognizing that human behavior is complex and generally determined by many traits, evidence of the predictive use of traits has been obtained (Brody, 1988; Hogan & Ones, 1997; McCrae & John, 1992). Important gains have been made in research on genetic contributions to personality and on physiological aspects of trait characteristics (Clark & Watson, 1999; Eysenck, 1990; Plomin et al., 1990; Zuckerman, 1990). Finally, important research programs are investigating the relation of traits to interpersonal behavior and psychopathology (Widier & Trull, 1992; Wiggins et al., 1989; Wiggins & Pincus, 1994). Over a decade ago, in response to situationist criticism, it was suggested that traits were alive and well (Epstein, 1977). If this was true at that time, then they are alive and doing even better now.

Interesting Hypotheses

At this point, a number of interesting hypotheses are emerging from proponents of the trait point of view. Some have already been discussed in this chapter. For example, there is the fundamental lexical hypothesis, suggesting that important individual differences will be encoded in language. Early studies have provided cross-cultural evidence in support of this hypothesis, although the results are less clear-cut when individuals using non-Western languages generate their own personality descriptions (Yang & Bond, 1990). Second, there is the interesting hypothesis that environments are important in personality development, but that it is the environment that is not shared by members of the same family that is crucial (Plomin & Daniels, 1987; Plomin et al., 1990).

Potential Ties to Biology

Theoretical and research work in relation to genetics, physiological functioning, and evolutionary theory suggests a link between personality psychology and biology that may hold promise for the future (Pickering & Gray, 1999). As will be discussed in the next chapter, the field of biology has made enormous gains over the past decade. As a minimum, concepts in personality cannot violate what is known about the biological functioning of humans. Beyond this, however, developments in biology may guide some of our research efforts. The trait model particularly, with its emphasis on personality structure and genetic influences, lends itself to the integration of biological findings into a comprehensive model of personality.

The above are some of the strengths of the trait position, gains both made and promised for the future. What of the limitations?

LIMITATIONS OF THE THEORY

Problems with the Method: Factor Analysis

The method of factor analysis is central to trait theory, in particular to development of the five-factor model. Just as Cattell suggested that factor analysis could be used to discover personality's equivalent of chemistry's periodic table of the elements, today's proponents suggest that it has resulted in discovery of the basic dimensions of personality traits—the Big Five (McCrae & John, 1992). At the same time, the method has its critics. Allport, although committed to trait theory, stated that the factors identified through this procedure "resemble sausage meat that has failed to pass the pure food and health inspection" (1958, p. 251). Others are equally critical, suggesting that the method is comparable to putting people through a centrifuge and expecting the "basic stuff" to come out (Lykken, 1971; Tomkins, 1962). Even more critically, Bandura (1999, p. 165) suggests: "Seeking the structure of personality by factor analyzing a limited collection of behavioral descriptors essentially reduces to a psychometric method in search of a theory.… This… is reminiscent of the debates of yesteryear about the correct number of instincts or cardinal motives."

If factor analysis is as powerful as its proponents suggest, essentially the same factors should be found in different studies. Although it has been stated that the five-factor model is a basic discovery of personality psychology and that five factors are "just right" (McCrae & John, 1992), some critics suggest that fewer than five are needed (Eysenck, 1990; Tellegen, 1991; Zuckerman, 1990) and others suggest that five is not nearly enough (A. H. Buss, 1988; Cattell, 1990; Waller, 1999). Beyond this, despite suggestions of a new consensus concerning the Big Five, many suggest that the degree of correspondence among studies has been less than ideal (Block, 1995). In the words of one supporter of trait theory, "the resemblance is more fraternal than identical" (Briggs, 1989, p. 248).

A further issue concerning factor analysis is one we reviewed earlier. The factors that one finds in studying the population cannot be assumed to exist in the psychological makeup of each individual in the population (Borsboom et al., 2003). Since a fundamental goal of personality theory is to explain the psychological experience of individual persons, this is a significant limitation. To appreciate its significance, suppose that one knew nothing about the workings of the human body but wanted to create a science of human biology. What would happen if we started by factor analyzing reports of physical characteristics and tendencies? Conceivably, we might get factors such as attractiveness (a dimension of unattractive versus attractive), athleticism (unathletic versus athletic people), and healthiness (chronically sickly versus healthy persons). Such factors clearly would provide valid information about individual differences; indeed, it would be hard to claim that one "knew about individual differences" in physical characteristics without knowing that people differ on these factors. Yet it is equally clear that one could not claim that individual persons possess "healthiness" or "athleticism" in the same manner that they possess, for example, lungs or a central nervous system. If one wanted to build a biological science that explained the workings of the individual person, one could not base it on the individual-difference variables. (If you currently are taking a biology class, it is unlikely that your textbook has chapters on attractiveness or athleticism.) Instead, one would have to explore biological systems that are discovered by dissecting individual biological beings, not by summarizing individual differences among these beings.

TRAIT APPROACHES AT A GLANCE

Structure	Process	Growth and Development
Traits	Dynamic traits, motives associated with traits	Contributions of heredity and environment to traits

Table 8.4   Summary of Strengths and Limitations of Trait Theory

Strengths	Limitations
1. Active research effort	1. The method: factor analysis
2. Interesting hypotheses	2. What does a trait include?
3. Potential ties to biology	3. What is left out or neglected?

These considerations suggest a view of trait theory that is well summarized by the Big Five researchers Saucier, Hampson, & Goldberg (2000, p. 28): "Clearly, the study of different lexicons [of personality description] can lead to a useful and highly generalizable classification system for personality traits, but this classification system should not be reified into an explanatory one. A model of descriptions does not provide a model of causes, and the study of personality lexicons should not be equated with a study of personality."

One way that one *could* provide an explanation of personality traits is not merely to rely on the lexicon of personality descriptors, but to explore underlying biological systems that contribute to personality and individual differences. We consider contemporary research on this topic in the next chapter.

Problems with the Trait Concept

The trait concept suggests a disposition to respond similarly across a variety of situations. At this point it might seem as if trait theorists agree about what a trait is and what it includes. Yet, as was suggested over 20 years ago, "what is to be included in a definition of traits is not self-evident" (Borgatta, 1968, p. 510). The existence of a trait is demonstrated by consistent patterns of behavior. The behavior generally referred to is overt behavior expressed in situations. Yet, of late, the trait concept has been broadened to include nonobservable behavior, emotions, motives, and attitudes (A. H. Buss, 1989; McCrae & Costa, 1990; McCrae & John, 1992). Indeed, from this standpoint, Henry Murray (Chapter 4) is considered to be a trait theorist!

Trait theorists can define the concept in any way they want, and include within it whatever they choose, but what is included and whether there is agreement in this regard does make a difference (Pervin, 1994). Particularly important is whether the distinction between a trait and a motive is at all useful (Winter et al., 1998). Murray's (1938) thinking is important here since he specifically contrasted the concept of need with that of trait. According to Murray, in contrast with traits, needs can be momentary or enduring and can be present within the organism without becoming manifest in behavior. Thus, Murray suggested that "according to my prejudice, trait psychology is over-

Pathology	Change
Extreme scores on trait dimensions (e.g., neuroticism)	(No formal model)

concerned with recurrences, with consistency, with what is clearly manifested (the surface of personality), with what is conscious, ordered, and rational" (1938, p. 715). These are not trivial differences, and they call attention to Murray's skepticism about people's ability to report accurately about themselves and his emphasis on a dynamic conceptualization of personality.

What Is Left Out or Neglected?

Does the trait concept and the five-factor model provide us with a comprehensive model of personality? In part, this question follows from the discussion of what is to be included in the trait concept. Even many trait theorists would suggest, however, that there is more to personality than the Big Five—for example, people's self-concepts, their identities, their cognitive styles, and the unconscious (A. H. Buss, 1988; McAdams, 1992).

Another question is, does the model say anything about the organization of personality? Is a person just a bundle of traits or is an important part of personality the way in which the traits are organized? It is interesting that Allport (1961) placed pattern and organization at the core of personality. Modern trait theorists would appear to agree that "the essence of personality is the organization of experience and behavior" (McCrae & Costa, 1990, p. 118). Yet, trait research is noticeably lacking in this regard. And, as noted, for a theory of individual differences there is a surprising paucity of studies of the individual. Thus, in the words of one recent critic: "The five-factor model is essentially a psychology of the stranger— a quick and simple portrait of someone" (McAdams, 1992, p. 333).

Finally, with the exception of Eysenck, trait theory is strangely lacking in regard to a theory of personality change. It is one thing to document the stability of personality and to suggest reasons for such stability—genetic (temperament) factors, selection and shaping of situations, stereotypes (self-confirming), and responses by others. It is another thing to omit an account of change. The McCrae group (2000) account of endogenous maturational changes is modeled on biological processes but is not yet very well specified.

Even with an emphasis on stability, relatively few trait theorists consider most aspects of personality as fixed and enduring as intelligence. And, even if one questions the efficacy of psychotherapy, a way of accounting for change that sometimes occurs would appear to be a reasonable requirement of a comprehensive theory of personality (Brody, 1988). As we have reviewed, research on these issues has begun to appear, with trait researchers attempting to predict how particular life experiences bring about systematic changes in personality traits (Caspi & Roberts, 1999).

In sum, trait theory is alive and well, but aches and pains remain. In what form the patient will survive remains to be seen.

MAJOR CONCEPTS

Big Five   In trait factor theory, the five major trait categories including emotionality, activity, and sociability factors.

Facets   Facets are the more specific traits (or components) that make up each of the broad Big Five factors. For example, facets of extraversion are activity level, assertiveness, excitement seeking, positive emotions, sregariousness, and warmth.

Five-factor model   An emerging consensus among trait theorists suggesting five basic factors to human personality: neuroticism, extraversion, openness, agreeableness, and conscientiousness.

Fundamental lexical hypothesis   The hypothesis that over time the most important individual differences in human interaction have been encoded as single terms into language.

NEO-PI-R   A personality questionnaire designed to measure people's standing on each of the factors of the five-factor model, as well as on facets of each factor.

OCEAN   The acronym for the five basic traits: openness, conscientiousness, extraversion, agreeableness, and neuroticism.

Person-situation controversy   A controversy between psychologists who emphasize the importance of personal (internal) variables in determining behavior and those who emphasize the importance of situational (external) influences.

REVIEW

1. A consensus among trait theorists is emerging around the Big Five or five-factor model (OCEAN). Support for the model comes from the factor analysis of trait terms in language, the factor analysis of ratings and questionnaire (e.g., NEO-PI) data, and the analysis of genetic (inherited) contributions to personality.

2. The fundamental lexical hypothesis suggests that over time the fundamental individual differences among people have been encoded into language.

3. The proposed theoretical five-factor model emphasizes the biological basis of basic tendencies and the development of these tendencies essentially independent of environmental influences (intrinsic maturation). There is evidence of stability of general trait structure and levels, the evidence being stronger for stability during adulthood than during childhood and adolescence. Similarly, there is evidence of stability in the relative positions of individuals on trait measures during development, again greater for adulthood than for childhood. Individual differences in such stability exist, and the limits of environmental influence on personality development and change remain to be determined. Evidence of change in personality trait levels, however, contradicts five-factor theory.

4. Proponents of the five-factor model suggest that it has important potential applications in areas such as vocational guidance, personality diagnosis, and psychological treatment. It was noted, however, that developments in this area are recent and remain to be evaluated. In addition, the model offers no specific recommendations concerning the process of personality change.

5. Critics of trait theory suggest that human behavior is very variable. Instead of emphasizing broad dispositions within the person, the importance of situational influences should be recognized. This has led to the person-situation controversy. There is evidence for longitudinal stability in personality and for cross-situational consistency where a broad range of situations and behaviors is sampled (aggregation). At the same time, there is evidence for variability in individual behavior, particularly where situations are very different from one another. The task remains to account for patterns of stability and variability in behavior.

6. An overall evaluation of current trait theory suggests strengths in research, the formulation of interesting hypotheses, and the potential for ties to biology in relation to work on genetic contributions to personality and evolutionary developments. At the same time, questions can be raised concerning the method of factor analysis, the clarity of meaning of the trait concept, the neglect of such important areas of psychological functioning as the self, and a theory of personality change.

9

BIOLOGICAL FOUNDATIONS OF PERSONALITY

TEMPERAMENT: VIEWS OF MIND-BODY RELATIONSHIPS FROM THE PAST TO THE PRESENT
  Constitution and Temperament: Early Views
  Constitution and Temperament: Longitudinal Studies
  Constitution and Temperament: Kagan's Research on Inhibited and Uninhibited Children

EVOLUTIONARY THEORY AND PERSONALITY: THE MODERN SYNTHESIS, PART I
  Social Exchange and the Detection of Cheating
  Sex Differences: Evolutionary Origins?
    Male-Female Mate Preferences
    Causes of Jealousy
    Evolutionary Origins of Sex Differences: How Strong Are the Data?
  Evolutionary Theory and the Big Five Personality Dimensions
  Evolutionary Explanations: Comment

GENES AND PERSONALITY: THE MODERN SYNTHESIS, PART II
  Behavioral Genetics
    Selective Breeding Studies
    Twin Studies
    Adoption Studies
    Heritability Coefficient
    Heritability of Personality: Findings
    Some Important Caveats
    Molecular Genetic Paradigms

  Environments and Gene-Environment Interactions
    Shared and Nonshared Environment
    Understanding Nonshared Environment Effects
    Three Kinds of Nature-Nurture Interactions
    Summary and Caveats
NEUROSCIENCE AND PERSONALITY
  Localizing Brain Functions: Amygdala
  Left and Right Hemispheric Dominance
  Neurotransmitter Functioning: Dopamine and Serotonin
  Neurobiology and the Three Major Temperament Dimensions
    Three Dimensions of Temperament: PE, NE, and DvC
    Emotional and Lifestyle Correlates of PE, NE, and DvC
    Biological Correlates of PE, NE, and DvC
    Biology and Personality Traits: Some Limitations
  Plasticity: Biological Processes Are Both Cause and Effect
  Summary
NEUROSCIENTIFIC INVESTIGATIONS OF "HIGHER-LEVEL" PSYCHOLOGICAL FUNCTIONS
  Brain and Self
  Brain and Moral Judgment
BIOLOGY AND SOCIOPOLITICAL ISSUES
MAJOR CONCEPTS
REVIEW

Chapter Focus

Why are some people generally happy and others sad, some energetic and others lethargic, some impulsive and others cautious, some excited and others calm, some optimistic and others pessimistic? Do we learn these styles of behavior? Or might they be part of our biological makeup? Often it is said that parents are believers in the importance of the environment, or nurture, when they have their first child, and believers in temperament differences, or nature, when they have their second child. Initial differences between children from the same family often are that great! Along similar lines, people looking into a nursery window generally are struck with the differences among the newly born—some active and others moving little, some spending a lot of time crying while others remain calm.

For centuries humans have tried to understand the relation between body and mind, between constitution and personality. And since the 1880s when Sir Francis Galton contrasted "nature" (heredity) with "nurture" (environment), psychologists have been concerned with the relation between the two. During the past few decades tremendous gains have been made in our understanding of biological processes. Are there biological processes that determine individual differences in temperament and personality? If so, which processes are key? The study of biological foundations of personality is a fast-moving field and in this chapter we will try to capture both the insights that have been gained and the questions that remain.

QUESTIONS TO BE ADDRESSED IN THIS CHAPTER

1. Are infants born with differences in temperament? If so, how stable are such differences, and what are the biological bases for them?

2. Are there universal aspects of personality functioning, and, if so, can evolutionary theory inform us about the roots of such processes?

3. What role do genes play in the formation of personality? How do they interact with the environment in the unfolding of personality?

4. Can relationships be established between personality functioning and brain processes? For example, can traits such as those considered in previous chapters be understood in terms of individual differences in brain functioning?

In his fascinating exploration of the relation between biology and personality, the eminent neurologist Antonio Damasio (1994) considers the case of Phineas Gage, a construction foreman who in 1848 survived a freak accident in which a three-and-a-half-foot iron rod passed through his head. Working on a railroad construction job, Gage undertook to blast a path through hard rock. He drilled a hole in the ground, filled it with explosive powder, and then inserted an iron rod. Next, a fuse was to be lit. Gage is described as a virtuoso

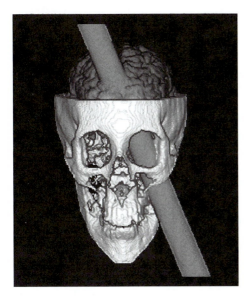

This illustration shows the location through which an iron rod blasted through the frontal cortex of Phineas Gage—who survived the accident, but experienced a profound change in his personality.

at this. However, on this occasion he was distracted and the charge blew up in his face, sending the iron rod through his left cheek, piercing the base of his skull, traversing the front of his brain, and exiting through the top of his head. Phineas Gage was stunned but, miraculously, not killed. He was able to walk and speak. Indeed, he could describe what happened in full detail and communicate in a rational way. However, as the story unfolds, "Gage's disposition, his likes and dislikes, his dreams and aspirations are all to change. Gage's body may be alive and well, but there is a new spirit animating it. Gage was no longer Gage" (Damasio, 1994, p. 7). No longer serious, industrious, energetic, and responsible, Gage now was irresponsible, thoughtless of others, lacking in planfulness, and indifferent to the consequences of his actions. The piercing iron rod had largely destroyed a part of Gage's frontal cortex.

Why the telling of this story? Damasio suggests that in this case we see the importance of the brain for unique human properties. The view that body and mind, biology and personality, are interconnected has a long history. Let us begin by tracing some of this history in relation to the concept of temperament, considered by many to be a fundamental aspect of our personality and clearly a part of Gage's personality that was changed when the iron rod pierced his brain.

You have about as much choice in some aspects of your personality as you do in the shape of your nose or the size of your feet. Psychologists call this biological, inborn dimension of personality "temperament."

Source: Hamer & Copeland, 1998, p. 7.

TEMPERAMENT: VIEWS OF MIND-BODY RELATIONSHIPS FROM THE PAST TO THE PRESENT

What is **temperament**? Psychologists generally use the term to refer to individual differences in mood or quality of emotional response. As suggested by the quote above, these differences are viewed as primarily inherited and biologically based: "The concept of temperament refers to any moderately stable, differentiating emotional or behavioral quality whose appearance in childhood is influenced by inherited biology, including differences in brain neuro-chemistry" (Kagan, 1994, p. xvii). Many aspects of personality clearly do not have their basis in inherited biology. We acquire social skills, our self-concept, personal goals in life, and so forth through interaction with the social world. But other features of personality—features such as an individual's typical mood, their chronic level of activity, or their degree of emotional reaction in response to particular types of environmental stimuli—may directly reflect individual differences in inherited biology. It is these individual differences in emotional quality that appear early, remain fairly stable, are inherited, and are based in biological processes that are referred to as temperament (Eisenberg, Fabes, Guthrie, & Reiser, 2000; Rothbart, Ahadi, & Evans, 2000).

CONSTITUTION AND TEMPERAMENT: EARLY VIEWS

As highlighted by scholarly reviews of the field (Kagan, 1994; Strelau, 1998), human beings have long been interested in the possibility that psychological differences among people have a biological basis. In ancient Greece, Hippocrates posited that variations in psychological characteristics reflect variations in bodily fluids (see Chapter 7, Figure 7.2). The Greeks believed that all of nature was composed of four elements: air, earth, fire, and water. Hippocrates and (centuries later) Galen suggested a similar fourfold analysis of bodily fluids and associated psychological characteristics. The four elements of nature were said to be represented in the human body by four humors (blood, black bile, yellow bile, phlegm), each corresponding to a temperament: sanguine, melancholic, choleric, phlegmatic. Individual differences in temperament corresponded to the predominance within the individual of one or another of the four humors. Similarly, diseases corresponded to excesses in one or another humor (e.g., too much black bile and depression). In other words, from these early times a classification of temperament types was proposed, one based on constitution or basic body chemistry.

The conceptions of the ancient Greeks were remarkably long-lasting. More than two millennia after Hippocrates, the great German philosopher Immanuel Kant turned his attention to questions of temperament. Kant, writing around 1800 A.D., thought some of the same things that Hippocrates thought in the fourth century B.C. Kant distinguished four types of temperament and felt that their basis was found in bodily fluids. He believed that variations in blood, rather than in the range of bodily fluids discussed by the Greeks, were the cause of variations in temperament. Yet the basic conceptualization remained curiously similar to that of the ancient Greeks. Needless to say, the details of these bodily fluid theories are completely rejected by all contemporary psychological scientists.

A very different—but equally unsatisfactory—theory of the biological bases of individual differences arose in the 19th century from the work of the German physician Franz Joseph Gall. Gall founded the field of **phrenology**, which tried to locate areas of the brain responsible for specific aspects of emotional and behavioral functioning (Figure 9.1). Gall did postmortem inspections of brains and attempted to relate differences in brain tissue to reports of the individual's capacities, dispositions, and traits before death. In particular, a possible relation between personality and bumps on the head was to be examined (the bumps purportedly being indicative of the development of

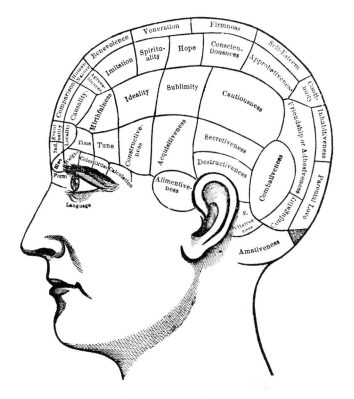

Figure 9.1 Gall's Localization of Personality Functions of the Brain.

underlying brain tissue). Phrenology gained great notoriety and popularity in the early 19th century. Gall's work was seen as a serious effort to locate aspects of personality functioning in specific parts of the brain. Subsequently, however, phrenology was utterly discredited. Contemporary research indicates that the brain simply does not work in the way that Gall assumed, with localized regions of brain being responsible for specific types of thought and social behavior. Instead, most complex actions and thought patterns are executed by the synchronized action of multiple, interconnected regions of the brain (Bressler, 2002; Edelman & Tononi, 2000).

Efforts of enduring value to science finally were seen in the mid-19th century. Three publications were proved to be critical: Charles Darwin's *The Origin of Species* (1859) and *The Expression of Emotions in Man and Animals* (1872), and Gregor Mendel's *Experiments on Plant Hybrids* (1865). Darwin's *Origin*, of course, was foundational to the contemporary science of biology. His *Expression of Emotions* documented numerous close relations between emotional expression in humans and emotional expression in other complex mammals; in so doing, it contributed indirectly to the study of temperament and also foreshadowed the development of contemporary evolutionary psychology (discussed later in this chapter). Mendel's work reported eight years of research on the breeding of pea plant characteristics and served as the foundation for modern genetics.

Also of great historical note are the efforts of Francis Galton, who was a cousin of Darwin. Galton explored the potential inherited basis of individual difference in both personality and intelligence. It so doing, he sparked a "nature-nurture" controversy that has flared up repeatedly throughout the history of the field.

It also was during this time that the eminent psychiatrist Emil Kraepelin, born in the same year as Freud and a rival as the founder of modern psychiatry, attempted a classification of mental disorders that were believed to be largely hereditary. Noteworthy here is Kraepelin's emphasis on disorders of mood such as manic-depressive illness, now known as bipolar disorder (Barondes, 1998). In sum, during this period there was evidence of considerable interest in biological processes generally and their relation to personality in particular.

In the 20th century, investigators in both Europe and the United States became intrigued by the possibility of systematic links between psychological temperament and body types. The German psychiatrist Ernst Kretschmer tried to relate body type to personality early in the century (*Physique and Character*, 1925). Kretschmer devised a method of measuring body type, resulting in a classification of three fundamental types: pyknic (plump, round physique), athletic (muscular, vigorous physique), and asthenic (frail, linear physique). These physiques were then found to differ in incidence of psychiatric disorder, a pyknic physique being associated with manic-depressive disorder and an asthenic physique being associated with schizophrenia. Beyond this, Kretschmer assumed a relation between physique and normal personality (e.g., pyknic and extraversion, asthenic and introversion), although no evidence was presented for such a relationship. Kretschmer's work suffered from faulty methodology (e.g., he did not correct for the fact that manic-depressive disorder tends to occur later in life than schizophrenia and people tend to become heavier and rounded with age) but it laid the foundation for later work in constitutional psychology.

In the U.S., a similar effort was carried out by William Sheldon (1940, 1942), who suggested that each person has an inherited basic biological structure (bodily physique, constitution) that determines his or her temperament. Sheldon defined three dimensions of physique that largely corresponded to those suggested by Kretschmer: endormorphy (soft and round), mesomorphy (hard and rectangular, muscular), and ectomorphy (linear and fragile, thin, lightly muscled). Like Kretschmer, he suggested that physique was systematically related to temperament. Although his research appeared to yield systematic relations between body type and personality, his work, like Kretchmer's, proved to be plagued with methodological problems; subsequent work indicated that the relation between body type and personality were quite weak (Strelau, 1998).

An effort of the early 20th century that proved of more lasting value was found in the work of Pavlov, whose research we discuss in detail in Chapter 10. Much of Pavlov's work examined how the nervous system of organisms is modified by experience (see Chapter 10), Yet Pavlov also developed a theory of stable individual differences in nervous-system functioning that highlighted the possibility of variations in the "strength" of the nervous system, that is, in the degree to which normal nervous system functioning could be maintained in the face of high levels of stimuli or stress (Strelau, 1998).

CONSTITUTION AND TEMPERAMENT: LONGITUDINAL STUDIES

The historical efforts to study temperament that we have just reviewed were hampered not only by conceptual shortcomings, but by limitations in the scientific methods employed. A defining feature of those psychological characteristics called "temperament" is that they are present early in life and are relatively stable across the life course. Yet none of aforementioned studies involved infants or longitudinal research (i.e., research that studies a group of persons over an extended period of time).

Beginning in the 1950s, things began to change. A pioneering scientific effort was the New York Longitudinal Study (NYLS) conducted by Alexander Thomas and Stella Chess (Thomas & Chess, 1977). These researchers followed over 100 children from birth to adolescence, using parental reports of infants' reactions to a variety of situations to define variations in infant temperament. On the basis of ratings of infant characteristics such as activity level, general mood, attention span, and persistence, they defined three infant temperament types: easy babies who were playful and adaptable, difficult babies who were negative and unadaptable, and slow-to-warm-up babies who were low in reactivity and mild in their responses. This study and subsequent studies found a link between such early differences in temperament and later personality characteristics (Rothbart & Bates, 1998; Shiner, 1998). For example, difficult babies were found to have the greatest difficulty in later adjustment whereas easy babies were found to have the least likelihood of later difficulties. In addition, Thomas and Chess suggested that the parental environment best suited for babies of one temperament type might not be best for those of a different temperament type; that is, there is a goodness-of-fit between infant temperament and parental environment.

Following the NYLS research, Arnold Buss and Robert Plomin (1975, 1984) used parental ratings of behavior to define four dimensions of temperament: Emotionality (ease of arousal in upsetting situations; general distress), Activity (tempo and vigor of motor movements; on the go all the time; fidgety), Sociability (responsiveness to other persons, makes friends easily versus shy), and Impulsivity (ability to inhibit or control behavior; impulsive; easily bored), creating the acronym, EASI. The last of these dimensions (Impulsivity) was dropped because it was not found as a clear dimension in subsequent factor analyses of questionnaires. However, research supported the view of Buss and Plomin that temperament shows evidence of continuity over time and of being largely inherited, the latter based on evidence of greater similarity of mothers' ratings of monozygotic (identical) twins than dizygotic (fraternal) twins. Although noteworthy in the use of factor analysis to define dimensions of temperament and in the study of twins to determine inheritance of temperament, the research was problematic in the use of parental ratings rather than more objective measures of observation. Contemporary researchers recognized that parents may be systematically biased when rating the personality of their own children; for example, parents tend to overestimate the similarity of identical twins and to underestimate the similarity of fraternal twins (Saudino, 1997).

Many contemporary efforts to characterize the nature of psychological temperament resemble the research strategy of Buss and Plomin (1984). Reseachers generally try to identify a small set of individual-difference dimensions that characterize major variations in temperament characteristics in the population at large (e.g., Goldsmith & Campos, 1982; Gray, 1991; Strelau, 1998). We do not dwell on the details of these efforts here because, in important respects, they are similar to the five-factor model we reviewed in detail in our previous chapter. Indeed, five-factor enthusiasts contend that the five per-

The developmental psychologist Jerome Kagan has identified early differences in temperament, conceptualized as inhibited and uninhibited types.

sonality traits are an adequate framework for conceptualizing individual differences in temperament (Costa & McCrae, 2001). Instead, we now consider an approach to the study of temperament that differs from many other efforts in two important respects: (1) it relies on direct measures of behavior and physiology rather than on questionnaire ratings, and (2) it does not assume that temperament can be characterized in terms of individual-difference dimensions; instead of a continuous dimension (like height), the investigators explore the possibility that temperament qualities vary categorically (like eye color). This novel work is the research program of Jerome Kagan and colleagues.

CONSTITUTION AND TEMPERAMENT: KAGAN'S RESEARCH ON INHIBITED AND UNINHIBITED CHILDREN

The need for the use of objective measures of temperament was recognized by the developmental psychologist Jerome Kagan (1994, 1999). Dating his ideas back to Galen's suggestion that each of us inherits a temperament that is based in our constitution or physiology, Kagan set out to use objective, laboratory measures of behavior and biological functioning to study the unfolding of temperament in childhood. Based on past observations of hundreds of children, Kagan was impressed with what appeared to be two clearly defined behavioral profiles in temperament, conceptualized by him as **inhibited** and **uninhibited**. Relative to the uninhibited child, the inhibited child reacts to unfamiliar persons or events with restraint, avoidance, and distress, takes a longer time to relax in new situations, and has more unusual fears and phobias. Such a child behaves timidly and cautiously, the initial reaction to novelty being to become quiet, seek parental comfort, or run and hide. By contrast, the uninhibited child seems to enjoy these very same situations that seem so stressful to the inhibited child. Rather than being timid and fearful, the uninhibited child responds with spontaneity in novel situations, laughing and smiling easily.

Struck by such dramatic differences, Kagan set out to address the following questions: How early do such differences in temperament emerge? How stable are these differences in temperament over time? Can some biological bases for such differences in temperament be suggested? His central hypothesis was that infants inherit differences in biological functioning that lead them to be more or less reactive to novelty and that these inherited differences tend to be stable during development. According to the hypothesis, infants born highly reactive to novelty should become inhibited children whereas those born with low reactivity should develop into uninhibited children.

How was this hypothesis investigated? Not trusting parental reports because parents often compare children with one another and interpret the same behavior in different ways, Kagan brought four-month-old infants into the laboratory and videotaped their behavior while they were exposed to familiar and novel stimuli (e.g., mother's face, voice of a strange female, colorful mobiles moving back and forth, a balloon popping). The videotapes then were scored on measures of reactivity such as arching of the back, vigorous flexing of limbs, and crying. About 20 percent of the infants were designated as high-reactive, characterized by arching of the back, intense crying, and an unhappy facial expression in response to the novel stimuli. The behavioral profile suggested that they had been overaroused by the stimuli, particularly

Research on temperament indicates that some children inherit a predisposition to become highly distressed in the presence of novel situations and people—even smiling, friendly ones!

since the responses stopped when the stimuli were removed. In contrast, the low-reactive infants, about 40 percent of the group, appeared to be calm and laid-back in response to the novel stimuli. The remaining infants, about 40 percent, showed various mixtures of response.

To determine whether, as predicted, the high-reactive infants would become inhibited children and the low-reactive infants uninhibited children, Kagan again studied the children when they were 14 months old, 21 months old, and 4 1/2 years old. Again the children were brought to the laboratory and exposed to novel, unfamiliar situations (e.g., flashing lights, a toy clown striking a drum, a stranger in an unfamiliar costume, the noise of plastic balls rotating in a wheel at the first two ages and meeting with an unfamiliar adult and unfamiliar children at the later age). In addition to behavioral observations, physiological measures such as heart rate and blood pressure in response to the unfamiliar situations were obtained.

Was consistency between early behavioral profiles of reactivity and later profiles expressive of inhibited and uninhibited types found? Kagan suggests that this indeed was the case. Thus, the high-reactive infants showed greater fearful behavior, heart acceleration, and increased blood pressure in response to the unfamiliar at 14 and 21 months of age than did the low-reactive infants. And, such differences were maintained at the later testing at age 4 1/2 years of age. At this point it was found that the children who had been high-reactive infants smiled and talked less with the unfamiliar adult, and were more shy with unfamiliar peers than was the case for the children who had been low-reactive infants. Further testing in the eighth year of life indicated continuing consistency, with a majority of the children assigned to each group at age four months retaining membership in that group. In sum, there was considerable evidence of temperament stability and suggestions of a possible biological basis for these differences in temperament. As we will observe later in the chapter, additional evidence of differences in biological functioning was obtained subsequently.

At the same time that consistency of temperament is emphasized, we should recognize that there also was evidence of the potential for change. Most of the high-reactive infants did not become consistently fearful. Change in these children seemed particularly tied to having mothers who were not overly protective and placed reasonable demands on them (Kagan, Arcus, & Snidman, 1993). And, some of the low-reactive infants lost their relaxed style. Despite an initial temperamental bias, environment played a role in the unfolding personality. Thus, according to Kagan, "any predisposition conferred by our genetic endowment is far from being a life sentence; there is no inevitable adult outcome of a particular infant temperament" (1999, p. 32). At the same time, Kagan points out that not one of the high-reactive infants became a consistently uninhibited child and it was very rare for a low-reactive infant to become a consistently inhibited child. Although change was possible, the temperamental bias did not vanish and appeared to set some constraints on the direction of development. According to Kagan, "it is very difficult to change one's inherited predisposition completely" (1999, p. 41).

Evidence directly bears on the question of whether temperament qualities vary dimensionally or categorically. Woodward, Lenzenweger, Kagan, Snidman, and Arcus (2000) employed statistical techniques that are designed to answer this question. These statistical methods are designed to identify categories or "classes" that may explain patterns of variation in data obtained from a large group of persons. To illustrate, suppose you did not know that some people are men and others are women. If you asked people a large number of questions about their personal habits, you might find out that there are distinct groups. A statistical analysis could indicate that some responses go together so strongly (e.g., people who say that they wear skirts also tend to say that they wear lipstick and own high-heel shoes) that they indicate a group of people that is a categorically distinct class (women). Woodward and colleagues (2000) found that the group of infants showing high reactivity (limb movements, crying) in response to novel situations is a distinct class. A distinct group of about 10 percent of a large population of children was found to be consistently more reactive than the population at large. This finding is important because it conflicts with an assumption that is commonly made by other researchers, namely, the assumptions that individual differences in personality characteristics exclusively involve continuous dimensions rather than distinct categories.

Contemporary research also sheds light on the precise brain regions that contribute to inhibited and uninhibited tendencies (Schmidt & Fox, 2002). More than one region appears to be involved, with behavioral tendencies reflecting interactions among the different neural systems. One important region is the amygdala, a region of brain that, as we note below, is centrally involved in fear response. A second region is the frontal cortex, which is involved in regulating emotional response, in part by influencing the functioning of the amygdala. Interestingly, the functioning of these brain regions is not entirely determined by inherited factors; social experiences appear to modify brain functioning and thus influence children's emotional tendencies (Schmidt & Fox, 2002).

A recent study provides particularly clear evidence of the role of amygdala functioning in inhibited versus uninhibited temperament (Schwartz, Wright, Shin, Kagan, & Rauch, 2003). In this work, the researchers studied a group of young adults who had been categorized as being highly inhibited or uninhibited when they were only two years old. The adults participated in a laboratory study in which they viewed pictures of human faces. A key portion of the experiment involved participants' reactions to familiar faces (i.e., pictures of people that the participant had seen previously, in an earlier portion of the

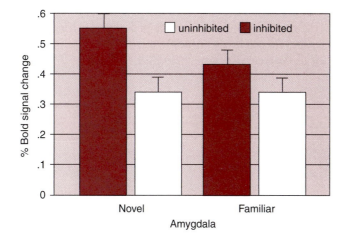

Figure 9.2   fMRI measures of brain reactivity to novel and familiar faces among people who had been classified as uninhibited and inhibited. *From Schwartz, Wright, Shin, Kagan, & Rauch (2003).*

experiment) versus novel faces (people had not been seen previously); it was predicted that inhibited people respond more to the novel, unfamiliar faces. A particularly valuable feature of the research was the measurement technique used. A brain imagining technique, fMRI (described in more detail later in this chapter), was employed to determine the exact brain regions that became active as people viewed the familiar and novel faces. The fMRI measures provided clear support for the hypothesis that uninhibited versus inhibited persons differ in amygdala functioning (Figure 9.2). When they viewed the novel faces, adults who—back when they were only two years old—had been identified as inhibited children showed higher levels of amygdala reactivity. The results, then, provide striking evidence of a specific biological basis of this temperament characteristic, and show that these differences in biology can be stable over long periods of life.

In summary, we have seen that there is clear evidence of a link between biological processes and aspects of personality functioning such as temperament. On the one hand, it seems inconceivable that such a link would not exist. Yet a few points are worthy of keeping in mind. First, evidence of inheritance does not mean that temperament is only inherited. As with all aspects of personality, environment is important as well. Second, as Kagan's research indicates, evidence of inheritance does not mean that change is impossible. We began this section with a quote suggesting that we have no choice in the temperament with which we are born. The authors go on to suggest the following: "Just because a person is born with a particular temperament, however, doesn't mean there is a simple set of instructions or blueprints. Nor does temperament mean that people are 'stuck' with their personalities from birth. On the contrary, one of the marvelous features of temperament is a built-in flexibility that allows us to adapt to life's hurdles and challenges.... Everyone has the ability to grow and to change at every stage of life" (Hamer & Copeland, 1998, p. 7). Finally, discussion in this section has focused on the effect of biological processes on personality as it is expressed in thought, emotion, and behavior.

At the same time, it is important to recognize that our thoughts, emotions, and behavior have effects on other biological processes. Thus, for example, our emotions can influence our immunological functioning in terms of greater or lesser resistance to disease (Cohen, 1996; Maier, Watkins, & Fleshner, 1994).

EVOLUTIONARY THEORY AND PERSONALITY: THE MODERN SYNTHESIS, PART I

This is natural selection: the non-random differential reproduction of genes. Natural selection has built us, and it is natural selection we must understand if we are to comprehend our own identities.

SOURCE: Trivers, 1976, p. v.

We are part of nature, but we like to see ourselves as otherwise.

SOURCE: Goldsmith, 1991, p. 104.

Biologists and psychologists distinguish between two kinds of explanation—**ultimate causes** and **proximate causes**. Ultimate causes refer to explanations associated with evolution, that is, why the behavior of interest evolved and the adaptive function it served. Darwin's theory of evolution serves as the foundation for such ultimate cause explanations of behavior. According to recent formulations of the theory, organisms that solve adaptive tasks pass their genes on to successive generations. Proximate cause explanations refer to biological processes operating in the organism at the time the behavior is observed. In other words, one kind of explanation takes a historical view of the development of the species, in this case an evolutionary view, whereas the other kind of explanation focuses on processes operating in the present. In this section we consider ultimate, evolutionary-based interpretations of personality functioning. In subsequent sections we consider proximate causes involving the action of genes and brain functions.

In recent years, many psychologists have tried to build such evolutionary explanations of psychological functioning. As a review by Linnda Caporael (2001) explains, these efforts have been of more than one type. Although all contemporary psychologists recognize the importance of analyzing evolutionary forces, their analyses differ. As a result, there exist "evolutionary psychologies" (Caporael, 2001). Main points of differences involve the degree to which psychological tendency is seen as "hardwired" (i.e., as a biologically fixed, inevitable aspect of human nature) versus being a tendency that arises as a result of interactions between biology and culture. The latter perspective leaves open the possibility that different cultures will produce different psychological tendencies (e.g., Nisbett, 2003).

In the past decade, writers who highlight the evolutionarily "hardwired" aspects of human nature have gained much prominence in personality psychology. Their work represents a startling challenge to many ways of thinking in the field. In this approach, contemporary human functioning is understood in relation to evolved solutions to adaptive problems faced by the species over millions of years (D. M. Buss, 1991, 1995, 1999). The idea is that basic psychological mechanisms are the result of evolution by selection, that is, they exist and have endured because they have been adaptive to survival and reproductive success. The fundamental components of human nature, then, can be understood in terms of **evolved psychological mechanisms** that have adaptive value in terms of survival and reproductive success. Such aspects of human nature, as our fundamental motives and emotions, can thereby be understood in terms of their adaptive value.

Four points about evolution and the human mind are highlighted in this approach to evolutionary psychology (Pinker, 1997; Tooby & Cosmides, 1992). First, the features of mind that evolved are ones that solve problems that are important to reproductive success. The critical feature in evolution is the passing on of genes. However, note that the reproduction-related problems do not merely involve acts of sexual reproduction. They include a wide range of problems relevant to the survival and reproduction of the organism. Consider the following simple example. Organisms need to see objects at a distance and to judge how near or far they are from objects. An organism that could not make these judgments commonly would be at a disadvantage (e.g., when hunting or trying to protect itself from a predator). To solve this problem, our nervous systems have evolved a solution: a pair of eyes that enables us to see in depth. The psychological capacity, depth perception, reflects a specific neural system that has evolved because of its usefulness in solving a recurrent problem faced throughout evolution. The intriguing feature of contemporary evolutionary psychology is that it extends this type of analysis to include patterns of social behavior that solve significant social problems faced across the eons of evolutionary history.

A second point is that the evolved mental mechanisms are adaptive to the way of life of hundreds of centuries ago, when our ancestors were hunters and gatherers (Tooby & Cosmides, 1992). An implication is that we may have evolved psychological tendencies that no longer are good for us. For example, our taste preference for fat was "clearly adaptive in our evolutionary past because fat was a valuable source of calories but was very scarce. Now, however, with hamburger and pizza joints on every street corner, fat is no longer a scarce resource. Thus, our strong taste for fatty substances now causes us to over-consume fat. This leads to clogged arteries and heart attacks, and hinders our survival" (D. M. Buss, 1999, p. 38).

Third, evolved psychological mechanisms are domain-specific. According to evolutionary psychologists, we do *not* evolve a general tendency "to survive." Instead, the body and mind consists of evolved mechanisms that solve specific problems that occur in specific types of settings, or domains. Fundamental aspects of human nature, such as specific motives and emotions, apply to specific problems and contexts. For example, evolution does not give us a general tendency to be afraid, but instead selects for psychological mechanisms that cause us to fear specific stimuli that have been threats to humans across the course of evolution. Similarly, evolution gives us specific emotions, such as jealousy, because these emotional reactions have proven adaptive in solving specific problems of social living. These domain-specific motives and emotions have remained as part of our human nature because they facilitated survival and reproductive success given the problems to be faced in our ancestral environment. Note that this makes evolutionary psychology quite different than the trait approaches we discussed in the previous two chapters. In trait theory, a context-free variable such as "agreeableness" might be seen as responsible for actions such as being agreeable on a date and being agreeable toward a young niece or nephew. In evolutionary psychology, these acts would be seen as merely superficially similar. Even though they might both be described as "agreeable" behaviors, they would be caused by different psychological mechanisms, since, throughout the course of evolution, attracting opposite-sex mates and caring for children were distinctly different problems of social life.

The fourth point concerns the components and overall structure of the mind, or what is commonly called the "architecture" of mental systems. One view of mental architecture is that the mind is like a computer. There is a central processing mechanism and all information, whatever its content, gets processed through this mechanism. If you are using your computer's word processor, the same processing mechanisms indeed will come into play whether you are writing a term paper or writing a love letter. Evolutionary psychologists reject this conception of mental architecture. Although they may view the mind as engaged in information processing, a core idea of evolutionary psychology is that the mind contains *multiple* information processing devices, each of which processes information from one specific domain of life (Pinker, 1997). Your computer may use the same mechanism to process a love letter and a term paper, but your brain does not. The task of attracting mates (through love letters or whatever other favored strategy you may have) is a distinct problem of great evolutionary significance. To solve it, we purportedly have evolved a mental system that comes into play when we face problems having to do with mate attraction. Since many different problems arise in different domains of life, the mind is said to consist of multiple domain-specific mental mechanisms. These mechanisms often are called mental "modules" (Fodor, 1983), a term that is meant to capture the fact that they are special-purpose mechanisms designed to carry out a domain-specific mental function.

SOCIAL EXCHANGE AND THE DETECTION OF CHEATING

A key question then is: Which psychological mechanisms have evolved through selection and which adaptive problems did they evolve to solve? Seminal work on this question was conducted by the evolutionary psychologist Leda Cosmides (1989). She explored a particular type of social setting and associated problem that, she reasoned, has been of significance throughout the course of evolution. The social setting involves "social exchange," that is, the exchange of goods and services. Throughout evolution, part of people's social interaction has involved the mutual exchange of beneficial goods. For example, a person may agree to help another with child-care tasks one day if that other person agrees to do the same on another day. People in a village that grows a large amount of a particular crop may agree to exchange some of their food with people from another village that produces a desired manufactured product. In any such exchange, it is important to avoid being cheated. The ability to detect cheating has survival value. If you chronically fail to notice that a person who needs change has just asked you for "two tens for a five" instead of "two fives for a ten," then you gradually run out of resources that are required for social living, survival, and reproduction. You must be able to detect cheaters. Cosmides reasoned that cheating detection is of such great survival value that the mind contains distinct systems for the detection of cheaters.

She tested this in a clever manner that illustrates the evolutionary psychologists' overall approach to questions of mental architecture. Her work

Figure 9.3 Schematic Illustration of Logical Problems Used in Cheating Detection Research. *Each card has two sides. The research participant sees one side and must decide whether to turn over the card to see the other side in order to test a logical rule. In the top problem, the rule is "if P then Q," that is, "if there is a P on one side of the card then there should be a Q on the other side." In the bottom problem (constructed for the present illustration), the rule is "if Made $ then Paid Taxes" (i.e., if a person made a certain amount of money in a given year, then they paid taxes). When asked to test the "if P then Q" rule, research participants commonly fail to turn over the not-Q card. However, in problems having the structure of the "if Made $ then Paid Taxes" problem, participants commonly do correctly turn over the Not-Paid Taxes card to see if the person might have been cheating (i.e., if the person might not have paid taxes even though they made money).*

involved a particular type of logical reasoning task. In the task, people are asked to solve an "if...then..." problem, that is, to test a problem of logical relations in which one has to determine if a rule of the sort "if P then Q" is accurate (Figure 9.3). As you might guess from this description, such abstract logical problems generally are difficult. People in psychology experiments commonly fail to solve them. However, Cosmides herself reasoned that people would be good at solving the problem if its content related to the detection of cheating. Although people might be poor at solving the problem "if P then Q?" they might be quite good at solving a problem such as "if person made a lot of money, did they pay taxes?" If the problem concerns potential cheating, then the particular subsystem of mind that processes information about social contracts and cheating should come into play, and people should be better at solving the problem. This is precisely what Cosmides (1989) found. Although a minority of people correctly solve abstract "P then Q" problems, a large majority correctly solve the same problem if the content of the problem involves the detection of cheating.

More recent work suggests that the ability to solve cheating problems is a human universal, precisely as evolutionary psychologists would expect. Cheating detection abilities are found not only among U.S. college students, but among nonliterate research participants living in cultures that are isolated from the industrialized world (Sugiyama, Tooby, & Cosmides, 2002). Other evidence has begun to identify specific brain regions that are involved in reasoning about social exchange. This work involved study of a neuropsychological patient who, in a bicycle accident, had incurred a head injury that damaged portions of his brain's frontal cortex and amygdala. When tested on a variety of logical reasoning tasks, the patient performed normally (i.e., in a manner similar to persons without brain injury) when reasoning in domains other than social exchange, but showed impaired performance when trying to solve problems involving social contracts (Stone, Cosmides, Tooby, Kroll, & Knight, 2002). The findings suggest, then, that there exists a specific neural subsystem of the brain that has evolved to solve such problems.

SEX DIFFERENCES: EVOLUTIONARY ORIGINS?

Another domain to which evolutionary psychologists have turned their attention is sex differences. The evolutionary psychologist's reasoning is that, throughout evolution, male and female human beings have had different roles to play as a natural result of biological differences between the sexes. Differences, of course, are found in physical stature, as well as in child care (e.g., pregnancy, breast feeding). Since these differences have been consistent across the course of evolution, is it reasoned that the human mind has evolved sex-specific psychological tendencies. In other words, men and women, as a result of facing somewhat different problems across the course of evolution, are predicted to have somewhat different brains that predipose them to different patterns of thinking, feeling, and action.

Before considering this research, we alert the reader to the fact that drawing conclusions about psychological differences between men and women is a very tricky matter. Even if one finds such differences, it is hard to interpret them. True, men and women differ biologically. So one interpretation is that biology causes sex differences. But men and women also differ socially; specifically, they often develop within societies that do not treat men and women equally. Men commonly earn more money than women and hold more positions of power in society. It may be that, irrespective of biological differences, any group within society that makes more money and holds more positions of power will differ, psychologically, from a group that earns less money and holds fewer positions of power. Sex differences, then, could be socially constructed, rather than being biologically caused. A core idea of evolutionary psychology, however, is that biology determines sex differences. Evolved psychological differences between men and women are seen as responsible for the gender differences we observe in society. This notion has been advanced most vigorously by the evolutionary psychologist David Buss (1989, 1999). He has considered sex differences in two aspects of male-female relationships: mate preferences and causes of jealousy.

Male-Female Mate Preferences

Do you like men who are rich and professionally successful? Do you like women who appear youthful and have "curvey" hips? If so, evolutionary psychologists think they know why. According to evolutionary theory, as introduced by Darwin, selection pressures across the course of human evolution have produced sex differences in preferences for mates. The particular features of men that are attractive to women, and the features of women that are attractive to men, are thought to be a product of evolution.

Two ideas underlie the contemporary evolutionary psychologist's analysis of sex differences. One is something called **parental investment theory** (Trivers, 1972). The theory is an analysis of the different costs, or investments, that men versus women have made in parenting throughout the ages. The core idea is that biological differences between the sexes cause women to invest more in parenting. Women can pass their genes on to fewer offspring than men potentially can. This is because of both the limited time periods during which they are fertile and, relative to men, the more limited age range during which they can produce offspring. In other words, parental investment is greater for females because of the greater "replacement costs" for them. Also, women of course carry the biological burden of pregnancy, which lasts for nine months. Men not only do not have to bear physical costs of pregnancy but, unlike women, in principle can be involved in multiple pregnancies at the same time. It follows that females will have stronger preferences about mating partners than will males and that males and females will have different criteria for the selection of mates (Trivers, 1972). Women need men to help with the burdens of pregnancy and child care, and thus should seek men who have the potential for providing resources and protection. Men, in contrast, should be less interested in protection; instead, they are expected to focus on the reproductive potential of a partner (the person's youth and other biological markers of reproductive fitness). Although these preferences evolved ages ago, they still are present in the human mind. Thus, they should be evident in current social patterns. For example, since women are more interested than are men in a partner who can provide resources, the evolutionary psychologist would expect that, when on a dinner date, men would be more likely to pay for the dinner. Paying for dinner is viewed as an evolved strategy through which men display financial resources and thus add to their attractiveness to women.

In addition to parental investment theory, a second line of reasoning concerns parenthood. Since women carry their fertilized eggs, they can always be sure that they are the mothers of the offspring. On the other hand, males cannot be so sure that the offspring is their own, and therefore must take steps to ensure that their investment is directed toward their own offspring and not those of another male (D. Buss, 1989, p. 3). Thus follows the suggestion that males have greater concerns about sexual rivals and place greater value on chastity in a potential mate than do females.

The following are some of the specific hypotheses that have been derived from parental investment and parenthood probability theories (Buss, 1989; Buss, Larsen, Westen, & Semmelroth, 1992):

1. A woman's "mate value" for a man should be determined by her reproductive capacity as suggested by youth and physical attractiveness. Chastity should also be valued in terms of increased probability of paternity.

2. A man's "mate value" for a woman should be determined less by reproductive value and more by evidence of the resources he can supply, as evidenced by characteristics such as earning capacity, ambition, and industriousness.

3. Males and females should differ in the events that activate jealousy, males being more jealous about sexual infidelity and the threat to paternal probability, and females more concerned about emotional attachments and the threat of loss of resources.

Buss (1989) obtained questionnaire responses from 37 samples, representing over 10,000 individuals, from 33 countries located on 6 continents and 5 islands. There was tremendous diversity in geographic locale, culture, ethnicity, and religion. What was found? First, in each of the 37 samples males valued physical attractiveness and relative youth in potential mates more than did females, consistent with the hypothesis that males value mates with high reproductive capacity. The prediction that males would value chastity in potential mates more than would females was supported in 23 out of the 37 samples, providing moderate support for the hypothesis. Second, females were found to value the financial capacity of potential mates more than did males (36 of 37 samples) and valued the characteristics of ambition and industriousness in a potential mate to a greater extent than males (29 of 37 samples), consistent with the hypothesis that females value mates with high resource-providing capacity.

Causes of Jealousy

In subsequent research, three studies were conducted to test the hypothesis of sex differences in jealousy (D. M. Buss et al., 1992). In the first study, undergraduate students were asked whether they would experience greater distress in response to sexual infidelity or emotional infidelity. Whereas 60 percent of the male sample reported greater distress over a partner's sexual infidelity, 83 percent of the female sample reported greater distress over a partner's emotional attachment to a rival.

In the second study, physiological measures of distress were taken on undergraduates who imagined two scenarios, one in which their partner became sexually involved with someone else and one in which their partner became emotionally involved with someone else. Once more males and females were found to have contrasting results, with males showing greater physiological distress in relation to imagery of their partner's sexual involvement and women showing greater physiological distress in relation to imagery of their partner's emotional involvement.

In the third study, the hypothesis that males and females who had experienced committed sexual relationships would show the same results as in the previous study but to a greater extent than would males and females who had not been involved in such a relationship was explored. In other words, actual experience in a committed relationship was important in bringing out the differential effect. This was found to be the case for males for whom sexual jealousy was found to be increasingly activated by experience with a committed sexual relationship. However, there was no significant difference in response to emotional infidelity between women who had and had not experienced a committed sexual relationship.

In sum, the authors interpreted the results as supportive of the hypothesis of sex differences in activators of jealousy. Although alternative explanations for the results were recognized, the authors suggested that only the evolutionary psychological framework led to the specific predictions.

Evolutionary Origins of Sex Differences: How Strong Are the Data?

Based on our coverage so far, evolutionary psychology appears to provide a quite convincing explanation of sex differences. Indeed, many contemporary psychologists find the theory convincing in this regard. However, in recent years new research findings have begun to raise questions about the validity of the theory as it applies to sex differences in social behavior.

In evaluating evolutionary psychology, a major question is whether patterns of sex differences are found universally, that is, across all cultures of the world. Evolutionary psychology expects that sex differences will be universal. People share the same brain and physical anatomy. Humans share a common evolutionary past; throughout most of our species' evolutionary history, all humans lived in the same region of the world, Africa. If evolved psychological mechanisms are the cause of sex differences in social behavior, then those sex differences should be similar in all regions of the world and all human cultures.

A contrasting idea is that sex differences are a product of features of the society in which people live. In societies that treat men and women very differently—for example, in which there are particularly large differences in the work opportunities available to men versus women and in the income that they earn—sex difference may be larger than in societies in which men and women share more equally in the goods of society. Such a result would contradict the predictions of evolutionary psychology.

Eagly and Wood (1999) have provided evidence on this question. They re-analyzed data from a multinational study of men's and women's preferences in mates. The evolutionary psychology prediction is that the same pattern of sex differences would be found in all cultures, with women preferring men who have the capacity to earn money and men preferring young women with domestic skills. On the one hand, some of Eagly and Wood's findings were consistent with evolutionary psychology. For example, when looking for a mate, men did tend to value the quality of being a good cook to a greater degree than did women. However, other findings contradicted evolutionary psychology by demonstrating the existence of variations in the nature of sex differences. Specifically, sex differences were found to be smaller within societies in which men and women have more similar roles within the overall social structure. In societies in which there was greater gender equality, women were less concerned with men's earning capacity, men were less concerned with women's housekeeping skills, and sex differences on these measures were smaller (Eagly & Wood, 1999). A subsequent review of anthropological research on sex differences similarly was "not very supportive of evolutionary psychology" (Wood & Eagly, 2002, p. 718). Instead of pointing to

Sex differences in mate preferences have been shown to be smaller in societies in which women's earning capacity is similar to men's.

universal patterns of sex differences that result from biology alone, the data were consistent with a biosocial view of sex differences. In a biosocial perspective, sex differences reflect interactions between biological qualities of men and women and social factors, particularly those involving economic conditions and the division of labor within society (Wood & Eagly, 2002).

Additional data also are damaging to the initial conclusions that evolutionary psychologists drew regarding sex differences. Some of this work involves the re-analysis of data sets that originally were interpreted as being supportive of evolutionary psychology predictions. Miller, Putcha-Bhagavatula, & Pedersen (2002) note that initial studies of sex differences in mate preferences by Buss and colleagues sometimes failed to compare men and women on all relevant psychological variables. When re-analyzing these mate-preference data, the Miller group (2002) found that "across the data, what men desired most in a mate women desired most in a mate. [There were] extraordinarily high correlations between men's and women's ratings for both short-term and long-term sexual partners" (p. 90).

The evolutionary psychologist's claim that men and women differ in the events that activate jealousy (Buss et al., 1992) is also contradicted by recent data (DeSteno, Bartlett, Braverman, & Salovey, 2002). These recent findings suggest that the original findings of evolutionary psychologists in this area may have resulted from a methodological artifact; an arbitrarily chosen feature of the research procedures may have artificially contributed to the results. Most of the evolutionary psychological original research on the topic involved a multiple-choice or "forced choice" method. Participants in research are asked if they would be more distressed if they found that their romantic partner (a) had sexual relations with another person or (b) formed a close emotional bond with another person. Note, first, that this is an odd question, particularly from an evolutionary psychological perspective. Over the course of human evolution, it cannot possibly be the case that people frequently were faced with learning simultaneously about a partner's sexual and emotional relations and then having to decide which is worse. Recognizing the oddity of this forced-choice procedure, DeSteno and colleagues (2002) also asked participants to consider the sexual and emotional scenarios one at a time and to indicate how upset they would be by each one. With this change in procedure, the sex differences in jealousy predicted by evolutionary psychology were no longer found. Instead, men and women were highly similar. Both were more distressed by sexual infidelity than by news of a partner's emotionally close nonsexual relationship.

Related findings come from the analysis of men's and women's physiological responses to imagining sexual versus emotional infidelity (Harris, 2000). If men and women possess different evolved modules of the sort suggested by parental investment theory, then they should respond differently to these two scenarios; men should react with stronger feelings of jealousy when imagining sexual infidelity and women should react more when envisioning emotional infidelity. In the careful research of Harris, women were *not* found to be more responsive to emotional (versus sexual) infidelity. Men did respond strongly to sexual infidelity but, as Harris points out, that may not have resulted from the infidelity but merely from the idea that sex occurred; men simply may respond relatively strongly to any scenario involving sexual content. On her physiological measures, Harris (2000) indeed found that men responded strongly to imagined sexual encounters whether *or not* infidelity was involved. Subsequent work similarly failed to find the sex differences predicted by evolutionary psychology when research participants were asked to contemplate actual instances of infidelity they had experienced, rather than the hypothetical instances of infidelity that some previous researchers had studied (Harris, 2002). The overall findings, then, contradict the evolutionary psychological account of sex differences in jealousy—an account that, as Harris (2000) noted, had previously been seen as a "showcase example of evolutionary psychology" (p. 1082).

In summary, then, current data do not provide consistent support for evolutionary psychological hypotheses about sex differences in mate attraction and jealousy. The exact nature of gender differences that might exist, and the roles of evolutionary hardwiring versus social structure in bringing them about, thus remain to be defined.

EVOLUTIONARY THEORY AND THE BIG FIVE PERSONALITY DIMENSIONS

Can the evolutionary perspective be related to modern trait theory? Many trait theorists now view the five-factor model, and traits generally, within an evolutionary perspective. There are three major components to this picture. First, returning to Goldberg's (1990) fundamental lexical hypothesis, there is the view that trait terms have emerged to help people categorize behaviors fundamental to the human condition. Which aspects of interaction would seem to be of particular importance? Goldberg (1981) argued that people ask five fundamental and universal questions when they interact with another person (X):

1. Is X active and dominant or passive and submissive (Can I bully X or will X try to bully me)?
2. Is X agreeable (warm and pleasant) or disagreeable (cold and distant)?
3. Can I count on X (Is X responsible and conscientious or undependable and negligent)?
4. Is X crazy (unpredictable) or sane (stable)?
5. Is X smart or dumb (How easy will it be for me to teach X)?

Not surprisingly, these five questions correspond to the Big Five trait factors.

Second, according to the evolutionary view, important individual differences exist because they have played some role in the processes of evolution by natural selection. Traits such as extraversion and emotional stability (as opposed to neuroticism) might be particularly important for mate selection (Kenrick, Sadalla, Goth & Trost, 1990), and conscientiousness and agreeableness might be particularly important in relation to group survival. Thus, the trait terms in our daily language might reflect individual differences important to the tasks humans have had to face in the long history of their evolutionary development.

Third, there is the view that humans are biologically similar to the great apes and therefore share certain characteristics with them. Indeed, more than 98 percent of our genes are shared in common. According to one view, seven traits are shared by humans and other primates: activity level, fearfulness, impulsiveness, sociability, nurturance, aggressiveness, and dominance (A. H.

EMOTIONS AND TRAITS:
HOW SIMILAR ARE HUMANS AND OTHER ANIMALS?

Darwin's *The Origin of Species* suggested a continuity between humans and other species. In his book *The Expression of the Emotions in Man and Animals* he suggested a continuity of expressions of emotions in animals and people, that is, that many of the same basic emotions and accompanying facial expressions exist in both. There is evidence of a similarity of expression of what are called basic emotions (e.g., anger, sadness, fear, joy) in nonhuman primates and humans, in infants as well as adults, and across cultures (Ekman, 1993, 1998). Evolutionary psychologists suggest a continuity in traits between humans and other species, a view bolstered by the fact that humans and the great apes share over 98 percent of the same genes. Is there evidence of such a continuity of traits?

Gosling and John (1998, 1999) set out to consider the question of whether there are dimensions of personality common to a wide range of species, raising the question: "What are the major dimensions of animal personality?" In a review of the literature of descriptions of 12 species, ranging from octopuses, guppies, and rats to gorillas and chimpanzees, they found evidence that three of the human five-factor dimensions showed generality across species—E, N, and A: "The evidence indicates that chimpanzees, various other primates, dogs, cats, donkeys, and pigs, even guppies and octopuses all show individual differences that can be organized along dimensions akin to E, N, and (with the exception of guppies and octopuses) A" (1999, p. 70). However, a separate C factor was found only in chimps (King & Figueredo, 1997), our closest relatives. This may be because traits related to C, such as following rules and norms, thinking before acting, and cognitively controlling impulses may be a relatively recent evolutionary development.

Are such similarities anthropomorphic projections on the part of humans or are they actual attributes of the animals? In a study of trait ratings of humans, dogs, and cats, Gosling and John again found evidence of three of the Big Five in dogs and cats as well as humans—E, N, and A, but no separate C factor. In a further study, they generated a list of "personality descriptors" of dogs, based on attributes human subjects most frequently used to describe dogs (e.g., affectionate, cuddly, energetic, happy, intelligent, nervous, lazy, loyal). One group of subjects then rated a human they knew on the "dog personality inventory" and another group of subjects rated a dog they knew on the same list of descriptors. Would the same factors emerge from the two groups of ratings, suggesting similar dimensions of personality for humans and dogs? Using the dog personality inventory for humans, they again found evidence of the Big Five: N, E, O, A, C. When the same rating items were applied to dogs, three factors similar to E, N, and A again emerged, with no separate C factor.

Overall, studies on animal personality suggested the following conclusions: (1) Animal personality can be assessed reliably. (2) The structure of personality traits in humans is quite similar to that of chimps. (3) Non-primate mammals like dogs and cats seem to have a less differentiated personality structure, with three dimensions showing considerable, although not perfect, generality across many species. (4) Personality descriptions of other species are not mere anthropomorphic projections; that is, such descriptions are not "all in the mind" of the human but instead reflect actual characteristics of the animal being rated. (5) Although only little research has been done, there is now some evidence for continuity of personality trait structure between humans and members of other species.

SOURCES: Ekman, 1993, 1998; Gosling & John, 1998, 1999; King & Figueredo, 1997.

Buss, 1997). Some of these traits relate to prosocial behavior, others to ways in which we attempt to handle conflict with others or struggle for power. Again, the relevance of many of these traits to the Big Five is apparent.

Nonetheless, one must note that any answers to the question of how the evolutionary view relates to the Big Five variables hinge on an issue we highlighted in the previous chapter, namely, whether one views the Big Five variables as (a) descriptions of people's psychological tendencies, or (b) structures that explain a person's behavior. The evolutionary view and the Big Five are quite compatible if one views the Big Five as descriptive. Evolutionary psychology potentially explains why these particular five individual differences are noticed and discussed when people observe and describe the psychological characteristics of others. However, it seems quite difficult to reconcile the perspective if one chooses to treat the Big Five as psychological structures that cause people's behavior, as is done in five-factor theory (McCrae & Costa, 1996). This is because the units of analysis in evolutionary psychology and in five-factor theory differ fundamentally. In evolutionary psychology, the basic units of analysis are domain-specific. Evolved psychological mechanisms solve domain-specific problems of living (attracting mates, detecting cheaters, etc.). In contrast, the units of analysis of five-factor theory are domain-general; a variable such as "extraversion" or "conscientiousness" does not make reference to any specific type of social domain in which the person is being extraverted or conscientious.

EVOLUTIONARY EXPLANATIONS: COMMENT

In earlier periods in the history of psychology, evolutionary explanations for human behavior either were ignored or fell into disfavor. Today, few psychologists question that an analysis of the evolution of our species can provide insight into the nature of the contemporary human mind. Investigators do differ greatly, however, in their beliefs about the degree to which evolutionary psychology can provide a basis for the analysis of personality.

On the one hand, some investigators are extremely enthusiastic. Buss, for example, suggests that an evolutionary framework offers virtually the only hope for bringing the field of psychology into some kind of theoretical order. He suggests that human behavior depends on psychological mechanisms and the only known cause of such mechanisms is evolution by natural selection. Thus, anyone interested in the social behavior of humans must take into account the evolutionary history of the behavior. According to this view, the biological roots of human nature, as expressed in the genes, are the link between evolution and behavior (Kenrick, 1994). Evolution is also seen to account for the social structures that other psychologists view as the causes of behavior; evolutionary psychologists suggest that culture itself is generated by evolved psychological mechanisms (Tooby & Cosmides, 1992).

At the same time, there are others who question how much evolutionary theory has to say about human functioning and who also caution about the implications that may be drawn from such a view. While not denying that we have an evolutionary history, these psychologists suggest humans have progressed to the point where they are much more free of genetically programmed responses. They caution us against interpreting social patterns as biologically based when they could reflect the influence of social forces. For example, Cantor (1990) suggests that in focusing on the problems of survival and reproduction, evolutionary psychologists have ignored much of the diversity of social interaction and efforts to solve contemporary problems. In addition, Eagly and Wood (1999) suggest that the sex differences in human behavior emphasized by Buss and others can be accounted for by the different roles demanded of men and women as much as by evolved dispositions. Many feminists are concerned about Buss's interpretation of data about sex differences, claiming that such an interpretation ignores cultural factors, suggests that male-female differences are inevitable, and thus potentially provides members of society with an excuse for engaging in gender-biased behavior.

It is particularly noteworthy that critics of evolutionary psychology do not merely include psychologists who are interested in the impact of social forces. The critics also include biologists who are intimately familiar with evolutionary theory, but who feel that evolutionary psychologists have overstated the impact of evolutionary mechanisms on human thought and action. Biologists recognize that organisms develop in environmental and social settings. The settings the organism experiences shape its biological nature (Ehrlich, 2000; Lewontin, 2000). The nervous system develops in interaction with the social world, with neural connections being established and weakened as a function of people's experiences (Edelman & Tononi, 2000). Evolutionary psychologists commonly have supported their views by arguing against individuals who disregard the role of biology in psychological functioning. But, increasingly, these arguments are irrelevant. The greater challenge for evolutionary psychologists is to defend their views against the arguments of biologists—scientists who are intimately familiar with principles of natural selection and the workings of the human organism, but who conclude that evolutionary psychologists have erred by underestimating the importance of interactions between the biological person and the social environment (Lewontin, 2000).

A final consideration is that, even if one accepts the principles of evolutionary psychology, these principles fail to address some topics that are of central concern to personality psychology (Cervone, 2000). For example, almost all personality theorists recognize that personality reveals itself when people interpret ambiguous social situations. The interpretation of ambiguity, then, is a core concern of the field. It was the central issue in the projective testing favored by psychodynamic theorists (Chapter 4); the tests present ambiguous stimuli and the personality psychologist is interested in individual differences in their interpretation. It is a central issue in the personal construct and social-cognitive theories discussed in subsequent chapters, which provide detailed analyses of how people assign meaning to ambiguous encounters (Chapters 12 and 13). In contrast, evolutionary psychology provides few if any tools for addressing this issue. Consider an example (Cervone, 2000). Suppose you are playing cards with a group of friends, one of whom is a member of the opposite sex who you find attractive and who also seems to be winning most of the hands in the card game.

What would the evolutionary psychologist predict about your behavior? Well, on the one hand, the prediction might be that your cheating-detection module will be activated. If so, you should engage in behavioral strategies to protect against cheating (e.g., staring at the person in a stern manner). On the other hand, the prediction might be that your mate-attraction module will be activated. If so, you should engage in strategies designed to make yourself attractive to the other person (flirting). The point of this example is that evolutionary psychology provides no tools for determining *which* of the two modules will be activated. The social situation is ambiguous. To some people, it may be a social exchange situation. To others, it may be an opportunity to attract a mate. It is obvious that people who interpret the situation one way versus another will subsequently engage in different behavioral strategies. The challenge for the personality psychologist is to explain why one person encodes the ambiguous situation as having to do with social exchange, whereas another person encodes it as an opportunity to attract mates. This inherently requires an analysis of mental processes that come into play *prior* to domain-specific mental modules. The person has to figure out what the domain is in the first place. Evolutionary psychology does not tell us how people do this. It is difficult to see how a theory that says little about how people interpret ambiguous stimuli can serve as a general framework for the psychology of personality.

In sum, it is clear that evolutionary psychology is a powerful theoretical framework of enormous importance to the psychology of personality. Yet it is difficult to determine whether, in the long run, the approach will be an organizing framework for the field, or merely will supplement other frameworks by providing insight into the distal evolutionary foundations of psychological capacities that develop through interaction with the social world.

What makes us all human is our DNA.

SOURCE: Hamer, 1997, p. 111.

GENES AND PERSONALITY: THE MODERN SYNTHESIS, PART II

Whatever we inherit that is common to us as humans, as well as what we inherit that makes us unique, exists through the action of genes. We inherit 23 pairs of chromosomes, one of each pair from each of our biological parents. The chromosomes contain thousands of genes. Genes are made up of a molecule called DNA and direct the synthesis of protein molecules. Genes may be thought of as sources of information, directing the synthesis of protein molecules along particular lines. It is the information contained in the genes that directs the biological development of the organism. It is this information that directs the biological development of the fertilized egg into a fetus, a fully formed neonate, an adolescent with secondary sex characteristics, and an elderly person with characteristics associated with the aged. The amount of information contained in the genes is truly remarkable.

In appreciating the relation of genes to behavior, it is important to understand that genes do not govern behavior directly. Thus, there is no "extraversion gene" or "introversion gene" and there is no "neuroticism gene." To the extent that genes influence the development of personality characteristics such as the Big Five, described in Chapter 8, they do so through the direction of the biological functioning of the body.

BEHAVIORAL GENETICS

The study of genetic contributions to behavior is called the field of **behavioral genetics**. Behavior geneticists employ a variety of techniques to estimate the degree to which variation in psychological characteristics is due to genetic factors. As we shall see, the methods of behavioral genetics also can, and do, provide evidence of environmental effects on personality. Behavioral geneticists employ three primary research methods: selective breeding studies, twin studies, and adoption studies.

Selective Breeding Studies

In **selective breeding** studies, animals with a desired trait for study are selected and mated. This selection and reproduction process is used with successive generations of offspring to produce a strain of animals that is consistent within itself for the desired characteristic. Selective breeding is not only a research technique, it is used, for example, to breed race horses or breeds of dogs with desired characteristics.

Once one has created different strains of animals through selective breeding, one not only can study their typical behavioral tendencies. It also is possible to subject the different strains to different experimentally controlled developmental experiences. Researchers then can sort out the effects of genetic differences and environmental differences on the observed later behavior. For example, the roles of genetic and environmental factors in later barking behavior or fearfulness can be studied by subjecting genetically different breeds of dogs to different environmental rearing conditions (Scott & Fuller, 1965).

Selective breeding research has enhanced our understanding of how genes contribute to problems that often are blamed solely on the individual. Consider work on alcoholism (Ponomarev & Crabbe, 1999). The researchers bred various strains of mice that proved to exhibit qualitatively different responses to alcohol. This work illustrated, then, that genes play a role in responsiveness to alcohol, addiction, and withdrawal. It contributed to a more complete understanding of the fact that genetic factors present some individuals with severe vulnerabilities to lifelong problems with alcohol (Hamer & Copeland, 1998).

Twin Studies

Even the most enthusiastic researcher realizes that selective breeding research cannot and should not be done with humans. Ethical factors force the researcher to consider alternatives. Fortunately for science, a ready alternative exists: human twins. Twins provide a naturally occurring experiment. What the scientist wants, ideally, is a circumstance in which there are known variations in degree of genetic similarity and/or environmental similarity. If two organisms are identical genetically, then any later observed differences can be attributed to differences in their environments. On the other hand, if two organisms are different genetically but experience the same environment, then any observed differences can be attributed to genetic factors. The existence of identical (monozygotic) twins and fraternal (dizygotic) twins offers a good approximation to this research ideal. Monozygotic (MZ) twins develop from the same fertilized egg and are genetically identical. Dizygotic (DZ) twins develop from two separately fertilized eggs and are as genetically similar as any pair of siblings, on the average sharing about 50 percent of their genes.

These identical twins were reared apart and met only after reaching college age. Research has demonstrated that identical twins are surprisingly similar in their personalities even if they do not grow up together.

Researchers capitalize on these systematic differences between MZ and DZ twins by conducting **twin studies** to gauge the degree to which genetic factors explain person-to-person variations in psychological characteristics.

Two logical considerations underpin the twin method. The first is that, since MZ twins are genetically identical, any systematic difference between them must be due to environmental effects. Interestingly, then, the study of genetically identical persons is particularly valuable for revealing the effects of environmental experience. Second, it is the difference in similarity between MZ twin pairs and DZ twin pairs that is crucial to estimating the effects of genetics. Specifically, we know that MZ twins are *more similar* to one another genetically than DZ twins are similar to one another genetically. If genetics influence a given personality characteristic, then MZ twins, as a result of being more similar genetically, also should be more similar on the given personality characteristic than are DZ twins. If they are not, then there is no genetic effect. When studying both MZ and DZ twin pairs, then, the researcher can compare them (MZ similarity compared to DZ similarity on a trait of interest) to determine the magnitude of the influence of genetic factors. This genetic influence usually is expressed numerically in terms of a heritability coefficient (described below).

The twin strategy usually is conduced with twins who grow up in the same household. However, circumstances sometimes force parents to give up children for adoption early in life. As a result, MZ and DZ twins sometimes are reared apart. This creates a circumstance of remarkable interest to the psychological scientist and the public at large, namely, biologically identical people who are raised in different environments. What happens? Does biology win out, with genetically identical twins being psychologically identical despite their different experiences? Or do social experiences win out, with people differing substantially despite their identical genes? These questions can be answered thanks to an international data set that features large numbers of reared-apart twins who have completed various psychological measures (Bouchard, Lykken, McGue, Segal, & Tellegen, 1990). Results provide clear evidence that the effects of biology endure across different circumstances. On multiple personality trait measures, MZ twins raised apart were found to be similar to a significant degree; twin correlations indicating the degree of similarity between the twins were in the .45 to .50 range. Of particular interest is that MZ twins raised apart were about as similar to one another as were MZ twins raised together (Bouchard et al., 1990). Being raised in the same household did *not* make the twins more similar on broad personality trait measures. We return to this fascinating finding, and its interpretations and implications, after reviewing further research findings below.

Adoption Studies

Studies of children who grow up with caregivers other than their biological parents are called **adoption studies**. (Adoption studies sometimes involve identical twins, as in the research reviewed in the paragraph immediately above, but commonly may involve non-twin siblings.) Adoption studies offer another method for studying genetic and environmental effects. When adequate records are kept, it is possible to consider the similarity of adopted children to their natural (biological) parents, who have not influenced them environmentally, and compare this with the similarity to their adoptive parents, who share no genes in common with them. The extent of similarity to their biological parents is indicative of genetic factors while the extent of similarity to their adoptive parents is indicative of environmental factors.

Finally, such comparisons can be extended to families that include both biological and adoptive children. Take, for example, a family of four children; two of the children are the biological offspring of the parents and two of the children have been adopted. The two biological offspring share a genetic similarity with one another and with the biological parents that is not true for the two adopted children. Assuming the two adopted children are unrelated, they share no genes in common but share a genetic similarity with their parents and any siblings who might exist in other environments. Thus, it is possible to compare different parent-offspring and biological sibling-adoptive sibling combinations in terms of similarity on personality characteristics. For example, one can ask whether the biological siblings are more similar to one another than are the adoptive siblings, whether they are more similar to the parents than the adoptive siblings, and whether the adoptive siblings are more similar to their biological parents than to their adoptive parents. A "yes" answer to such questions would be suggestive of the importance of genetic factors in the development of the particular personality characteristic.

It should now be clear that in twin and adoption studies we have individuals of varying degrees of genetic similarity being exposed to varying degrees of environmental similarity. By measuring these individuals on the characteristics of interest, we can determine the extent to which their genetic similarity accounts for the similarity of scores on each characteristic. For example, we can compare the IQ scores of MZ and DZ twins reared together and apart, biological (nontwin) siblings reared together and apart, adoptive siblings and biological siblings with parents, and adoptive siblings with their biological and adoptive parents. Some representative correlations are presented in Table 9.1. The data clearly suggest a relationship between greater genetic similarity and greater similarity of IQ.

Heritability Coefficient

How, exactly, does the behavioral geneticist determine the degree to which genetic variations determine variations among people in a personality characteristic? This usually is done by computing what is called a **heritability** coeffi-

Table 9.1 Average Familial IQ Correlations (*R*)

As genetic similarity increases, so does the magnitude of the correlations for IQ, suggesting a strong genetic contribution to intelligence.

Relationship	Average R	Number of Pairs
REARED-TOGETHER BIOLOGICAL RELATIVES		
MZ twins	.86	4,672
DZ twins	.60	5,533
Siblings	.47	26,473
Parent–offspring	.42	8,433
Half-siblings	.35	200
Cousins	.15	1,176
REARED-APART BIOLOGICAL RELATIVES		
MZ twins	.72	65
Siblings	.24	203
Parent–offspring	.24	720
REARED-TOGETHER NONBIOLOGICAL RELATIVES		
Siblings	.32	714
Parent–offspring	.24	720

NOTE: MZ, monozygotic; DZ, dizygotic
SOURCE: Adapted from "Familial Studies of Intelligence: A Review," by T. J. Bouchard and M. McGue, 1981, *Science, 250*, p. 1056. © American Association for the Advancement of Science. Reprinted from McGue et al., 1993, p. 60.

cient, or h^2 (it is h "squared' because numbers are squared when computing variations around an average score). The heritability coefficient represents the proportion of observed variance in scores that can be attributed to genetic factors. In a study involving both MZ and DZ twins, h^2 is based on the difference between the MZ and DZ correlations. If MZ twins (who share all their genes) are no more similar to one another than are DZ twins (who share half their genes), then there is no genetic effect: h^2 is zero. If MZ twins differ greatly from DZ twins, h^2 is large; its upper limit is 1.0, or 100% of the total variance. To the extent that h^2 is less than 1.0, there exists variance that is not accounted for by genetic factors; this remaining variance is explained by environmental variation.

Note that the heritability coefficient refers to variation *in the population examined in a given study*. There are two implications of this point. First, different heritability coefficients, for the same psychological trait, may be observed in different populations; for example, if one is studying a population in which many people have been subjected to environmental effects that exert a particular large influence on them (e.g., stress from disease or war), then the environmental effects in this group will be relatively large and h^2 will be relatively small (Grigorenko, 2002). Second, the heritability coefficient does not indicate the degree to which genetics accounts for the fact that a particular individual has a particular characteristic. It is a measure of variation in the population. For some attributes (e.g., a biological feature or psychological capacity possessed by all humans), there may be no person-to-person variation. The h^2 would be zero—even if genetics explains why all people have the attribute. For other attributes (e.g., your ability to read), the attribute may be explained by an interaction of genetic and social factors, and it may make little sense to say that genetics versus the environment each accounted for X percent of the attribute. The h^2 is an estimate associated with a population and not a definitive measure of the action of genes.

Heritability of Personality: Findings

We now consider additional behavior genetic findings and the conclusions about personality to which they lead. An interesting feature of work in this area is that findings are often relatively consistent from study to study. This enables the behavior geneticist to summarize results with confidence. Here are two quotes featuring key summaries: "It is difficult to find psychological traits that reliably show no genetic influence" (Plomin & Neiderhiser, 1992) and "For almost every behavioral trait so far investigated, from reaction time to religiosity, an important fraction of the variation among people turns out to be associated with genetic variation. This fact need no longer be subject to debate" (Bouchard et al., 1990). These quotes reflect findings from numerous twin and adoption studies. These studies have been conducted on a wide variety of personality variables, often with large samples of research participants, and with the work extending over significant periods of time. The evidence of genetic influence is sometimes startling, as when identical twins reared apart and brought together as adults are found not only to look and sound alike but to have the same attitudes and share the same hobbies and preferences for pets (Lykken, Bouchard, McGue, & Tellegen, 1993). But beyond such almost eerie observations is a pattern of results strongly suggesting an important role for heredity in almost all aspects of personality functioning (Plomin & Caspi, 1999). Recent estimates of the overall heritability of personality traits converge on roughly 40 percent. Table 9.2 presents heritability estimates for a wide variety of characteristics. For comparative purposes, heritability estimates for height and weight are included, as well as a few other characteristics that may be of interest.

A criticism made of behavior-genetic research on personality is that most studies are based on self-report questionnaire methods. A recent study is important in this regard in that two independent peer reports as well as self-reports on the NEO Five-Factor Inventory were collected on a sample of 660 MZ twins and 304 DZ twins (200 same sex and 104 opposite sex). The investigators found good evidence of reliability of ratings in terms of peer-peer rating agreement, good evidence of the accuracy of self-report in terms of self-peer rating agreement, and general support for earlier findings concerning genetic influence on all of the Big Five personality factors (Table 9.3) (Riemann, Angleitner, & Strelau, 1997).

Some Important Caveats

Before concluding this section, it is important to be aware of two inappropriate conclusions that can be drawn from the behavioral genetic data, conclusions that no behavioral geneticist would make. First, it is possible to draw the inappropriate conclusion that the heritability estimate indicates the extent to which a characteristic is determined by heredity. Even were one to accept the overall heritability estimate of 40 percent for personality, this would not mean that 40 percent of one's personality is inherited, or that 40 percent of some aspect of one's personality is inherited, or that 40 percent of the difference in personality between two individuals or groups of people is inherited. Similarly, a heritability estimate of 80 percent for IQ does not mean that 80

Table 9.2 Heritability Estimates

The data indicate a strong genetic contribution to personality (overall estimate of 40% of the variance), a contribution not as large as that for height, weight, or IQ but larger than that for attitudes and behaviors such as TV viewing.

Trait	h^2 estimate
Height	.80
Weight	.60
IQ	.50
Specific cognitive ability	.40
School achievement	.40
BIG FIVE	
Extraversion	.36
Neuroticism	.31
Conscientiousness	.28
Agreeableness	.28
Openness to Experience	.46
EASI TEMPERAMENT	
Emotionality	.40
Activity	.25
Sociability	.25
Impulsivity	.45
ATTITUDES	
Conservatism	.30
Religiosity	.16
Racial integration	.00
TV viewing	.20

NOTE: EASI = Four dimensions of temperament identified by Buss and Plomin (1984). E, emotionality; A, Activity; S, Sociability; I, Impulsivity.
SOURCES: Bouchard et al., 1990; Dunn & Plomin, 1990; Loehlin, 1992; McGue et al., 1993; Pedersen et al., 1998; Pedersen et al., 1992; Plomin, 1990; Plomin et al., 1990; Plomin & Rende, 1991; Tellegen et al., 1998; Tesser, 1993; Zuckerman, 1991.

Table 9.3 Peer-Peer, Self-Peer, MZ and DZ (Self-Report), and MZ and DZ (Average Peer Report) Correlations on the NEO Five-Factor Inventory

	Peer-Peer	Self-Peer Self-Report			Averaged Peer Report	
			MZ	DZ	MZ	DZ
N	.63	.55	.53	.13	.40	.01
E	.65	.60	.56	.28	.38	.22
O	.59	.57	.54	.34	.49	.30
A	.59	.49	.42	.19	.32	.21
C	.61	.54	.54	.18	.41	.17
Mean	.61	.55	.52	.23	.40	.18

NOTE: MZ, monozygotic; DZ, dizygotic
SOURCE: Adapted from Riemann, Angleitner, and Strelau, 1997, pp. 460, 461, 462.

percent of intelligence is inherited, or that 80 percent of one's own intelligence is inherited, or that 80 percent of group differences in intelligence is due to heredity. Remember that the heritability estimate is a population statistic that varies with the characteristic measured, how the characteristic is measured, the age and other characteristics of the population investigated, and whether twin or adoption data are used. Again, the heritability index is an estimate of the proportion of the variance in a characteristic, measured in a particular way, in a specific population, that can be attributed to genetic variance.

A second inappropriate conclusion concerning heritability estimates would be the suggestion that because a characteristic has an inherited component, it cannot be changed. There is a very common assumption that if something is biological and inherited, it is fixed. Even sophisticated individuals, well aware of the flaw in this view, slip into making such a connection. Even if something is altogether determined by heredity, this does not mean that it cannot be altered by the environment. Dogs can be bred for specific characteristics but this does not mean that a particular environment cannot alter the characteristic. Similarly, as noted earlier, individuals may be born with certain temperaments but this does not mean that their temperaments are set for life (Kagan, 1999). Height is significantly determined by genes but can be influenced by the environment in terms of nutrition.

Molecular Genetic Paradigms

In recent years, researchers have begun to move beyond the traditional behavior-genetic paradigm. Instead of merely comparing different types of twins, they have turned to a direct examination of the underlying biology. This work employs molecular genetic techniques in an effort to identify specific genes that are linked with personality traits (Plomin & Caspi, 1999). By examining the genetic material of different individuals, researchers hope to show how genetic variations, or alleles, relate to individual differences in personality functioning. Ideally, one might be able to show how a genetic variation codes for alternative forms of a biological substance or system that, in turn, has psychological effects.

Initial research reported the discovery of a gene linked to the trait of novelty seeking, similar to Eysenck's P factor, and to low C on the Big Five (Benjamin et al., 1996; Ebstein et al., 1996). However, this finding has not been replicated uniformly in follow-up studies (Grigorenko, 2002). Perhaps more promising, researchers recently have identified an interaction between a specific genetic mechanism and the social environment. This research studied the effects of maltreatment in childhood on the development of antisocial behavior later in life (Caspi et al., 2002). Despite such unfortunate maltreatment, some children have good developmental outcomes; they seem to be resilient in the face of early life stress. The question, then, was whether there might be a genetic basis to this resilience.

To answer this question, the researchers identified a subset of the study's population of participants who possessed a gene that has an important property: it codes for an enzyme that lowers the activity of certain neurotransmitters in the brain that are linked to aggressive behavior. Among those who had experienced maltreatment in childhood, people with this genetic variation were found to differ from others (Figure 9.4). Specifically, people who experienced severe maltreatment *but* who had the gene that produced high levels of the enzyme were less likely to display antisocial behavior in adulthood. The genetic variation, in other words, seemed to lower the negative impact of maltreatment. This exciting finding requires replication. However, it suggests a promising feature for molecular-genetic research on personality.

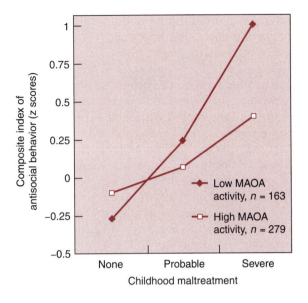

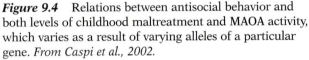

Figure 9.4 Relations between antisocial behavior and both levels of childhood maltreatment and MAOA activity, which varies as a result of varying alleles of a particular gene. *From Caspi et al., 2002.*

Subsequent work by this same research team has discovered molecular-genetic factors that make individuals more or less vulnerable to becoming depressed (Caspi et al., 2003). The genetic factor that was studied is one that influences levels of serotonin in the brain; specifically, the researchers studied a naturally-occurring genetic variation that involves two different versions of a gene that affects serotonergic activity. The researchers' expectation was *not* that possessing a particular genetic background would lead inevitably to the experience of depression. Instead, they again expected an interaction: Genes should predict the onset of depression only in people who have certain types of environmental experiences. The environmental experiences they investigated were those that involve high levels of stress. Adults were surveyed to determine the degree to which they recently had experienced stressful life events involving factors such as finances, health, employment, and interpersonal relationships. The expectation of a gene-X-environment interaction was confirmed. Individuals who were genetically predisposed to have lower levels of serotonergic activity *and* who experienced numerous stressful life events were much more likely to become depressed than were other individuals (Caspi et al., 2003). Again, then, molecular-genetic research indicates that genes affect psychological outcomes in interaction with environmental experiences.

ENVIRONMENTS AND GENE-ENVIRONMENT INTERACTIONS

Genetic researchers realized early on that genetic and environmental influences are inextricably linked and interact in their influence on personality and behavior in adulthood. A classic study by Cooper and Zubek (1958) nicely illustrates such gene-environment interactions using the selective breeding research. In previous research, strains of maze-bright and maze-dull rats had been bred so that the strain of "bright" ones were much more likely to learn how to navigate a maze than were the "dull" ones. The researchers wanted to study how early environment experiences would influence the adult problem solving capacity of these genetically different rats. Thus, they raised one group of each strain in an enriched, stimulating environment and another group of each strain in an impoverished environment. What happened? Compared to the normal lab environment, the enriched environment improved later learning ability in the dull rats but did not help the bright ones. Conversely, the impoverished environment markedly handicapped the bright rats but did not impair the dull group. Thus, even these rats were not "prisoners" of their genetic predispositions—the environment interacted with their genes in a crucial way, modifying the way these predispositions were expressed.

For human personality, if the behavioral genetic data indicate that roughly 40 to 50 percent of the variance for single personality characteristics and personality overall are determined by genetic factors, then the rest of the population variance is made up of some combination of environmental effects and measurement error. Indeed, one of the interesting aspects of recent developments in behavioral genetics has been the effort to use twin and adoption data to determine environmental effects on personality variables. Thus, although Plomin (1990) suggests that "genetic influence is so ubiquitous and pervasive in behavior that a shift in emphasis is warranted: ask not what is heritable; ask instead what is not heritable" (p. 112), at the same time he suggests that the "other message is that the same behavioral genetic data yield the strongest available evidence for the importance of environmental influence" (p. 115).

Shared and Nonshared Environment

In his book *Nature and Nurture*, Plomin (1990) suggests that behavioral genetics has two messages: nature and nurture. Behavioral genetics research leads to evidence concerning the importance of genes and of the environment. What behavioral geneticists are doing is not only estimating the proportion of the population variance of a characteristic that is due to heredity, but estimating the proportion that is due to different kinds of environments. A distinction is made between shared environments and nonshared environments. **Shared environments** consist of those environments shared by siblings as a result of growing up in the same family. **Nonshared environments** consist of those environments that are not shared by siblings growing up in the same family. For example, siblings may be treated differently by parents because of sex differences, birth order differences, or life events unique to a particular child (e.g., illness in the child or financial difficulties during the youth of one child). In addition, each child typically grows up with a different peer group, an influence emphasized by some as of even greater importance for adult personality development than the family (Harris, 1998).

In behavioral genetics research the issue of shared and nonshared environment effects is studied by assessing degree of resemblance in personality as a function of both degree of genetic similarity and degree of shared family environment. If shared environments are important, then biological siblings raised together will be much more similar than biological siblings raised apart. They also should be much more similar to their biological parents than are the siblings raised apart. In essence, biological siblings raised together should resemble one another, and their parents, beyond the degree that could be accounted for by common genes alone. In addition, if shared environments are important, then two adopted siblings raised together should be more similar than if they were raised apart. If nonshared environments are important, then these relationships should not hold. In essence, if nonshared environ-

Robert Plomin

ments are important, then biological siblings raised together will be no more similar than if they were raised apart.

Although we recognize sibling differences, and sometimes ask how two siblings raised in the same family can be so different, generally we say: "You know that they came from the same household." Yet, in one of the most striking findings from behavioral genetics, there is considerable evidence that shared environmental effects—experiences shared as members of the same family—are not nearly as important as nonshared environmental effects. Put differently, the unique experiences siblings have inside and outside the family appear to be far more important for personality development than the shared experiences resulting from being in the same family. In a groundbreaking paper in this area, the question asked was: "Why are children from the same family so different (Plomin & Daniels, 1987)?" The answer: nonshared environments! The suggestion made is that in addition to the 40 percent or so of personality that is due to genetic factors, approximately 35 percent is due to the effects of nonshared environments and only 5 percent due to shared environments, the rest being due to measurement error (Dunn & Plomin, 1990).

A recent study by Loehlin, McCrae, Costa, and John (1998) examined genetic and environmental effects in three different measures of the Big Five, with results generally consistent with the above conclusions. Three findings stood out. First, all five of the Big Five dimensions showed substantial genetic influences of the same magnitude; that is, individual differences in A, C, and O were just as heritable as individual differences in E and N, which had been studied extensively in the context of Eysenck's model of these two superfactors (see Chapter 7). Second, these findings were independent of the effects of intellectual ability, which had also been measured and were controlled in the behavior-genetic analyses; that is, Openness was found to be a personality dimension independent of intelligence, with its own genetic basis. Third, from a methodological perspective, having available three measures for each Big

Why Children from the Same Family Are So Different: *Each sibling experiences a different, unique family environment.*

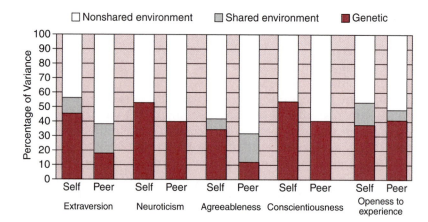

Figure 9.5   Genetic (green), shared environment (gray), and nonshared environment (white) components of variance for self-report ratings and peer ratings for the Big Five personality traits. Nonshared environment effects include error of measurement. *(Plomin & Caspi, 1999, p. 253.) Copyright © Guilford Press. Reprinted by permission.*

Five factor made it possible to test generalizability across instruments and estimating error separately, rather than including it with the estimate of non-shared environment as in some previous research.

In an analysis of the data from the self-peer ratings of MZ and DZ twins on the NEO scale (Riemann, Angleitner, & Strelau, 1997), Plomin calculated the percentage of the variance due to genetic factors, shared environments, and nonshared environments (including measurement error) for both self and peer ratings on the Big Five. The resulting percentages closely approximate those reported earlier, although the percentages for genetic factors tend to be lower for peer ratings than self ratings (Figure 9.5) (Plomin & Caspi, 1999, p. 253).

Understanding Nonshared Environment Effects

These findings suggest that differences among families seem to matter less for the development of children than do differences within families. Recent research (Reiss, 1997; Reiss, Neiderhiser, Hetherington, & Plomin, 1999) has begun to focus on the particular processes linking genetic, family, and social influences on personality development during the important years of adolescence. This work focuses on the unique relationship between the parent and each adolescent sibling in terms of conflict and negativity, warmth and support, and so forth. In other words, the research seeks to separate out the effects of parenting common to siblings in a family from the effects of parenting unique to each sibling. The evidence to date shows substantial differences in the way siblings are treated by their parents. What is striking, however, is that much of the parenting unique to each child seems to be due to the genetic characteristics of that child. That is, differences in the way parents treat each child seem to be due to different behaviors evoked in the parent by that child, in line with earlier suggestions that children from the same family grow up to be different in part because of genetic differences that lead them to be treated differently by the parents. Most students with siblings can readily testify to such differences in parental treatment!

Does the suggestion that children from the same family are different because of the effects of nonshared environments mean that family experiences are unimportant? Does this mean that early experiences are unimportant for personality development, in contrast with what psychoanalysts would have us believe? Although such conclusions have been drawn by some, this is not in fact what is suggested. Rather, the interpretation is that family influences are important, as are experiences outside the family, but it is the experiences unique to each child that are important rather than the experiences shared by children in the same family. Rather than the family unit being important for investigation, it is the unique experiences of each child in the family that are important.

Three Kinds of Nature-Nurture Interactions

Until now we have considered the effects of genes and environment on personality separately. However, nature and nurture always are interacting with one another: "The critical point to remember in all of this is that in the dance of life, genes and environment are absolutely inextricable partners" (Hyman, 1999, p. 27). Along with the continuous unfolding of the effects of genes and experience, three particular forms of gene-environment interactions have been distinguished (Plomin, 1990; Plomin & Neiderhiser, 1992). First, the same environmental experiences may have different effects on individuals with different genetic constitutions. For example, the same behavior on the part of an anxious parent may have different effects on an irritable, unresponsive child than on a calm, responsive child. Rather than a straightforward effect of parental anxiety that is the same for both kinds of children, there is an interaction between parental behavior and child characteristic. In this case the individual is a passive recipient of environmental events. Genetic factors are interacting with environmental factors but only in a passive, reactive sense.

In a second kind of nature-nurture interaction, individuals with different genetic constitutions may evoke different responses from the environment. For example, the irritable, withdrawn child may evoke a different response from the parent than will a calm, responsive child. Within the same family, siblings can evoke different parental behaviors that then set in motion two completely different patterns of parent-child interaction. Such differences were indicated in the research considered earlier on differential parental treatment of siblings associated with genetic differences in the children. Beyond this, differences in inherited characteristics lead to different responses from peers and others in the environment outside the family. Attractive children call forth different peer responses than do less attractive children. Athletic children call forth different responses than do unathletic children. In each case, a genetically determined characteristic evokes a differential response from the environment.

In the third form of gene-environment interaction, individuals with different constitutions select and create different environments. Once the individual is able to take an active form of interaction with the environment, which occurs at a fairly early age, genetic factors influence the selection and creation of environments. The extravert seeks out different environments than does the introvert, the athletic individual different environments than the unathletic individual, and the musically gifted individual different environments than the individual gifted in visual imagery. These effects increase over the course of time as individuals become increasingly able to select their own environments. By a certain point in time it is impossible to determine the extent to which the individual has been the "recipient" of an environmental effect as opposed to the "creator" of the environmental effect.

CURRENT APPLICATIONS

ARE CRIMINALS BORN OR MADE?

The extent to which personality characteristics are inherited is an important question for psychologists and one with potential social applications. Some people suggest that there is an "aggressive personality" and that criminals are born, not made. Others suggest otherwise.

A fair amount of evidence, based on twin studies and adoption studies, suggests that perhaps heredity accounts for as much as 40 percent of individual differences in the trait

Criminality: *Although there is evidence of a genetic link to antisocial behavior, social conditions also play a role.*

of aggressiveness. Further, there is growing evidence of a genetic contribution to criminality. For example, identical twins are twice as likely as fraternal twins to be similar in their criminal activity. Also, a close relationship has been found between antisocial behavior in adopted children and such behavior in their biological parents. Sarnoff Mednick, one major investigator, concludes: "These studies all suggest that we should take seriously the idea that some biological characteristics that can be genetically transmitted may be involved in causing a person to become involved in criminal activity."

Does this mean that criminal behavior is inevitable in some people? Not necessarily. When a biological parent but not an adoptive parent had a record of conviction, only a minority of the children later had a record of court convictions. In addition, some cultures and environments are known to foster more criminality than others. Thus, although genetic influences play a role in the development of criminal behavior, parental behavior and social conditions also influence the likelihood of such a development.

SOURCES: Lykken, 1995; *Psychology Today*, March 1985.

Summary and Caveats

Individuals can be relatively passive recipients of environments, they can play a role in environmental events through the responses they evoke, and they can play an active role in selecting and creating environments. In each case, there is a nature-nurture, gene-environment interaction. In considering the nature and nurture of personality, we must keep in mind that the development of personality is always a function of the interaction of genes with environments, that there is no nature without nurture and no nurture without nature. We can separate the two for purposes of discussion and analysis, but the two never operate independent of one another. Indeed, genetic factors and environmental experiences are so intertwined that the usual formulation—"nature *versus* nurture"—may not even make sense any more. Instead, it may be better to think of "*via* nurture" (Ridley, 2003). The basic nature of genetic material, in other words, is that "creates now possibilities for the organism" (Ridley, 2003, p. 250) that are realized only if the organism encounters particular environments—that is, only if it is nurtured in a particular way.

As an approach to the question of biology and personality, work in both evolutionary psychology and behavior genetics has one frustrating feature: There isn't much biology. Evolutionary psychologists provide relatively little evidence regarding specific brain systems underlying personality functioning. Twin studies tell us that genetic influences are relevant to personality, but they don't specify what exactly the biological influences are.

NEUROSCIENCE AND PERSONALITY

An alternative strategy, which avoids such frustration, is to directly explore brain and other bodily systems. Contemporary work on the neuroscience of personality seeks to understand how neural systems (specific parts of the brain as well as interconnected parts that work together), neurotransmitters (chemical substances that transmit information from one neuron to another), and hormones (chemical substance that travel through the bloodstream and affect the activity of bodily organs) contribute to psychological characteristics in behavior, and the interplay between psychological and bodily processes. Some of this work complements the trait theories of personality (Chapters 7 and 8) by discovering biological underpinnings of emotions that are central to personality traits. Other work is beginning to identify the neural foundations of higher-level psychological functions involving self-concept and reasoning about the social world.

LOCALIZING BRAIN FUNCTIONS: AMYGDALA

Much has been learned about parts of the brain that have specific functions. For example, the limbic system, in particular the amygdala (Figure 9.6) plays an important role in motivation and emotion (Adolphs, Russell, & Tranel, 1999; LeDoux, 1999). The amygdala appears to be important in the processing of all

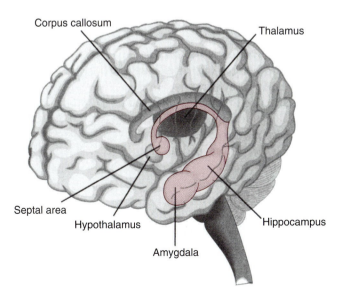

Figure 9.6 The Limbic System. *The limbic system, located within the cerebrum, consists of the septal area, amygdala, and hippocampus.*

emotional stimuli but is particularly important in relation to negative (e.g., fearful, avoidance) stimuli. Ordinarily the amygdala plays a central role in fear conditioning and unconscious emotional memories. On the other hand, individuals with amygdala damage have difficulty being conditioned to fear stimuli and difficulty remembering past conditioned fear responses (LeDoux, 1999). Because of its connection to emotion, one might suspect a connection between the amygdala and individual differences in emotions such as fearfulness. Indeed, Kagan (1999) suggests that the inhibited child has a low threshold of excitability of the amygdala; that is, such a child reacts with avoidance and distress because its limbic system is too easily aroused by unfamiliarity.

LEFT AND RIGHT HEMISPHERIC DOMINANCE

Another aspect of brain system functioning that appears to be central to emotion and motivation is the anterior region of the right and left cerebral hemispheres. Of particular interest is research suggesting that dominance by the left or right cerebral hemisphere plays a role in emotion, with dominance of activation in the left frontal region associated with arousal of approach-related (typically positive) emotion and dominance of the right frontal region associated with arousal of withdrawal-related (typically negative) emotion; that is, there is an association between brain functioning (i.e., hemispheric lateralization) and emotional style (Davidson, 1994, 1995, 1998).

According to Davidson (1998), individual differences in lateralization are associated with differences in general mood and tendencies to respond to stimuli with positive or negative emotion. In one study demonstrating such differences, measures of hemispheric activity were taken before and during the showing of film clips designed to elicit positive or negative emotion. In addition, subjects rated their mood at baseline, prior to being shown the film clips, and their emotional experiences during each film clip. Individual differences in prefrontal asymmetry were found to be associated with baseline mood (left hemispheric dominance with positive affect and right hemispheric dominance with negative affect) and with emotional responses to the films, even after the contribution of baseline mood was statistically removed: "Those individuals with more left-sided prefrontal activation at baseline reported more positive affect to the positive film clips and those with more right-sided prefrontal activation reported more negative affect to the negative film clips. These findings support the idea that individual differences in electrophysiological measures of prefrontal activation asymmetry mark some aspect of vulnerability to positive and negative emotion elicitors" (Davidson, 1998, p. 316).

In relation to emotional disorders, research indicates that currently depressed and previously depressed individuals have decreased left-anterior cortical activity relative to nondepressed individuals (Allen, Iacono, Depue, & Arbisi, 1993). And, individuals with damage to the left-anterior brain region are likely to become depressed whereas those with damage to the right-anterior brain region are likely to become manic (Robinson & Downhill, 1995). Finally, research on infants suggests a relation between individual differences in measures of prefrontal activation and affective reactivity, with infants experiencing greater distress upon separation from their mothers showing greater right-sided prefrontal activation and lesser left-sided prefrontal activation than infants who showed little distress in this situation (Davidson & Fox, 1989). In line with this, Kagan

(1994) reports evidence that inhibited children show more reactivity in their right hemisphere and uninhibited children dominance in the left hemisphere.

NEUROTRANSMITTER FUNCTIONING: DOPAMINE AND SEROTONIN

One of the areas in neuroscience receiving the greatest attention is that of **neurotransmitter** functioning, in particular the neurotransmitters dopamine and serotonin. We know that an excess in the neurotransmitter dopamine is implicated in schizophrenia while an underproduction of dopamine is implicated in Parkinson's disease. Dopamine also is associated with pleasure, being described as a "feel good" chemical (Hamer, 1997). Animals will perform responses that lead to administration of dopamine (Wise, 1996). Thus, dopamine appears to be central to the functioning of the reward system: "One way of characterizing the job of this dopamine circuit is that it's a reward system. It says, in effect, "That was good, let's do it again, and let's remember exactly how we did it" (Hyman, 1999, p. 25). Addictive drugs such as cocaine are viewed as "masquerading" as the neurotransmitter dopamine, leading to the experience of pleasure upon taking the drug but also to the experience of a low as the cocaine stops coming and the dopamine level drops.

The neurotransmitter serotonin also is involved in the regulation of mood. Modern drugs, known as SSRIs, selective serotonin reuptake inhibitors, are thought to alleviate depression through their prolongation of the action of serotonin at the synapses of neurons. SSRIs administered to normal individuals have been found both to reduce negative affective experience and to increase social, affiliative behavior (Knutson et al., 1998). Finally, we know that the hormone cortisol is associated with the stress response. Again returning to Kagan's (1994) research, inhibited children at the age of five were found to be high in reactivity to threat, as measured by cortisol response, although this was not as true at age seven.

NEUROBIOLOGY AND THE THREE MAJOR TEMPERAMENT DIMENSIONS

What kinds of insights currently are available into the relation between neurobiological functioning and personality (Table 9.4)? This is a complex area. Pioneering work was done by Eysenck (1990). A number of subsequent efforts have been made by personality psychologists to establish trait models and tie them to specific biological processes (Cloninger, Svrakic, & Przybeck, 1993; Depue, 1995, 1996, Depue & Collins, 1999; Eysenck, 1990; Gray, 1987; Pickering & Gray, 1999; Tellegen, 1985; Zuckerman, 1991, 1996). Although similarities appear among almost all of these models, and many are similar to the five-factor model described in Chapter 8, they do not always overlap in clear ways with one another. Thus, rather than exploring a number of such models, we will follow the lead of Lee Anna Clark and David Watson (1999; Watson, 2000) in their analysis of personality temperament.

Three Dimensions of Temperament: PE, NE, and DvC

According to Clark and Watson's (1999) model, individual differences in temperament can be summarized in terms of three big superfactors similar to those suggested by Eysenck and also corresponding, roughly, to three of the

Table 9.4 Suggested Links Between Biology and Personality

Amygdala   Part of the primitive limbic system, the brain's emotional response center. Particularly important for aversive emotional learning.

Hemispheric Lateralization   Dominance of the right frontal hemisphere associated with activation of negative emotions and personality traits of shyness and inhibition; dominance of the left frontal hemisphere associated with activation of positive emotions and personality traits of boldness and disinhibition.

Dopamine   A neurotransmitter associated with reward, reinforcement, pleasure. High dopamine levels are associated with positive emotions, high energy, disinhibition, and impulsivity. Low dopamine levels are associated with lethargy, anxiety, and constriction. Animals and people will self-administer drugs that trigger the release of dopamine.

Serotonin   A neurotransmitter involved in mood, irritability, and impulsivity. Low serotonin levels are associated with depression but also with violence and impulsivity. Drugs known as SSRIs (selective serotonin reuptake inhibitors) (e.g., Prozac, Zoloft, Paxil) are used to treat depression as well as phobias and obsessive-compulsive disorders. Exactly how they operate is not totally clear.

Cortisol   A stress-related hormone secreted by the adrenal cortex that facilitates reactions to threat. Although adaptive in relation to short-term stress, responses to long-term, chronic stress can be associated with depression and memory loss.

Testosterone   A hormone important in the development of secondary sex characteristics and also associated with dominance, competitiveness, and aggression.

SOURCES: Hamer & Copeland, 1998; Sapolsky, 1994; Zuckerman, 1995.

Big Five dimensions: NE (Negative Emotionality), PE (Positive Emotionality), and DvC (Disinhibition versus Constraint). Individuals high on the NE factor experience elevated levels of negative emotions and see the world as threatening, problematic, and distressing, whereas those low on the trait are calm, emotionally stable, and self-satisfied. The PE factor relates to the individual's willingness to engage the environment, with high scorers (like extraverts) enjoying the company of others and approaching life actively, with energy, cheerfulness, and enthusiasm, whereas low scorers (like introverts) are reserved, socially aloof, and low in energy and confidence. It is important to note that although NE and PE have opposite sounding qualities, they are independent of one another; that is, an individual can be high or low on each (Watson & Tellegen, 1999; Watson, Wiese, Vaidya, & Tellegen, 1999). This is because they are under the control of different internal biological systems. The third factor, DvC, does not involve affective tone, as was true for the first two factors, but rather relates to style of affective regulation, with high DvC scorers being impulsive, reckless, and oriented toward feelings and sensations of the moment whereas low scorers are careful, controlled by long-term implications of their behavior, and avoiding risk or danger.

Emotional and Lifestyle Correlates of PE, NE, and DvC

Are there emotional, behavioral, and biological correlates of these three factors? In terms of mood, not surprisingly individuals high on NE report such negative emotional states as fear, sadness, anger, guilt, contempt, and disgust whereas individuals high on PE report such positive feelings as joy, interest, attentiveness, excitement, enthusiasm, and pride. Since these two are, as noted, independent of one another, there are individuals who experience high levels of both positive and negative mood states as well as individuals who experience neither. The DvC factor, reflecting style of affective regulation, is not significantly associated with either positive or negative mood.

In terms of lifestyle, individuals scoring high on DvC tend to obtain poorer grades and receive poorer job performance ratings, even when the effects of intelligence are removed: "Poor grades early in college are more likely to be obtained by those who lack discipline and prefer to live day-to-day rather than planning carefully for the future" (Clark & Watson, 1999, p. 414). In addition, high DvC scorers drink alcohol more, smoke marijuana more, and are more active sexually (both frequency and variety) than low scorers. Such differences in lifestyle are not associated with scores on the other two factors. Number of hours of sleep does not differ for the three factors. However, sleeping patterns do. High scorers on DvC tend to be "night owls" who go to sleep late and arise late whereas high scorers on PE tend to be "morning larks" who rise early and retire early. One can perhaps already imagine the problems when a person high on DvC is a roommate or partner of someone high on PE!

Biological Correlates of PE, NE, and DvC

Given such striking differences, are there biological correlates of the three factors? It is suggested that this indeed is the case with, as noted, different biological processes being key for each. According to the model, influenced by the thinking of Depue (1996, Depue & Collins, 1999), PE is associated with the action of dopamine, the "feel good" chemical. In animal research, high dopamine levels are associated with approach behaviors whereas deficits in this neurotransmitter are associated with deficits in incentive motivation. In all, Clark and Watson suggest that "individual differences in the sensitivity of this biological system to the signals of reward that activate incentive motivation and positive affect, and supportive cognitive processes, form the basis of the PE dimension of temperament" (1999, p. 414). Differences in hemispheric lateralization, with high PE scores being associated with left hemispheric dominance, may also be involved (Davidson, 1992, 1994, 1998).

Turning to DvC, Clark and Watson suggest that the biological basis of this factor is serotonin. According to them, humans low in this neurotransmitter tend to be aggressive and to show increased use of dopamine-activating drugs such as alcohol. Alcoholism also is associated with reduced serotonin functioning. Hamer (1997) also associates the neurotransmitter dopamine with thrill seeking, impulsivity, and disinhibition. There also is evidence that high levels of the hormone testosterone are associated with competitiveness and aggressiveness, both linked with high scores on DvC.

Clark and Watson suggest that less is known about the neurobiology underlying NE. However, there is a relation between low serotonin levels at the neuron synapses and depression, anxiety, and obsessive-compulsive symptoms. Hamer and Copeland (1998) relate low serotonin levels to a dark view of the world, analogous to Galen's melancholic temperament. Depue (1995) reports that animals low in serotonin are excessively irritable and Hamer (1997) describes serotonin as the "feel bad" chemical. In addition, there is the evidence noted of a relation between right hemispheric lateralization and the tendency to experience negative emotions. Finally, there is evidence that excessive sensitivity of the amygdala likely plays a role in the tendency to experience high levels of anxiety and distress (LeDoux, 1995, 1999).

Biology and Personality Traits: Some Limitations

At the same time that these relationships are suggested, it is clear that there is no one-to-one correspondence between biological processes and personality traits. Rather, each biological component appears to be associated with the expression of more than one trait and the expression of each trait is influenced by more than one biological factor: "Models of personality based on only one neurotransmitter are clearly too simplistic and will require the addition of other modifying factors" (Depue & Collins, 1999, p. 513). Thus, it is difficult to integrate all these neurobiological findings into the **three-dimensional temperament model** because we risk oversimplifying the neurobiology we know so far. The links between biology and temperament suggested in Table 9.4 are best described as initial hypotheses, as our best guesses of how things might hang together, to be tested further and revised as more data become available.

In addition, although brain localization of functions has advanced significantly, it is important to consider the brain as a total system. According to Damasio (1994), Gall was correct in suggesting that the brain consists of subsystem parts that are specialized in the function they play, as opposed to being one large, undifferentiated mass. However, not only was Gall not able to identify correctly the parts and functions, he was unaware of how the brain functions as a system. As Damasio puts it: "I am not falling into the phrenological trap. To put is simply: The mind results from the operation of each of the separate components, and from the concerted operation of the multiple systems constituted by those separate systems" (1994, p. 15). There is both differentiation-localization and organization-system. In sum, personality traits are linked with the functioning of the patterning of elements in the biological system rather than by single elements: "Psychobiology is not for seekers of simplicity" (Zuckerman, 1996, p. 128).

PLASTICITY: BIOLOGICAL PROCESSES ARE BOTH CAUSE AND EFFECT

There is a tendency to think of biological processes as fixed and determining personality emotions and behaviors, as if the former is cause and the latter is effect, and there is little room for change. It is true that individual differences in biology associated with temperament tend to be stable and play an influential role in the unfolding of personality. However, there also is evidence of **plasticity** in the system; that is, the potential for change in the neurobiological system as a result of experience. We are continuing to learn about the plasticity of aspects of neurobiological functioning as well as that of temperament (Gould, Reeves, Graziano, & Gross, 1999). Although Kagan (1994) emphasizes the stability of temperament, he also reports that many children change from inhibited to uninhibited and vice versa.

Plasticity in neurobiological functioning is clear in relation to neurotransmitters and hormones. For example, although leadership in a monkey hierarchy is associated with high levels of serotonin, if the troop is reorganized so that leadership ranks are reversed, the new leaders develop higher levels of serotonin than when they were on the bottom (Raleigh & McGuire, 1991).

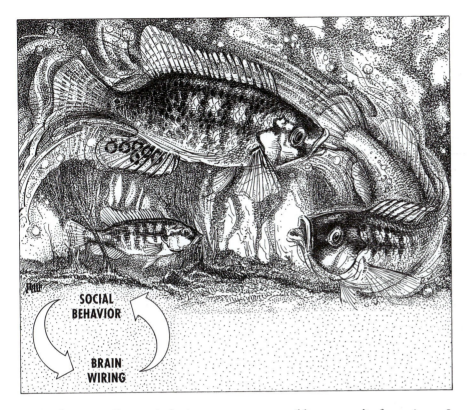

Brain Plasticity: *Changes in brain structure are possible as a result of experience. In cichlid fish, dominant males have larger cells in the hypothalamus than do nondominant males. However, if defeated, the cells shrink along with changes in breeding behavior. (Illustration by Dimitry Schidlovsky.)*

Similarly, the relation between testosterone and aggression or competitiveness is bidirectional, with high testosterone facilitating greater aggression and competitivenss but competition and aggression also leading to higher testosterone levels (Dabbs, 2000). For example, not only does losing a competitive sports event result in lower testosterone levels but being a fan of a losing team does as well (McCaul, Gladue, & Joppe, 1992). In fact, just winning in a coin toss can result in an increase in testosterone level (Gladue, Boechler, & McCaul, 1989). These effects are so strong that Hamer and Copeland (1998) are led to conclude that "from song birds to squirrels, and mice to monkeys, an aggressive encounter changes testosterone levels. Winners get a blast of testosterone; losers get a drain. Humans are the same" (p. 112).

SUMMARY

We have considered possible biological linkages to the Three temperament factors found in questionnaire research and behavioral observations. The view that biological processes provide the basis for these factors is supported by evidence of the heritability of these traits and the identification of specific genes associated with them (Hamer & Copeland, 1998). At the same time, it is worth repeating a number of points of caution in drawing relevant conclusions. (1)

Any gene found, or likely to be found, that is associated with a personality trait accounts for but a small proportion of the variance in the expression of that trait. (2) Personality traits reflect the expression of multiple genes. (3) Personality traits always reflect the interaction of genes with environments. As we have seen, this is true for biological processes as well. (4) Relationships between personality traits and biological processes are quite complex, with much remaining to be discovered. (5) There is a bidirectional relationship between biological processes and experience. This bidirectionality is part of the more general plasticity characteristic of our neurobiological functioning.

NEUROSCIENTIFIC INVESTIGATIONS OF "HIGHER-LEVEL" PSYCHOLOGICAL FUNCTIONS

The work we have just reviewed primarily addressed emotional and motivational processes. Investigators related biological systems to psychological phenomena involving moods, basic impulses, and emotions such as fear. But what about the rest of personality functioning? Specifically, what about "higher-level" psychological functions (e.g., self-concept, morality, etc.) that are at the heart of personality functioning and social behavior? Those psychological functions also require a biological brain. In principle, then, neuroscience can shed light on these complex psychological functions. We now turn to some recent research that attempts to do just that.

BRAIN AND SELF

A uniquely human capacity is the ability to reflect on the self: one's features, potentials, appearance to others, and so forth. A question of basic research interest concerns the nature of this capacity. Does it reflect people's overall cognitive capabilities; in other words, is the self just "one of those things we happen to think about?" Or is it unique? Might there be functionally distinct systems in the brain that come into play when we are thinking about ourselves as opposed to thinking about other people or things?

Recent work (Kelley et al., 2002) has investigated this question by using a brain imaging technique, **fMRI**. An fMRI (or functional magnetic resonance imaging) enables researchers to identify specific regions of the brain that are active when people perform a given task. This is done by analyzing changes in blood flow during task performance. If there is a particularly large change in blood flow in a given brain region during task performance, this provides evidence that the brain region is somehow involved in the performance of that task.

The task that participants performed in the research of Kelley and colleagues (2002) involved the rating of trait adjectives (dependable, polite, etc.). Participants made three types of ratings about the words. They judged (1) whether the adjective (when presented to them) was presented in uppercase letters, (2) whether the adjective described George W. Bush, and (3) whether the adjective described themselves. The idea, then, is that there might be some brain regions that are uniquely active when people think about themselves ("am I dependable?") as opposed to another person ("is Bush dependable?") or cues unrelated to a person ("is the word 'dependable' in uppercase type?"). An alternative possibility is that thinking about the self is no different than thinking about other people.

Kelley and colleagues (2002) found that, yes, there are regions of brain that appear to be uniquely involved in judgments about the self. An area near the

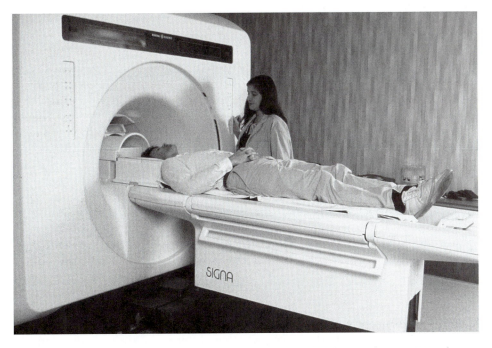

Participant taking part in magnetic resonance imaging (MRI) procedure. MRI techniques have greatly advanced science's understanding of brain systems involved in personality functioning.

front of the brain—specifically, the medial prefrontal cortex, or MPFC—was "selectively engaged during self-referential judgments" (Kelley et al., p. 790). Compared to baseline recordings, fMRI recordings during task performance indicated that when participants were not performing the trait rating task, the MPFC was more involved in judgments about the self than judgments about Bush or about the typeface of the letters.

Such findings of course do not mean that this particular region of the frontal cortex is the biological "home of the self." Judging oneself with respect to trait adjectives is only one aspect of self-concept, and multiple brain regions surely come into play when people engage in any complex mental activity involving self-reflection. Yet, the findings provide intriguing initial evidence that neuroscientific research can inform complex questions about personality functioning. Future years are sure to see growing interest, and scientific evidence, on the question of the neural foundations of self-concept (see, e.g., Churchland, 2002).

BRAIN AND MORAL JUDGMENT

Personality theorists have long been interested in moral judgment. As you have learned, Freud proposed an entire structure of personality, the superego, to explain people's tendency to evaluate the actions of themselves and others according to moral and ethical standards.

Moral judgments seem unique not only to the professional personality theorist, but probably also to you, the intuitive personality theorist. Suppose someone says the following two things: "5 + 5 = 11" and "poor people who need emergency medical care should be denied care unless they can pay for it." Both statements seem "wrong." But they seem wrong in different ways. The latter statements seem wrong in a deep, emotional way. Your sense that this opinion is morally wrong seems to engage emotional processes in a way that your knowledge that "11" was the wrong answer to "5 + 5" does not.

If moral judgments are, in fact, different from other judgments, then it might be possible to identify specific brain regions that come into play specifically when people engage in moral reasoning tasks. This possibility was pursued in a study by Greene, Somerville, Nystrom, Darley, & Cohen (2001). Like Kelley and colleagues (2002), these researchers used fMRI to investigate the possible link between brain functioning and an aspect of personality functioning. In the work of Greene and colleagues, research participants were asked to consider a series of difficult choices, or dilemmas. Some of the choices were moral dilemmas; they involved issues such as the correctness of keeping money that one has found or harming someone if the harm resulted in a benefit to a large number of other people. Other choices were non-moral; they involved decisions such as whether to take a bus versus a train to get to a given location. Participants were asked to judge whether or not a given course of action was appropriate as a response to each of the moral and non-moral problems. The question, then, was whether different brain regions would be involved when people thought about the moral versus non-moral tasks.

The researchers indeed did find that there was different involvement of brain regions in moral versus non-moral reasoning. Of particular interest is that the brain regions involved in moral reasoning were those that, in previous research, had been shown to be involved also in the generation of emotional experiences (Greene et al., 2001). The fMRI data, in other words, confirmed the intuition stated above: The difference between moral and non-moral reasoning is that moral reasoning is not "cold" factual thinking. Instead, it involves emotional responses that directly influence people's decision-making capabilities. These findings are part of a wide range of recent data demonstrating the role of the brain's emotional systems in psychological functions that previously had been thought of as purely "cognitive" in nature (Bechara, Damasio, & Damasio, 2000; Sanfrey et al., 2003). More generally, they demonstrate the power of neuroscientific research to inform questions about social thinking processes and personality that are a primary focus of theories that we will consider later in this text (Chapters 11 to 13).

BIOLOGY AND SOCIOPOLITICAL ISSUES

The role of biology in personality historically has been controversial. When Galton framed the issue in terms of "nature versus nurture" and concluded that "nature prevails," he set the tone for controversy over the 100 years. The enduring controversial issues are not only scientific, but also political and social (Baumrind, 1993; Jackson, 1993; Pervin, 1984; Scarr, 1992, 1993).

The popularity of different positions on these issues has varied over the years. During the 1930s and 1940s, views emphasizing genetic factors became extremely unpopular, in part because of their association with views prevalent in Nazi Germany (Degler, 1991). More recently, there has been a return to an interest in evolutionary and genetic contributions to human psychological functioning.

Remembering the past, scholars who explore the role of biology in personality and social behavior are careful to explain that the study of biology does not necessarily imply the adoption of a conservative social agenda (Pinker, 2002).

In recent years, the emphasis on genetic factors has become so great that some warn that the proverbial pendulum of opinion may have swung too far in this direction: "Despite the reluctance of the behavioral sciences to acknowledge genetic influences even through the 1970s, genetic influence has become increasingly accepted during the 1980s. It is good for the field of personality that it has moved away from simple-minded environmentalism. The danger, now, however, is that the rush from environmentalism will carom too far—to a view that personality is almost completely biologically determined" (Plomin, Chipuer, & Loehlin, 1990, p. 225).

Given the tendency to frame the issue in either-or terms, for the pendulum to swing in one or the other direction, and for views to become polarized and politicized, it is necessary to chart a balanced and differentiated course. In charting this course, it is important to understand exactly what concepts do and do not mean and which implications and conclusions can and cannot be drawn from the data. Humans do differ in personality, and these differences are based, to one extent or another, on biological factors. We cannot be afraid to study such factors or appreciate their significance. At the same time, we have to appreciate and be aware of, indeed on guard against, some of the directions these views have taken people in the past.

MAJOR CONCEPTS

Adoption studies   An approach to establishing genetic-behavior relationships through the comparison of biological siblings reared together with biological siblings reared apart through adoption. Generally combined with twin studies.

Behavioral genetics   The study of genetic contributions to behaviors of interest to psychologists, mainly through the comparison of degrees of similarity among individuals of varying degrees of biological-genetic similarity.

Evolved psychological mechanisms   The view that basic psychological mechanisms are the result of evolution by selection, that is, they exist and have endured because they have been adaptive to survival and reproductive success.

fMRI (functional magnetic resonance imaging   A brain imaging technique that identifies specific regions of the brain that are involved in the processing of a given stimulus or the performance of a given task; the technique relies on recordings of changes in blood flow in the brain.

Heritability   The proportion of observed variance in scores in a specific population that can be attributed to genetic factors.

Inhibited-Uninhibited temperaments   Relative to the uninhibited child, the inhibited child reacts to unfamiliar persons or events with restraint, avoidance, and distress, takes a longer time to relax in new situations, and has more unusual fears and phobias. The uninhibited child seems to enjoy these very same situations that seem so stressful to the inhibited child. The uninhibited child responds with spontaneity in novel situations, laughing and smiling easily.

Neurotransmitters   Chemical substances that transmit information from one neuron to another (e.g., dopamine and serotonin).

Parental investment theory   The view that women have a greater parental investment in offspring than do men because women pass their genes on to fewer offspring.

Phrenology   The early 19th century attempt to locate areas of the brain responsible for various aspects of emotional and behavioral functioning. Developed by Gall, it was discredited as quackery and superstition.

Plasticity   The ability of parts of the neurobiological system to change, temporarily and for extended periods of time, within limits set by genes, to meet current adaptive demands and as a result of experience.

Proximate causes   Explanations for behavior associated with current biological processes in the organism.

Selective breeding An approach to establishing genetic-behavior relationships through the breeding of successive generations with a particular characteristic.

Shared and nonshared environments The comparison in behavior genetics research of the effects of siblings growing up in the same or different environments. Particular attention is given to whether siblings reared in the same family share the same family environment.

Temperament Individual differences in general mood or quality of emotional response that appear early, remain fairly stable, are inherited, and are based in biological processes.

Three-dimensional temperament model The three superfactors describing individual differences in temperament: Positive Emotionality (PE), Negative Emotionality (NE), and Disinhibition vs. Constraint (DvC).

Twin studies An approach to establishing genetic-behavior relationships through the comparison of degree of similarity among identical twins, fraternal twins, and nontwin siblings. Generally combined with adoption studies.

Ultimate causes Explanations for behavior associated with evolution.

REVIEW

1. Psychologists have long been interested in individual differences in temperament, relating such differences to constitutional factors. Advances in temperament research have come in the form of longitudinal studies and objective measures of behavior and constitutional-biological variables. Kagan's research on inhibited and uninhibited children is illustrative of such developments.

2. Evolutionary theory concerns ultimate causes of behavior, that is, why the behavior of interest evolved and the adaptive function it served. Work in the area of male-female mate perferences, emphasizing sex differences in parental investment and parenthood probability, and in male-female differences in causes of jealousy illustrate research associated with evolutionary interpretations of human behavioral characteristics.

3. Three methods used to establish genetic-behavior relationships are selective breeding, twin studies, and adoption studies. Twin and adoption studies lead to significant heritability estimates for intelligence and most personality characteristics. The overall heritability for personality has been estimated to be .4 to .5, that is, 40 to 50 percent of the variance in personality characteristics is due to genetic factors. However, there is evidence that heritability estimates are influenced by the population studied, personality characteristic studied, and measures used.

4. Associations between findings in neuroscience and personality have focused on the functioning of neurotransmitters such as dopamine and serotonin, individual differences in hemispheric lateralization and emotional style, demonstrated in the work of Davidson, and on the functioning of parts of the brain such as the amygdala in relation to the processing of emotional stimuli and emotional memories. The three-dimensional temperament model proposed by Clark and Watson represents one attempt to systematize relations between the findings in neuroscience and personality. Many such links are suggested, although at this time a comprehensive model of biological processes and personality traits remains to be formulated.

5. Although there is a tendency to think of biological processes as fixed, there is considerable evidence of plasticity or potential for change in the neurobiological system as a result of experience.

6. In recent years, researchers in neuroscience have begun to identify specific brain regions that are involved in complex aspects of personality functioning such as judgments about the self and judgments of the morality of actions. This work generally relies on brain imaging techniques, particularly fMRI.

7. In considering the issues addressed in this chapter, in particular those in relation to genes and personality, it is important to be aware of the possible sociopolitical implications of alternative views and the potential for ideology to bias interpretations of findings.

8. In the course of this chapter, a number of notes of caution have been suggested that are worthy of repeating: (a) All psychological processes have a biological component to them. For example, genes determine the operation of biological processes that, in conjunction with environmental events, determine the unfolding of personality. There is no "nature" without "nurture" and no personality without biology or "mind" without "body." (b) Multiple genes are involved in most, probably all, personality characteristics. (c) Multiple biological processes (e.g., neurotransmitters, hormones) are involved in most, probably all, personality characteristics. In sum, we are unlikely to find simple one-to-one relationships between biological processes and personality traits.

10

BEHAVIORISM AND THE LEARNING APPROACHES TO PERSONALITY

THE BEHAVIORISTIC VIEW OF THE SCIENCE OF PERSONALITY
  Environmental Determinism and Its Implications for the Concept of Personality
  Experimental Rigor, Observable Variables, and the Study of Simple Systems
WATSON, PAVLOV, AND CLASSICAL CONDITIONING
  Watson's Behaviorism
  Pavlov's Theory of Classical Conditioning
    Principles of Classical Conditioning
  Psychopathology and Change
    Conditioned Emotional Reactions
    The "Unconditioning" of Fear of a Rabbit
    Additional Applications of Classical Conditioning
    Systematic Desensitization
  A Reinterpretation of the Case of Little Hans
  Further Developments

SKINNER'S THEORY OF OPERANT CONDITIONING
  A View of the Theorist
  Skinner's Theory of Personality
    Structure
    Process: Operant Conditioning
    Growth and Development
    Psychopathology
    Behavioral Assessment
      ABA Research Design
      Sign and Sample Approaches to Assessment
    Behavior Change
    Free Will?

A COMPARISON OF LEARNING APPROACHES WITH EARLIER VIEWS

CRITICAL EVALUATION
  Strengths of Learning Approaches
  Limitations of Learning Approaches

MAJOR CONCEPTS

REVIEW

Chapter Focus

Have you ever dated someone who did something that really annoyed you? A woman was particularly bothered by her boyfriend's constant complaining about how much schoolwork he had to do. She grew tired of constantly providing him with attention and sympathy—after all, she had just as much work! One day she was struck with a new idea: What if she simply ignored her boyfriend every time he complained? It worked! When she stopped pampering him, his complaining gradually disappeared; in the language of behaviorism, her attention to his problems had been serving as a "positive reinforcement" that had taught him to complain in the first place.

Without realizing it, this woman was using some of the basic principles of learning theory to change her boyfriend's behavior. This chapter considers approaches to personality that are based on theories of learning, and the overall approach to psychological science known as behaviorism. According to behaviorism, people gradually acquire their personality styles as a result of their experiences with the environment. Associated theories of learning specify the exact processes through which people are shaped by environmental experiences.

In this chapter, you will learn about two main theories in the history of the psychological study of learning: Pavlov's classical conditioning and Skinner's operant conditioning. These theories both share a commitment to the experimental testing of clearly defined hypotheses. Approaches to assessment and change are then considered, along with an overall critical evaluation of these approaches to personality.

QUESTIONS TO BE ADDRESSED IN THIS CHAPTER

1. How does a focus on laboratory research and cause-effect relationships lead to different observations and different theories than those associated with clinical research and correlational research?

2. To what extent can basic principles of learning, often based on the study of learning in nonhuman animals, provide the basis for a theory of personality?

3. To what extent is our behavior controlled by reinforcers (i.e., rewards and punishments)? Can abnormal behaviors be understood in terms of learning principles?

4. If normal behavior is learned or acquired like all other behavior, can therapeutic change occur as the result of the application of learning principles? To what extent, then, is psychopathology more a problem of faulty learning than of a disease or illness?

5. If our behavior is ultimately determined by the environment, as claimed by the behaviorists, what are the implications for the common assumption that people have "free will" that enables them to choose one versus another course of action?

The two theories of learning discussed in this chapter—Pavlov's classical conditioning and Skinner's operant conditioning—are not opposing views. Instead, they highlight different aspects of the ways in which people learn from the environment. In combination, they provide the groundwork for the behaviorist view of personality and human nature.

During the middle of the 20th century, behaviorism was the predominant school of thought in scientific psychology. It subsequently experienced a precipitous decline. Despite this, there is much to be learned from a review of behaviorism. Developing a comprehensive scientific theory of personality is no easy feat. It is instructive to see where past efforts have succeeded and failed. Furthermore, despite whatever conceptual limitations it may have, the behaviorist school of thought gave rise to therapeutic methods of unquestioned value; we will consider some of them in this chapter. An additional point is that, in recent years, a number of researchers who would not label themselves "behaviorists" have nonetheless explored some of the themes that are defining of the behavioral approach. These include the ideas that much of our action is controlled directly by stimuli in the environment (Bargh & Ferguson, 2000; Bargh & Gollwitzer, 1994) and that our intuition that we are in conscious control of our behavior (rather than the environment being in control of us) is simply a "trick" (Wegner, 2003, p. 65) that our mind plays on us. Ideas that were originally highlighted by the behaviorists endure in the contemporary field.

THE BEHAVIORISTIC VIEW OF THE SCIENCE OF PERSONALITY

Behaviorism differs enormously from the theories we discuss elsewhere in this book. The approach introduces radically new perspectives on both human nature and scientific strategies for learning about people. The behavioristic learning theory approach to personality has two basic assumptions (Table 10.1). The first is that behavior must be explained in terms of the causal influence of the environment on the person. The second is that an understanding of people should be built upon objective scientific research in which variables are carefully controlled in laboratory experiments. An aspect of this research that might strike you as particularly unusual is that, although the behaviorist is ultimately interested in understanding people, their laboratory experiments commonly involve animals.

ENVIRONMENTAL DETERMINISM AND ITS IMPLICATIONS FOR THE CONCEPT OF PERSONALITY

The trait theorists Eysenck and Cattell were interested in learning. They viewed learning as part of the broader field of personality. Behaviorism, in

Table 10.1 Basic Points of Emphasis of Learning Approaches to Personality

1. Empirical research is the cornerstone of theory and practice.
2. Personality theory and applied practice should be based on principles of learning.
3. Behavior is responsive to reinforcement variables in the environment and is more situation specific than suggested by other personality theories (e.g., trait, psychoanalytic).
4. Rejection of the medical symptom-disease view of psychopathology and emphasis instead on basic principles of learning and behavior change.

contrast, takes the opposite view. Behaviorists view the study of personality as merely a branch of the broader field of learning. Indeed, to the behaviorist, the study of general laws of learning would, if successful, completely eliminate the need for a distinct field of study called "personality theory."

The behaviorists' reasoning behind this position goes as follows. We human beings are physical objects in a physical universe. As such, we are subject to physical laws that can be understood through scientific analysis. Ever since the beginnings of modern physics hundreds of years ago, the behaviorists reason, scientists have recognized that the way to explain the behavior of any physical object is to identify the forces in the environment that act upon it, causing its behavior. Suppose we throw a rock into the air and observe its behavior: It travels in a curving, parabolic path back to earth. How do we explain this? We don't say that the rock "enjoys traveling in parabolic paths" or that it has "the trait of fallingness." Instead, we recognize that the behavior of a rock is fully determined by lawful environmental forces (the force and direction of our throw, plus gravity and perhaps air pressure). To the behaviorist, the behavior of people should be explained in exactly this same way. Just as environmental forces determine the trajectory of the rock, environmental forces determine the trajectories of our lives as we come into contact with, and are influenced by, one environmental factor after another. To the behaviorist, then, there is no more need to explain a person's behavior in terms of his or her attitudes, feelings, or personality traits than there is to explain the rock's behavior in terms of its attitudes, feelings, or rock traits. The rock doesn't fall to earth because it decided to fall, but because gravity caused it to fall. Similarly, people do not act as they do because they decided to act that way, but because environment forces cause them to do so.

Behaviorists recognize that people have thoughts and feelings. But they view thoughts and feelings as "behaviors" that also are caused by the environment. If you say that "I took this personality psychology class because I thought it would be interesting" or "I broke up with my boyfriend because I felt our relationship wouldn't work out," a behaviorist would say that you were wrong. You didn't identify the right factor in your "because." To the behaviorist, the environment caused your behavior of taking the class. Furthermore, the environment caused your behavior of saying that you thought the class would be interesting! Similarly, features of the environment caused your feelings in the relationship and caused your decision to end it.

The most radical feature of the behaviorist worldview, then, is that it does not explain a person's actions in terms of their thoughts and feelings. Instead, it explains people's actions, thoughts, and feelings in terms of environmental forces that shape the individual. This, to the behaviorist, is the only way to build a scientifically credible study of behavior. Suppose, by analogy, that we were studying evolution and wanted to explain why primates who once walked on four legs later evolved into upright primates who walked on two legs. We would never explain this by saying that the four-legged walkers "got tired of walking on all fours" or "decided to stand straight up." Such explanations would be absurd. They would have no scientific utility. The evolved change from four- to two-legged walking was, we recognize, caused entirely by adaptive pressures in the evolutionary environment. To the behaviorist, saying that people act a certain way "because they decided to" has no more scientific value than saying that the primates evolved because they decided to do so. Instead of such nonscientific explanations, behaviorists urge us to identify the environmental factors that are the true cause of people's feelings, thoughts, and actions. The behaviorist B. F. Skinner states this thesis with the greatest clarity:

> We can follow the path taken by physics and biology by turning directly to the relation between behavior and the environment and neglecting supposed mediating states of mind. Physics did not advance by looking more closely at the jubilance of a falling body, or biology by looking at the nature of vital spirits, and we do not need to try to discover what personalities, states of mind, feelings, traits of character, plans, purposes, [or] intentions...really are in order to get on with a scientific analysis of behavior.
>
> SOURCE: Skinner (1971) *Beyond Freedom & Dignity*, p. 15.

Note the implications of this viewpoint for our typical conception of personality. To the behaviorist, terms for talking about personality—whether the terms come from psychoanalysis, trait theory, or some other theory—do not refer to real psychological entities that are in the person's head and cause their behavior. Instead, the personality terms are simply descriptive labels. They are descriptive patterns of psychological experience that are, in reality, caused by the environment. If the environment causes a person to feel hostility toward a same-sex parent and attraction toward an opposite-sex parent, the psychoanalyst labels this an "Oedipal complex." If the environment causes a person to engage in energetic, outgoing, sociable behaviors, the trait theorist labels the person an "extravert." In these and an infinity of other cases, the personality term does not identify the cause of the person's behavior. The behaviorist instead views the term as merely a label for a pattern of action that is caused by the environment.

To the behaviorists, then, an understanding of the laws of learning promises to replace any and all personality theories. If behavior can be explained by the laws of learning, and if "personality" is just a label that describes the type of behavior a person has learned to do, then there is no need for a scientific theory of personality that is distinct from learning theory. Behaviorists were quite explicit about this. They looked forward to a day when theories of personality would be "regarded as historical curiosities" (Farber, 1964, p. 37).

The behavioral emphasis on external environmental determinants has a number of significant implications. One is that it highlights the potential **situational specificity** of behavior. Since environmental factors are the causes of behavior, people's behavioral style is expected to vary significantly from one environment to another. Note how this expectation differs from the approach of the trait theories (Chapters 7 and 8). Trait variables corresponded to *consistent* styles of behavior; these variables were meant to explain why a person acts in a consistent manner across diverse situations. In contrast, behaviorists expect that there will be substantial variability in action as people adapt to situations that present different rewards and punishments for different types of behavior.

The behavioristic view of learning processes also has significant implications for the understanding and treatment of psychopathology. Psychopathology is not understood as an internal problem—an illness in the person's mind. Instead, the behaviorist assumes that maladaptive, "abnormal" behavior is caused by maladaptive environments to which the person has been exposed. The implication of this assumption is profound. It implies that the task of therapy is not to analyze underlying conflicts or to reorganize the individual's personality. Instead, the goal is to provide a new environment, that is, new learning experiences for the client. The new environment should cause the client to learn new and more adaptive patterns of behavior, as we discuss later in this chapter.

EXPERIMENTAL RIGOR, OBSERVABLE VARIABLES, AND THE STUDY OF SIMPLE SYSTEMS

The second defining feature of the behavioral-learning perspective is its approach to scientific research. The behaviorists' research strategy follows naturally from their emphasis on environment influences. If behavior is determined by the environment, then the way to do research is to manipulate environmental variables and determine their exact influence on behavior. The behaviorist seeks to base the entire study of human nature on the results of such carefully controlled experiments.

An advantage of this method is that environmental variables and behavior are both observable. The researcher can see the variables, and thus can measure them with accuracy and systematically relate environmental factors to behavior. This advantage commonly is not found in other theories. One cannot directly observe the id, an Oedipal conflict, an extraverted tendency, a motive to self-actualize, and so forth. The behaviorist argues that these other theories simply do not lend themselves to convincing scientific tests because they contain variables that one cannot even observe.

The desire to study personality through experimental methods poses a severe challenge. It often may be impractical, as well as unethical, to manipulate environmental variables that may substantially affect people's everyday behaviors. Also, day-to-day human actions may be determined by such a large number of variables, and these variables may be so complexly related to one another, that it is difficult to sort out the potentially lawful relations between any one environmental factor and behavior.

These difficulties lead the behaviorist to adopt the following research strategy. Rather than researching complex social actions, the behaviorist commonly studies simple responses. And rather than study complex human beings, the behaviorist studies simpler organisms, such as rats and pigeons. The original body of data upon which behavioral principles are based consists almost entirely of laboratory research on laboratory animals.

This research strategy may strike you as strange. "Why," you may be thinking, "would anyone think that they can learn about *person*ality by studying animals?" This is a very good question. It is important, as one begins to learn about the behavioral approach, to recognize that the behaviorist's research strategy is not one that is unique to them. Instead, it is common in the sciences. It is the strategy of studying simple systems.

Suppose you were designing an airplane and were wondering if your craft would fly safely in windy weather. One strategy for answering this question would be to build an entire real plane, fill it with people, launch it into the sky, and see if it crashes when the wind kicks up. Of course, you would not do that. This strategy for learning about the flight characteristics of the plane is very costly and completely unethical. You would, instead, study something simpler than a real plane: perhaps a model plane in a wind tunnel, or a computer simulation of an airline and wind flows. You would recognize that this simpler system is not the same thing as a real plane. Yet you would reason that it contains important features that are the same as the features of the system in which you are really interested, that is, the real plane. A similar strategy might be adopted by biologists seeking to understand the side effects of a new drug. Although the researchers are interested in the effects of the drug on people, they would first study its effects on laboratory animals, under the assumption that there is enough similarity in the makeup of animals and people that the animal study will, at the very least, provide some valuable information about the effects of the drug on people. Even if we do not think about it explicitly, we all recognize the value of studying simple systems. None of us would get on a new plane if we learned that a model of the plane had repeatedly crashed in a wind tunnel, or we would try a new headache medicine if we learned that it had killed a bunch of laboratory rats.

This, then, is the simple system strategy. It is a research strategy in which, for both practical and ethical reasons, one conducts scientific studies on a system that is simpler than the one in which the researcher fundamentally is interested.

It is this strategy that is adopted by the behaviorist. Behaviorists are fundamentally interested in the complex social behavior of people. But, in order to run large numbers of ethical and logistically feasible laboratory experiments, they study relatively simple organisms and relatively simple responses that can easily be observed in the lab. In many ways, this strategy proved to be a great success. Research on learning processes generated some of the most robust and reliable findings in the history of experimental psychology. The question, of course, is whether the results of these experiments generalize from animals in the laboratory to humans in the social world.

Table 10.1 summarizes the basic points of emphasis in behaviorism that we have reviewed. With this background, we now begin our coverage of theories that were developed within this behavioral approach to psychological science. Specifically, we start where the approach itself began historically, with the ideas of John Watson and the associated research contributions of Ivan Pavlov.

WATSON'S BEHAVIORISM

WATSON, PAVLOV, AND CLASSICAL CONDITIONING

John B. Watson (1878–1958) was the founder of the approach to psychology known as **behaviorism.** He began his graduate study at the University of Chicago in philosophy and then switched to psychology. During these years he took courses in neurology and physiology and began to do a considerable amount of animal research. Some of this research concerned the increased complexity of behavior in the rat and the associated development of the central nervous system. During the year before he received his doctorate, Watson had an emotional breakdown and had sleepless nights for many weeks. He described this period as useful in preparing him to accept a large part of Freud (Watson, 1936, p. 274). The graduate work at Chicago culminated in a dissertation on animal education and was associated with the development of an important attitude regarding the use of human subjects.

At Chicago, I first began a tentative formulation of my later point of view. I never wanted to use human subjects. I hated to serve as a subject. I didn't like the stuffy, artificial instructions given to subjects. I always was uncomfortable and acted unnaturally. With animals I was at

John B. Watson

home. I felt that, in studying them, I was keeping close to biology with my feet on the ground. More and more the thought presented itself: Can't I find out by watching their behavior everything that the other students are finding by using O's (human subjects)?

SOURCE: Watson, 1936, p. 276.

Watson left Chicago in 1908 to become a professor at Johns Hopkins University, where he served on the faculty until 1919. During his stay there, which was interrupted by a period of service during World War I, Watson developed his views on behaviorism as an approach to psychology. He first stated these views forcefully in a landmark paper published in psychology's leading journal, *Psychological Review*, in 1913. Public lectures and a book published in 1914 (Watson's *Behavior*) called further attention to a view of psychology that emphasized the study of observable behavior and rejected the use of introspection (observing one's own mental states) as a method of research. Watson's arguments were received enthusiastically by American psychologists. He was elected president of the American Psychological Association for 1915. He quickly expanded the theoretical base of his work by drawing on the findings of the Russian physiologist Pavlov, incorporating them into his most significant book, *Psychology from the Standpoint of a Behaviorist* (1919). In 1920, he published a revolutionary study of the learning of emotional reactions with his student Rosalie Rayner (Watson & Rayner, 1920). At that time, he clearly was poised to be the dominant American psychologist of the 20th century.

This, however, is not how his career unfolded. In 1919, Watson divorced his wife and subsequently married his student, Rayner. This scandalous turn of events forced his resignation from Johns Hopkins and caused him to entirely abandon his research career. Instead, he entered the business world, spending his years in advertising studying potential sales markets. Watson appeared to take this turn of events in good spirit, reporting "that it can be just as thrilling to watch the growth of a sales curve of a new product as to watch the learning curve of animals or men" (Watson, 1936, p. 280). After 1920, Watson did write some popular articles and a book, *Behaviorism* (1924). But his career as a theorist and experimenter had ended.

PAVLOV'S THEORY OF CLASSICAL CONDITIONING

Ivan Petrovich Pavlov (1849–1936) was a Russian physiologist who, in the course of his work on the digestive process, developed a procedure for studying behavior and a principle of learning that profoundly affected the field of psychology. Around the beginning of the 20th century, Pavlov was involved in the study of gastric secretions in dogs. As part of his research, he placed some food powder inside the mouth of a dog and measured the resulting amount of salivation. He noticed that after a number of such trials the dog began to salivate, even before the food was put in its mouth, to certain stimuli: the sight of the food dish, the approach of the person who brought the food, etc. Stimuli that previously did not elicit salivation (called neutral stimuli) could now elicit the salivation response because of their association with the food powder that automatically caused the dog to salivate. To animal owners this may not seem to be a startling observation. However, it led Pavlov to conduct significant research on the process known as **classical conditioning**.

Ivan Petrovich Pavlov

Pavlov explored a broad range of scientific issues. In addition to his work on basic conditioning processes, he studied individual differences among his dogs, thereby stimulating a new field of temperament research (Strelau, 1997). He made important contributions to the understanding of abnormal behavior, using animal experiments to study disorganized behavior in dogs and human patients to study neuroses and psychoses, providing the foundation for forms of therapy based on principles of classical conditioning. In 1904 he was awarded the Nobel Prize for his work on digestive processes. His methods and concepts remain important today; they are among the most important in the history of psychology (Dewsbury, 1997).

Principles of Classical Conditioning

The essential characteristic of classical conditioning is that a previously neutral stimulus becomes capable of eliciting a response because of its association with a stimulus that automatically produces the same or a similar response. In other words, the dog salivates to the first presentation of the food powder. One need not speak of a conditioning or learning process at this point. The food can be considered to be an unconditioned stimulus (US) and the salivation an unconditioned response (UR). This is because the salivation is an automatic, reflex response to the food. A neutral stimulus, such as a bell, will not lead to salivation. However, if on a number of trials the bell is sounded just before the presentation of the food powder, the sounding of the bell itself without the subsequent appearance of food may have the potential to elicit the salivation response. In this case, conditioning has occurred since the presentation of the bell alone is followed by salivation. At this point, the bell may be referred to as a conditioned stimulus (CS) and the salivation as a conditioned response (CR).

In a similar way, it is possible to condition withdrawal responses to previously neutral stimuli. In the early research on conditioned withdrawal, a dog was strapped in a harness and electrodes were attached to his paw. The delivery of an electric shock (US) to the paw led to the withdrawal of the paw (UR), which was a reflex response on the part of the animal. If a bell was repeatedly presented just before the shock, eventually the bell alone (CS) was able to elicit the withdrawal response (CR).

The experimental arrangement designed by Pavlov to study classical conditioning allowed him to investigate a number of important phenomena. For example, would the conditioned response become associated with the specific neutral stimulus alone or would it become associated with other similar stimuli? Pavlov found that the response that had become conditioned to a previously neutral stimulus would also become associated with similar stimuli, a process called **generalization**. In other words, the salivation response to the bell would generalize to other sounds. Similarly, the withdrawal response to the bell would generalize to sounds similar to the bell.

What are the limits of such generalization? If repeated trials indicate that only some stimuli are followed by the unconditioned stimulus, the animal recognizes differences among stimuli, a process called **discrimination**. For example, if only certain sounds but not others are followed by shock and reflexive paw withdrawal, the dog will learn to discriminate among sounds. Thus, whereas the process of generalization leads to consistency of response across similar stimuli, the process of discrimination leads to increased specificity of response. Finally, if the originally neutral stimulus is presented repeatedly without being

CURRENT APPLICATIONS

DEATH BY HEROIN OVERDOSE: A CLASSICAL CONDITIONING EXPLANATION

Dwayne Goettel, 31, keyboardist and programmer for the influential industrial band Skinny Puppy, died from an apparent heroin overdose on August 23, 1995, in a bathroom at his parents' house. How could this have happened? As a bandmate told *Rolling Stone* magazine, Goettel had just returned to his parents' house to kick his habit.

Goettel is one of hundreds of heroin addicts who die each year of a reaction typically known as an "overdose." Yet, how these deaths happen still remains unclear. Why do some long-term heroin users die from a dose that would not be expected to be fatal for them? Research by Sheppard Siegel and his colleagues suggests that some instances of heroin overdose may result from a failure of tolerance. How does a heroin addict, who has spent years building up a tolerance to heavy doses of the drug, experience such a failure of tolerance? Pavlov's theory of classical conditioning provides the basis for an answer to this question.

Pavlov proposed that drug administration constitutes a conditioning trial. The unconditioned stimulus (US) is the bodily effect of the drug, and the unconditioned response (UR) is how the body compensates for those effects. Conditioning occurs when the US (the effect of the drug) becomes associated with a conditioned stimulus (CS)—such as environmental cues present when the drug is taken. In other words, as heroin users establish an addiction, they learn to associate the effects of the drug with the environment in which they usually take it. Soon, the environmental cues alone can bring about the compensatory effects even before the drug is taken. Thus, the environmental cues serve as a signal to the body that the effects of the drug are about to take place. In preparation, the body reacts to the

cues in a manner that helps compensate for the anticipated effects of the drug. This conditioned response (CR) builds tolerance to the drug by lessening the drug's effects.

This Pavlovian model of drug tolerance has an important implication: heroin addicts are at risk for overdose when they take the drug in an environment that has not previously been associated with the drug. If the environmental cues typically associated with the drug are absent, the conditioned response cannot occur, causing a failure of tolerance. The heroin user takes a heavy dose of the drug and the body is left unprepared for its effects.

Is there empirical evidence for this explanation? In an animal study, rats received daily injections of increasing dosages of heroin in one of two environments. In the final session of the experiment, all the rats were administered a dose of heroin; for this injection, half of the rats were in the same environment in which they had been administered heroin in the past (same-environment rats) and the other half were in an environment in which they had never been administered heroin before (different-environment rats). The different-environment rats were significantly more likely to die from the injection than the same-environment rats. Why? The different-environment rats had lower tolerance to heroin because they were in an environment not previously associated with the drug. Unlike the same-environment rats, they did not have the conditioned response stimulated by cues in the environment to prepare them for the effects of the drug.

The rat experiment supports the model, but does the same phenomenon occur in humans? For obvious reasons, the parallel experiment cannot be conducted on people, so we must rely on what heroin users who have survived an overdose tell us about their experience. This is exactly what Siegel did to complement the results of the rat experiment. He interviewed former heroin addicts who had been hospitalized for drug overdoses. The majority of the survivors reported that the setting in which the overdose episode occurred was atypical. For example, one person reported that he injected the drug in the bathroom of a car wash—for him, an unusual place to take the drug. These reports from human victims show that the Pavlovian model of drug tolerance is relevant and useful in understanding such tragic deaths as that of the musician Dwayne Goettel in his parents' bathroom.

SOURCES: *Rolling Stone*, Oct. 1995, p. 25; Siegel, 1984; Siegel et al., 1982.

followed at least occasionally by the unconditioned stimulus, there is an undoing or progressive weakening of the conditioning or association, a process known as **extinction**. Whereas the association of the neutral stimulus with the unconditioned stimulus leads to the conditioned response, the repeated presentation of the conditioned stimulus without the unconditioned stimulus leads to extinction. For example, for the dog to continue to salivate to the bell, there must be at least occasional presentations of the food powder with the bell.

Although the illustrations used relate to animals, the principles can apply to humans as well. For example, consider a child who is bitten or merely treated roughly by a dog. The child's fear of this dog may now be extended to all dogs—the process of generalization. Suppose, however, by getting help, the child begins to discriminate among dogs of various kinds and begins to be afraid only of certain dogs. We can see here the process of discrimination. Over time, the child may have repeated positive experiences with all dogs, leading to the extinction of the fear response altogether. Thus, the classical conditioning model may be potentially very helpful in understanding the development, maintenance, and disappearance of many of our emotional reactions.

PSYCHOPATHOLOGY AND CHANGE

Pavlov not only did basic research on generalization, discrimination, and extinction. He also did research that suggested explanations for other phenomena of great interest, such as conflict and the development of neuroses. A classic example explored what came to be known as experimental neuroses in animals. In this research, a dog was conditioned to salivate to the image of a circle. Differentiation between a circle and a similar figure, an ellipse, was then conditioned; this was done by not reinforcing the response to the ellipse, while response to the circle continued to be reinforced. Then, gradually, the ellipse was changed in shape. Its shape was made to be closer and closer to a circle. At first, the dog could still discriminate between the circle and the ellipse. But then, as the figures became extremely similar, it no longer could tell them apart. What happened to the dog? Its behavior became disorganized; as Pavlov himself described:

After three weeks of work upon this discrimination not only did the discrimination fail to improve, but it became considerably worse, and finally disappeared altogether. The hitherto quiet dog began to squeal in its stand, kept wriggling about, tore off with its teeth the apparatus for mechanical stimulation of the skin, and bit through the tubes connecting the animal's room with the observer, a behavior which never happened before. On being taken into the experimental room the dog now barked violently, which was also contrary to its usual custom; in short, it presented all the symptoms of a condition of acute neurosis.

SOURCE: Pavlov, 1927, p. 291.

Conditioned Emotional Reactions

Pavlov's work on the conditioning process clearly defined stimuli and responses and provided an objective method for the study of learning phenomena. It therefore played an influential role in the thinking of later behaviorists such as Watson. For example, shortly after the publication of *Psychology from the Standpoint of a Behaviorist* (1919), Watson reported on the conditioning of emotional reactions in an infant. The research on Albert, an 11-month-old child, has become a classic in psychology. In this research, the experimenters, Watson and Rayner (1920), trained the infant to fear animals and objects that previously were not feared. They found that striking a hammer on a suspended steel bar produced a startle and fear response in the infant. They then found that if the bar was struck immediately behind Albert's head just as he began to reach for a rat, he began to fear the rat, whereas previously he had not shown this response. After doing this a number of times, the experimenters found that the instant the rat alone (without the sound) was shown to Albert, he began to cry. He had developed what is called a **conditioned emotional reaction**.

At this point, Albert now feared the rat because of its emotional association with the frightening sound. Furthermore, there was evidence that Albert began to fear other objects that somewhat resembled the rat, such as objects that were white and furry. Despite some evidence that Albert's emotional reaction was not as strong or as general as expected (Harris, 1979), Watson and Rayner concluded that many fears are conditioned emotional reactions. On this basis they criticized the more complex psychoanalytic interpretations.

> The Freudians twenty years from now, unless their hypotheses change, when they come to analyze Albert's fear of a seal skin coat will probably tease from him the recital of a dream upon which their analysis will

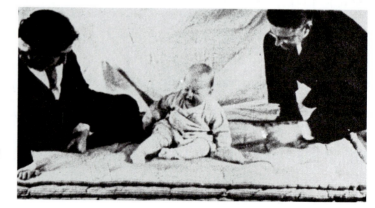

John Watson and Rosalie Raynor conducting research on the classic conditioning of emotional reactions with the 11-month-old Little Albert.

show that Albert at three years of age attempted to play with the pubic hair of the mother and was scolded violently for it. If the analyst has sufficiently prepared Albert to accept such a dream when found as an explanation of his avoiding tendencies, and if the analyst has the authority and personality to put it over, Albert may be fully convinced that the dream was a true revealer of the factors which brought about the fear.

SOURCE: Watson and Rayner, 1920, p. 14.

The "Unconditioning" of Fear of a Rabbit

For many psychologists, the classical conditioning of emotional reactions plays a critical role in the development of psychopathology and a potentially important role in behavioral change. Behavior therapy based on the classical conditioning model emphasizes the extinction of problematic responses, such as conditioned fears, or the conditioning of new responses to stimuli that elicit such undesired responses as anxiety.

An early use of this approach, one that followed Watson and Rayner's (1920) study of the conditioning of the fear emotional response in Albert, was the effort of Jones (1924) to remove a fear under laboratory conditions. In this study of systematic utilization of behavior therapy, described as one of the earliest, if not the first, Jones attempted to treat the exaggerated fear reaction in a boy, Peter, who then was two years and ten months old. Peter was described as a generally healthy, well-adjusted child with a fear of a white rat that also extended to a rabbit, fur coat, feather, and cotton wool. Jones carefully documented the nature of the child's fear response and the conditions that elicited the greatest fear. She then set out to determine whether she could "uncondition" the fear response to one stimulus and whether such unconditioning would then generalize to other stimuli. Jones chose to focus on Peter's fear of the rabbit since this seemed even greater than his fear of the rat. She proceeded by bringing Peter to play at a time when the rabbit was present, as well as three other children who were selected because they were fearless toward the rabbit. Gradually Peter moved from almost complete terror at the sight of the rabbit to a completely positive response. The steps noted along the way to this progress are presented in Figure 10.1.

Peter's progression through these steps was not even or unbroken, and fortunately Jones gives us a careful, explicit accounting of a fascinating chain of events. Peter had progressed through the first nine steps listed in Figure 10.1 when he was taken to the hospital with scarlet fever. After a delay of two months, Peter returned to the laboratory with his fear response at the original level. Jones describes the cause of this relapse as follows:

This was easily explained by the nurse who brought Peter from the hospital. As they were entering a taxi at the door of the hospital, a large dog, running past, jumped at them. Both Peter and the nurse were very much frightened. This seemed reason enough for this [to] precipitate descent back to the original fear level. Being threatened by a large dog when ill, and in a strange place and being with an adult who also showed fear, was a terrifying situation against which our training could not have fortified him.

Thus, at this point Jones began anew with another method of treatment, "direct conditioning." Here Peter was seated in a chair and given food he liked

1. Rabbit anywhere in the room in a cage causes fear reactions.
2. Rabbit 12 feet away in cage tolerated.
3. Rabbit 4 feet away in cage tolerated.
4. Rabbit 3 feet away in cage tolerated.
5. Rabbit close in cage tolerated.
6. Rabbit free in room tolerated.
7. Rabbit touched when experimenter holds it.
8. Rabbit touched when free in room.
9. Rabbit defied by spitting at it, throwing things at it, imitating it.
10. Rabbit allowed on tray of high chair.
11. Squats in defenseless position beside rabbit.
12. Helps experimenter to carry rabbit to its cage.
13. Holds rabbit on lap.
14. Stays alone in room with rabbit.
15. Allows rabbit in play pen with him.
16. Fondles rabbit affectionately.
17. Lets rabbit nibble his fingers.

Figure 10.1   Steps in the "Unconditioning'" of Peter's Fear of a Rabbit. (M. C. Jones, 1924)

as the experimenter gradually brought the rabbit in a wire cage closer to him: "Through the presence of pleasant stimulus (food) whenever the rabbit was shown, the fear was eliminated gradually in favor of a positive response." In other words, the positive feelings associated with food were counterconditioned to the previously feared rabbit. However, even in the later sessions the influence of other children who were not afraid of the rabbit seemed to be significant. And what of the other fears? Jones notes that after the unconditioning of Peter's fear of the rabbit, he completely lost his fear of the fur coat, feathers, and cotton wool as well. Despite the lack of any knowledge concerning the origins of Peter's fears, the unconditioning procedure was found to work successfully and to generalize to other stimuli as well.

Additional Applications of Classical Conditioning

Another important early procedure was one developed by Mowrer and Mowrer (1928) for the treatment of bedwetting. In general, bedwetting in children occurs because the child does not respond to stimuli from the bladder in time to awaken and urinate in the bathroom. To deal with this condition, Mowrer and Mowrer developed a device based on the classical conditioning model. This consisted of an electrical device in the child's bed. If the child urinated, the device activated a bell that awakened the child. Gradually stimuli from the bladder became associated with the awakening response. Eventually, the response was anticipated so that bedwetting no longer took place.

The classical conditioning procedure also has been used in treating alcoholics. For example, an aversive stimulus such as shock or a nausea-inducing agent is applied immediately after the alcoholic takes a drink. The aversive stimulus acts as an unconditioned stimulus, and the avoidance response is conditioned to the alcohol (Nathan, 1985).

CURRENT APPLICATIONS

WHAT MAKES SOME FOODS A TREAT AND OTHERS DISGUSTING?

Most people love some odors and food tastes and are disgusted by others. Often these responses date back to childhood and seem nearly impossible to change. Can classical conditioning help us to understand them and their power?

Consider some research on food tastes. What makes some foods so unpleasant—even disgusting—that we have emotional reactions to just the thought of them? Eating worms, or drinking milk that has a dead fly or dead cockroach in it are examples. The interesting thing about some of these reactions is that a food that evokes disgust in one culture can be considered a delicacy in another, and disgust might be evoked by a dead fly or cockroach in the milk even if one is told that the insect was sterilized before it was put in the milk. Having seen the dead insect in the milk, one might not even be prepared to drink a different glass of milk; the disgust reaction now having generalized to the milk itself.

According to the researchers of such reactions, a possible explanation lies in the strong emotional reaction that becomes associated with a previously neutral object. In classical conditioning terms, the disgust response becomes associated with, or conditioned to, a previously neutral object such as milk or another food: "We believe that Pavlovian conditioning is alive and well, in the flavor associations of billions of meals eaten each day, in the expression of affects of billions of eaters as they eat away, in the association of foods and offensive objects, and in the association of foods with some of their consequences."

If this is the case, then it suggests that many things that we like, perhaps even feel addicted to, are the result of classical conditioning. This being the case, it may be possible to change our emotional reactions to certain objects through the process of classical conditioning.

Conditioned food responses: *Many strong and persisting emotional responses to foods, such as a disgust response to worms, are acquired through the process of classical conditioning. (Copyright © 1985 American Psychological Association. Reprinted by permission from* Psychology Today.*)*

SOURCE: *Psychology Today*, July 1985; Rozin & Zellner, 1985. Copyright © 1985 American Psychological Association. Reprinted by permission from Psychology Today.

Systematic Desensitization

based on the concept of classical conditioning

By far the most influential development in this area has been that of Joseph Wolpe's method of **systematic desensitization**. Interestingly, this method of therapy was developed by a psychiatrist rather than a psychologist, and by someone who originally practiced within a psychoanalytic framework. After a number of years of practice, however, Wolpe read and was impressed by the writings of Pavlov. He came to believe that a neurosis is a persistent, maladaptive learned response that is almost always associated with anxiety. Therapy, then, involves the inhibition of anxiety through the counterconditioning of a competing response. In other words, therapy involves the conditioning of responses that are antagonistic to or inhibitory of anxiety. A variety of anxiety-inhibiting responses can be used for counterconditioning purposes. However, the one that has received most attention is deep muscle relaxation. Through the process of systematic desensitization, the patient learns to respond to certain previously anxiety-arousing stimuli with the newly conditioned response of relaxation.

Systematic desensitization involves a number of phases (Wolpe, 1961). First, there is a careful assessment of the therapeutic needs of the patient. After determining that the patient's problems can be treated by systematic desensitization, the therapist trains the patient to relax. A detailed procedure is described for helping the patient to relax first one part of the body and then all parts. Whereas, at first, patients have limited success in freeing themselves from muscle tension, after about six sessions most are able to relax the entire body in seconds. The next phase of treatment involves the construction of an anxiety hierarchy. This is a procedure in which the therapist tries to obtain from the patient a list of stimuli that arouse anxiety. These anxiety-arousing stimuli are grouped into themes such as fear of heights or fear of rejection. Within each group or theme, the anxiety-arousing stimuli are then arranged in order from most disturbing to least disturbing. For example, a theme of claustrophobia (fear of closed spaces) might involve placing the fear of being stuck in an elevator at the top of the list, an anxiety about being on a train in the middle of the list, and anxiety in response to reading of miners trapped underground at the bottom of the list. A theme of death might involve being at a burial as the most anxiety-arousing stimulus, the word death as somewhat anxiety-arousing, and driving past a cemetery as only slightly anxiety-arousing. Patients can have many or few themes and many or few items within each anxiety hierarchy.

With the construction of the anxiety hierarchies completed, the patient is ready for the desensitization procedure itself. The patient has learned to calm the self by relaxation, and the therapist has established the anxiety hierarchies. Now the therapist encourages the patient to achieve a deep state of relaxation and then to imagine the least anxiety-arousing stimulus in the anxiety hierarchy. If the patient can imagine the stimulus without anxiety, then he or she is encouraged to imagine the next stimulus in the hierarchy while remaining relaxed. Periods of pure relaxation are interspersed with periods of relaxation and imagination of anxiety-arousing stimuli. If the patient feels anxious while imagining a stimulus, he or she is encouraged to relax and return to imagining a less anxiety-arousing stimulus. Ultimately the patient is able to relax while imagining all stimuli in the anxiety hierarchies. Relaxation in relation to the imagined stimuli generalizes to relaxation in relation to these stimuli in everyday life. "It has consistently been found that at every stage a stimulus that evokes no anxiety when imagined in a state of relaxation will also evoke no anxiety when encountered in reality" (Wolpe, 1961, p. 191).

A number of clinical and laboratory studies have indicated that systematic desensitization can be a useful treatment procedure. These successful results

"Leave us alone! I am a behavior therapist! I am helping my patient overcome a fear of heights!"

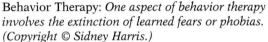

Behavior Therapy: *One aspect of behavior therapy involves the extinction of learned fears or phobias. (Copyright © Sidney Harris.)*

led Wolpe and others to question the psychoanalytic view that, as long as the underlying conflicts remain untouched, the patient is prone to develop a new symptom in place of the one removed (symptom substitution) (Lazarus, 1965). According to the behavior therapy point of view, no symptom is caused by unconscious conflicts. There is only a maladaptive learned response, and once this response has been eliminated, there is no reason to believe that another maladaptive response will be substituted for it.

A REINTERPRETATION OF THE CASE OF LITTLE HANS

In this section the application of the learning theory approach will be observed in a case presented by Wolpe and Rachman (1960) that gives us an excellent opportunity to compare the behavioral approach with that of psychoanalysis. In fact, it is not a case in the same sense as other cases that have been presented. Rather, it is a critique and reformulation of Freud's case of Little Hans.

As we learned in Chapter 4, the case of Little Hans is a classic in psychoanalysis. In this case, Freud emphasized the importance of infantile sexuality and Oedipal conflicts in the development of a horse phobia, or fear. Wolpe and Rachman are extremely critical of Freud's approach to obtaining data and of his conclusions. They make the following points: (1) Nowhere is there evidence of Hans's wish to make love to his mother. (2) Hans never expressed fear or hatred of his father. (3) Hans consistently denied any relationship between the horse and his father. (4) Phobias can be induced in children by a simple conditioning process and need not be related to a theory of conflicts or anxiety and defense. The view that neuroses have a purpose is highly questionable. (5) There is no evidence that the phobia disappeared as a result of Hans's resolution of his Oedipal conflicts. Similarly, there is no evidence that insight occurred or that information was of therapeutic value.

Wolpe and Rachman feel handicapped in their own interpretation of the phobia because the data were gathered within a psychoanalytic framework.

They do, however, attempt an explanation. A phobia is regarded as a conditioned anxiety reaction. As a child, Hans heard and saw a playmate being warned by her father that she should avoid a white horse lest it bite her: "Don't put your finger to the white horse." This incident sensitized Hans to a fear of horses. Also, there was the time when one of Hans's friends injured himself and bled while playing with horses. Finally, Hans was a sensitive child who felt uneasy about seeing merry-go-round horses being playfully beaten. These factors set the condition for the later development of the phobia. The phobia itself occurred as a consequence of the fright Hans experienced while watching a horse fall down. Whereas Freud suggested that this incident was an exciting cause that allowed the underlying conflicts to be expressed in terms of a phobia, Wolpe and Rachman suggest that this incident was the cause.

Wolpe and Rachman see a similarity here to Watson's conditioning of fear in Little Albert. Hans was frightened by the event with a horse and then generalized his fear to all things that were similar to or related to horses. The recovery from the phobia did not occur through the process of insight, but probably through a process of either extinction or counterconditioning. As Hans developed, he experienced other emotional responses that inhibited the fear response. Alternatively, it is suggested that perhaps the father's constant reference to the horse in a nonthreatening context helped to extinguish the fear response. Whatever the details, it appears that the phobia disappeared gradually, as would be expected by this kind of learning interpretation, instead of dramatically, as might be suggested by a psychoanalytic, insight interpretation. The evidence in support of Freud is not clear, and the data, as opposed to the interpretations, can be accounted for in a more straightforward way through the use of a learning theory interpretation.

FURTHER DEVELOPMENTS

Most of the work on classical conditioning has focused on relatively simple reflex mechanisms that humans share with other animals. However, Pavlov also recognized the importance of speech and thought in what he called the second signal system. The concept of the second signal system provides for an understanding of much more complex organizations of stimuli and responses. The importance of this concept is illustrated by Razran's (1939) research on semantic conditioning. In this research with human subjects, Razran paired the visual presentation of the words *style, urn, freeze,* and *surf* with food reinforcement, leading to the development of a salivary response to the words. He then tested whether the conditioned response would generalize to words that sounded similar (*stile, earn, frieze,* and *serf*) or to words that sounded different but were similar in meaning (*fashion, vase, chill,* and *wave*). What would one expect to find—generalization to sound or to meaning? Razran found a significant difference in terms of the latter, suggesting that conditioning processes can be influenced by meaning or semantics. Pavlov himself did relatively little research on the second signal system, but it has continued to be a major area of investigation in Russian psychology, including developmental studies of changes in the factors controlling conditioning processes.

The concepts of conditioned emotional responses and a second signal system considerably expand the interpretation of the importance of classical conditioning in human behavior. For example, it has been suggested that people acquire motives or goals by associating positive and negative affect with stimuli, including symbols (Pervin, 1983; Staats & Burns, 1982).

For some time interest in classical conditioning declined among personality psychologists. However, recently there has been increased recognition of the potential contributions of concepts and procedures associated with classical conditioning theory. One illustrative area of research is the use of classical conditioning procedures to demonstrate that people can unconsciously develop fears and attitudes toward others (Krosnick, Betz, Jussim, & Lynn, 1992; Ohman & Soares, 1993). For example, a stimulus, such as a picture with positive or negative affective value, can be presented subliminally (i.e., below the threshold of awareness) in association with another stimulus, such as another photo. Thus, a person will come to dislike a photo unconsciously associated with negative emotion and come to like a photo unconsciously associated with positive emotion. One can speculate in this regard how many of our attitudes and preferences are classically conditioned on a subliminal or unconscious basis. Consider, for example, the following conclusion of a leading social psychologist: "The aversive prejudice, once created, may be difficult to consciously eliminate." People can have egalitarian beliefs and still act prejudicial in certain situations—their impulsive, automatic reaction when faced with a member of that minority group may be negative. This doesn't mean that people are lying about nonprejudicial attitudes. It's that these attitudes reside coincidentally with a conditioned aversive reaction learned early in childhood (Cacioppo, 1998, p. 10).

To attach even greater significance to this process, there now is evidence that, whereas conditioned responses may readily generalize across contexts, the extinction of these responses may be very context-specific (Bouton, 1994). Thus, you may learn a fear or disgust response in one context and have it generalize to many other contexts. However, extinguishing the response in one context does not mean that it will be extinguished in other contexts as well. The person who has acquired a fear of authority figures in one context may find the fear generalizing to other contexts as well. However, in extinguishing the fear in one context the person may be surprised to find that the fear remains in other contexts. This suggests that the extinction of strongly conditioned and widely generalized problematic responses, often the goal in psychotherapy, may be a particularly difficult enterprise.

Another effort in relation to classical conditioning is investigation of the conditioning of health-related responses (Ader & Cohen, 1993). For example, patients undergoing repeated chemotherapy for cancer often develop a classically conditioned nausea and vomiting response, that is, the nausea and vomiting associated with the chemotherapy become conditioned to stimuli associated with the chemotherapy. Anticipatory nausea and vomiting develops , just as Pavlov's dog developed an anticipatory salivation response to the bell that preceded the food stimulus. Another example of research in this area involves exploration of the classical conditioning of the immune system. Here the question is whether unconditioned responses of the body's disease-fighting system can be conditioned to other stimuli. There is some evidence that this is the case, raising the potential for the use of classical conditioning procedures to enhance the immune-system functioning of the body. In sum, classical conditioning procedures are being used to investigate important aspects of social behavior and health functioning.

The developments we have just reviewed primarily involve applications of conditioning principles to questions of human behavior. However, another major development concerns the study of basic neural and biochemical processes that mediate classical conditioning. Put simply, the question is "What actually happens in the brain when an organism acquires a new response to a stimulus?" Although many contemporary scientists contribute to an understanding of this issue, an investigator of particular note is Eric Kandel of Columbia University in New York, who was awarded the Nobel Prize in medicine in 2000 for his research on the topic. Kandel's research is a classic example of the "simple systems" strategy we overviewed earlier. In order to understand what happens in the brain when an organism learns a new response, Kandel studied an organism much simpler than the one studied by Pavlov (the dog). Kandel studied a type of sea slug called Aplysia. Aplysia have relatively few nerve cells, which makes it easier to study the role of specific individual cells in classical conditioning. Aplysia also exhibit a simple response, the gill-withdrawal reflex, that can be modified through conditioning. Kandel's findings reveal that the conditioning process, at the neural level, involves changes in the strength of connections among neurons (Kandel, 2000). The synapses of neurons that comprise the gill-withdrawal reflex become more strongly associated as a result of conditioning. Kandel's work is an exceptionally good example of how basic research in the neurosciences can inform the study of learning.

SKINNER'S THEORY OF OPERANT CONDITIONING

Although John Watson dropped out of the field of psychology, numerous other investigators picked up the banner of behaviorism during the middle of the 20th century. These included historically significant figures such as Clark Hull, who developed a highly systematic drive theory of learning, and John Dollard and Neal Miller, who attempted to show how Hull's theory could address phenomena involving drives and intrapsychic conflicts that were of interest to psychoanalysts. Even these important contributions, however, were eventually overshadowed by those of another researcher who became one of the most influential figures in all of 20th century psychology.

The most influential behavioral researcher, theorist, and spokesperson was the Harvard psychologist B. F. Skinner (1904–1990). Indeed, Skinner is probably the most well-known American psychologist of the last century; a recent quantitative analysis of the impact of individual psychologists on the field as a whole ranked Skinner as the singularly most eminent psychologist of the 20th century (Haggbloom et al., 2002). Skinner's eminence reflects his exceptional skill at articulating the broad implications of behavioral principles. In Skinner's hands, behaviorism was not just an approach to the psychology of learning. It was an all-encompassing philosophy that promised a comprehensive account of human behavior, as well as technologies for improving the human experience.

A VIEW OF THE THEORIST

The scientist, like any organism, is the product of a unique history. The practices which he finds most appropriate will depend in part upon his history.

B. F. Skinner

SOURCE: Skinner, 1959, p. 379.

In this passage, Skinner takes the point of view that has been argued in each of the theory chapters in this book, that is, that psychologists' orientations and research strategies are, in part, consequences of their own life history and expressions of their own personalities.

B. F. Skinner was born in Pennsylvania, the son of a lawyer who was described by his son as having been desperately hungry for praise and a mother who had rigid standards of right and wrong. Still, Skinner (1967) described his home during his early years as a warm and stable environment. He reported a love for school and showed an early interest in building things. This desire to build things is particularly interesting in relation to the behavioral emphasis on laboratory equipment in the experimental setting, and because it contrasts with the absence of such an interest in the lives and research of the clinical personality theorists.

At about the time Skinner entered college, his younger brother died. Skinner commented that he was not much moved by his brother's death and that he probably felt guilty for not being moved. Skinner went to Hamilton College and majored in English literature. At that time, his goal was to become a writer, and at one point he sent three short stories to Robert Frost, from whom he received an encouraging reply. After college, Skinner spent a year trying to write, but concluded that at that point in his life he had nothing to say. He then spent six months living in Greenwich Village in New York City. During this time he read Pavlov's *Conditioned Reflexes* and came across a series of articles by Bertrand Russell on Watson's behaviorism. Russell thought that he had demolished Watson in these articles, but they aroused Skinner's interest in behaviorism.

Although Skinner had not taken any psychology courses in college, he had begun to develop an interest in the field and was accepted for graduate work in psychology at Harvard. He justified his change in goals as follows: "A writer might portray human behavior accurately, but he did not therefore understand it. I was to remain interested in human behavior, but the literary method had failed me; I would turn to the scientific" (Skinner, 1967, p. 395). Psychology appeared to be the relevant science. Besides, Skinner had long been interested in animal behavior (recalling his fascination with the complex behaviors of a troupe of performing pigeons). Furthermore, there would now be many opportunities to make use of his interest in building gadgets.

During his graduate school years at Harvard, Skinner developed his interest in animal behavior and in explaining this behavior without reference to the functioning of the nervous system. After reading Pavlov, he disagreed with Pavlov's contention that, in explaining behavior, one could go "from the salivary reflexes to the important business of the organism in everyday life." However, Skinner believed that Pavlov had given him the key to understanding behavior. "Control your conditions (the environment) and you shall see order!" During these and the following years, Skinner (1959) developed some of his principles of scientific methodology: (1) When you run into something interesting, drop everything else and study it. (2) Some ways of doing research are easier than others. A mechanical apparatus often makes doing research easier. (3) Some people are lucky. (4) A piece of apparatus breaks down. This presents problems, but it can also lead to (5) serendipity—the art of finding one thing while looking for something else.

After Harvard, Skinner moved first to Minnesota, then to Indiana, and then returned to Harvard in 1948. During this time he became, in a sense, a sophis-

Figure 10.2   "Boy, have I got this guy conditioned! Every time I press the bar down he drops a piece of food." *(Skinner, 1956.)*

ticated animal trainer; he was able to make organisms engage in specific behaviors at specific times. He turned from work with rats to work with pigeons. Finding that the behavior of any single animal did not necessarily reflect the average picture of learning based on many animals, he became interested in the manipulation and control of individual animal behavior. Special theories of learning and circuitous explanations of behavior were not necessary if one could manipulate the environment so as to produce orderly change in the individual case. In the meantime, as Skinner notes, his own behavior was becoming controlled by the positive results being given to him by the animals "under his control" (Figure 10.2).

The basis of Skinner's **operant conditioning** procedure is the control of behavior through the manipulation of rewards and punishments in the environment, particularly the laboratory environment. However, his conviction concerning the importance of the laws of behavior and his interest in building things led Skinner to take his thinking and research far beyond the laboratory. He built a "baby box" to mechanize the care of a baby, teaching machines that used rewards in the teaching of school subjects, and a procedure whereby pigeons could be used militarily to land a missile on target. He committed himself to the view that a science of human behavior and the technology to be derived from it must be developed in the service of humankind. His novel, *Walden Two* (1948), describes a utopia based on the control of human behavior through positive reinforcement (reward).

Skinner was considered by many to be the greatest contemporary American psychologist. He received many awards, including the American Psychological Association's award for Distinguished Scientific Contribution (1958) and the National Medal of Science (1968). In 1990, shortly before his death, he became the first recipient of the American Psychological Association's Citation for Outstanding Lifetime Contribution to Psychology.

SKINNER'S THEORY OF PERSONALITY

Let's begin our discussion of Skinner's theory of personality by contrasting its general qualities with those of the theories you already have learned about in the previous chapters. Each of the previous theories (and, to give you a preview, each of the ones discussed subsequently in this book) emphasize structural concepts. Freud used structural concepts such as id, ego, and superego; Rogers used concepts such as self and ideal self; and Allport, Eysenck, and

Cattell used the concept of traits. Each theorist, then, inferred the existence of a psychological structure in the head of the individual that accounted for the person's consistent styles of emotion and behavior. In contrast, Skinner's behavioral approach greatly *de*emphasizes structure. This is for two reasons. First, behaviorists view behavior as an adaptation to situational forces. They thus expect situational specificity in behavior: if the situational forces change, so does the behavior. If behavior varies from one situation to another, then there is little need to propose structural concepts to explain the supposed consistency of personality. The second reason involves a general approach to constructing a theory. As we explained earlier, the behaviorists wanted to build a theory based on observable variables. They felt that only observable variables could be verified by basic research. Inferring the existence of invisible personality structures was seen by Skinner, then, as a way of thinking that was not properly scientific.

The fact that Skinner does not propose a series of personality structures makes his work entirely different than the other personality theories. In fact, Skinner rejected the view that his ideas constituted a personality theory. He saw himself as replacing the personality theories with a new way of thinking about behavior.

Structure

The key structural unit for the behavioral approach in general, and Skinner's approach in particular, is the response. A response may range from a simple reflex response (e.g., salivation to food, startle to a loud noise) to a complex piece of behavior (e.g., solution to a math problem, subtle forms of aggression). What is critical to the definition of a response is that it represents an external, observable piece of behavior that can be related to environmental events. The learning process essentially involves the association or connection of responses to events in the environment.

In his approach to learning, Skinner distinguishes between responses elicited by known stimuli, such as an eyeblink reflex to a puff of air, and responses that cannot be associated with any stimuli. These responses are emitted by the organism and are called **operants**. Skinner's view is that stimuli in the environment do not force the organism to behave or incite it to act. The initial cause of behavior is in the organism itself. "There is no environmental eliciting stimulus for operant behavior; it simply occurs. In the terminology of operant conditioning, operants are emitted by the organism. The dog walks, runs, and romps; the bird flies; the monkey swings from tree to tree; the human infant babbles vocally. In each case, the behavior occurs without any specific eliciting stimulus.... It is in the biological nature of organisms to emit operant behavior" (Reynolds, 1968, p. 8).

Process: Operant Conditioning

Before discussing some of the processes that this theory views as underlying behavior, it is important to consider the concept of the **reinforcer**. The Skinnerians define a reinforcer as an event (stimulus) that follows a response and increases the probability of its occurrence. If a pigeon's pecking at a disk, which is a piece of operant behavior, is followed by a reinforcer such as food, the probability of its pecking at the disk is increased. According to this view, a reinforcer strengthens the behavior it follows, and there is no need to turn to biological explanations to determine why a stimulus reinforces behavior. Stimuli that originally do not serve as reinforcers can come to do so through their association with other reinforcers. Some stimuli, such as money, become **generalized reinforcers** because they provide access to many other kinds of reinforcers.

It is important to observe here that a reinforcer is defined by its effect on behavior, an increase in the probability of a response. Often it is difficult to know precisely what will serve as a reinforcer for behavior, as it may vary from individual to individual or from organism to organism. Finding a reinforcer may turn out to be a trial-and-error operation. One keeps trying stimuli until one finds a stimulus that can reliably increase the probability of a certain response.

The Skinnerian approach focuses on the qualities of responses and their relationships to the rates and intervals at which they are reinforced, or schedules of reinforcements. A simple experimental device, the Skinner box, is used to study these relationships. In this kind of box there are few stimuli, and behaviors such as a rat's pressing of a bar or a pigeon's pecking of a key are observed. It is here, according to Skinner, that one can best observe the elementary laws of behavior. These laws are discovered through the control of behavior, in this case the bar-pressing activity of the rat or the key-pecking activity of the pigeon. Behavior is understood when it can be controlled by specific changes in the environment. To understand behavior is to control it. Behavior is controlled through the choice of responses that are reinforced and the rates at which they are reinforced. Schedules of reinforcement can be based on a particular time interval or a particular response interval. In a time interval schedule, the reinforcement appears after a certain period, say every minute, regardless of the number of responses made by the organism. In a response interval, or a response ratio schedule, reinforcements appear after a certain number of responses (e.g., presses of a bar, pecks of a key) have been made.

Thus, reinforcements need not be given after every response, but can instead be given only sometimes. Furthermore, reinforcements can be given on a regular or fixed basis—always after a certain period of time or after a certain number of responses—or they can be given on a variable basis—sometimes after a minute and sometimes after two minutes, or sometimes after a few responses and sometimes after many responses. Each **schedule of reinforcement** tends to stabilize behavior in a different way.

In a sense, operant learning represents a sophisticated formulation of the principles of animal training. Complex behavior is shaped through a process of **successive approximation**; that is, complex behaviors are developed by reinforcing pieces of behavior that resemble the final form of behavior one wants to produce.

> Operant conditioning shapes behavior as a sculptor shapes a lump of clay. Although at some point the sculptor seems to have produced an entirely novel object, we can always follow the process back to the original undifferentiated lump, and we can make the successive stages by which we return to this condition as small as we wish. At no point does anything emerge which is very different from what preceded it.... An

operant is not something which appears full grown in the behavior of the organism. It is the result of a continuous shaping process.

SOURCE: Skinner, 1953, p. 91.

The process of shaping or successive approximation is seen most clearly in the work of animal trainers. The difficult tricks performed by circus animals are not learned as complete wholes. Rather, the trainer gradually builds up sequences of learned responses through the reinforcement of particular behaviors that are then linked or chained to one another. What started off as the learning of individual behaviors ends up as the display of a complex series of acts before a circus audience. The animal ultimately is rewarded for its behavior, but the final reward is made dependent, or contingent, on the performance of the series of previously learned behaviors. In a similar way, complex behaviors in humans may be developed through the process of successive approximation.

Although operant conditioning primarily emphasizes the use of positive reinforcers such as food, money, or praise, Skinnerians also emphasize the importance of reinforcers based on the organism's escape from, or avoidance of, aversive (unpleasant) stimuli. In such cases responses are reinforced by the removal or avoidance of an unpleasant stimulus rather than by the appearance of a pleasant stimulus. In all these cases the effect is to reinforce or increase the strength of the response. Such response-outcome contingencies can be contrasted with the case of punishment. In punishment, an aversive stimulus follows a response, decreasing the probability of that response occurring again. However, the effect of punishment is temporary and it appears to be of little value in eliminating behavior. For this reason, Skinner has emphasized the use of positive reinforcement in shaping behavior.

Growth and Development

The Skinnerian view of growth and development continues to emphasize the importance of schedules of reinforcement in acquiring and performing behavior. As the child develops, responses are learned and remain under the control of reinforcement contingencies in the environment. The emphasis is on specific responses as they are influenced by specific environmental reinforcers. Children become self-reliant through the reinforcement of acts in which they take care of themselves, for instance, in eating and dressing. The child is reinforced immediately after completing those acts, both by material rewards such as food and by social rewards such as praise. In learning to tolerate delay of gratification the child may first be reinforced after a brief period of delay and then gradually may be reinforced for longer periods of delay. After a while, delay behavior becomes stabilized, and one can say that the child has developed an ability to tolerate delays in gratification.

What of children who imitate the behavior of parents, siblings, and others? Are such behaviors tied to the same principles of reinforcement? Behaviors can be imitated without being directly reinforced (Skinner, 1990). However, this occurs only where imitation has been reinforced many times; through generalization, imitation itself takes on the qualities of a reinforcer. Whereas initially the child is reinforced for imitating specific responses, the child is now reinforced to be generally imitative and a generalized imitative response tendency has developed. Thus, from the Skinnerian point of view, new behaviors may be acquired through the process of successive approximations or through the development of a generalized imitative repertoire. In either case, the behaviors are under the control of reinforcement contingencies in the environment.

Psychopathology

The learning theory position on psychopathology may be stated as follows: the basic principles of learning provide a completely adequate interpretation of psychopathology. Explanations in terms of symptoms with underlying causes are not necessary. According to the behavioral point of view, behavioral pathology is not a disease. Instead, it is a response pattern learned according to the same principles of behavior as are all response patterns.

The Skinnerians argue against any concept of the unconscious or a "sick personality." Individuals are not sick, they merely do not respond appropriately to stimuli. Either they fail to learn a response or they learn a **maladaptive response**. In the former case, there is a behavioral deficit. For example, individuals who are socially inadequate may have had faulty reinforcement histories in which social skills were not developed. Having failed to be reinforced for social skills during socialization as children, as adults they have an inadequate response repertoire with which to respond to social situations.

Reinforcement is important not only for the learning of responses but also for the maintenance of behavior. Thus, one possible result of an absence of reinforcement in the environment is depression. According to this view, depression represents a lessening of behavior or a lowered response rate. The depressed person is not responsive because positive reinforcement has been withdrawn (Ferster, 1973).

When a person learns a maladaptive response, the problem is that a response has been learned that is not considered acceptable by society or by others in the person's environment. This may be because the response itself is considered unacceptable (e.g., hostile behavior) or because the response occurs under unacceptable circumstances (e.g., joking at a formal business meeting). Related to this situation is the development of superstitious behav-

Superstitious Behavior: *Skinner suggested that superstitious behavior is based on an accidental relationship between a response and reinforcement.*

ior (Skinner, 1948). Superstitious behavior develops because of an accidental relationship between a response and reinforcement. Thus, Skinner found that if he gave pigeons small amounts of food at regular intervals regardless of what they were doing, many birds came to associate the response that was coincidentally rewarded with systematic reinforcement. For example, if a pigeon was coincidentally rewarded while walking around in a counterclockwise direction, this response might become conditioned even though it had no cause-effect relationship with the reinforcement. The continuous performance of the behavior would result in occasional, again coincidental, reinforcement. Thus, the behavior could be maintained over long periods of time.

In sum, people develop faulty behavior repertoires, what others call "sick" behavior or psychopathology, because of the following: they were not reinforced for adaptive behaviors, they were punished for behaviors that later would be considered adaptive, they were reinforced for maladaptive behaviors, or they were reinforced under inappropriate circumstances for what would otherwise be adaptive behavior. In all cases there is an emphasis on observable responses and schedules of reinforcement rather than on concepts such as drive, conflict, unconscious motives, or self-esteem.

Behavioral Assessment

The emphasis on specific behaviors tied to defined situational characteristics forms the basis for what has come to be known as **behavioral assessment**. Heavily influenced by the thinking of Skinner, the behavioral approach to assessment emphasizes three things: (1) identification of specific behaviors, often called **target behaviors** or target responses; (2) identification of specific environmental factors that elicit, cue, or reinforce the target behaviors; and (3) identification of specific environmental factors that can be manipulated to alter the behavior. Thus, a behavioral assessment of a child's temper tantrums would include a clear, objective definition of temper tantrum behavior in the child, a complete description of the situation that sets off the tantrum behavior, a complete description of the reactions of parents and others that may be reinforcing the behavior, and an analysis of the potential for eliciting and reinforcing other nontantrum behaviors (Kanfer & Saslow, 1965; O'Leary, 1972). This **functional analysis** of behavior, involving the effort to identify the environmental conditions that control behavior, sees behavior as a function of specific events in the environment. The approach has also been called the **ABC assessment**: one assesses the Antecedent conditions of the behavior, the Behavior itself, and the Consequences of the behavior.

Behavioral assessment generally is closely tied to treatment objectives. For example, consider the task of assisting a mother who came to a clinic because she felt helpless in dealing with her four-year-old son's temper tantrums and general disobedience (Hawkins, Peterson, Schweid, & Bijou, 1966). The psychologists involved in this case followed a fairly typical behavioral procedure to assessment and treatment. First, the mother and child were observed in the home to determine the nature of the undesirable behaviors, when they occurred, and which reinforcers seemed to maintain them. The following nine behaviors were determined to constitute the major portion of the boy's objectionable behavior: (1) biting his shirt or arm; (2) sticking out his tongue; (3) kicking or biting himself, others, or objects; (4) calling someone or something a derogatory name; (5) removing or threatening to remove his clothing; (6)

saying "NO!" loudly and vigorously; (7) threatening to damage objects or persons; (8) throwing objects; and (9) pushing his sister. Observation of the mother-child interaction suggested that the objectionable behavior was being maintained by attention from the mother. For example, often she tried to distract him by offering him toys or food.

The treatment program began with a behavioral analysis of how frequently the boy expressed one of the objectionable behaviors during one-hour sessions conducted in the home two to three times a week. Two psychologists acted as observers to ensure that there was high reliability or good agreement concerning recording of the objectionable behavior. This first phase, known as a baseline period, lasted for 16 sessions. During this time, mother and child interacted in their usual way. Following this careful assessment of the objectionable behavior during the baseline period, the psychologists initiated their intervention, or treatment program. Now the mother was instructed to tell her son to stop or to put him in his room by himself without toys each time he emitted an objectionable behavior. In other words, there was a withdrawal of the positive reinforcer for objectionable behavior. At the same time, the mother was instructed to give her son attention and approval when he behaved in a desirable way. In other words, the positive reinforcers were made contingent on desirable behavior. During this time, known as the first experimental period, the frequency of objectionable behaviors was again counted. As can be seen in Figure 10.3, there was a marked decline in the frequency of objectionable behavior. In the preexperimental baseline phase, dozens of objectionable behaviors commonly were observed during any given one-hour period. In contrast, during the first experimental period, only 1 to 8 such responses per session were observed.

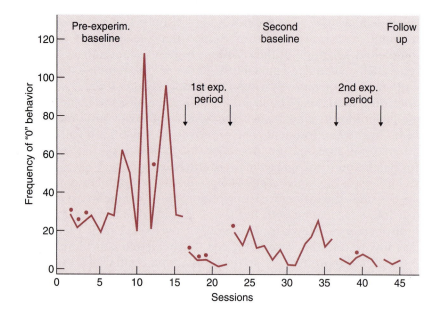

Figure 10.3   Number of 10-second Intervals per 1-hour Session, in Which Objectionable Behavior Occurred. Dots indicate sessions in which reliability was tested. *(Hawkins et al., 1966) Copyright © 1966 by Academic Press, Inc. Reprinted by permission*

Following the first experimental treatment period, the mother was instructed to return to her former behavior to determine whether it was the shift in her reinforcement behavior that was determining the change in her son's behavior. During this second baseline period, her son's objectionable behavior ranged between 2 and 24 per session (Figure 10.3). There was an increase in this behavior, though not a return to the former baseline level. However, the mother reported that she had trouble responding in her previous way because she now felt more "sure of herself." Thus, even during this period she gave her son more firm commands, gave in less after denying a request, and gave more affection in response to positive behaviors in her son than was previously the case. Following this there was a return to a full emphasis on the treatment program, resulting in a decline in objectionable behavior (second experimental period). The rate of objectionable behavior was found to remain low after a 24-day interval (follow-up period), and the mother reported a continuing positive change in the relationship.

ABA Research Design　In sum, in this case it was possible to assess the target responses in the home environment as well as their reinforcers, and then to specify a treatment regimen that resulted in measurable changes in the frequency of these behaviors. As well as illustrating behavioral assessment, this study illustrates an interesting variant of the experimental method—the Skinnerian **ABA research** design or own-control design (Krasner, 1971). Basically the ABA, own-control research design involves the experimental manipulation of a specific behavior and the demonstration that changes in behavior can be attributed directly to specific changes in environmental events. One subject is used and serves as his or her own control relating to variations in experimental conditions. In the first, or baseline phase (A) of this design, the current rate of occurrence of the behavior of interest is recorded. In the second or reinforcement phase (B), a reinforcer following the behavior of interest is introduced to increase the frequency of that behavior. Once the behavioral response has been established at the desired frequency, the reinforcer may be withdrawn (A phase) to see whether the behavior returns to the original (baseline period) rate. This is called the nonreinforcement period. Instead of comparing a subject who is reinforced with one who is not, the subject is treated differently in the various phases—he is his own control. In some research, a fourth phase is also included in which the reinforcer is reintroduced to reestablish the desired behavior (see Figure 10.3). Also, some experiments may begin with the reinforcement phase and then move to nonreinforcement and then reintroduction of reinforcement. This approach is typical when it does not make sense to begin with a baseline period, such as when a new behavior is being taught.

Sign and Sample Approaches to Assessment　As can be seen, in behavioral assessment there is emphasis on single variables (specific target behaviors) and the gathering of reliable, objective data. What is different about behavioral assessment in comparison to some other personality measures is that the behavior itself is of interest, not some theoretical construct (ego strength, extraversion) presumed to be expressed in the behavior. Mischel (1968, 1971) has contrasted these differences in terms of sign and sample approaches to assessment. In the **sign approach**, traits are inferred from test behavior. Test items are assumed to be adequate to reflect personality characteristics, and interpretations are made of test behavior relative to assumed underlying traits. There is, in other words, a high level of inference from test behavior to interpretations concerning personality characteristics. In the **sample approach**, interest is in the behavior itself and how it is affected by alterations in environmental conditions. Interest is in overt behavior, and it is assumed that one must understand the surrounding stimulus conditions to understand the relevant behavior. There is a low level of inference from test behavior to other similar behaviors in the individual. The sign approach asks about motives and traits that act together to result in observed behavior; the sample approach asks about environmental variables that affect behaviors in terms of their frequency, intensity, and duration.

Behavior Change

Use of the principles of operant conditioning to regulate behavior can be seen in a **token economy** (Ayllon & Azrin, 1965). Under a token economy, the behavioral technician rewards, with tokens, the various patient behaviors that are considered desirable. The tokens, in turn, can be exchanged by the patient for desirable products, such as candy and cigarettes. Thus, for example, hospitalized psychiatric patients could be reinforced for activities such as serving meals or cleaning floors. In a tightly controlled environment, such as a state hospital for long-term psychiatric patients, it is feasible to make almost anything that a patient wants contingent on the desired behaviors.

Research evidence supports the effectiveness of token economies. They are effective in increasing behaviors such as social interaction, self-care, and job performance in severely disturbed patients and mentally retarded individuals. They also have been used to decrease aggressive behavior in children and to decrease marital discord (Kazdin, 1977).

Token economy programs represent a very straightforward application of operant conditioning principles to the problem of behavior change. Target behaviors are selected and reinforcement is made contingent on performance of the desired responses. This is completely consistent with the behavioral emphasis on how the environment acts upon people, as opposed to how people act upon the environment. The behaviorist working on human behavior change is, in essence, a social engineer. The scientific technology developed in the behavioral laboratory is applied directly to real-world problems of behavior change. Watson suggested that through control of the environment he could train an infant to become any type of specialist he might select. Skinnerian social engineers take this principle one step further. As seen in the development of token economies, as well as in the development of communes based on Skinnerian principles, there is an interest in the design of environments that will control broad aspects of human behavior.

Free Will?

Skinner's operant behaviorism seems to have uplifting implications. By studying the influence of the environment on behavior, behaviorism gives rise to a technology of behavior change that can be usefully applied to the solution of human problems.

Yet Skinner's behaviorism also has an implication that is disturbing. It is one that Skinner was quite aware of, and that he explained in detail in a book titled *Beyond Freedom and Dignity* (Skinner, 1971). The implication is that people do not have free will. If the environment is the cause of our action, then we ourselves cannot be the cause of our behavior. And if we ourselves are not the cause of our behavior, then we do not truly have freedom to act. We do not make free choices. We do not have free will.

Skinner was quite aware that people *believe* that they have free will. But he concluded that this belief is an illusion. To illustrate how this could be, consider the following circumstances. Suppose that you are speeding down a highway in your red sports car, as you see a police car up ahead, you slow down to avoid a ticket. If a passenger asks you "Why did you slow down?," you are not likely to say "Because I have free will and decided to." Instead, you will recognize that the environment caused your behavior. The presence of the police officer was an environmental cause of your slowing down. Now suppose a passenger asks "Why did you buy a red sports car?" Here you are *not* likely to cite environmental causes. Instead, you are likely to say "because I decided to" or "because I like red sports cars." You feel you had free will regarding your car purchase. But here is where Skinner says you are wrong. In Skinner's behaviorism, your behavior of slowing down and your behavior of buying a red sports car are both caused by the environment. But in the former case, the environment is simple, immediate, and obvious. You cannot miss the fact that the police officer is the cause of your slowing down. But in the latter case, the environmental causes are complex and extended over a long period of time. Dozens of previous experiences (previous reinforcements and punishments) might have contributed to your behavior of buying a red sports car. It is impossible for you to remember all of them and assess their effects on your decision. But that does not mean that they were not there. In these cases, in which the environmental causes of behavior are complex, people essentially lose track of the multifaceted environmental causes and erroneously conclude that their behavior was caused by a single factor: themselves. Skinner concluded that people live with an illusion of free will—a conclusion similar to that reached by some contemporary research psychologists (Wegner, 2003).

Skinner did not argue against the notion of free will merely to disturb people. Quite the opposite. He felt that the solution of personal and social problems required a systematic application of behavioristic technology. Furthermore, he felt that people would not accept this technology if they thought that it infringed on their free will. Skinner recognized that people do not like to think that their behavior is being controlled, and therefore that they would argue against an application of behavioral technology. But Skinner turned this argument on its head by contending that behavior is *always* controlled by the environment. Recognizing this fact, and rejecting traditional notions of free will would, Skinner argued, open the door to a humane application of behavioral technology.

Before leaving this topic, we caution that many scholars have rejected Skinner's arguments about free will. Phenomenological theorists felt that Skinner's view underestimated human being's inherent capacities; indeed, Rogers (1956) engaged in written debate with Skinner on the topic. More recent personality theorists (see Chapters 12 and 13) similarly have contended that Skinner underestimated people's capacity to exert free will by thinking in a constructive manner about the environment that they face—a capacity lacked by the rats and pigeons who were Skinner's research subjects. Philosophers have noted that Skinner provided an insufficient analysis of the concept of free will itself, arguing that even if one accepts Skinner's basic principles, people still have capacities that enable them to engage in many thoughts and actions that deserve to be called acts of free will (Dennett, 1984). The recognition that the brain is a bodily organ that evolved and functions according to deterministic scientific principles is not incompatible with the idea that people have a significant capacity for free will and thus have personal responsibility for their actions (Dennett, 2003).

Perhaps the most devastating critique of behaviorist principles comes from the famed linguist and political scientist Noam Chomsky (1987). Chomsky notes that there is a very large gap between the experimental evidence that Skinner has at his disposal and the arguments he is making. Skinner's arguments concern the environmental control of human social behavior. But his database consists of animals in boxes. Skinner's discussions of human behavior thus are not a simple application of scientific evidence. Instead, they are a substantial step beyond the scientific evidence that actually is available. "Claims [of the sort Skinner makes] must be evaluated in terms of the evidence presented for them," Chomsky writes. "In the present instance [Skinner's *Beyond Freedom and Dignity*], this is a simple task. No evidence is presented" (Chomsky, 1987, p. 160). Chomsky's point is that Skinner did not in any way demonstrate, scientifically, that people do not have free will. Instead, he used an experimental database involving small animals, plus a philosophical position about the causes of behavior, to construct an argument against the notion of human free will. Cogent counter-arguments are available.

A COMPARISON OF LEARNING APPROACHES WITH EARLIER VIEWS

This chapter has considered learning-behavioral approaches, in particular those based on principles of classical conditioning and operant conditioning. Perhaps the most significant comparison between the theories presented in this chapter and those considered previously is the emphasis on processes of learning rather than on structures, such as motives, traits, or the self-concept. In part following from this, learning-behavioral approaches tend to emphasize the importance of specific behaviors rather than general personality characteristics. In addition, there is an interest in general laws of learning rather than in individual differences. Also, in terms of method of research, there is an emphasis on laboratory experiments rather than clinical investigation or the use of questionnaires. Finally, there tends to be a difference in the extent to which the focus is on variables internal to the organism as opposed to those external to it. Compared with the views presented earlier, the theories considered in this chapter emphasize the importance of variables in the environment in the regulation and control of behavior (Table 10.2).

In total, these principles give us a view of human personality that contrasts starkly with all the approaches we have discussed previously. Consider a behaviorist view of the previous theories. Psychoanalysis is seen as utterly nonscientific, because it deals entirely with unseen internal variables that cannot be observed and measured systematically. Phenomenological theory is seen as a soft-headed approach that falls into the trap of viewing people as the causes of their behavior, rather than recognizing the influence of the environ-

Table 10.2   Contrasting General Points of Emphasis of Learning Views and Traditional Theories of Personality

Learning Views	*Traditional Personality Theory*
Processes of learning	Personality structures
Specific behaviors	General characteristics
General laws	Individual differences
Laboratory data	Clinical data & questionnaires
Environmental variables	Internal variables

ment. Trait theory is seen as dealing merely with descriptions of behavior, rather than with its causes. If behaviorism had been fully successful, it would have swept all these other theories aside.

We have now covered considerable ground, including a variety of theoretical and applied approaches. It is time to take stock of learning-behavioral approaches to personality. **CRITICAL EVALUATION**

STRENGTHS OF LEARNING APPROACHES *Record*

Three major contributions have been made by learning approaches: (1) a commitment to systematic research and theory development; (2) a recognition and exploration of the role of situational and environmental variables in influencing behavior; and (3) a pragmatic approach to treatment leading to important new developments (Table 10.3).

Learning psychologists share a commitment to empiricism or systematic research. Whatever the differences in theory, the various approaches are characterized by a respect for scientific methodology and for evidence in support of a new point of view. In contrast with the development of psychoanalysis—and to a certain extent with that of phenomenology and humanistic approaches—learning approaches have been largely tied to academic departments where the emphasis is on clarity in defining constructs and on replicability in verifying data. Although at times this may limit what is studied and how phenomena are conceptualized, it also sets some useful boundaries on armchair speculation and quasi-religious debate. Thus, to a greater extent than most other approaches considered to this point, the learning approach emphasizes laboratory research that leads to the establishment of causal relationships.

The second contribution and strength of learning approaches is a recognition of the role of environmental and situational variables in behavior. Most learning approaches emphasize the importance of regulating or maintaining conditions in the environment; all emphasize the importance of situational analysis. For some time, traditional personality theory and assessment gave minimal attention to such variables. The importance of the situation or environment was noted by psychoanalytic and trait theorists, but there was no active exploration or conceptual development. In many ways, it has been unfortunate that the emphasis on situational variables and situation-specific aspects of performance became associated with the person-situation controversy. As most personality psychologists now recognize, both person and situation variables enter into behavior, and we must try to understand how they relate to one another. The learning approach has called attention to the variability and flexibility that are characteristic of much human behavior, as well as to the diversity of skills that are relevant to specific tasks.

3) Related to this has been a pragmatism that has led to the development of important procedures for behavior change. In contrast with many traditional treatment programs, which focused on young, verbal, intelligent, and successful patients, many behavior modification programs started by treating individuals on whom almost everyone else gave up—the chronic schizophrenic, the autistic child, the retarded, the addicted, and so on. Traditional therapy programs were not working and new approaches were required. Behavior therapists filled the void, in particular with the application of Skinnerian principles in behavior modification programs. These programs have raised moral and ethical issues concerning the control of human behavior, but on the whole significant gains have been made in assisting people who otherwise would have been left untouched.

LIMITATIONS OF LEARNING APPROACHES

If the strengths outlined above seem significant, the limitations to be detailed are no less noteworthy. In some cases, they speak to the same issues already covered, suggesting that the reality is not always as pretty as the picture presented. For example, with its concern for objectivity and rigor, the learning approach has oversimplified personality and neglected important phenomena.

There are many components to the criticism that learning theorists oversimplify behavior. One component is the claim that the principles of learning used are derived from research on rats and other subhuman animals. Are the same principles involved in human learning? In other words, can rat laws function as human laws? A second component of this criticism is the claim that the behaviors studied by learning theorists are superficial. In their effort to gain experimental control over relevant variables, learning theorists have limited themselves to simple, specific responses and have avoided complex behaviors. We may recall here Cattell's argument that the bivariate method limits investigators to the study of a few variables, and this means that they must ignore behaviors that cannot be produced in the laboratory.

A third and critical component of the criticism regarding oversimplification concerns cognitive behavior. Cognitive behavior involves the way in which the individual receives, organizes, and transmits information. The work of many psychologists demonstrates the importance of understanding cognitive behavior. Yet, for a long time behaviorists avoided considering these phenomena. Perhaps because of a reluctance to look at internal processes or to consider complex processes, learning theorists clung to their attempts to understand all behavior in terms of stimulus-response bonds or in terms of operants and successive approximation.

Critics of the approaches considered in this chapter also emphasize that there is no agreed-on theory of learning and that a large gap exists between theory and practice. Some time ago a supporter of behavior therapy suggested that it is a group of techniques rather than a theory-based scientific procedure: "When you eliminate the polemics and politics and gratuities, however, what remains of the theory to define the field and to tell you what it is about?

Table 10.3   Summary of Strengths and Limitations of Learning Approaches   *Record — need to know*

Strengths	Limitations
1. Committed to systematic research and theory development.	1. Oversimplifies personality and neglects important phenomena.
2. Recognizes the role of situational and environmental variables in influencing behavior.	2. Lacks a single, unified theory; gap between theory and practice.
3. Takes a pragmatic approach to treatment which can lead to important new developments.	3. Requires further evidence to support claims of treatment effectiveness.

Not a whole lot" (London, 1972, p. 916). Further, although there is evidence that procedures can be effective, such as with systematic desensitization, there is a question concerning the processes involved—that is, such a procedure may be working for reasons other than those suggested by behavior therapists (Kazdin & Wilson, 1978; Levis & Malloy, 1982).

Questions also have been raised about the effectiveness of behavior therapy. These include the issue of whether results obtained in the laboratory or clinic are maintained in the natural environment (Bandura, 1972; Kazdin & Bootzin, 1972). In addition, some studies suggest that in many patients gains are eventually lost (Eysenck & Beech, 1971). Finally, techniques found to be useful with mild problems in the laboratory may be far less significant when applied to clients with more serious difficulties.

Two final criteria seem particularly damning for behaviorism. The first concerns behaviorists' view of science. A central idea was that science involves the study of observables. Only by sticking to observable, measurable variables could there be scientific progress. Although this was a bedrock principle of behaviorism since the time of Watson, it is plainly wrong as a general statement about the nature of scientific progress. Many mature sciences (such as chemistry or physics) routinely posit variables that are unseen. Newton could not observe gravity. He inferred the existence of a gravitational force based on systematic observations of the world. Similarly, contemporary theoretical physicists commonly posit unseen subatomic particles and forces. Sticking to observable variables would be far too restrictive in other sciences—and may be too restrictive in a science of personality. Thus, one big problem for behaviorism was that it rested on a very limited view of the nature of scientific inquiry (Harré & Second, 1972).

The other problem concerns the notion of generativity: a valuable theory is one that generates new, valuable observations of the world. An unarguable fact about contemporary psychological science is that few of its interesting new observations of the world are inspired by behaviorism. Instead, other theoretical frameworks have guided the field's most valuable research programs. Many psychologists found that they could learn more about human psychology by abandoning the dictums of behaviorism than by adhering to them. In particular, beginning in the late 1950s, psychologists found that they could learn a lot about people by adopting a cognitive framework, that is, a scientific perspective that explores the ways in which people acquire, remember, and use knowledge about the world. It is the cognitive revolution in psychology

LEARNING APPROACHES AT A GLANCE

	Structure	Process	Growth and Development
	Response	Classical conditioning; instrumental conditioning; operant conditioning	Imitation; schedules of reinforcement and successive approximations

that ultimately overthrew behaviorism. In the chapters that follow we will consider the personality theories that are a part of this revolution.

MAJOR CONCEPTS

ABA (own-control) research   A Skinnerian variant of the experimental method consisting of exposing one subject to three experimental phases: (A) a baseline period, (B) introduction of reinforcers to change the frequency of specific behaviors, and (A) withdrawal of reinforcement and observation of whether the behaviors return to their earlier frequency (baseline period).

ABC assessment   In behavioral assessment, an emphasis on the identification of antecedent (A) events and the consequences (C) of behavior, and (B) a functional analysis of behavior involving identification of the environmental conditions that regulate specific behaviors.

Behavioral assessment   The emphasis in assessment on specific behaviors that are tied to defined situational characteristics (e.g., ABC approach).

Behaviorism   An approach within psychology, developed by Watson, that restricts investigation to overt, observable behavior.

Classical conditioning   A process, emphasized by Pavlov, in which a previously neutral stimulus becomes capable of eliciting a response because of its association with a stimulus that automatically produces the same or a similar response.

Conditioned emotional reaction   Watson and Rayner's term for the development of an emotional reaction to a previously neutral stimulus, as in Little Albert's fear of rats.

Discrimination   In conditioning, the differential response to stimuli depending on whether they have been associated with pleasure, pain, or neutral events.

Extinction   In conditioning, the progressive weakening of the association between a stimulus and a response; in classical conditioning because the conditioned stimulus is no longer followed by the unconditioned stimulus; and in operant conditioning because the response is no longer followed by reinforcement.

Functional analysis   In behavioral approaches, particularly Skinnerian, the identification of the environmental stimuli that control behavior.

Generalization   In conditioning, the association of a response with stimuli similar to the stimulus to which the response was originally conditioned or attached.

Generalized reinforcer   In Skinner's operant conditioning theory, a reinforcer that provides access to many other reinforcers (e.g., money).

Maladaptive response   In the Skinnerian view of psychopathology, the learning of a response that is maladaptive or not considered acceptable by people in the environment.

Operant conditioning   Skinner's term for the process through which the characteristics of a response are determined by its consequences.

Operants   In Skinner's theory, behaviors that appear (are emitted) without being specifically associated with any prior (eliciting) stimuli and are studied in relation to the reinforcing events that follow them.

Reinforcer   An event (stimulus) that follows a response and increases the probability of its occurrence.

Sample approach   Mischel's description of assessment approaches in which there is an interest in the behavior itself and its relation to environmental conditions, in contrast to sign approaches that infer personality from test behavior.

Pathology	Change	Illustrative Case
Maladaptive learned response patterns	Extinction; discrimination learning; counterconditioning; positive reinforcement; imitation; systematic desensitization; behavior modification	Peter; Reinterpretation of Little Hans

Schedule of reinforcement   In Skinner's operant conditioning theory, the rate and interval of reinforcement of responses (e.g., response ratio schedule and time intervals).

Sign approach   Mischel's description of assessment approaches that infer personality from test behavior, in contrast with sample approaches to assessment.

Situational specificity   The emphasis on behavior as varying according to the situation, as opposed to the emphasis by trait theorists on consistency in behavior across situations.

Successive approximation   In Skinner's operant conditioning theory, the development of complex behaviors through the reinforcement of behaviors that increasingly resemble the final form of behavior to be produced.

Systematic desensitization   A technique in behavior therapy in which a competing response (relaxation) is conditioned to stimuli that previously aroused anxiety.

Target behaviors (target responses)   In behavioral assessment, the identification of specific behaviors to be observed and measured in relation to changes in environmental events.

Token economy   Following Skinner's operant conditioning theory, an environment in which individuals are rewarded with tokens for desirable behaviors.

REVIEW

1. The learning approach to personality emphasizes principles of learning and the experimental testing of clearly defined hypotheses. Associated with this is an emphasis on the situational specificity of behavior, the application of principles of learning to behavior change, and rejection of the medical symptom-disease model of psychopathology.

2. Watson spelled out the rationale for a behaviorist approach to psychology.

3. Pavlov's work on classical conditioning illustrates how a previously neutral stimulus can become capable of eliciting a response because of its association with a stimulus that produces the same or a similar response (e.g., the dog salivates to the bell stimulus associated with the food powder). Generalization, discrimination, and extinction are three important processes studied by Pavlov.

4. The classical conditioning procedure suggests that many abnormal behaviors are the result of conditioning responses to inappropriate stimuli. Watson and Rayner's case of Little Albert illustrates such a conditional emotional reaction. The application of principles of classical conditioning is seen in the classic case of Peter's fear of a white rabbit, in the treatment of bedwetting in children, and in the method of systematic desensitization. In systematic desensitization the relaxation response is counterconditioned to a graded, imagined hierarchy of stimuli that formerly were associated with anxiety.

5. Freud's case of Little Hans has been reinterpreted according to the principles of classical conditioning. The phobia is viewed as a conditioned anxiety reaction precipitated by his viewing a horse fall down, rather than as an expression of underlying conflicts.

6. Skinner, considered by many to be the greatest contemporary American psychologist, developed the principles of operant conditioning. The emphasis here is on responses emitted by the organism (operants) and the schedules of reinforcement that shape behavior. Complex behavior is shaped through successive approximation.

7. The Skinnerian interpretation of psychopathology emphasizes behavioral deficits and the development of maladaptive responses that are maintained

by reinforcers in the environment. Behavioral assessment includes an analysis of the Antecedent conditions of the behavior of interest, and Behavior itself, and the Consequences of the behavior—the ABCs of behavioral assessment. A distinction is drawn between sign and sample approaches to assessment. Whereas in sign approaches personality is inferred from test responses, in sample approaches interest is in the behavior itself and how it is affected by environmental conditions.

8. Although there is no single method of behavior therapy or behavior modification, its procedures emphasize principles of learning theory. In behavior modification involving Skinnerian principles of operant conditioning, desired behaviors are shaped through stages of successive approximation. The ABA or own-control design can be used to demonstrate that the reinforcers being manipulated are the causal agents in the change process. The application of these principles to behavior regulation in an institutional setting is seen in a token economy.

9. Learning approaches are diverse in their specifics. As a group, however, they can be contrasted with traditional personality theories in terms of their greater emphasis on specific behaviors and general laws of learning.

10. Learning approaches share a commitment to research and generally are open to theoretical developments. Additional strengths are recognition of the importance of environmental variables and a pragmatic approach to treatment that has fostered the development of new procedures for behavior change. At the same time, these approaches tend to oversimplify personality and neglect important phenomena. In addition, there is still no unified theory of learning, and further evidence is required to support claims of treatment effectiveness.

11

A COGNITIVE THEORY OF PERSONALITY: GEORGE A. KELLY'S PERSONAL CONSTRUCT THEORY OF PERSONALITY

GEORGE A. KELLY (1905–1966): A VIEW OF THE THEORIST

KELLY'S VIEW OF THE SCIENCE OF PERSONALITY

KELLY'S VIEW OF THE PERSON

THE PERSONALITY THEORY OF GEORGE A. KELLY

Structure
Constructs and Their Interpersonal Consequences
Types of Constructs and the Construct System
The Role Construct Repertory (Rep) Test
Unique Information Revealed by Personal Construct Testing
Cognitive Complexity/Simplicity

Process
Anticipating Events
Anxiety, Fear, and Threat

GROWTH AND DEVELOPMENT

CLINICAL APPLICATIONS
Psychopathology
Change and Fixed-Role Therapy

THE CASE OF JIM
Rep Test: Personal Construct Theory
Comments on the Data

RELATED POINTS OF VIEW AND RECENT DEVELOPMENTS
Contemporary Analyses of Person/Situation Beliefs

CRITICAL EVALUATION: STRENGTHS AND LIMITATIONS OF PERSONAL CONSTRUCT THEORY

SUMMARY

MAJOR CONCEPTS

REVIEW

Chapter Focus

You've just finished a novel that you thoroughly enjoyed. Excitedly, you call a friend to recommend the book, telling him about the exquisitely detailed descriptions of the characters and the settings. To your dismay, your friend informs you that he has already read the book—and hated it! "Thin plot, slow moving," he complains. How could this be? Your "environment" (the book) was the same, yet you had utterly different experiences. You had completely different thoughts about exactly the same environmental stimulus.

This is what George Kelly's personal construct theory is all about: how each individual uniquely perceives, interprets, and conceptualizes the world. Just as you and your friend differed in your reading of the book, people differ in the way they "read" the persons and events of social life. To Kelly, these differences are at the heart of personality functioning. Our thoughts, emotional reactions, moods, goals, behavioral tendencies—virtually everything of interest to the personality psychologist—are, to Kelly, a product of our interpretations of the world. Individual differences in emotion and action, then, derive from individual differences in these interpretations. These ideas were the foundation of a cognitive theory of personality, a method of personality assessment, and an approach to therapy that were developed by one of the most innovative and impactful figures in the history of personality psychology: George Kelly.

Kelly – Consistency Model

QUESTIONS TO BE ADDRESSED IN THIS CHAPTER

1. What is the personality scientist doing when constructing a personality theory? How does Kelly's analysis of science inform us about this question?

2. In what ways are your thoughts, in your daily life, similar to the mental activities of a scientist? What did Kelly mean by suggesting that people are like scientists (his "person-as-scientist" metaphor)?

3. Can one explain motivated human behavior without using explanatory concepts such as "motive"?

4. How can an analysis of personal constructs explain psychological distress and inform the practice of psychotherapy?

In earlier chapters, you learned about two theories of personality that had their origins in clinical work: Freud's psychoanalysis and Rogers's phenomenological theory. This chapter considers a third theory that developed primarily out of contact with clients in therapy. Work as a therapist naturally directs one's attention to the "whole person." In other words, rather than focusing on one psychological variable or another, the therapist must confront whole, complex, intact individuals who experience multiple goals and feelings that cohere in meaningful ways. Like the clinician/theorists Freud and Rogers, George Kelly aimed to understand the whole individual.

Although sharing these characteristics with Freud and Rogers, Kelly's overall theory differs from their work. Freud emphasized animalistic forces in the unconscious. Kelly highlights the uniquely human capacity to reflect on oneself, the world, and the future. Regarding Rogers, Kelly's and Rogers's contributions are similar in some respects; both were concerned with creating a theory of the whole, coherent person. But Kelly explored in much greater detail the particular cognitive processes through which people categorize people and things and construct meaning out of the events of their day.

Why is his work called "personal construct" theory? Kelly used the word "construct" to refer to the ideas or categories that people use to interpret their world. Some of these categories are universal. For example, if you and a friend both stare out the window during a boring moment in your professor's lectures and spot a 20-foot-tall green-and-brown leafy object, you probably will both categorize it as "a tree." We all have in our head the category "tree" and we all apply this category to 20-foot-tall green-and-brown leafy objects. But some categories vary from person to person. People differ in whether they possess the given category and in where they use it. Suppose your professor sees you and your friend staring out the window at the tree, stops the lecture, and asks you both to start paying attention to class. You may categorize the professor as an "attentive teacher" whereas your friend may see her as a "condescending intellectual." In the language of Kelly's personal construct theory, you two will have used different personal constructs ("attentive teacher," "condescending intellectual") to interpret your professor's behavior. The use of these constructs would have great implications for your subsequent thoughts and feelings. You may admire the professor for her attention, whereas your friend may feel insulted by her condescension. To Kelly, an individual's personality can be understood in terms of the collection of personal constructs— or the *personal construct system*—that he or she uses to interpret the world.

In this text we label Kelly's work a "cognitive" theory, a term that derives from the Latin verb that means "to know" and that, in contemporary psychology, generally refers to thinking processes. A "cognitive" theory of personality, then, is a theory that places the analysis of human thinking processes at the centerpoint of the analysis of personality and individual differences. Kelly himself did not use the term "cognitive" to describe his theory, thinking it was too restrictive and that it suggested an artificial division between cognition (thinking) and affect (feeling). However, "cognitive" remains the most popular classification of Kelly's theory, and for good reason (Neimeyer, 1992; Winter, 1992). The constructs that people possess comprise their knowledge of the world, and these constructs are used in the acquisition of new knowledge. People apply their constructs to the interpretation of daily events through mental procedures that generally are termed "cognitive processes"; these include categorizing people and things, attributing meaning to events, and predicting events.

Kelly's most important work in personality theory was published in 1955. At that point, Kelly was ahead of his time in emphasizing human cognition. In the 1950s, behaviorism dominated academic psychology. Contemporary cognitive psychology had not yet been developed. Kelly's work, then, anticipated subsequent developments in the field. Throughout the last quarter of the 20th century—that is, years after Kelly's death—psychologists increasingly interpreted human behavior in terms of cognitive processes through which people interpret and understand their world. A supporter of personal construct theory has noted that "Kelly's theory enjoys the irony of becoming increasingly contemporary with age" (Neimeyer, 1992, p. 995).

Kelly provided not only an abstract theory but an approach to life. He challenged people—both the people he saw in therapy and the people who were his contemporaries in psychology—to think in new terms, to view the world in new ways, to "try on new constructs." He similarly would invite and challenge you, the student, to "try on" the novel ideas of personal construct theory.

GEORGE A. KELLY (1905–1966): A VIEW OF THE THEORIST

The nature of George Kelly, the person, comes through in his writing. He appears to have been the kind of person he encouraged others to be—an adventuresome soul who is unafraid to think unorthodox thoughts and who dares to explore the unknown.

Kelly's philosophical and theoretical positions stem, in part, from the diversity of his experience (Sechrest, 1963). Kelly grew up in Kansas and obtained his undergraduate education there at Friends University and at Park College in Missouri. He pursued graduate studies at the University of Kansas, the University of Minnesota, and the University of Edinburgh, and received his Ph.D. from the State University of Iowa in 1931. He developed a traveling clinic in Kansas, was an aviation psychologist during World War II, and was a professor of psychology at Ohio State University and Brandeis University.

Kelly's early clinical experience was in the public schools of Kansas. While there, he found that teachers referred pupils to his traveling psychological clinic with complaints that appeared to say something about the teachers themselves. Instead of verifying a teacher's complaint, Kelly decided to try to understand it as an expression of the teacher's construction or interpretation of events. For example, if a teacher complained that a student was lazy, Kelly did not look at the pupil to see if the teacher was correct in the diagnosis; rather he tried to understand the behaviors of the child and the way the teacher perceived these behaviors—that is, the teacher's construction of them—that led to the complaint of laziness. This was a significant reformulation of the problem. In practical terms, it led to an analysis of the teachers as well as the pupils, and to a wider range of solutions to the problems. Furthermore, it led Kelly to the view that there is no objective, absolute truth—phenomena are meaningful only in relation to the ways in which they are construed or interpreted by the individual.

George Kelly, then, was a person who refused to accept things as black or white, right or wrong. He was a person who liked to test new experiences; who dismissed truth in any absolute sense, and therefore felt free to reconstrue or reinterpret phenomena; who challenged the concept of objective reality and felt free to play in the world of make-believe; who perceived events as occurring to individuals and, therefore, was interested in the interpretations of these events by individuals; who viewed his own theory as only a tentative formulation and who, consequently, was free to challenge views that others accepted as fact; who experienced the frustration and challenge, the threat and joy, of exploring the unknown.

To a greater extent than any other personality theorist, Kelly based his theory of personality on an extremely explicit view of science and the nature of scientific inquiry. The fundamental question to consider here is "What are scientists doing when they are constructing theories?" One view is that the scientist is searching for truth. Maybe there is a "true" theory out there and, armed with the methods of the sciences, the diligent scientist can find it. This conception implies that all theories can be evaluated as being true or false. A different view, adopted by Kelly (and many contemporary scientists and philosophers of science, e.g., Proctor & Capaldi, 2001) is that "true versus false" is not the right question to ask about a scientific theory. The problem is that any complex and well-formulated theory is likely to seem true in some respects but not others. An alternative question to ask, then, is whether and how a theory is *useful*. Does the theory enable one to do some useful things that one could not do without the theory? This question does raise another one: How does one evaluate a theory's usefulness? Kelly reasoned that scientists often are interested in predicting events; they find it useful to be able to predict how events will turn out. This reasoning converts questions about utility into questions about prediction: What important events can one predict using a given theory?

The simple idea of evaluating a theory according to its usefulness for making predictions has a significant implication. Different theories may enable one to make different types of predictions. Thus, different theories each may be uniquely useful. This implies that one does not need to choose between theories, accepting one as right and seeing the others as wrong. Instead, it may be valuable to see the world through the lens of different theories, each of which may enable one to see something interesting. Kelly called this idea **constructive alternativism**: alternative scientific constructs each may provide a useful view of the world. According to this position, there is no objective reality or absolute truth to discover. Instead, there are efforts to construe events—to interpret phenomena in order to make sense of them. There are always alternative constructions available from which to choose.

In Kelly's view, then, the enterprise of personality science is not concerned with the discovery of truth or, as Freud might have suggested, the uncovering of things in the mind previously hidden. Rather, it is an effort to develop scientific construct systems that are useful in predicting events. Different personality theories each may make unique and valid predictions about persons.

Kelly developed these ideas in part because he was concerned about the tendency toward dogma in psychology. He thought psychologists believed that constructs of inner states and traits actually existed rather than understanding them as "things" in a theoretician's head. If someone is described as an introvert, we tend to check to see whether he is an introvert, rather than checking the person who is responsible for the statement. Kelly's position against "truth" and dogma is of considerable significance. It allows one to establish an "invitational mood" in which one is free to invite many alternative interpretations of phenomena and to entertain propositions that initially may seem absurd. The invitational mood is a necessary part of the exploration of the world, for the professional scientist as well as for the patient in therapy.

According to Kelly, it is this invitational mood that allows one the freedom to develop creative hypotheses. A hypothesis should not be asserted as a fact,

[handwritten margin note:] Kelly is a "constructivist" — we are bound by our own "constructs" of ourselves"

1. There is no objective reality and there are no "facts." Different theories have different constructions of phenomena. These theories also have different ranges of convenience and different foci of convenience.
2. Theories should lead to research. However, an extreme emphasis on measurement can be limiting and lead to viewing concepts as "things" rather than as representations.
3. The clinical method is useful because it leads to new ideas and focuses attention on important questions.
4. A good theory of personality should help us to solve the problems of people and society.
5. Theories are designed to be modified and abandoned.

Figure 11.1 Some Components of Kelly's View of Science.

but instead should allow the scientist to pursue its implications as if it were true. Kelly viewed a theory as a tentative expression of what has been observed and of what is expected. A theory has a **range of convenience**, indicating the boundaries of phenomena the theory can cover, and a **focus of convenience**, indicating the points within the boundaries where the theory works best. Different theories have different ranges and different foci of convenience.

For Kelly, theories were modifiable and ultimately expendable. A theory is modified or discarded when it stops leading to new predictions or leads to incorrect predictions. Among scientists, as well as among people in general, how long one holds onto a theory in the face of contradictory information is partly a matter of taste and style.

Kelly's view of science is not unique, yet its clarity of expression and points of emphasis remain important (Figure 11.1). In addition to highlighting the utility of a theory (rather than its truth versus falsity), Kelly also questioned other traditional assumptions. These include psychologists' extreme emphasis on measurement. In Kelly's time, and today, much work in personality psychology is devoted to the precise measure of individual differences in one versus another psychological construct. Kelly felt that this emphasis on measurement leads personality theorists erroneously to view theoretical concepts as if they are real things in people's heads. The psychologist inadvertently becomes a technician whose primary expertise is in statistics, rather than being a scientist whose primary expertise is in the study of the human mind. A third feature of Kelly's view of science is that it leaves room for clinical as opposed to purely experimental methods. He considered the clinical method useful because it speaks the language of hypothesis, because it leads to the emergence of new variables, and because it focuses on important questions. Here we have a fourth significant aspect of Kelly's view of science: it should focus on important issues. Kelly felt that psychologists often feared doing anything that might not be recognized as science. This fear caused them to avoid studying important aspects of human experience that are difficult to test scientifically. Kelly urged that psychologists stop trying to look scientific and get on with the job of understanding people. He believed that a good scientific theory should encourage the invention of new approaches to the solution of the problems of people and society.

We have reviewed Kelly's view of science in detail because it is intimately connected to his view of persons. Kelly felt that scientists and laypersons (i.e., nonscientists in their everyday life) are engaged in the same task. They both use constructs to predict events. The scientists' constructs surely may differ from those of the layperson; they may be stated in a more precise manner and (depending on the science) may involve mathematical concepts rather than words. Yet the scientists' and laypersons' tasks are fundamentally similar. Both try to develop ideas (i.e., constructs) that enable them to predict events. The personality scientist may have a formal theory that enables her to make some types of predictions (e.g., a trait theorist might be able to predict your scores on personality traits 5 years from now based on your scores today). But your wise grandmother may have an informal, "nonscientific" theory that enables her to make a different set of predictions (e.g., whether one versus another type of discussion will cheer you up if you're having a down day). In both cases, the person is using accumulated knowledge to make predictions.

This reasoning underlies a metaphor that is central to Kelly's view of persons. It is the "person-as-scientist" metaphor. To Kelly, the central features of everyday life involve our attempts to develop ideas that enable us to predict significant events in our daily life. We want to be able to predict whether we will, for example, pass an upcoming exam, succeed in getting a date, or get out of a state of depression. We also want to predict which types of experiences might help us to achieve these goals. In making these predictions, Kelly argues, we operate as scientists. Like scientists, we develop theories ("maybe I'm the sort of person who needs to work with friends when studying for exams"), we test hypotheses ("this time I'll try a different strategy of asking for a date and see what happens"), and we weigh evidence ("last time I tried to relieve my depression by eating a lot of desserts, but that didn't work").

The person-as-scientist view has two further consequences. First, it highlights the fact that people are essentially oriented toward the future. "It is the future which tantalizes man, not the past. Always he reaches out to the future through the window of the present" (Kelly, 1955, p. 49). Much of human thinking indeed is directed toward future events. Of the personality theories we have discussed so far, Kelly's is the one that most directly confronts this basic fact of mental life.

The second consequence is the following. If scientists can usefully adopt different theories to make different types of predictions, then so can laypersons. Just as there can be constructive alternativism in the domain of scientific constructs discussed previously, there can be constructive alternativism in the domain of personal constructs. People have the capacity to think constructively about the environment—to "re-think" their usual ways of construing the world. The individual can develop alternative theoretical formulations, can "try on different constructs," and in so doing can devise novel strategies for dealing with the challenges and conflicts of life.

This view of people's capacity to think constructively about the world yields a new understanding of an issue discussed in our previous chapter of this book, namely, free will and determinism. To behaviorists such as Skinner, people merely responded to the environment. They thus were controlled by environmental forces and lacked free will. To Kelly, however, people do not respond passively to the environment. They think actively about it. Not only that, people actively think about their own thought processes. These thinking capacities make human beings both free and determined. "This personal construct system provides him [humankind] with both freedom of decision and limitations of action—freedom, because it permits him to deal with the meaning of events rather than forces him to be helplessly pushed about by them, and limitation, because he can never make choices outside the world of alternatives he has erected for himself" (Kelly, 1958, p. 58). Having "enslaved" ourselves with these constructions, we are able to win freedom again and again by reconstruing the environment and life. Thus, we are not victims of past history or of present circumstances—unless we choose to construe ourselves in that way.[*]

These points are the general principles upon which Kelly built a theory of personality structures and processes. We now turn to the details of that theory.

THE PERSONALITY THEORY OF GEORGE A. KELLY

STRUCTURE

The key structural variable in Kelly's theory of personality is the personal *construct*. A **construct** is a concept used to interpret, or construe, the world. People use these concepts to categorize events and to chart a course of behavior. According to Kelly, a person anticipates events by observing patterns and regularities. A person experiences events, interprets them, and places a structure and a meaning on them. In experiencing events, individuals notice that some events share characteristics that distinguish them from other events. Individuals distinguish similarities and contrasts. They observe that some people are tall and some are short, that some are men and some are women, that some things are hard and some are soft. It is this construing of a similarity and a contrast that leads to the formation of a construct. Without constructs, life would be chaotic—we wouldn't be able to organize our worlds, to describe and classify events, objects, and people.

According to Kelly, at least three elements are necessary to form a construct: two of the elements must be perceived as similar to each other, and the third element must be perceived as different from these two. The way in which two elements are construed to be similar forms the **similarity pole** of the construct; the way in which they are contrasted with the third element forms the **contrast pole** of the construct. For example, observing two people helping someone and a third hurting someone could lead to the construct kind/cruel, with kind forming the similarity pole and cruel the contrast pole. Kelly stressed the importance of recognizing that a construct is composed of a similarity/contrast comparison. This suggests that we do not understand the nature of a construct when it uses only the similarity pole or the contrast pole. We do not know what the construct respect means to a person until we know what events the person includes under this construct and what events are viewed as being opposed to it.

A construct is not dimensional in the sense of having many points between the similarity and contrast poles. Subtleties or refinements in construction of

---

[*]Kelly's references to "man the scientist" and "man the biological organism" may strike students as sexist. It should be remembered that Kelly was writing in the 1950s, prior to efforts to remove sexism from language.

events are made through the use of other constructs, such as constructs of quantity and quality. For example, the construct black/white in combination with a quantity construct leads to the four-scale value of black, slightly black, slightly white, and white (Sechrest, 1963).

Constructs and Their Interpersonal Consequences

It is fascinating as well as enlightening to think of the constructs people use. Often they are part of the person's everyday language, though the individual might be surprised to learn that these are only constructs and that alternative ways of viewing the world are possible. Think, for example, of the constructs that are part of your own construct system. What are the terms or characteristics you use to describe people? Does each term include an opposite one to form a similarity/contrast pair, or is one end of the construct missing in some cases? Can you think of constructs that people you know use to say something about themselves as individuals? What constructs are shared by members of one social class or culture and not shared by members of a different social class or culture? Finally, consider Kelly's suggestion that whatever constructs one applies to others are potentially applicable to the self. "One cannot call another person a bastard without making bastardy a dimension of his own life also" (Kelly, 1955, p. 133).

Differences in construct systems are often part of the problem in communications between groups. In fact, consider a specific application of this point: Can you think of constructs that people use and that often result in problems in interpersonal relationships? For example, a frequent problem in marital relationships is when both partners emphasize the core construct guilty/innocent. Typically, each then argues that he or she is the "innocent" party and their partner is "to blame" for the difficulties. Both may initially see the counselor as a judge who will render a verdict rather than as someone who may help them to view things in another light or revise their constructs.

Another example concerns a friend of one of the authors who once said: "Isn't there a winner and a loser in every relationship?" That person was obviously unaware that "winner/loser" is a possible, but not a necessary, construct. Another person might have used the construct compromising/uncompromising person or compassionate/uncompassionate person. Such different constructions would lead to very different patterns of relationships. Many marital relationships run into trouble because they are construed in power terms and tests of will rather than in terms of help and empathy. Thus, although seemingly abstract, constructs can be seen as very much influencing basic aspects of our daily lives.

Types of Constructs and the Construct System

We need not assume from this discussion that constructs are verbal or that they are always verbally available to a person. Although Kelly emphasized the cognitive aspects of human functioning—the ones that Freudians would call the conscious—he did take into consideration phenomena described by Freudians as being unconscious. Kelly did not use the conscious-unconscious construct; however, he did use the **verbal/preverbal construct** to deal with some of the elements that are otherwise interpreted as conscious or unconscious. A verbal construct can be expressed in words, whereas a preverbal con-

HAVING WORDS FOR WHAT YOU SEE, TASTE, AND SMELL

"Why are we so inarticulate about these things?" said a student in referring to tastes, odors, and touch sensations. What would the implications be if we had a greater vocabulary for experience, that is, if we had more constructs for such phenomena? Can having more taste constructs develop one's sense of taste? More odor constructs one's sense of smell? Is the secret to becoming a food connoisseur the development of one's construct system?

At one time it was thought that language determines how we perceive and organize the

Unity of Constructs: *Having a relevant constructs may facilitate sensitivity to tastes and odors.*

world. In light of today's evidence, such a view seems too extreme. We are capable of sensing and recognizing many things for which we have no name or concept. However, having a concept or construct may facilitate experiencing and recalling some phenomena. For example, research on odor identification suggests that having the right words to describe an odor facilitates recognition of the odor: "People can improve their ability to identify odors through practice. More specifically, they can improve it through various cognitive interventions in which words are used to endow odors with perceptual or olfactory identity." A name for a smell helps to transform it from vague to clear. Not just any word will do, since some words seem to capture better the sensory experience than others do. The important fact, however, is that cognition does play an important role in virtually all aspects of sensory experience.

In sum, expanding one's sensory construct system alone may not provide for increased sensitivity to sensory experience but, together with practice, it can go a long way toward doing so. Want to become a food connoisseur? Practice, but also expand your construct system.

SOURCE: *Psychology Today*, July 1981.

struct is one that is used even though the person has no words to express it. A preverbal construct is learned before the person develops the use of language. Sometimes, one end of a construct is not available for verbalization; it is characterized as being **submerged**. If a person insists that people do only good things, one assumes that the other end of the construct has been submerged since the person must have been aware of contrasting behaviors to have formed the "good" end of the construct. Thus, constructs may not be available for verbalization, and the individual may not be able to report all the elements that are in the construct. In spite of the recognized importance of preverbal

Core Constructs: *Marital difficulties can revolve around the use of core constructs such as guilty/innocent.*

and submerged constructs, ways of studying them have not been highly developed by personal construct psychologists.

The constructs used by a person in interpreting and anticipating events are organized as part of a system. Each construct within the system has a range of convenience and a focus of convenience. A construct's range of convenience comprises all those events for which the user would find application of the construct useful. A construct's focus of convenience comprises the particular events for which application of the construct would be maximally useful. For example, the construct caring/uncaring, which might apply to people in all situations where help is given (range of convenience), would be particularly applicable in situations where special sensitivity and effort are required (focus of convenience). In addition, some constructs are more central to the person's construct system than are others. Thus, there are **core constructs** that are basic to a person's functioning and can be changed only with great consequences for the rest of the construct system, and **peripheral constructs** that are much less basic and can be altered without serious modification of the core structure.

The construct system is also organized in terms of a hierarchy. An example of a hierarchy in the animal kingdom is ANIMAL/Dog/golden retriever. In a hierarchy, the broadest and most inclusive constructs are the superordinate constructs at the top of the hierarchy (e.g., ANIMAL). These **superordinate constructs** include more narrow and specific constructs, such as dog, cat, and giraffe in our example. In turn, each of these middle-level constructs includes a large number of even more narrow **subordinate constructs** (e.g., golden retriever, German shepherd, poodle, etc.). Constructs, then, differ in their breadth and inclusiveness.

It is important to recognize that the constructs within the person's construct system are interrelated. Behavior, then, expresses the construct *system* rather than a single construct. Change in one construct can trigger changes in other parts of the system. Although constructs generally are consistent with one another, some constructs conflict with others, which produces strain and difficulties for a person in making choices (Landfield, 1982).

To summarize, according to Kelly's theory of personal constructs, an individual's personality is made up of his or her construct system. A person uses constructs to interpret the world and to anticipate events. The constructs a person uses thus define his or her world. People naturally differ from one another in the constructs they use and in the organization among constructs in their overall system of knowledge. If you want to understand a person, you must know something about the constructs that person uses, the events subsumed under these constructs, the way in which these constructs tend to function, and the way in which they are organized in relation to one another to form a system (Adams-Webber, 1998).

The Role Construct Repertory (Rep) Test

Knowing other people, then, is knowing how they construe the world. How does one gain this knowledge of a person's constructs? Kelly's answer is direct—ask them to tell you what their constructs are. "If you don't know what is going on in a person's mind, ask him; he may tell you" (1958b, p. 330). Instead of using tests that had been developed by others in relation to different theoretical systems, Kelly developed his own assessment technique—the **Role Construct Repertory Test (Rep test)**. As an assessment technique the Rep test is probably more closely related to a theory of personality than is any other comprehensive personality test. The Rep test was developed out of Kelly's construct theory and was designed to be used as a way of eliciting personal constructs.

Basically the Rep test consists of two procedures—(a) the development of a list of actual persons based on a Role Title List and (b) the development of constructs based on the comparison of triads of persons. In the first procedure, the subject is given a Role Title List or list of roles (figures) believed to be of importance to all people. Illustrative role titles are mother, father, a teacher you liked, or a neighbor you find hard to understand. Generally, 20 to 30 roles are presented and subjects are asked to name a person they have known who fits each role. Following this, the examiner picks three specific figures from the list and asks the subject to indicate the way in which two are alike and are different from the third. The way in which two of the figures are seen as alike is called the similarity pole of the construct, and the way in which the third is different is called the contrast pole of the construct. For example, a subject might be asked to consider the persons named for Mother, Father, and Liked Teacher. In considering the three, the subject might decide that the people associated with the titles Father and Liked Teacher are similar in being outgoing and different from Mother, who is shy. Thus, the construct outgoing/shy has been formed. The subject is asked to consider other groups of three persons (triads), usually 20 to 30 of them. With each presentation of a triad, the subject generates a construct. The construct given may be the same as a previous one or a new construct. Illustrative constructs given by one person are presented in Table 11.1.

The structure of the Rep test follows directly from Kelly's theory. The test elicits people's constructs—or ways of perceiving the world—based on their consideration of the way in which two things are similar to each other and different from the third. It is particularly attractive since subjects are completely free to express how they construe the world. At the same time, however, it makes a

Table 11.1   Role Construct Repertory Test: Illustrative Constructs

Similar Figures	Similarity Construct	Dissimilar Figure	Contrasting Construct
Self, Father	Emphasis on happiness	Mother	Emphasis on practicality
Teacher, Happy person	Calm	Sister	Anxious
Male friend, Female friend	Good listener	Past friend	Trouble expressing feelings
Disliked person, Employer	Uses people for own ends	Liked person	Considerate of others
Father, Successful person	Active in the community	Employer	Not active in the community
Disliked person, Employer	Cuts others down	Sister	Respectful of others
Mother, Male friend	Introvert	Past friend	Extravert
Self, Teacher	Self-sufficient	Person helped	Dependent
Self, Female friend	Artistic	Male friend	Uncreative
Employer, Female friend	Sophisticated	Brother	Unsophisticated

number of important assumptions. First, it is assumed that the list of roles presented to the subjects is representative of the important figures in their lives. Second, it is assumed that the constructs verbalized by the subject are, indeed, the ones used to construe the world. In turn, this assumes that the subjects can verbalize their constructs and that they feel free to report them in the testing situation. Finally, it is assumed that the words the subjects use in naming their constructs are adequate to give the examiner an understanding of how the subjects have organized their past events and how they anticipate the future.

One of the remarkable features of the Rep test is its tremendous flexibility. By varying the role titles or instructions, one can determine a whole range of constructs and meanings. For example, a modification of the Rep test has been used to determine the constructs consumers use in purchasing cosmetics and perfumes. These constructs are then used by advertisers to develop advertisements that will appeal to consumers (Stewart & Stewart, 1982). In another study, a Sex Rep was developed to measure the meanings men and women associate with the concepts of masculinity and femininity. Earlier research on sex role stereotypes had found that both men and women perceive personality characteristics associated with the concept of masculinity more positively than they do characteristics associated with the concept of femininity. In contrast with such results, research using the Sex Rep suggested that women could see themselves as feminine and still be high on self-esteem and health. In other words, the cultural image or stereotype of the concepts masculinity and femininity may be quite different from the personal meanings associated with these concepts (Baldwin, Critelli, Stevens, & Russell, 1986). At the stereotype level, the personality characteristics associated with the concept of masculinity may be more favorable or desirable for both men and women. At the personal level, however, psychological health may be reflected in men seeing themselves as masculine and women seeing themselves as feminine, with neither being perceived as intrinsically better than the other. The Rep test offers a method for arriving at such personal meanings.

Unique Information Revealed by Personal Construct Testing

As you can tell from the description above, the Rep test is rather complicated. Administering and scoring the test is a more complex, time-consuming procedure than, for example, merely giving people a small set of standard person-

CURRENT APPLICATIONS

A REP TEST FOR CHILDREN: HOW DO THEY CONSTRUE PERSONALITY?

What kinds of constructs do you use to differentiate among people you know? For example, how are your mother and father similar to each other but different from yourself? Has the way you construe the similarities and differences between your parents and yourself changed since you were a child? A study by Donahue (1994) suggests that your construct system has changed both in content and in form. Donahue used a simplified version of Kelly's Rep test to elicit the constructs eleven-year-olds use to describe personality. The children nominated nine individuals: self, best friend, an opposite-sex peer "who sits near you at school," a disliked peer, mother (or mother figure), father (or father figure), a liked teacher, the ideal self, and a disliked adult. The individuals' names were written on cards, and presented in sets of three. For example, to elicit the first construct, the children had to consider the self, the best friend, and the liked teacher. They then generated a word or phrase to describe how two of the individuals were alike, and an opposite word to describe how the third person was different from the other two. In this way, each child generated nine constructs.

What kinds of constructs did the children use? In terms of content, Donahue categorized the constructs according to the "Big Five" dimensions of personality description—extraversion, agreeableness, conscientiousness, emotional stability, and openness to experience (see Chapter 8). Although the children used constructs from all Big Five

domains, the vast majority of their constructs dealt with Agreeableness (e.g., "is nice" versus "gets into fights") and Extraversion ("wants to be in charge" versus "likes to play quiet"). In contrast to the personality descriptions of adults, the children used the other three Big Five dimensions much less frequently. Thus, most of their constructs were interpersonal in nature—reflecting the importance of getting along with their peers, parents, and teachers.

In terms of form, Donahue coded six distinct ways of structuring or expressing personal constructs: facts ("from Oklahoma"), habits ("eats lots of sweets"), skills ("is the marble champion"), preferences ("likes comic books"), behavioral trends ("always in trouble with the teacher"), and traits ("shy"). As expected, the children used fewer trait descriptors and many more facts than adults. These findings suggest that children's construct systems are more concrete and become more abstract and psychological as they mature into adults.

These findings show that the Rep test allows us to see how personal construct systems are defined across ages in terms of both content and form. Of course, many other interesting comparisons are possible. For example, how do you think the construct systems of women and men differ? What about those of different ethnic groups or cultures? The Rep test allows us to explore both what is unique and what is shared in the way we construe the world around us.

SOURCE: Donahue (1994).

ality trait tests and computing Big Five scores (see Chapter 8). Is the effort worth it? Does one actually learn unique information about the individual being tested by following the procedures suggested by Kelly? Or might it be possible to get the same information by using simpler procedures based on trait theory?

This question has been examined systematically in research by Grice (in press). He administered two types of tests to a sample of research participants: (1) an idiographic grid procedure that was modeled closely after Kelly's Rep test for assessing personal constructs, and (2) a nomothetic grid technique in which people made personality ratings using a fixed set of Big Five markers, rather than using the potentially unique personality descriptors that are revealed by Kelly's procedure. The question, then, is the degree to which the idiographic personal construct procedure reveals information that is unique, that is, information that is not revealed by the nomothetic Big Five procedure.

This question was addressed by statistical analyses of these two forms of personality assessment. The findings revealed that the procedures overlapped only partly. Specifically, about half of the variation in personality ratings made in personal construct testing was predictable from Big Five scores, whereas the other half was unique (Grice, in press). Kelly's personal construct method would, then, appear to be well worth the effort. Half of the information that is learned about individuals through Kelly's test would be lost if one employed merely Big Five testing methods. As Grice (in press) explains, "when left to their own devices" in Kelly's idiographic procedure, people commonly go "beyond personality traits (viz. the Big Five) to describe themselves and other people" (msp. 26).

Cognitive Complexity/Simplicity

As noted, one can describe people not only in terms of the content of their constructs but also in terms of the structure of the construct system. Both the Rep test and modifications of it have again proved to be useful in this regard. An early effort to look at structural aspects of the construct system was Bieri's (1955) study of **cognitive complexity**. Bieri designated the degree to which a construct system is broken down (levels in the hierarchy) or differentiated as reflecting the system's cognitive complexity/simplicity. A cognitively complex system contains many constructs and provides for considerable differentiation in perception of phenomena. A cognitively simple system contains few constructs and provides for poor differentiation in perception of phenomena. A cognitively complex person sees people in a differentiated way, as having a variety of qualities, whereas a cognitively simple person sees people in an undifferentiated way, even to the extent of using only one construct (e.g., good/bad) in construing others. Using a modified Rep test, Bieri compared cognitively complex and cognitively simple subjects in relation to their accuracy in predicting the behavior of others and in relation to their ability to discriminate between themselves and others. As predicted, it was found that cognitively complex subjects were more accurate in predicting the behavior of others than were cognitively simple subjects. Furthermore, cognitively complex subjects were more able to recognize differences between themselves and others. Presumably the greater number of constructs available to complex subjects allows for both greater accuracy and greater potential for recognition of differences.

Bieri went on to construe cognitive complexity/simplicity as a dimension of personality, defining it as an information-processing variable: "Cognitive complexity may be defined as the capacity to construe social behavior in a multidimensional way" (Bieri et al., 1966). In one study of the way in which individuals process information, it was found that subjects high in complexity differed from subjects low in complexity in the way that they handled inconsistent information about a person. Subjects high in complexity tended to try to use the inconsistent information in forming an impression, whereas subjects low in complexity tended to form a consistent impression of the person and to reject all information inconsistent with that impression (Mayo & Crockett, 1964). Later research has also indicated that more complex individuals are better able to take the role of others (Adams-Webber, 1979, 1982; Crockett, 1982). In terms of the Big Five dimensions described in Chapter 8, complexity is related most strongly to the fifth factor, openness to new experiences (Tetlock, Peterson, & Berry, 1993).

Thus, the Rep test can be used to determine the content and structure of an individual's construct system, as well as to compare the effects of different construct system structures. The Rep test has the advantages of arising from a theory and of allowing subjects to generate their own constructs, instead of forcing subjects to use dimensions provided by the tester. In sum, Kelly posits that the structure of personality consists of the construct system of the individual. An individual is what he construes himself and others to be, and the Rep test is a device to ascertain the nature of these constructions.

Contemporary researchers continue to study the complexity versus simplicity of cognitive construct systems. They are particularly interested in the complexity of beliefs about the self, or "self-complexity". Much of this interest was spurred by seminal research conducted by Patricia Linville (1985). Linville reasoned that people may differ significantly in their levels of self-complexity. Some people may possess a small number of central beliefs about the self that come into play repeatedly in one or two central circumstances in their lives. Other people may be involved in numerous life roles and may possess a rich array of different skills and personal tendencies, each of which comes into play in different settings. For example, you might have two friends, one of whom is a pre-med student who studies 60 hours a week and describes himself as being "smart" and "diligent," and the other of whom is a student, parent, church volunteer, part-time employee, and a weekend athlete, and who sees herself as having a distinct personal style in each of these different settings. The latter person would be seen as being higher in self-complexity.

Research by Linville (1985, 1987) indicated that higher levels of complexity serve as a buffer against stress. People with high self-complexity, in other words, seemed emotionally better off when things were particularly stressful in their lives. For example, if a student high in self-complexity were to fail a test, the existence of other life roles (parent, employee, etc.) seemed to serve as a useful cognitive distraction that helped them to avoid prolonged negative mood. A recent review indicates, however, that self-complexity is not consistently found to be a buffer against stress, and suggests that improvements in the measurement of self-complexity are needed (Rafaeli-Mor & Steinberg, 2002).

Finally, another promising area of contemporary study is "social identity complexity" (Roccas & Brewer, 2002). Social identity complexity refers to the complexity of people's mental representations of the social groups to which they belong. People who live in a multicultural society may recognize complex interrelations among multiple group identities.

In sum, then, the study of cognitive complexity versus simplicity stands as the most highly investigated aspect of individual differences in personal construct systems.

CURRENT APPLICATIONS

COGNITIVE COMPLEXITY, LEADERSHIP, AND INTERNATIONAL CRISES

A series of fascinating studies suggests that cognitive style, in particular the dimension of cognitive complexity-simplicity, may have important implications for leadership and international relations. For example, would one suspect that greater or lesser cognitive complexity would be advantageous for a revolutionary leader? In a study of successful and unsuccessful leaders of four revolutions (American, Russian, Chinese, Cuban), it was found that low cognitive complexity was associated with success during the phase of revolutionary struggle but high complexity was associated with success in the poststruggle consolidation phase. The suggestion made was that a categorical, single-minded approach is desirable during the early phase but that a more flexible and integrated view is necessary during the later phase. Cognitive complexity would also appear to be valuable in exercising leadership in a large corporation. Thus, successful corporate leaders are able to develop flexible plans, to include various kinds of information in their decisions, and to make connections between decisions.

How would such a characteristic relate to international relations? Evidence suggests that diplomatic communications prior to international crises are lower in cognitive complexity than are those prior to crises that do not result in war. For example, communications between the United States and the Soviet Union were much less complex prior to the outbreak of the Korean War than prior to the Berlin blockade or the Cuban missile crisis. Also, analysis of samples of Israeli and Arab speeches delivered to the United Nations General Assembly found that complexity was significantly reduced prior to each of the four wars in the Middle East (1948, 1956, 1967, 1973). Can such measures be used to predict and possibly avoid future wars or would deception be too easy?

SOURCE: Suedfeld & Tetlock, 1991.

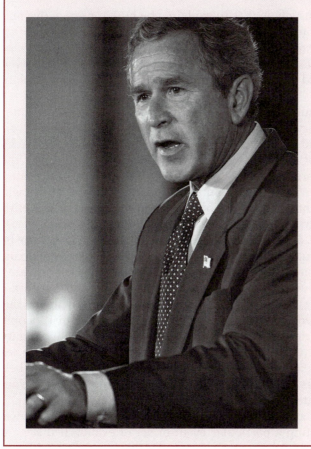

Many Americans view George W. Bush as a strong leader who is able to deal well wih crises, despite the fact that—or maybe because—his approach to problems can be characterized as low cognitive complexity.

PROCESS

The process aspects of Kelly's personal construct theory radically departed from traditional theories of motivation available in his time. As already mentioned, the psychology of personal constructs does not interpret behavior in terms of motivation, drives, and needs. For personal construct theory, the term *motivation* is redundant. This term assumes that a person is inert and needs something to get started. But, if we assume that people are basically active, the controversy as to what prods an inert organism into action becomes a dead issue. "Instead, the organism is delivered fresh into the psychological world alive and struggling" (Kelly, 1955, p. 37). Kelly contrasted other theories of motivation with his own position in the following way:

> Motivational theories can be divided into two types, push theories and pull theories. Under push theories we find such terms as drive, motive, or even stimulus. Pull theories use such constructs as purpose, value, or need. In terms of a well-known metaphor, these are the pitchfork theories on the one hand and the carrot theories on the other. But our theory is neither of these. Since we prefer to look to the nature of the animal himself, ours is probably best called a jackass theory.
>
> SOURCE: Kelly, 1958a, p. 50.

Anticipating Events

A basic task for scientific psychology is to explain why humans are active and why they direct their actions toward one goal versus another. In Kelly's time, the traditional way to explain such human capacities was in terms of "motives." Different motives presumably powered different forms of behavior. Kelly, as we noted, rejected the concept of motive. How, then, did he explain the direction of activity?

Kelly addressed this issue in what he termed the "fundamental postulate" of personal construct theory. According to this postulate, people's psychological processes are channeled by the ways in which they anticipate events. Kelly felt that the entire range of psychological outcomes that are of interest to the personality psychologist are shaped by people's anticipations of the future. People use their personal construct system to anticipate what the future will bring. Thus, the fundamental postulate links the structure aspects of Kelly's theory (the personal construct system) to ongoing dynamic processes.

In experiencing events, an individual observes similarities and contrasts, thereby developing constructs. On the basis of these constructs, individuals, like true scientists, anticipate the future. As we see the same events repeated over and over, we modify our constructs so that they will lead to more accurate predictions. Constructs are tested in terms of their predictive efficiency. But what accounts for the direction of behavior? Again, like the scientist, people choose the course of behavior that they believe offers the greatest opportunity for anticipating future events. Scientists try to develop better theories, theories that lead to the efficient prediction of events, and individuals try to develop better construct systems. Thus, according to Kelly, a person chooses the alternative that promises the greatest further development of the construct system.

In making a choice of a particular construct, the individual, in a sense, makes a "bet" by anticipating a particular event or set of events. If there are inconsistencies in the construct system, the bets will not add up; they will cancel each other out. If the system is consistent, a prediction is made that can be tested. If the anticipated event does occur, the prediction has been upheld and the construct validated, at least for the time being. If the anticipated event does not occur, the construct has been invalidated. In the latter case, the individual must develop a new construct or must loosen or expand the old construct to include the prediction of the event that took place.

In essence, then, individuals make predictions and consider further changes in their construct systems on the basis of whether those changes have led to accurate predictions. Notice that individuals do not seek reinforcement or the avoidance of pain; instead, they seek validation and expansion of their construct systems. If a person expects something unpleasant and that event occurs, he or she experiences validation regardless of the fact that it was a negative, unpleasant event. Indeed, a painful event may even be preferred to a neutral or pleasant event if it confirms the predictive system (Pervin, 1964).

One should understand that Kelly is not suggesting that the individual seeks certainty, such as would be found in the repetitive ticking of a clock. The boredom people feel with repeated events and the fatalism that comes as a result of the inevitable are usually avoided wherever possible. Rather, individuals seek to anticipate events and to increase the range of convenience or boundaries of their construct systems. This point leads to a distinction between the views of Kelly and the views of Rogers. According to Kelly, individuals do not seek consistency for consistency's sake or even for self-consistency. Instead, individuals seek to anticipate events, and it is a consistent system that allows them to do this.

Anxiety, Fear, and Threat

Thus far, Kelly's system appears to be reasonably simple and straightforward. The process view becomes more complicated with the introduction of the concepts of **anxiety, fear**, and **threat**. Kelly defined anxiety in the following way: Anxiety is the recognition that the events with which one is confronted lie outside the range of convenience of one's construct system. One is anxious when one is without constructs, when one has "lost his structural grip on events," when one is "caught with his constructs down. People protect themselves from anxiety in various ways. Confronted by events they cannot construe—that is, that lie outside their range of convenience—individuals may broaden a construct and permit it to apply to a greater variety of events, or they may narrow their constructs and focus on minute details. For example, suppose an individual who has the construct caring person/selfish person and considers herself a caring person finds herself acting in a selfish way. How can she construe herself and events? She can broaden the construct caring person to include selfish behavior, or—probably more easily in this case—restrict the construct caring person to important people in her life, rather than people generally. In the latter case, the construct applies to a more limited set of people or events.

In contrast to anxiety, one experiences fear when a new construct appears to be about to enter the construct system. Of even greater significance is the experience of threat. Threat is defined as the awareness of imminent comprehensive change in one's core structure. A person feels threatened when a major shakeup in the construct system is about to occur. One feels threatened by death if it is perceived as imminent and if it involves a drastic change in one's core constructs. Death is not threatening when it does not seem imminent or when it is not construed as being fundamental to the meaning of one's life.

Encountering people from different cultures is an experience that may expand one's construct system.

Threat, in particular, has a wide range of ramifications. Whenever people undertake some new activity, they expose themselves to confusion and threat. Individuals experience threat when they realize that their construct system is about to be drastically affected by what has been discovered. "This is the moment of threat. It is the threshold between confusion and certainty, between anxiety and boredom. It is precisely at this moment when we are most tempted to turn back" (Kelly, 1964, p. 141). The response to threat may be to give up the adventure—to regress to old constructs to avoid panic. Threat occurs as we venture into human understanding and when we stand on the brink of a profound change in ourselves.

Threat, the awareness of imminent comprehensive change in one's core structure, can be experienced in relation to many things. Consider, for example, the experience of music majors who are going to perform before a music jury that will determine whether they pass for the semester. To what extent can they be expected to experience threat associated with the possibility of failure? Why should some music majors experience more performance anxiety than others? Following Kelly, two psychologists tested the hypothesis that students would feel threatened by the possibility of failure by a music jury to the extent that such failure implied reorganization of the self-construal component of their construct system. To test this hypothesis, at the beginning of the semester, music majors were administered a Threat Index consisting of 40 core constructs (e.g., competent/incompetent, productive/unproductive, bad/good) in relation to which they first rated the self and then the self-if-performed-poorly on the jury. The Threat Index score consisted of the number of core constructs on which the self and self-if-performed-poorly were rated on opposite poles. Anxiety was measured through the use of a questionnaire at the beginning of the semester and three days before the onset of the music juries. Consistent with personal construct theory, those students who reported that failure on the jury would result in the most comprehensive change in self-construal were also those who reported the greatest increase in anxiety as the date of the jury approached (Tobacyk & Downs, 1986).

Unfortunately, the investigators in this study used the concept of anxiety in a way that was not necessarily consistent with Kelly's views. Even more significant, what was not studied in this case was the experiences of students anticipating the possibility of performing much better before the jury than would be expected on the basis of their self-construal; that is, would comprehensive change as a result of unexpected exceptional performance also be associated with threat? This is important since in Kelly's view it is the awareness of imminent comprehensive change in the construct system that is threatening, not failure per se.

Some personal construct psychologists have focused their research attention on attitudes toward death, both in terms of the ways in which death is construed and the amount of threat associated with death (Moore & Neimeyer, 1991; Neimeyer, 1994). In terms of how death is construed, research suggests that people use constructs such as purposeful/purposeless, positive/negative, acceptance/rejection, anticipated/unanticipated, and final/afterlife. In terms of the amount of threat associated with death, research has involved measurement of the discrepancy between the ways in which individuals construe themselves and the ways in which they construe death. In other words, in personal construct theory terms, death threat is high when the person is unable to construe death as relevant to the self. As measured by the Threat Index, individuals rate themselves and their own death on constructs such as healthy/sick, strong/weak, predictable/random, and useful/useless. An individual's threat score represents the difference between the two sets of ratings. Presumably in the case of a large self/death discrepancy, interpretation of the death construct as relevant to the self would involve comprehensive change in one's construct system. Death threat, as defined in this way, has been found to be lower in hospice patients than general hospital patients, lower in individuals open to feelings as opposed to those who repress feelings, and lower in self-actualizing individuals as opposed to individuals less oriented toward growth and self-actualization.

What makes the concepts of anxiety, fear, and threat so significant is that they suggest a new dimension to Kelly's view of human functioning. The dynamics of functioning can now be seen to involve the interplay between the individual's wish to expand the construct system and the desire to avoid the threat of disruption of that system. Individuals always seek to maintain and enhance their predictive systems. However, in the face of anxiety and threat, individuals may rigidly adhere to a constricted system instead of venturing out into the risky realm of expansion of their construct systems.

To summarize the process aspects of personal construct theory, Kelly assumes an active organism, and he does not posit any motivational forces. For Kelly, people behave as scientists in construing events, in making predictions, and in seeking expansion of the construct system. Sometimes, not unlike the scientist, we are made so anxious by the unknowns and so threatened by the unfamiliar that we seek to hold on to absolute truths and become dogmatic. On the other hand, when we are behaving as good scientists, we are able to adopt the invitational mood and to expose our construct systems to the diversity of events that make up life.

Kelly was never explicit about the origins of construct systems. He stated that **GROWTH AND** constructs are derived from observing repeated patterns of events. But he did **DEVELOPMENT** little to elaborate on the kinds of events that lead to differences like the ones between simple and complex construct systems. Kelly's comments relating to

Development of the Construct System. *Being exposed to many stimuli facilitates development of the construct system. Aware of this, some parents try to develop "superbabies."*

growth and development are limited to an emphasis on the development of preverbal constructs in infancy and the interpretation of culture as involving a process of learned expectations. People belong to the same cultural group in that they share certain ways of construing events and have the same kinds of expectations regarding behavior.

Developmental research associated with personal construct theory generally has emphasized two kinds of change. First, there has been exploration of increases in complexity of the construct system associated with age (Crockett, 1982; Hayden, 1982; Loevinger, 1993). Second, there has been exploration of qualitative changes in the nature of the constructs formed and in the ability of children to be more empathic or aware of the construct systems of others (Adams-Webber, 1982; Donahue, 1994; Morrison & Cometa, 1982; Sigel, 1981). In terms of construct system complexity, there is evidence that as children develop they increase the number of constructs available to them, make finer differentiations, and show more hierarchical organization or integration. In terms of empathy, there is evidence that as children develop they become increasingly aware that many events are not related to the self and increasingly able to appreciate the constructs of others (Sigel, 1981).

Two studies have been reported that are relevant to the question of the determinants of complex cognitive structures. In one study, the subjects' level of cognitive complexity was found to be related to the variety of cultural backgrounds to which they had been exposed in childhood (Sechrest & Jackson, 1961). In another study, parents of cognitively complex children were found to be more likely to grant autonomy and less likely to be authoritarian than were the parents of children low in cognitive complexity (Cross, 1966). Presumably, the opportunity to examine many different events and to have many different experiences is conducive to the development of a complex structure. One

[handwritten margin notes: admits no new content into it Impermeable — fixed, rigid / permeable — allows almost any new content into it]

would also expect to find that children who experience a long-standing and severe threat from authoritarian parents would develop constricted and inflexible construct systems.

The question of factors determining the content of constructs and the complexity of construct systems is of critical importance. In particular, it is relevant to the field of education, since a part of education appears to be the development of complex, flexible, and adaptive construct systems. Unfortunately, Kelly himself made few statements in this area. Kelly's theory simply did not treat questions of development as thoroughly as would have been ideal. Relatively little contemporary research on personality development is directly guided by the postulates of personal construct theory.

PSYCHOPATHOLOGY

[handwritten: know]

According to Kelly, psychopathology is a disordered response to anxiety. As in the theories of Freud and Rogers, the concepts of anxiety, fear, and threat play a major role in Kelly's theory of psychopathology. However, it must be kept in mind that these concepts, although retained, have been redefined in terms relevant to personal construct theory.

For Kelly, psychopathology is defined in terms of disordered functioning of a construct system. Only a poor scientist retains a theory and makes the same predictions despite repeated research failures. Similarly, abnormal behavior involves efforts to retain the content and structure of the construct system despite repeated incorrect predictions or invalidations. At the root of this rigid adherence to a construct system are anxiety, fear, and threat. Kelly stated that one could construe human behavior as being directed away from ultimate anxiety. Psychological disorders are disorders involving anxiety and faulty efforts to reestablish the sense of being able to anticipate events:

> There is a sense in which all disorders of communication are disorders involving anxiety. A "neurotic" person casts about frantically for new ways of construing the events of his world. Sometimes he works on "little" events, sometimes on "big" events, but he is always fighting off anxiety. A "psychotic" person appears to have found some temporary solution for his anxiety. But it is a precarious solution, at best, and must be sustained in the face of evidence which, for most of us, would be invalidating.
>
> Source: Kelly, 1955, pp. 895–896.

Fundamental to Kelly's view of psychopathology, then, are people's efforts to avoid anxiety (the experience that one's construct system is not applicable to events) and to avoid threat (the awareness of imminent comprehensive change in the construct system). To protect against anxiety and threat, an individual employs protective devices. This view resembles that of Freud. Indeed, Kelly suggested that in the face of anxiety, individuals may act in ways that will make their constructs unavailable for verbalization, that is, not consciously available. Thus, for example, in the face of anxiety, individuals may submerge one end of a construct or suspend elements that do not fit well into a construct. These are responses to anxiety that seem very similar to the concept of repression.

CHANGE AND FIXED-ROLE THERAPY

The process of positive change is discussed by Kelly in terms of the development of better construct systems. If sickness represents the continued use of constructs in the face of consistent invalidation, psychotherapy is the process of helping clients to improve their predictions. In psychotherapy, clients are trained to be better scientists. Psychotherapy is a process of reconstruing—of reconstructing the construct system. This means that some constructs need to be replaced and some new ones added; some need to be tightened, others loosened; and some need to be made more permeable, others less permeable. Whatever the details of the process, *psychotherapy is the psychological reconstruction of life.*

Kelly developed a specific technique for developing better construct systems that he called **fixed-role therapy**. Fixed-role therapy assumes that, psychologically, people are what they represent themselves to be and that people are what they do. Fixed-role therapy encourages clients to represent themselves in new ways, to behave in new ways, to construe themselves in new ways, and thereby to become new people. The purpose of this entire procedure is to reestablish the spirit of exploration, to establish the construction of life as a creative process. Kelly was wary of the emphasis on "being oneself" as Rogers had suggested (see Chapters 5 and 6); how could one be anything else but oneself? To Kelly, remaining what one is seemed uninteresting and unadventurous. Instead he suggested that people should feel free to make believe, to play, and thereby to become.

In fixed-role therapy, clients are presented with a new personality sketch that they are asked to act out. On the basis of some understanding of the client, a group of psychologists gets together to write a description of a new

Fixed-Role Therapy. *In Kelly's fixed-role therapy clients are encouraged to behave and represent themselves in new ways. Drawing by Lippman; Copyright © 1972 The New Yorker Magazine, Inc.*

person. The task for the clients is to behave as if they were that person. The personality sketch written for each client involves the development of a new personality. Many characteristics presented in the sketch are in sharp contrast with the person's actual functioning. In the light of construct theory, Kelly suggested that it might be easier for people to play up what they believe to be the opposite of the way they generally behave than to behave just a little bit differently. Design of the sketch involves setting in motion processes that will have effects throughout the construct system. Fixed-role therapy does not aim at the readjustment of minor parts. Instead, it aims to reconstruct a personality. It offers a new role, a new personality for the client in which new hypotheses can be tested; it offers the client the opportunity to test out new ways of construing events under the full protection of make-believe.

How does the process of fixed-role therapy work? After a personality sketch is drawn up, it is presented to the client. The client decides whether the sketch sounds like someone he would like to know, and whether he would feel comfortable with such a person. This is done to make sure that the new personality will not be excessively threatening to the client. In the next phase of fixed-role therapy, the therapist invites the client to act as if he were that person. For about two weeks, the client is asked to forget who he is and to be this other person. If the new person is called Tom Jones, then the client is told the following: "For two weeks, try to forget who you are or that you ever were. You are Tom Jones. You act like him. You think like him. You talk to your friends the way you think he would talk. You do the things you think he would do. You even have his interests and you enjoy the things he would enjoy." The client may resist, he may feel that this is playacting and that it is hypocritical, but he is encouraged, in an accepting manner, to try it and see how it works. The client is not told that this is what he should eventually be, but he is asked to assume the new personality. He is asked to give up being himself temporarily so that he can discover himself.

> During the following weeks, the client eats, sleeps, and feels the role. Periodically, he meets with the therapist to discuss problems in acting the role. There may be some rehearsing of the personality sketch in the therapy session so that the therapist and client will have a chance to examine the functioning of the new construct system when it is actually in use. The therapist must be prepared to act as if he or she were various persons and to accept the invitational mood. The therapist must at every moment "play in strong support of an actor—the client—who is continually fumbling his lines and contaminating his role."
>
> SOURCE: Kelly, 1955, p. 399

Fixed-role therapy was not the only therapeutic technique discussed or used by Kelly (Bieri, 1986). However, it is one that is particularly associated with personal construct theory, and it does exemplify some of the principles of the personal construct theory of change. The goal of therapeutic change is the individual's reconstruction of the self. The individual drops some constructs, creates new ones, does some tightening and loosening, and develops a construct system that leads to more accurate predictions. The therapist encourages the client to make believe, to experiment, to spell out alternatives, and to reconstrue the past in the light of new constructs. The process of therapy is complex. Different clients must be treated differently, and the resistance to change must be overcome. However, positive change is possible in a situation where a good director assists in the playing of the human drama or a good teacher assists in the development of a creative scientist.

THE CASE OF JIM

Rep Test: Personal Construct Theory

Jim took the group form of Kelly's Rep test separately from the other tests (Figure 11.2). Here we have a test that is structured in terms of the roles given to the subject and the task of formulating a similarity-contrast construct. However, the subject is given total freedom in the content of the construct formed. As noted in Chapter 10, the Rep test is derived logically from Kelly's theory of personal constructs. Two major themes appear in these constructs. The first theme is the *quality of interpersonal relationships*. Basically this involves whether people

CONSTRUCT	CONTRAST
Self-satisfied	Self-doubting
Uninterested in communicating with students as people	Interested in communicating with students as people
Nice	Obnoxious
Sensitive to cues from other people	Insensitive to cues
Outgoing–gregarious	Introverted–retiring
Introspective–hung up	Self-satisfied
Intellectually dynamic	Mundane and predictable
Outstanding, successful	Mediocre
Obnoxious	Very likable
Satisfied with life	Unhappy
Shy, unsure of self	Self-confident
Worldly, openminded	Parochial, closeminded
Open, simple to understand	Complex, hard to get to know
Capable of giving great love	Somewhat self-oriented
Self-sufficient	Needs other people
Concerned with others	Oblivious to all but his own interests
So hung up that psychological health is questionable	Basically healthy and stable
Willing to hurt people in order to be "objective"	Unwilling to hurt people if he can help it
Closeminded, conservative	Openminded, liberal
Lacking in self-confidence	Self-confident
Sensitive	Insensitive, self-centered
Lacking social poise	Secure and socially poised
Bright, articulate	Average intelligence

Figure 11.2   Rep Test Data—Case of Jim.

are warm and giving or cold and narcissistic. This theme is expressed in constructs such as *gives love/is self-oriented, sensitive/insensitive, and communicates with others as people/is uninterested in others*. A second major theme concerns *security* and is expressed in constructs such as *hung up/healthy, unsure/self-confident*, and *satisfied with life/unhappy*. The frequency with which constructs relevant to these two themes appear suggests that Jim has a relatively constricted view of the world—that is, much of Jim's understanding of events is in terms of the warm/cold and secure/insecure dimensions.

How do the constructs given relate to specific people? On the sorts that involved himself, Jim used constructs expressing insecurity. Thus, Jim views himself as being like his sister (so hung up that her psychological health is questionable), in contrast to his brother, who is basically healthy and stable. In two other sorts of constructs, he sees himself as lacking self-confidence and social poise. These ways of construing himself contrast with those involving his father. His father is construed as being introverted and retiring, but also as self-sufficient, open-minded, outstanding, and successful.

The constructs used in relation to Jim's mother are interesting and again suggest conflict. On the one hand, his mother is construed to be outgoing, gregarious, and loving; on the other, she is construed to be mundane, predictable, close-minded, and conservative. The close-minded, conservative construct is particularly interesting since, in that sort, Jim's mother is paired with the person with whom he feels most uncomfortable. Thus, the mother and the person with whom he feels most uncomfortable are contrasted with his father, who is construed to be open-minded and liberal. The combination of sorts for all persons suggests that Jim's ideal person is someone who is warm, sensitive, secure, intelligent, open-minded, and successful. The women in his life—his mother, sister, girlfriend, and previous girlfriend—are construed as having some of these characteristics but also as missing others.

Comments on the Data

The Rep test gives us valuable data about how Jim construes his environment. With it we continue to use the phenomenological approach discussed in relation to Rogers, and again find that Jim's world tends to be perceived in terms of two major constructs: warm interpersonal/cold interpersonal relationships and secure, confident/insecure, unhappy people. Through the Rep test we gain an understanding of why Jim is so limited in his relationships to others and why he has so much difficulty in being creative. His restriction to only two constructs hardly leaves him free to relate to people as individuals and instead forces him to perceive people and problems in stereotyped or conventional ways. A world filled with so little perceived diversity can hardly be exciting, and the constant threat of insensitivity and rejection can be expected to fill Jim with a sense of gloom.

The data from the Rep test, like Kelly's theory, are tantalizing. What is there seems so clear and valuable, but one is left wondering about what is missing. There is a sense of the skeleton for the structure of personality, but one is left with only the bones. Jim's ways of construing himself and his environment are an important part of his personality. Assessing his constructs and his construct system helps us to understand how he interprets events and how he is led to predict the future. But where is the flesh on the bones—the sense of an individual who cannot be what he feels, the person struggling to be warm amid feelings of hostility and struggling to relate to women although confused about his feelings toward them?

RELATED POINTS OF VIEW AND RECENT DEVELOPMENTS

Psychology is different today than it was in Kelly's time. In his day, Kelly's emphasis on human cognitive processes was radical. Today, such an emphasis is mainstream. It is in this sense that Kelly anticipated future developments in the field. As we will see in the next chapter, contemporary social-cognitive approaches to personality embrace many of the same assumptions about human nature that are found in personal construct theory.

Although Kelly's theory attracted considerable attention when it was presented in 1955, it differed so greatly from the field's traditions that it spawned little research in the following decade. It was only in later years that many leads suggested by personal construct theory were explored (Neimeyer & Neimeyer, 1992). A major focus has been the Rep test and the structure of construct systems. Studies of the reliability of the Rep test suggest that the responses of individuals to the role title list and constructs used are reasonably stable over time (Landfield, 1971). Beyond this the Rep test has been used to study a variety of individuals with psychological problems, the construct systems of married couples, and people with varied interpersonal relationships (Duck, 1982). Modifications of the Rep test have been used to study the structural complexity of construct systems, the perception of situations, and, as noted, the use of nonverbal constructs. Almost every aspect of Kelly's theory has received at least some study (Mancuso & Adams-Webber, 1982). The organization of the construct system and changes in this organization associated with development are particularly noteworthy topics (Crockett, 1982). The developmental principles emphasized suggest many similarities in the developmental theories of Kelly and Piaget: (1) an emphasis on progression from a global, undifferentiated system to a differentiated, integrated one; (2) increasing use of abstract structures to handle more information more economically; (3) development in response to efforts to accommodate new elements in the cognitive system; and (4) development of the cognitive system as a system, as opposed to a simple addition of new parts or elements.

Other relevant research has roots in Kelly's personal construct theory, although it is conducted within the framework of more contemporary approaches to personality (Chapters 12 and 13). For example, the psychologist Tory Higgins (1999) has developed an approach to cognitive constructs and personality functioning that is highly compatible with Kelly's, and the social-cognitive theorist Walter Mischel has directly extended Kelly's analysis of encoding constructs as a core feature of personality (Chapter 12). Other investigators have recently considered a question to which Kelly devoted relatively little attention, namely, the possibility of cultural differences in the constructs used and how constructs are formed (Chapter 14). These contemporary developments relate to personal construct theory, but only in an indirect way. The contemporary personality psychologist has, at his or her disposal, a battery of findings, theoretical concepts, and research methods in the study of human cognition that were unavailable to Kelly. Contemporary investigators commonly use these tools to analyze precisely the same phenomena that interested Kelly. Yet they rarely do so by using the precise terms and theoretical formulations of personal construct theory. Even though Kelly remains an extraordinarily respected figure, today the details of his theory often are viewed as expendable—precisely as Kelly himself might have anticipated.

CONTEMPORARY ANALYSES OF PERSON-SITUATION BELIEFS

One illustration of this point is found in contemporary analyses of person-situation beliefs, where current research is highly compatible with the principles of personal construct theory, even though it is not directly guided by the precise ideas formulated by Kelly.

As you will recall from our coverage of the Rep test, Kelly was interested in capturing the ways in which people's beliefs come into play as they think about particular people who are significant to them. The idea is that it is not sufficient to study the person's beliefs in a manner that is isolated from life contexts. Personal constructs do not merely "sit in the head." They are *used* to make sense of the social world. Kelly explored the ways in which people use personal constructs to categorize the persons and relationships of their lives.

A similar emphasis is seen in contemporary research on relationship schemas. A "schema" is an elaborate body of knowledge about a person or thing. People use such knowledge to make judgments, quickly and efficiently, about ongoing events. For example, if you spend a lot of time listening to contemporary music, you may have an elaborate body of knowledge about musicians, bands, and musical styles—you have a "music schema." Using this schema, you can quickly make decisions about music (whether you like a particular band, a particular song, etc.). As studied in particular by Mark Baldwin (1999), a relationship schema, then, is a well-developed belief about interpersonal relationships. A relationship schema is an integration of different types of knowledge. People mentally integrate knowledge about themselves, knowledge about other people or types of people (parents, teachers, romantic partners, etc.), and knowledge about social settings (family get-togethers, classes, dates, etc.) into coherent bodies of knowledge. This integrated body of knowledge—the relationships schema—then guides people's anticipations of future events. Recent findings indicate that relationship schemas influence people's expectancies about interpersonal relationships, and that these expectancies influence people's thoughts and feelings in social encounters (Baldwin, 1999)—precisely as Kelly would have predicted.

Other recent work has explored a particular feature of people's overall construct system, namely, the degree to which a person's knowledge is highly integrated versus "compartmentalized." This line of research focuses on people's constructs about themselves and whether these constructs are evaluative positive or negative (i.e., good or bad). Everybody recognizes that there are both positive and negative features to their personality. But, as analyzed by Carolin Showers (2002), people differ in the degree to which constructs representing these features are grouped together, or compartmentalized. As Showers illustrates (Table 11.2), some people group together their positive features, seeing them as separate from negative aspects of self. "Harry" (Table 11.2) associated positive constructs with his "Renaissance scholar" self and negative constructs with his self-as-test-taker. "Sally," in contrast, views herself in terms of a mix of positive and negative constructs in different social settings. Research suggests that different types of compartmentalization have different implications for people's emotional experiences. Importantly, the effects here are not simple ones. It is *not* the case that people who show high versus low degrees of compartmentalization are, in general, significantly happier or sadder than others. Instead there is an interaction between features of the personal construct system and features of the environment. When people encounter situations that bring to mind positive features of the self, individuals who compartmentalize their constructs experience more positive moods. It appears that, since positive features of self are grouped together, thoughts about one positive aspect of self activate other positive thoughts, lifting people's mood. However, when people encounter situations that bring to mind negative features of self, then individuals who do *not* compartmentalize have more positive (or perhaps less negative) emotional experiences. In these negative situations, an integrated organization of positive and negative constructs (as shown by Sally, Table 11.2) is beneficial because negative thoughts are associated with positive constructs that serve to protect one against extremely negative emotional experiences (Showers, 2002).

Research such as that of Baldwin (1999) and Showers (2002) explores the psychological processes of interest to Kelly. The nature and organization of people's personal constructs are found to explain significant features of personality functioning. In this regard, the results can be seen as supporting personal construct theory. Yet this contemporary research is not grounded in personal construct theory. These contemporary scientists, in other words, do not turn specifically to Kelly's theorizing as a basis for their research. (Indeed, they do not find it necessary even to refer to Kelly's theory in the papers that we have cited here.) Instead, reflecting developments in the contemporary

Table 11.2   Examples of Compartmentalized Organization ("Harry") and Integrative Organization ("Sally") for Identical Items of Information about Self as Student

"Harry": Compartmentalized organization		"Sally": Integrative organization	
Renaissance scholar (+)	*Taking tests, grades (–)*	*Humanities classes (+/–)*	*Science classes (+/–)*
+ Curious	– Worrying	+ Creative	+ Disciplined
+ Disciplined	– Tense	– Insecure	+ Analytical
+ Motivated	– Distracted	+ Motivated	– Competitive
+ Creative	– Insecure	– Distracted	– Worrying
+ Analytical	– Competitive	+ Expressive	+ Curious
+ Expressive	– Moody	– Moody	– Tense

NOTE: A positive or negative valence is indicted for each category and each item. The symbol +/– denotes a mixed-valence category.

SOURCE: Adapted from Showers (1992a). Copyright © 1992 by the American Psychological Associated. Adapted by permission.

field, they ground their research in social-cognitive analyses of personality functioning—analyses to which we turn in our subsequent chapters.

CRITICAL EVALUATION: STRENGTHS AND LIMITATIONS OF PERSONAL CONSTRUCT THEORY

Kelly's structural model of personality was a significant contribution to personality theory. The interpretation of behavior in terms of the individual's construing of events is useful in theory and in practice. It allows one to consider the unique aspects of the behavior of individuals, as well as the lawfulness or regularity of much of this behavior. The Rep test, which has the advantage of being derived from the theory, is an important assessment device. Although it has been criticized by some as being so flexible as to be unmanageable (Vernon, 1963), it is recognized by others as an extremely imaginative technique, quite amenable to quantification (Kleinmuntz, 1967; Mischel, 1968). A remaining unresolved problem for the Rep test, as well as for the theory as a whole, is that it requires the individual to use words even though the theory recognizes that preverbal or submerged constructs exist. Given the clinical significance of such constructs, the lack of means for assessing them remains a serious limitation.

The process view of Kelly has several interesting facets. It clearly represents a departure from the drive-reduction or tension-reduction views of Freud and other theorists. However, the process view leaves open a number of issues. The basis for action of an individual is not really clear. For example, how does the individual know which construct will be the best predictor? How does one know which end of the construct (similarity or contrast) to use?

In his review of Kelly's theory, Bruner (1956) referred to it as the single greatest contribution of the decade between 1945 and 1955 to the theory of personality functioning. Clearly, much of the theory was new and worthwhile. However, some areas of psychology appear to be more within the range of convenience of the psychology of personal constructs than other areas. For example, until recently the theory has had little to say about growth and development. Kelly's theory offers an interesting analysis of anxiety, but it has almost nothing to say about the important emotion of depression. In fact, for all its worthwhile emphasis on cognition, the theory offers a limited view of the person. Although Kelly denied the charge, the theory is noticeably lacking in emphasis on human feelings and emotions. In his review, Bruner stated that people may not be the pigs that reinforcement theory makes of them, but he wondered also whether people are only the scientists that Kelly suggests. Bruner commented further: "I rather suspect that when some people get angry or inspired or in love, they couldn't care less about their systems as a whole! One gets the impression that the author is, in his personality theory, overreacting against a generation of irrationalism" (Bruner, 1956, p. 356). Despite efforts to come to grips with the area of human emotions (McCoy, 1981), many interpretations within the context of personal construct theory seem strained and, on the whole, human emotions remain an area outside of its range of convenience.

Two additional relevant issues are worthy of consideration. First, although construct systems have been widely studied, there is little evidence that measures of these systems that specifically were developed by Kelly are related to overt behavior (Crockett, 1982; Duck, 1982). The theory would certainly suggest that this is the case, but evidence is needed. Second, Kelly's theory of motivation remains problematic. As noted, Kelly failed to be specific about the basis for many decisions people make in terms of their construct systems. Beyond

KELLY AT A GLANCE

	Structure	Process	Growth and Development
	Constructs	Processes channelized by anticipation of events	Increased complexity and definition to construct system

this, more traditional views of motivation enter the discussion of personal construct theorists. For example, it is suggested that people do not like boredom or surprise (Mancuso & Adams-Webber, 1982). However, emphases on intermediate degrees of novelty or stimulation have typically been associated with pleasure, reinforcement, or hedonic theories of motivation. An emphasis on emotion or pleasure often enters clinical discussions. For example, Landfield (1982) suggests that a person chooses that end of a construct that is positively valued. Furthermore, in his discussion of a case he suggests that the patient stopped having an affair for emotional rather than purely cognitive reasons: "After all, she did like her husband better than her lover" (p. 203).

A final note in the evaluation of Kelly's theory concerns its current status as a basis for active research. Clearly there has been activity and interest. However, two reviews of these efforts question whether much progress is being made or whether development is being held back by reverence, insularity, and orthodoxy (Rosenberg, 1980; Schneider, 1982). As noted by a follower of Kelly, without new ideas no theory of personality can survive (Sechrest, 1977). As we have emphasized, other theoretical frameworks have begun to supplant Kelly's. A review of personal construct psychology has concluded that, except among a group of enthusiasts, Kelly's ideas often are neglected (Jankowicz, 1987). This is less true in England, where Kelly's ideas are widely known and are part of the training of most clinicians. However, in the United States, the high respect accorded to Kelly's ideas by those who know them well is not matched by a high degree of overall attention and impact on the field. This is true with regard to both research and clinical practice (Winter, 1992).

SUMMARY

In sum, personal construct theory has both strengths and limitations (Table 11.3). On the positive side, there is the following: (1) The theory makes a significant contribution by bringing to the forefront of personality the importance of cognition and construct systems. (2) It is an approach to personality that attempts to capture both the uniqueness of the individual and the lawfulness of people generally. (3) It has developed a new, interesting, and theoretically relevant assessment technique, the Rep test.

On the negative side, there is the following: (1) The theory shows relative neglect of certain important areas such as emotion and motivation. (2) Despite Kelly's view that theories are there to be reformulated and abandoned, no one since 1955 has formulated any significant new theoretical developments in personal construct theory. (3) It has remained outside of mainstream research relating work in cognitive psychology to personality. Many of these approaches give lip service to Kelly's contributions but proceed along independent lines.

Pathology	Change
Disordered functioning of the construct system	Psychological reconstruction of life; invitational mood; fixed-role therapy.

Table 11.3 Summary of Strengths and Limitations of Personal Construct Theory

Strengths	*Limitations*
1. Places emphasis on cognitive processes as a central aspect of personality.	1. Has not led to research that *extends* the theory.
2. Presents a model of personality that provides for both the lawfulness of general personality functioning and the uniqueness of individual construct systems.	2. Leaves out or makes minimal contributions to our understanding of some significant aspects of personality (growth and development, emotions).
3. Includes a theory-related technique for personality assessment and research (Rep test).	3. Is not as yet connected with more general research and theory in cognitive psychology.

[handwritten annotations: How do we get our Constructs? / Know permeable Construct / impermeable Construct / Know Construction + dilation aggression / Hostility]

MAJOR CONCEPTS

Anxiety An emotion expressing a sense of impending threat or danger. In Kelly's personal construct theory, anxiety occurs when the person recognizes that his or her construct system does not apply to the events being perceived.

Cognitive complexity/simplicity An aspect of a person's cognitive functioning that is defined at one end by the use of many constructs with many relationships to one another (complexity) and at the other end by the use of few constructs with limited relationships to one another (simplicity).

Construct In Kelly's theory, a way of perceiving, construing, or interpreting events.

Constructive alternativism Kelly's view that there is no objective reality or absolute truth, but only alternative ways of construing events.

Contrast pole In Kelly's personal construct theory, the contrast pole of a construct is defined by the way in which a third element is perceived as different from two other elements that are used to form a similarity pole.

Core construct In Kelly's personal construct theory, a construct that is basic to the person's construct system and cannot be altered without serious consequences for the rest of the system.

Fear In Kelly's personal construct theory, fear occurs when a new construct is about to enter the person's construct system.

Fixed-role therapy Kelly's therapeutic technique that makes use of scripts or roles for people to try out, thereby encouraging people to behave in new ways and to perceive themselves in new ways.

Focus of convenience In Kelly's personal construct theory, those events or phenomena that are best covered by a construct or by the construct system.

Peripheral construct In Kelly's personal construct theory, a construct that is not basic to the construct system and can be altered without serious consequences for the rest of the system.

Preverbal construct In Kelly's personal construct theory, a construct that is used but cannot be expressed in words.

Range of convenience In Kelly's personal construct theory, those events or phenomena that are covered by a construct or by the construct system.

Role Construct Repertory Test (Rep test) Kelly's test to determine the constructs used by a person, the relationships among constructs, and how the constructs are applied to specific people.

Similarity pole In Kelly's personal construct theory, the similarity pole of a construct is defined by the way in which two elements are perceived to be similar.

Submerged construct In Kelly's personal construct theory, a construct that once could be expressed in words, but now either one or both poles of the construct cannot be verbalized.

Subordinate construct In Kelly's personal construct theory, a construct that is lower in the construct system and is thereby included in the context of another (superordinate) construct.

Superordinate construct In Kelly's personal construct theory, a construct that is higher in the construct system and thereby includes other constructs within its context.

Threat In Kelly's personal construct theory, threat occurs when the person is aware of an imminent, comprehensive change in his or her construct system.

Verbal construct In Kelly's personal construct theory, a construct that can be expressed in words.

REVIEW

1. The personal construct theory of George Kelly emphasizes the way in which the person construes or interprets events.

2. Kelly viewed the person as a scientist—an observer of events who formulates concepts or constructs to organize phenomena and uses these constructs to predict the future.

3. According to the position of constructive alternativism, there is no absolute truth. Rather, people choose among alternative constructs and always are free to reconstrue events.

4. Kelly viewed personality in terms of the person's construct system—the types of constructs the person formed and how they were organized. Constructs are formed on the basis of observations of similarities among events. Core constructs are basic to the system, whereas peripheral constructs are less important. Superordinate constructs are higher in the hierarchy and include other constructs under them, whereas subordinate constructs are lower in the hierarchy.

5. Kelly developed the Role Construct Repertory Test (Rep test) to assess the content and structure of the person's construct system. The Rep test has been used to study the extent to which the person can be described as cognitively complex or simple, indicating the extent to which the person can view the world in differentiated terms.

6. Kelly did not feel the need for a motive concept. Instead, he assumed that people are active, and postulated that people anticipate events and seek to predict the future. Change in the construct system is dictated by efforts to improve prediction.

7. According to Kelly, the person experiences anxiety when aware that events lie outside the construct system, experiences fear when a new construct is about to emerge, and experiences threat when there is the danger of comprehensive change in the construct system. Disordered responses to anxiety can be seen in the way constructs are applied to new events (excessively permeable or impermeable), in the way constructs are used to make predictions (excessive tightening or loosening), and in the organization of the entire construct system (constriction or dilation).

8. For Kelly, psychotherapy is the process of reconstructing the construct system. In Kelly's fixed-role therapy, clients are encouraged to represent themselves in new ways, behave in new ways, and construe themselves in new ways.

9. Research on personal construct theory has focused mainly on the Rep test. Recent research has shown that Kelly's idiographic assessment procedures reveal much information about the individual that is not revealed by nomothetic tests based on trait theory. Other work has explored the complexity/simplicity of construct systems in a manner that is related to, yet not directly guided by, the postulates of personal construct theory.

10. An evaluation of personal construct theory recognizes its strengths in emphasizing cognitive processes, in developing a way of suggesting broad principles while capturing the uniqueness of the individual, and in developing an assessment device and a method of therapy directly related to the theory. At the same time, the theory neglects some important areas, fails to come to grips with some fundamental questions, and has had a limited impact on the research and therapeutic efforts of others.

12

SOCIAL-COGNITIVE THEORY: BANDURA AND MISCHEL

RELATING SOCIAL-COGNITIVE THEORY TO THE PREVIOUS THEORIES

A VIEW OF THE THEORISTS
    Albert Bandura (1925–)
    Walter Mischel (1930–)
    Impact of the Theorists

VIEW OF THE PERSON

VIEW OF THE SCIENCE OF PERSONALITY

SOCIAL-COGNITIVE THEORY OF PERSONALITY: STRUCTURE
    Competencies and Skills
    Beliefs and Expectancies
        The Self and Self-Efficacy Beliefs
        Self-Efficacy and Performance
    Goals
    Evaluative Standards
    The Nature of Social-Cognitive Personality
        Structures

SOCIAL-COGNITIVE THEORY OF PERSONALITY: PROCESS
    Reciprocal Determinism
    Personality as a Cognitive-Affective Processing System (CAPS)
    Observational Learning (Modeling)
        Acquisition versus Performance
        Vicarious Conditioning
    Self-Regulation and Motivation
        Self-Efficacy, Goals, and Self-Evaluative Reaction
    Self-Control and Delay of Gratification
        Learning Delay of Gratification Skills
        Mischel's Delay of Gratification Paradigm
        Social-Cognitive View of Growth and Development

MAJOR CONCEPTS

REVIEW

Do you remember your first day of high school? Perhaps you don't care to! What could be more unnerving than not knowing how to act, especially in an environment where "fitting in" is paramount? Although she was really anxious and unsure of what to expect, one young woman decided to approach the first day of high school as an opportunity to learn. Her plan was to model herself after the most successful seniors in the school. She paid close attention to what they talked about, what they wore, where they went and when they went there. Soon, she was the coolest freshman in the class.

This young woman was very influenced by her new environment, but she was also an active agent in choosing how to respond to that influence. This idea, that behavior is the result of an interaction between the person and the environment, is a key concept in the social-cognitive theory of personality. This theory is distinctive in its emphasis on the social origins of behavior and the importance of cognition (thought processes) in human functioning. People are viewed as capable of actively directing their own lives and learning complex patterns of behavior in the absence of rewards. Social-cognitive theory has developed considerably during the past few decades and today is an important force in the science of personality.

QUESTIONS TO BE ADDRESSED IN THIS CHAPTER

1. How do people learn patterns of social behavior?
2. Can people control, or regulate, their own motivation?
3. How should the personality scientist analyze the causes of behavior?
4. What does it mean to think of personality as being a cognitive and affective "system"?

Social-cognitive theory has its historical origins in the behavioral/learning tradition (Chapter 10). Beginning in the 1950s, some theorists tried to capitalize on the virtues of the learning approach while shifting learning theory's focus of attention away from the behavior of animals in boxes and toward the behavior of human beings in the social world. Reflecting these origins, the social-cognitive approach originally was known as "social learning" theory. During the past quarter century, however, investigators generally have adopted the "social-cognitive" label. The change in terminology is significant. It calls attention to the two central features of contemporary theorizing: (1) that human thought processes, or "cognitive" processes, should serve as the centerpoint in the analysis of personality; and (2) that thinking develops in social context; in other words, people acquire their thoughts about themselves and the world through social interaction. The theory thus, is "social-cognitive."

RELATING SOCIAL-COGNITIVE THEORY TO THE PREVIOUS THEORIES

Social-cognitive theory is the last personality theory that we will introduce in this book. Since you now have learned a lot about the other theories, it is valuable here, in beginning our coverage of social-cognitive theory, to relate this new theory to the previous ideas. Social-cognitive theorists have been critical of central features of each of the theories we have presented previously (see Bandura, 1986, 1999; Mischel & Shoda, 1998, 1999).

To the social-cognitivist, psychoanalysis overemphasizes unconscious forces and the influence of the early childhood environment. Social-cognitive theory, in contrast, explores people's capacities to use conscious reasoning processes to guide their behavior. It highlights people's ability to develop and grow across the entire course of life.

Social-cognitive theorists also criticize the ideas of trait theory. They conclude that trait theory places too great an emphasis on the consistency of behavior across situations. Social-cognitivists recognize that people display not only consistency but also meaningful variability in action. Individuals vary their behavior in a strategic manner from one situation to another, according to how their personal goals and capabilities relate to the opportunities and demands in the different settings. Social-cognitive theory reasons that this variability in action is as meaningful as is consistency in action, and thus tries to explain both consistency and variability (see, Anderson & Chen, 2002; Mischel & Shoda, 1995; Mischel, 1999; Shoda, 1999).

Evolutionary psychology also is seen as an inadequate basis for the psychology of personality. Among other problems, social-cognitive theorists note that evolutionary psychology, which explains behavior in terms of biological factors that are unchanged from one generation to the next, cannot explain the vast changes in social life that are observed from one historical period to the next (Bussey & Bandura, 1999). A century ago, evolutionary psychologists might have explained why women, compared to men, are evolutionarily predisposed to stay at home rather than entering the workforce. Now that women have entered the workforce in massive numbers, such an "explanation" is simply pointless.

Finally, social-cognitive theory rejects the basic tenets of behaviorism. Behaviorism depicts organisms as being controlled by environmental rewards and punishments. Social-cognitive theorists, in contrast, argue that people are at least partly "in control." People's thinking abilities give them the capacity to motivate and guide their own actions and experience. Social-cognitive theory is fundamentally concerned with this unique human capacity for self-direction, or personal agency (Bandura, 1997, 2001). Another contrast between behaviorism and social-cognitive theory also is important. Social-cognitive theory provides a novel analysis of how people learn new patterns of behavior. Rather than emphasizing reinforcement principles, as the behaviorists did, social-cognitive theory explores people's capacity to learn by observation, even in the absence of rewards (Table 12.1).

The two previous theories that are most similar to contemporary social-cognitive theory are phenomenological theory and personal construct theory. Social-cognitive theory shares their interest in how people construct personal meaning out of the events of their lives, and how beliefs about the self contribute to these processes of meaning construction. Although social-cogni-

Table 12.1 Distinguishing Features of Social-Cognitive Theory

1. Emphasis on people as active agents.
2. Emphasis on social origins of behavior.
3. Emphasis on cognitive (thought) processes.
4. Emphasis on behavior as situation-specific.
5. Emphasis on systematic research.
6. Emphasis on the learning of complex patterns of behavior in the absence of rewards.

tivists spend a lot of their time in psychological laboratories running experiments, they also are humanists. They emphasize people's capacity to influence their destinies and try to develop methods to help people achieve their potentials (Bandura, 2001). Despite these similarities, social-cognitive theory differs from these two older theories. A big difference is that social-cognitivists provide a lot of critical details about specific cognitive processes in personality functioning that are missing in the phenomenological and personal construct approach. They are able to do this by drawing on contemporary research findings that were unavailable to earlier theorists.

A final way in which social-cognitive theory differs from previous approaches is subtle, yet significant. It concerns the relation between personality theory and the rest of psychological science. Most of the prior personality theories developed outside of the mainstream of scientific psychology. The personality theorist commonly was a lone investigator. Working independently, the theorist would construct an elaborate theoretical structure whose assumptions and terminology often bore little resemblance to ideas found elsewhere in the field. In contrast, social-cognitive theorists have tried to break this isolation. They explicitly try to capitalize on scientific advances in other branches of psychology, as well as other sciences that study human nature and social behavior (Cervone & Mischel, 2002). From this perspective, personality psychologists have an integrative task (Caprara & Cervone, 2000). A personality theory should integrate knowledge from diverse branches of psychology—developmental, social, cognitive, cultural, and so forth—and synthesize this knowledge into a coherent portrait of human nature and the differences among persons. This is a fundamental goal of the social-cognitive theorist.

Many contemporary personality psychologists pursue this goal. Numerous personality scientists have made, and are making, theoretical and empirical contributions to social-cognitive theory (reviewed, for example, in Cervone & Shoda, 1999b). However, two people have made extraordinarily seminal contributions that mark them as the primary social-cognitive personality theorists. These theorists are Albert Bandura and Walter Mischel. As you read about these two individuals and their ideas, you should understand that their work is complementary. In previous chapters, we commonly have highlighted differences between theoretical views. However, in the case of Bandura and Mischel, the similarities greatly outweigh the differences. Although they have focused on somewhat different aspects of personality functioning, their theoretical ideas complement one another and contribute to a coherent body of theorizing that constitutes the contemporary social-cognitive perspective on personality.

A VIEW OF THE THEORISTS

ALBERT BANDURA (1925–)

Albert Bandura grew up in northern Alberta, Canada and went to college at the University of British Columbia. After graduation he chose to do graduate work in clinical psychology at the University of Iowa because it was known for its excellence in research on learning processes. Even then, Bandura was interested in the application of learning theory to clinical phenomena. In an interview, Bandura indicated that he "had a strong interest in conceptualizing clinical phenomena in ways that would make them amenable to experimental test, with the view that as practitioners we have a responsibility for assessing the efficacy of a procedure, so that people are not subjected to treatments before we know their effects" (quoted in Evans, 1976, p. 243). At Iowa he was influenced by Kenneth Spence, a follower of the behaviorist Clark Hull, and by the general emphasis on careful conceptual analysis and rigorous experimental investigation. During that time he was also influenced by the writings of Neal Miller and John Dollard, who had begun to apply behavioral principles to the study of personality and social behavior.

Albert Bandura

After obtaining his Ph.D. at Iowa in 1952, Bandura went to Stanford University, where he spent his entire academic career. At Stanford, Bandura began to work on interactive processes in psychotherapy, as well as on family patterns that lead to aggressiveness in children. The work on familial causes of aggression, conducted in collaboration with Richard Walters—his first graduate student—identified the central role of modeling influences (learning through observation of others) in personality development. These findings and consequent laboratory investigations of modeling processes resulted in the books *Adolescent Aggression* (Bandura & Walters, 1959) and *Social Learning and Personality Development* (Bandura & Walters, 1963); the latter volume, in particular, laid the foundations for the social-cognitive perspective on personality that developed throughout the latter third of the 20th century. In 1969, Bandura published the volume *Principles of Behavior Modification*, a book that reformulated the practice of behavior therapy by directing therapists' attention to the thinking processes of their clients, rather than to the environmental factors and conditioning processes emphasized by behaviorists (Chapter 10).

During the past quarter century, Bandura has devoted much of his attention to "self-processes," that is, to thinking processes involving personal goals, self-evaluation, and beliefs about one's own capabilities for performance (1977, 1997). This focus makes Bandura's social-cognitive theory an "agentic" conception of human nature (Bandura, 1999, 2001). People are seen as causal agents who can shape their own personal development. Bandura does not analyze the individual in isolation. Instead, he addresses societal factors, such as social and economic conditions, that influence people's beliefs about their ability to influence events (Bandura, 2001).

Bandura describes himself as conducting a multifaceted research program aimed at clarifying aspects of human capability that should be emphasized in a comprehensive theory of human behavior. His most significant effort to formulate such a theory is the monumental volume *Social Foundations of Thought and Action* (Bandura, 1986). This book organizes a vast body of psychological knowledge about personality processes and structures into a coherent conceptual framework, and stands as the definitive statement of Bandura's theoretical position.

Bandura has received a number of distinguished scientific achievement awards. In 1974 he was elected president of the American Psychological Association, and in 1980 he received the Association's Distinguished Scientific Contribution Award "for masterful modeling as researcher, teacher, and theoretician."

WALTER MISCHEL (1930–)

Walter Mischel was born in Vienna and lived his first nine years "in easy playing distance of Freud's house." He describes the possible influence of this period as follows:

Walter Mischel

When I began to read psychology Freud fascinated me most. As a student at City College (in New York, where my family settled after the Hitler-caused forced exodus from Europe in 1939), psychoanalysis seemed to provide a comprehensive view of man. But my excitement fizzled when I tried to apply ideas as a social worker with "juvenile delinquents" in New York's Lower East Side: somehow trying to give those youngsters "insight" didn't help either them or me. The concepts did not fit what I saw, and I went looking for more useful ones.

SOURCE: Mischel, 1978, personal communication.

The experience with juvenile delinquents is of particular interest for two reasons. First, it probably relates to Mischel's long-standing interest in the psychological mechanisms underlying delay of gratification and self-control. Second, there is a similarity to Bandura in that both did their early clinical work with aggressive youngsters.

Mischel did his graduate work at Ohio State University, where he came under the influence of the personal construct theorist George Kelly, as well as the personality theorist Julian Rotter, who tried to extend behavioral principles to the study of human behavior by exploring people's expectations about environmental reinforcements. Kelly's influence is seen in Mischel's study of the constructs through which people encode information about their experience and themselves. Rotter's influence is seen in Mischel's emphasis on the importance of outcome expectancies and outcome values for determining action in a situation (expectancy-value theory) (Mischel, 1999). He describes their influence as follows:

George Kelly and Julian Rotter were my dual mentors and each has enduringly influenced my thinking. I see my own work both with cognition and with social learning as clearly rooted in their contributions, a focus on the person both as construer and actor, interacting with the vicissitudes of the environment, and trying to make life coherent even in the face of all inconsistencies.

SOURCE: Mischel, 1978, personal communication.

After completing his graduate work at Ohio State, Mischel spent a number of years at Harvard University and then, like Bandura, joined the faculty of Stanford University. During this time (1965) he participated in a Peace Corps assessment project that had a profound influence on him. In this project it was found that global trait measures did a poor job of predicting performance; in fact, they did less well than self-report measures. This increased Mischel's skepticism concerning the utility of traditional personality theories, such as trait and psychoanalytic theory, that emphasize stable and broadly generalized personality characteristics (Mischel, 1990). The definitive statement of this skepticism was the 1968 book *Personality and Assessment*, mentioned in Chapter 8. This book is probably the single most influential volume in personality psychology in the last 40 years. It challenged the entire body of theoretical assumptions and methodological practices that were associated with both psychoanalysis and trait theory. Mischel's arguments became the cornerstone of the "person-situation controversy" that was central to the field in the 1970s and 1980s (Chapter 8). Mischel describes his skepticism concerning the utility of broadly generalized personality variables, such as global trait constructs, as follows:

> Characterizations of individuals on common trait dimensions (such as "Conscientiousness" or "Sociability") provided useful overall summaries of their average levels of behavior but missed, it seemed to me, the striking discriminativeness often visible within the same person if closely observed over time and across situations. Might the same person who is more caring, giving, and supportive than most people in relation to his family also be less caring and altruistic than most people in other contexts? Might these variations across situations be meaningful stable patterns that characterize the person enduringly rather than random fluctuations? If so, how could they be understood and what did they reflect? Might they be worth taking into account in personality assessment for the conceptualization of the stability and flexibility of human behavior and qualities? These questions began to gnaw at me and the effort to answer them became a fundamental goal for the rest of my life.
>
> SOURCE: Mischel, as quoted in Pervin, 1996, p. 76.

In addition to critiquing previous approaches, in 1973 Mischel provided an alternative: a set of cognitive-social personal variables (Mischel, 1973). More recently, Mischel and colleagues have broadened their theoretical perspective by explaining how these variables can be understood as a complex, interconnected system of cognitive and affective processes that underlies human individuality (Mischel & Shoda, 1995).

In 1978 Mischel received the Distinguished Scientist Award from the Clinical Psychology Division of the American Psychological Association and in 1983 was cited by the Association for his outstanding contributions to personality theory and assessment. Since 1984 he has been a professor of psychology at Columbia University. In 1999, he accepted a position as editor of the *Psychological Review*, the most important publication outlet for theoretical papers in the field of psychology. In 2002–2003 he served as president of the Association for Research in Personality.

IMPACT OF THE THEORISTS

In addition to these biographical details, it is noteworthy to consider the overall impact of Bandura's and Mischel's scientific contributions. A recent review (Haggbloom et al., 2002) assessed the scientific impact of the psychologists of the 20th century. This assessment included a systematic analysis of the frequency with which psychologists' work was cited in scientific journals and psychology textbooks. Through this measure, the authors were able to construct an objective ranking of the most impactful, eminent psychologists of the past century. Both Bandura and Mischel were ranked among the centuries' top 25 most impactful psychologists. Indeed, the work of only three psychologists was ranked as more influential than Bandura's: Skinner, Piaget, and Freud.

A different perspective on these rankings is to note that, at the time of the writing of this edition of this textbook, there are only four living individuals who were ranked among the 25 most eminent psychologists of the previous century. Two of them were the social-cognitive personality theorists Bandura and Mischel. Thus,

Bandura and Mischel are not only among the most significant contributors to personality psychology; they are among the most significant contributors to the field of psychology at large.

VIEW OF THE PERSON

Both Bandura and Mischel recognize the importance of articulating a clear and explicit view of human nature. Clarity is important because views of human nature have significant practical implications. As Bandura notes, "views about human nature influence which aspects of psychological functioning are studied most thoroughly and which remain unexamined. Theoretical conceptions similarly determine the paradigms used to collect evidence which, in turn, shape the particular theory" (1977b, p. vi). In other words, there is a back-and-forth relationship between a view of the person, a program of research, and a theory of personality.

The simplest way to understand the social-cognitive theory view of persons is by considering the following question: What is a person? In other words, what makes some beings "persons" and other beings "not persons"? There are three interlocking psychological qualities that are essential defining features of persons: (1) Persons are beings who can reason about the world using language. (2) This reasoning can involve reflection not only on present circumstances, but on the distant past and on hypothetical events in the future. (3) This reasoning commonly involves reflection on the self—the being who is doing the reasoning. People, then, are beings who can use language to reason—in past, present, and future tense—about themselves and the world (Harré and Secord, 1973). It is these core human qualities, and the psychological capabilities to which they give rise, that are the essential focus of social-cognitive theory.

This view of persons may seem so obvious that it did not even need to be stated. But note that this emphasis differs from some of the earlier theories. Psychoanalytic theory highlighted animalistic impulsive forces in the unconscious. Behaviorists based a theory of persons on the study of animals. Trait theorists are happy to report that the Big Five model of human personality differs little from the model one obtains when studying individual differences among dogs or other non-human species (Gosling & John, 1999). The social-cognitivist recognizes that people and complex mammals share many neuroanatomical features and behavioral capacities. But at the same time, social-cognitive theory severely questions whether these shared features can or should be the basis of the study of human personality. The study of personality is about persons, and it is the uniquely human-cognitive capacities of persons that are the focus of social-cognitive theory.

Centering a personality theory on human-cognitive capacities (Bandura, 1999) has numerous implications. It draws attention to people's role as active agents who can causally contribute to their experiences and their development. Since people can reason about future events, they can select which events they will experience and can prepare themselves for future challenges. This emphasis differs markedly from other approaches. Psychoanalysts saw people as being controlled by unconscious emotions. Behaviorists saw us as being controlled by the environment. A focus on human-cognitive capacities brings a different view. Even if unconscious emotional forces can influence us, people have the cognitive capacity to overcome them when they are felt (Metcalfe & Mischel, 1999). Even if the environment does affect us, we may be able to exert self-control by avoiding some environments, choosing to enter into others, and shaping features of the physical and social environment that we experience (Bandura, 1986).

Mischel describes the emerging image of the human being as follows:

> The image is one of the human being as an active, aware problem-solver, capable of profiting from an enormous range of experiences and cognitive capacities, possessing great potential for good or ill, actively constructing his or her psychological world, and influencing the environment but also being influenced by it in lawful ways.... It is an image that has moved a long way from the instinctual drive-reduction models, the static global traits, and the automatic stimulus-response bonds of traditional personality theories. It is an image that highlights the short-comings of all simplistic theories that view behavior as the exclusive result of any narrow set of determinants, whether these are habits, traits, drives, reinforcers, constructs, instincts, or genes and whether they are exclusively inside or outside the person.
>
> SOURCE: Mischel, 1976, p. 253.

VIEW OF THE SCIENCE OF PERSONALITY

Like most of the theorists we have discussed, both Bandura and Mischel are committed to the goal of building a theory of personality on a firm base of empirical research. They strive to present theoretical concepts in a clear manner. Such clarity fosters systematic research that can be used to evaluate the theoretical ideas. Thanks in part to this theoretical clarity, social-cognitive theory has probably generated a more diverse array of basic and applied research in recent decades than has any other theoretical perspective in personality psychology.

In addition to this general orientation, the social-cognitive theory view of personality science has three defining features. One, mentioned already, is the idea that a personality theory should be integrative. The theorist should try to integrate scientific knowledge from diverse fields of study into a comprehensive model of persons. Social-cognitive theorists commonly draw on work in cognitive psychology, developmental psychology, neuroscience, and especially social psychology in their efforts to build a comprehensive model of the individual and of differences between individuals.

A second feature is the social-cognitive theorists' belief that the science of personality must focus on individual persons. Using a term introduced earlier (Chapter 7), social-cognitive theorists have employed not only "nomothetic" but also "idiographic" research methods. They have tried to develop theories and research methods that speak to the idiosyncrasies of the unique individual.

Thirdly, Bandura and Mischel have been intensely interested in the practical applications of their theoretical ideas. They have stressed that a basic "bottom line" for evaluating a theory is whether the theoretical ideas help psychologists, and society at large, to develop practical tools that prove to benefit human welfare (e.g., Bandura, 1969). Social-cognitive investigators commonly have turned their attention to applied questions on topics such as education, clinical behavior change, or the reduction of societal aggression.

In sum, social-cognitive theory is concerned with developing a personality psychology that is scientifically rigorous, is integrative, and that has applied benefits. There is a concern with both the subjective qualities of inner mental life and the need to study such qualities through systematic, reliable research methods. In all likelihood it is this blend of concern with important human events and scientific respectability that most accounts for the theory's current popularity.

<table>
<tr><td>

SOCIAL-COGNITIVE THEORY OF PERSONALITY: STRUCTURE

</td><td>

The stage has been set for considering the details of the social-cognitive theory of personality. In doing so, we must keep in mind the importance of cognitive processes in human motivation, emotion, and action, as well as the social origins of human behavior.

The personality structures emphasized by social-cognitive theory mainly involve cognitive processes. Four structural concepts are particularly noteworthy: competencies and skills, expectancies and beliefs, behavioral standards, and personal goals.

</td></tr>
</table>

COMPETENCIES AND SKILLS

The first type of personality structure in social-cognitive theory is skills or **competencies**. The core insight of the theory is that differences between people who we observe may not be caused by differences in emotions or motivational impulses, as other theories have emphasized. Instead, the differences may reflect variations in people's skill in executing different types of action. Some people may, for example, act in an introverted manner because they lack the social skills that are required to execute socially effective extraverted acts. Others may be conscientious because they have acquired a large degree of cognitive skills that enable them to adhere to social norms.

Of particular interest to social-cognitive theorists, then, are cognitive competencies and skills in solving problems and coping with the problems of life (Cantor, 1990; Mischel & Shoda, 1998, 1999). Competencies involve both ways of thinking about life problems and behavioral skills in executing solutions to them. They involve two types of knowledge: procedural and declarative knowledge (Cantor & Kihlstrom, 1987). Declarative knowledge is knowledge that we can state in words. Procedural knowledge refers to cognitive and behavioral capacities that a person may have without being able to articulate the exact nature of those capacities; the person can execute the behavioral "procedure" without being able to say how they did it. For example, you may be good at cheering up a friend who is feeling depressed, yet may not be able to say in words precisely what it is that you do that enables you to succeed at this task. Competencies, then, involve a combination of declarative and procedural knowledge.

A focus on competencies has two implications. The first involves **context specificity**. The term refers to the fact that psychological structures that are relevant to some social situations, or contexts, may be irrelevant to others. Context specificity is a natural feature of skills (Cantor & Kihlstrom, 1987). A person may have excellent study skills, but these are of little use when it comes to getting a date or resolving an argument. Different contexts present different types of challenges and thus require different competencies. A person who is competent in one context may not be competent in another. This emphasis on context specificity (also see Chapter 14) differentiates social-cognitive theory from trait approaches (Chapters 7 and 8), which feature context-free personality variables. Social-cognitive theory generally rejects context-free variables—particularly when discussing cognitive competencies. The last thing that the social-cognitivist would want to do is to assume that one person is "generally more competent" than another. Instead, it is recognized that any given individual's competencies may vary considerably from one domain of life to another.

The second implication involves psychological change. Competencies are acquired through social interaction and observation of the social world (Bandura, 1986). A person who is lacking skills in a particular area of life can change. They can engage in new interactions and new observations of the world and thereby acquire new competencies. The ideas of social-cognitive theory therefore can be applied directly to clinical applications that are designed to boost people's life skills (Chapter 13).

BELIEFS AND EXPECTANCIES (Structure)

The other three social-cognitive structures can be understood by considering three different ways that people may think about the world (Cervone, 2004). One set of thoughts involve beliefs about what the world *actually is like* and what things probably will be like in the future. These thoughts are called beliefs and—when the beliefs are directed to the future—**expectancies**. A second class of thinking involves thoughts about what things *should* be like. These thoughts are **evaluative standards**, that is, mental criteria (or standards) for evaluating the goodness or worth of events. A third class of thinking involves thoughts about what one *wants to achieve in the future*. These thoughts are called personal **goals**. In addition to competencies, then, the other three main social-cognitive personality structures are beliefs and expectancies, evaluative standards, and goals. We first will consider beliefs and expectancies, which we will refer to simply as "expectancies" here because social-cognitive theory so strongly emphasizes the role in personality functioning of people's beliefs about prospective future events.

Social-cognitive theory contends that a primary determinant of our actions and emotions is our expectations about the future. People have expectancies concerning topics such as the likely behavior of other people, the rewards or punishments that may follow a certain type of behavior, or their own ability to handle the stress and challenges. It is this system of thoughts about the future that constitutes the person's expectancies.

As was the case with skills and competencies, a person's expectations may vary considerably from one situation to another. Everyone expects that the same action might elicit different reactions in different situations (e.g., loud, jovial behavior at a party versus a church). People naturally discriminate between situations, expecting different opportunities, rewards, and constraints in different settings. Although researchers sometimes do study generalized expectations, most social-cognitive investigators study expectancies in a domain-linked manner. In other words, they assess people's expectancies with regard to specific areas, or domains, of their life. Social-cognitive theorists recognize that the capacity to vary expectations and behavior from one situation to another is basic to survival. No animal could survive if it failed to make such discriminations. Humans, because of their tremendous cognitive capacity, make an incredible variety of discriminations among situations.

A key point in the social-cognitive approach is that, when forming expectancies, people may group together situations in ways that are highly idiosyncratic. One person may group together situations involving school versus social life, and perhaps have high expectations in one domain and low expectations in the other. Another person may think of situations in terms of relaxing circumstances versus circumstances that make them anxious—where both relaxing and anxiety-provoking circumstances could occur both at school and in social life. Yet anther person may possess a cognitive category that involves "opportunities to get a date"—where those opportunities could be relaxing or anxiety-provoking, and could arise in social settings or at school. People naturally "slice up" the situations of their life in different ways, and thus, may display idiosyncratic patterns of expectancies and social behavior. According to social-cognitive theorists, the essence of personality lies in these differing ways in which unique individuals perceive situations, develop expectations about future circumstances, and display distinct behavior patterns as a result of these differing perceptions and expectations.

This focus on expectancies differentiates social-cognitive theory from behaviorism. In behaviorism, behavior was understood as being caused by reinforcements and punishments in the environment. In social-cognitive theory, in contrast, behavior is explained in terms of people's *expectations about* rewards and punishments in the environment (Bandura, 1969, 1986; Mischel, 1973). This is an important difference. The shift to studying expectations, as opposed to merely environmental events, enables the social-cognitive theorist to explain why two different people may react differently to the same environment. The two people may experience similar environmental events, yet develop different expectations about what is likely to happen in the future.

The Self and Self-Efficacy Beliefs

Although some of our expectations concern other people, expectations of particular importance to personality functioning involve the self. Bandura (1997, 2001) has been at the forefront in emphasizing that people's expectations about their own capabilities for performance are the key ingredient in human achievement and well-being. He refers to these expectations as perceptions of self-efficacy. **Perceived self-efficacy**, then, refers to people's perceptions of their own capabilities for action in future situations.

Why are self-efficacy perceptions so important? It is because self-efficacy perceptions influence a number of different types of behavior that, in turn, are necessary for human achievement. Consider some area of life in which you have achieved success. For example, if you are a reader of this textbook, you probably were quite successful in high school and thereby succeeded in gaining admission to college. What was required for this success? You had to: (1) decide to commit yourself to college admission, (2) persist in study in order to learn material in high school and achieve high grades, and when taking important exams you had to (3) remain calm and (4) think in a highly analytical manner. It is precisely these four behavioral mechanisms that are influenced by self-efficacy perceptions (Bandura, 1997). People with a higher sense of self-efficacy are more likely to decide to attempt difficult tasks, to persist in their efforts, to be calm rather than anxious during task performance, and to

Self-efficacy Beliefs: *Self-efficacy beliefs are based in part on experiences with success and failure. Mark Wohlers was a successful pitcher until he lost control, to the extent that he bounced the ball to the plate or threw it over the batter's head. His confidence plummeted from what had been a very high level to near zero. Trying to regain his confidence, he said: "Confidence comes with success. The way I pitched the other day built a little more confidence.... It's just getting out there and having success."* (New York Times, *March 9, 1997, p. D7)*

organize their thoughts in an analytical manner. In contrast, people who question their own capabilities for performance may fail even to attempt valuable activities, may give up when the going gets rough, tend to become anxious during task performance, and often become "rattled" and fail to think and act in a calm, analytical manner (colloquially speaking, one might say that a person with a low sense of self-efficacy tends to "choke" on difficult activities).

These influences of self-efficacy are spelled out further throughout this chapter and later in this book. For now, however, it is important to consider in a little more detail how Bandura conceptualizes perceived self-efficacy and how his strategy for assessing perceived self-efficacy follows from this conceptualization. Perceived self-efficacy differs from what may appear to be similar concepts. Perceived self-efficacy differs from self-esteem. Self-esteem refers to people's overall (or "global") evaluation of their personal worth. Perceived self-efficacy, in contrast, refers to people's appraisals of what they are capable of accomplishing in a given setting. Thus, perceived self-efficacy differs from self-esteem in two ways: (1) perceived self-efficacy is not a global variable; instead, it is recognized that people commonly will have different self-efficacy perceptions in different situations, and (2) perceived self-efficacy is not an abstract sense of personal worth, but a judgment of what one can do. Imagine that you have a big math exam coming up. You may have a perfectly high sense of self-esteem. Yet, at the same time, you may have a low sense of self-efficacy for getting a high grade on the exam. Social-cognitive theory would predict that you would be anxious about the exam, even though you may have a high sense of overall self-esteem. These theoretical differences have proven to be quite significant in practice. Although the relations between self-esteem measures and performance are often quite weak (Baumeister, Campbell, Krueger, & Vohs, 2003), a large and diverse set of research findings indicates that the relation between measures of perceived self-efficacy and performance is strong (Bandura & Locke, 2003; Stajkovic & Luthans, 1998).

A second distinction of importance concerns the difference between self-efficacy expectations and outcome expectations (Bandura, 1977a). Outcome expectations are beliefs about the rewards and punishments that will occur if one performs a given type of behavior. Self-efficacy expectations are beliefs about whether one can perform the behavior in the first place. Suppose you are considering what major to choose in college. You might believe that there are high rewards (e.g., high financial income in the future) if you were to major in electrical engineering. You would, then, have high outcome expectations with respect to electrical engineering. But you might also think that you are not personally capable of executing the behaviors (e.g., passing all the math, physics, and engineering courses) required to major in electrical engineering. You would have low self-efficacy expectations with respect to electrical engineering. Social-cognitive theory contends that efficacy expectations generally are more important than are outcome expectations as a determinant of behavior. If people lack a sense of efficacy for accomplishing something, the rewards associated with accomplishing that goal are probably irrelevant to them. You are unlikely to select electrical engineering as your major, despite its financial attractions, if you have a low sense of self-efficacy for completing the required courses.

In terms of assessment, Bandura emphasizes what he calls a **microanalytic research** strategy. According to this strategy, detailed measures of perceived self-efficacy are taken before performance of behaviors in specific situations. Specifically, people are asked to indicate their degree of certainty in performing specific behaviors in designated contexts. A self-efficacy scale for athletic performance in, for example, the sport of basketball would *not* ask a vague question such as "Do you think you are a good basketball player?" (The question is vague because the word "good" is so ambiguous: good compared to your teammates?; Compared to member of the NBA a collegiate basketball player? Compared to your little brother?) Instead, test items would describe specific actions and accomplishments and ask people to indicate their confidence in attaining them. For example, "How confident are you that you can make at least 75% of your free throws during a basketball game?"; or "How confident are you that you can dribble upcourt with a basketball even if you are covered by a skilled defensive player?" This assessment strategy follows directly from the theoretical considerations above. In terms of theory, Bandura recognizes that self-efficacy perceptions may vary, for any individual, from one situation to another. In terms of assessment methods, then, situation-specific measures are employed in order to capture this variability. Such measures are much better for capturing the psychological characteristics of the individual. Global self-concept measures are criticized because they "[do] not do justice to the complexity of self-efficacy perceptions, which vary across different activities, different levels of the same activity, and different situational circumstances" (Bandura, 1986, p. 41).

Self-Efficacy and Performance

A basic claim of social-cognitive theory is that self-efficacy perceptions causally influence behavior. If you think critically about such claims, you may already have a counter-argument: Maybe self-efficacy perceptions do not really play a causal role. Maybe some other factor is really the cause. One possible other factor is people's actual level of skill. Skill levels might influence both self-efficacy perceptions and behavior, and account for the relation between perceived self-efficacy and motivated action. For example, everyone has a high sense of self-efficacy for picking up a 5-pound weight (we're confident that we can do it) and a low sense of self-efficacy for picking up a 500-pound weight (we perceive ourselves as incapable of doing it). But there's no need to appeal to the notion of perceived self-efficacy to explain why we actually can lift the light weight and not the heavy one. Our behavior can be understood simply in terms of our inherent physical capacities. How, then, do we know that we ever need to appeal to the notion of perceived self-efficacy to explain behavior?

Social-cognitivists have addressed this question through experimental strategies. The idea is to experimentally manipulate perceived self-efficacy while holding other factors—such as people's actual skills—constant. Once self-efficacy perceptions are manipulated experimentally, one can see whether the variations in perceived self-efficacy causally influence behavior.

Of course, one needs a strategy for manipulating perceived self-efficacy. Ideally, the manipulation would be simple and subtle, to ensure that it influenced perceived self-efficacy but did not also influence people's actual skills on the task.

One research strategy has been to employ a technique known as "anchoring" manipulations. Anchoring refers to a thinking process that comes into play when people try to figure out the answer to a problem. What often happens is that the final answer that people reach is greatly influenced by whatever people happen to think of *first* when they try to solve the problem; their final answer is "anchored on" their initial guess. Surprisingly, this occurs even when the initial guess is determined by factors that are completely random and obviously irrelevant to the problem (Tversky & Kahneman, 1974). For example, imagine you are trying to guess a numerical quantity such as the population in millions of the nation of Russia. Suppose that just before you make your estimate someone pulls a random number out of a hat; reads it aloud: "639"; and then asks "do you think there are more or less that 639 million people living in Russia?" You would know that 639 is way too high, and you would know that it also is irrelevant to the real answer because it was chosen randomly. Nonetheless, if you respond like most research participants in anchoring studies, when you then guessed the actual population your guess would be much higher than if you never had been exposed to the random value. ("Hmm," you might think, "it can't be 639 million. Um…maybe it's 400 million.") Your final guess would be "anchored" in the direction of the large number. Conversely, if you first were exposed to a *low* anchor value (e.g., in our population example, the value 20 million), your final guess would probably end up lower ("Hmm, 20 million, that can't be right. Maybe it's, um…70 million"). The presentation of random anchor values, then, is a way of experimentally manipulating people's judgments.

Cervone and Peake (1986) applied anchoring techniques to the question of self-efficacy judgment and behavior. Prior to performing a task that had a series of items, participants were asked to judge whether they could solve "more or less than X" of the items. In high and low anchor conditions, the "X" was a number that corresponded to a high versus low level of performance. This number appeared to be random, literally drawn out of a hat. People then judged exactly how many items they could solve (their level of self-efficacy on the task). Findings indicated that the anchoring manipulation affected perceived self-efficacy; participants exposed to high and low random numbers had

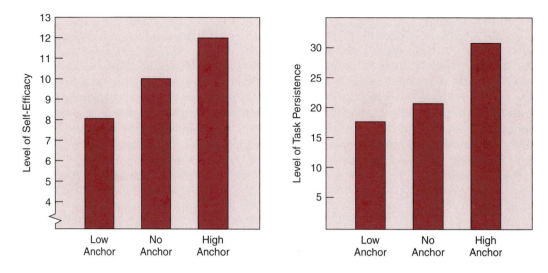

Figure 12.1   Mean levels of perceived self-efficacy and behavior as a function of exposure to apparently random high versus low anchor values. *From Cervone & Peake, 1986.*

high and low self-efficacy perceptions (Figure 12.1, left panel). This circumstance, then, is exactly what one needs to test the claim that self-efficacy causally influences behavior; thanks to the anchoring manipulation, people *differ* in perceived self-efficacy while being the *same* on other factors, such as actual skills on the task. To provide this test, the experimenters asked people to work on the task and measured their behavioral persistence (i.e., how long they tried working on the problems before giving up). Variations in self-efficacy were found to create corresponding variations in behavior (Figure 12.1, right panel). The groups that had high versus low self-efficacy perceptions differed in their subsequent behavior—even though the high versus low differences were created experimentally, and merely by presenting random anchor values.

Such findings provide strong evidence for a central aspect of social-cognitive theory, namely, that people's subjective perceptions of themselves have a unique causal influence on their own behavior. Even when a seemingly irrelevant situational factor causes people to have relatively high or low judgments of self-efficacy, these judgments can affect subsequent decisions and actions.

Note that this sort of finding provides strong evidence *against* a behavioral view of cognition and behavior. Recall that, in behaviorism (Chapter 10), behavior was explained in terms of environmental events rather than cognitive processes. When looking at Bandura's self-efficacy research, a behaviorist might argue that a person's actions *and* their self-efficacy perceptions are both caused by the environment. In this behaviorist view, self-efficacy perceptions would *not* be seen as a cause of behavior but merely as a thinking process that happens to be correlated with the environmental events that are the true causes of people's behaviors. By analogy, the behaviorist might point out that the hood of your car gets hot when you drive at high speed, yet the heating of the hood is not a cause of the car's high speed. It merely is an event that happens to be correlated with the true causes. The counter-argument, from social-cognitive theory, is that if you manipulate self-efficacy perceptions experimentally, then you find changes in subsequent behavior. This strongly suggests that

CURRENT APPLICATIONS

SELF-EFFICACY AND CONDOM USE: HOW TO CHANGE BEHAVIOR

The AIDS epidemic has complicated sexual relations, particularly for young people. In effect, sex education has become a form of preventive medicine. Awareness is definitely a step in the right direction, and knowing the facts about HIV, AIDS, and risky behavior is certainly important. But is it enough to influence young people's behavior? One study suggests not. This research tested whether an intervention program based on social-cognitive theory could improve HIV prevention. More specifically, would it help to increase safe-sex self-efficacy?

Bandura (1992) had proposed a conceptual model linking social-cognitive theory and perceived self-efficacy to the control of sexual activities that would put individuals at risk for HIV infection and AIDS. Essentially, Bandura's model promotes the idea that how we perceive our ability to cope with a situation and to control its outcome is the key to influencing actual behavior.

A study by Basen-Engquist (1994) tested Bandura's model with a quasi-experimental field study involving college students. The subjects were divided into three groups. One group participated in a safe-sex efficacy workshop, another group heard a didactic lecture on HIV, and the third group was a control who heard a lecture about an unrelated topic. As expected, an immediate post-test showed that the first and second groups scored higher on safe-sex self-efficacy and were more likely to report the intention to use a condom than the control group. The follow-up two months later, however, revealed that the group in the safe-sex efficacy workshop was more likely than both other groups to have increased in actual condom use. In other words, it was the manipulation of safe-sex self-efficacy, not mere information about HIV, that produced the change in behavior.

This research demonstrates that HIV prevention efforts must consider the psychology of safe-sex behavior. So much attention has been placed on increasing awareness through education that the question of how information is actually used by young people has been obscured. The discrepancy between intended and actual condom use in the group who received the HIV lecture suggests that information does not get translated into actual behavior as readily as educators would hope. Social-cognitive theory, and perceived self-efficacy in particular, may provide the important psychological link between education and behavior change.

SOURCE: Basen-Engquist (1994).

self-efficacy perceptions do play a causal role, rather than merely being correlated with other factors that are the "true causes" of behavior. If you heat up the hood of your car, it doesn't suddenly go faster. But if you increase people's perceptions of self-efficacy, then changes in behavior do, in fact, result.

GOALS

The third type of personality structure in social-cognitive theory is goals. A goal is a mental representation of the aim of an action or course of actions. A basic belief of social-cognitive theory is that people's ability to envision the future enables them to set specific goals for action and thus, to motivate and direct their own behavior. Goals, then, contribute to the human capacity for self-control. Goals guide us in establishing priorities and in selecting among situations. They enable us to go beyond momentary influences and to organize our behavior over extended periods of time.

A person's goals are organized in a system. In a goal system, some goals are more central or important than others. Goal systems often are understood as having a hierarchical structure. Goals at a higher level in the hierarchy (e.g., get accepted into law school) organize lower-level goals (e.g., get good grades in college) which, in turn, organize lower-level aims (e.g., study for exams). Goal systems, however, are not rigid or fixed. People may select among goals, depending on what seems most important to them at the time, what the opportunities in the environment appear to be, and their judgments of self-efficacy for goal attainment.

People's goals on a task may differ in a variety of ways (Locke & Latham, 1990, 2002). One obvious variation is in the level of challenge, or difficulty, of goals. For example, in a college class, some people may have the goal merely of passing the course, whereas other may adopt the challenging goal of getting an A in the class. Another variation involves the nearness, or proximity, of goals. One person may set a proximal goal, that is, a goal that involves an aim that is coming up soon. Others may set distal goals, that is, goals that specify achievements that are far in the future. For example, if one's goal is to lose weight, a proximal goal might be losing 1 pound each week, whereas a distal goal would be losing 12 pounds in the next 3 months. Research findings indicate that proximal goals often have a bigger influence on one's current behavior than do distal goals (Bandura & Schunk, 1981; Stock & Cervone, 1990). In part, this is because distal goals allow one to "slack off" in the present. For example, the person who wants to lose 12 pounds in 3 months might convince herself that she can go off her diet one week and still meet the long-term aim.

In addition, goals may differ in a manner that involves the subjective meaning of an activity. On any challenging task, some people may have the goal of developing more knowledge and skills on the task; the meaning of the task is that it is an opportunity to learn. Others, in contrast, may be more concerned with goals such as not embarrassing themselves in front of others. These differences between "learning" and "performance" goals (Dweck & Leggett, 1988) are discussed in Chapter 13.

Goals are related to the previous social-cognitive personality construct expectancies. The relationship is a back-and-forth, or reciprocal, one. Expectancies influence the process of goal setting. When selecting goals in an important area of life, people generally reflect on their expectations about their performance. People with higher perceptions of self-efficacy often set higher goals and remain more committed to them (Locke & Latham, 2002). Conversely, goals may influence expectancies and may interact systematically with expectancies as people work on tasks and receive feedback on their performance (Grant & Dweck, 1999). For example, suppose you take an exam and learn that your score was identical to the average score in the class. If your goal was merely to learn something about the course material and to earn a passing grade, then you might be perfectly satisfied with your performance. However, if your goal was to perform exceptionally well in the course in order to impress your friends and your professor, then you might interpret the average grade very negatively and become discouraged, especially if your expectations are that you no longer can achieve your ultimate aims in the course.

EVALUATIVE STANDARDS

The fourth personality structure in social-cognitive theory is **evaluative standards**. A mental "standard" is a criterion for judging the goodness, or worth, of a person, thing, or event. The study of evaluative standards, then, addresses the ways in which people acquire criteria for evaluating events and how these evaluations influence their emotions and actions.

Of particular importance in social-cognitive theory are evaluative standards concerning one's self, or "personal standards." Personal standards are fundamental to human motivation and performance. Social-cognitive theory recognizes that people commonly evaluate their ongoing behavior in accordance with internalized personal standards. As an example, imagine that you are writing a term paper for a course. What are you thinking about? On the one hand, you have in mind the content of the material for the paper: the main facts you have to cover, the thesis you are trying to develop, and so forth. On the other hand, inevitably you will find yourself thinking of something else. You will be thinking about the quality of your own writing. You will evaluate whether the sentences you have written are good enough or have to be revised. In other words, you have in mind evaluative standards that you use to judge the goodness or worth of your own behavior. Much of the writing and revising process is one in which you try to alter your own behavior (i.e., your writing) to bring it in line with your own personal standards for writing.

Evaluative standards often trigger emotional reactions. We react with pride when we meet our standards for performance and we are dissatisfied with ourself when we fail to meet our own standards. Bandura refers to such emotions as **self-evaluative reactions**; we evaluate our own actions and then respond in an emotionally satisfied or dissatisfied way toward ourselves as a result of this self-evaluation (Bandura, 1986).

The study of evaluative standards is the theoretical tool through which social-cognitive theory addresses moral behavior and violations of moral standards (Bandura, 1986). Some of the evaluative standards that we learn involve ethical and moral principles concerning the treatment of other people. Although everyone in a given society may be familiar with such principles, sometimes people do not use them to regulate their own behavior. For example, everyone knows that it is wrong to steal things from a store or to include plagiarized material in a term paper, yet some people still do these things; they selectively "disengage" their moral standards when it is to their personal advantage to do so (Bandura, Barbaranelli, Caprara, & Pastorelli, 1996).

This focus on personal standards for evaluation is another point that differentiates social-cognitive theory from behaviorism. In a behavioristic experiment, evaluative standards are determined by the experimenter. The experimenter decides that a given number of lever presses by a rat, for example, are enough presses to receive a reinforcement. Social-cognitive theorists note that such experiments fail to address a basic fact of human life. In the human case, evaluative standards are not always set by an outside agent. They are determined by the individual. People have their own personal standards for evaluating their own behavior. There certainly are external influences on these internal standards. Personal standards have social foundations; people commonly acquire standards for performance by observing the performances of others (Bandura, 1986). But once they are acquired, standards and self-evaluative reactions serve as a kind of "internal guidance system" through which people direct their own actions. Ongoing behavior, then, is determined by this internal psychological system, not by forces in the environment, as the behaviorists had argued.

THE NATURE OF SOCIAL-COGNITIVE PERSONALITY STRUCTURES

In social-cognitive theory, the four personality structures we have reviewed—beliefs and expectancies, goals, evaluative standards, and competencies and skills—are not treated as four independent "objects" in one's head. Instead, these four personality structures should be understood as referring to distinct classes of thinking. Each of the four is a cognitive subsystem within the overall system of personality. The theoretical claim is that cognitions about what the world actually is like (beliefs), about one's aims for the future (goals), and about how things normatively should be (standards) play distinct roles in personality functioning and thus, should be treated as distinct personality structures. Similarly, the declarative and procedural knowledge that gives people the capacity to act in an intelligent, skilled manner (competencies) is seen as being psychologically distinct from beliefs, goals, and evaluative standards, and thus, as constituting a distinct personality structure.

Given this view of cognition and personality, the social-cognitive theorist would never assign to a person a single score that is supposed to represent "how much" of each variable they have. Social-cognitive theorists believe that personality is far too complex to be reduced to any simple set of scores. Instead, each of these four personality structures refers to a complex system of social cognition. People have a large number of goals, a wide spectrum of beliefs, an array of evaluative standards, and a diversity of skills. Different personality structures come into play in different social situations. By studying this complex system of social-cognitive structures, and its interaction with the social world, the social-cognitive theorist tries to grapple with the true complexity of the individual.

SOCIAL-COGNITIVE THEORY OF PERSONALITY: PROCESS

Social-cognitive theory addresses the dynamics of personality processes in two different ways. The first involves general theoretical principles. Social-cognitive theorists have presented two theoretical principles that they think scientists should use when analyzing the dynamics of personality processes. One is an analysis of the causes of behavior that is called reciprocal determinism. The other is a framework for thinking about internal personality processes, which is called a cognitive-affective processing system (CAPS) framework.

After we review these two ideas—reciprocal determinism and the CAPS model—we will consider the second way in which social-cognitive theory addresses personality processes. By way of preview, it is by analyzing psychological functions that are of particular importance in a scientific analysis of personality and individual differences. Three types of psychological functions have received particular attention; these are (1) observational learning (or learning through "modeling"), (2) motivation, and (3) self-control.

RECIPROCAL DETERMINISM

Bandura (1986) has introduced a theoretical principle known as **reciprocal determinism**. This principle addresses the issue of cause-and-effect in the study of personality processes.

The problem Bandura is trying to solve is the following. When analyzing a person's behavior, there generally are three factors to consider: the person, his or her behavior, and the environmental setting in which the person acts. In this three-part system, how are we to analyze causes and effects? What causes what? Should one say that the person, with his or her personality attributes, is the cause of behavior (as implied in some trait theories of personality)? Should one say that the environment is the real cause of behavior (as argued by the behaviorists)? Bandura thinks we should not say either of these things because both statements are too simplistic. Instead, he argues that causality is a "two-way street." Stated more formally, causality is reciprocal. Each of the three factors under consideration—behavior, personality characteristics, and the environment—are causes of one another. The factors are reciprocal determinants. Bandura's principle of reciprocal determinism, then, contends that personality, behavior, and the environment must be understood as a system of forces that mutually influence one another across the course of time (Figure 12.2).

To understand this principle intuitively, imagine yourself in conversation with someone who you find attractive. You might smile, look attentive, and try to alter the topics of conversation in a manner that makes a good impression on the other person. Now, from the perspective of a personality scientist, how are we to understand causality in this conversation? What causes what? On the one hand, one could say that the environment causes your behavior. The other person's physical and social attractiveness has caused you to act in a certain way. This is not incorrect; yet it is insufficient. The environment is something that you interpreted, and your particular interpretations are influenced by beliefs and feelings of yours—that is, your personality characteristics. Further, your ability to make a good impression depends on your social skills—another feature of your personality. In addition, your behavior alters the environment you experience. If you skillfully make a good impression, then the other person will be in a better mood, will like you more, will be smiling, will be attentive to you, and so on. In other words, through your own actions, you will have created a more positive social environment. Finally, if you are successful, your behavioral success may alter your mood and your

Figure 12.2 Schematic representation of Bandura's principle of reciprocal determinism, which posits that personality, behavior, and the environment must be understood as a system of forces that mutually influence one another. *From Bandura (1997).*

sense of self; there will be an influence of your own behavior on your own personality. It is futile to isolate one factor as "the cause" and the other as "the effect" in such a system. Instead, personality, behavior, and the environment must be understood as factors that reciprocally determine one another.

The principle of reciprocal determinism constitutes a rejection of the views of other theories. Some theories explain behavior primarily in terms of inner forces: the inner conflicts of psychoanalysis, the motive for self-actualization of the phenomenological theories, the genetically determined dispositions of the trait theories, and the evolved psychological modules of evolutionary psychology. Others explained behavior in terms of external forces—behaviorism being the paradigm case. Bandura rejects this entire discourse about "inner versus outer" or "internal versus external" forces as woefully inadequate because it fails to recognize the person's internal psychology and the social environment influence one another reciprocally. People are influenced by environmental forces, but they also choose how to behave. The person is both responsive to situations and actively constructs and influences situations. People select situations as well as being shaped by them; the capacity to choose the type of situation that one will encounter is seen by social-cognitive theorists as a critical element of people's capacity to be active agents who influence the course of their own development.

PERSONALITY AS A COGNITIVE-AFFECTIVE PROCESSING SYSTEM (CAPS)

In recent years, social-cognitive theorists increasingly have emphasized that personality should be understood as a system. The term "system" generally refers to something that has a large number of parts that interact among each other. The behavior of the system reflects not only the isolated parts, but the ways in which the parts are interconnected. Systems with a very large number of highly integrated parts often exhibit highly complex and coherent forms of behavior, even if the parts are relatively simple. Dynamic interactions among the parts give rise to the system's complexity. An example of this is the brain. It performs remarkably complex actions despite the fact that its parts—neurons—are relatively simple. The complex interconnections among the parts give rise to the brain's complex capabilities (Damasio, 1994; Edelman & Tonini, 2000).

Social-cognitive theory views personality as a complex system. Social-cognitive variables do not operate in isolation from one another. Instead, the various cognitions and affects interact with one another in an organized fashion; as a result, there is an overall coherence to personality functioning (Cervone & Shoda, 1999b).

A systems view of structure has been articulated by Mischel and Shoda (1995). They present a **cognitive-affective processing system** (CAPS) model of personality (Figure 12.3). The CAPS model has three essential features. First, cognitive and emotional personality variables are seen as being complexly linked to one another. It is not merely the case that people have a goal (e.g., get more dates), a level of competency (e.g., low dating skills), a particular expectancy (e.g., low perceived self-efficacy for dating), and certain evaluative standards and self-evaluative reactions (e.g., feeling emotionally dissatisfied with oneself when it comes to dating). Instead, their personality system features these cognitions and affects *and* interrelations among them. Thoughts about one's goals may trigger thoughts about skills, which in turn

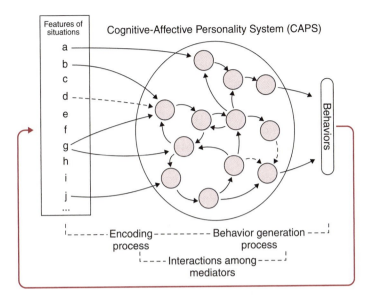

Features of situations

Cognitive-Affective Personality System (CAPS)

a
b
c
d
e
f
g
h
i
j
...

Behaviors

Encoding process — Behavior generation process
Interactions among mediators

Figure 12.3 Schematic representations of the cognitive-affective processing system (CAPS) theory of Mischel and Shoda. *From Mischel and Shoda (1995).*

trigger thoughts about self-efficacy, all of which may affect one's self-evalua-tions and emotions.

The second key feature of the **CAPS** model concerns the social environ-ment. In this model, different aspects of social situations, or "situational fea-tures," activate subsets of the overall personality system. For example, a situ-ation in which you are in a conversation with someone about a date they had last weekend may activate the system of goals and expectancies involving dates outlined in the paragraph above. In contrast, a conversation about poli-tics, sports, or classes at school may activate an entirely different set of cog-nitions and affects.

The third feature follows naturally from the second one. If different situation-al features activate different parts of the overall personality system, then people's behavior should *vary* from one situation to another. Suppose, hypothetically, that an individual's personality system contains negative thoughts and feelings about their dating skills but positive thoughts and feelings about their academic abili-ties. Situational features that activate one versus the other concern (dating ver-sus academic performance) should produce, in the individual, entirely different patterns of emotion and action. Although the individual's personality system is stable, their experiences and action nonetheless should change from one situa-tion to another as different subsets of their overall personality system become active. This is perhaps the most distinctive feature of the **CAPS** model (Mischel & Shoda, 1995). It contends that not only average levels of behavior but also *vari-ations* in behavior are a defining aspect of personality.

Empirical research by Mischel and his associates illustrates the CAPS approach (Shoda, Mischel, & Wright, 1994). In this work, children were observed in various settings during a 6-week period at a summer camp; illus-trative settings were woodworking, cabin meeting, classroom, mealtime, play-ground, and watching TV. Within these settings, situations were defined in terms of whether the interaction involved a peer or an adult counselor and whether the interaction was positive or negative in nature (e.g., the child was praised versus punished by a counselor or teased by a peer). For each child, observations were made regularly on the basis of the frequency with which each of five types of behavior occurred in each of the defined situations: verbal aggression (teased, provoked, or threatened); physical aggression (hit, pushed, physically harmed); whined or displayed babyish behavior; complied or gave in; talked prosocially. These observations were made on an hourly basis, 5 hours a day, 6 days a week, for 6 weeks—an average of 167 hours of observation per child. This yielded an unusually large amount of observation of each child in terms of behaviors expressed in a variety of situations over the course of time.

When analyzing these data, the investigators plotted *if...then...*profiles. In an *if...then...*profile analysis, one plots an individual person's behavior in each of a variety of different situations. One then determines if the individual's behavior varies systematically from one person to another. One might be able to determine that "if" the person encounters a particular type of situation, "then" they tend to act in a certain manner. The "if's" and "then's" may vary from one person to another. The profile analysis thus captures idiosyncratic tendencies exhibited by unique individuals.

What, then, were the findings? Of course there was evidence of considerable differences in behaviors expressed in different situations. People do behave differently in different types of situations. In general, behavior is different on the playground than in the classroom, in a cabin meeting than in woodworking. And, of course there were individual differences in average expressions of each of the five observed types of behavior. As trait theorists suggest, there are individual differences in average expressions of behavior across situations. However, the more critical question for social-cognitive theory is whether individuals can be described in terms of their distinctive patterns of situation-behavior relationships. In other words, do individuals differ in their patterns of behavior even if their overall levels are the same? Can two individuals express the same average level of aggressive behavior, be the same on a trait such as aggressiveness, but differ in the kinds of situations in which they express their aggressiveness? Mischel and his associates indeed found clear evidence that individuals have distinctive, stable profiles of expressing particular behaviors in specific groups of situations. Consider, for example, the verbal aggression profiles of two individuals in relation to five types of psychological situations (Figure 12.4). Clearly the two differ in their profiles of expressing verbal aggression across the various situations. Each behaves reasonably consistently within specific groups of situations but differently between groups of situations. Averaging behavior across situations would mask such distinctive patterns of situation-behavior relationships.

What can be concluded from this research? Mischel and his associates suggest that individuals have distinctive profiles of situation-behavior relationships, what are called **behavioral signatures**. "It is this type of intraindividual stability in the pattern and organization of behavior that seems especially central for a psychology of personality ultimately devoted to understanding and capturing the uniqueness of individual functioning" (Shoda, Mischel, & Wright, 1994, p. 683). Mischel and colleagues emphasized that these unique patterns of behavior would be completely overlooked if one merely asked about people's overall, average behavioral tendencies. Two people who, for example,

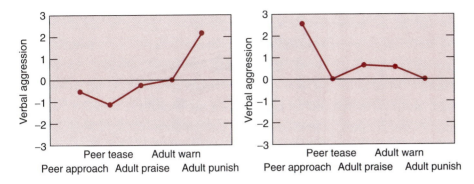

Figure 12.4   Illustrative intraindividual profiles of verbal aggression for two individuals across five types of psychological situations. *(Adapted from Shoda, Mischel, & Wright, 1994, p. 6.)*

display the same average level of anxiety may be fundamentally different people. An *if...then...*profile analysis might reveal that one person is anxious in achievement settings and the other is anxious when it comes to romantic relationships. The analysis would indicate that the different people have different personality dynamics—despite the fact that they might happen to get the same score on "global trait anxiety" if a researcher averages together their responses in the different situations of their life. The basic message of Mischel and colleagues, then, is: Don't average together the different situations of their life! Instead, look closely at individuals and the potentially unique patterns of action that they display as they adapt to different life circumstances.

OBSERVATIONAL LEARNING (MODELING)

So far, we have outlined four personality structures that are central to social-cognitive theory and have reviewed two theoretical principles that Bandura and Mischel use to understand the nature of personality and the causes of behavior. We now can see these theoretical ideas put into action. Social-cognitive theorists use these theoretical principles to understand two main psychological activities, or what we will call here two psychological functions: (1) acquiring new knowledge and skills, particularly through processes of observational learning; and (2) exerting control over, or self-regulating, one's own actions and emotional experiences.

The first of these two psychological functions concerns the question of how people acquire knowledge and skills. How do we learn social skills? How do we acquire particular beliefs, goals, and standards for evaluating our behavior? Previous theories commonly have overlooked these questions. There is little explicit discussion of the acquisition of beliefs and social skills in most of the previous theories we have discussed. The theory that addressed the topic most explicitly was behaviorism. As you will recall, behaviorists claim that people learn things through a trial-and-error learning process called shaping, or successive approximation. Over a large series of learning trials, reinforcements gradually shape a complex pattern of behavior. Although there are lots of errors at first, through reinforcement processes behavior gradually approximates a desired pattern.

Observational Learning: *Aggressive behavior can be learned from the observation of such behavior on television. (Etta Hulme, reprinted by permission of NEA, Inc.)*

In a profoundly important development for psychology, Albert Bandura succeeded in explaining the shortcomings of this behavioral theory and in providing psychology with an alternative theoretical explanation. In retrospect, the shortcomings of the behavioral approach seem obvious. Sometimes learning simply cannot occur by a trial-and-error because the errors are too costly. As an example, consider the first time you ever drove a car. According to the behaviorists, reinforcements and punishments would gradually shape safe driving behavior on your part. On Day 1 of driving you might get into 9 or 10 traffic accidents, but due to reinforcement processes on Day 2 you might only have 5 or 6 accidents, and after a few more trials the errors would disappear and the environment would have shaped safe driving behavior. Is this what actually happened? We sure hope not! In reality, the first time you sat behind the wheel—before you ever had been reinforced or punished for specific driving behaviors—you already were able to drive a car fairly adequately. What needs to be explained is the human capacity to learn such skills in the absence of prior rewards and punishments.

Social-cognitive theory explains that people can learn merely by observing the behaviors of others. The person being observed is called a model, and this **observational learning** processes is also known as "modeling." People's cognitive capacities enable them to learn complex forms of behavior merely by observing a model perform these behaviors. As Bandura (1986) has detailed, people can form an internal mental representation of the behavior they have observed, and then can draw upon that mental representation at a later point in time. Learning by modeling is evident in innumerable domains of life. A child may learn language by observing parents and other people speaking. You may have learned some of the basic skills for driving (where to put your hands and feet, how to start the car, how to turn the wheel) merely by observing other drivers. People learn what types of behavior are acceptable and unacceptable in different social settings by observing the actions of others.

This modeling process can be much more complex than simple imitation or mimicry. The notion of "imitation" generally implies the exact replication of a narrow response pattern. In modeling, however, people may learn general rules of behavior by observing others. They then can use those rules to self-direct a

Modeling: *Social learning theorists emphasize the importance of observing others in the acquisition of behavior. (Drawing by Opie; © 1978 The New Yorker Magazine, Inc.)*

variety of types of behavior in the future. Bandura's conceptualization of modeling also is narrower than the psychodynamic notion of identification. Identification implies an incorporation of broad patterns of behavior exhibited by a specific other individual. Modeling, in contrast, involves the acquisition of information through the observation of others, without implying that the observer internalizes entire styles of action exhibited by the other individual.

The individual who is observed in the process of observational learning (i.e., the model) need not be someone who is physically present. In contemporary society, much modeling occurs through the media. We may learn styles of thought and action from people who we never meet, but who we merely observe on television or other media sources. A social concern is that television often models antisocial behavior such as aggression; research indicates that exposure to high levels of aggression in the media when one is a child can cause people to learn aggressive patterns of behavior that are evident later in life. Huesmann and colleagues (Huesmann, Moise-Titus, Podolski, & Eron, 2003) performed a long-term longitudinal study on the question of whether exposure to violence in the media during childhood leads to higher levels of aggression later in life. Among both men and women, people who saw high levels of violence when they were 6 to 10 years old turned out to be more aggressive in early adulthood. The link between media violence in childhood and aggression in adulthood held up even when the researchers statistically controlled for factors other than media exposure (e.g., socioeconomic status) that might possibly be correlated with levels of aggression. Bandura's research on modeling clearly has important social implications.

Acquisition versus Performance

An important part of the theory of modeling is the distinction between **acquisition** and **performance**. A new, complex pattern of behavior can be learned or acquired regardless of reinforcers, but whether or not the behavior is per-

DON'T BLAME ME; IT WAS THAT VIDEO GAME!

In November 2002, a teenager in the state of Wisconsin was arrested for auto theft. This was no minor case of theft; the teen was charged with stealing about 100 vehicles! What could cause such behavior? Hostile impulses buried deep in the teen's unconscious? A lifelong trait of criminality?

As reported by the Associated Press, the teenager himself had a much simpler explanation: "He had been inspired by the video game 'Grand Theft Auto.'" In the game, players control animated figures who violently battle law enforcement officials as they go on crime rampages, including the theft of autos. As the local police chief in Wisconsin reported, after playing this game for many hours the teenager felt that stealing real cars would be "challenging and fun." In the language of social-cognitive theory, the game provided psychological models of illegal behavior, including the anticipated benefits (fun, challenge) of that behavior.

This, of course, is just a single, isolated case. It does not provide scientific evidence that playing video games actually contributed to this particular teenager's behavior. Nor does it answer the key question: In general, does playing a lot of violent video games cause a person to act more violently in the real world?

This question can be answered. It can be done by evaluating a large number of cases in which one can measure both game playing and real-world aggression. One then can determine the overall degree to which exposure to violent and criminal acts in video games is related to real-world aggressive behavior.

The psychologists Craig Anderson and Brad Bushman have provided an analysis of this sort. They analyzed the results obtained in 35 research reports examining the relation

between violent video game playing and various measures of real-world aggression. Their sample included more than 4,000 participants who had taken part in both correlational studies (i.e., studies correlating game playing and aggression) and experimental studies (i.e., studies in which exposure to violence in video games was controlled experimentally).

As the authors themselves summarize, the results of their analyses "clearly support the hypothesis that exposure to violent video games poses a public-health threat to children and youths, including college-age individuals" (Anderson & Bushman, 2001, p. 358). In both experimental and non-experimental studies, higher exposure to violence in video games was linked to higher levels of aggression, as well as to lower levels of prosocial behavior. The overall correlation between levels of violent game playing and levels of aggression was a little under .2. Although a correlation of this size means that there are many people who play violent video games yet are not violent in other aspects of their life, it nonetheless is large enough to indicate unequivocally that violent game playing can have a detrimental effect on large numbers of people.

Subsequent research by the authors indicates one way in which game playing has its effects (Bushman & Anderson, 2002). Playing violent games produces a "hostile expectation bias." In this experimental research, people played either a nonviolent or a violent video game. They subsequently were asked whether various interpersonal conflicts depicted in stories (that were not part of the game) involved feelings of aggression and hostility on the part of the story characters. People who had played the violent game subsequently were biased to think that the story charac-

ters were feeling and acting aggressively and were having aggressive thoughts. This result implies that people who play violent video games frequently may, in their day-to-day life, more frequently think that other people around them are having hostile, aggressive thoughts. This, of course, could contribute to hostile feelings and actions on their part.

It appears, then, that "fun" and "challenge" are not the only feelings created by violent video games.

SOURCES: Anderson & Bushman, 2001; Associated Press, Nov. 14, 2002. Bushman & Anderson, 2002.

formed will depend on rewards and punishments. Consider, for example, the classic study by Bandura and his associates to illustrate this distinction (Bandura, Ross, & Ross, 1963). In this study three groups of children observed a model express aggressive behavior toward a plastic Bobo doll. In the first group, the aggressive behavior by the model was not followed by any consequences (No Consequences). In the second group, the model's aggressive behavior was followed by rewards (Reward), and in the third group it was followed by punishment (Punishment). Following observation of the model's aggressive behavior, children from the three groups were presented with two conditions. In the first condition, the children were left alone in a room with many toys, including a Bobo doll. They were then observed through a one-way mirror to see if they would express the aggressive behaviors of the model (No Incentive condition). In the next condition, the children were given attractive incentives for reproducing the model's behavior (Positive Incentive condition).

Two relevant questions can be asked. First, did the children behave aggressively when they were given an incentive to do so as opposed to when they were not? Many more imitative aggressive behaviors were shown in the Incentive condition than in the No Incentive condition (Figure 12.5). In other words, the children had learned (acquired) many aggressive behaviors that were not performed under the No Incentive condition but were performed under the Incentive condition. This result demonstrated the use of the distinction between acquisition and performance. Second, did the consequences to the model affect the children's display of aggressive behavior? Observation of behavior in the No Incentive condition indicated clear differences; children who observed the model being punished performed far fewer imitative acts than did children in the Model Rewarded and No Consequences groups (Figure 12.5). This difference, however, was wiped out by offering the children attractive incentives for reproducing the model's behavior (Positive Incentive). In sum, the consequences to the model had an effect on the children's performance of the aggressive acts but not on the learning of them.

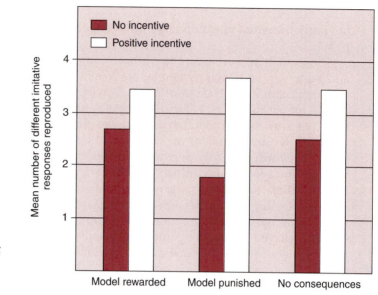

Figure 12.5   Mean Number of Different Imitative Responses Reproduced by Children as a Function of Response Consequences to the Model and Positive Incentives. *(Bandura, 1965) Copyright 1965 by the American Psychological Association. Reprinted by permission.*

Vicarious Conditioning

A number of other studies have since demonstrated that the observation of consequences to a model affects performance but not acquisition. The difference between acquisition and performance suggests, however, that in some way the children were being affected by what happened to the model; that is, either on a cognitive basis, on an emotional basis, or both, the children were responding to the consequences to the model. The suggestion here is that the children learned certain emotional responses by sympathizing with the model, that is, vicariously by observing the model. Not only can behavior be learned through observation, but emotional reactions such as fear and joy can also be conditioned on a vicarious basis: "It is not uncommon for individuals to develop strong emotional reactions toward places, persons, and things without having had any personal contact with them" (Bandura, 1986, p. 185).

The process of learning emotional reactions through observing others, known as **vicarious conditioning**, has been demonstrated in both humans and animals. Thus, human subjects who observed a model expressing a conditioned fear response were found to develop a vicariously conditioned emotional response to a previously neutral stimulus (Bandura & Rosenthal, 1966; Berger, 1962). Similarly, in an experiment with animals it was found that an intense and persistent fear of snakes developed in younger monkeys who observed their parents behave fearfully in the presence of real or toy snakes. What was particularly striking about this research is that the period of observation of their parents' emotional reaction was sometimes very brief. Further, once the vicarious conditioning took place, the fear was found to be intense, long-lasting, and present in situations different from those in which the emotional reaction was first observed (Mineka, Davidson, Cook, & Kleir, 1984).

Although observational learning can be a powerful process, one should not think that it is automatic or that one is bound to follow in the footsteps of others. Children, for example, have multiple models and can learn from parents, siblings, teachers, peers, and television. In addition, they learn from their own direct experience. Beyond this, as children get older they may actively select which models they will observe and attempt to emulate.

SELF-REGULATION AND MOTIVATION

As we have just reviewed, one central personality process in social-cognitive theory is the acquisition of knowledge and skills, which is commonly accomplished through observational learning. A second process concerns putting that knowledge into action. In other words, it involves questions of human motivation.

Social-cognitive theory addresses human motivation primarily by examining the motivational impact of thoughts related to oneself, or self-referent thinking. The general idea is that people commonly guide and motivate their own actions through their thinking processes. Key thinking processes often involve the self. Consider your own motivational processes as they relate to this course in personality psychology. You may have enrolled in the course because you expected that you would find the material interesting. You may have calculated an expected grade you could earn in the course; in selecting this course, you may have avoided other course options in which you expected that you might earn a low grade. During the time you have been in the course, you may have set personal goals for performance in the class and may have guided your own studying by reminding yourself that "I've got to finish reading these chapters before the mid-term exam!" It is these personal expectations, personal goals, and talking-to-oneself that social-cognitive theory sees as being at the heart of human motivation.

The general term for personality processes that involve the self-directed motivation of behavior is **self-regulation**. The term is meant to imply that people have the capacity to motivate themselves: to set personal goals, to plan strategies, to evaluate and modify their ongoing behavior. Self-regulation involves not only getting started in goal attainment, but avoiding environmental distractions and emotional impulses that might interfere with one's progress.

The process of self-regulation inherently involves all of the social-cognitive personality structures that we have reviewed thus far. People regulate their behavior by setting personal goals and by evaluating their ongoing behavior according to evaluative standards for performance. Expectancies also are critical; in particular, high expectations of self-efficacy may be necessary if people are to persevere in their goals despite running into setbacks along the way.

In its study of self-regulation, social-cognitive theory emphasizes the human capacity for foresight—our ability to anticipate outcomes and make plans accordingly (Bandura, 1990). Thus, according to Bandura, "most human motivation is cognitively generated" (1992, p. 18). People vary in the standards they set for themselves. Some individuals set challenging goals, others easy goals; some individuals have very specific goals, others ambiguous goals; some emphasize short-term, proximal goals while others emphasize long-range, distal goals (Cervone & Williams, 1992). In all cases, however, it is the anticipation of satisfaction with desired accomplishments and dissatisfaction with insufficient accomplishments that provides the incentives for our efforts. In this analysis, people are seen as proactive rather than as merely reactive. People set their own standards and goals, rather than merely responding to demands from the environment. Through the development of cognitive mechanisms such as expectancies, standards, and self-evaluation we are able to establish goals for the future and gain control over our own destiny (Bandura, 1989a,b, 1999).

Self-Efficacy, Goals, and Self-Evaluative Reactions

Research in social-cognitive theory has examined how these multiple personality processes—self-efficacy perceptions, goals, and self-evaluation of one's ongoing behavior—combine to contribute to self-regulation. Bandura and Cervone (1983) studied the effects of goals and performance feedback on motivation. The hypothesis tested was that performance motivation reflects both the presence of goals and the awareness of how one is doing relative to standards: "Simply adopting goals, whether easy or personally challenging ones, without knowing how one is doing seems to have no appreciable motivational effects" (1983, p. 123). The assumption was that greater discrepancies between standards and performances would generally lead to greater self-dissatisfaction and efforts to improve performance. However, a critical ingredient of such efforts is self-efficacy judgments. Thus, the research tested the hypothesis that self-efficacy judgments, as well as self-evaluative judgments, mediate between goals and goal-directed effort.

In this research, subjects performed a strenuous activity under one of four conditions: goals with feedback on their performance, goals alone, feedback alone, and absence of goals and feedback. Following this activity, described as part of a project to plan and evaluate exercise programs for postcoronary rehabilitation, subjects rated how self-satisfied or self-dissatisfied they would be with the same level of performance in a following session. In addition, they recorded their perceived self-efficacy for various possible performance levels. Their effortful performance was then again measured. In accord with the hypothesis, the condition combining goals and performance feedback had a strong motivational impact, whereas neither goals alone nor feedback alone had comparable motivational significance (Figure 12.6). Also, subsequent effort was most intense when subjects were both dissatisfied with substandard performance and high on self-efficacy judgments for good attainment. Neither dissatisfaction alone nor positive self-efficacy judgments alone had a comparable effect. Often effort was reduced where there was both low dissatisfaction with performance and low perceived self-efficacy. The authors concluded that there was clear evidence in support of the theory that goals have motivating power through self-evaluative and self-efficacy judgments.

Performance feedback and self-efficacy judgments have been found to be particularly important in the development of intrinsic interest. Thus, psychologists have been able to enhance the interest of students in learning and their level of performance by helping them to break down tasks into subgoals, helping them to monitor their own performance, and providing them with feedback that increased their sense of self-efficacy (Bandura & Schunk, 1981; Morgan, 1985; Schunk & Cox, 1986). Intrinsic interest thus develops when the person has challenging standards that provide for positive self-evaluation when met, and the sense of self-efficacy in the potential for meeting those standards. It is such intrinsic interest that facilitates effort over extended periods of time in the absence of external rewards. Conversely, it is difficult to sus-

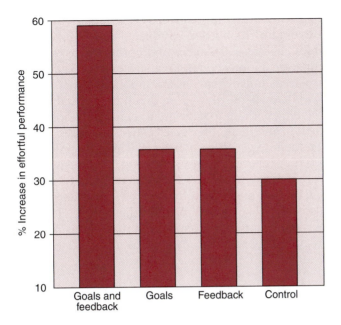

Figure 12.6 Mean Percentage Increase in Effortful Performance under Conditions Varying in Goals and Performance Feedback. *(Bandura & Cervone, 1983) Copyright © 1983 by the American {Psychological Association. Reprinted by permission.*

tain motivation where one feels that the external or internal self-evaluative rewards are insufficient, or where one's sense of efficacy is so low that a positive outcome seems impossible. Self-perceived inefficacy can nullify the motivating potential of even the most desirable outcomes. For example, no matter how attractive it might seem to become a movie star, people will not be motivated in that direction unless they feel that they have the necessary skills. In the absence of such a sense of self-efficacy, becoming a movie star remains a fantasy rather than a goal that is pursued in action.

The effects of self-efficacy beliefs on effort and performance can be so great as to wipe out otherwise large differences in ability. For example, in one study males and females engaged in a competitive muscular leg endurance task. Self-efficacy beliefs of the subjects were manipulated by telling some that they were competing against an individual with a knee injury (high self-efficacy) and others that they were competing against a varsity track athlete (low self-efficacy). Not surprisingly, high self-efficacy subjects clearly performed better than low self-efficacy subjects and male subjects generally performed better than female subjects. What was particularly striking, however, was that subjects in the female, high self-efficacy group performed slightly better than subjects in the male, low self-efficacy group on the strength task. In other words, shifts in self-efficacy beliefs wiped out earlier large sex differences in physical strength (Weinberg, Gould, & Jackson, 1979).

Self-efficacy beliefs also influence how people cope with disappointments and stress in the pursuit of life goals. Research generally suggests that human functioning is facilitated by a personal sense of control (Schwarzer, 1992). Self-efficacy beliefs represent one aspect of such a sense of control. A study of women coping with abortion demonstrated the importance of self-efficacy beliefs in coping with stressful life events (Cozzarelli, 1993). In this research, women about to obtain an abortion completed questionnaire measures of personality variables such as self-esteem and optimism, as well as a self-efficacy scale measuring expectations concerning successful post-abortion coping. For example, the scale included items asking about whether the women thought they would be able to spend time around children or babies comfortably and whether they would continue to have good sexual relations following abortion. Following abortion, and then, three weeks later, measures of mood and depression were obtained (e.g., the degree to which the women were feeling depressed, regretful, relieved, guilty, sad, good). The results clearly supported the hypothesis that self-efficacy was a key determinant of post-abortion adjustment. The contribution of personality variables such as self-esteem and optimism were also related to post-abortion adjustment. However, their effects appeared to occur through their contribution to feelings of self-efficacy.

In sum, perceptions of self-efficacy have been shown to have diverse effects on experience and action, in the following ways:

Selection   Self-efficacy beliefs influence the goals individuals select (e.g., individuals with high self-efficacy beliefs select more difficult, challenging goals than do those who are low self-efficacy beliefs).

Effort, Persistence, and Performance   Individuals with high self-efficacy beliefs show greater effort and persistence, and perform better relative to individuals with low self-efficacy beliefs (Stajkovic & Luthans, 1998).

Emotion   Individuals with high self-efficacy beliefs approach tasks with better moods (i.e., less anxiety and depression) than individuals with low self-efficacy beliefs.

Coping   Individuals with high self-efficacy beliefs are better able to cope with stress and disappointments than are individuals with low self-efficacy beliefs. Bandura summarizes the evidence concerning the effects of self-efficacy beliefs on motivation and performance as follows: "Human betterment has been advanced more by persisters than by pessimists. Self-belief does not necessarily ensure success, but self-disbelief assuredly spawns failure" (1997, p. 77).

To summarize the social-cognitive view of motivation, a person develops goals or standards that serve as the basis for action. People consider alternative courses of action and make decisions on the basis of the anticipated outcomes (external and internal) and the perceived self-efficacy for performing the necessary behaviors. Once action has been taken, the outcome is assessed in terms of the external rewards from others and one's own internal self-evaluations. Successful performance may lead to enhanced self-efficacy and either a relaxation of effort or the setting of higher standards for further effort. Unsuccessful performance or failure may lead to giving up or continued striving, depending on the value of the outcome to an individual and to his or her sense of self-efficacy in relation to further effort.

Illustrating these concepts in relation to academic work, it is possible to remain motivated in one's studies when one has high standards, positive outcomes, feelings of pride associated with meeting those standards, and the sense that one is capable of meeting them. On the other hand, boredom and low motivation are likely when standards are low and few external or internal rewards are expected for accomplishment, or when one perceives successful performance as impossible.

SELF-CONTROL AND DELAY OF GRATIFICATION

The research on motivational processes that we have just reviewed was concerned with the following type of situation. Sometimes you need to *do* something, but you can't get yourself to do it. For example, you might need to start working on a term paper that is due at the end of the semester, but for some reason you can't get yourself to start actually doing the writing. It is under these circumstances that clear goals and standards for performance, and a strong sense of self-efficacy, are beneficial.

Now we turn to a different type of psychological problem. Sometimes you need to *stop* doing something. There may be some behavior that you find quite enjoyable, but that is socially inappropriate and/or potentially harmful to yourself or others. Smoking, overeating, and driving your car down the highway at 100 mph are obvious examples. Here, the psychological challenge is the opposite of the one we analyzed above. You need to curtail the intrinsically enjoyable behavior. You need to control your impulsive reactions because, in the long run, it is better if you do not give in to them. When these cases of self-control involve putting off something good in the present in order to attain something better in the future (e.g., not having "that extra piece of pie" now so that, in the future, one will be in better health), the phenomenon is referred to as "delay of gratification."

Learning Delay of Gratification Skills

Research in social-cognitive theory suggests that people's capacity to delay gratification has a social basis. Modeling and observational learning are important to the development of performance standards for success and reward that serve as a basis for delay of gratification. Children exposed to models who set high standards of performance for self-reward tend to limit their own self-rewards to exceptional performance to a greater degree than do children who have been exposed to models who set lower standards or to no models at all (Bandura & Kupers, 1964). Children will model standards even if they result in self-denial of available rewards (Bandura, Grusec, & Menlove, 1967) and will also impose learned standards on other children (Mischel & Liebert, 1966). Children can be made to tolerate greater delays in receiving gratification if they are exposed to models exhibiting such delay behavior.

The effects of a model on delay behavior in children are well illustrated in research by Bandura and Mischel (1965). Children found to be high and low in delay of gratification were exposed to models of the opposite behavior. In a live-model condition, each child individually observed a testing situation in which an adult model was asked to choose between an immediate reward and a more valued object at a later date. The high-delay children observed a model who selected the immediately available reward and commented on its benefits, whereas the low-delay children observed a model who selected the delayed reward and commented on the virtues of delay. In a symbolic-model condition, children read verbal accounts of these behaviors, the verbal account again being the opposite of the child's pattern of response. Finally, in a no-model condition, children were just appraised of the choices given the

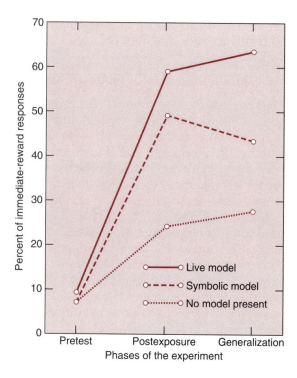

Figure 12.7   Mean Percentage of Immediate-Reward Responses by High-Delay Children on Each of Three Test Periods for Each of Three Experimental Conditions. *(Bandura & Mischel, 1965) Copyright © by the American Psychological Association. Reprinted by permission.*

adults. Following exposure to one of these three procedures, the children were again given a choice between an immediate reward and a more valuable reward. The results were that the high-delay children in all three conditions significantly altered their delay-of-reward behavior in favor of immediate gratification. The live-model condition produced the greatest effect (Figure 12.7). The low-delay children exposed to a delay model significantly altered their behavior in terms of greater delay, but there was no significant difference between the effects of live and symbolic models. Finally, for both groups of children, the effects were found to be stable when the tests were readministered four to five weeks later.

As mentioned previously, the performance of observed behaviors clearly is influenced by the observed consequences to the model. For example, children who watch a film in which a child is not punished for playing with toys that were prohibited by the mother are more likely to play with prohibited toys than are children who see no film or see a film in which the child is punished (Walters & Parke, 1964). The old saying "Monkey see, monkey do" is not completely true. It would be more appropriate to say "Monkey sees reward or is not punished, monkey does." After all, the monkey is no fool.

Mischel's Delay of Gratification Paradigm

In addition to the issue of social influences such as modeling on delay of gratification, another question involves the exact cognitive processes that enable someone to control their impulses. What can you do if you want to control your impulses? What mental strategies enable people to delay gratification? Much insight into this question comes from an exceptionally informative line of research pioneered by Mischel (1974; Metcalfe & Mischel, 1999).

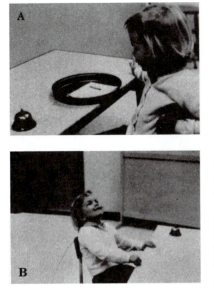

Photos depict a child in the delay of gratification research of Mischel and colleagues (see text). The child is shown a reward (a small pretzel is depicted) and can ring the bell if she cannot wait for the experimenter to return. As depicted in the lower photo, children generally are more successful at waiting if they look away from the rewards and distract themselves from the frustration of having to wait.

In Mischel's **delay of gratification** paradigm, an adult who is interacting with a young child (usually one of preschool age) informs the child that she needs to leave the child alone for a few minutes. Before leaving, the adult teaches the child a game. The game involves two different rewards. If the child can wait patiently until the adult comes back, she will get a large reward (e.g., a few marshmallows). If the child simply cannot wait for the adult to return, the child can ring a bell and the adult will return immediately; however, if this happens, the child earns only a smaller reward (e.g., one marshmallow). The child, then, can earn a small reward immediately but a larger reward by delaying gratification. The dependent measure in the study is how long children are able to wait before ringing the bell.

A critical experimental manipulation in this setting is whether children can see the reward—or, phrased more technically, whether the rewards are available for attention. In one experimental condition, children could see the rewards. In another, the rewards were not available for attention; they simply were covered up. This simple experimental manipulation proved to have a huge effect on children's delay abilities (Figure 12.8). When the rewards were covered up, most children were able to wait a relatively long time. But when the children were looking at the rewards, they had an enormously hard time controlling their impulses. It appears that looking at rewards that one is not supposed to have primarily is a frustrating experience that children have a hard time handling (Mischel, 1974). Being unable to look at the rewards, then, makes the situation easier to handle.

Subsequent work showed that the critical factor in delay of gratification is what is going on in children's heads as they try to wait for the large reward. Children do well at the task if they employ cognitive strategies that distract them from the attractive qualities of the rewards. For example, if children are taught to think about how marshmallows resemble some non-food object (e.g., clouds), or are asked to form mental images in which they think of the rewards as if they are merely photos rather than are real things, or are taught

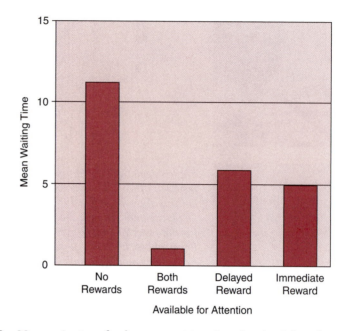

Figure 12.8   Mean minutes of voluntary waiting time for the delayed reward in each attention condition. *(From Mischel & Ebbesen, 1970).*

to sing songs to themselves or play other mentally distracting games during the delay period, then they are able to delay gratification even if the rewards are in sight (Mischel & Baker, 1975; Mischel & Moore, 1973; Moore, Mischel, & Zeiss, 1976). "Thus, what is in the children's heads—not what is physically in front of them—crucially affects their ability to purposefully sustain delay in order to achieve their preferred but delayed goals.... If the children imagine the real objects as present they cannot wait long for them. In contrast, if they imagine pictures of the objects, they can wait for long time periods" (Mischel, 1990, p. 123). Imagining a mere picture of the object is a "cool" encoding (Metcalfe & Mischel, 1999), that is, a way of thinking about the stimulus that does not activate "hot," impulsive emotional systems. People seem more capable of controlling their emotional reactions, then, when they focus their attention on less emotional features of a given situation; the impact of "hot" versus "cool" encoding for interpersonal behavior is reviewed in Chapter 14.

Mischel's delay of gratification findings vividly illustrates the human capacity for self-control. In this regard, it again is instructive to contrast this social-cognitive research with behaviorism. The behaviorist looking at Mischel's paradigm might have argued that the reward contingencies would be the main determinant of children's behavior. The problem with that argument is that children in the different experimental conditions (Figure 12.8) all face exactly the same reward contingencies. They all get the same small and large rewards based on the same behavior. Mischel's research, then, illustrates the power of something that classic behaviorism never thought of, namely, the behavioral influence of people's *mental representations of* rewards. People have the capacity to overcome the potential frustration of the delay of gratification situation by employing mental strategies.

Table 12.2   Illustrative Correlations Between Preschool Delay Time and Parental Ratings of Their Children's Competences and Information on Their SAT Scores

Parental Responses to Questionnaire Items (Adolescence)	Preschool Delay Measure
1. Likelihood of being sidetracked by minor setbacks	-.30[*]
2. Likelihood of exhibiting self-control in frustrating situations	.58[***]
3. Ability to cope with important problems	.31[*]
4. Ability to do well academically when motivated	.37[*]
5. Likelihood of yielding to temptation	-.50[***]
6. Likelihood of settling for immediate but less desirable choice	-.32[*]
7. Ability to pursue goals when motivated	.38[*]
8. Ability to exhibit self-control in tempting situations	.36[*]
9. Ability to concentrate	.41[**]
10. Ability to exhibit self-control when frustrated	.40[**]
11. SAT Verbal	.42[*]
12. SAT Quantitative	.57

[*] $p < .05$ [**] $p < ,01$ [***] $p < .001$ (Sample size for items 1 – 10 = 43, for 11 – 12 = 35)

(Adapted from Shoda, Mischel, & Peake, 1990, p. 983).

Since this research involves children, one may wonder about the implication of the results for later personality development. Mischel investigated this question by relating the delay of gratification scores of preschool children to measures of their cognitive and social competence in adolescence, covering a time span of approximately 10 years. Adolescent competence scores were based on parental ratings of their children's cognitive and self-control skills. In addition, parents were asked to provide their children's SAT verbal and quantitative scores, information that was found to be reliable when checked against score information provided by the Educational Testing Service. The results indicated considerable continuity between preschool measures of delay in a laboratory situation and measures of cognitive and social competence obtained in adolescence (Table 12.2) (Shoda, Mischel, & Peake, 1990). Mischel concludes that the results "give a general picture of the child who delayed in preschool developing into an adolescent who is seen as attentive, able to concentrate, able to express ideas well, responsive to reason, competent, skillful, planful, able to think ahead, and able to cope and deal with stress maturely.... Perhaps most important, the attributes suggested by the adolescent ratings are consistent with the cognitive competencies essential for delay revealed by the experimental research, namely the ability to divert and control attention strategically in the pursuit of one's goal" (1999, p. 484).

SOCIAL-COGNITIVE VIEW OF GROWTH AND DEVELOPMENT

In addition to the importance of direct experience, social-cognitive theory emphasizes the importance of models and observational learning in personality development. Individuals acquire emotional responses and behaviors through observing the behaviors and emotional responses of models (i.e., the processes of observational learning and vicarious conditioning). Whether acquired behaviors are performed similarly depends on directly experienced consequences and the observed consequences to models. Through the experiencing of **direct external consequences**, individuals learn to expect rewards and punishments for specific behaviors in specific contexts. Through **vicarious experiencing of consequences** to others, individuals acquire emotional reactions and learn expectancies without going through the often painful step of experiencing consequences directly. Thus, through direct experience and observation, through direct experiencing of rewards and punishments and through vicarious conditioning, individuals acquire such important personality characteristics as competencies, expectancies, goals-standards, and self-efficacy beliefs. In addition, through such processes individuals acquire self-regulatory capacities. Thus, through the development of cognitive competencies and standards people are able to anticipate the future and reward or punish themselves for relative progress in meeting chosen goals. The latter **self-produced consequences** are of particular significance in maintaining behavior over extended periods of time in the absence of external reinforcers.

It is important to recognize that social-cognitive theory is opposed to views that emphasize fixed stages of development and broad personality types. According to Bandura and Mischel, people develop skills and competencies in particular areas. Rather than developing consciences or healthy egos, they develop competencies and motivational guides for action that are attuned to specific contexts. Such a view emphasizes the ability of people to discriminate among situations and to regulate behavior flexibly according to internal goals and the demands of the situation.

SUMMARY

This chapter has reviewed the basic principles of the social-cognitive approach to personality. They include three main ideas.

Personality is conceptualized in terms of four types of variables: competencies, beliefs and expectancies, goals, and evaluative standards. These cognitive personality structures develop as a result of social experience, and thus are called "social-cognitive."

Personality is understood as a cognitive-affective processing system. The notion of *system* is critical; different social-cognitive structures and processes are highly interconnected and organized, and thus work together as a coherent system. This personality system develops and functions through reciprocal interactions with the social environment.

Social-cognitive theory explores a variety of personality processes that are central to everyday social behavior. These include (a) modeling, or observational learning; (b) motivation, which involves the self-regulation of behavior as people work toward goals; and (c) the control of impulses, where research on delay of gratification shows that what children pay attention to while trying to control their impulses determines self-control ability.

In the next chapter, we continue to explore contemporary social-cognitive theory. We do so by examining not only the contributions of Bandura and Mischel and their colleagues, but those of other contemporary researchers who contribute to an understanding of social-cognitive processes in personality. We also consider applications of the theoretical ideas to real-world problems, including applications in the psychological clinic.

MAJOR CONCEPTS

Acquisition   The learning of new behaviors, viewed by Bandura as independent of reward and contrasted with performance—which is seen as dependent on reward.

Behavioral signatures   Individually distinctive profiles of situation-behavior relationships.

Cognitive-affective processing system (CAPS)   A theoretical framework developed by Mischel and colleagues in which personality is understood as containing a large set of highly interconnected cognitive and emotional processes; the interconnections cause personality to function in an integrate, coherent way, or as a "system."

Competencies   A structural unit in social-cognitive theory reflecting the individual's ability to solve problems or perform tasks necessary to achieve goals.

Context specificity   The idea that a given personality variable may come into play in some life settings, or contexts, but not others, with the result that a person's behavior may vary systematically across contexts.

Delay of gratification   The postponement of pleasure until the optimum or proper time, a concept particularly emphasized in social-cognitive theory in relation to self-regulation.

Direct external consequences   In social-cognitive theory, the external events that follow behavior and influence future performance, contrasted with vicarious consequences and self-produced consequences.

Evaluative standards   Criteria for evaluating the goodness or worth of a person or thing. In social-cognitive theory, people's standards for evaluating their own actions are seen as being involved in the regulation of behavior and the experience of emotions such as pride, shame, and feelings of satisfaction or dissatisfaction with oneself.

Expectancies   In social-cognitive theory, what the individual anticipates or predicts will occur as the result of specific behaviors in specific situations (anticipated consequences).

Goals   In social-cognitive theory, desired future events that motivate the person over extended periods of time and enable the person to go beyond momentary influences.

Microanalytic research   Bandura's suggested research strategy concerning the concept of self-efficacy in which specific rather than global self-efficacy judgments are recorded.

Observational learning (modeling)   Bandura's concept for the process through which people learn merely by observing the behavior of others, called models.

Perceived self-efficacy   In social-cognitive theory, the perceived ability to cope with specific situations.

Performance   The production of learned behaviors, viewed by Bandura as dependent on rewards, in contrast with the acquisition of new behaviors, which is seen as independent of reward.

Reciprocal determinism   The mutual, back-and-forth effects of variables on one another; in social-cognitive theory, a fundamental causal principle in which personal, environmental, and behavioral factors are viewed as causally influencing one another.

Self-evaluative reactions   Feelings of dissatisfaction versus satisfaction (pride) in oneself that occur as people reflect on their actions.

Self-regulation   Psychological processes through which persons motivate their own behavior.

Self-produced consequences   In social-cognitive theory, the consequences to behavior that are produced personally (internally) by the individual and that play a vital role in self-regulation and self-control.

Vicarious conditioning   Bandura's concept for the process through which emotional responses are learned through the observation of emotional responses in others.

Vicarious experiencing of consequences   In social-cognitive theory, the observed consequences to the behavior of others that influence future performance.

REVIEW

1. Social-cognitive theory centers its analyses of personality on uniquely human-cognitive capacities. Thanks to their ability to think about themselves, their past, and their future, individuals are seen to have the capacity to influence their own experiences and development. Since these thinking processes develop through interaction with the social environment, they are called "social-cognitive." The two main representatives of the social-cognitive approach are Albert Bandura and Walter Mischel.

2. The personality structures emphasized in social-cognitive theory are competencies and skills, expectancies and beliefs, behavioral standards, and personal goals. These four personality variables refer to four distinct classes of cognition; they thus can be seen as distinct subsystems within the overall system of personality. Any given person may have different skills, beliefs, standards, and goals in different situations. Thus, behavior naturally varies across situations in a meaningful manner that reflects the individual's personality characteristics.

3. Social-cognitive theory addresses personality processes in a number of different ways. Processes of reciprocal determinism examine the back-and-forth influences between personality and the environment. The notion that personality is a cognitive-affective processes system captures the internal dynamics of personality processing. Much research attention on personality processes has explored observational learning, self-regulation, and self-control.

4. The social-cognitive theory analysis of observational learning emphasizes that people's knowledge and skills primarily are acquired by observing others. Observational learning processes also include the learning of emotional reactions through observation of models, a process known as vicarious conditioning. An important distinction is made between acquiring patterns of behavior in the absence of rewards and performing those behaviors, the latter being dependent on expected consequences (i.e., expected rewards and punishments).

5. The social-cognitive theory analysis of motivation emphasizes the motivational impact of people's thoughts about themselves. Self-efficacy judgments, or the perceived ability to perform tasks relevant to a situation, play a key role in motivation through their influence on selection of goals, effort and persistence toward achieving the goal, the emotions with which tasks are approached (i.e., anxiety and depression associated with low self-efficacy), and success in coping with stress and negative events. In addition, much work examines processes of goal setting, and the role that people's evaluations of their own actions play in goal-directed motivation.

6. Research on the development of cognitive and behavioral competencies associated with delay in gratification illustrates the social-cognitive principles of growth and development. Standards are learned through the observation of models and through reinforcement. The ability to delay gratification involves the development of cognitive and behavioral competencies that are acquired through observation of others and through direct experience. Delay behavior, then, is influenced by outcome expectancies, including both responses from others and self-evaluative responses.

7. Throughout social-cognitive theory there is an emphasis on the development of cognitive skills and competencies in particular areas. The emphasis is on the ability of the person to discriminate among situations and regulate behavior according to internal goals and external demands. Thus, once more, there is a shift from context-free traits to functioning in specific situations. The overall goal is to explain both consistency and variability in personality functioning in terms of a common set of psychological mechanisms.

SOCIAL-COGNITIVE THEORY: EXTENSIONS, APPLICATIONS, AND EVALUATION

COGNITIVE COMPONENTS OF PERSONALITY: BELIEFS, GOALS, AND EVALUATIVE STANDARDS
  Beliefs about the Self and Self-Schemas
    Self-Schemas and Reaction-Time Methods
    Self-Based Motives and Motivated Information Processing
  Learning versus Performance Goals
    Causes of Learning versus Performance Goals: Implicit Theories
  Standards of Evaluation
    Self-Standards and Self-Discrepancies
    A "General Principles" Approach to Personality

CAUSAL EXPLANATIONS AND ATTRIBUTIONS
  Consequences of Causal Attributions

CLINICAL APPLICATIONS
  Stress and Coping
  Pathology and Change
    Ellis's Rational-Emotive Therapy
    Beck's Cognitive Therapy for Depression
    The Cognitive Triad of Depression
    Research on Faulty Cognitions
    Cognitive Therapy

Psychopathology: Modeling, Self-Conceptions, and Perceived Self-Efficacy
    Self-Efficacy, Anxiety, and Depression
    Self-Efficacy and Health
    Therapeutic Change: Modeling and Guided Mastery

THE CASE OF JIM
  Social-Cognitive Theory: Goals, Reinforcers, and Self-Efficacy Beliefs
  Comment
  Additional Assessments

COMPARATIVE ANALYSIS: RELATING SOCIAL-COGNITIVE THEORY TO THE PREVIOUS APPROACHES

CRITICAL EVALUATION
  Strengths
    Systematic Research on Important Phenomena and Evidence
    A Theory Open to Change
    View of the Person and Social Concern
  Limitations
    Not Yet a Systematic, Unified Theory
    Relative Neglect of Important Areas

MAJOR CONCEPTS

REVIEW

Chapter Focus

A college senior was trying to work on his medical school applications late one evening, but found himself so paralyzed by anxiety that he could get nothing accomplished. How could he cope with the possibility of not getting accepted anywhere? His family is counting on him to be a doctor! His friends would think he was a big braggart if he didn't get in to a medical school after his years of talk about being premed! These thoughts so preoccupied him that he failed to complete his applications by the deadlines. He eventually sent them in, but by being late he significantly worsened his chances of getting into medical school. Thus, his own behavior had increased the likelihood that the unwanted outcome would become a reality.

This young man is doing something that is extremely common. When working on a task, people often think about not only the task at hand (the admissions information, in this case) but about themselves (their goals, hopes, and fears). These thoughts may cause one to do worse; they distract people from the task at hand, create anxiety, and thus undermine performance. A psychologist might say that these thoughts are "dysfunctional": they work (or "function") badly for people, undermining their efforts to succeed.

Basic research in social-cognitive theory has explored the impact of beliefs, goals, and standards on people's emotions and behavior, including negative emotions that undermine performance. In clinical applications of this research, psychologists have developed ways to alter dysfunctional beliefs. These extensions and applications of social-cognitive theory are examined in this chapter. In concluding sections of the chapter, we evaluate social-cognitive theory, in part by comparing it to personality theories you learned about previously in the text.

QUESTIONS TO BE ADDRESSED IN THIS CHAPTER

1. How can the study of knowledge structures, or "schemas," inform the understanding of personality and self-concept?

2. How do people's goals and standards for performance affect their motivation and emotional life?

3. How can a social-cognitive analysis of personality contribute to the development of effective psychotherapies?

4. Can psychotherapy rely on cognitive processes alone, or is actual experience a necessary component of therapeutic change?

In Chapter 12, you learned that social-cognitive theory explains personality in terms of basic thinking—or "cognitive"—capacities. The main theorists, Albert Bandura and Walter Mischel, worked to develop a systematic personality theory whose core variables described primary aspects of thinking that influence people's emotions and social behavior. In other words, the "units of analysis" of the theory (see Chapter 1) are thinking processes that develop through social interaction. As you will recall from the previous chapter, three of these cognitive personality variables were (1) *beliefs* about the self and the world around one, (2) personal aims or *goals*, and (3) evaluative *standards* that people use to judge the goodness or worth of our own actions and those of others. The basic idea of social-cognitive theory is that beliefs, goals, and standards—as well as competencies for performing behaviors—contribute to the uniqueness and coherence of our personality.

In this chapter, we review contemporary research on each of these three social-cognitive components of personality. As you will see, some of the research programs that we review will be ones that were spearheaded by Bandura or Mischel, the primary social-cognitive theorists reviewed in Chapter 12. But other research programs have been initiated by other personality scientists. Numerous researchers in the contemporary field analyze personality by examining the role of social-cognitive processes and structures. Their efforts extend and complement the work of Bandura and Mischel and, in so doing, contribute to a broad social-cognitive tradition in contemporary personality psychology.

BELIEFS ABOUT THE SELF AND SELF-SCHEMAS

People possess a wide range of beliefs about the physical and social world. A subset of beliefs that are of particular importance to personality are beliefs about the self. Self-referent beliefs are important because a wide range of phenomena—emotions, motivation, the flow of ideas that constitute our mental life—are affected by our thoughts about our selves. Events elicit emotional reactions and become motivating when they are seen as relevant to our sense of self (Lazarus, 1991).

As we have noted previously, the study of self-concept was relatively neglected during significant portions of psychology's history. As we have seen, traditional psychoanalysts were more interested in id processes than self processes. Behaviorists tried to explain behavior without reference to the self. None of the central variables in the trait theories (other than the theory of Allport) directly concerned aspects of self-concept. During much of the cognitive revolution of the 1960s and early 1970s, the concept of self received little attention. In part this was due to the use of a computer metaphor in cognitive psychology; how could a computer model make sense out of such a concept? Rogers's phenomenological theory, of course, directly addressed self-concept; yet Rogers, writing primarily in the 1950s and early 1960s, could not capitalize on contemporary developments in psychological science that inform the study of self processes. For the first three-quarters of the 20th century, then, psychological researchers did a rather poor job of developing a science of the self.

In a remarkable coincidence of timing, the intellectual scene shifted in 1977. A number of scientists, working independently, published seminal papers in which aspects of self-concept figured prominently. One such paper was Bandura's (1977) initial statement of self-efficacy theory, discussed in Chapter 12. Other work included social psychological studies demonstrating that information that is relevant to the self is more memorable than other types of information (Rogers, Kuiper, & Kirker, 1977). Finally, a paper that proved to be of enormous significance to the study of personality, and that we

COGNITIVE COMPONENTS OF PERSONALITY: BELIEFS, GOALS, AND EVALUATIVE STANDARDS

Hazel Markus

will now discuss, was published by the psychologist Hazel Markus (1977), who explored self-schemas.

The idea that the mind contains **schemas** has a long history. The 18th century German philosopher Immanuel Kant recognized that we make sense out of new experiences by interpreting events in terms of preexisting ideas in the mind (Watson, 1963). These preexisting mental structures are what he referred to as schemas. Schemas are knowledge structures that we use to bring order to what otherwise might be a chaotic jumble of stimuli. To illustrate, suppose you listen to a new song on the radio. In terms of the physical stimuli involved, the sound might seem chaotic: there's some banging on a drum, some noises from a synthesizer, a few guitar chords, somebody singing something, somebody else singing something else. And all these different sounds occur at the same time! Chaos! Yet, of course, it isn't chaos. It sounds to you like an ordered, structured, meaningful piece of music. It sounds this way because you have acquired mental schemas for song structures, and these schemas guide your interpretation of the information (i.e., the sounds that comprise the song). The role of schemas becomes clear if you hear music of a musical form with which you are not at all familiar, that is, music for which you are lacking a musical schema. If, for example, you hear music from a different culture or contemporary symphonic music that is not written according to traditional harmonies, rhythms, and melodic structures, it might sound chaotic to you—even though it surely sounds structured and orderly to its composer. This is because you lack the musical schemas that are necessary to make sense of the sounds.

Schemas, then, are structures of the mind that we use to make sense of the world around us. Phrased more technically, schemas are knowledge structures that guide and organize the processing of information. A schema, then, is far more than just a stored list of facts. A schema instead is an organized network of knowledge (Fiske & Taylor, 1991; Smith, 1998) that commonly is of such complexity that it may be impossible for a person to state its contents. For example, you may not be able to state in words all the knowledge of music that you possess (the sounds of instruments, patterns of rhythm and melody, etc.). Yet you surely can use that knowledge to understand and evaluate new songs.

Markus (1977) recognized that many of our most important schemas concern ourselves. In a key step forward in the study of social cognition and personality, she suggested that the self is a concept or category like any other concept or category, and that people form cognitive generalizations about the self just as they do about other things. People, then, develop self-schemas. Through interaction with the social world, we develop generalized knowledge structures concerning ourselves. These elements of self-knowledge guide and organize information processing when we encounter new situations.

Importantly, different people—with their different interpersonal, social, and cultural life experiences—develop different self-schemas, that is, schemas with different content. For example, one person might have an independence/dependence self-schema; in other words, they might commonly think of themselves as an independent person, might possess a lot of knowledge about this personality characteristic of theirs, and might interpret situations according to their relevance to independence. Another person might possess a schema organized around the concept of guilt/innocence, and use this schema to interpret many situations, even though a guilt/innocence schema might not even be present in most other persons. Self-schemas, then, may account for the relatively unique ways in which idiosyncratic individuals think about the world around them.

Self-Schemas and Reaction-Time Methods

An important aspect of Markus' work was that she not only provided theoretical ideas about self-schemas. She also provided methodological tools to study self-schemas. A key research method employed by Markus (1977) was *reaction-time* (or response latency) measures. Reaction-time measures are experimental methods in which an experimenter records not only the content of a person's response (e.g., whether they say "yes" or "no" in response to a question), but also how long it takes the person to respond to the question. Reaction-time measures are directly relevant to the central idea associated with the notion of self-schemas. The idea is that schemas guide information processing. People who possess a self-schema with regard to a given domain of social life should, then, be faster in responding to questions regarding that life domain. Reaction-time measures, then, provide the index of speed of response that is necessary to test this theoretical idea.

To illustrate the logic of reaction-time methods, suppose you happen to be someone who spends hours a week doing volunteer service in which you are helpful to other individuals in your community. As a result, you may have developed a self-schema regarding your "helpfulness." Now suppose that both you and another person, who rarely does volunteer service, are in a study in which you are asked the question "Are you a helpful person?" Both of you may say "yes." Even the other person, who only occasionally volunteers, may say that, "yes," he or she is helpful. However, despite your similar "yes" responses, self-schema theory would expect that you would differ in the *speed* with which you make your responses. Compared to the other person, you should be faster to say that, "yes," you are helpful. Your preexisting self-schema regarding helpfulness should speed your information processing.

This is exactly the sort of result that Markus (1977) found and that has been replicated by subsequent investigators. Markus (1977) first identified people who possessed a self-schema regarding independence (the attribute she happened to use in her study). She did this by using a two-step method in which participants (1) rated themselves as high or low on independence and (2) indicated the degree to which the personality characteristic was important to them. Only people who had an extreme high or low self-rating and thought that independence/dependence was important to their personality were judged as being schematic for the attribute; the idea is that we tend to develop schemas about personal attributes that we view as socially important to our lives. Subsequently, participants were asked to rate whether a series of adjectives (some of which were semantically related to independence/dependence) were descriptive of themselves. Exactly as predicted, participants who possessed a schema made these judgments faster. Specifically, independent-schematic participants rated independent adjectives more quickly than dependent adjectives, and dependent-schematic persons identified dependent adjectives faster than independent traits (Markus, 1977).

Research on self-schemas by Markus and others suggests that, once we have developed ways of thinking about ourselves (our self-schemas), there is a strong tendency for them to be maintained. We seem to be biased to pay attention to, to remember, and to judge as being true information that is consistent with our schemas about ourselves. Schemas, then, not only guide the processing of information. In so doing, they also create self-confirming biases.

An illustration of how self-schemas are not only related to the processing of information but to action as well comes from research on schemas, sexual behavior, and romantic involvement. The researchers in this study investigated the hypothesis that women with differing sexual self-schemas would process interpersonal information differently and function differently in their sexual and romantic relationships (Andersen & Cyranowski, 1994). Women were asked to rate themselves on a list of 50 adjectives, 26 of which were used to form a Sexual Self-Schema Scale (e.g., uninhibited, loving, romantic, passionate, direct). Since the relevant items were embedded in the longer list, subjects did not know of the existence of the specific scale, believing instead that they were making general self-ratings. The women were also asked to respond to sexuality measures selected to sample sexual experiences and romantic involvement. Clear evidence was found that women with high scores on the Sexual Self-Schema Scale, particularly those with positive sexual self-schemas, were more sexually active, experienced greater sexual arousal and sexual pleasure, and were more able to be involved in romantic love relationships relative to women with low scores on the scale. "Co-schematics," that is, women who had both positive schemas organized around their ability to experience sexual passion and negative schemas involving sexual conservatism or embarrassment, were found to experience high levels of involvement with sexual partners yet also to experience relative high levels of sexual anxiety (Cyranowski & Andersen, 1998). These experiences, in turn, could further influence views about the self, creating a self-confirming bias in which schemas contribute to experiences that, in turn, confirm the original schemas.

In this emphasis on the self, it should be clear that any given individual does *not* possess merely one self-schema. Instead, people tend to live complex lives in which they develop a number of different views of themselves. For example, it may not be the case that you are either a hard-working student, or a loyal friend, or a good dancer at parties, or an anxious test-taker. Instead, you well could be all four of these things; that is, you may possess self-schemas concerning all four of these aspects of self. The different self-schemas would tend to come to mind in different settings. Different situational cues may cause different self-schemas to enter working memory and thus, to be part of the **working self-concept** (Markus & Wurf, 1987), that is, the subset of self-concept that is in working memory at any given time (Figure 13.1). Self-concept thus is dynamic; the information about the self that is in consciousness, and guides behavior, at any given time changes dynamically as people interact with the ever-changing events of the social world.

Contemporary research on social cognition and self-concept (e.g., Banaji & Prentice, 1994), then, suggests that the self is not a single, unitary thing. Instead, people commonly possess multiple self-schemas. The different self-schemas frequently are related to one another; for example, using the example above, there may be links between your view of yourself as hard-working and as someone who is anxious when it comes to taking tests, and friendship and dancing at parties may provide an important break from the academic routine of college life. Recognizing these relations, investigators have suggest-

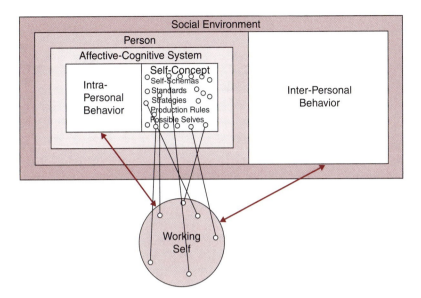

Figure 13.1   Schematic representation of the Working Self, which consists of a subset of mental representations that make up the overall self-concept. *The central idea in this model is that different social circumstances activate different subsets of a person's overall self-knowledge; in other words, different situations bring different information into working memory, creating different "working selves" in different settings. From Markus and Wurf (1987).*

ed that, rather than a single self-schema, people tend to possess a "family of selves" (Cantor & Kihlstrom, 1987), that is, a collection of self-views that may be as diverse as are different members of the same family, yet that may share some family resemblances. According to this view, you are many things, in many places, with many people. Thus, you have many contextualized selves, each with a set of features. The features of these contextualized selves, this family of selves, will overlap in some ways and be distinctive in others. Each of us, then, has a family of selves, the contents and organization of which are unique. Within this family of selves there may be a prototypic self, a self-concept in relation to which we say, "This is what I am really like." And within this family of selves there may be fuzzy selves, or parts of us that we are not sure how they fit in relation to the other selves.

Self-Based Motives and Motivated Information Processing

Self-schemas do not merely provide information that is used in thinking, in the way that an encyclopedia might provide information that is used in answering a trivia question. Self-schemas also motivate people to process information in particular ways. Motivational processes, then, are often self-based (Banaji & Prentice, 1994; Higgins, 1996, 1997; Kunda, 1990). Two motives in relation to the self have been emphasized in research social cognition and personality. They are motives for **self-enhancement** and for **self-verification**.

Your intuitions may tell you that people are biased toward seeing themselves in a positive light. For example, when you get a bad grade on an exam, you might be prone to think of how poorly written or unfair the exam was; con-

SOURCES OF SELF-ESTEEM FOR MEN AND WOMEN: HOW DO SELF-SCHEMAS OPERATE?

Do men and women differ in their self-schemas? Josephs, Markus, and Tafarodi (1992) think so. Their work sheds light on the nature of gender differences in self-concept and also illustrates how self-schemas operate—how they organize and guide the processing of self-related information.

The basic idea for this research is that culture provides us with norms about gender-appropriate behavior (i.e., behavior considered correct for each sex), and both men and women learn and represent these norms in their self-schemas for gender-appropriate behavior. What is the content of these schemas? An extensive literature review suggested that one important content domain is the degree to which men and women see themselves as separate from, or connected with, others. Men are more likely to have "individualist," "independent," and "autonomous" schemas for the self, and other individuals are represented not as part of the self but as separate and distinct from it. Women, in contrast, are more likely to have "collectivist," "ensembled," and "connected" schemas for the self, and relations with others are thought to be basic elements of the self.

Josephs and colleagues then hypothesized that how we feel about ourselves should depend on how successfully we measure up to our gender-appropriate self-schemas. Thus, for men thinking of self as independent and unique should be associated with self-esteem; for women, in contrast, thinking of self as connected should be associated with self-esteem. To test this idea, Josephs and colleagues conducted three studies. In Study 1, subjects were asked to indicate the percentage of other people who are as good as they are with respect to various skills or abilities. As predicted, men with high self-esteem, in

contrast to men with low self-esteem and women in general, construed themselves as having uniquely superior abilities in comparison to others.

Study 2 was based on the idea that the better one's memory for particular kinds of information, the more important is this information for the self-schema. Subjects learned to "encode," or associate, words either with themselves or with other people important to them. As predicted, high self-esteem women—in contrast with low self-esteem women and men in general—had better memory for words they had encoded with respect to others. These findings fit the hypothesis: supposedly, the high self-esteem women had better memory for words related to others because relationships with others are important or self-relevant to them.

Finally, Study 3 examined reactions to threatening information about the self. Subjects completed a bogus personality test and then received manipulated feedback regarding their (a) individual attainment and (b) interpersonal attainment. As predicted, when high self-esteem men received negative feedback about their individual attainment, they compensated for this threat to their self-worth by predicting they would improve on a future test. Similarly, when high self-esteem women received negative feedback on interpersonal attainment, they compensated for this threat to their self-worth by predicting improvement. These findings show both men and women feel threatened in their self-worth when they fail to confirm their self-schemas; however, they differ in the content of these schemas, with independence and individual attainment more central for men and connection and interdependence more central for women.

Together, the results of these three studies demonstrate that gender norms influence how we establish self-esteem. The studies also illustrate how self-schemas influence the way we process information: how we compare ourselves to others (Study 1), what information we remember (Study 2), and how we compensate for threatening information (Study 3). These are all important cognitive processes in which our self-schemas play a crucial role.

SOURCE: Josephs, Markus, & Tafarodi, 1992.

versely, when you get a good grade, the professor might seem like an exam-writing genius. Much research is consistent with such intuitions. People often are biased toward positive views of the self (Tesser, Pilkington, & McIntosh, 1989).

These biases can be explained by positing a self-enhancement motive. According to this theorizing, people seek to establish and maintain positive self-images. We prefer positive feedback to negative feedback. Without necessarily being narcissists (Chapter 4), we overestimate our positive attributes and underestimate the negative attributes. Further, we compare ourselves favorably with those below us and try to associate ourselves with those perceived to have desirable features (Wood, 1989).

At the same time, people may seek a world that is consistent and predictable. They often seem to have a self-verification motive (Swann, 1991, 1992), that is, a motive to solicit from others information that confirms aspects of their self-concept. People may present themselves in ways that will elicit such evidence. For example, if you see yourself as an extremely shy person, even if you are not happy about your shyness, you may present yourself in ways that maintain your own shy behavior and reputation (e.g., by avoiding social roles in which you would have to be very outgoing). The reason for this, according to Swann, is that people have a need for consistency and predictability. Self-confirmation affords a degree of predictability and control that is not possible when events, such as feedback from others, violate our self-schemas.

This may seem obvious, but the nonobvious part of Swann's view is the suggestion that people even seek self-confirmation when they have negative schemas. That is, a person with a negative self-schema will seek out information and social feedback that confirms the negative self-schema, becoming in a sense his or her own worst enemy. For example, depressives who have negative self-schema can seek out self-verifying information which serves to maintain their negative self-image and their depression (Giesler, Josephs, & Swann, 1996). More generally, in accord with his emphasis on self-verification, Swann presents evidence to the effect that people gravitate toward relationships with people who see them as they see themselves. Thus, not only are persons with positive self-concepts more committed to spouses who think highly of them than to spouses who think poorly of them, but persons with negative self-concepts are more committed to spouses who think poorly of them than to spouses who think well of them (De La Ronde & Swann, 1998; Swann, De La Ronde, & Hixon, 1994). In the words of the comedian Groucho Marx: "I'd never join a club that would have me as a member."

What happens, then, when the two motives conflict? If push comes to shove, do we prefer accurate feedback or positive feedback, the disagreeable truth or what fits our fancy, to be known for who we are or to be adored for who we would like to be (Strube, 1990; Swann, 1991)? In other words, what happens when our cognitive need for consistency or self-verification conflicts with our affective need for self-enhancement, what Swann has called the cognitive-affective crossfire (Swann et al., 1987, 1989)? A complete answer to this question is not at hand. The evidence to date suggests, however, that generally we prefer positive feedback but prefer negative feedback in relation to negative self-views. In line with this, there is evidence that life events inconsistent with the self-concept can lead to physical illness, even if these events are positive (Brown & McGill, 1989). In other words, positive life events can be bad for one's health if they conflict with a negative self-concept and disrupt one's negative identity. At the same time, there are individual differences in this regard and we may be more oriented toward self-enhancement in some relationships and self-verification in other relationships. For example, there is evidence that self-enhancement is more important during the early stages of a relationship but self-verification becomes increasingly important as the relationship becomes more intimate (Swann, De La Ronde, & Hixon, 1994).

Another illustration of how self-schemas can have motivational properties is Markus's concept of possible selves (Markus & Nurius, 1986). Possible selves represent what people think they might become, what they would like to become, and what they are afraid of becoming. In this sense, possible selves not only serve to organize information but also have a powerful motivational influence, directing us toward becoming certain things and away from becoming other things (Markus & Ruvolo, 1989). In relation to this, possible selves help us understand why people experience difficulties in self-control or willpower. According to Markus, we are able to carry out our intentions when the desired end state is experienced as self-relevant or a definite possible self. On the other hand, we are blocked in carrying out our intentions when the end state is not experienced as a possible self. Thus, for example, in attempting to diet, there must be an overlap between the "diet concept" and the self-concept, a sense of "me feeling lighter" and "me giving away clothes that are too big" : "If the anticipation of satisfaction from wearing clothes two sizes smaller results in more, or more intense, cognitive, affective, or somatic self-representations than the anticipation of the delicious tastes and immediate gratification, the mandate to restrain oneself from eating for another hour can be more easily formulated" (Cross & Markus, 1990, p. 729).

LEARNING VERSUS PERFORMANCE GOALS

Self-schemas, discussed above, concern people's beliefs about their personal qualities. Other elements of personality that are important to social-cognitive approaches to personality are people's goals for behavior. As we discussed in our previous chapter, goals, which are mental representations of the aim of an action or course of actions, are seen as central to human motivation by social-cognitive personality theorists.

In our previous chapter, we discussed research showing that the presence versus absence of clear goals on a task greatly affects people's motivation (see pages 446–49). Here we discuss contemporary research on a phenomenon that is related, yet slightly different. On any given activity, people may possess different *types of* goals. Different people may think about an activity differently; different thoughts about goals to be achieved may run through people's minds as they perform the same task. These different goals may lead to different patterns of thought, emotion, and behavior; the goals, in other words, may be the cause of what one would interpret as different personality styles. Although a number of useful distinctions among types of goals have been drawn, one particularly valuable distinction differentiates "learning" goals from "performance" goals.

In their social-cognitive theory of personality and achievement motivation, Carol Dweck and her colleagues (Dweck & Leggett, 1988; Grant & Dweck, 1999) have differentiated between **learning goals** and **performance goals**. The distinction can perhaps best be understood by reflecting on thoughts that may run through your mind when you are trying to achieve something. Suppose that you are working on a group project in a class that you are taking; perhaps you and a group of people are in a psychology research methods course and you are trying to design an experiment to answer a particular research question. There are at least two ways of thinking about your goals in this situation. On the one hand, you may think about the task and all you can learn from it: the different types of research designs, different ways of analyzing data, conclusions you can draw from the research, and the overall educational experience you will have from this activity. If you are thinking this way, you have what Dweck would refer to as a "learning goal." On the other hand, you might have a very different pattern of thinking. You might have the aim of showing other people in the group how smart you are, of avoiding embarrassment when you don't know some information, of making a good impression on the professor, and so forth. If you are thinking this way, you have what Dweck would call a "performance goal"; that is, you have a goal that involves "putting on a good performance" for other people who may be evaluating you.

Carol Dweck

People with learning versus performance goals tend to have very different experiences on tasks, particularly if they have doubts about their capabilities or experience setbacks. In an initial experimental test of this idea, Elliott and Dweck (1988) induced learning versus performance goals among grade school students performing a cognitive task. The students were given different information about the task, with the information being designed to induce one versus the other type of goal. In one experimental condition, students were told that they were performing a task that would sharpen their mental skills; this information was designed to induce learning goals, since the task appeared merely to be one in which people would learn mental skills that might be useful at some later point. In another condition, they were told that they were performing a task that would be evaluated by experts who would examine how well they were doing; this condition, of course, induced performance goals. Students' beliefs in their ability on the task were also manipulated through provision of bogus feedback on a prior activity.

This study (Elliott & Dweck, 1988) yielded two types of results of great interest. First, people who had a combination of performance goals and low beliefs in their ability performed poorly (Table 13.1); specifically, they were less likely than others to develop useful strategies on the task. The second type of finding involved a "think aloud" data-collection procedure, that is, a procedure in which experimenters ask people to think out loud while they are trying to solve a problem. When thinking out loud, most people, of course, voice thoughts about the task they are trying to solve. However, some people think not only about the task, but about themselves and their feelings. For example, Elliott and Dweck (1988) recorded the degree to which people spontaneously

Table 13.1   Percentage of Participants for Whom Task Strategies Improved and Percentage of Participants Who Spontaneously Expressed Negative Affect during a Task, as a Function of Having a Learning versus Performance Goal and Having Low versus High Perceptions of Ability.

	Condition			
	Learning Goal		Performance Goal	
	Low Perceived Ability	High Perceived Ability	Low Perceived Ability	High Perceived Ability
Strategy improves	22.2	20.8	8.7	37.0
Negative affect	3.7	0.0	30.4	3.7

expressed negative emotions while working on the task. It turned out that people who had performance goals and low beliefs in their ability were much more likely to make such statements (Table 13.1). Students who had the goal of making a good impression on others (i.e., performance-goal participants) expressed much tension and anxiety when performing the task; for example, one participant, instead of thinking solely about the problems, spontaneously said "My stomach hurts" (Elliott & Dweck, 1988, p. 10). Learning goals, then, can cause people to have negative thoughts and feelings that interfere with their performance.

This research by Dweck and colleagues provides insight into what we commonly call "test anxiety." As you may know intuitively, some people become highly anxious when taking a test and, as a result, perform more poorly than they would have if they had remained calm. What is so interesting about Dweck's approach to this problem is that she does not hand out a scale of "test anxiety" that describes who might become anxious when taking a test. Instead, she explores a pattern of thinking that is an underlying cause of the emotions and actions that we call "test anxiety." Such an approach is particularly useful if one is interested in developing interventions to help people to become less test anxious. Dweck's social-cognitive analysis suggests that one might intervene by trying to change people's patterns of thinking.

Causes of Learning versus Performance Goals: Implicit Theories

In light of the results we have reviewed, a question that may have crossed your mind is: Why do some people adopt learning goals on tasks, whereas others adopt performance goals? What are the causes of different goal orientations? Fortunately, this question also has crossed the mind of Dweck and colleagues, who have examined this issue systematically. A primary factor they have considered is that different people may have different **implicit theories** about human attributes, including human abilities, and that these different implicit theories contribute to different goal orientations.

"Implicit theories" are those we possess, that guide our thinking, but that we may not usually state in words—that is, we usually do not explicitly articulate the ideas. They are "theories" in that they do not involve just simple facts, but more complex ideas about how things work. Clearly, people have many implicit theories. We believe that gravity pulls objects down to earth (even though we may state this explicitly only when taking a physics class). We

Test anxiety that occurs when people become concerned with how they are being evaluated by others can lower performance on academic tests.

believe that people have certain fundamental rights (even though we may only state this explicitly when taking a government class).

The particular implicit theories of interest to Dweck and colleagues are theories about whether or not psychological attributes are changeable. In a series of studies, Dweck and her colleagues investigated the implications of children having one or the other of two kinds of beliefs, the two sets of beliefs differing in how malleable or fixed the relevant trait is believed to be (Dweck, 1991, 1999; Dweck, Chiu, & Hong, 1995). According to one set of beliefs, known as an entity theory, a particular characteristic or trait is viewed as fixed. According to the other set of beliefs, known as an incremental theory, a particular characteristic or trait is believed to be malleable or open to change. For example, an entity view of intelligence suggests that intelligence is a fixed trait; in this view, people simply "have" more or less intelligence. On the other hand, an incremental view of intelligence suggests that intelligence is a malleable trait that can be increased; in this view, educational experiences contribute to knowledge and make one a more intelligent person.

Differences in views concerning the nature of a trait such as intelligence have implications for goals that are set and responses to failure (Dweck & Leggett, 1988). For example, children with an entity view of intelligence tend to set performance goals. If one thinks that intelligence is a fixed entity, then it is only natural to interpret activities as a test of one's intelligence—that is, as a "performance" in which one's intelligence is evaluated. Conversely, children with an incremental view of intelligence tend to set learning goals. If intelligence can be increased, then, it is natural to set the learning goal of acquiring experiences that increase one's intelligence. Different implicit theories, then, lead people to set different goals that, in turn, have different implications for emotion and motivation.

Before concluding this discussion of goal orientations, two points should be noted. First, Dweck's analysis does not apply merely to achievement tasks of the sort one encounters in school. It can apply to other characteristics as well; for example, if one sees oneself as being a "lazy" person, one might view this either as a fixed quality or as something that might change for the better over the course of your personal development. Grant and Dweck (1999) use the more general term "judgment goals" and "development goals" (analogous to performance goals and learning goals, respectively), to capture the fact that any of a variety of characteristics may be viewed as either a fixed trait or as changeable. Bear in mind that they are not asking whether, in reality, the characteristic is fixed or changeable. The personality variable of interest is people's subjective beliefs about the degree to which their personality characteristics can change. More recent research has shown that different goal orientations are important not only to achievement tasks, but also to interpersonal behavior (Erdley et al., 1997).

The second point to recognize is that Dweck's is not the only distinction that has been drawn between different types of goals. For example, many investigators (e.g., Carver & Scheier, 1998; Emmons, 1989; Emmons & Kaiser, 1996; Elliot & Sheldon, 1998) distinguish between approach and avoidance goals. Some people may be oriented toward achieving positive outcomes ("I want to get at least a B in this class") whereas others may be oriented toward the avoidance of negative outcomes ("I want to avoid getting less than a B in this class"). Adopting avoidance goals often seems to induce more negative emotional experiences. A somewhat different distinction is drawn by the psychologist Tory Higgins (1997, 1999), who distinguishes what he refers to as two different forms of regulatory focus. Some people focus on "promotion," that is, on positive outcomes (either attaining them or avoiding the loss of ones that have been attained). Others have a prevention focus, that is, they psychologically focus on preventing the occurrence of (or gaining an absence of) negative outcomes. Different motivation processes come into play when people are promotion versus prevention focused (Shah & Higgins, 1997).

STANDARDS OF EVALUATION

As we noted in our previous chapter, another social-cognitive mechanism that is central to personality functioning is evaluative standards, that is, criteria for evaluating the goodness or a person, a person's actions, or other events in the world. Standards are related to, yet differ from, goals (Boldero & Francis, 2002; Cervone, 2004). Goals represent aims that we hope to achieve in the future. Standards are criteria that we use to evaluate outcomes in the present. For example, if you are watching an ice skating performance, you might evaluate the performance as good or bad according to standards you have used for judging the performance of skaters. You might have these standards whether or not you, personally, have the goal of being a figure skater. Goals and standards, then, are psychologically distinct mechanisms.

As you just saw in our review of the work of Dweck and colleagues, in the study of goals it is valuable to draw qualitative distinctions among different types of goals, or different (learning versus performance) goal orientations. The same is true in the study of performance standards. There exist different types of performance standards that have different implications for personality functioning. Particularly valuable distinctions have been drawn by Tory Higgins (1987, 1990).

Self-Standards and Self-Discrepancies

Higgins (1987, 1989, 1996) has investigated what he refers to as self-guides. Self-guides are personal standards that individuals wish to meet. In other words, they are mental representations of types of performance that one wants to attain in the future; they are "guides" in that these mental representations guide one's performance toward their attainment. Self-guides are thought to result from early social learning experiences that are associated with emotional consequences for meeting or failing to meet standards.

Torny Higgins.

Higgins and colleagues recognize that there exist different types of self-guides. Specifically, some self-guides represent standards of achievement that people ideally would like to reach. For example, although you might see yourself as a shy individual, you ideally might like to be a more outgoing and socially confident person. If so, standards representing socially outgoing behavior would function for you as an *ideal* self-guide, or as part of what Higgins would call your "ideal self." Alternatively, you might hold some standards that represent duties or obligations, rather than personal ideals. For example, even though you may like being a laidback individual, you might feel some responsibility to be a more conscientious person who plans for the future. If so, standards involving conscientiousness and planfulness would represent *ought* standards, or elements of the ought self. A primary distinction recognized by Higgins, then, differentiates between *actual* and *ought* standards.

Higgins's analysis of personal standards provides not only an understanding of different types of cognition. It also is the foundation for an analysis of emotion. Different standards make people vulnerable to different types of emotional experiences (Higgins, 1987, 1996). There are two steps to Higgins' reasoning. First is that people experience negative emotions when they detect a discrepancy between how things really are going for them—or their "actual self"—and one of their self-guides. These **self-discrepancies** are, then, central to emotional experience. Second, discrepancies with *different* (ideal versus ought) self-guides trigger *different* emotions. Discrepancies between the actual and ideal self cause people to feel sad or dejected; failing to meet one's ideal standards is a loss of positive outcomes that brings on sadness. In contrast, discrepancies between the actual and ought self cause agitation and anxiety, because the possibility of not achieving one's obligations is generally perceived as an impending threat.

A key point here is that different people may have different (ideal versus ought) standards and thus may interpret precisely the same event in different ways. Imagine that you know two psychology majors in this personality class you are taking, one of whom has chosen the major because her parents are psychologists and want her to go into the field, whereas the other has chosen a psych major because she ideally would like to pursue a career as a psychology professor at a prestigious university. Now imagine that both people get the same low score on an exam in the class. Higgins's analysis would suggest that these two people might have different emotional reactions despite experiencing the same event. The person whose parents are psychologists might have ought standards that induce anxiety, whereas the budding professor might possess mostly ideal standards that foster sadness.

To test these ideas, Higgins, Bond, Klein, & Strauman (1986) first assessed individual differences in self-descrepancies. Their goal was to identify one set of people who predominantly have actual/ideal discrepancies, and a second set who predominantly have actual/ought discrepancies. To do this, Higgins and colleagues (1986) employed an open-ended assessment procedure in which participants listed attributes they believed they (a) actually possessed, (b) ideally would like to possess, and (c) believed they should, or ought to, possess. In a subsequent experimental session, these people's emotional reactions were assessed as they envisioned themselves experiencing a negative life event. Although all participants envisioned the same event, they experienced different emotions. People whose self-descriptions featured many actual/ideal discrepancies became sad but not anxious when thinking about the negative outcome. People whose self-described attributes featured mostly actual/ought discrepancies became anxious but not sad.

These findings, then, suggest that self-discrepancies are a cognitive basis for individual differences in emotional experience. However, you might be thinking that the findings are not entirely convincing. They are only correlational; different types of self-discrepancies are correlated with different emotional reactions. As we discussed back in Chapter 2, experimental—rather than merely correlational—research would provide evidence that is more convincing.

A great advantage of Higgins's work is that he is able to provide such experimental evidence. Ought and ideal standards are elements of knowledge, and elements of knowledge can be experimentally primed (that is, made more mentally salient through a procedure that activates the knowledge). A second study, then, experimentally manipulated self-discrepancies through priming. People who possessed both actual/ideal and actual/ought self-discrepancies were assigned at random to conditions that primed either ideal standards or ought standards. Priming alternative standards led to different emotional reactions (Table 13.2). When ideal self-discrepancies were primed, participants felt dejected. When ought standards were primed, they felt agitated. Thus, an experimental manipulation of cognition led to changes in emotion.

Much subsequent research has yielded evidence consistent with Higgins's core idea that discrepancies with ideal versus ought standards lead to different emotional experiences. This includes clinical research with social phobics and clinically depressed patients, who exhibit predominantly actual/ought and

Table 13.2 Mean Change in Dejection Emotions and Agitation Emotions as a Function of Level of Self-Discrepancies and Type of Priming

| | Ideal Priming | | Ought Priming | |
Level of Self-Discrepancies	Dejection Emotions	Agitation Emotions	Dejection Emotions	Agitation Emotions
High actual: ideal and actual: ought discrepancies	3.2	−0.8	0.9	5.1
Low actual: ideal and actual: ought discrepancies	−1.2	0.9	0.3	−2.6

NOTE: Each of 8 dejection emotions and 8 agitation emotions was measured on a 6-point scale from *not at all* to *a great deal*. The more positive the number, the greater the increase in discomfort.
SOURCE: Higgins et al., 1986, Study 2.

actual/ideal discrepancies, respectively (Straumann, 1989). Higher levels of neuroticism and lower levels of subjective well-being are experienced by people whose self-descriptions indicate a discrepancy between how they really think they are and how they judge who they think they ought to be (Pavot, Fujita, & Deiner, 1997). The existence of self-discrepancies has health implications, having been found to decrease the effectiveness of the functioning of our immunological system in fighting disease (Strauman, Lemieux, & Coe, 1993). Clinical researchers have begun to develop therapeutic techniques to reduce discrepancies between the actual and ideal self (Strauman et al., 2001).

A "General Principles" Approach to Personality

Higgins's (1999) analysis of cognition, emotion, and individual differences has a theoretical advantage that is a bit subtle, yet highly significant. It concerns the explanation of consistencies in behavior as opposed to variations in behavior from one situation to another. As we have discussed previously, some personality psychologists treat consistencies in behavior as an indication of an individual's personality, whereas variations are explained in terms of the power of situations to influence behavior. In this approach, "personality variables" explain what people do on average, and "situational factors" explain variations around the average. As Higgins recognizes, this sort of thinking yields a very unsatisfying science of persons. It is unsatisfying because different, and seemingly unrelated, theoretical principles have to be invoked to explain one versus another behavior by the same person.

In contrast, Higgins's work yields general principles; he describes it as a **general principles approach** to understanding personality and situational influences. People's knowledge—including their ideal and ought standards for performance—explains consistencies in their emotion and behavior, since knowledge is an enduring aspect of personality. But knowledge mechanisms also explain situational influences. Different situations activate different aspects of knowledge and, in so doing, bring about different emotional and motivational patterns. Thus, one obtains an integrated account of personal and situational influences on emotion and behavior in which one set of common, general principles explains both consistency in thought and action that results from personal influences and variability in thought and action that results from situational influences.

CAUSAL EXPLANATIONS AND ATTRIBUTIONS

In preceding sections we discussed how people organize information relevant to situations and people (including themselves). In this section we are concerned with how people organize information about the causes of events. We see someone hit or yell at another person and we infer some reason for the action. Is the person generally hostile? Was something malicious done to him? We see someone act in a strange way. Was she not feeling well? Was our previous picture of these people inaccurate, and must we now view them in a new way? These inferences about the causes of events are called **attributions**; they involve attributing a causal factor that is responsible for an observed event.

Weiner (1990, 1996, Weiner & Graham, 1999) suggests that there are three dimensions relevant to causal explanations. The first dimension, related to the

Table 13.3   Possible Causal Attributions for Success and Failure

Cause	Internal	External
Stable	Ability	Task difficulty
Variable	Effort	Chance or luck

Source: Weiner, 1979

work of Rotter on locus of control, concerns whether causes are perceived as coming from within (internal) or from outside (external) the person. This dimension has been named a *locus of causality*. A second dimension of causality, stability, concerns whether the cause is stable and relatively fixed as opposed to being unstable or variable. The implications for causal attributions from combining these two dimensions can be seen in Table 13.3. Accordingly, we can attribute success or failure to ability ("I am bright"), effort ("I tried hard"), task difficulty ("The test was easy"), or chance or luck ("I was lucky in guessing right"). The third dimension, controllability, has to do with whether events are subject to control or influence through additional effort. For example, social rejection because of physical unattractiveness might be attributed to internal, stable, and uncontrollable causes, whereas social rejection because of obnoxious behavior might be attributed to internal, stable, and controllable causes. In each case it is the beliefs and causal ascriptions of the person that are important. Thus, for example, one person might see her physical appearance as uncontrollable, whereas another might see it as controllable. One person might see her intellectual performance as due to fixed intelligence, whereas another might see it as due to effort and acquired knowledge (Dweck, 1991, 1999; Dweck, Chiu, & Hong, 1995).

CONSEQUENCES OF CAUSAL ATTRIBUTIONS

The practical implications of differing attributions for performance are illustrated in a study of college freshmen (Wilson & Linville, 1985). In this study, freshmen whose grades were below the median and who indicated that they were worried about their academic performance were put into one of two groups. Those in one group were given information suggesting that the causes of their poor performance were unstable. This information consisted of statistics indicating that grades typically improve after the first year and videotaped interviews of upper-class students who reported improved performance following poor grades during their freshman year. Students in the second group were given general information that did not relate to grade improvement and saw videotaped interviews in which there was no mention of grades. The hypothesis tested was that the attribution of poor grades to unstable causes would reduce anxiety about academic performance and increase expectations about future grades, leading to improvement in actual performance. Indeed, it was found that students in the first (unstable attribution) group improved in their subsequent grade performance significantly more than did subjects in the second (control) group. In addition, a smaller proportion of the students in the first group left college the following semester. Thus, the authors of the study concluded that showing college freshmen that the causes of low grades are temporary can greatly benefit academic performance.

CURRENT APPLICATIONS

GIVING UP ADDICTIONS AND AVOIDING RELAPSE

Millions of people suffer from compulsive behavior patterns that have an addictive quality: smoking, overeating, gambling, drinking, drug abuse. Often they give up the troublesome behavior for a period of time, only to find that it returns. What accounts for the relapse, and how can its risks be minimized?

Although many people claim a physiological basis for addictive behavior, two points are noteworthy: (1) In some of these compulsive patterns, no true physiological addiction exists. Yet a psychological craving remains. Generally, periods of intense craving are associated with feelings of threat and inability to cope with events. (2) Many people are able to go through an extended period of abstinence, only to experience a relapse of overeating after weight loss, habitual smoking after abstinence, and so on. Researchers in this area have identified a common element in the relapse process. Those who are able to maintain abstinence perceive themselves as more able to cope with and affect events than those

who relapse. They have better self-efficacy judgments. Many people show occasional lapses from total abstinence. Those who relapse, however, treat the event as a statement about themselves and their efficacy. Thus, they make statements such as "I'm a failure" or "I just can't do it" or "I have no willpower." Already feeling vulnerable in relation to the task at hand, they treat occasional lapses in a way that only serves to further damage their beliefs in themselves.

In treating addictions and compulsive patterns of behavior, getting people to abstain is only part of the job. In many cases, this turns out to be easier than helping them to remain abstinent. Evidently, changing the way they interpret occasional lapses and enhancing their feeling of self-efficacy concerning abstinence are an important part of the work that needs to be done.

SOURCE: Marlatt, Baer, & Quigley, 1995; Marlatt & Gordon, 1980; *New York Times*, February 23, 1983, C1.

Additional dimensions have been suggested, but the point here is that people make causal attributions, and that such attributions have important psychological implications. For example, such attributions have important implications for motivation. A person is more likely to persist at a task if it is viewed as one involving effort than if success or failure is viewed as being due to chance. Similarly, persons will behave differently if they believe health or illness is due to internal or external causes ("I am a sickly person" versus "The flu bug got me") and if they believe in the efficacy of self-care ("Basic health principles prevent illness" versus "One can do little to prevent illness") (Lau, 1982). Causal attributions also are important aspects of stereotypes. For example, success in men and failure in women tend to be attributed to ability, whereas failure in men and success in women tend to be attributed to effort or luck (Deaux, 1976). Differences in causal attribution also have important implications for emotion. As noted in relation to learned helplessness, depression is seen as resulting from an internal, stable, global attribution. Other illustrations of emotional consequences of causal attributions are pride following success and a causal attribution to ability, and guilt following failure and a causal attribution to effort (Weiner, 1990; Weiner & Graham, 1999). Finally, causal attributions have important implications for moral judgments. For example, to the extent that we see failure as due to lack of effort we see punishment as appropriate, whereas this is not the case if failure is perceived to be due to lack of ability. And, to the extent that we see someone's "illness" as due to circumstances beyond their control we view it as a sickness and respond with sympathy, whereas if we view it as due to controllable influences we view it as a sin and respond with moral condemnation and anger (Weiner, 1993, 1996; Weiner & Graham, 1999). Illustrative here would be differing views concerning the causes of alcoholism, drug abuse, and AIDS. In sum, it is suggested that attributions cause many of our emotions, motivations, and behaviors.

CLINICAL APPLICATIONS

Thus far in discussing social-cognitive theory, we primarily have reviewed core theoretical principles and basic research that supports them. We now turn to a key area of application of this theory and research: the psychological clinic. Clinical applications of cognitive theory have been of enormous significance in the past quarter-century. Indeed, in many clinical settings and training programs, the cognitive approach has become the most predominant of all theoretical orientations.

There is no one theory or technique of cognitive therapy. Instead, there are different approaches, often tailored to specific problems, that share some common assumptions:

1. Cognitions (attributions, beliefs, expectancies, memories concerning the self and others) are viewed as critical in determining feelings and behaviors. Thus, there is an interest in what people think and say to themselves.

2. The cognitions of interest tend to be specific to situations or categories of situations, though the importance of some generalized expectancies and beliefs is recognized.

3. Psychopathology is viewed as arising from distorted, incorrect, maladaptive cognitions concerning the self, others, and events in the world. Different forms of pathology are viewed as resulting from different cognitions or ways of processing information.

4. Faulty, maladaptive cognitions lead to problematic feelings and behaviors, and these in turn lead to further problematic cognitions. Thus, a self-fulfilling cycle may set in whereby persons act so as to confirm and maintain their distorted beliefs.

5. Cognitive therapy involves a collaborative effort between therapist and patient to determine which distorted, maladaptive cognitions are creating the difficulty and then to replace them with other more realistic, adaptive cognitions. The therapeutic approach tends to be active, structured, and focused on the present.

6. In contrast with other approaches, cognitive approaches do not see the unconscious as important, except insofar as patients may not be aware of their routine, habitual ways of thinking about themselves and life. Further, there is an emphasis on changes in specific problematic cognitions rather than on global personality change.

STRESS AND COPING

The work of cognitively oriented psychologists has been very important in the area of stress, coping, and health. Lazarus, whose work has been very influential in this area, suggests that psychological stress depends on cognitions relating to the person and the environment (Lazarus, 1990). In this cognitive approach to stress and coping, stress is viewed as occurring when the person views circumstances as taxing or exceeding his or her resources and endangering well-being. Involved in this are two stages of cognitive appraisal. In primary appraisal, the person evaluates whether there is anything at stake in the encounter, whether there is a threat or danger. For example, is there potential harm or benefit to self-esteem? Is one's personal health or that of a loved one at risk? In secondary appraisal, the person evaluates what, if anything, can be done to overcome harm, prevent harm, or improve the prospects for benefit. In other words, secondary appraisal involves an evaluation of the person's resources to cope with the potential harm or benefit evaluated in the stage of primary appraisal.

There are different ways of coping with any given situation. A key distinction is one that differentiates between **problem-focused coping**, which refers to attempts to cope by altering features of a stressful situation, and **emotion-focused coping**, which is coping in which an individual strives to improve his or her internal emotional state, for example, by emotional distancing or the seeking of social support. Research by Folkman, Lazarus, and colleagues has developed a questionnaire to assess coping, the Ways of Coping Scale, and has explored the health implications of different coping strategies. This research suggests the following conclusions (Folkman, Lazarus, Gruen, & DeLongis, 1986; Lazarus, 1993):

1. There is evidence of both stability and variability in the methods individuals use to cope with stressful situations. Although the use of some coping methods appears to be influenced by personality factors, the use of many coping methods appears to be strongly influenced by the situational context.

2. In general, the greater the reported level of stress and efforts to cope, the poorer the physical health and the greater the likelihood of psycho-

The experience of stress in daily life can be reduced through cognitive strategies that help people to cope with everyday stressors.

logical symptoms. In contrast, the greater the sense of mastery, the better is the physical and psychological health.

3. Although the value of a particular form of coping depends on the context in which it is used, in general, planful problem solving ("I made a plan of action and followed it" or "Just concentrate on the next step") is a more adaptive form of coping than escape avoidance ("I hoped a miracle would happen" or "I tried to reduce tension by eating, drinking, or using drugs") or confrontative coping ("I let my feelings out somehow" or "I expressed anger to those who caused the problem").

In addition to this conceptual analysis of stress and coping, the therapist requires practical procedures to reduce stress. Such a procedure has been developed by Don Meichenbaum (1995), whose **stress inoculation training** procedure is based on a cognitive view of stress. In accord with Lazarus's view, Meichenbaum suggests that stress be viewed in cognitive terms; that is, stress involves cognitive appraisals, and individuals under stress often have a variety of self-defeating and interfering thoughts. In addition, such self-defeating cognitions and related behaviors have a built-in self-confirmatory component (e.g., people get others to treat them in an overprotective way). Finally, events are perceived and recalled in ways that are consistent with a negative bias. Meichenbaum's stress inoculation procedure is designed to help individuals cope better with stress and is seen as analogous to medical inoculation against biological disease.

Stress inoculation training involves teaching clients the cognitive nature of stress, followed by instruction in procedures to cope with stress and change faulty cognitions and, finally, training in the application of these procedures in actual situations. In terms of the cognitive nature of stress, the effort is to have the client become aware of such negative, stress-engendering, automatic thoughts as "It is such an effort to do anything" and "There is nothing I can do to control these thoughts or change the situation." The important point here is that the person may not be aware of having these automatic thoughts, and thus, must be taught to be aware of them and their negative effects. In terms of coping procedures and correction of faulty cognitions, clients are taught relaxation as an active coping skill and taught cognitive strategies such as how to restructure problems so that they appear more manageable. In addition, clients are taught problem-solving strategies, such as how to define problems, generate possible alternative courses of action, evaluate the pros and cons of each proposed solution, and implement the most practicable and desirable one. Clients also are taught to use coping self-statements such as "I can do it," "One step at time," "Focus on the present; what is it I have to do?" "I can be pleased with the progress I'm making," and "Keep trying; don't expect perfection or immediate success." Finally, through imagery rehearsal and practice in real-world situations clients are taught to feel comfortable with the utilization of these procedures. In imagery rehearsal the client imagines various stressful situations and the use of the coping skills and strategies. Practice involves role-playing and modeling involving the therapist as well as practice in real-world situations.

The stress inoculation training procedure is active, focused, structured, and brief. It has been used with medical patients about to undergo surgery, with athletes to help them deal with the stress of competition, with rape victims to help them deal with the trauma of such assaults, and in the work environment

Imagery: *Cognitive therapists encourage patients to imagine scenes to determine the nature of their fears and develop positive courses of action.*

to teach workers more efficient coping strategies and to help worker management teams consider organizational change.

PATHOLOGY AND CHANGE

The cognitive, information processing view holds that psychopathology results from unrealistic, maladaptive cognitions. Therapy, then, involves efforts to change such cognitive distortions and replace them with more realistic, adaptive cognitions.

Ellis's Rational-Emotive Therapy

Albert Ellis was a former psychoanalyst who developed a therapeutic system of personality change known as rational emotive-therapy (RET) (Ellis, 1962, 1987; Ellis & Harper, 1975). According to his theory, the causes of psychological difficulties are irrational beliefs or irrational statements we make to ourselves that we must do something, that we have to feel some way, that we should be a certain kind of person, that we cannot do anything about our feelings or situation in life.

What kinds of maladaptive cognitions do people have? About as many different kinds as there are cognitive processes. Consider the following possibilities:

Irrational beliefs. "If good things happen, bad things must be on the way." "If I express my needs, others will reject me."

Faulty reasoning. "I failed on this effort, so I must be incompetent." "They didn't respond the way I wanted them to, so they must not think much of me."

Dysfunctional expectancies. "If something can go wrong for me, it will." "Catastrophe is just around the corner."

Negative self-views. "I always tend to feel that others are better than me." "Nothing I do ever turns out right."

Maladaptive attributions. "I'm a poor test taker because I am a nervous person." "When I win, it's luck; when I lose, it's me."

Memory distortions. "Life is horrible now and always has been this way." "I've never succeeded in anything."

Maladaptive attention. "All I can think about is how horrible it will be if I fail." "It's better not to think about things; there's nothing you can do anyway."

Self-defeating strategies. "I'll put myself down before others do." "I'll reject others before they reject me and see if people still like me."

Obviously there is overlap among the above maladaptive cognitions. Often important maladaptive cognitions have more than one flawed aspect. However, they illustrate the kinds of cognitions that create problematic feelings and situations for people. Through the use of logic, argument, persuasion, ridicule, or humor, an effort is made to change the irrational beliefs causing the difficulties. Although Ellis's views were long neglected by behavior therapists, with their emphasis on overt motor behavior, they have received greater interest with the development of cognitive therapy (Dobson & Shaw, 1995; Meichenbaum, 1995).

Beck's Cognitive Therapy for Depression

Like Albert Ellis, Aaron Beck is a former psychoanalyst who became disenchanted with psychoanalytic techniques and gradually developed a cognitive approach to therapy. His therapy is best known for its relevance to the treatment of depression, but it has relevance to a wider variety of psychological disorders. According to Beck (1987), psychological difficulties are due to automatic thoughts, dysfunctional assumptions, and negative self-statements.

The Cognitive Triad of Depression

Beck's cognitive model of depression emphasizes that a depressed person systematically misevaluates ongoing and past experiences, leading to a view of the self as a loser, the view of the world as frustrating, and the view of the future as bleak. These three negative views are known as the cognitive triad and include negative views of the self such as "I am inadequate, undesirable, worthless," negative views of the world such as "The world makes too many demands on me and life represents constant defeat," and negative views of the future such as "Life will always involve the suffering and deprivation it has for me now." In addition, a depressed person is prone to faulty information processing, such as in magnifying everyday difficulties into disasters and overgeneralizing from a single instance of rejection to the belief that "Nobody likes me." It is these thinking problems, these negative schemas and cognitive errors, that cause depression.

Research on Faulty Cognitions

Considerable research has attempted to determine the role of faulty cognitions in depression and other psychological difficulties. Generally there is support for the presence of Beck's cognitive triad, as well as other faulty cognitions (Segal & Dobson, 1992). In particular, compared to nondepressed indi-

Aaron T. Beck

viduals, those who are depressed appear to focus more on themselves (Wood, Saltzberg, & Goldsamt, 1990), to have more accessible negative self-constructs (Bargh & Tota, 1988; Strauman, 1990), and to have a bias toward pessimism rather than optimism, particularly in relation to the self (Epstein, 1992; Taylor & Brown, 1988). What is not clear from this research, however, is whether such cognitions cause depression, as opposed to being part of depression. And, even if they play a causal role, the question of how such faulty cognitions develop remains to be determined.

One of the puzzling questions for psychologists who emphasize the role of faulty cognitions in depression is the following: What happens to the faulty cognitions when the depression has lifted? The reason that this question is important is that once having experienced a serious depression, there is a tendency toward relapse or the likelihood of experiencing another depression. Why should this be the case if the faulty cognitions are gone? There is some growing evidence that the answer to the question is the following: The faulty cognitions that make the person vulnerable to depression are latent and only become manifest under conditions of stress (Alloy, Abramson, & Francis, 1999; Dykman & Johll, 1998; Ingram, Miranda, & Segal, 1998; Wenzlaff & Bates, 1998). In other words, faulty cognitions can have varying degrees of strength and greater or lesser availability to awareness. People vulnerable to depression may retain negative attitudes toward the self that only become manifest and operational when they experience blows to their self-esteem. The task of therapy, then, is to affect fundamental change in these cognitions as well as to make the person aware of the conditions under which they become operational.

Cognitive Therapy

Cognitive therapy of depression is designed to identify and correct distorted conceptualizations and dysfunctional beliefs (Beck, 1993; Brewin, 1996). Therapy generally consists of 15 to 25 sessions at weekly intervals. The approach is described as involving highly specific learning experiences designed to teach the patient to monitor negative, automatic thoughts, to recognize how these thoughts lead to problematic feelings and behaviors, to examine the evidence for and against these thoughts, and to substitute more reality-oriented interpretations for these biased cognitions. The therapist helps the patient to see that interpretations of events lead to depressed feelings. For example, the following exchange between therapist (T) and patient (P) might occur:

P: I get depressed when things go wrong. Like when I fail a test.

T: How can failing a test make you depressed?

P: Well, if I fail I'll never get into law school.

T: So failing the test means a lot to you. But if failing a test could drive people into clinical depression, wouldn't you expect everyone who failed the test to have a depression? Did everyone who failed get depressed enough to require treatment?

P: No, but it depends on how important the test was to the person.

T: Right, and who decides the importance?

P: I do.

Source: Beck, Rush, and Shaw, 1979, p. 146.

In addition to the examination of beliefs for their logic, validity, and adaptiveness, behavioral assignments are used to help the patient test certain maladaptive cognitions and assumptions. This may involve the assignment of activities designed to result in success and pleasure. In general, the therapy focuses on specific target cognitions that are seen as contributing to the depression. Beck contrasts cognitive therapy with traditional analytic therapy in terms of the therapist's being continuously active in structuring the therapy, in the focus on the here and now, and in the emphasis on conscious factors.

Beck's cognitive therapy has been expanded to include the treatment of other psychological difficulties, including anxiety, personality disorders, drug abuse, and marital difficulties (Beck, 1988; Beck & Freeman, 1990; Beck, Wright, Newman, & Liese, 1993; Clark, Beck, & Brown, 1989; Epstein & Baucom, 1988; Young, 1990). The basic view is that each difficulty is associated with a distinctive pattern of beliefs. For example, whereas in depression these concern failure and self-worth, in anxiety they concern danger. There is evidence for the effectiveness of cognitive therapy (Antonuccio, Thomas, & Danton, 1997; Craighead, Craighead, & Ilardi, 1995; Hollon, Shelton, & Davis, 1993; Robins & Hayes, 1993). Although the distinctive therapeutic features of cognitive therapy and whether changes in beliefs are the key therapeutic ingredients remain to be determined (Dobson & Shaw, 1995; Hollon, De Rubeis, & Evans, 1987), recent evidence suggests that therapeutic change indeed follows cognitive change (Tang & De Rubeis, 1999a,b).

PSYCHOPATHOLOGY: MODELING, SELF-CONCEPTIONS, AND PERCEIVED SELF-EFFICACY

According to social-cognitive theory, maladaptive behavior results from dysfunctional learning. Like all learning, maladaptive responses can be learned as a result of direct experience or as the result of exposure to inadequate or "sick" models. Thus, Bandura suggests that the degree to which parents themselves model forms of aberrant behavior is often a significant causal factor in the development of psychopathology. Again, there is no need to look for traumatic incidents in the early history of the individual or for the underlying conflicts. Nor is it necessary to find a history of reinforcement for the initial acquisition of the pathological behavior. On the other hand, once behaviors have been learned through observational learning, it is quite likely that they have been maintained because of direct and vicarious reinforcement. Recall the research on the vicarious conditioning of emotional responses. Monkeys who observed their parents express a fear of snakes developed a conditioned emotional response that was intense, long-lasting, and generalized beyond the context in which it was first learned. Thus, it is suggested that observational learning and vicarious conditioning may account for a great proportion of human fears and phobias.

Although the learning of specific overt behaviors and emotional reactions is important in psychopathology, increasingly social-cognitive theory has come to emphasize the role of **dysfunctional expectancies** and self-conceptions. People may erroneously expect painful events to follow some events or pain to be associated with specific situations. They then may act so as to avoid certain situations or in a way that creates the very situation they were trying to avoid. An example is the person who fears that closeness will bring pain and then acts in a hostile way, resulting in rejection by others and presumably confirming the expectancy that closeness leads to disappointment and rejection.

Cognitive processes also play a role in psychopathology in terms of **dysfunctional self-evaluations**, in particular in terms of perceived low self-efficacy or perceived inefficacy. Remember that perceived self-efficacy is the perception that one can perform the tasks required by a situation or cope with a situation. In perceived inefficacy, one feels that one cannot perform the necessary tasks or cope with the demands of the situation. Thus, according to social-cognitive theory, it is perceived inefficacy that plays a central role in anxiety and depression (Bandura, 1997).

Self-Efficacy, Anxiety, and Depression

Let us first consider the role of perceived self-efficacy in anxiety. According to social-cognitive theory, people with perceptions of low self-efficacy in relation to potential threats experience high anxiety arousal. It is not the threatening event per se but the perceived inefficacy in coping with it that is fundamental to anxiety. Research indicates that those who believe they cannot manage threatening events experience great distress. They may also develop further dysfunctional cognitions such as a preoccupation with what may happen. In other words, the anxious person may focus attention on the disaster that lies ahead, and on his or her inability to cope with it, rather than focusing on what might be done to cope with the situation. The perception of inability to cope with the situation may then be complicated further by the perceived inability to cope with the anxiety itself, a fear-of-fear response that can lead to panic (Barlow, 1991).

Whereas perceived inefficacy in relation to threatening events leads to anxiety, perceived inefficacy in relation to rewarding outcomes leads to depression; that is, depression represents the response to perceived inability to gain desired rewarding outcomes. Part of the problem with depressives, however, may be their excessively stringent standards. In other words, individuals prone to depression impose upon themselves excessively high goals and standards. When they fall short of these exacting standards, they blame themselves and their lack of ability or competence for what has happened. Excessive self-criticism is, in fact, often a major feature of depression. In sum, although perceived self-inefficacy to fulfill desired goals is fundamental to depression, part of the problem may be the excessive goals themselves. In addition, the low self-efficacy beliefs may contribute to diminished performance, leading to falling even further below standards and additional self-blame (Kavanagh, 1992). Just such a relationship was found in a study of childhood depression. In this study, perceived social and academic inefficacy was found to contribute to depression directly as well as indirectly through problem behaviors that interfered with future social and academic success (Bandura, Pastorelli, Barbaranelli, & Caprara, 1999). Thus, a self-defeating cycle was established wherein low self-efficacy contributed to depression and problem behaviors, which in turn contributed to further perceived inefficacy and depression.

Bandura (1992) raises the interesting point that discrepancies between standards and performance can have varied effects that can lead to greater effort, to apathy, or to depression. What determines which effect will occur? According to Bandura, discrepancies between performance and standards lead to high motivation when people believe they have the efficacy to accomplish the goal. Beliefs that the goals are beyond one's capabilities because they are unrealistic will lead to abandoning the goal and perhaps to apathy, but not to depression. For example, a person may say "This task is just too hard" and give up, perhaps becoming frustrated and angry, but not depressed. Depression occurs when a person feels inefficacious in relation to a goal but believes the goal to be reasonable; therefore that person feels he or she must continue to strive to meet the standard. Thus, the effects of a discrepancy between standards and performance on effort and mood depend on self-efficacy beliefs and whether the standard is perceived to be reasonable, possible to achieve, and important.

The relationships between depressed mood and discrepancies between standards and performance is a two-way street. Not only do these discrepancies create depressed emotions; depressed emotions contribute to the existence of these discrepancies. Evidence on this point comes from research that experimentally manipulates people's moods (Cervone, Kopp, Schaumann, & Scott, 1994; Scott & Cervone, 2002), as well as work that compares depressed and non-depressed persons (Tillema, Cervone, & Scott, 2001). The findings indicate that when people are feeling bad, they tend to have more perfectionistic standards. When in a bad mood, routine outcomes seem less satisfactory; as a result, people are satisfied only with superior attainments. These higher standards for performance commonly exceed the level of performance people think they actually can attain (Cervone et al., 1994).

Self-Efficacy and Health

One of the most active areas of social-cognitive research has been on the relation between self-efficacy beliefs and health (Bandura, 1997). The results of this research can be easily summarized: Strong, positive self-efficacy beliefs are good for your health. Conversely, weak and negative self-efficacy beliefs are bad for your health (Schwarzer, 1992). There are two major ways in which self-efficacy beliefs affect health. These ways are the beliefs' effects on health-related behaviors and their effects on physiological functioning (Contrada, Leventhal, & O'Leary, 1990; Miller, Shoda, & Hurley, 1996). Self-efficacy beliefs affect both the likelihood of developing various illnesses and the process of recovery from illness (O'Leary, 1992).

Self-efficacy beliefs have been related to such varied behaviors as cigarette smoking, alcohol use, and condom use with relation to pregnancy and AIDS. For example, perceptions of self-efficacy to practice safer sexual behavior have been related to the probability of adopting safer sexual practices. Modeling, goal-setting, and other techniques have been used to increase self-efficacy beliefs and thereby reduce risky behavior (O'Leary, 1992). Changes in self-efficacy beliefs also have been found to be of importance in relation to the process of recovery from illness. For example, in recovery from a heart attack it is important to have an appropriate amount of physical activity. That is, sometimes individuals recovering from a heart attack may have unrealistically high self-efficacy beliefs and exercise beyond what is constructive for them. In these cases patients must monitor their self-efficacy beliefs to bring them into more accord with reality and, correspondingly, to bring their exercise into healthier patterns (Ewart, 1992).

Turning to the relation between self-efficacy beliefs and bodily functioning, there is evidence that high self-efficacy beliefs buffer the effects of stress and enhance the functioning of the body's immune (disease-fighting) system.

CURRENT APPLICATIONS

SELF-EFFICACY AND HEALTH

According to social-cognitive theory, perceptions of self-efficacy have important implications for emotional reactions to situations and motivations to undertake various behaviors. Such a concept would appear to have important implications for health in terms of understanding people's emotional and behavioral responses to stressful conditions and health-related programs.

Recent research by Bandura and others suggests that this is indeed the case. A variety of studies indicate that feelings of low self-efficacy are associated with increased stress responses, poorer responses to pain, and low motivation to pursue health-related programs. Conversely, increased feelings of self-efficacy are associated with lower self-reported stress, decreased physiological responses indicative of stress, increased coping, and increased involvement in programs prescribed by health-care workers. In one treatment program, arthritic patients were given treatment to enhance their perceived self-efficacy in coping with their difficulty. The treatment not only accomplished this but also resulted in reduced pain and joint inflammation, as well as in improved psychosocial functioning. In another treatment program with bulimics—or individuals who binge eat and then vomit to purge themselves of the food—increases in self-efficacy were found to be associated with greater self-control in eating and decreases in vomiting frequency. Finally, in a third program, changes in perceived self-efficacy for walking were found to be associated with increased exercise in an activity program prescribed for patients at risk for heart disease.

Research to date suggests that self-efficacy theory has important implications for such diverse health-related behaviors as smoking cessation, pain experience and management, control of eating and weight, and adherence to preventive health programs.

SOURCES: Bandura, 1997; Miller, Shoda, & Hurley, 1996; Schneider, O'Leary, & Agras, 1987; Schwarzer, 1992.

There is evidence that excessive stress can lead to impairment of the immune system, whereas improvement of the ability to ameliorate stress can enhance its functioning (O'Leary, 1990). In an experiment designed to examine the impact of perceived self-efficacy of control over stressors on the immune system, Bandura and his associates found that perceived self-efficacy indeed enhanced immune system functioning (Wiedenfeld et al., 1990).

In this research, subjects with a phobia (excessive fear) of snakes were tested under three conditions: a baseline control phase involving no exposure to the phobic stressor (snake), a perceived self-efficacy acquisition phase during which subjects were assisted in gaining a sense of coping efficacy, and a perceived maximal self-efficacy phase once they had developed a complete sense of coping efficacy. During these phases, a small amount of blood was drawn from the subjects and analyzed for the presence of cells that are known to help regulate the immune system. For example, the level of helper T cells, known to play a role in destroying cancerous cells and viruses, was measured. These analyses indicated that increases in self-efficacy beliefs were associated with increases in enhanced immune system functioning, as evidenced, for example,

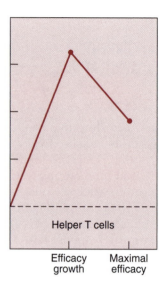

Figure 13.2   Changes in helper T Cells during exposure to phobic stressor while acquiring perceived coping self-efficacy and after perceived coping self-efficacy develops to maximal level. *(Wiedenfeld et al., 1990) Copyright © 1990 by the American Psychological Association. Adapted by permission.*

by the increased level of helper T cells (Figure 13.2). Thus, although the effects of stress can be negative, the growth of perceived efficacy over stressors can have valuable adaptive properties at the level of immune system functioning.

Therapeutic Change: Modeling and Guided Mastery

Bringing about beneficial behavior change is a critical goal to Bandura and other social-cognitivists. Bandura pursues this goal while warning that it should be pursued cautiously; therapeutic procedures should be applied clinically only after the basic mechanisms involved are understood and after the effects of the methods have been adequately tested.

According to Bandura, the change process involves not only the acquisition of new patterns of thought and behavior, but also their generalization and maintenance. The social-cognitive view of therapy consequently emphasizes the importance of changes in the sense of efficacy. The treatment approach most emphasized by social-cognitive theory is the acquisition of cognitive and behavioral competencies through modeling and **guided mastery**. In the former, desired activities are demonstrated by various models who experience positive consequences, or at least no adverse consequences. Generally, the complex patterns of behavior to be learned are broken down into subskills and increasingly difficult subtasks so as to ensure optimal progress. In guided mastery the individual not only views a model performing beneficial behaviors; clients also are assisted in performing the behaviors themselves. The first-hand experience of behavioral success is expected, in social-cognitive theory, to produce the most rapid increases in self-efficacy and performance. In sum, in contrast with therapeutic approaches that emphasize verbal communication, social-cognitive theory prescribes mastery experiences as the principle vehicle of personal change (Bandura, 1997).

Much research on therapeutic modeling and guided participation has been carried out, beginning with work by Bandura and colleagues on the problem of snake phobias (Bandura, 1977). A small percentage of the population suffers from an extreme, irrational fear of snakes that can interfere with their daily life. Bandura hypothesized that therapeutic treatments would help peo-

Guided Mastery: *Bandura emphasizes the role of modeling and guided participation in behavior change. Here, individuals afraid of snakes are helped to overcome their fear by a therapist who models the desired behavior.*

ple to overcome their fears only if they increased people's self-perceptions of their personal capability to cope with the situation that makes them afraid. The hypothesized psychological mechanism that is key to change, in other words, is perceived self-efficacy.

Bandura and colleagues tested this hypothesis through their microanalytic research strategy. They conducted an experiment in which chronic snake phobics were assigned to one of three conditions: participant modeling (the therapist models the threatening activities and subjects gradually perform the tasks, with therapist assistance, until they can be performed alone); modeling (subjects observe the therapist perform the tasks but do not engage in them); and a control condition (Bandura, Adams, & Beyer, 1977). Both before and after these conditions, the subjects were tested on a Behavioral Avoidance Test (BAT), consisting of 29 performance tasks requiring increasingly threatening interactions with a red-tailed boa constrictor. The final task involved letting the snake crawl in their laps while holding their hands at their sides. To determine the generality of change, subjects were also tested after treatment with a dissimilar threat—a corn snake. To test the role of perceived self-efficacy, the researchers conducted a highly detailed assessment in which they measured snake phobics' perceived self-efficacy for performing each of a series of increasingly challenging behaviors with a snake (e.g., walking to within five feet of a snake, touching a snake, picking up a snake, etc.). The self-efficacy assessments were taken before treatment, after treatment but before the second administration of the BAT, following the second administration of the BAT, and again one month following the completion of treatment.

The results indicated that, as expected, participant modeling produced the strongest changes in behavior (Figure 13.3). More important, for the study of perceived self-efficacy, changes in self-efficacy perceptions and changes in

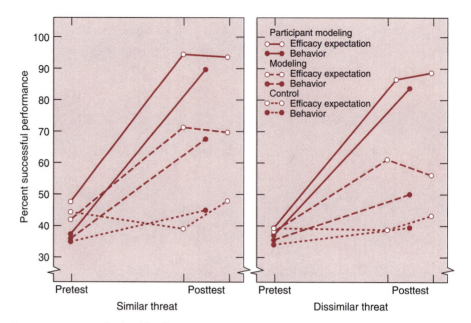

Figure 13.3   Level of Self-Efficacy and Approach Behavior Displayed by Subjects Toward Different Threats After Receiving Vicarious (Modeling) or Performance-based Participant Modeling Treatments or No Treatment. *(In the post-test phase, level of self-efficacy was measured prior to and after the behavioral avoidance tests with the two subjects.) (Bandura, Adams, & Beyer, 1977). Copyright © 1977 American Psychological Association. Reprinted by permission.*

behavior were extremely closely related. This was true at both the between-group level (i.e., one experimental group versus another) and the within-group level (i.e., one individual versus another, within the same experimental condition). At the between-group level, the groups that achieve the greatest changes in self-efficacy perceptions also achieved the greatest changes in behavior (Figure 13.3). At the individual level, self-efficacy judgments (before the second BAT) were uniformly accurate predictors of performance; that is, strong self-efficacy judgments were associated with higher probabilities of successful task performance. The self-efficacy/behavior relations were remarkably large; Bandura and colleagues (1977) report a correlation of .84 between level of self-efficacy and subsequent approach behavior. Self-efficacy expectations were even better predictors of future performance than was past performance! Follow-up data indicated that the subjects not only maintained their gains in self-efficacy and approach behavior but achieved further improvements. In sum, the data supported the utility of guided participation and the social-cognitive view that treatments improve performance because they raise expectations of personal efficacy (also see Bandura & Adams, 1977; Bandura, Adams, & Beyer, 1977; Bandura, Reese, & Adams, 1982; Williams, 1992).

This social-cognitive approach subsequently has been used in the treatment of a wide variety of difficulties. For example, studies have demonstrated the utility of developing coping skills and increased self-efficacy in handling test anxiety (Smith, 1989) and of vulnerability to assault in women (Ozer & Bandura, 1990; Weitlauf, Cervone, & Smith, 2001). In the latter case, women who participated in a modeling program in which they mastered the physical

GENERAL VIEW

Psychological procedures, whatever their format, serve as ways of creating and strengthening expectations of personal effectiveness. Social-cognitive therapy emphasizes the acquisition of cognitive and behavioral competencies through modeling and guided participation.

ATTRIBUTES OF GOOD MODELS: RELEVANCE AND CREDIBILITY

Models who compel attention, who instill trust, who appear to be realistic figures for self-comparison, and whose standards seem reasonable to the learner will be good sources for therapeutic modeling effects. These attributes may be summarized in terms of the positive functions of relevance and credibility.

SOME ILLUSTRATIVE RULES FOR INDUCING AND MAINTAINING DESIRED CHANGES

1. Structure the tasks to be learned in an orderly, stepwise sequence.
2. Explain and demonstrate general rules or principles. Check client's understanding and provide opportunities for clarification.
3. Provide guided simulated practice with feedback concerning success and error.
4. Once the desired behavior is established, increase opportunities for self-directed accomplishment.
5. Test newly acquired skills in the natural environment under conditions likely to produce favorable results.
6. Test skills in increasingly more demanding situations until a satisfactory level of competence and self-efficacy has been obtained.
7. Provide opportunity for therapist consultation and feedback during periods of increased independent mastery.

THERAPEUTIC EFFECTS OF MODELING

1. *Development of New Skills*. Through observing models and through guided participation people acquire new patterns of behavior and new coping strategies. For example, submissive clients learn to model assertive behavior.
2. *Changes in Inhibitions About Self-Expression*. As a result of modeling, responses already available to the person may be weakened or strengthened. For example, inhibitory effects can occur as a result of observing models receive negative consequences for certain behaviors. Disinhibitory effects, which are more common in therapy, result from observing models perform behaviors without adverse consequences or with positive consequences. Fears may be overcome in this way.
3. *Facilitation of Preexisting Patterns of Behavior*. Behaviors already available to the person and that are not associated with anxiety may occur more often as a result of modeling influences. For example, learners may be aided to become more skillful conversationalists.
4. *Adoption of More Realistic Standards for Judging One's Own Performance*. Observing models reward themselves for varying levels of performance can affect the learner's self-standards. For example, rigid self-demands characteristic of depressed people can be relaxed as a result of modeling.

CONCLUSION

"A burgeoning literature confirms the value of modeling treatments for redressing deficits in social and cognitive skills, and for helping to remove defensive avoidance behavior."

Figure 13.4 Summary of Social-Cognitive Therapy. *(Rosenthal & Bandura, 1978, p. 622)*

skills needed to defend themselves against unarmed sexual assailants gained increased freedom of action and decreased avoidant behavior. Fundamental to all of these studies is the experience of mastery that leads to a therapeutic increase in perceived self-efficacy (Figure 13.4).

Of particular significance for any therapeutic approach is the degree to which the positive effects endure and generalize to other aspects of the person's functioning. Skeptics of modeling and guided mastery approaches might expect there to be little evidence of enduring change or of generalization beyond, for example, the specific phobia treated. However, research suggests that the effects often are enduring and transfer to self-efficacy beliefs in other areas as well (Cervone & Scott, 1995; Williams, 1992). Bandura describes such effects as follows:

> Psychological treatments have traditionally attempted to change human behavior by talk. In the sociocognitive view, human functioning can be enhanced more dependably and fundamentally by mastery experiences than by conversation. In translating this notion to therapeutic practice for phobic disorders, my students and I evolved a powerful guided mastery treatment. It eradicates phobic behavior and biochemical stress reactions, eliminates phobic ruminations and recurrent nightmares, and creates positive attitudes toward formerly dreaded threats. These striking changes are achieved by everyone in a brief period. The changes endure. In follow-up assessments we discovered that the participants not only maintained their therapeutic gains, but made notable improvements in domains of functioning quite unrelated to the treated dysfunction. Thus, for example, after mastering an animal phobia, participants had reduced their social timidity, expanded their competencies in different spheres, and boosted their venturesomeness in a variety of ways. Success in overcoming, within a few hours of treatment, a phobic dread that had constricted and tormented their lives for twenty or thirty years produced a profound change in participants' beliefs in their personal efficacy to exercise better control over their lives. They were putting themselves to the test and enjoying their successes much to their surprise.
>
> SOURCE: Bandura, as quoted in Pervin, 1996, p. 82.

THE CASE OF JIM

Social-Cognitive Theory: Goals, Reinforcers, and Self-Efficacy Beliefs

Twenty years ago Jim was assessed from various theoretical points of view: psychoanalytic, phenomenological, personal construct, and trait. At the time, social-cognitive theory was just beginning to evolve, and thus he was not considered from this standpoint. Later, however, it was possible to gather at least some data from this theoretical standpoint as well. Although comparisons with earlier data may be problematic because of the time lapse, we can gain at least some insight into Jim's personality from this theoretical point of view. We do so by considering Jim's goals, reinforcers he experiences, and his self-efficacy beliefs.

Jim was asked about his goals for the immediate future and for the long-range future. He felt that his immediate and long-term goals were pretty much the same: (1) getting to know his son and being a good parent; (2) becoming more accepting and less critical of his wife and others; and (3) feeling good about his professional work as a consultant. Generally he feels that there is a good chance of achieving these goals but he is guarded in that estimate, with some uncertainty about just how much he will be able to "get out of myself" and thereby be more able to give to his wife and child.

Jim also was asked about positive and aversive reinforcers, things that were important to him that he found rewarding or unpleasant. Concerning positive reinforcers, Jim reported that money was "a biggie." In addition he emphasized time with loved ones, the glamor of going to an opening night, and generally going to the theater or movies. He had a difficult time thinking of aversive reinforcers. He described writing as a struggle and then noted, "I'm having trouble with this." When his concerns about rejection were mentioned, Jim responded: "Oh, to be sure. I agree. Somehow I'm blanking. I think there's more there, but I don't know." Relatedly, Jim discussed his competencies or skills, both intellectual and social. In the intellectual area he reported that he considered himself to be very bright and functioning at a very high intellectual level. He felt that he had no real intellectual deficiencies, though he distinguished between tight, logical thinking and loose, creative thinking, and felt that he was somewhat weak in the latter. Similarly, he felt that he writes well from the standpoint of a clear, organized presentation, but he had not written anything that is innovative or creative.

In the social area, Jim felt that he was very skilled: "I do it naturally, easily, well. I can pull off anything and have a lot of confidence in myself socially. If I was meeting with President Reagan tomorrow I could do it easily. I am at ease with both men and women, in both professional and social contexts." The one social concern noted was his constant struggle with "how egocentric I should be, how personally to take things." He felt that sometimes he takes things too personally. For example, he often feels hurt, offended, and disappointed if someone doesn't call him, wondering why they don't care about him and whether he's done something to offend them. He related this to the time he lived in a commune when he would, on a nightly basis, go over a checklist of people in the commune and wonder how he was doing with each of them: "My security is based on how I'm doing with others. I put a lot of energy into friendships, and when I'm relating well I feel good."

In terms of self-efficacy beliefs, it is clear that Jim has many positive views of himself. He believes that he does most things well; he is a good athlete, a competent consultant, bright, and socially skilled. Does he have areas of low self-efficacy? Jim mentioned three such areas. First, he feels that he does not genuinely accept his wife. He tends to be critical of others generally and of his wife in particular. Related to this is the second area mentioned, a difficulty in "getting out of myself so that I can be genuinely devoted to others." He is particularly concerned about this in relation to whether he will be able to maintain the parental interest and commitment that he would like. This is a high priority for him, but he is concerned that he will not want to be inconvenienced or put out by the new addition to the household. Finally, the third area of low self-efficacy concerned creativity: "I know I'm not good at being creative, so I don't try it."

Whereas Bandura emphasizes the situation-specific aspects of self-efficacy beliefs, Jim felt that these represented fairly broad, consistent areas of high and low self-efficacy and could not pick out more specific situations expressive of his beliefs in this area.

Comment

In many ways the social-cognitive data on Jim are more limited than those associated with the previous theories of personality. We learn about important aspects of Jim's life, but clearly there also are major gaps. There are two reasons for this. First, only a limited amount of time was available for assessment. Second, and perhaps more important, social-cognitive theorists have not developed comprehensive personality assessment tests; only recently have social-cognitive investigators turned their attention explicitly to questions of personality assessment (Cervone, Shadel, & Jencius, 2001). In part, the previous lack of attention reflected social-cognitive theory's conviction that systematic research and the testing of hypotheses, rather than the in-depth study of individuals, is critical to building a scientifically valid personality theory. It perhaps also reflected the social-cognitive criticism of traditional approaches to assessment that emphasize broad personality consistencies across many domains. In this regard, it is interesting that Jim had difficulty articulating out differences in his functioning in various areas. In this sense, he functions much more like a traditional personality theorist than like a social-cognitive theorist, although with further questioning he probably would have been able to specify ways in which his goals, reinforcers, competencies, and self-efficacy beliefs varied from context to context.

Additional Assessments

Although assessments of Jim that are based directly on the principles of social-cognitive theory are limited, the results of other assessment devices that were conducted in Jim's case are of relevance to the theoretical approach. For example, the results of the Role Construct Repertory Test (Rep test) concerning Jim's constructs, in particular those relating to the self (or self-schema), would be of great interest. In addition, there would be interest in his goals and self-efficacy beliefs, assessed in relation to social-cognitive theory. Finally, we were able to obtain from Jim some estimate of his cognitions, attributions, dysfunctional thoughts, and coping strategies.

Jim was asked about specific or general beliefs he held. He noted that he believes in hard work, earning things, and being responsible for what one does. He believes that some people are natural winners and others are losers, the former making life easy for themselves and the latter making life difficult for themselves. Generally he feels that he likes life the easy way and enjoys being a winner. Other beliefs about himself are that he is intelligent, hardworking, personable, humorous, in need of approval, and possessing a depressive streak. Ideally he would like to be more selfless and generous, take setbacks more easily, and relax more. In terms of generalized expectancies, the Life Orientation Test (Scheier & Carver, 1985) was given to Jim as a measure of generalized optimism and pessimism. His responses indicated a strongly pessimistic orientation that fits with his depressive streak. For example, he strongly disagreed with the statements "I'm a believer in the idea that 'every cloud has a silver lining'" and "I'm always optimistic about my future." In contrast to these statements, he strongly disagreed with the statement "I hardly ever expect things to go my way," which probably reflects his clear belief that control is possible and desirable. Thus, he had an extremely high score on the Desirability of Control Scale (Burger & Cooper, 1979).

Jim gave the following as categories he used to view the world: successful/not successful, wealthy/not wealthy, attractive/not attractive, bright/not bright, interesting/not interesting, kind and loving/unloving, patient/impatient, generous/not generous, and deep/shallow. In terms of attributions, he again emphasized his belief in control and responsibility as opposed to belief in luck, chance, or fate. Jim filled out the Attributional Style Questionnaire; his responses reflected a general tendency toward internal, stable, and global attributions. Such an attributional style would fit with his tendency toward depressive streaks and belief in the desirability of control. However, an analysis of the subsections of this questionnaire reveals that this pattern holds more for positive events than for negative ones. In particular, his internal and stable attributions tend to be much more true for positive events than for negative ones. Thus, his belief that positive events can be controlled by his own efforts and can remain stable, reflected in the generalized expectancy that things can work out the way he wants, probably helps him to be less depressed than might otherwise be the case. In addition, his responses indicate a greater internal attribution for interpersonal events than for events having to do with professional achievement.

Finally, let us consider the area of irrational beliefs, dysfunctional thoughts, and cognitive distortions. One important point here is what Jim describes as his tendency to overpersonalize: "This is a problem of mine. If someone doesn't call, I attribute it to a feeling state in relation to me. I can feel terribly injured at times." Although he could not come up with any irrational beliefs or dysfunctional thoughts in the interview, his responses to the Automatic Thoughts Questionnaire (Hollon & Kendall, 1980) shed some light on this area of his functioning. He reported having the following thoughts frequently: "I've let people down," "I wish I were a better person," "I'm disappointed in myself," and "I can't stand this." These frequent thoughts have to do with his not being as loving or generous as he would like, his being very demanding of himself professionally and in athletics, his obsession about things that might go wrong, and his intolerance of things not going his way. For example, he cannot stand to be in traffic and will say: "I can't stand this. This is intolerable." Although Jim does not think much of Ellis's work and in the interview suggested that he didn't have many irrational beliefs, on the questionnaire he checked four out of nine items as frequent thoughts of his: "I must have love or approval," "When people act badly, I blame them," "I tend to view it as a catastrophe when I get seriously frustrated or feel rejected," and "I tend to get preoccupied with things that seem fearsome." He also described his tendency to catastrophize if he is going to be late for a movie: "It's a calamity if I'm going to be one minute late. It becomes a life and death emergency. I go through red lights, honk the horn, and pound on the wheel." This is in contrast to his own tendency to be at least a few minutes late for virtually all appointments, though rarely by more than a few minutes.

When asked about his coping methods, Jim responded: "Heavy-duty compulsivity. It's part of my character in everything, clean ash-trays in the car, the bed made in the morning, everything in the apartment in place. Order is very important. It's pervasive. Also intellectualization and humor." Jim also filled out the Ways of Coping Scale (Folkman, et al., 1986). His responses to this scale indicate that his primary modes of coping with stressful events are to accept responsibility ("Criticize or lecture myself," "Realize I brought the problem on myself") and to engage in problem solving ("Just concentrate on what I had to do next," "Draw on my past experiences; I was in a similar position before"). In general, he tends to remain self-controlled and to think about the problem rather than use escape-avoidance methods, engage in risky solutions, or seek social support and sympathy from others. The latter reflects his not being forgiving of himself for getting into difficulty. Although there appear to be some positive aspects to his coping, other responses indicate that he feels he does not change or grow as a person as a result of these coping methods.

From a social-cognitive perspective, what can be said about Jim as he approaches midlife? We see that in general Jim has a strong sense of self-efficacy in relation to intellectual and social skills, though he feels less efficacious in relation to creative thought and the ability to be loving, generous, and giving to people who are dear to him. He values money and financial success but has settled more on family intimacy and the quality of his work as a consultant as goals for the future. He has a strong sense of individual responsibility and belief in personal control over events. His attributions tend to be internal, stable, and global, and there is a streak of pessimism and depression to him. He is bothered by concerns about the approval of others, by his perfectionism and impatience, and by a tendency to worry about things. He tends to be self-controlled in coping with stress rather than avoiding problems or escaping from them. Generally he sees himself as a competent person and is guardedly optimistic about his chances of achieving his goals in the future.

COMPARATIVE ANALYSIS: RELATING SOCIAL-COGNITIVE THEORY TO THE PREVIOUS APPROACHES

At the outset of our previous chapter, we noted some relations between social-cognitive theory and the other theories of personality covered in this text. We now return you to this topic, armed with the detailed knowledge of social-cognitive theory that you have acquired through these two chapters. We relate social-cognitive theory to psychoanalysis, phenomenological theory, personality construct theory, behaviorism, and trait theory, in turn, below.

Social-cognitive theorists, especially Bandura, are critical of psychoanalysis for its reliance on concepts that cannot be studied experimentally and on therapeutic procedures that have not demonstrated their effectiveness in changing actual psychosocial functioning. Bandura suggests that laboratory investigations have "failed to unearth an unconscious agency of the type assumed by psychodynamic theory" (1986, p. 3) and that "insight into dubious unconscious psychodynamics has little effect on behavior" (p. 5). Regarding anxiety, Bandura emphasizes perceived inefficacy in coping with potentially aversive events rather than on intrapsychic conflict or the threat of unconscious impulses. Therapeutically, he emphasizes the value of behavioral mastery over one's fears, rather than dialogue with one's therapist that is aimed at uncovering unconscious conflicts.

The overall social-cognitive theory view of personality functioning also differs from that of psychoanalysis. Social-cognitive theorists are critical of the psychoanalytic emphasis on broad personality dispositions (character types) and the relative fixity of behavior established during the early years. Instead, social-cognitive theory suggests that behavior varies systematically according to context. Rather than broad stages of development, development in particular areas is emphasized; rather than generalized dynamics and defenses, specific expectancies and self-evaluations are emphasized; rather than early traumatic experiences, observational learning and vicarious conditioning are emphasized; rather than insight into unconscious dynamics, changes in conscious cognitive functioning are emphasized.

Turning to phenomenological theory, one finds significant points of overlap between social-cognitive theory and the work of phenomenologists such as Rogers. In particular, both highlight human potentials and the concept of self. Yet points of agreement are overshadowed by fundamental differences. According to social-cognitive theory, people have a complex system of self-conceptualizations and self-evaluations, with subsets of this self-system coming into play in different contexts. This view contrasts with the phenomenological emphasis on a generalized self-concept: "A global self-conception does not do justice to the complexity of self-efficacy percepts, which vary across different activities, different levels of the same activity, and different circumstances" (Bandura, 1986, p. 410). Other differences are that members of the human potential movement tended to ignore research, particularly laboratory research, whereas such research is the foundation of social-cognitive theory. With regard to therapy, Rogers emphasized the therapeutic climate as the primary ingredient of change, whereas social-cognitive theory highlights skill development and the effect of behavioral mastery on self-efficacy beliefs.

As we noted earlier, the previous approach that is most similar to social-cognitive theory is Kelly's personal construct approach. Both view people as active constructors of psychological meaning, and see these meaning construction processes as central to personality functioning. They also share an emphasis on the utility of behavioral experiences in changing constructs or cognitions. Despite this, and despite Kelly's acknowledged influence on Mischel, followers of the two approaches tend to go their own ways and Bandura virtually ignores the work of Kelly. Why should this be the case? It reflects in part the differing roots of the two approaches and in part their different groundings. Whereas Kelly set his views apart from traditional psychology, social-cognitive theory originally was based on learning theory and continues to be rooted in developments throughout the psychological sciences. Personal construct theory focuses more heavily on thinking processes and the dynamics of inner psychological life than social-cognitive theory, which places much of its effort on analyzing relations between thought and overt action. Whereas personal construct theorists have tended to limit themselves to the study of constructs and to the use of the Rep test as a measuring device, the social-cognitive theory approach to research has been much broader. In this regard, social-cognitive theory can be seen as moving beyond the personal construct approach and, in its greater breadth, supplanting it.

Social-cognitive theory had its roots in learning theory. It continues to share the behaviorist emphasis on rigorous experimentation and on the importance of learned behavior in relation to specific situations or contexts. Both theories reject the medical symptom/disease model and emphasize therapy as the learning of new patterns of thinking and behaving rather than as a cure for some underlying problem. However, as should be clear from this chapter and the previous one, social-cognitive theory's emphasis on cognitive processes as causes of behavior differentiate it fundamentally from behaviorism. In contrast to behaviorism, social-cognitive theory believes that causally, people influence their own action through their capacities to think—especially about themselves. Bandura and other social-cognitive theorists view self-reports about cognition as a valuable source of evidence, again in contrast to the behavioral approach.

Finally, we consider the relation between social-cognitive theory and trait theory. Here one finds perhaps the sharpest points of disagreement on points of substance—despite complete agreement with regard to goals and some research methods. Regarding the points of agreement, both trait theorists and social-cognitive theorists seek to build a comprehensive model of personality on a systematic base of research data. Both value correlational and experimental methods, though social-cognitivists have placed greater emphasis on the role of laboratory experimentation, with trait theorists relying more on correlational techniques and factor analysis.

The differences between social-cognitive theory and trait theory are twofold. One concerns the notion of personality "dispositions"—that is, the things people tend to do, and that distinguish people from one another. Trait theorists construe dispositions in terms of broad psychological tendencies: agreeable tendencies, conscientious tendencies, and so forth. A person's score on a given trait represents his or her average tendency to display the actions that are seen as manifestations of the trait. In adopting this conception, trait theory suggests that behavior is fairly consistent across situations and over time. In contrast, as we have seen, social-cognitive theorists believe that studying mean-level, average tendencies is insufficient. This is because personality often reveals itself in changes in behavior across situations and time. Social-cognitive theorists thus strive to go "beyond traits" (Cervone & Shoda, 1999a), that is, to account for both average tendencies and variation in action. This expands the notion of "disposition" to include systematic variations in action.

The second difference concerns the causes of behavior. When contrasting social-cognitive theory and trait theory in this regard, one must recall that there is no one singular trait theory. Instead, as you learned, some researchers in the trait approach viewed personality traits merely as descriptive terms, whereas others (e.g., McCrae & Costa, 2003; Chapter 8) claimed that traits also were causes of behavior. Social-cognitive theorists disagree strongly with this latter claim (Bandura, 1999; Cervone, 1999), feeling that an explanation of social behavior must be grounded in an understanding of cognitive and emotional systems and the social contexts with which these personality systems interact. In this view, a personality trait term—conscientious, friendly, agreeable, etc.—*describes* how a person acts, but it does *not explain* why a person acts this way. It must be emphasized again that many researchers who study traits and temperament would agree with social-cognitive theorists on this point; they would contend that treating traits as "descriptive categories and not aspiring to equip [them] with explanatory values is fully admissible" whereas if a trait is treated as an "internal property which is a 'cause' of a given behavior" then "criticism of such a meaning…is justified" (Eliasz & Klonowicz, 2001, p. 37).

In summary, then, social-cognitive theory emphasizes what a person can do, particularly in specific contexts, whereas trait theorists emphasize what a person has in terms of context-free traits; social-cognitive theorists emphasize learned cognitive expectancies and competencies, whereas trait theorists emphasize broad dispositions that tend to be genetically based; social-cognitive theorists emphasize adaptation to changing circumstances, whereas trait theorists emphasize stable factor structures; although both accept the value of self-report, social-cognitive theorists emphasize the assessment of ongoing thoughts and feelings in relation to specific situations rather than global self-assessments of general functioning.

STRENGTHS

Social-cognitive theory is perhaps the current favorite among academic personality psychologists. Many clinicians also would label themselves social-cognitive psychologists. What accounts for the theory's growth in popularity and influence? Probably the major factors have been its attention to experimentation and its parallel consideration of important human phenomena. Beyond this, there is an impressive openness to change, as well as a continuing concern with other points of view. These strengths will be considered in greater detail.

Systematic Research on Important Phenomena

Developments in social-cognitive theory have been grounded in careful experimental research. Bandura and Mischel have defined theoretical concepts in ways that leave them open to empirical verification and have always conducted active research programs. The variety of phenomena investigated and the research methods used are impressive. For example, the research on modeling has systematically investigated a wide range of behaviors including aggression, moral judgments, setting of standards, vicarious conditioning of fears, delay of gratification, and helping behavior. Children and adults have been found to be influenced by a wide range of models: live humans, filmed humans, verbally presented models of behavior, and cartoons. The process of modeling has been studied in terms of the influences of model characteristics, observer characteristics, and observed consequences to the model of the demonstrated behavior. The concept of self-efficacy has been studied in terms of its determinants, implications for a wide range of behaviors, and potential for change—an impressive record of research.

Most of this social-cognitive research has been conducted with the social behaviors of humans. Thus, in considering the evidence, we are not asked to make large extrapolations from animal research to humans and from simple behaviors to complex human processes. Social-cognitive theory investigates and attempts to account for the very phenomena that are of interest to most people aggression: the effects of parents and mass media on children, the change of dysfunctional behaviors, the development of self-regulatory capacities, and the increase of control over one's life.

A Theory Open to Change

Social-cognitive theory has changed and evolved over the years. A comparison of *Social Learning and Personality Development* (1963) by Bandura and Walters with the latest formulations of social-cognitive theory (Bandura, 1999, 2001; Mischel & Morf, 2002; Mischel & Shoda, 1999) gives ample testimony to the changes that have come about. The theory's original emphasis on behavior, observational learning, and the importance of social reinforcers in maintaining behavior has not been lost, yet there has been a greatly increased emphasis on self-regulatory processes and the human capacity for personal agency. In the process of reciprocal determinism we not only have environmental contingencies shaping people but also people shaping environmental contingencies. There is an emphasis not only on behavior but on cognition and emotion as well, including relationships between thinking and emotion. Social-cognitive theorists have tried to remain informed about developments in other areas of psychology and to adjust their position so that it remains consistent with these developments. Beyond this, social-cognitive theory itself has influenced and contributed to other parts of psychology. Although social-cognitive theory draws on advances in fields such as cognition and development, it also contributes to these advances. As noted by one reviewer: "Bandura's contributions to a theoretical understanding of human development have been of major significance for the field. Social-cognitive theory has evolved over the years in a way that is responsive to new data" (Grusec, 1992, p. 784).

While developing their own theory in this manner, social-cognitive theorists have played a valuable role in criticizing other theoretical positions (psychoanalytic, trait, Skinnerian). Mischel, in particular, has been influential in drawing attention to the problems associated with views that overemphasize trait factors, and both Bandura and Mischel have argued that one cannot build a comprehensive, explanatory scientific theory of personality on the principle of behaviorism, psychoanalysis, or trait theory. Whatever one's exact opinion on the issues, their critiques have lead to a more realistic assessment of the complex, interacting causes of behavior.

View of the Person and Social Concern

Social-cognitive theory offers a view of the person that is more reasonable than a robot or telephone switchboard and suggests possible solutions to problems of genuine social concern. The overall view highlights human capabilities for growth and self-direction (Bandura, 2001). There is a systematic analysis of the psychological mechanisms that underlie human potentials (Caprara & Cervone, 2000, 2003). Rather than studying primarily what people "are like" (their typical tendencies or dispositions), social-cognitive theorists argue that a complete conception of human personality must include the study of what people can become (their potentials).

This focus on human capabilities and the potential for change often has been directed to issues of social concern. Bandura (1977a), for example, considers the soundness of a legal system of deterrence, the potential for creating environments conducive to learning and intellectual development, and the interplay between personal freedom and limits on conduct that must exist in every society. Interestingly enough, he concludes his book with the following: "As a science concerned with the social consequences of its applications, psychology must promote public understanding of psychological issues that bear on social policies to ensure that its findings are used in the service of human betterment" (p. 213). As we have seen, and will see again in the next chapter, significant practical benefits of social-cognitive research have been demonstrated.

LIMITATIONS

Given these significant strengths, what are the limitations of social-cognitive theory? Some of these are associated with new developments and the fact that many of the approaches are recent. Social-cognitive theory has shown a constructive openness to change but has not followed a path that has led to a carefully integrated network of theoretical assumptions. Social-cognitive theory still appears to ignore important phenomena that are recognized by other approaches. These points will be considered in greater detail.

Not Yet a Systematic, Unified Theory

Social-cognitive theory is not yet a systematic, unified theory in the sense of there existing an overall network of assumptions that ties together all elements of the approach. This lack of overall theoretical coherence has some drawbacks. Occasionally diverse concepts seem to be lumped together. In other instances, the social-cognitive view functions more as an overarching strategy or framework for studying personality, rather than being a well-specified theory. In attempting to go beyond a simplistic emphasis on internal (person) or external (environment) determinants and a simplistic emphasis on cognition, affect, or overt behavior as all important, social-cognitive theory represents an important contribution. However, it often presents as a general view or orientation rather than a fully worked out statement of relationships.

Recent years have seen greater efforts at systematization. These include work that presents a systematic organization of social-cognitive personality variables (Cervone, 2004). Even at the time of Bandura's landmark 1986 volume, commentators acknowledged the degree to which an overall theory of personality had started to be achieved, noting of Bandura's work that the outline of a "grand theory" of human behavior is there, and "what more can we ask from a single colleague and scholar" (Baron, 1987, p. 415). Future work should bring greater systematization and scope to social-cognitive theory.

Relative Neglect of Important Areas

It is impossible for a theory of personality to be truly all-encompassing at this time. Accepting such qualifications, it would still appear that social-cognitive theorists ignore or give minimal attention to significant aspects of human functioning. Without accepting all of the viewpoint of stage theorists, biological forces of maturation would appear to be important in the feelings people expe-

SOCIAL-COGNITIVE THEORY AT A GLANCE

Theorist or Theory	Structure	Process
Social-Cognitive Theory	Competencies, Beliefs, Goals, Evaluative Standards	Cognitive and affective processing system functions in reciprocal interaction with the social environment, especially in observational learning, self-regulated motivation, and self-control

rience and in the way they process information. Sexual feelings do become increasingly important at particular times in the life cycle, and the thinking of a child is fundamentally different from that of an adult in a variety of ways. Social-cognitive theorists recognize that biological temperament is important to personality and individual differences, but have not sufficiently integrated these temperament factors into their theoretical formulations. Specifically, the ways in which temperament and social experience interact to influence the individual's development of personal goals, standards, and efficacy beliefs is poorly understood, and stands as a particularly promising area for future research.

Beyond this, although social-cognitive theory recognizes the importance of motivational factors and conflict, only recently has it begun to give serious attention to these processes. The concepts of standards and goals represent an important development in the social-cognitive view of motivation. At the same time, this is an area in need of further development. In particular, there is need for study of the kinds of goals people have, the basis for their acquisition, and people's phenomenological experience as they pursue their goals. Bandura seems to equate goals with standards, as if the only thing that motivates people is standards. But don't people pursue other goals? Similarly, Bandura suggests that people are motivated by the discrepancy between performance and a standard, but aren't people also motivated by the desire to achieve the goal itself rather than to close a discrepancy between performance and a standard?

Turning to the concept of conflict, Bandura recognizes that most behavior is determined by multiple goals, yet he strangely ignores the concept of conflict.

Table 13.4 Summary of Strengths and Limitations of Social Cognitive Theory

Strengths	Limitations
1. Has impressive research record.	1. Is not a systematic, unified theory.
2. Considers important phenomena.	2. Contains potential problems associated with the use of verbal self-report.
3. Shows consistent development and elaboration as a theory.	3. Requires more exploration and development in certain areas (e.g., motivation, affect, system properties of personality organization).
4. Focuses attention on important theoretical issues.	4. Provides findings concerning therapy that are tentative rather than conclusive.

Growth and Development	Pathology	Change
Social learning through observation and direct experience; development of self-efficacy judgments and standards for self-regulation	Learned response patterns; excessive self-standards; problems in self-efficacy	Modeling; guided mastery; increased self-efficacy

Most people can readily think of situations where they felt in conflict between goals. For some people conflict is a fundamental part of their lives. Thus, it seems strange that such a seemingly important concept would be so neglected.

In sum, there are good grounds both for enthusiasm about social-cognitive theory and for caution, even skepticism. Social-cognitive theory represents a major development. It is still evolving, and its further efforts are worthy of careful attention (Table 13.4).

MAJOR CONCEPTS

Attributions   Beliefs about the causes of events.

Dysfunctional expectancies   In social-cognitive theory, maladaptive expectations concerning the consequences of specific behaviors.

Dysfunctional self-evaluations   In social-cognitive theory, maladaptive standards for self-reward that have important implications for psychopathology.

Emotion-focused coping   Coping in which an individual stresses to improve his or her internal emotional state, for example, by emotional distancing or the seeking of social support.

General principles approach   Higgins's term for an analysis of personal and situational influences on thought and action in which a common set of causal principles is used to explain both cross-situational consistency in thought and action that results from personal influences and variability in thought and action that results from situational influences.

Guided mastery   A treatment approach emphasized in social-cognitive theory in which a person is assisted in performing modeled behaviors.

Implicit theories   Broad, generalizable beliefs that we may not be able to state explicitly in words, yet that influence our thinking.

Learning goals   In Dweck's social-cognitive analysis of personality and motivation, a goal of trying to enhance one's knowledge and personal mastery of a task.

Performance goals   In Dweck's social-cognitive analysis of personality and motivation, a goal of trying to make a good impression on other people who may evaluate you.

Problem-focused coping   Attempts to cope by altering features of a stressful situation.

Schemas   Complex cognitive structures that guide information processing.

Self-discrepancies   In theoretical analyses of Higgins, incongruities between beliefs about one's current psychological attributes (the actual self) and desired attributes that represent valued standards or guides.

Self-enhancement   A motive to maintain or enhance positive views of the self.

Stress inoculation training   A procedure to reduce stress developed by Meichenbaum in which clients are taught to become aware of such negative, stress-inducing cognitions.

Self-schemas   Cognitive generalizations about the self that guide a person's information processing.

Self-verification   A motive to obtain information that is consistent with one's self-concept.

Working self-concept The subset of self-concept that is in working memory at any give time; the theoretical idea is that different social circumstances may activate different aspects of self-concept.

REVIEW

1. Much research in the social-cognitive tradition has explored three cognitive components of personality: beliefs, goals, and evaluative standards. The study of beliefs has included research on the role of cognitive generalizations about the self, or self-schemas. Research on goals has explored differences between types of goals, including learning versus performance goals. Work on evaluative standards has explored discrepancies between people's views of their actual self and standards representing ideals versus oughts, or obligations.

2. Research has established that people's thoughts about the causes of significant life events, or attributions about the events, significantly influence motivation and emotional reactions.

3. In clinical applications, social-cognitive theory rejects the medical symptom/disease model of psychopathology, emphasizing instead the dysfunctional learning of behaviors, expectancies, standards for self-reward, and, most significantly, self-efficacy beliefs. Dysfunctional learning can occur through the observation of models, in particular through vicarious conditioning, or through direct experience.

4. According to social-cognitive theory, there are two key points in bringing about psychological change in therapy. One is that low levels of perceived self-efficacy contribute to a wide variety of psychological dysfunctions, including anxiety and depression. The other is that self-efficacy perceptions can be increased therapeutically, especially through modeling and guided mastery therapies. In modeling, models demonstrate the skills and subskills necessary in specific situations. In guided participation, the person is assisted in performing these modeled behaviors. Research supports the use of these procedures in raising the perception of self-efficacy.

5. In relation to the theories considered previously, (a) social-cognitive theory emphasizes conscious cognitive processes and experimental data as opposed to the psychoanalytic emphasis on unconscious processes and clinical data; (b) social-cognitive theory emphasizes the specificity of self-efficacy beliefs as opposed to the global self-conceptions emphasized by Rogers; and (c) social-cognitive theory emphasizes the situational specificity and variability of behavior as opposed to the broad dispositions emphasized by trait theorists, and treats trait constructs merely as summary descriptions of observed behavior, not as causes of that behavior.

6. Social-cognitive theory's strengths include its ability to bring systematic research to bear on important problems of personality functioning and social behavior. Its primary limit is that it is not yet a wholly unified, systematic theory. A primary challenge to social-cognitive theory is to relate the development of social-cognitive structures to inherited biological qualities that contribute to individual differences.

14

PERSONALITY IN CONTEXT: INTERPERSONAL RELATIONS, CULTURE, AND DEVELOPMENT ACROSS THE COURSE OF LIFE

INTERPERSONAL RELATIONSHIPS
    Rejection Sensitivity
        "Hot" and "Cool" Focus
    Transference in Interpersonal
        Relationships
**STRATEGIES FOR MEETING
ACADEMIC AND SOCIAL CHALLENGES:
OPTIMISTIC STRATEGIES AND
DEFENSIVE PESSIMISM**
**KNOWLEDGE, APPRAISAL, AND
CROSS-SITUATIONAL COHERENCE**
**PERSONALITY DEVELOPMENT IN
SOCIOECONOMIC CONTEXT**
    Causes and Effects of Personality
        Attributes
    Personality, Gender, and Historical Context
**PERSONALITY FUNCTIONING ACROSS
THE LIFE SPAN**
    Psychological Resilience in the Later Years

    Emotional Life in Older Adulthood:
        Socioemotional Selectivity
PERSONS IN CULTURES
**Two Strategies for Thinking about
Personality and Culture**
    Strategy #1: Personality...and Culture?
    Strategy #2: Culture and Personality
**Personality and Self as Socially
Constructed within Culture**
    Independent and Interdependent Views of
    Self
**PERSONALITY PROCESSES AND
SOCIAL CHANGE**
    Media Modeling of Prosocial Behavior
        Literacy
        HIV/AIDS Prevention
SUMMARY
MAJOR CONCEPTS
REVIEW

"I wish I was like you. You're always so optimistic about everything."

"Yeah, right. I just broke up with Pete."

"Oh no! What happened?"

"Well, I thought for sure that he was going to break up with me, so I challenged him on it, and we had a big fight."

"What made you think you'd break up?"

"That's what always happens, isn't it?"

"No. I mean, I've been with Sam for two years, and I'm sure we're going to stick together."

"Well, then you're the optimist I guess. Except for how weird you get about exams."

"I'm telling you, I'm going to fail the final in this personality class."

"That's ridiculous. You said the same thing before the mid-term and then you got an A!"

Are both of these people "optimists"? Or are both "pessimists"? Or might there be a deeper lesson to be learned from this dialogue?

To many contemporary personality psychologists, the lesson is that personality must be understood "in context." We learn about someone's personality as we observe them interact with the social situations—the "contexts"—of their life. Even if the two people in the dialogue above are both "moderately optimistic" on average, this characterization does not tell you much about the differences in their personalities. A deeper understanding is obtained only if one explores how they cope with the different situations of their lives. The nature of their uniqueness and of the differences between them cannot be discovered by yanking their personality out of the life contexts in which they live—for example, by asking them how they tend to act in general, irrespective of context, or by requiring them to perform some laboratory puzzles that bear no relation to the textures of their everyday life. Instead, we can only understand *who* they are by asking *where* they are when they display the distinctive patterns of experience and action that are the hallmarks of their personality.

This chapter, then, considers the question of personality in context. We address a range of issues: interpersonal relationships; socioeconomic contexts within which persons develop; personality development across the life span and the ways in which one's stage of life serves as a context that influences social motives; interactions among personality and culture; and the possibility that principles of personality theory can foster beneficial social change. Although the topics will vary, as you read the chapter you will detect a consistent theme. In each case, scientific progress in understanding persons is made through a careful study of both persons and the contexts of their lives.

Why are personality psychologists interested in social context? It is not because they are "closet social psychologists" or "closet sociologists." Instead, the interest is driven, to a large degree, by a different consideration. It is that personality functioning involves processes of meaning construction. People make sense of—i.e., construct meaning out of—the social and personal events they encounter. As you read the pages of this book, your mental life cannot be characterized merely in terms of perceptual information processing (e.g., "your visual system detects lines, curves, and angles on a white background," etc.). Instead, you are engaged also in an activity imbued with social meaning; you are "cramming for a final exam," perhaps "to graduate on time," so that "your family doesn't think you're a big failure," or maybe so that "you can achieve your dream of a college degree" and "move on to a job where you finally earn some real money." This sort of "imposition of meaning on life is the major end and primary condition of human existence" (Geertz, 1973, p. 434). What does meaning construction have to do with "personality in context"? Processes of meaning construction inherently involve social context. We rarely sit around thinking "things are OK in general" or "I'm very disappointed, but not with anything in particular." Instead, our thoughts are directed to the world. We are preoccupied with specific persons, situations, relationships, and life challenges. Personality, then, involves psychological systems through which people assign meaning to the significant contexts of their lives.

In terms of the personality theories, in this chapter we draw significantly on the social-cognitive approaches of Bandura, Mischel, and related investigators that were discussed in Chapters 12 and 13. Yet we take an even broader view by capitalizing on a variety of research traditions in contemporary personality psychology that address the ways in which people make sense of their social world.

QUESTIONS TO BE ADDRESSED IN THIS CHAPTER

1. In contexts that involve interpersonal relationships, why do some people experience anxiety about the relationship even when it seems to be going well?

2. In what ways does personality involve "strategies" for coping with life challenges, and how might people differ in the strategies they invoke?

3. How does people's knowledge about themselves and about social situations contribute to consistent styles of response that are evidenced across social contexts?

4. How is personality development influenced by socioeconomic conditions—and how does it influence them?

5. Through what personality processes are older adults able to maintain a strong sense of psychological well-being in the later years of life?

6. What is the nature of the relation between personality and culture?

7. Can personality theory contribute to widespread, beneficial social change?

INTERPERSONAL RELATIONSHIPS

The most significant contexts in most people's lives are ones that involve other people. Although individuals face many financial, professional, and academic demands, challenges that involve relationships with others—friends, family, romantic partners, ex-romantic partners, prospective romantics partners—have a particular power to capture our attention and to bring us either happiness or distress. In recent years, personality psychologists increasingly have recognized that "close relationships provide the most central context for our daily lives" (Cooper, 2002, p. 758). In exploring personality-in-context, then, the first context we consider is that of interpersonal relations.

Interpersonal relations are a particularly interesting setting in which to study the influence of personality factors because these influences are "two-sided." On the one hand, different personality characteristics may cause people to engage in actions that are helpful or harmful to relationships. For example, someone lacking in self-control over inappropriate sexual desires may engage in infidelities that harm a relationship. On the other hand, personality qualities may influence someone's *interpretation of* their partner's behavior irrespective of what their partner actually does. Biases in perception may cause a person to fail to notice a positive action by their partner, or perhaps to infer that a partner was being critical even when that was not the partner's intent.

Research exploring day-to-day interactions between relationship partners reveals this two-pronged impact of personality on the quality of relationships (Gable, Reis, & Downey, 2003). Positive behaviors (e.g., being affectionate) and negative behaviors (e.g., being critical or inattentive) by a relationship partner do have positive and negative effects, respectively, on the other person's satisfaction and happiness with the relationship. However, inaccurate perceptions of one's relationship partner are found to have an effect, too. People are less satisfied with their relationship when they infer that their partner has engaged in a negative behavior toward them—even if their partner reports that he or she never did the behavior in the first place (Gable et al., 2003). Personality factors that influence people's perceptions of their partner, then, may have a big effect on the quality of interpersonal relationships. We begin our discussion of personality in its interpersonal context, then, by reviewing one specific individual-difference variable that appears to have this influence.

REJECTION SENSITIVITY

Consider again the dialogue that opened this chapter. One of the speakers—the one who broke up with Pete—displayed a style of personality-in-context that is fairly well understood due to contemporary research on a personality quality known as **rejection sensitivity**.

As studied by the psychologist Geraldine Downey and her colleagues (e.g., Downey and Feldman, 1996; Ayduk, Mischel, & Downey, 2002), rejection sensitivity refers to a particular style of thinking. This thinking style is characterized by anxious expectations of rejection in interpersonal relationships. The idea is that some people seem particularly prone to expect that a relationship, such as with a boyfriend or girlfriend, will break up. Even if the relationship is going quite well, the person may dwell on the hypothetical possibility that they will be rejected. This thinking style is important because such anxious thoughts may affect the relationship itself. People who inaccurately expect

Research on rejection sensitivity reveals that some people are particularly concerned that relationships they are in will break up – even when the relationship appears to be going very well.

that their partner is going to reject them might, as a result of these expectations, create interpersonal tension that harms what originally had been a strong, positive relationship. Anxious expectations of rejection, then, can be a self-fulfilling prophecy, that is, something that turns out to be true because one expects it to be true.

Downey and Feldman (1996) assess individual differences in rejection sensitivity through the *Rejection Sensitivity Questionnaire (RSQ)*. Respondents are presented with a list of interpersonal circumstances (e.g., asking a boyfriend/girlfriend to move in with you, asking someone out on a date). For each circumstance, people are asked to indicate their subjective sense of the likelihood that the other person would accept versus reject their request (i.e., the request of moving in, going out on a date, etc.). They also indicate how concerned or anxious they would be regarding the other person's response in each circumstance. People who frequently say that there is a high likelihood of their being rejected, and who also say that they would be very anxious about being rejected, are classified as high in rejection sensitivity.

The potential impact of rejection sensitivity on interpersonal relationships has been documented in research involving first-year college students (Downey & Feldman, 1996). This was a longitudinal study in which key measures were taken at two different points in time. First, early in the academic year, a large sample of participants completed the RSQ. Four months later, the researchers identified a subset of people who had begun a romantic relationship only *after* completing the RSQ. At this time point, the researchers asked these individuals to report on this new, ongoing relationship. Specifically, participants completed a measure tapping attributions of hurtful intent in the new relationship. In this measure, people were presented with hypothetical acts that could have a number of different causes (e.g., your boyfriend/girlfriend begins spending less time with you), and were asked whether each act was an indication that the relationship partner was being intentionally hurtful. By designing the research in this manner, with the relationship occurring only after the RSQ was completed, the researchers could be sure that RSQ responses were not themselves a reaction to the specific relationship that people reported on four months into the academic year. Thus, this research design

Table 14.1   Correlations between Dispositional Variables and Rejection Sensitivity Questionnaire (RSQ) and Attributions of Hurtful Intent for the Behavior of a Subsequent Romantic Partner

Dispositional Variables	Correlation of RSQ with Attributions Partialling Out the Dispositional Variable	Correlation of Dispositional Variable with Attributions
Neuroticism	.34[*]	.06
Introversion	.35[*]	.08
Self-esteem	.34[*]	−.13
Social avoidance	.30[*]	.17
Social distress	.31[*]	.16
Interpersonal sensitivity	.35[**]	.06
Secure attachment	.40[**]	.04
Resistant attachment	.42[**]	−.12
Avoidant attachment	.43[**]	−.07

$p < .05, p < .01$

NOTE: "Partialling out" a variable refers to a statistical technique in which one examines the relation between two variables while controlling statistically for the effects of a third variable. The significant correlations in the center column thus indicate that RSQ scores are significantly correlated with attributions of hurtful intent even after one controls for the effects of the dispositional variables listed in the left column of the table.

SOURCE: Downey & Feldman, 1996

enabled Downey and Feldman to determine whether rejection sensitivity would contribute to thoughts about the subsequent relationship.

Findings revealed that rejection sensitivity indeed did predict beliefs about the new relationship (Table 14.1, left column). People who were higher in rejection sensitivity before their relationship began were more likely to infer hostile intent on the part of their partner after the relationship was underway. Since the thought that "my partner is intentionally being hostile to me" obviously can be bad for the health of a relationship, this implies that the personality characteristic of rejection sensitivity can be consequential to the quality and longevity of relationships.

A second feature of the results reported in Table 14.1 speaks to the overall theme of this chapter: the importance of studying personality in context. Rejection sensitivity is a *contextual* personality variable. It refers to a pattern of thinking (anxious expectations) that occurs in a specific context (interpersonal settings in which there is some possibility of not being socially accepted by someone you care about). Contrast this to *decontextual* or "global" personality variables. A personality variable such as "neuroticism" (see Chapters 7 and 8) is decontextualized in that it refers to a generalized, overall tendency to experience anxiety and related psychological distress. Whether one is anxious about a relationship, an exam, one's health, or global military conflict, the anxiety might be interpreted as a manifestation of neuroticism by a psychologist who adopts a theoretical framework in which actions are explained in terms of global personality variables.

Recognizing the difference between contextualized and decontextual personality constructs, Downey and Feldman (1996) did not merely ask whether their contextualized variable, rejection sensitivity, predicted people's thoughts about hostility on the part of their romantic partner. They asked whether rejection sensitivity predicted thoughts about hostility *after accounting for* the relation between these thoughts and a variety of global personality constructs. (This is accomplished through statistical procedures that determine the degree to which two variables are related while controlling for the impact of a third variable.) As you can see from the left column of Table 14.1, the contextualized variable, rejection sensitivity, predicted thoughts about hostility after controlling for the decontextualized trait variables. In contrast, as you can see in the right column of Table 14.1, none of the decontextualized, global variables significantly predicted people's thoughts about their relationships. This result clearly highlights the value of studying personality in context.

Subsequent work has indicated that individual differences in rejection sensitivity are related not only to attributions of hostility, but to long-term relationship outcomes. Both rejection-sensitive individuals and their romantic partners have been found to experience less satisfaction with their relationships, as compared to persons low in rejection sensitivity (Downey & Feldman, 1996). As one might suspect, the relationships of people who are high in rejection sensitivity also are more likely to break up than are the relationships of people who are not prone to anxious expectations of rejection (Downey, Freitas, Michaelis, & Khouri, 1998).

"Hot" and "Cool" Focus

Ideally, the personality psychologist would not only be able to describe the fact that people high and low in rejection sensitivity have different experiences in relationships. An ideal scientific outcome would be one in which researchers identified specific psychological processes that are associated with rejection sensitivity, as well as associated thoughts about hostility in relationships. Identifying these psychological processes would provide knowledge that could be used by the applied psychologist who might wish to develop strategies for teaching people to control their negative emotions and improve their relationship experiences.

Recent work has taken up this challenge. Researchers have explored cognitive strategies through which anyone (i.e., people low or high on rejection sensitivity) might be able to control excessive feelings of hostility in interpersonal encounters. The specific psychological process that is studied is attentional focus. In any complex social situation, there are lots of different things that one might pay attention to. Focusing on one versus another feature of the situation might have different effects on one's thoughts and emotions. This point was already illustrated in Chapter 12, where we discussed research on delay of gratification. Children were found to be more capable of controlling their emotional impulses when they focused their attention on relatively unemotional features of the environment. As you will recall in the delay of gratification paradigm children were able to control their impulsive emotions when they focused on the appearance of food (a "cool" encoding) rather than focusing on its taste (a "hot" encoding).

Ayduk, Mischel, and Downey (2002) have extended this reasoning about **hot versus cool attentional focus** to the study of interpersonal rejection and hostility. In this research, participants were asked to recall an experience from their past that had made them feel rejected by another person. Then, depending on the experimental condition to which they were assigned, participants were asked to think about this rejection experience in different ways. In a hot-focus condition, they thought about their emotions during the rejection experience (e.g., "How did your heart beat? How did your face feel", Ayduk et al., 2002, p. 445). In a cool-focus condition, participants' attention was directed to features of the situation that did not involve emotional experience, such as the physical setting in which the experience occurred (e.g., "Where were you standing with respect to the people and the objects around you?", Ayduk et al., 2002, p. 445).

Focusing attention on "hot" versus "cool" aspects of the past experience had a variety of effects (Ayduk et al., 2002). When asked to describe their mood after thinking about the rejection experience, people who focused on "cool" aspects of the experience described themselves as being less angry than people in the hot-focus condition or people in a control condition in which there were no "hot" or "cool" instructions. When participants wrote an essay describing their thoughts and feelings while thinking about the experience, cool-focus participants composed essays featuring less angry, emotional content. A third dependent measure in the experiment involved reaction-time measures (see Chapter 13). All participants engaged in a lexical decision task, which is a task in which both words and strings of letters that do not form words are presented on a computer screen and the research participant is asked to decide, as quickly as possible, whether a given letter string actually is a word. In this research (Ayduk et al., 2002), participants were presented with some words that related to hostility (e.g., "enraged," "vengeance"). Participants who earlier had focused their attention on "hot" features of their past interpersonal rejection were found to be the quickest to recognize that the hostility words were, in fact, words. The interpretation of this finding is that focusing attention on one's emotional reactions ("How did your heart beat?", etc.) activated thoughts about hostility, with that greater activation being revealed in the fast reaction times of the hot-focus participants. In summary, then, people who thought about the same type of interpersonal encounter but who focused their attention on different aspects of the encounter had substantially different psychological experiences.

As Ayduk and colleagues (2002) note, the ability to identify a specific psychological process, attentional focus, that contributes to hostile reactions has a significant applied implication. People who are particularly vulnerable to experiencing hostile emotions that interfere with their interpersonal relationships could be taught "cooling strategies." In principle, psychological interventions could teach people to gain greater control over their emotional life by focusing their attention on "cool" rather than "hot" aspects of interpersonal encounters.

TRANSFERENCE IN INTERPERSONAL RELATIONSHIPS

Have you ever met someone new who vaguely reminded you of someone from your past? Have you ever had the intuition that your reactions toward someone were identical toward your reactions to someone else who you have known? In Chapter 4, we learned that this possibility was of much interest to psychoanalysts. In psychoanalytic theory, a central component of the therapy process is that patients duplicate, in therapy, their past interactions with significant figures from their past. This experience of attitudes toward the analyst that are based in attitudes toward such figures was called "transference."

Contemporary experimental research suggests that transference processes may not be limited to the therapeutic setting. Many of our everyday reactions to people that we meet may be influenced by a key contextual factor: the degree to which the new person we meet happens to resemble significant people in our past.

Highly informative research on this topic has been done by Susan Andersen and her colleagues. They have developed a social-cognitive analysis of transference in interpersonal relationships (Andersen & Chen, 2002). In other words, although Andersen is interested in the same phenomenon as was Freud, she tries to explain the phenomenon using contemporary social-cognitive theory and methods, rather than the theoretical model employed by Freud.

Rather than seeing transference as reflecting mysterious forces in the unconscious, Andersen suggests that the phenomenon of transference is a natural by-product of basic social-cognitive processes of the sort we reviewed in our previous two chapters. The specific idea is the following. Much research already established two facts about individuals' interpretations of people and events (Higgins, 1996). First, we interpret events by using previously stored knowledge. For example, if we see someone standing in the street wearing blue pants and a blue shirt and blowing a whistle, we interpret this person as being "a police officer" thanks to the fact that we already have, stored in our head, knowledge about police officers. Our thoughts and expectations about the person are then guided by our preexisting knowledge about police officers. Second, we use a given piece of stored knowledge to interpret an event when that knowledge overlaps with information in the situation we are interpreting. In our example, if there had been less overlap between our knowledge of police officers and the person in the street—for example, if he had not been wearing blue pants and a blue shirt—then we might not have interpreted the person as a police officer, but merely as some nut standing in the street blowing a whistle.

Andersen and Chen (2002) recognize that these basic processes of social-cognition might explain the phenomena that Freud had recognized as transference. Suppose you meet a new person who happens to have qualities that resemble those of someone you have known well in your past. For example, the person might have a similar hairstyle or manner of speaking, or a similar set of interests and hobbies. This informational overlap between the new person and your past acquaintance may activate knowledge about the individual in your past. This activated knowledge about the past acquaintance may then influence your thoughts and feelings toward the new individual. You may assume—even without realizing that you are doing so—that the new individual possesses qualities that actually are those that were possessed by your past acquaintance. In other words, you will "transfer" your beliefs from your past acquaintance to the new person.

Evidence of such transference processes comes from an experimental paradigm in which, in an initial experimental session, participants write a description of a person with whom they have had a personally significant relationship. In a subsequent session, participants are asked to read descriptions of various target persons. Some of these descriptions include information that overlaps with their earlier description of their significant other. Later, participants are asked to try to recall information from the descriptions. The key dependent measure is "false positives," that is, the "remembering" of information about the target person that was not actually in the description of the target person, but was a characteristic of the significant other; these false-positive memories are the evidence of the transference of information from the past relationships to the new person. Findings indicate that people are much more likely to exhibit false-positive memories when target persons resemble significant others from their past than when they resemble either less significant acquaintances from their own past or significant figures from someone else's past experience (Andersen & Cole, 1990; Andersen, Glassman, Chen, & Cole, 1995). Emotional reactions and desires to establish a close relationship with a new acquaintance also are influenced by transference processes triggered by overlapping features between the new person and a significant figure from one's past (Andersen & Baum, 1994; Andersen, Reznik, & Manzella, 1996).

Like the work on rejection sensitivity reviewed earlier, research on social-cognitive processes in transference also illustrates this chapter's theme. In this case, the key contextual variable in understanding "personality in context" is the relation between the attributes of an old and a new acquaintance. When these attributes overlap, a person's experiences and actions cannot be explained in terms of their general, average behavioral tendencies. Instead, they must be understood in terms of context-specific thoughts that link an old and a new acquaintance. Thanks to these transference processes, then, even after you break up with a person, that person may "live on in one's head" and influences your future relationships.

STRATEGIES FOR MEETING ACADEMIC AND SOCIAL CHALLENGES: OPTIMISTIC STRATEGIES AND DEFENSIVE PESSIMISM

Research on rejection sensitivity sounds a general theme that is heard in many lines of psychological research: People who have negative thoughts about an upcoming situation may "shoot themselves in the foot." Their negative expectations about what might happen turn out to be a cause of the bad outcomes that they experience. But is this always the case? Is "negative thinking produced negative outcomes" a basic law of personality psychology? One important line of research suggests that the answer to this question is "no."

The psychologists Nancy Cantor, Julie Norem, and their colleagues have studied different strategies that people use to cope with challenging events. A "strategy" is a coherent set of behavioral and cognitive methods that people employ in order to achieve a valuable life goal (Cantor & Kihlstrom, 1987; Sanderson & Cantor, 1999). The basic idea of their work is that within any given context (e.g., a context such as coping with academic pressures at college) different people may use qualitatively different strategies. Two different strategies they have studied are strategic **"optimism"** and **"defensive pessimism"** (Cantor, Norem, Neidenthal, Langston, & Brower, 1987; Norem, 2001).

Optimists are people who hold relatively realistic expectations about their capabilities; if they have the skills required to handle a challenge, they generally will say so—to others and to themselves—and experience relatively little pre-performance anxiety. Defensive pessimists, however, are different (Norem, 2001). They are people who seem to use negative thinking as a strategy. Their chronic strategy for coping with stress is to expect the worst. Even after experiencing success, the defensive pessimist may express low expectations and much anxiety about the future. The defensive pessimist is that person portrayed in the passage that opened this chapter: the person who is worried about the final exam despite getting an A on the mid-term.

A key idea in research on defensive pessimism is that, for people who typically use this strategy, pessimism may not be all that bad a thing. There may be some "positive power" in "negative thinking" (Norem, 2001). For some people, in some contexts, negative thinking may be an effective coping strategy that ultimately enables people to motivate themselves to attain high levels of performance.

Key research on strategic optimism and defensive pessimism (Cantor et al., 1987) has examined a life transition that is of relevance to many readers of this text. It is the transition from high school to college. In the senior year of high school, people often settle into comfortable routines. They have well-established friendship patterns, know many of the school's teachers and administrators, and have figured out how to achieve decent grades. Moving on to college, in contrast, can be like having "the rug pulled out from under you." Suddenly your firm foundation of friends, family, and familiar classes is gone. You are confronted with new challenges: meeting new friends, staying in touch with old friends, keeping up with academics, becoming involved in social activities on campus.

Though such life transitions may simply be hectic to the student, they are of much scientific interest to the personality psychologist. Precisely because they are challenging, they are revealing of individual differences in coping skills and strategies. Just as a challenging IQ-test item is more revealing of differences in analytic intelligence than the question "What is 2 + 2?," challenging social situations are more revealing of individual differences in "social intelligence" and the ways in which people use their social intelligence to develop strategies for coping with challenges and stress (Cantor & Kihlstrom, 1987).

In this research, then, the investigators conducted a longitudinal study in which students were studied throughout their first year in college (Cantor et al., 1987). At the beginning of the year they administered a questionnaire designed to assess people's typical patterns of optimistic versus defensive pessimistic thinking about various life challenges. Based on the questionnaire responses, they identified a group of "academic pessimists" and a group of "academic optimists;" in other words, they identified people who used pessimistic versus optimistic strategies when confronting the task of getting good grades at college. They then assessed additional patterns of thinking on which optimists and pessimists might differ. These included expectations about one's GPA as well as "self-discrepancies," that is, thoughts that there is a negative discrepancy between one's actual self and one's ideal self-image in the domain of academics (Higgins, 1987; see Chapter 13). Finally, students' GPA at the end of the year was recorded.

Findings indicated that academic optimists and defensive pessimists did equally well at school. The groups did not differ in their overall GPA. However, they did differ in another way. They appeared to travel along different psychological paths to academic success (Cantor et al., 1987). This is revealed by analyses in which personality predictors of GPA were computed separately for the two groups (Figure 14.1). Academic optimists, those people who expected to do particularly well and who experienced relatively few self-discrepancies at the beginning of the academic year, were found to earn higher grades by the end of the year. Among optimists, then, positive thinking predicted academic success. However, the findings for the defensive pessimists were very different. In this group, expectations about academic performance at the beginning of the year were unrelated to end-of-year grades. If the defensive pessimist said "I'm going

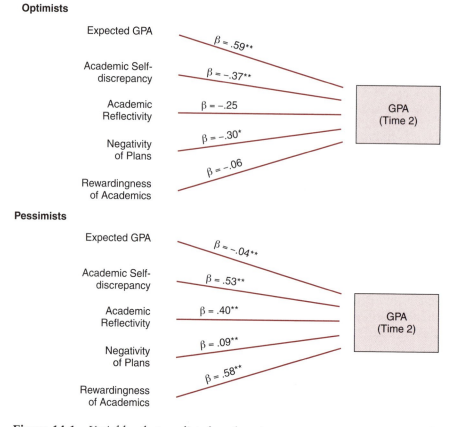

Figure 14.1 *Variables that predicted grade point average among two groups of people: academic optimists and academic defensive pessimists. The same personality variables predict performance differently for the two groups. From Cantor et al. (1987).*

to get a low GPA," this did *not* predict low levels of subsequent performance. Furthermore, among defensive pessimists, large actual-ideal self-discrepancies predicted *higher*, not lower, academic attainment. The defensive pessimists' negative thinking thus appeared to motivate toward higher achievement.

Another aspect of this research further highlights the importance of studying personality in context. Optimism versus pessimism did not turn out to be a generalized strategy that was evident in all aspects of a given student's life. Even if a student was a pessimist with regard to getting good grades, he or she may have been an optimist with regard to a different life context. Cantor and colleagues (1987) studied academic optimists' and pessimists' cognitions in two contexts: grade attainment and making new friends. In the domain of grade attainment, the groups differed enormously on cognitive factors such as their perceptions of the difficulty, controllability, and stress associated with academics. But when contemplating the challenge of making friends, they did not differ at all! When asked about the difficulty, controllability, and stress associated with the challenge of establishing new friendships at college, academic optimists and pessimists did not differ.

In summary, research on the personality strategies of optimism and defensive pessimism indicates that different people adopt distinctly different approaches for coping with life challenges. These different strategies foster qualitatively distinct patterns of experience as people cope with stressors. These cognitively-based individual differences can only be understood by considering both persons and the social contexts within which they employ optimistic versus pessimistic strategies for coping with life's challenges.

KNOWLEDGE, APPRAISAL, AND CROSS-SITUATIONAL COHERENCE

Our analysis of personality-in-context has so far highlighted ways in which people may respond *differently* to one versus another social setting. Yet there is a flip side to this coin. Sometimes people may respond in a *similar* manner to situations that superficially appear very different. Part of the story of personality-in-context is that people's responses in seemingly different contexts may go together in a meaningful way, or cohere. We have considered this issue of cross-situational coherence and consistency a number of times already, particularly in relation to trait theories of personality. We now return to it one last time, but from a somewhat different angle, namely, by considering cognitive processes that may be responsible for cross-situational coherence.

Consider the following situations: telling a joke at a party, jogging with friends, taking an exam for this class, and talking with people about political issues during lunch. The situations seem quite different. Yet now, as a hypothetical example, consider someone who seems himself or herself as being very competitive. To this person, the different situations may be meaningfully related. The person may view them as similar because they each involve competition with someone else: competition to tell the best joke, run the fastest, get the best grade, or make the best arguments in discussion. Once the person groups together the situations in this way, he or she may respond to the different settings with similar types of behavior.

A more formal way of analyzing this example involves a theoretical distinction between two aspects of cognition: knowledge and appraisal (Cervone, 2004; Lazarus, 1991). Knowledge refers to stored information that we carry around with us: information about our personal characteristics, our goals, other people's personal characteristics, their goals, objects in the world, types of social situations, and so on. The term *appraisal*, in contrast, refers to evaluations of the relationship between ourselves and some particular social encounter. These evaluations concern personal meaning: whether and how the encounter is relevant to our personal goals, whether and how it is consistent with our standards for good behavior, and whether and how we can cope with the situation.

Now let us return to the example above, with this knowledge/appraisal distinction in mind. Our competitive person presumably carries around with him knowledge about competitiveness. This knowledge might, for example, include enduring goals for exceeding other people and self-schemas involving the self as a competitor. When thinking about each of the situations, the person may categorize the situation in terms of this competition-related knowledge. As a result the person would appraise the core mean of each situation as involving competition against others, and respond in a similar style across the different contexts.

This reasoning underlies a recent analysis of what has been termed **personality architecture** (Cervone, 2004). This term refers to the overall design and operating characteristics of those psychological systems that contribute to personality functioning. The proposed model of personality architecture distinguishes between knowledge and appraisal, and thus is termed a **knowledge-and-appraisal personality architecture (KAPA)**. In the KAPA model, any given aspect of knowledge may come to mind in numerous settings, and contribute to cross-situational coherence in appraisals of situations.

Knowledge and appraisal processes have been studied in research in which participants take part in a series of assessment sessions (Cervone, 1997, 1999, 2004; Cervone et al., 2001). In the first two sessions, researchers assess two aspects of knowledge. One is knowledge about the self, or self-schemas; these are assessed primarily by asking people to write descriptions of their personality characteristics, including characteristics that they view as personal strengths and weaknesses. The other aspects of knowledge is beliefs about social situations. Situational beliefs are measured by giving people a list of common situations (similar to the sorts of situations described earlier: tell a joke at party; discuss political issues; etc.) and asking them to judge how relevant each of the situations is to each of their self-schemas.

In the third experimental session, there is a measure of situation-specific appraisals. Each of a large number of situations are described, and participants are asked to appraise their capabilities for executing a particular behavior in the situation—what you already have learned to call self-efficacy appraisals (Bandura, 1997). The situations in sessions 2 and 3 are systematically related. As a result, information from the first two sessions can be used to identify sets of situations—specifically, situations related to self-schemas involving personal strengths and personal weaknesses—in which people are expected to have relatively high and low self-efficacy appraisals. The underlying hypothesis is that when a positive self-schema comes to mind as people think about schema-related situations, the positive self-knowledge will cause people to feel a higher sense of self-efficacy for coping with the circumstance.

Data from one research participant illustrates the results of Sessions 1 and 2 (Figure 14.2). This person's self-schemas included the belief that she is a

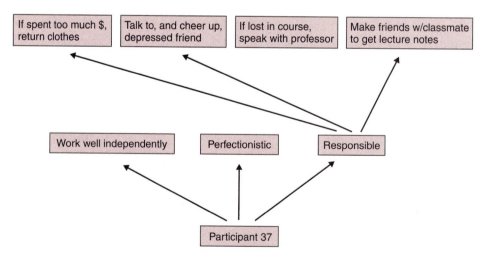

Figure 14.2　Diagram displays three self-schemas of a research participant and situations that the person related to one of these self-schemas, namely, her belief that she is a "Responsible" person. *From Cervone (2004).*

"responsible" person. The situations that she believed to be related to the characteristic of responsibility were interesting in that they were idiosyncratic. Some of them were typical of the traditional definition of the term (e.g., saving money). However, this person judged that a circumstance that might be construed as a negative, calculating act—making friends with someone who "looks smart" so you can get their lecture notes—was an instance of "responsible" action for a college student. In contrast, a potentially prototypic act of responsibility—speaking to a professor if one is lost in a course—was judged as irrelevant to this attribute by Participant 37.

What about the self-efficacy judgments? As Figure 14.3 illustrates, very large differences in self-efficacy appraisal were found across situations that participants believed to be highly related to positive versus negative self-schemas. Thus, schematic self-knowledge indeed appeared to influence self-efficacy appraisals, with positive self-knowledge bringing about consistently high appraisals of self-efficacy. It is also of relevance that, as predicted by the KAPA model, null results were found when participants made the same ratings but with traits for which they were not schematic, that is, for which they did not have a significant degree of self-knowledge.

Note that these results turn the tables on the typical arguments of the "person-situation controversy" (Chapters 8 and 12). Originally, social-cognitive theorists were thought to have expected merely cross-situational variability in action, whereas trait theorists expected consistency. Yet these results (Cervone, 2004) show that social-cognitive processes can cause people to group seemingly different situations together, and thus to respond to the situations in a consistent manner.

More generally, the results highlight something that is critical to understanding personality in context. It concerns how one thinks about context. In the physical sciences, contextual factors can be thought of as having fixed

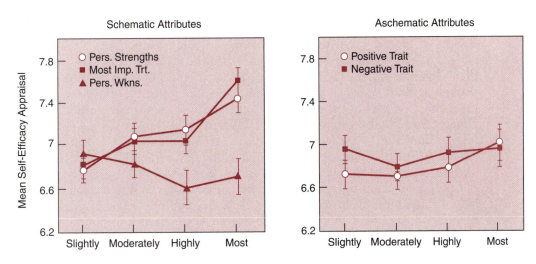

Figure 14.3 Mean self-efficacy appraisals plotted as a function of type of personality attribute *(self-schemas versus non-schematic, or aschematic, attributes)* and situational knowledge *(i.e., participants beliefs about the relevance of the attribute to situations). From Cervone (2004).*

properties. If we heat different substances to 50 degrees centigrade and ask if they melt, the contextual factor of temperature can be seen as being the same from one substance to another. If we drop a series of objects to see how fast they fall, the force of gravity is fixed; it is the same from one object to another. Situational factors can be viewed as distinct from objects that exist in the given situation, and the situational factors can be viewed as having properties that are fixed, or constant, from the vantage point of one versus another object in that environment. In the study of personality, however, things are different. This is because people generally must interpret situations in order to respond to them. They have to figure out what the situation means. Once one recognizes this fact, it is clear that a great many situations do not have a fixed meaning. The critical feature of a social situation—what it means to the people who are in it—may vary from one person to another. To you, telling jokes at a party may be fun. To someone else, it is a competition. To yet another person, it may be an anxiety-provoking test of social skills. This means that personality qualities and situational factors are not separate forces. Instead, they dynamically interact. Personality factors partly determine what a situation means to the individual who is in it.

PERSONALITY DEVELOPMENT IN SOCIOECONOMIC CONTEXT

A fundamental fact of life is that citizens of the world experience widely different socioeconomic conditions. Even within the world's industrialized and relatively rich nations, one finds great disparities in income and associated social opportunities. In many parts of the world, economic gaps between rich and poor have only widened in recent years.

Of what relevance are socioeconomic circumstances to the development of personality? Based on what you have learned about personality psychology so far, you might think that the answer is "little relevance." Historically, personality theorists have devoted relatively little attention to the socioeconomic conditions of the persons about whom they are theorizing. Theorists working in psychoanalytic, behavioral, and trait-theory traditions explicitly have sought to identify general principles of personality functioning that would transcend particular social circumstances (in the same the way that, for example, a biologist might try to identify basic principles of human anatomy and physiology that transcend social circumstances). Recent work, however, suggests that this traditional approach to the study of personality might be inadequate. Specifically, different personality attributes appear to have different implications for the individual in different socioeconomic settings. Important advances on this topic come from the work of Caspi, Elder, and their colleagues (Caspi, 2002; Caspi, Bem, & Elder, 1989).

Consider a seemingly simple question: What are the implications of individual differences in impulsivity for social development? For example, if we identify adolescents who differ in the degree to which they are impulsive, will we find that more impulsive individuals experience more problems of social development, such as delinquency? One possibility is that adolescents who are less able to control their emotional impulses (i.e., "high impulsivity" adolescents) inevitably will experience more social difficulties in their teenage years; this might occur because the avoidance of such problems (e.g., drug and alcohol use, physical aggression, vandalism) requires that one control one's

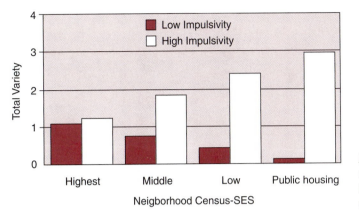

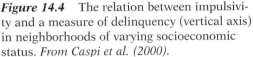

Figure 14.4 The relation between impulsivity and a measure of delinquency (vertical axis) in neighborhoods of varying socioeconomic status. *From Caspi et al. (2000).*

impulses. However, another possibility is that the effects of impulsivity are not inevitable. Instead, the implications of high versus low impulsivity perhaps can only be understood by examining personality in its socioeconomic context. In poor neighborhoods, adolescents may experience a relatively large number of circumstances that have the potential to trigger antisocial acts while, at the same time, benefiting from relatively few community structures that might help them to develop self-control skills. In contrast, in affluent neighborhoods, there are fewer opportunities for delinquency and there are more social supports.

Findings indicate that these differences between affluent and poor neighborhoods are highly consequential. The relation between impulsivity and delinquency is found to vary in the different socioeconomic contexts. Lynam and colleagues (2000) studied a large sample of 13-year-olds in Pittsburgh, Pennsylvania. These individuals lived in widely varying socioeconomic circumstances that ranged from neighborhoods high in socioeconomic status (SES) to neighborhoods that were poverty-stricken, including ones in which people lived in public housing that featured many factors that might foster delinquency. Using various laboratory measures that were administered when research participants were 13 years of age, the researchers determined whether each participant was high or low in impulsivity. With measures of both impulsivity and socioeconomic circumstances, Lynam and colleagues could determine whether the personality factor had different implications in different circumstances. It did. Among adolescents living in poor neighborhoods, high-impulsive individuals were more likely than low-impulsive individuals to become involved in delinquent behaviors (Figure 14.4). In contrast, in the affluent neighborhoods, adolescents who were either high or low in impulsivity did not differ in delinquency. Community resources in affluent neighborhoods appeared to buffer the potentially negative effects of the personality characteristic.

CAUSES AND EFFECTS OF PERSONALITY ATTRIBUTES

Other work has examined an issue that is particularly important, yet also particularly difficult to "untangle." It commonly is found that people living in lower-class neighborhoods experience higher levels of psychological distress

Some personality characteristics have a particularly large impact on life outcomes among people who live in lower socioeconomic conditions.

(e.g., anxiety, depression). If, at this point in your education in personality, you are "thinking like a psychologist," you will immediately recognize that such a finding is ambiguous: It is not clear whether people's personality characteristics cause them to end up in lower-class neighborhoods or if, conversely, living in lower-class neighborhoods causes psychological distress.

Caspi (2002) and colleagues have been able to study this issue by working with a very large sample of persons who are studied at multiple points in time. This research setting enables the personality scientist to use statistical methods that can disentangle the different potential causal influences. Specifically, Caspi and colleagues have worked with data from the Dunedin study, which is a project that has carefully followed the lives of 1000 individuals living in Dunedin, New Zealand, over a 30-year period. This project has yielded evidence that is of great interest not only to applied concerns regarding psychological distress, but to core issues in personality theory. A key finding is that questions about cause-and-effect relationships (i.e., is personality a causal influence on social class, or vice versa?) *vary* from one personality characteristic to another. For example, anxiety and social circumstances were closely related. Children who grew up in low-SES families became relatively more anxious adolescents. Furthermore, adolescents who received relatively less education became more anxious adults. Life conditions, then, causally influenced levels of anxiety, but anxiety did not causally appear to influence social class outcomes. In contrast, analyses of antisocial disorders yielded a different result. Engaging in antisocial conduct did have an effect on social class. People who engaged in antisocial behavior experienced more academic failure that, in turn, contributed to lower-class economic outcomes. Finally, analyses of depression yielded even more different results; social class variables was not a cause of depression, and depression did not influence social class (Caspi, 2002).

A key implication of these findings for personality theory is that one can learn about the relations among personality and social context only by studying relatively *specific* personality characteristics. Suppose that, instead of studying relatively specific variables (anxiety, depression, antisocial conduct), the researchers instead had studied a global trait variable such as neuroticism or negative affectivity (i.e., a generalized tendency to experience negative emotions). You will recall from Chapters 7 and 8 that measures of these generalized trait constructs combine a variety of specific emotional qualities into a global trait score; for example, in five-factor theory (Chapter 8), measures of anger, depression, and anxiety are combined into a single neuroticism score (Costa & McCrae, 1992). As Caspi and colleagues (2002) emphasize, this sort of global personality construct has a big drawback. It can obscure the actual relations between specific personality qualities and social context. Results from the Caspi group research suggest that this can occur because the global measures jumble together personality attributes that have different causes and effects.

PERSONALITY, GENDER, AND HISTORICAL CONTEXT

Caspi, Bern, and Elder (1989) provide related research on the interplay between personality and socioeconomic conditions. These investigators analyzed data describing the lives of American research participants who grew up during the Great Depression. In the late 1940s these people reached the age at which one might enter the workforce.

A personality characteristic of particular interest in this group was ill-temperedness, which is the tendency to display uncontrolled bouts of anger, including temper tantrums, verbal outbursts, and aggression. Ill-temperedness was assessed in childhood using interviews with mothers who described their child's emotional tendencies. The researchers then related high versus low ill-temperedness to later life outcomes.

Findings revealed that high versus low ill-temperedness was significantly related to economic outcomes in adulthood (Caspi et al., 1989). Importantly, results differed for male and female research participants. Male research participants who were ill-tempered as children were found to have lower occupational status at age 40. Amazingly, the effects of the personality variable were as large as the effects of a key socioeconomic variable, namely, the economic class in which people grew up as children. In general, people who grow up in higher-class households tend to end up with higher occupational status in adulthood. In the data analyzed by the Caspi group (1989), this typical result did hold among men who were low in ill-temperedness; in this group, men from higher-class backgrounds had higher-status jobs as adults. However, among men who were high in ill-temperedness, things were different. Ill-tempered men from higher social-class backgrounds essentially lost the advantages of their social class. Their occupational status in adulthood was no higher than that of men from lower-class backgrounds. Additional results indicated why this happened. Ill-tempered men tended to have lower educational achievement and educational achievement, in turn, affected adult occupational status (Caspi et al., 1989).

Note that these results were obtained when examining the lives of men. Among women, ill-temperedness was unrelated to occupational status. If one considers historical circumstances, this result is not surprising. In the United States during the 1940s women had limited job opportunities, so personal qualities that might potentially affect job status under other circumstances would have little effect. However, among women, high versus low ill-temperedness still was consequential. It was related to the occupational status of women's husbands. Women who were *low* in ill-temperedness were more likely to marry men with *higher* occupational status. In other words, women who were *high* in ill-temperedness in childhood "fared less well in the marriage market" (Caspi et al., 1989, p. 388). Note that they fared less well in a particular marriage market, namely, that of mid-20th century America. As Caspi and colleagues emphasize, different results might be obtained in different sociohistorical contexts during which women had greater economic opportunities. The work of Caspi, Elder, and colleagues suggests, then, that the historical period during which one conducts a study can itself function as an important context for understanding personality and its consequences.

PERSONALITY FUNCTIONING ACROSS THE LIFE SPAN

Research in psychology has focused to a very large degree on the young. In the study of personality, the historical tradition established by Freud (Chapter 3) suggested that personality structure was established in the first few years of life. In the study of cognition, much effort has been directed to understanding the growth of cognitive functions in children (e.g., Flavell, 1999). Critics of psychological research commonly have complained that a disproportionately large amount of the field's research involves young adults in college.

In many respects, a focus on childhood, adolescence, and young adulthood is quite reasonable. These are critical periods of personal development. However, this focus does conflict with a basic fact of 21st-century life: The world contains ever-larger percentages of older adults. Thanks to advances in medicine, people are living much longer than in the past. The changes in life span are quite dramatic. Historians remind us that "before the nineteenth century, wherever he lived, man could only count on a short expectation of life, with a few extra years in the case of the rich" (Braudel, 1981, p. 90). The life span was so much shorter centuries ago that it apparently was not an unusual event when a ruler of France in the 14th century took the throne at age 17 and abdicated it at age 42 while holding the reputation of a wise elder statesman (Braudel, 1981). Today, of course, large numbers of people in the industrialized world live into their 70s, 80s, and beyond. This is a circumstance unknown in prior human history.

PSYCHOLOGICAL RESILIENCE IN THE LATER YEARS

The growth of older-adult populations suggests a new research agenda for psychology: the study of personality functioning later in life. In the past decade, psychologists have responded to this agenda. Extensive research programs have examined psychological functioning in the later years of life (e.g., Baltes & Mayer, 1999).

A repeated finding in this area of research is one that is somewhat surprising. Since old age is accompanied by many difficulties and challenges—retirement, physical declines, the death of peers and same-generation family members—one might expect that the psychological experience of older adults would be primarily negative. However, this is not the case. On objective measures of self-esteem, a sense of personal control, and psychological well-being versus depression, researchers commonly find that older adults are *not* worse off than middle-age and younger adults (Baltes & Graf, 1996; Brändtstadter & Wentura, 1995). Rather than being characterized by despondency, in the later years of life individuals commonly report deeply satisfying, rich positive emotional experiences (Carstensen & Charles, 2003).

Older adults, then, exhibit much psychological "resilience." They commonly are able to withstand the difficulties that accompany the later years and to maintain a remarkably strong sense of self and personal well-being. A challenge for the personality scientist, then, is to understand the processes through which many older adults maintain a positive sense of self.

A core insight into this issue comes from the work of the German psychologist Paul Baltes and his associates (Baltes, 1997; Baltes & Baltes, 1990; Baltes & Staudinger, 2000). They recognize that development inherently involves trade-offs. When moving from one stage of life to another, people lose some psychological qualities but gain others. For example, early in life children gain logical reasoning capacities but may lose some capacities for fantasy life. In the later years, older adults may experience a decline in some basic cognitive functions yet may gain in personal wisdom (Baltes & Staudinger, 2000). The gains in knowledge and wisdom that people acquire with age often enable them to compensate for any losses in cognitive capacities.

The analysis by Baltes suggests a general model of psychological development and resilience in the later years of life (Baltes, 1997). In the Baltes model, people can maintain psychological well-being by selecting particular domains of life on which they focus their energies and knowledge. Although it may be difficult for the older adult to maintain a diverse array of life activities—work, clubs, athletic pursuits, hobbies, the development of new social networks, etc.—he or she may be extremely capable of maintaining high levels of functioning and well-being within selected life domains. By focusing their energies on a few important aspects of life, older adults may be able to compensate for physical or cognitive declines and maintain a high sense of well-being.

Evidence of the beneficial impact of wise selection processes comes from a very large-scale study of adults in Berlin (Freund & Baltes, 1998). Participants completed a self-reported questionnaire that assessed the degree to which they engaged in selection processes to optimize their functioning in the face of physical declines in old age. This questionnaire measured people's tendency to select a small number of significant life goals on which to concentrate their energies, as well as their capacity to draw on family and social-network resources to cope with life challenges. Even after controlling for other personality variables, people who more frequently employed these strategies for social living were found to have a higher sense of personal well-being and to experience more positive emotions in their daily life (Freund & Baltes, 1998).

EMOTIONAL LIFE IN OLDER ADULTHOOD: SOCIOEMOTIONAL SELECTIVITY

One illustration of selection processes comes from the research of Laura Carstensen and her colleagues (Carstensen, 1995; 1998; Carstensen, Isaacowitz, & Charles, 1999). Carstensen's **socioemotional selectivity theory** examines the ways in which social motivations shift across the course of life. The basic idea is that people are aware of the opportunities and constraints associated with different points in the life course. For example, a 20-year-old likely recognizes that many decades of family and professional life lay ahead, whereas an 85-year-old recognizes that he or she is likely entering, or already in, the last decade of life. This awareness of time influences one's life goals. For the younger adult, it makes sense to focus on the future, investing energy in long-term goals that involve the acquisition of information and skills that will prove useful in the decades ahead (e.g., skills of the sort acquired in college) or the development of one's self and sense of identity. In contrast, if one sees oneself as being near the end of life, it makes little sense to focus on such long-term goals. Instead, it is more reasonable to select one or two goals that have an immediate positive impact on one's life, and to focus one's energies on them. Thus, socioemotional selectivity theory predicts that goals involving meaningful emotional experiences become relatively more important in older adulthood. The older adult is predicted to be relatively less motivated to gain information about the world and to start new social networks, and relatively more motivated to have positive emotional experiences, which may be achieved by maintaining personally meaningful relationships with family and long-term friends (Figure 14.5). In sum, Carstensen's theory predicts that the older adult will be more likely than the younger adult to invest energy into a small, select set of social relationships that enhance emotional experience.

Research supports this hypothesis. For example, Carstensen and Fredrickson (1998) tested socioemotional selectivity theory in a study involving a large and ethnically diverse sample of adults ranging in age from 18 to 88. Their goal was to test the hypothesis that older adults would focus their attention on the enhancement of current emotional experiences, whereas younger adults would focus on possibilities for the future, such as meeting new people from whom new things about the world could be learned. To test this idea, they gave younger- and older-adult research participants a long list of different types of people (e.g., a long-time close friend, the author of a book you have just read). They asked the participants to make ratings that would reveal the dimensions (i.e., the features that differentiated the individuals in

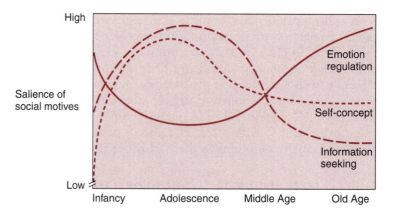

Figure 14.5   Schematic representation of socioemotional selectivity theory's predictions about variations in social motives across the life course. *From Carstensen (1995).*

the list) that were most important to them as they thought about the different people on the list. As predicted, older adults seemed to focus their thoughts on the emotional qualities of the people on the list, and to pay lesser attention to whether a meeting with a given person might provide information that would be valuable in the future. In contrast, younger adults focused less on people's emotional qualities, and more on the possibility of informative meetings with new people—whether or not those meetings involved experiences that were emotionally positive. Older adults, recognizing that they are in the latter years of life, thus seemed to be far more attentive to social experiences that would bring immediate emotional rewards. Interestingly, a subsequent study found similar results among HIV-positive men with symptoms of AIDS; though not elderly, these men faced the possibility of a limited life span and, in a manner similar to older adults, focused heavily on the immediate emotional qualities of social relationships (Carstensen & Fredricksen, 1998).

In earlier sections of this chapter on personality in context, the "contexts" we have examined have primarily been social settings. The work of Baltes, Carstensen, and colleagues indicates that age, and especially the number of years that one feels on has remaining in life, is another critical "context" for personality functioning.

There is no such thing as a human nature independent of culture. Men without culture would not be clever savages…nature's noblemen [or] intrinsically talented apes who had somehow failed to find themselves. They would be unworkable monstrosities with very few useful instincts, fewer recognizable sentiments, and no intellect: mental basket cases. As our central nervous system—and most particularly its crowning curse and glory, the neocortex—grew up in great part in interaction with culture, it is incapable of directing our behavior or organizing our experience without the guidance provided by systems of significant symbols.

Source: Geertz, 1973, p. 49

PERSONS IN CULTURES

TWO STRATEGIES FOR THINKING ABOUT PERSONALITY AND CULTURE

Strategy #1: Personality…and Culture?

There are two strategies for thinking about personality and culture. The first is one that you already have seen a number of times in this text. It is a strategy that begins with a particular theoretical conception or theory-driven hypothesis, and then asks whether the idea happens to apply across cultures. Since so much of 20th-century psychological science was a product of the Western world (the United States and Europe), in practice this strategy is one in which (1) a personality scientist starts with an idea about human nature that is based in Western culture and that reflects research findings or clinical experiences involving U.S. or European citizens, and then (2) asks whether this conception of personality receives support when research is conducted in non-Western cultures. You saw this strategy back in Chapter 6, when learning about the phenomenological theory of personality and self developed by the American psychologist Carl Rogers. After reviewing his theory, we summarized contemporary research on the question of whether Rogerian self-processes occur in Asian cultures. You saw this strategy again in Chapter 8, where we asked whether the Big Five model of personality traits (another product of Western personality psychology) replicates cross-culturally.

In this strategy for thinking about personality and culture, questions of culture and personality boil down to what the research psychologist calls questions of "generalizability." The issue is whether a given psychological finding holds, or generalizes, from one setting to another. Just as one can ask whether a given research result generalizes across genders, socioeconomic circumstances, or age groups, one can ask whether it generalizes across cultures.

It is important to determine whether research findings generalize across cultures. This first strategy, then, is a good one. But it is not good enough. It has two significant limitations. First, it may fail to identify aspects of personality that are important in other cultures but not in one's own. If researchers simply import a Western conception of personality into a non-Western culture, they may completely overlook aspects of personhood that are key features in the non-Western culture but are relatively unimportant in their own. As an example, consider the efforts of researchers studying the Big Five model of personality (Chapter 8) to characterize the basic units of language that individuals use to describe themselves and other persons. When researchers import the five-factor structure to non-Western cultures, they indeed do obtain evidence that these personality dimensions are recognized by members of these cultures as significant ways that individuals differ (McCrae & Costa, 1997); it should be noted, however, that significant culture variations in the language of individual differences are also found (Saucier & Goldberg, 2001). Yet this research still could be overlooking important aspects of other cultures' language of human nature. For example, consider Buddhist cultures. In this cultural context, a primary term for thinking about persons and their actions is *karma*, which refers to the positive and negative effects of actions on one's stream of consciousness, where that consciousness can extend from one physical lifetime to another through reincarnation (Chodron, 1990). This conception of karma is not prevalent in the Western cultures in which the Big Five were first studied. Questionnaires designed to measure the five personality dimensions thus do not contain many (if any) items that are directly relevant to the conception of karma. As a result, if these Western-world, English-language questionnaires are imported into to a Buddhist culture, researchers probably would fail to "find karma." The notion of karma will be overlooked, despite the fact that it is important to the non-Western culture, because it is not a component of the Western-world research instrument.

There is a second limitation to the strategy of asking merely whether a given research finding generalizes from one cultural context to another. It is that, implicitly, it treats culture as peripheral to the study of human nature. It implies that the personality theorist first can develop a culture-free model of core aspects of personality and individual differences, and then—as a kind of afterthought—can ask whether the model has to be "tweaked" here or there to account for cultural variation. Such an approach treats issues of culture as an optional supplement to personality psychology's core concern with basic human nature.

The quote that opened this section of our chapter, from the anthropologist Clifford Geertz, suggests that this way of thinking is backwards. To Geertz's thinking, there is no culture-free personality in the first place. Instead, psychological functioning is inherently cultural. People think about the world using languages and related communication systems that they acquire from their culture and that are themselves the products of generations of cultural experience. The things that people think about—other people, social settings, future possibilities, themselves—take on personal significance within meaning systems that are based on cultural and social practices, where those practices might vary from one cultural context to another.

Strategy #2: Culture and Personality

This way of thinking suggests a different strategy for conceptualizing personality and culture. In this alternative approach, culture is not on the periphery of personality psychology. It is at the core. Persons are seen as acquiring their sense of personhood through interactions with their culture.

This way of thinking about personality-culture relations has important implications for how one thinks not only about personality, but culture as well. Cultures consist of those very same persons who acquired their sense of personhood from that culture. Culture and personality, in other words, "make each other up" (Shweder & Sullivan, 1990, p. 399). "The practices and meanings of culture, and the psychological processes and structures of each member of the culture, are *mutually constitutive*" (Kitayama & Markus, 1999, p. 250).

In this view, then, there is no culture-free personality on the one hand and person-free culture on the other. Instead, there are persons who function psychologically by using cultural tools, including language and related meaning systems. And there are cultures whose practices are maintained by those very same people who inhibit them. For more than a decade, this way of thinking has been advanced within a field known as cultural psychology (Shweder & Sullivan, 1993). Cultural psychology is concerned with whether research findings generalize from one culture to another (the main question of what we have called Strategy #1). Yet it asks deeper questions about human nature, with a particular focus on the human capacity to use conscious reflection to make sense of the world of experience (Shweder & Sullivan, 1990).

The argument that one should view human experience through a cultural lens is made compelling by examples in which people of a given culture seem to lead lives that differ deeply from one's own. Consider, first, your own experiences and actions in a setting in which you meet a new acquaintance, for example at a party. If you are a member of the Western world, you are likely to introduce yourself by stating your name, and if the conversation continues and the two of you want to get to know each other better, you are likely to talk about your own interests, hobbies, personal background, or goals in life. If, the next day, you describe your new acquaintance to an old friend, you are likely to use personality trait terms that describe personal qualities that differentiate the individual from others (you might see your new acquaintance as "somewhat extraverted," "very open-minded", etc.). This probably strikes you as obvious. Isn't it always like this? Don't people present themselves and talk about each other in this manner no matter where in the world you go? Apparently not. Detailed analyses of personhood within traditional culture on the island of Bali (Geertz, 1973) indicate that our own ways of being a person are not universal.

In Bali, the label that people use to describe themselves is not a unique, personal name. Personal names are treated as very private; they are "treated as

Social practices in Bali suggest that Balinese culture emphasizes the relations among a person and the generations of his or her family, rather than highlighting the distinctive, unique features of the isolated individual, as is more common in Western cultures.

though they are military secrets" (Geertz, 1973, p. 375). Instead, people are differentiated using labels that make reference to the individual's place within family and community systems. Terms for referring to people make reference to family members (a person is "Mother-of-_____"), social status (which strongly defines how the person should be treated), or social roles (e.g., village chief). This system reflects a broader cultural conception in which persons are not primarily thought of as unique, idiosyncratic individuals, but as elements of a larger, eternal social order. Their cultural practices "[mute] the more idiosyncratic, merely biographical, and, consequently, transient aspects of . . . existence as a human being (what, in our more egoistic framework, we call "personality") in favor of some rather more typical, highly conventionalized, and, consequently, enduring ones" (Geertz, 1973, p. 370).

PERSONALITY AND SELF AS SOCIALLY CONSTRUCTED WITHIN CULTURE

The implications of cultural psychology for the study of personality are vividly illustrated by research on conceptions of self in American and Japanese culture conducted by Shinobu Kitayama and Hazel Markus (Kitayama & Markus, 1999; Cross & Markus, 1999). A central idea in this work is that there may be variations from culture to culture in people's implicit conceptions of self (Markus & Kitayama, 1991; Triandis, 1995). People's beliefs about what it is to be a "self" or a person may not be the same throughout the world. Different cultures may feature different beliefs about the rights, duties, possibilities, and most central features associated with personhood. Note that such beliefs are not necessarily explicit; in other words, it might be that many members of a culture do not explicitly put into words these culturally shared beliefs about the nature of personality. Yet, even if they do not stop to think about it explicitly, everyone does have conceptions about the most basic aspects of personality. It is these conceptions that appear to differ across cultures.

Independent and Interdependent Views of Self

Specifically, differences are found when contrasting European-American and East Asian cultures. In European-American cultures, the self is primarily construed as being **independent**. In an independent view, the individual is viewed as possessing a set of psychological qualities (personality traits, goals, etc.) that are distinct from, or independent of, those of other people. Individuals also are construed in terms of independent rights, such as the right to pursue personal happiness. In an independent view of self, then, a person is an entity that can be characterized as a kind of "container" within which are stored a collection of psychological traits that are the cause of the person's actions.

This perspective contrasts with a view of self found in East Asian cultures (Markus & Kitayama, 1991; Triandis, 1995). Here one finds an **interdependent** conception of self. In an interdependent view, people are construed in terms of their roles with family and social relationships. The cultural system emphasizes the responsibilities that are inherent in one's position within these relationships, rather than highlighting the individual person's self-centered pursuit of happiness. In interdependent cultures, behavior is not explained in terms of autonomous mental traits that reside in the person's head. Instead, people explain behavior in terms of networks of social obligations. It is the person's location within such social systems that are seen as the causes of

Research suggests that individuals in Asian cultures are more likely than are persons in Western cultures to possess interdependent views of self that highlight the interrelations among members of a community, as well as individuals' obligations to family and society.

behavior. For example, a person's chronic expression of "conscientious" behavior might be explained in terms of social obligations that compel the person to act conscientiously, rather than by saying that the person possesses a trait of conscientiousness.

How might these different conceptions of self have developed historically? How are they maintained in the contemporary world? Kitayama and Markus (1999) address these questions through a "collective-constructionist theory" of the self (Figure 14.6). This theory addresses three interlocking factors: broad philosophical traditions that arise in a given culture and that provide a framework within which social groups and individuals functions; social practices that are characteristic of a given culture and that take on meaning within that cultural system; and psychological processes and structures of the individual person, which develop through interaction with those social practices. Note that the paths of influence in this theory (Figure 14.6) run in two directions. Just as personality develops through social practices that occur within a cultural context, culture itself is maintained by social practices that are enacted by persons.

In this theory, the existence of independent versus interdependent conceptions of self is understood in terms of broad historical trends that have characterized European-American versus East Asian cultures. Drawing on the work of the social theorist Max Weber, Kitayama and Markus note that the history of the West (Figure 14.6, middle panel) includes a Protestant ethic in which individuals pursue a "calling," with industrious pursuit of this calling being a course of action that is thought to increase the glory of God. This belief system fosters a capitalistic set of social practices in which individuals work industriously to maximize their personal gain. Once these practices are in place, they become self-maintaining; in other words, social practices involving the industrious pursuit of wealth continue even when they no longer have any connection to their religious origins. Finally, individual people develop through engagement with these social practices. When social practices concern the maximization of personal gain, individuals tend to set goals for personal achievement, to think of life's possibilities in terms of costs and benefits, and to be concerned with personal qualities such as individual conscientiousness, which relates to personal achievement.

In contrast, in the East, social practices have their origin in a different ethos. Confusionism, Taoism, and Zen Buddhism provide a philosophical

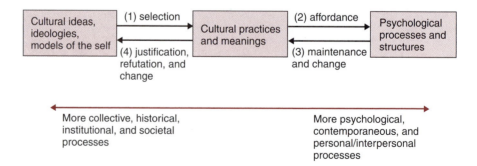

Figure 14.6   Representation of the "collective-constructionist theory" of the self. *From Kitayama & Markus (1999).*

backdrop that differs markedly from the Protestant ethic (Kitayama & Markus, 1999). Within Japanese culture, these philosophical systems function to highlight hierarchies in the social order, the interconnectedness of individuals within and across those hierarchies, and feelings of compassion toward others (Figure 14.6, bottom panel). This cultural context fosters two types of social practices. In formal or official social settings (or the "official frame"), strict social hierarchies dictate rules of acceptable behavior. In informal, personal settings (or the "personal frame"), empathic emotions such as sympathy and compassion figure centrally in social relations. The individual who develops within this two-part system of social practices develops two aspects of self-concept. One, which comes into play in the official frame, centers on a motive for self-improvement and feelings of self-criticism when one's actions do not contribute sufficiently to the welfare of society. The other, which is pertinent to the personal frame, centers on feelings of empathy toward others.

The notion that Eastern and Western cultures feature interdependent and independent senses of self is consistent with a range of empirical findings. As we reviewed in Chapter 6, psychological processes involving self-esteem differ from one cultural to another. East Asians are less likely to make efforts to maintain a high sense of personal esteem (Heine et al., 1999). Instead, self-criticism functions as a salient motive (Kitayama et al., 1997). Unlike findings in the Western world, in East Asia people are not more intrinsically motivated to engage in tasks when they choose them personally; instead, they experience greater intrinsic motivation when choices are made by authority figures or trusted peers (Iyengar & Lepper, 1999). Consistent with the notion that Western conceptions of the self draw attention to internal personal qualities that function as causes of behavior, Americans are found to over-attribute the causes of action to personal rather than situational factors (Ross, 1977). People in Japan, India, and China are less likely to exhibit this attributional bias (Kitayama & Masuda, 1997; Miller, 1984; Morris & Peng, 1994). Studies of subjective well-being also reveal interesting cross-cultural variations. When predicting people's ratings of satisfaction with their life, the pleasantness of everyday emotional experiences is a stronger predictor in Western than in Eastern cultures (Suh, Diener, Oishi, & Triandis, 1998). Each of these findings, then, is consistent with the contention that people in Eastern versus Western cultures have different, interdependent versus independent, construals of self.

The interplay of culture and personality also is revealed in studies of people who move from one cultural context to another. For example, consider what happens when people move from an Eastern culture to the West. Western social practices, more than Eastern ones, emphasize the asserting of one's personal attributes. Becoming engaged in these new social practices should cause people to become more extraverted, as they learn to fit in with their new culture. There is evidence that this does indeed occur. McCrae, Yik, Trapnell, Bond, & Paulhus (1998) studied Chinese students enrolled in a Canadian university. Some of these students had been in North America for many years, whereas others had immigrated only a few years before the study was conducted. People who had longer exposure to Canadian culture tended to have higher extraversion scores (McCrae et al., 1998).

The role of cognitive processes in these cultural differences is further revealed by studies of bicultural individuals. These are persons who have lived long enough in each of two different cultures that they have internalized the belief systems of both (Hong, Morris, Chiu, & Martinez, 2000). Such people are capable of "frame switching"; they can change the culturally grounded framework through which they interpret any given event. Interestingly, stimuli that cognitively prime one versus another cultural frame can thereby influence the bicultural individual's subsequent thinking processes. Cultural frameworks have been primed by exposing people to symbols representative of Chinese versus American culture (e.g., an American flag, a picture of a Chinese dragon). Compared to when they view Chinese symbols, bicultural individuals are more likely to attribute the causes of actions to internal causes after viewing symbols of American culture (Hong et al., 2000). Such findings suggest that cultural variations in cognition can be understood within the general theoretical framework provided by social-cognitive analyses (Chapters 12 and 13).

In sum, the study of culture and personality has advanced rapidly in recent years, and these advances have proven to have profound implications for the science of personality. The existence of substantial differences in the nature of personhood that are found when Eastern and Western cultures are compared has substantial ramifications for anyone who wishes to construct a universally applicable scientific theory of human nature.

PERSONALITY PROCESSES AND SOCIAL CHANGE

With the end of our coverage of personality theories on the horizon, we, the authors of this text, hope that you have become intellectually engaged with the field's theoretical issues. Twenty-first century personality psychologists address theoretical puzzles about human nature that have intrigued humankind since at least fourth-century B.C. Athens. The ability to think deeply and systematically about these issues is perhaps the most basic intellectual skill that you should have acquired in your course on personality. Even after you have forgotten the names of all the factors of the Big Five trait model or the results of some experiment testing Freud's ideas about the unconscious, you should retain the ability to ask critical questions about theoretical conceptions of human nature put forth by social scientists, philosophers, and public intellectuals.

Yet many readers may also have a practical bent. "Sure, I can evaluate these theories," you may be thinking to yourself, "but I have a different question: What can one *do* with these theories? Is there anything practical that can be achieved?"

If you are in fact asking this, then to you we would say "Congratulations!" This question is appropriate and enormously important. One of the most important ways of evaluating a theory or set of theories is not by scrutinizing their theoretical elegance, but by asking what practical goals they can achieve. This practical criterion becomes particularly important in light of contemporary critiques of the nature of theorizing. The personality theorist hopes to discover truths about human nature. Yet he or she inherently is engaged in a task in which the discovery of eternal truths may be so unlikely that "truth-seeking" is not even the best way to characterize the activity of theory construction. Scholars recognize that theorists in any scientific field work with a set of constraints (Gergen, 2001). They employ whatever knowledge, languages, and ways of thinking happen to be available to them at the particular historical time and social place in which they live. These cognitive systems are the theorists' tools. It is very unlikely that, at any particular point in history, these tools will be perfect, enabling the theorist to construct a scientific model that perfectly mirrors reality. All theories, then, will be limited by the intellectual tools available at the time that the theory is constructed. At best, then, one can hope that a scientific theory will provide a good model of some aspects of the world, while recognizing that it may provide a poor model of other aspects and may fail even to address some issues of importance (Giere, 1999).

If the entire odyssey of theory constructing is limited in this manner, then that is all the more reason for asking a practical, here-and-now question: "Sure, these theories may not be perfect, yet is there anything practical that one can do with them?"

We have, of course, addressed this question at numerous points earlier in the text. We generally have done so by reviewing clinical applications. As you have seen, there is no shortage of cases in which theoretical insights have been translated into clinical applications of practical significance.

Yet you may rightly ask whether there is anything more that the personality psychologist can do. The citizens of the world face incredible challenges: a large percentage of the world continues to live in poverty (3 billion people live on $2 or less a day), much of the world receives little formal education (e.g., in 35 African and South Asian nations, half of current teenagers from poor households never completed even the first grade), and the spread of HIV/AIDS is a medical catastrophe of incredible proportions (the disease strikes 14,000 new persons a *day*, with more than 60 million cases of HIV worldwide) (All figures from United Nations Population Fund, 2002.) Admittedly, many of the causes of these problems involve socioeconomic and political factors that are beyond the reach of the personality psychologist. Yet other problems have significant behavioral components. HIV/AIDS rates, for example, can be lowered through avoidance of high-risk behaviors. Behavioral change similarly can influence the risk of medical maladies such as cancer and heart disease.

A challenge for personality theorists, then, is to show how their theorizing might contribute to society-wide changes in behavior that are of widespread benefit. How could this be done? In an ideal world, one might first identify a theory that could be applied to issues of social change. One then would design an intervention that is based on the principles of this theory. Next (the hard part) one would have to figure out a way for *large* numbers of people—tens or hundreds of thousands of people in a community, geographic region, or nation—to be exposed to the intervention. Finally, a systematic statistical analysis of the behavior of the population in the study would have to be conducted to see if the intervention beneficially changed the behavior of the population. In short, one would have to run a giant theory-based psychology experiment. Sound like science fiction? It's not. It's science. Such experiments already have been conducted, and with great success.

MEDIA MODELING OF PROSOCIAL BEHAVIOR

Numerous investigators, working in different parts of the world, have drawn upon the principle of Bandura's social-cognitive theory when designing interventions for social change (Smith, October 2002). As you learned earlier (Chapter 12), social-cognitive theory highlights the influence of psychological models on people's thoughts and actions. By observing other people, we acquire skills, learn about features of the social world, and develop attitudes and expectations about the benefits of alternative courses of action. As you also learned (Chapter 13), psychologists already have devised modeling-based interventions to change behavior; these interventions generally have been applied in the treatment of individual clients or in studies with small groups of people.

The problem, then, is to figure out a way to bring well-established interventions based on social-cognitive theory to large populations of persons. The solution: TV. The same medium that brings us professional wrestling and infomercials can also deliver entertainment that fosters beneficial society-wide change.

Literacy

As summarized by Bandura (2002; also see Smith, October 2002), the first individual who recognized this potential and implemented it for social good was the Mexican television executive Miguel Sabido. Sabido's goal was to increase adult literacy in his nation. Although the Mexican government had designed adult literacy programs and established centers at which citizens could obtain literacy booklets, these efforts initially proved insufficient. The educational program itself was fine; the problem was that insufficient numbers of people were taking advantage of the program. What was needed was an intervention that would motivate individuals to go to the literacy center, acquire the educational materials, and invest the considerable effort that is required to develop literacy in adulthood. Obstacles in the way of this goal included people being unaware of exactly how to obtain the educational materials, lacking a sense of self-efficacy for becoming literate, and in some cases not feeling worthy of having an educated government official devote time to their own educational development (Bandura, 2002).

Sabido's tool for overcoming these obstacles was a televised soap opera. A year-long televised drama depicted the lives of characters who were participating in a literacy study group. Using social-cognitive theory principles regarding the effects of different types of psychological models (Bandura, 1986), Sabido made the program's message relevant to the widest possible audience by including in the show characters who represented persons of varying social status, age, and language skills. To provide concrete information about the government's literacy program, the show's characters were shown picking up actual literacy materials in actual distribution centers in Mexico City. As the weeks and months of programming unfolded, then, characters modeled the possibility of attaining literacy, the motivation and effort required to do so, and the benefits that literacy brings. Such modeling has the potential of shifting social norms, making it seem more appropriate and socially acceptable to embark on literacy education later in life.

Sabido's intervention proved to be a huge success. The show had millions of viewers, and they responded to the program's message. Although fewer than 100,000 people had enrolled in the Mexican government's literacy program in the year prior to the programming, after Sabido's program was viewed more than 800,000 people enrolled during a one-year period (Bandura, 1986, 2002). Sabido, then, had done it: He created an intervention based on the social cognitive theory of personality, applied that intervention to a huge audience, and produce a widespread, beneficial social change.

HIV/AIDS Prevention

In addition to using modeling to bring about social change among formerly non-literate citizens of Mexico, Sabido proved himself to be a role model to other psychological researchers. In the years since Sabido initiated education-entertainment broadcasting based on principles of social-cognitive theory, many others have followed in his footsteps. A particularly critical application has aimed to reduce the prevalence HIV/AIDS in the East African nation of Tanzania (Vaughn, Rogers, Singhal, & Swalehe, 2000; Mohammed, 2001).

For more than five years, from 1993 to 1999, citizens of Tanazia were able to hear a radio soap opera entitled *Twende na Wakati (Let's Go with the Times)*. In some ways, this was a typical entertainment series, with multiple characters whose lives unfolded gradually over the course of the drama. Yet the program had another element. It was designed by the Tanzanian government, working in collaboration with a non-profit organization called Population Communications International (PCI), to provide not only entertainment but education about HIV/AIDS risk behaviors.

Such education was particularly critical in this nation. Before the program began, the nation's citizens were relatively uninformed about the actual causes of HIV infection. The majority did not know how to prevent HIV. Many people suffered from misinformation as a result of rumors such as that the young could not contract the disease, that condoms were ineffective, and that it was possible by casual observation to determine whether a potential sexual partner had the virus (Vaughn et al., 2000). The society also suffers from a gender imbalance, with women being less likely to receive HIV/AIDS counseling and testing than men (United Nations Population Fund, 2002). The context for all these concerns is that Tanzania also suffers from one of the world's highest rates of HIV infection, with the vast majority of infections being caused by unprotected sexual intercourse (Vaughn et al., 2000).

Since radio is a particularly important source of information in Tanzania, investigators chose to use an education-entertainment radio broadcast in an attempt to foster behaviors in the population that would reduce the prevalence of HIV/AIDS. To this end *Twende na Wakati* featured characters who modeled the full range of positive and negative possibilities regarding HIV/AIDS, so that listeners would be aware not only of the benefits of taking HIV-preventive steps but the costs of not taking them. Negative models (e.g., a promiscuous truck driver who failed to use condoms and acquired HIV) exemplified the consequences of high-risk behavior. Positive models provided medically accurate information and counseling to other characters. Perhaps most important, the show featured "transitional" models. These were characters who, at first, were not engaging in safe-sex behaviors but who gradually adopted those behaviors as a result of the interventions of other characters. Social-cognitive theory and research (Bandura, 1986, 1997) indicate that such transitional models are particularly important in building a high sense of self-efficacy, since listeners can first identify with the character and his or her struggles and then, after this sense of identification, can observe the person succeeding.

The Tanzanian government took the remarkably valuable step not only of broadcasting this series, but of conducting an experiment to determine precisely whether the broadcast had its intended effect on the adoption of safe-sex practices. From 1993 to 1995, the program was broadcast in some regions

Photos depict researchers and radio actors who, working with the organization Population Communications International, are developing and recording radio dramas that are designed to foster beneficial social change.

of the country but not others; it subsequently was broadcast nationwide. The different regions could then be compared to gauge the effectiveness of the program. This was done through interview/surveys that asked people about their practice of specific behaviors that present HIV infection (Vaughn et al., 2000).

The broadcasting of *Twende na Wakati* proved to have a number of beneficial effects. Based on listener self-reports in a survey that was conducted, people engaged in more interpersonal communication about HIV risks as a result of listening to the program (Vaughn et al., 2000); analyses indicate that these communications are quite important, with part of the overall effect of the program being due to its influence of people's tendency to discuss more openly the problem of HIV/AIDS prevention (Mohammed, 2001). The program also affected attitudes and beliefs about HIV/AIDS. A valuable indication of this examined the percentage of people who reported having one or more HIV/AIDS risk factors (e.g., multiple sexual partners, unprotected sex) yet who felt that they personally were not at risk for getting the infection. During the 1993–1995 period, the percentage of such people in the region in which *Twende na Wakati* was broadcast fell from 21% to 10%; in contrast, in the region in which the show was not broadcast, the percentage of people who believed they were not at risk increased during the same period (Vaughn et al., 2000). Thus, the radio broadcast significantly influenced this critical HIV-related belief. Most importantly, the modeling of safe-sex practices on the radio show significantly affected people's actual sexual practices. In the broadcast region, both men and women reported declines in their number of sexual partners during the years 1993 to 1995. (People in the region in which the show initially was not broadcast showed such declines after the show was beamed to their area.) Further, condom use increased in the broadcast regions more rapidly than it did in the regions that were not exposed to the radio soap opera (Vaughn et al., 2000).

In summary, the broadcast had its intended effect. By applying principles of social-cognitive theory to the design of an intervention that can bring about behavioral change, and by devising a way of delivering that intervention to large numbers of persons, the researchers were able to bring about societal-wide changes in HIV/AIDS risk behaviors. To anyone asking whether psychologists actually can do something socially useful with their theories of personality, the work in Tanzania and Mexico provides a resounding "yes."

SUMMARY

In this chapter, you have learned about a series of research programs in contemporary personality psychology. The research topics were diverse. Yet they illustrated a common theme. Each concerned the interaction between persons and the social contexts in which they live. Questions about interpersonal relations, cross-situational coherence in experience and action, personality development in its socioeconomic context, development across the life span, personality and culture, and personality processes and social change were answered by research strategies that attended carefully both to personality and to social context.

At a very general level, this chapter's tour of contemporary research on personality in context conveys a message about the scientific field. It illustrates advances that have been made over the years in the scientific study of personality. A generation ago, many investigators construed persons and situations as two separate, independent forces. Each presumably exerted a separate effect—a person effect and a situation effect—on behavior. As you saw in our coverage of the person-situation controversy, investigators debated the relative size of person and situation effects (Chapter 8), sometimes computing statistical indices of the size of each separate factor (e.g., Funder & Ozer, 1983).

The research reviewed in this chapter shows how much the science of personality has advanced since that earlier era. Current research findings indicate that "person" and "context" are not independent forces. Instead, persons and contexts interact dynamically. They "make each other up" (Shweder & Sullivan, 1990, p. 399). Contexts are comprised primarily of persons, and the meaning of a social situation is constructed by the people who are in it. This may seem like an abstract theoretical point. Yet, as we have seen, recognizing it has practical advantages. It opens the door to a psychology of personality that can shed light on how people try to cope with the everyday challenges of their lives—and that can help them to do so.

MAJOR CONCEPTS

Independent versus interdependent construals of self
Alternative implicit beliefs about self-concept in which the self is viewed either as possessing a set of psychological qualities that are distinct of other people (independent self) or is viewed in terms of roles in family, social, and community relationships (interdependent self).

Defensive pessimism   A coping strategy in which people use negative thinking as a way of coping with stress.

Hot versus cool attentional focus   The focusing of one thought on emotionally arousing (hot) versus less arousing (cool) aspects of a situation or stimulus.

Knowledge-and-appraisal personality architecture (KAPA)   Theoretical analysis of personality architecture that distinguishes two aspects of cognition in personality functioning: enduring knowledge and dynamic appraisals of the meaning of encounters for the self.

Optimism   A coping strategy that features relatively realistic expectations about one's capabilities.

Personality architecture   A term to describe the overall design and operating characteristics of those psychological systems that underlie personality functioning.

Rejection sensitivity   A thinking style is character-ized by anxious expectations of rejection in interper-sonal relationships.

Socioemotional selectivity theory   Theoretical analysis by Carstensen that examines the ways in which social motivations shift across the course of life.

REVIEW

1. Contemporary research shows how personality can be understood by examining interactions between persons and the contexts in which they live. The first example of this general point involved interpersonal relations, which the context of romantic relationships was seen to elicit nega-tive, pessimistic, and ultimately self-defeating thoughts among a group of people with the per-sonality characteristic of rejection sensitivity. Other research showed how people may transfer thoughts and feelings from a past relationship onto a new relationship partner.

2. Research on the coping strategies of optimism and defensive pessimism showed how people may address the same social stressor with very differ-ent—yet sometimes equally effective—strategies that involve optimistic versus pessimistic styles of thinking.

3. Research on knowledge, appraisal, and cross-situ-ational coherence illustrated how a given aspect of knowledge may come into play across seemingly diverse contexts, and thus produce consistent self-appraisals in the different settings

4. Work on personality development in context illus-trated how socioeconomic circumstances can affect personality development. Findings included research showing how a given personality charac-teristic can have different implications for devel-opment in economically affluent versus poor con-texts.

5. Research on personality and culture shows how the meaning of personality and of the self may vary from one culture to another; major differ-ences involve self-construals that are independent versus interdependent.

6. Principles from social-cognitive theory have been applied to bring about large-scale social change. Research applying modeling techniques to enhance literacy and HIV/AIDS prevention were reviewed.

15

AN OVERVIEW OF
PERSONALITY THEORY,
ASSESSMENT, AND RESEARCH

**COMMON GROUND AND
REMAINING CHALLENGES**
    Philosophical View of the Person
    Internal and External Causes of Behavior
    The Unity of Behavior and the Concept of
        the Self
    Varying States of Awareness and the
        Concept of the Unconscious
    Relationships among Cognition, Affect, and
        Overt Behavior
    Influences of the Past, Present, and Future
        on Behavior
**PERSONALITY THEORY AS AN
ANSWER TO THE QUESTIONS OF
WHAT, HOW, AND WHY**
    Personality Structure

Process
Growth and Development
Psychopathology
Change
Biological Foundations and Levels of
    Explanation
Relationships among Theory, Assessment,
    and Research

THE CASE OF JIM
    Comparison of the Assessment Data on
        Different Theories
    Stability and Change Over Time
    Jim's Reflections on the Data

OVERVIEW AND A FINAL SUMMING UP

REVIEW

Chapter Focus

You might think of the many theories presented in this book as pieces in the complicated puzzle we call personality. Let's take a step back and consider how all these pieces might fit together. Ultimately, there may be several different ways of putting the puzzle together. In this final chapter, then, our goal is a deeper understanding of the issues in personality research. Through the process of contrast and comparison, we aim for a greater appreciation of the theories covered in this book. First, we return to some of the issues that divide personality theorists. Second, we provide an overview of the concepts that each theory uses to explain the what, how, and why of human behavior. Finally, we again consider relations among theory, assessment, and research. Throughout, we emphasize the distinctive contributions each theory can make toward a more complete understanding of human personality.

QUESTIONS TO BE ADDRESSED IN THIS CHAPTER

1. How can we understand the existence of the many different theories of personality covered in the text?

2. What can we conclude about the major issues on which the theories covered in the text disagree?

3. How can we make sense of the various pictures of Jim derived from the different theories and their preferred assessment instruments?

What theorists believe people to be influences which determinants and mechanisms of human functioning they explore most thoroughly and which they leave unexamined. The view of human nature embodied by psychological theories is more than just a philosophical issue.

Source: Bandura, 1986, p. 1.

We are nearing the end of our long journey through the land of personality theory and research. We have considered an extraordinarily wide range of theoretical conceptions and a range of research methodologies—case studies, questionnaire studies, laboratory experiments with humans, laboratory experiments with animals, twin studies, cross-cultural studies, brain imaging studies—that seems even wider. Hopefully you have gained an understanding of the interplay between psychological theory and research. Research findings contribute to, and modify, theoretical ideas. Yet, as the quote from Bandura illustrates, personality theory is enduringly important because theoretical conceptions determine the aspects of human nature that become the subject of research.

Having now covered this ground, in this final chapter we take stock of where we have been. We consider some points of "common ground" that personality scientists have reached, and turn particular attention to unresolved questions that remain as challenges for future researchers in the field—including, we hope, some of you, the readers of this text.

The pages of this text commonly have highlighted contrasts between different personality theorists. This was fitting on a number of grounds. The differences between theoretical views sometimes was stark. Scientific activity and genuine progress in the field often have been motivated by conflicts among theoretical perspectives. Another reason for exploring the contrasts among theories is the following. Although a great many of you who are the readers of this text will not go on to a research career in this field, you nonetheless will live in a world in which much debate, and some decisions of social importance, will be based on one or another conception of human nature. Familiarity with contrasting views of human nature, and with research that supports and sometimes fails to support them, makes you a more well-informed citizen and decision maker in this world.

Despite these contrasts, there are many points of agreement in the contemporary field of personality science. The interplay among contrasting theoretical ideas and research programs has, to a significant degree, achieved the promise that was articulated at the very conclusion of our first chapter: The different theories have "force[d] deep-going reconsiderations upon one another" (Geertz, 2000, p. 199). With some exceptions, theoretical conceptions generally have become less extreme in their focus over the years. For example, in the contemporary field, no personality researcher would deny the importance of both conscious and unconscious processes to personality functioning. Virtually everyone would recognize that humans are a product of evolution, yet that cultural factors—which are a part of humans' evolutionary history—are critical to understanding the individual. On the classic issue of nature versus nurture, only the most extreme trait positions (McCrae & Costa, 1996) argue against an interactionist approach in which more personality structures develop through processes that involve reciprocal interactions between individuals and the contexts in which they live (Magnusson, 1999). Theoretical positions often have become more nuanced. In so doing, they probably have moved somewhat closer to the subtlety and complexity of their target of investigation.

Despite these moves, there is no one, single theoretical paradigm in the contemporary field. A number of critical issues continue to divide personality scientists. Let us return to these issues, which we introduced back in Chapter 1, in the light of our subsequent discussion of the major personality theories.

PHILOSOPHICAL VIEW OF THE PERSON

We have seen that implicit in most theories of personality is a general, philosophical view of human nature. The theorists covered in this text present a diversity of views: Freud's view of the person as an energy system; Rogers's view of the person as a self-actualizing organism; Kelly's view of the person as a scientist; the Skinnerian view of the person as responding to environmental reinforcement contingencies; the social-cognitive view of the person as a problem-solving organism; the computer model of the person as a complex information processor. Of course, other views are possible and within any single orientation, such as trait theory, different views can emerge. Furthermore, such capsule descriptions fail to do justice to the complexity inherent in each view. At the same time, these capsule descriptions capture a distinctive element in each theoretical perspective and help to make us aware of the differ-

**CURRENT
QUESTIONS**

THE RISE AND FALL OF SCHOOLS IN PSYCHOLOGY: WHICH SCHOOL HAS BEEN MOST PROMINENT?

Since the birth of scientific psychology more than a century ago, many schools of thought have risen and fallen from prominence. One popular contention is that the cognitive perspective now dominates scientific psychology, having prevailed over psychoanalysis and behaviorism. In contrast, others argue that no such cognitive revolution has occurred: "The repeated declaration of a revolution may be more a reflection of the enthusiasm many cognitive psychologists have for their subdiscipline than of actual events" (Friman, Allen, Kerwin, & Larzelere, 1993, p. 662).

Despite the passionate claims and heated arguments, there have been few attempts to document these trends empirically. A recent study by Robins, Gosling, and Craik (1999) moves beyond mere speculation on this issue, measuring historical trends in the prominence of psychoanalysis, behaviorism, and cognitive psychology. (Note that this analysis studied the whole field of psychology, rather than personality psychology in particular; therefore, the trait approach was not included as a separate school.)

Prominence implies that a school's scientific achievements are capturing the attention of the rest of the field. Thus, Robins and colleagues. argued, prominence in mainstream scientific psychology can be measured by what is cited and published in the most influential general psychology publications. These "flagship" publications (e.g., *Psychological Review* and the *American Psychologist*) serve dual roles in the field: they reflect current trends and they define the agenda for the future. Thus, a school of thought's prominence in the flagship journals should be reflected in the number of articles published on topics relevant to that school. For example, if cognitive psychology has been increas-

ing in scientific prominence, we would expect to find an increase in articles on cognitive topics appearing in the flagship publications.

To determine the number of relevant articles, Robins and colleagues used keywords to represent topics of central concern to each school, and then determined the frequency with which these keywords appeared in articles published since 1967. For each school, they calculated the percentage of articles published in the flagship publications that included at least one of the keywords selected to represent that school.

Figure 15.1 shows the publication trends from 1967 to 1994. Articles relevant to cognitive psychology have appeared with increasing frequency in the flagship publications, while the number of articles relevant to behavioral psychology has been decreasing. Note that Figure 15.1 also shows that psychoanalytic articles were almost nonexistent throughout the period examined. Over the past three decades, the percentage of flagship articles devoted to cognitive psychology has more than doubled from 1967 to the present (from less than 7 percent to more than 16 percent), whereas the percentage of articles devoted to behavioral psychology declined over this period to less than a third of its 1967 value (from about 9 percent to about 2.5 percent). In contrast, psychoanalysis did not show any substantial changes.

Also represented in Figure 15.1 is the publication trend for articles relevant to neuroscience that have appeared in the flagship publications. Much to the surprise of the authors, and the disbelief of their colleagues, there was not evidence of a strong rise in the neuroscience perspective within psychology. To check on this, Robins and colleagues, performed a number of other analyses, leading

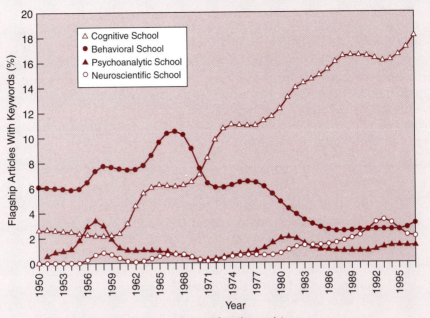

Note: A smoothing function was used to transform the raw data.

Figure 15.1 Percentage of Articles Published in the Flagship Publications that Include Keywords Relevant to the Cognitive, Behavioral, Psychoanalytic, and Neuroscience Schools. *(Copyright © 1999 American Psychological Association, reprinted by permission.)*

to the conclusion that although there are signs that the neuroscience perspective is growing, "the analyses lead us to conclude that the growth of neuroscience within mainstream psychology is weak when compared with the rise of cognitive psychology" (p. 123). At the same time, the Robins group note that the widespread belief in the growth of the field of neuroscience is not mistaken. Here they cite the number of new neuroscience journals and the dramatic increase of citations of articles published in these journals within articles published in other highly regarded scientific journals. Thus, it is clear that the biological developments noted in Chapter 9 are of considerable importance and will have to be incorporated into mainstream psychology generally and future personality theories in particular.

These data suggest four major conclusions. (1) Cognitive psychology has overtaken behaviorism as the most prominent of the three major schools in scientific psychology. (2) Despite claims to the contrary, behavioral psychology seems to be on the decline. (3) Mainstream scientific psychology has paid little attention to psychoanalytic research and articles pertaining to the psychoanalytic school have been virtually nonexistent in the flagship publications over the past three decades. Although psychoanalytic ideas continue to influence research in psychology, contemporary psychoanalytic writing is not assimilated directly into scientific psychology. (4) Findings in neuroscience have not yet become part of mainstream scientific psychology but their importance suggests that this is a step that must be taken in the future.

How do these trends fit into the broader context of psychology as a science? Interpreted within a Kuhnian perspective, the findings of Robins and colleagues might be taken to suggest that the cognitive school is the most recent in a succession of dominant paradigms. But that conclusion may be premature because additional evidence is required before a Kuhnian revolution can be declared. For example, Kuhn's emphasis on the socialization process within science would require that all textbooks of scientific psychology adopt the cognitive orientation, and that most young scientists work on cognitive topics. Certainly, this is not (yet) the case, as the present textbook amply demonstrates. Whether cognitive psychology will evolve into the dominant paradigm or remain a competing perspective, which both informs other perspectives and is informed by them, remains to be seen.

SOURCES: Robins, Gosling, & Craik, 1999; Friman, Allen, Kerwin, & Larzelere, 1993.

ing views that do exist. Of particular interest here is the emphasis on cognition found in so many recent theoretical developments (psychoanalytic ego psychology, social-cognitive theory, and cognitive information-processing personality theory).

Each view of the organism opens up certain avenues of thought, research, and analysis. Each also potentially closes off other important lines of emphasis and investigation. The early behavioristic view of the person inhibited recognition of the importance of cognitive functions. The current cognitive emphasis may correct this imbalance, but it may also lead us to ignore other important areas of experience such as motivation and emotion. The point here is not that one view is right or wrong but that such views exist and that it is important to be aware of them in understanding each theory, as well as in assessing its strengths and limitations.

INTERNAL AND EXTERNAL CAUSES OF BEHAVIOR

A second, related issue is whether the causes of behavior are inside the person or in the environment. In Chapter 1, Freud and Skinner were contrasted as representing extreme positions on this issue. We have also discussed how the questions asked by researchers have changed over the years. First, researchers asked whether behavior is caused by the person or by the situation, then to what extent behavior is caused by person and situation factors, and finally how person and situation factors interact with one another to determine behavior.

In the theories covered, this issue emerged most clearly in relation to trait theory and social-cognitive theory. At one extreme, trait theory has been characterized as suggesting that people are stable and consistent in their behavior over time and across situations. Psychoanalytic theory, with its similar emphasis on personality structure, has been seen as emphasizing internal causes of behavior and general stability in personality functioning. At the other extreme, learning theory has been characterized as emphasizing environmental determinants of behavior and the variability or situational specificity of behavior. Such characterizations are useful in highlighting important theoretical differences. At the same time, it should be clear that none of these theories emphasizes only one set of causes. To a certain extent, they are all interactionist in their emphasis; they all emphasize the interaction between individual and environment, or person and situation, in determining behavior. Trait theory, for example, does recognize the importance of situational factors in affecting which traits are activated as well as affecting the moods of the individual. It is inconceivable that a trait theorist or a psychoanalytic theorist would expect a person to behave the same way in all situations. On the other hand, social-cognitive theory recognizes the importance of person factors in terms of concepts such as goals, cognitive and behavioral competencies, self-efficacy, and self-regulation. Indeed, the concept of reciprocal determinism or the mutually causal relationship between person and situation is a cornerstone of social-cognitive theory.

As with other issues in the field, emphasis often shifts in one direction or another, in this case in terms of relative emphasis on internal, person factors or on external, environmental factors. At one point considerable evidence was presented to suggest that human behavior is quite variable. Such evidence was used to challenge traditional trait and psychodynamic views of personality structure and personality dispositions (Mischel, 1968). More recently, evidence has been presented to suggest that human behavior is more consistent than had been suggested previously (Epstein, 1983; Pervin, 1985). Such consistency does not seem to be explained by unchanged environmental circumstances. Indeed, we often are impressed with how resistant some behavior is to change despite dramatic changes in environmental circumstances. Thus, whereas at one point situational determinants were emphasized, many psychologists are again emphasizing dispositions or reaction tendencies within individuals.

Although important differences remain in the relative emphasis on internal (person) and external (situation) causes, all theories of personality recognize that both are important in understanding behavior. Perhaps we can now expect to find theorists who increasingly will address questions in terms of both sets of causes rather than with an almost exclusive emphasis on one or another set of causes. All personality theorists recognize that there is both consistency and variability to individual behavior. The task, then, is to account for the pattern of stability and change that characterizes people.

THE UNITY OF BEHAVIOR AND THE CONCEPT OF THE SELF

There is movement in human organisms, as living systems, toward integrated functioning and the reduction of conflict. Personality theories differ in the extent to which they emphasize the patterned, unified system aspects of human functioning. An emphasis on the unity of behavior is greatest in the clinical theories of Freud, Rogers, and Kelly. With the exception of Allport, it is much less prominent in trait theories and learning theories. Why should this be? Undoubtedly the reasons are complex and varied, but a number of points can be considered. First, clinical theories are based on observations of many behaviors of a single individual. The theories of Freud, Rogers, and Kelly evolved out of these clinical observations. Their efforts were directed toward understanding relationships among thoughts, behaviors, and feelings. Almost of necessity, they were struck with the issues of conflict and threats to the coherence of the system, as reported to them by their patients. Although clinical approaches based on learning theory exist and are important, they evolved out of theories rather than initially serving as the basis for them.

A second point to be considered is the emphasis in trait theories and learning theories on exploring particular variables. The belief here is that human behavior can be understood through the systematic study of particular variables or processes. The strategy is to study phenomena systematically and to build from the simple to the complex. Pattern and organization become important when one has a clear enough grasp of the parts that constitute the pattern or organization.

The concept of self traditionally has been used to express the patterned, organized aspects of personality functioning. In psychoanalytic theory, the concept of ego expresses the "executive" or integrative aspects of system functioning. Although sometimes portrayed as a person or homunculus inside the individual ("The ego seeks to reduce conflict"), it actually describes processes going on within the person. For both Rogers and Kelly the concept of self plays an important integrative function. For Rogers, the person seeks self-actualization and to make the self and experience congruent with one another. For Kelly, the constructs associated with the self and how they are organized play a central role in the person's functioning. The emphasis on the concept of self as an organizing entity is perhaps most clearly expressed in the view of Allport. The concept of self, or proprium, as he called it, gave testimony to the complex, organized aspects of the mature human system.

In their efforts to avoid the vague, romantic, and fanciful, many theorists have avoided the concept of self. In particular, the self as a homunculus within the person that determines action has been criticized. Still, as we have witnessed, recent developments in social-cognitive theory place heavy emphasis on the concept of self. This is a somewhat different concept of self, however, involving standards for self-praise and self-criticism as well as other self-regulatory functions. Nevertheless, it is a self-concept. The concept of efficacy, or ability to perform the behavior necessary for certain outcomes, an increasingly important part of Bandura's theory, involves cognitions or beliefs about the self. It is seen as a broadly integrative concept that can account for diverse findings. Thus, at this point, social-cognitive theory also has come to emphasize both the organized aspects of the human personality and the importance of the self-concept in such organization. Finally, the organizing and directing functions of self-schemas are clearly articulated in the cognitive information-processing view. Just as any complex system may have higher-order control units, so the self may be viewed as consisting of schemas or constructs that organize and integrate the functioning of other parts of the system. It is noteworthy, however, to reemphasize the view of a multiplicity or family of selves rather than a single, all-encompassing self-concept.

Although the utility and necessity of the concept of self continue to be debated, theories of personality are drawn to it continuously. In one form or another, the concept of self enters into most theories and attests to the important ways in which we experience ourselves, to the myriad ways in which we understand ourselves, and to the organized aspects of our functioning.

VARYING STATES OF AWARENESS AND THE CONCEPT OF THE UNCONSCIOUS

Interest in varying states of awareness has been increasing in psychology. As noted at the outset, many theorists are uncomfortable with the concept of the unconscious as formulated by Freud. The notion of things buried in the unconscious or of unconscious forces striving for expression is too metaphorical for most systematic thinkers. Yet, if we accept the view that we are not always aware of factors affecting our behavior, how are we to conceptualize such phenomena? Is it merely that we do not attend to them and that focusing our attention brings them into awareness? Is it the case, as some cognitive theorists suggest, that what others view as unconscious processes actually consist of rehearsed behaviors that flow automatically, that they consist of overlearned responses? In other words, is there no need to consider special processes and label them as unconscious?

As we have seen, both Rogers and Kelly avoided the concept of the unconscious. Instead, they emphasized concepts that involve aspects of functioning that are not available to awareness. Rogers stated that experiences incongruent with the self-concept may be distorted or denied. Threatening feelings may be unavailable to awareness but experienced through the process of subception. Kelly suggested that one or both poles of a construct may be submerged and unavailable to awareness. Each of these theories describes a defensive process resulting in important aspects of personality functioning being unavailable to awareness. Although initially expressing little interest in unconscious processes, cognitive theorists have recently been concerned with them albeit not necessarily in the terms suggested by psychoanalytic theorists.

The problem of evaluating the importance of such phenomena and conceptualizing them remains. If much of our behavior is governed by reinforcements, both from within ourselves and from others, are we always aware of what these reinforcers are? If not, why not? Is it because some of them were learned in infancy, prior to the development of verbal labels? Is it because some are so much a part of our daily lives that we no longer attend to them? Or is it because often we choose not to be aware of things that make us anxious and uncomfortable? How much attention is paid to these phenomena and how they are interpreted continue to be important issues on which theories of personality differ.

RELATIONS AMONG COGNITION, AFFECT, AND OVERT BEHAVIOR

As we have seen, personality theories differ in the attention given to cognitive, affective, and behavioral processes. Understanding the intricate relations among them remains a significant task. Although Freud emphasized cognitive and drive processes, he assigned a central role to affects in his conceptualization of human behavior. This is seen most clearly in relation to the affect of anxiety, but he and his followers also were concerned with other affects such as anger, depression, guilt, shame, and jealousy. There is interest in overt behavior, but only as an expression of the workings of drive processes. Rogers and Kelly both emphasized the person as an active construer of events, but for Rogers the "felt experience" was central, whereas for Kelly emotions followed from cognitive interpretations. The latter emphasis also is found in current attribution and other cognitive theories. In these theories cognitive properties are central and primary to feelings and overt behavior. Radical behaviorism, of course, focused exclusively on overt behavior. However, behavior therapists increasingly have become concerned with cognitive processes and, even more recently, with the influences of affective processes.

Historically, many issues in psychology initially are framed in either or terms. Is it heredity or environment? Person or situation? Then there is debate about which is more important. Finally, there is recognition that the issues are more complex than "either or" and "more important than" solutions. There is recognition that multiple factors enter into complex functioning, each of them contributing to a greater or lesser extent at different times and in different situations. The critical question then becomes one of understanding relationships among variables, rather than choosing among them. Thus, the question becomes how heredity and environment interact, and how person and situation variables mutually affect one another. Similarly, we are coming to understand that people are always thinking, feeling, and behaving, and that what remains to be understood is how these processes interact in the ongoing stream of human functioning.

INFLUENCES OF THE PAST, PRESENT, AND FUTURE ON BEHAVIOR

When we think of Freud, we almost automatically think of behavior being governed by the past. When we think of Kelly, we think of a person as striving to anticipate the future. Prediction becomes the key to understanding behavior. Skinner's emphasis on past reinforcement contingencies can be contrasted with social-cognitive theory's emphasis on expectancies. Is behavior regulated by the past or by our expectations of the future?

This is yet another issue that divides personality theorists. Often the differences among theorists are subtle but important in their implications. For example, Bandura's suggestion that past reinforcements are important for what has been learned but that expectancies about future reinforcement are important for what is performed is a subtle but important distinction. It involves not only the important distinction between the acquisition and the performance of behavior but also an important emphasis on cognitive functioning. In fact, there appears to be a close relationship between an emphasis on the future and an emphasis on cognitive processes. This is not surprising, since the development of higher mental processes and the capacity for language are necessary for an organism to be able to construct a future world.

In reality, of course, past events and our anticipation of future events affect one another, as well as our experiences in the present. How we anticipate the future is inevitably linked to our past. However, it is probably also the case that how we view the future influences our construction of the past. For example, if we are depressed about the future we may feel bound by our past, whereas if we are optimistic about the future we may perceive the past as having been liberating. Our views of the past, present, and future are all parts of our experience. An understanding of the relationships among these views, then, becomes the task of each theory of personality.

PERSONALITY THEORY AS AN ANSWER TO THE QUESTIONS OF WHAT, HOW, AND WHY

In Chapter 1 it was stated that a theory of personality should answer the questions of what, how, and why. In later chapters, the concepts and principles used by various theorists to account for human personality were considered. Some of the major concepts relevant to each theory are given in Table 15.1. At this point, let us review some of these concepts, consider the similarities among the theories, and raise some remaining questions.

PERSONALITY STRUCTURE

Each theory that has been studied here suggests concepts relevant to the structure of personality. The theories differ not only in the content of these units but also in their level of abstraction and in the complexity of the structural organi-

Table 15.1 Summary of Major Theoretical Concepts

Theorist, Theory, or Approach	Structure	Process	Growth and Development	Pathology	Change
Freud	Id, ego, superego; unconscious, preconscious, conscious	Sexual and aggressive instincts; anxiety and the mechanisms of defense	Erogenous zones; oral, anal, phallic stages of development; Oedipus complex	Infantile sexuality; fixation and regression; conflict; symptoms	Transference; conflict resolution; "Where id was, ego shall be"
Rogers	Self; ideal self	Self-actualization; congruence of self and experience; incongruence and defensive distortion and denial	Congruence and self-actualization versus incongruence and defensiveness	Defensive maintenance of self; incongruence	Therapeutic atmosphere: congruence, unconditional positive regard, empathic understanding
Trait Approaches	Traits	Dynamic traits; motives associated with traits	Contributions of heredity and environment to traits	Extreme scores on trait dimensions (e.g., neuroticism)	(No formal model)
Learning Approaches	Response	Classical conditioning; instrumental conditioning; operant conditioning	Schedules of reinforcement and successive approximations	Maladaptive learned response patterns	Extinction; discrimination learning; counter-conditioning; positive reinforcement; systematic desensitization; behavior modification
Kelly	Constructs	Processes channelized by anticipation of events	Increased complexity and definition to construct system	Disordered functioning of construct system	Psychological reconstruction of life; invitational mood; fixed-role therapy
Social Cognitive Theory	Beliefs; standards; goals; competencies	Observational learning; vicarious conditioning; self-evaluative and self-regulatory processes	Social learning through observation and direct experience; development of self-efficacy judgments and standards for self-regulation	Learned response patterns; excessive self-standards; problems in self-efficacy	Modeling; guided participation; increased self-efficacy; cognitive therapy

zation. Freud's structural units are at a very high level of abstraction. One cannot observe an id, ego, or superego, or a conscious, preconscious, or unconscious. In trait theory, the five-factor model posited core units of analysis that were very different in nature, yet similarly abstract. Somewhat less abstract are the structural units used by Rogers and Kelly. More concrete still are the units of analysis of social-cognitive theory, which typically refer to relatively well-defined aspects of cognition that can be measured through self-report or indexed through other laboratory methods. Few contemporary investigators seek the almost complete absence of abstraction found in behaviorism, which developed during an historical period in which investigators were wary of making any claims whatsoever about unseen, internal psychological mechanisms.

In addition to differences in their level of abstraction, theories differ in the complexity of structural organization. This complexity may be considered in terms of the number of units involved and whether they are formed in some kind of hierarchical arrangement in relation to one another. For example, consider the fairly simple structure described by most learning theorists. There are few categories of responses; no suggestion that behavior generally involves the expression of many units at the same time; and a bias against the concept of personality types, which implies a stable organization of many different responses. Contrast this with the psychoanalytic framework, which includes many structural units and almost unlimited possibilities for interrelationships among the units. Or consider Kelly's system, which allows for a complex system involving many constructs, some superordinate and others subordinate.

These differences in complexity of structural organization can be related to differences in the general importance attached to structure in behavior. The concept of structure generally is used to account for the more stable aspects of personality and for the consistency of individual behavior over time and over situations. To consider two extremes: psychoanalytic theory places great emphasis on the stability of behavior over time, whereas learning theory does not; psychoanalytic theory places great emphasis on the consistency of behavior across situations, whereas learning theory does not. At one extreme, psychoanalytic theory involves abstract units and a complex structural organization. At the other extreme, learning theory involves concrete units and little emphasis on their organization. In other words, there appears to be a relationship between the importance attributed to structure by a theory and the theory's emphasis on stability and consistency in human behavior.

PROCESS

Our review of process aspects of personality theories—the parts of the theories that addressed the "why" of behavior—revealed much diversity. For Freud, the individual's efforts are directed toward expressing the sexual and aggressive instincts and, thereby, toward the reduction of the tension associated with these instincts. For Rogers, the individual is more forward looking, seeking growth and self-actualization even at the cost of increased tension. Rogers also places emphasis on a third motivational force: consistency. The particular kind of consistency emphasized by Rogers is a congruence between self and experience. For Kelly, who also emphasizes consistency, the relevant variables are different. According to Kelly, it is important that the individual's constructs be consistent with one another, so that the predictions from one do not cancel out the predictions from another. It is also important that predictions be consistent with experiences, in other words, that events confirm and validate the construct system. For Skinner, processes of personality involved reinforcements. He found no use for concepts of drive or tension. Social-cognitive theory similarly did not invoke drive variables, but instead saw dynamic cognitive processes, particularly involving goals and the self, as being central to human motivation.

Notice that these motivational models conflict with one another only if we assume that all behavior must follow the same motivational principles. In relation to structure, we need not assume that an individual only has drives, that one only has a concept of the self, or that one only has personal constructs. In the same way, we need not assume that an individual is always reducing tension, or always striving toward actualization, or always seeking consistency. It may be that all three models of motivation are relevant to human behavior. An individual may at some points be functioning to reduce tension, at other times to actualize his or her self, and at other times to achieve cognitive consistency. Another possibility is that, at one time, two kinds of motivation are operating, but they are in conflict with one another. For example, an individual may seek to relieve aggressive urges by hitting someone, but he or she may also like the person involved and view this behavior as out of character. A third possibility is that two kinds of motivation may combine to support one another. Thus, to make love to someone can represent the reduction of tension from sexual urges, an actualizing expression of the self, and an act consistent with the self-concept and with predictions from one's construct system. If room is left for more than one process model, it becomes the task of psychologists to define the conditions under which each type of motivation will occur and the ways in which the different types of motivation can combine to determine behavior.

GROWTH AND DEVELOPMENT

As a general rule, the theories we covered commonly devoted less attention to the question of growth and development than would have been ideal. Trait theorists have done important work on the influences of heredity and environment, and on age trends in personality development. Psychoanalytic theory gives attention to the role of biological and environmental factors in personality development, but in most cases this remains speculative. It is disappointing that Rogers and Kelly have so little to say in this area. Finally, although the learning theorists have done a great deal to interpret the processes through which cultural, social class, and familial influences are transmitted, they have seriously neglected biological factors. Important progress has been made by social-cognitive theorists such as Bandura, who has long explored the role of modeling in personality development, and Mischel, who has explored longitudinal consistency in delay of gratification. To be clear, the research domain of personality development is a vibrant area of study (e.g., Bergman, Magnusson, & El-Khouri, 2003; Pulkkinen & Caspi, 2002). The concern is that the classic personality theories have not incorporated a developmental perspective as fully as would be optimal.

In considering the theorists covered in this text, differences concerning two questions about development become apparent. The first concerns the utility of the concept of stages of development, and the second concerns the importance of early experiences for later personality development. Psychoanalytic theory attaches great importance to the early years and to the concept of stages of development. In relation to the early years, they emphasize particular experiences within the family. Such a view can be contrasted with the trait emphasis on heredity and the importance of the nonshared environment, including experiences outside the home. The psychoanalytic emphasis can be contrasted as well with the social-cognitive criticism of the concept of stages of development and of suggestions that personality is relatively fixed by developments during the early years. Social-cognitive theorists emphasize, instead, the potential for different parts of personality to develop in different ways and much greater potential for change as a result of later experience.

PSYCHOPATHOLOGY

The forces producing psychopathology are interpreted differently by the theorists. However, the concept of conflict is essential to a number of them. This is most clearly the case in psychoanalytic theory. According to Freud, psychopathology occurs when the instinctive urges of the id come into conflict with the functioning of the ego. Although Rogers does not emphasize the importance of conflict, one can interpret the problem of incongruence in terms of a conflict between experience and the self-concept. Learning theory offers a number of explanations for psychopathology, and at least one of these explanations emphasizes the importance of approach avoidance conflicts. And, although cognitive theorists do not emphasize the importance of conflict, one can think of the implications of goal conflicts and conflicting beliefs or expectancies. In addition, as cognitive theorists consider motivational questions, they come to recognize the potential for conflict between the motives for self-verification and self-enhancement.

Many complex questions concerning psychopathology remain unanswered. For example, we know that cultures vary in the incidence of various forms of psychopathology. Depression is rare in Africa but is common in the United States. Why? Conversion symptoms, such as hysterical paralysis of the arm or leg, were quite common in Freud's time but are observed much less frequently today. Why? Are there important differences in the problems that people in different cultures face? Or do they face the same problems but cope with them differently? Or is it just that some problems are more likely to be reported than others and that this pattern varies with the culture? If people today are more concerned with problems of identity than with problems of guilt, if they are more concerned with the problem of finding meaning than of relieving sexual urges, what are the implications for psychoanalysis and the other theories of personality?

Psychopathology is a major concern for clinical theories of personality. In Kelly's terms, this is a major focus of convenience for these theories. However, we have seen that interpretations of the nature of psychopathology vary considerably among them. And, although other theories of personality are derived from observations outside the therapeutic setting, they have nonetheless recognized the importance of explaining psychopathology. The issue here is not whether personality theory should offer some understanding of psychopathology, but rather how central this topic is for the theory and the variables that are emphasized. It is fascinating to observe how each theory of personality, with its own set of structural units and process concepts, can come up with such varying interpretations of the same phenomena.

CHANGE

The following questions concerning change are given varying amounts of attention by each theorist: What is changed? What are the conditions for change? What is the process in change? Psychoanalytic theory, in its emphasis on changes in the relationship between the unconscious and the conscious and between the ego and the id, is particularly concerned with structural change. Kelly, in his analysis of psychotherapy as the psychological reconstruction of life, also deals with structural change. In contrast, Rogers is most concerned with the conditions that make change possible. Although his research has attended to structural change (e.g., changes in self-ideal, self-discrepancy), this has been for the purpose of having a criterion against which he could measure the effectiveness of different variables (e.g., congruence, unconditional positive regard, empathic understanding). Kelly pointed out the importance of an atmosphere of experimentation and invitational mood, but there is little research to suggest the variables critical in establishing this atmosphere or mood.

The process of change is a particular focus of convenience for learning theory. The following learning processes are used to account for a wide range of changes related to a variety of forms of psychotherapy: extinction, discrimination learning, counterconditioning, positive reinforcement, and imitation. Whereas initially learning concepts were used to explain treatment effects associated with other theories, more recently these concepts have been used to develop learning-based treatment methods. A clear illustration of therapeutic technique as an outgrowth of theory is Bandura's work on modeling and guided participation. It is also interesting to note here that although therapy or psychological change has not been a major aspect of social-cognitive theory, it is becoming an increasingly important part of it. In fact, Bandura suggests that developments in this area may well serve as a general test of the theory.

There are, of course, basic and important differences in the theories concerning the potential for change. At one extreme is psychoanalytic theory, which suggests that fundamental personality change is quite difficult, and some versions of trait theory, which contend that traits are relatively unchanged by environmental experience. However, as we have seen, research findings provide new evidence of change. Recognizing this, various theorists now pursue the exciting challenge of explaining the how's and why's of personality change across the life course. In considering the question of how people change, we again recognize the extent to which theories of personality emphasize different processes of change, different conditions for change, and change in different aspects of personality functioning. Some of these differences may well represent competing and conflicting points of view, and others merely various terms for similar processes. Finally, some differences may result from attending to different aspects of the person. Sorting these out is a task for both students and professionals in the field.

BIOLOGICAL FOUNDATIONS AND LEVELS OF EXPLANATION

As indicated in Chapter 9, enormous gains have been made in the field of biology, particularly in the area of neuroscience. As was made clear in that chapter, these gains have important implications for the field of personality. An issue that will need to be addressed in the future concerns how we will integrate findings from neuroscience and other parts of biology into our more traditional explanations for the phenomena of interest to personality psychologists. We come here to the question of levels of explanation and to the risks of reductionism, on the one hand, and rejection of important findings, on the other.

The issue of levels of explanation involves the level at which we will try to study, understand, and explain the phenomena of interest. Explanations for phenomena can be at a low level, involving small parts and low levels of complexity of organization, or at a high level, involving larger parts and high levels of complexity of organization. For example, we can understand emotions in terms of various levels ranging from what is going on in the relevant neurons, to the brain level in terms of the role of the amygdala, to the brain system level in terms of the role of memory in emotion, to the person level in terms of how various memories and emotions are structured in relation to one another, to the sociocultural level in terms of how the rules for perceiving and expressing emotions are learned by members of each culture. To take another example, we can understand problems such as those of alcoholism and drug abuse at the level of genes and heredity, at the level of cell receptors, at the level of learning (e.g., classical conditioning), at the level of family and other environmental stressors, to the level of sociocultural factors such as peer influences and cultural beliefs.

Most psychologists would suggest that each of these is a legitimate level for analysis and the conduct of research. However, some would argue for one or another of two extreme positions. At one extreme, some would argue that everything of interest to personality psychologists ultimately will be explained in terms of the functioning of the brain and other parts of the human biological system. At the other extreme, some would argue that such explanations are reductionistic, in the sense of offering explanations at a lower level for phenomena at a higher level that require analysis in terms of different concepts and principles of organization. Currently there is considerable debate, for example, about the best level for understanding consciousness, with some seeking explanations at the level of brain functioning and others seeking explanations at the level of meaning.

The position taken in this book is in accord with that articulated by Cacioppo (1999; Berntson & Cacioppo, 2000; Cacioppo & Berntson, 1992) in terms of support for a multilevel, integrative approach to understanding the phenomena of interest to personality psychologists. According to this view, each level of analysis has its own strengths and limitations, with distinctive contributions to make to understanding and explanation. No single level of explanation is best for understanding the phenomena of interest and appreciation of the contributions from all levels is desirable. Thus, for example, understanding, and treatment, of the problems of drug and alcohol abuse requires an appreciation of each of the levels described earlier: gene, cell, learning, family, and sociocultural environment. As expressed by Zuckerman (1998): "All types of phenomena may be studied at different levels, from the most molecular to the most molar. Each level has its own methods, constructs, and limitations. An analysis at one level may be perfectly compatible with one at another level. The cognitive, behavioral, and biological are complementary and not conflicting modes of explanation" (p. 150).

According to one scientist, different scientists prefer one or another level of analysis: "Basically, some people like reductive analysis into component particles. Others revel in complex wholes" (Jolly, 1999, p. 231). Such preferences are understandable and, from the standpoint of scientific advancement, desirable. The task for us as students of the field is to appreciate the contributions that can be made by each level of analysis. The task for future personality psychologists will be to bridge the gap that can exist between the different levels and to develop conceptual models that provide for the distinctive contributions of each (Klein & Kihlstrom, 1998).

RELATIONSHIPS AMONG THEORY, ASSESSMENT, AND RESEARCH

At various times in this book, theory, assessment, and research have been considered separately. However, an attempt has been made to keep in mind the intimate relationships among them. Indeed, this has been a major theme throughout the book.

In Chapter 1, theory as an attempt to fit together and explain a wide variety of facts with a few assumptions was considered. In Chapter 2 the tools that personality psychologists use to observe and measure behavior in a systematic way were discussed. It is clear that research involves the use of assessment techniques to develop and test theory. What of the relationships among theory, assessment, and research? Here we can note a relationship between the assumptions basic to theories and the techniques of assessment generally associated with these theories. For example, a psychodynamic theory such as psychoanalysis is associated with the Rorschach test, phenomenological theory such as that of Rogers with the interview and measures of the self-concept, factor-analytic theory with psychometric tests, a learning theory approach with objective tests, and cognitive theories with ways in which people process information and organize their worlds.

Are the observations obtained similar when assessment techniques associated with the different theories are applied to the same individual? Recall here the story of the wise blind men and the elephant. Each wise man examined a part of the elephant and assumed that he knew what it was. None knew that it was an elephant, and each came to a different conclusion on the basis of his observations. One felt the tail and thought it was a snake, another a leg and thought it was a tree, another a trunk and thought it was a hose, and another a body and thought it was a wall. Do the theories refer to different parts of the same individual, each representing an interesting though incomplete picture of the whole and describing the same qualities but in different terms? Or do the theories picture very different individuals?

The case of Jim has given us the opportunity to follow an individual over the course of 20 years and to compare the observations gained from different theoretical perspectives. Let us compare the observations from the different tests, as well as those obtained at different times. Finally, we can consider Jim's impressions of the personality tests.

THE CASE OF JIM

Comparison of the Assessment Data on Different Theories

A number of themes emerge consistently across the various tests administered to Jim when he was a college student. First, all of the tests show evidence of tension, insecurity, and anxiety. Second, they present evidence of difficulties in relating to women. Third, they show evidence of difficulties in interpersonal relationships, particularly in experiencing and expressing warmth. Finally, the tests present consistent evidence of rigidity, inhibition, compulsivity, and difficulty in being creative.

At the same time, the pictures that emerge from the different approaches are qualitatively different from one another, although not necessarily in conflict. For example, the vampires and "Count Dracula sucking blood" images on the Rorschach are qualitatively different from Jim's self-reports of problems in interpersonal relationships, and the evidence of sadism on the projectives is qualitatively different from the self-reports of difficulties in this area.

Finally, it is important to note that each assessment device seems able to pick up aspects of Jim's personality not necessarily detected by the other tests, or to highlight an aspect of his personality left vague on the other tests. For example, the projectives highlighted some of his conflicts and defenses; the 16 P.F. his somatic complaints and mood swings; and the interview and autobiography his perception of himself as deep, sensitive, kind, and basically good.

Stability and Change Over Time

We have been able to follow Jim over the course of 20 years, from a struggling college student undecided about his career to an established professional, husband, and father. During this period we have also been able to administer new personality tests as they have evolved in association with new theoretical developments in the field. The picture that emerges gives considerable evidence of stability in Jim's personality. Twenty years later, evidence remains of tension-neuroticism; difficulties in being as warm and tender as he would like to be, particularly in relation to his wife; and evidence of compulsive characteristics leading him to be less creative than he would like to be.

At the same time, important developments have occurred, developments that are spelled out in the interview and in responses to other tests. Twenty years later, Jim is a happier person, with a greater sense of self-efficacy in intellectual and social areas and a greatly reduced concern about his sexual adequacy. He is more able to get out of himself, though this still remains somewhat of a struggle. As he approaches midlife, Jim feels that he is moving in the right direction and is committed to the goals of being a good husband and father, as well as further development of his professional skills.

The picture that emerges is one of both stability and change, of continuity with the past although not a complete duplication of it. In all likelihood, it would have been difficult to predict the developments that have occurred; on the other hand, one can look back and see why his life has unfolded as it has.

Jim's Reflections on the Data

How did Jim view the various tests and personality sketches? Jim felt that the projective data did a good job of pointing out his conflicts and defenses, but that they overemphasized the insecurities present at the time. He believed that the phenomenological data (semantic differential, Rep test) gave an accurate picture of him at the time, although he has now become more aware of similarities to his mother. In addition, he felt that he now has a less constricted view of people and of the world, and can express more warmth. As with the other approaches, Jim felt that the trait approach captured a part of him that was present at the time, and in relation to which there have been changes. He is less insecure now, though he still has concerns about being liked and still has mood swings.

What of the cognitive approach considered at this time? As a psychologist Jim was somewhat aware of this general orientation, but he was not very familiar with it. Thus, in a sense, this was a professional learning experience for him. At the same time, it should be noted that he came to the material with a mixed psychodynamic and humanist slant. Thus, he said of the cognitive, information-processing approach: "It picked up some interesting things but we're not cut from the same cloth. There's something valuable in it but I don't see it as a whole approach. It captures a part of the truth, a part of me, but somehow it seems like a denuded frame of reference. It misses some of the power and drama of life."

What was his overall view of the alternative approaches? In general Jim felt that the various approaches captured different aspects of him, highlighting different aspects of his personality while picking up some consistent themes. In addition, he commented that he felt that different approaches to therapy could be useful with different people or as different ways of gaining access to people.

The emphasis here has not been on whether one or another approach to theory, assessment, and research is right or wrong. Rather we have focused on relations among the three approaches and on the strengths and limitations of each. It would appear that different aspects of personality are studied with greater or lesser ease in different settings and with greater or lesser accuracy with different assessment devices. Each research approach and assessment device appears to have its own special contribution to make, as well as its own potential for sources of error or bias. Thus, if we limit ourselves to one approach to research or assessment, we may restrict our observations to phenomena directly relevant to a specific theoretical position. Alternatively, we can appreciate the contributions that different theories, research procedures, and assessment devices can make to our understanding of human behavior. Like Jim, we can consider the possibility that each approach captures a glimpse of the person, highlighting different aspects of personality while picking up common themes.

As we said in our opening pages, in a certain sense every person is a psychologist. Every person develops a view of human nature and a strategy for predicting events. The theory and research presented in this book represent the efforts of psychologists to systematize what is known about human personality and to suggest areas for future exploration. We have tried to highlight

OVERVIEW AND A FINAL SUMMING UP

similarities in what different psychologists have been trying to do as well as differences in what they view as the best mode of conducting research. Although psychologists as a group are more explicit about their view of the person than is the average layperson, and although they are more systematic in their efforts to understand and predict human behavior, there are individual differences among them. In this book we have considered the theories of a number of psychologists in detail. They represent the major theories in the field although they are not the only ones, and they are representative of the diversity of approaches that can be considered reasonable and useful.

An effort has been made in this text to demonstrate that theory, assessment, and research are related to one another. In most cases some consistency can be found in the nature of theory proposed, the types of tests used to obtain data, and the problems selected for investigation. At the same time, it can be suggested that the theories of personality covered need not be considered mutually exclusive. In a very real sense, each represents a glimpse of the total picture. Human behavior is like a very complex jigsaw puzzle. The theories of personality considered have offered us many possible pieces for solution of the puzzle. Although some pieces may have to be discarded as not fitting the puzzle at all, and many remain outstanding, undoubtedly many of the pieces offered will be there when the final picture is put together.

REVIEW

1. Personality theories have repeatedly confronted basic problems, the solutions to these problems going far to define the basic nature of the theory. These issues are the philosophical view of the person; the relation between internal and external causes of behavior; consistency across situations and over time; the unity of behavior and the concept of the self; the concept of the unconscious; relations among cognition, affect, and overt behavior; and the relative importance of the past, present, and future.

2. All theories of personality seek to organize what is known and to advance our knowledge of what is not yet known. In doing so, the theories use concepts in relation to the following areas: structure, process, growth and development, psychopathology, and personality change. The theories covered can be compared in terms of the concepts emphasized in each of these areas (Table 15.1).

3. A multilevel approach is suggested in terms of integrating findings from neuroscience and other parts of biology into more traditional explanations for the phenomena of interest to personality psychologists.

4. It is again emphasized that theory, assessment, and research are generally closely linked with one another, with different observations leading to different theories that in turn suggest different approaches to assessment and research.

5. It is suggested that each of the theories covered in the text presents a glimpse of the complex totality that is personality.

ABA (own-control) research A Skinnerian variant of the experimental method consisting of exposing one subject to three experimental phases: (A) a baseline period, (B) introduction of reinforcers to change the frequency of specific behaviors, and (A) withdrawal of reinforcement and observation of whether the behaviors return to their earlier frequency (baseline period).

ABC assessment In behavioral assessment, an emphasis on the identification of antecedent (A) events and the consequences (C) of behavior (B); a functional analysis of behavior involving identification of the environmental conditions that regulate specific behaviors.

Ability, temperament, and dynamic traits In Cattell's trait theory, the categories of traits that capture the major aspects of personality.

Acquisition The learning of new behaviors, viewed by Bandura as independent of reward and contrasted with performance—which is seen as dependent on reward.

Adoption studies An approach to establishing genetic-behavior relationships through the comparison of biological siblings reared together with biological siblings reared apart through adoption. Generally combined with twin studies.

Anal personality Freud's concept for a personality type that expresses a fixation at the anal stage of development and relates to the world in terms of the wish for control or power.

Anal stage Freud's concept of that period of life during which the major center of bodily excitation or tension is the anus.

Anxiety An emotion expressing a sense of impending threat or danger to oneself.

Attachment behavioral system (ABS) Bowlby's concept emphasizing the early formation of a bond between infant and caregiver, generally the mother.

Attributions Beliefs about the causes of events.

Authenticity The extent to which the person behaves in accord with their self as opposed to behaving in terms of roles that foster false self-presentations

Bandwidth The area to which a theory or technique of assessment is applicable.

Behavioral assessment The emphasis in assessment on specific behaviors that are tied to defined situational characteristics (e.g., ABC approach).

Behavioral genetics The study of genetic contributions to behaviors of interest to psychologists, mainly through the comparison of degrees of similarity among individuals of varying degrees of biological-genetic similarity.

Behavioral signatures Mischel's concept for individually distinctive profiles of situation-behavior relationships.

Behaviorism An approach within psychology, developed by Watson, that restricts investigation to overt, observable behavior.

Bivariate method Cattell's description of the method of personality study that follows the classic experimental design of manipulating an independent variable and observing the effects on a dependent variable.

Cardinal trait Allport's concept for a disposition that is so pervasive and outstanding in a person's life that virtually every act is traceable to its influence.

Case studies An approach to research in which one studies an individual person in great detail. This study is commonly associated with clinical research, that is, research conducted by a therapist in the course of in-depth experience with a client.

Castration anxiety Freud's concept of the boy's fear, experienced during the phallic stage, that the father will cut off the son's penis because of their sexual rivalry for the mother.

Catharsis The release and freeing of emotion through talking about one's problems.

Central trait Allport's concept for a disposition to behave in a particular way in a range of situations.

Classical conditioning A process, emphasized by Pavlov, in which a previously neutral stimulus becomes capable of eliciting a response because of its association with a stimulus that automatically produces the same or a similar response.

Client-centered therapy Rogers's term for his earlier approach to therapy in which the counselor's attitude is one of interest in the ways in which the client experiences the self and the world.

Clinical method Cattell's description of the method of personality study in which there is an interest in complex patterns of behavior as they occur in life, but variables are not assessed in a systematic way.

Cognitive-affective processing system (CAPS) A theoretical framework developed by Mischel and colleagues in which personality is understood as containing a large set of highly interconnected cognitive and emotional processes; the interconnections cause personality to function in an integrate, coherent way, or as a "system."

Cognitive complexity/simplicity   An aspect of a person's cognitive functioning that is defined at one end by the use of many constructs with many relationships to one another (complexity) and at the other end by the use of few constructs with limited relationships to one another (simplicity).

Collective unconscious   Carl Jung's term for inherited, universal, unconscious features of mental life that reflect the evolutionary experience of the human species.

Competencies   A structural unit in social-cognitive theory that refers to an individual's capacity to solve problems or perform tasks necessary to achieve specific goals.

Conditioned emotional reaction   Watson and Rayner's term for the development of an emotional reaction to a previously neutral stimulus, as in Little Albert's fear of rats.

Congruence   Rogers's concept expressing an absence of conflict between the perceived self and experience. Also one of three conditions suggested as essential for growth and therapeutic progress. See also "Empathic understanding" and "Unconditional positive regard".

Conscious   Those thoughts, experiences, and feelings of which we are aware.

Construct   In Kelly's theory, a way of perceiving, construing, or interpreting events.

Constructive alternativism   Kelly's view that there is no objective reality or absolute truth, but only alternative ways of construing events.

Context specifity   The idea that a given personality variable may come into play in some life settings, or contexts, but not others, with the result that a person's behavior may vary systematically across contexts.

Contingencies of self-worth   The positive and negative events on which one's feelings of self-esteem depends.

Contrast pole   In Kelly's personal construct theory, the contrast pole of a construct is defined by the way in which a third element is perceived as different from two other elements that are used to form a similarity pole.

Core construct   In Kelly's personal construct theory, a construct that is basic to the person's construct system and cannot be altered without serious consequences for the rest of the system.

Correlational coefficient   A numerical index that summarizes the degree to which two variables are related linearly.

Correlational research   An approach to research in which existing individual indifferences are measured and related to one another, in contrast with the experimental approach to research.

Death instinct   Freud's concept for drives or sources of energy directed toward death or a return to an inorganic state.

Defense mechanisms   Freud's concept for those devices used by the person to reduce anxiety. They result in the exclusion from awareness of some thought, wish, or feeling.

Defensive pessimism   A coping strategy in which people use negative thinking as a way of coping with stress.

Delay of gratification   The postponement of pleasure until the optimum or proper time, a concept particularly emphasized in social-cognitive theory in relation to self-regulation.

Demand characteristics   Cues that are implicit (hidden) in the experimental setting and influence the subject's behavior.

Denial   The defense mechanism in which a painful internal or external reality is denied.

Direct external consequences   In social-cognitive theory, the external events that follow behavior and influence future performance, contrasted with vicarious consequences and self-produced consequences.

Discrimination   In conditioning, the differential response to stimuli depending on whether they have been associated with pleasure, pain, or neutral events.

Distortion   According to Rogers, a defensive process in which experience is changed so as to be brought into awareness in a form that is consistent with the self.

Dysfunctional expectancies   In social-cognitive theory, maladaptive expectations concerning the consequences of specific behaviors.

Dysfunctional self-evaluations   In social-cognitive theory, maladaptive standards for self-reward that have important implications for psychopathology.

Ego   Freud's structural concept for the part of personality that attempts to satisfy drives (instincts) in accordance with reality and the person's moral values.

Emotion-focused coping   Coping in which an individual strives to improve his or her internal emotional state, for example, by emotional distancing or the seeking of social support.

Empathic understanding   Rogers's term for the ability to perceive experiences and feelings and their meanings from the standpoint of another person. One of three therapist conditions essential for therapeutic progress. See also "Congruence" and "Unconditional positive regard."

Energy system   Freud's view of personality as involving the interplay among various forces (e.g., drives, instincts) or sources of energy.

Erogenous zones   According to Freud, those parts of the body that are the sources of tension or excitation.

Evaluative standards Criteria for evaluating the goodness or worth of a person or thing. In social-cognitive theory, people's standards for evaluating their own actions are seen as being involved in the regulation of behavior and the experience of emotions such as pride, shame, and feelings of satisfaction or dissatisfaction with oneself.

Evolved psychological mechanisms The view that basic psychological mechanisms are the result of evolution by selection, that is, they exist and have endured because they have been adaptive to survival and reproductive success.

Existentialism An approach to understanding people and conducting therapy, associated with the human potential movement, that emphasizes phenomenology and concerns inherent in existing as a person. Derived from a more general movement in philosophy.

Expectancies In social-cognitive theory, what the individual anticipates or predicts will occur as the result of specific behaviors in specific situations (anticipated consequences).

Experimental research An approach to research in which the experimenter manipulates the variable and is interested in general laws, in contrast with the correlational approach to research.

Experimenter expectancy effects Unintended experimenter effects involving behaviors that lead subjects to respond in accordance with the experimenter's hypothesis.

Extinction In conditioning, the progressive weakening of the association between a stimulus and a response; in classical conditioning because the conditioned stimulus is no longer followed by the unconditioned stimulus; and in operant conditioning because the response is no longer followed by reinforcement.

Extraversion In Eysenck's theory, one end of the introversion-extraversion dimension of personality characterized by a disposition to be sociable, friendly, impulsive, and risk taking.

Facets In the five-factor model and on the NEO-PI-R, facets represent subcomponents or subscales of the five factors (see Five-factor model).

Factor analysis A statistical method for determining those variables or test responses that increase and decrease together. Used in the development of personality tests and of some trait theories (e.g., Cattell, Eysenck).

Fear In Kelly's personal construct theory, fear occurs when a new construct is about to enter the person's construct system.

Fidelity The area to which a theory or technique of assessment is particularly applicable.

Five-factor model An emerging consensus among trait theorists suggesting five basic factors to human personality: neuroticism, extraversion, openness, agreeableness, and conscientiousness.

Fixation Freud's concept expressing a developmental arrest or stoppage at some point in the person's psychosexual development.

Fixed-role therapy Kelly's therapeutic technique that makes use of scripts or roles for people to try out, thereby encouraging people to behave in new ways and to perceive themselves in new ways.

fMRI (functional magnetic resonance imaging) A brain imaging technique that identifies specific regions of the brain that are involved in the processing of a given stimulus or the performance of a given task; the technique relies on recordings of changes in blood flow in the brain.

Focus of convenience In Kelly's personal construct theory, those events or phenomena that are best covered by a construct or by the construct system.

Free association In psychoanalysis, the patient's reporting to the analyst of every thought that comes to mind.

Functional analysis In behavioral approaches, particularly Skinnerian, the identification of the environmental stimuli that control behavior.

Functional autonomy Allport's concept that a motive may become independent of its origins; in particular, motives in adults may become independent of their earlier basis in tension reduction.

Fundamental lexical hypothesis The hypothesis that over time the most important individual differences in human interaction have been encoded as single terms into language.

Generalization In conditioning, the association of a response with stimuli similar to the stimulus to which the response was originally conditioned or attached.

General principles approach Higgins's term for an analysis of personal and situational influences on thought and action in which a common set of causal principles is used to explain both cross-situational consistency in thought and action that results from personal influences and variability in thought and action that results from situational influences.

Generalized reinforcer In Skinner's operant conditioning theory, a reinforcer that provides access to many other reinforcers (e.g., money).

Genital stage In psychoanalytic theory, the stage of development associated with the onset of puberty.

Goals In social-cognitive theory, desired future events that motivate the person over extended periods of time and enable the person to go beyond momentary influences.

Guided mastery A treatment approach emphasized in social-cognitive theory in which a person is assisted in performing modeled behaviors.

Habit   In Hull's theory, an association between a stimulus and a response.

Heritability   The proportion of observed variance in scores in a specific population that can be attributed to genetic factors.

Hierarchy   A relation between entities in which one of them is an example of, or serves the purpose of, the other. In any given personality theory, different variables often are related hierarchically.

Hot versus cool attentional focus   The focusing of one thought on emotionally arousing (hot) versus less arousing (cool) aspects of a situation or stimulus.

Human potential movement   A group of psychologists, represented by Rogers and Maslow, who emphasize the actualization or fulfillment of individual potential, including an openness to experience.

Id   Freud's structural concept for the source of the instincts or all of the drive energy in people.

Ideal self   The self-concept the individual would most like to possess. A key concept in Rogers's theory.

Identification   The acquisition, as characteristics of the self, of personality characteristics perceived to be part of others (e.g., parents).

Implicit theories   Broad, generalizable beliefs that we may not be able to state explicitly in words, yet that influence our thinking.

Incongruence   Rogers's concept of the existence of a discrepancy of conflict between the perceived self and experience.

Independent versus interdependent construals of self   Alternative implicit beliefs about self-concept in which the self is viewed either as possessing a set of psychological qualities that are distinct of other people (independent self) or is viewed in terms of roles in family, social, and community relationships (interdependent self).

Inhibited-Uninhibited temperaments   Relative to the uninhibited child, the inhibited child reacts to unfamiliar persons or events with restraint, avoidance, and distress, takes a longer time to relax in new situations, and has more unusual fears and phobias. The uninhibited child seems to enjoy these very same situations that seem so stressful to the inhibited child. The uninhibited child responds with spontaneity in novel situations, laughing and smiling easily.

Internal working model   Bowlby's concept for the mental representations (images), associated with emotion, of the self and others that develop during the early years of development.

Introversion   In Eysenck's theory, one end of the introversion-extraversion dimension of personality characterized by a disposition to be quiet, reserved, reflective, and risk avoiding.

Isolation   The defense mechanism in which emotion is isolated from the content of a painful impulse or memory.

Knowledge-and-appraisal personality architecture (KAPA)   Theoretical analysis of personality architecture that distinguishes two aspects of cognition in personality functioning: enduring knowledge and dynamic appraisals of the meaning of encounters for the self.

Latency stage   In psychoanalytic theory, the stage following the phallic stage in which there is a decrease in sexual urges and interest.

L-data   Life-record data, that is data that involves records of behavior in everyday life situations.

Learning goals   In Dweck's social-cognitive analysis of personality and motivation, a goal of trying to enhance one's knowledge and personal mastery of a task

Libido   The psychoanalytic term for the energy associated first with the life instincts and later with the sexual instincts.

Life instinct   Freud's concept for drives or sources of energy (libido) directed toward the preservation of life and sexual gratification.

Maladaptive response   In the Skinnerian view of psychopathology, the learning of a response that is maladaptive or not considered acceptable by people in the environment.

Mechanism   An intellectual movement of the 19th century which argued that basic principles of natural science could explain not only the behavior of physical objects, but human thought and action.

Mechanisms of defense   See "Defense mechanisms."

Microanalytic research   Bandura's suggested research strategy concerning the concept of self-efficacy in which specific rather than global self-efficacy judgments are recorded.

Modeling   Bandura's concept for the process of reproducing behaviors learned through the observation of others.

Multivariate method   Cattell's description of the method of personality study, favored by him, in which there is study of the interrelationships among many variables at once.

Need for positive regard   See "Positive regard, need for."

NEO-PI-R   A personality questionnaire designed to measure people's standing on each of the factors of the five-factor model, as well as on facets of each factor.

Neuroticism   In Eysenck's theory, a dimension of personality defined by stability and low anxiety at one end and by instability and high anxiety at the other end.

Neurotransmitters   Chemical substances that transmit information from one neuron to another (e.g., dopamine and serotonin).

Nomothetic (strategies) Strategies of assessment and research in which the primary goal is to identify a common set of principles or laws that apply to all members of a population of persons.

Observational learning Bandura's concept for the process through which people learn merely by observing the behavior of others, called models.

OCEAN The acronym for the five basic traits: Openness, Conscientiousness, Extraversion, Agreeableness, and Neuroticism.

O-data Observer data (i.e., specific observations or ratings by knowledgeable observers such as parents, friends, or teachers based on observations).

Oedipus complex Freud's concept expressing the boy's sexual attraction to the mother and fear of castration by the father, who is seen as a rival.

Operant conditioning Skinner's term for the process through which the characteristics of a response are determined by its consequences.

Operants In Skinner's theory, behaviors that appear (are emitted) without being specifically associated with any prior (eliciting) stimuli and are studied in relation to the reinforcing events that follow them.

Optimism A coping strategy that features relatively realistic expectations about one's capabilities.

Oral personality Freud's concept of a personality type that expresses a fixation at the oral stage of development and who relates to the world in terms of the wish to be fed or to swallow.

Oral stage Freud's concept for that period of life during which the major center of bodily excitation or tension is the mouth.

OT-data In Cattell's theory, objective test data or information about personality obtained from observing behavior in miniature situations.

Parental investment theory The view that women have a greater parental investment in offspring than do men because women pass their genes on to fewer offspring.

Penis envy In psychoanalytic theory, the female's envy of the male's possession of a penis.

Perceived self-efficacy In social-cognitive theory, the perceived ability to cope with specific situations.

Perception without awareness Unconscious perception or perception of a stimulus without conscious awareness of such perception.

Perceptual defense The process by which an individual defends (unconsciously) against awareness of a threatening stimulus.

Performance The production of learned behaviors, viewed by Bandura as dependent on rewards, in contrast with the acquisition of new behaviors, which is seen as independent of reward.

Performance goals In Dweck's social-cognitive

analysis of personality and motivation, a goal of trying to make a good impression on other people who may evaluate you.

Peripheral construct In Kelly's personal construct theory, a construct that is not basic to the construct system and can be altered without serious consequences for the rest of the system.

Permeable construct In Kelly's personal construct system, a construct that allows new elements into it.

Person-situation controversy A controversy between psychologists who emphasize the importance of personal (internal) variables in determining behavior and those who emphasize the importance of situational (external) influences.

Personality architecture Term to describe the overall design and operating characteristics of those psychological systems that underlie personality functioning.

Phallic character Freud's concept of a personality type that expresses a fixation at the phallic stage of development and strives for success in competition with others.

Phallic stage Freud's concept for that period of life during which excitation or tension begins to be centered in the genitals and during which there is an attraction to the parent of the opposite sex.

Phenomenal field Rogers's concept for the individual's conscious and unconscious perceptions of the self and the world.

Phenomenology An approach within psychology that focuses on how the person perceives and experiences the self and the world.

Phrenology The early 19th century attempt to locate areas of the brain responsible for various aspects of emotional and behavioral functioning. Developed by Gall, it was discredited as quackery and superstition.

Plasticity The ability of parts of the neurobiological system to change, temporarily and for extended periods of time, within limits set by genes, to meet current adaptive demands and as a result of experience.

Pleasure principle According to Freud, psychological functioning based on the pursuit of pleasure and the avoidance of pain.

Positive regard, need for Rogers's concept expressing the need for warmth, liking, respect, and acceptance from others.

Preconscious Freud's concept for those thoughts, experiences, and feelings of which we are momentarily unaware but can readily bring into awareness.

Preverbal construct In Kelly's personal construct theory, a construct that is used but cannot be expressed in words.

Primary process In psychoanalytic theory, a form of thinking that is not governed by logic or reality testing and that is seen in dreams and other expressions of the unconscious.

Problem-focused coping   Attempts to cope by altering features of a stressful situation.

Process   In personality theory, the concept that refers to the motivational aspects of personality.

Projection   The defense mechanism in which one attributes to (projects onto) others one's own unacceptable instincts or wishes.

Projective test   A test that generally involves vague, ambiguous stimuli and allows subjects to reveal their personalities in terms of their distinctive responses (e.g., Rorschach Inkblot Test, Thematic Apperception Test).

Proximate causes   Explanations for behavior associated with current biological processes in the organism.

Psychoticism   In Eysenck's theory, a dimension of personality defined by a tendency to be solitary and insensitive at one end and to accept social custom and care about others at the other end.

Q-data   In Cattell's theory, personality data obtained from questionnaires.

Q-sort   An assessment device in which the subject sorts statements into categories following a normal distribution. Used by Rogers as a measure of statements regarding the self and ideal self.

Range of convenience   In Kelly's personal construct theory, those events or phenomena that are covered by a construct or by the construct system.

Rationalization   The defense mechanism in which an acceptable reason is given for an unacceptable motive or act.

Reaction formation   The defense mechanism in which the opposite of an unacceptable impulse is expressed.

Reality principle   According to Freud, psychological functioning based on reality in which pleasure is delayed until an optimum time.

Reciprocal determinism   The mutual effects of variables on one another (e.g., Bandura's emphasis on personal and environmental factors continuously affecting one another).

Regression   Freud's concept expressing a person's return to ways of relating to the world and the self that were part of an earlier stage of development.

Reinforcer   An event (stimulus) that follows a response and increases the probability of its occurrence.

Rejection sensitivity   A thinking style is characterized by anxious expectations of rejection in interpersonal relationships.

Reliability   The extent to which observations are stable, dependable, and can be replicated.

Repression   The primary defense mechanism in which a thought, idea, or wish is dismissed from consciousness.

Response style   The tendency of some subjects to respond to test items in a consistent, patterned way that has to do with the form of the questions or answers rather than with their content.

Role   Behavior considered to be appropriate for a person's place or status in society. Emphasized by Cattell as one of a number of variables that limit the influence of personality variables on behavior relative to situational variables.

Role Construct Repertory Test (Rep test)   Kelly's test to determine the constructs used by a person, the relationships among constructs, and how the constructs are applied to specific people.

Sample approach   Mischel's description of assessment approaches in which there is an interest in the behavior itself and its relation to environmental conditions, in contrast to sign approaches that infer personality from test behavior.

Schedule of reinforcement   In Skinner's operant conditioning theory, the rate and interval of reinforcement of responses (e.g., response ratio schedule and time intervals).

Schema   A cognitive structure that organizes information and thereby influences how we perceive and respond to further information.

S-data   Self-report data or information provided by the subject.

Secondary disposition   Allport's concept for a disposition to behave in a particular way that is relevant to few situations.

Secondary process   In psychoanalytic theory, a form of thinking that is governed by reality and associated with the development of the ego.

Selective breeding   An approach to establishing genetic-behavior relationships through the breeding of successive generations with a particular characteristic.

Self-actualization   The fundamental tendency of the organism to actualize, maintain, and enhance itself. A concept emphasized by Rogers and other members of the human potential movement.

Self-concept   The perceptions and meaning associated with the self, me, or I.

Self-consistency   Rogers's concept expressing an absence of conflict among perceptions of the self.

Self-discrepancies   In theoretical analyses of Higgins, incongruities between beliefs about one's current psychological attributes (the actual self) and desired attributes that represent valued standards or guides.

Self-enhancement   A motive to maintain or enhance positive views of the self.

Self-evaluative reactions   Feelings of dissatisfaction versus satisfaction (pride) in oneself that occur as people reflect on their actions.

Self-schemas Cognitive generalizations about the self that guide people's information processing.

Self-experience discrepancy Rogers's emphasis on the potential for conflict between the concept of self and experience—the basis for psychopathology.

Self-produced consequences In social-cognitive theory, the consequences to behavior that are produced personally (internally) by the individual and that play a vital role in self-regulation and self-control.

Self-regulation Bandura's concept for the process through which persons regulate their own behavior.

Self-verification A motive to obtain information that is consistent with one's self-concept.

Shared and Nonshared Environments The comparison in behavior genetics research of the effects of siblings growing up in the same or different environments. Particular attention is given to whether siblings reared in the same family share the same family environment.

Sign approach Mischel's description of assessment approaches that infer personality from test behavior, in contrast with sample approaches to assessment.

Similarity pole In Kelly's personal construct theory, the similarity pole of a construct is defined by the way in which two elements are perceived to be similar.

Situational specificity The emphasis on behavior as varying according to the situation, as opposed to the emphasis by trait theorists on consistency in behavior across situations.

Socioemotional selectivity theory Theoretical analysis by Carstensen that examines the ways in which social motivations shift across the course of life.

Source trait In Cattell's theory, behaviors that vary together to form an independent dimension of personality, which is discovered through the use of factor analysis.

State Emotional and mood changes (e.g., anxiety, depression, fatigue) that Cattell suggested may influence the behavior of a person at a given time. The assessment of both traits and states is suggested to predict behavior.

Stress inoculation training Meichenbaum's procedure for training individuals to cope with stress by changing their cognitions about stressful events.

Structure In personality theory, the concept that refers to the more enduring and stable aspects of personality.

Subception A process emphasized by Rogers in which a stimulus is experienced without being brought into awareness.

Sublimation The mechanism of defense in which the original expression of the instinct is replaced by a higher cultural goal.

Subliminal psychodynamic activation The research procedure associated with psychoanalytic theory in which stimuli are presented below the perceptual threshold (subliminally) to stimulate unconscious wishes and fears.

Submerged construct In Kelly's personal construct theory, a construct that once could be expressed in words, but now either one or both poles of the construct cannot be verbalized.

Subordinate construct In Kelly's personal construct theory, a construct that is lower in the construct system and is thereby included in the context of another (superordinate) construct.

Successive approximation In Skinner's operant conditioning theory, the development of complex behaviors through the reinforcement of behaviors that increasingly resemble the final form of behavior to be produced.

Superego Freud's structural concept for the part of personality that expresses our ideals and moral values.

Superfactor A higher-order or secondary factor representing a higher level organization of traits than the initial, primary factors derived from factor analysis.

Superordinate construct In Kelly's personal construct theory, a construct that is higher in the construct system and thereby includes other constructs within its context.

Surface trait In Cattell's theory, behaviors that appear to be linked to one another but do not in fact increase and decrease together.

Symptom In psychopathology, the expression of psychological conflict or disordered psychological functioning. For Freud, a disguised expression of a repressed impulse.

System A collection of highly interconnected parts that function together; in the study of personality, distinct psychological mechanisms may function together as a system that produces the psychological phenomena of personality.

Systematic desensitization A technique in behavior therapy in which a competing response (relaxation) is conditioned to stimuli that previously aroused anxiety.

Target behaviors (target responses) In behavioral assessment, the identification of specific behaviors to be observed and measured in relation to changes in environmental events.

T-data Test data or information obtained from experimental procedures or standardized tests.

Temperament Individual differences in general mood or quality of emotional response that appear early, remain fairly stable, are inherited, and based in biological processes.

Threat In Kelly's personal construct theory, threat occurs when the person is aware of an imminent, comprehensive change in his or her construct system.

Three-dimensional temperament model The three superfactors describing individual differences in temperament: Positive Emotionality (PE), Negative Emotionality (NE), and Disinhibition vs. Constraint (DvC).

Token economy Following Skinner's operant conditioning theory, an environment in which individuals are rewarded with tokens for desirable behaviors.

Trait A disposition to behave in a particular way, as expressed in a person's behavior over a range of situations.

Transference In psychoanalysis, the patient's development toward the analyst of attitudes and feelings rooted in past experiences with parental figures.

Twin studies An approach to establishing genetic-behavior relationships through the comparison of degree of similarity among identical twins, fraternal twins, and nontwin siblings. Generally combined with adoption studies.

Type The classification of people into a few groups, each of which has its own defining characteristics (e.g., introverts and extraverts).

Ultimate causes Explanations for behavior associated with evolution.

Unconditional positive regard Rogers's term for the acceptance of a person in a total, unconditional way. One of three therapist conditions suggested as essential for growth and therapeutic progress. (See also " Congruence" and "Empathic understanding").

Unconscious Those thoughts, experiences, and feelings of which we are unaware. According to Freud, this unawareness is the result of repression.

Undoing The defense mechanism in which one magically undoes an act or wish associated with anxiety.

Units of analysis A concept that refers to the basic variables of a theory; different personality theories invoke different types of variables, or different basic units of analysis, in conceptualizing personality structure.

Validity The extent to which our observations reflect the phenomena or variables of interest to us.

Verbal construct In Kelly's personal construct theory, a construct that can be expressed in words.

Vicarious conditioning Bandura's concept for the process through which emotional responses are learned through the observation of emotional responses in others.

Vicarious experiencing of consequences In social-cognitive theory, the observed consequences to the behavior of others that influence future performance.

Working self-concept The subset of self-concept that is in working memory at any give time; the theoretical idea is that different social circumstances may activate different aspects of self-concept.

REFERENCES

ADAMS-WEBBER, J. R. (1979). *Personal construct theory: Concepts and applications.* New York: Wiley.

ADAMS-WEBBER, J. R. (1982). Assimilation and contrast in personal judgment: The dichotomy corollary. In J. C. Mancuso & J. R. Adams-Webber (Eds.), *The construing person* (pp. 96–112). New York: Praeger.

ADAMS-WEBBER, J. R. (1998). Differentiation and sociality in terms of elicited and provided constructs. *American Psychological Society, 9,* 499–501.

ADER, R., & COHEN, N. (1993). Psychoneuro-immunology: Conditioning and stress. *Annual Review of Psychology, 44,* 53–85.

ADOLPHS, R., RUSSELL, J. A., & TRANEL, D. (1999). A role for the human amygdala in recognizing emotional arousal from unpleasant stimuli. *Psychological Science, 10,* 167–175.

AINSWORTH, A., BLEHER, M., WATERS, E. & WALL, S. (1978). *Patterns of attachment: A psychological study of the strange situation.* Hillsdale, NJ: Erlbaum.

AINSWORTH, M. D. S., & BOWLBY, J. (1991). An ethological approach to personality development. *American Psychologist, 46,* 333–341.

AINSWORTH M. D., BLEHAR, M., WATERS, E., & WALL. S. (1978). *Patterns of attachment.* Hillsdale, NJ: Erlbaum.

ALEXANDER, F., & FRENCH, T. M. (1946). *Psychoanalytic therapy.* New York: Ronald.

ALLEN, J. J., IACONO, W. G., DEPUE, R. A., & ARBISI, P. (1993). Regional electroencephalographic asymmetries in bipolar seasonal affective disorder before and after exposure to bright light. *Biological Psychiatry, 33,* 642–646.

ALLOY, L. B., ABRAMSON, L. Y., & FRANCIS, E. L. (1999). Do negative cognitive styles confer vulnerability to depression? *Current Directions in Psychological Science, 8,* 128–132.

ALLPORT, F. H., & ALLPORT, G. W. (1921). Personality traits: Their classification and measurement. *Journal of Abnormal and Social Psychology, 16,* 1–40.

ALLPORT, G. W. (1937). *Personality: A psychological interpretation.* New York: Holt, Rinehart & Winston.

ALLPORT, G. W. (1958). What units shall we employ? In G. Lindzey (Ed.), *Assessment of human motives* (pp. 239–260). New York: Holt, Rinehart & Winston.

ALLPORT, G. W. (1961). *Pattern and growth in personality.* New York: Holt, Rinehart, & Winston.

ALLPORT, G. W. (1967). Autobiography. In E. G. Boring & G. Lindzey (Eds.), *A history of psychology in autobiography* (pp. 1–26). New York: Appleton-Century-Crofts.

ALLPORT, G. W., & ODBERT, H. S. (1936). Trait-names: A psycholexical study. *Psychological Monographs, 47* (Whole No. 211).

AMERICAN PSYCHOLOGICAL SOCIETY OBSERVER, The accuracy of recovered memories. July 1992, p. 6.

ANDERSEN, B. L., & CYRANOWSKI, J. M. (1994). Women's sexual self-schema. *Journal of Personality and Social Psychology, 67,* 1079–1100.

ANDERSEN, S. M., & BERK, M. S. (1998). The social-cognitive model of transference: Experiencing past relationships in the present. *Current Directions in Psychological Science, 7,* 109–115.

ANDERSEN, S. M., & CHEN, S. (2002). The relational self: An interpersonal social-cognitive theory. *Psychological Review, 109,* 619–645.

ANDERSEN, S. M., & COLE, S. W. (1990). "Do I know you?": The role of significant others in general social perception. *Journal of Personality & Social Psychology, 59,* 384–399.

ANDERSEN, S. M., GLASSMAN, N. S., CHEN, S., & COLE, S. W. (1995). Transference in social perception: The role of chronic accessibility in significant-other representations. *Journal of Personality & Social Psychology, 69,* 41–57.

ANDERSEN, S. M., REZNIK, I., & MANZELLA, L. M. (1996). Eliciting facial affect, motivation, and expectancies in transference: Significant-other representations in social relations. *Journal of Personality & Social Psychology, 71,* 1108–1129.

ANDERSON, C. A., & BUSHMAN, B. J. (2001). Effects of violent video games on aggressive behavior, aggressive cognition, aggressive affect, physiological arousal, and prosocial behavior: A meta-analytic review of the scientific literature. *Psychological Science, 12,* 353–359.

ANDERSON, N., & ONES, D. S. (2003). The construct validity of three entry level personality inventories used in the UK: Cautionary findings from a multiple-inventory investigation. *European Journal of Personality, 17,* S39–S66.

ANTONUCCIO, D. O., THOMAS, M., & DANTON, W. G. (1997). A cost-effectiveness analysis of cognitive behavior therapy and fluoxetine (Prozac) in the treatment of depression. *Behavior Therapy, 28,* 187–210.

APA ETHICAL PRINCIPLES OF PSYCHOLOGISTS. (1981). *American Psychologist, 36,* 633–638.

APA MONITOR. (1982). The spreading case of fraud, 13, 1.

APA MONITOR. (1990). The risk of emotion suppression, July 14.

ARONSON, E., & METTEE, D. R. (1968). Dishonest

behavior as a function of differential levels of induced self-esteem. *Journal of Personality and Social Psychology, 9,* 121–127.

ASENDORPF, J. B., BANSE, R., & MÜCKE, D. (2002). Double dissociation between implicit and explicit personality self-concept: The case of shy behavior. *Journal of Personality and Social Psychology, 83,* 380–393.

ASENDORPF, J. B., CASPI, A., & HOFSTEE, W. K. B. (Eds.) (2002). The puzzle of personality types. Special Issue, *European Journal of Personality, 16,* Issue S1.

ASENDORPF, J. B., & VAN AKEN, M. A. G. (1999). Resilient, overcontrolled, and undercontrolled personality prototypes in childhood: Replicability, predictive power, and the trait-type issue. *Journal of Personality and Social Psychology, 77,* 815–832.

ASHTON, M. C., LEE, K., & PAUNONEN, S. V. (2002). What is the central feature of extraversion? Social attention versus reward sensitivity. *Journal of Personality and Social Psychology, 83,* 245–252.

ASPINWALL, L. G., & STAUDINGER, U. M. (Eds.) (2002). *A psychology of human strengths: Perspectives on an emerging field.* Washington, DC: American Psychological Association.

AYDUK, O., MISCHEL, W., & DOWNEY, G. (2002). Attentional mechanisms linking rejection to hostile reactivity: The role of "hot" versus "cool" focus. *Psychological Science, 13,* 443–448.

AYLLON, T., & AZRIN, H. H. (1965). The measurement and reinforcement of behavior of psychotics. *Journal of the Experimental Analysis of Behavior, 8,* 357–383.

BAKERMANS-KRANENBURG, M. J., & VAN IZENDOORN, M. H. (1993). A psychometric study of the Adult Attachment Interview: Reliability and discriminant validity. *Developmental Psychology, 29,* 870–879.

BALAY, J., & SHEVRIN, H. (1988). The subliminal psychodynamic activation method. *American Psychologist, 43,* 161–174.

BALAY, J., & SHEVRIN, H. (1989). SPA is subliminal, but is it psychodynamically activating? *American Psychologist, 44,* 1423–1426.

BALDWIN, A., CRITELLI, J. W., STEVENS, L. C., & RUSSELL, S. (1986). Androgyny and sex role measurement: A personal construct approach. *Journal of Personality and Social Psychology, 51,* 1081–1088.

BALDWIN, A. L. (1949). The effect of home environment on nursery school behavior. *Child Development, 20,* 49–61.

BALDWIN, M. W. (1999). Relational schemas: Research into social-cognitive aspects of interpersonal experience. In D. Cervone & Y. Shoda (Eds.), *The coherence of personality: Social-cognitive bases of consistency, variability, and organization* (pp. 127–154). New York: Guilford Press.

BALTES, P. B. (1997). On the incomplete architecture of human ontogeny: Selection, optimization, and, compensation as foundation of developmental theory. *American Psychologist, 52,* 366–380.

BALTES, P. B., & BALTES, M. M., (1990). *Successful aging. Perspective from the Behavioral Sciences.* Cambridge, UK: Cambridge University Press.

BALTES, P. B., & GRAF, P. (1996). Psychological aspects of aging: Facts and frontiers. In D. Magnusson (Ed.), *The lifespan development of individuals: Behavioral, neurobiological, and psychosocial perspectives* (pp. 427–460). Cambridge, UK: Cambridge University Press.

BALTES, P. B., & MAYER, K. U. (1999). *The Berlin aging study: Aging from 70 to 100.* Cambridge, UK: Cambridge University Press.

BALTES, P. B., & STAUDINGER, U. M. (2000). Wisdom: A metheuristic (pragmatic) to orchestrate mind and virtue toward excellence. *American Psychologist, 55,* 122–136.

BALTES, P. B., STAUDINGER, U. M., & LINDENBERGER, U. (1999). Lifespan psychology: Theory and application to intellectual functioning. *Annual Review of Psychology, 50,* 471–507.

BANAJI, M., & PRENTICE, D. A. (1994). The self in social-contexts. *Annual Review of Psychology, 45,* 297–332.

BANDURA, A. (1965). Influence of models' reinforcement contingencies on the acquisition of imitative responses. *Journal of Personality and Social Psychology, 1,* 589–595.

BANDURA, A. (1969). *Principles of behavior modification.* New York: Holt, Rinehart and Winston.

BANDURA, A. (1972). The process and practice of participant modeling treatment. Paper presented at the Conference on the Behavioral Basis of Mental Health, Ireland.

BANDURA, A. (1977a). Self-efficacy: Toward a unifying theory of behavioral change. *Psychological Review, 84,* 191–215.

BANDURA, A. (1977b). *Social learning theory.* Englewood Cliffs, NJ: Prentice Hall.

BANDURA, A. (1986). *Social foundations of thought and action: A social cognitive theory.* Englewood Cliffs, NJ: Prentice Hall.

BANDURA, A. (1989a). Social cognitive theory. *Annals of Child Development, 6,* 1–60.

BANDURA, A. (1989b). Self-regulation of motivation and action through internal standards and goal systems. In L. A. Pervin (Ed.), *Goal concepts in personality and social psychology* (pp. 19–85). Hillsdale, NJ: Erlbaum.

BANDURA, A. (1990). Self-regulation of motivation through anticipatory and self-reactive mechanisms. *Nebraska Symposium on Motivation, 38,* 69–164.

BANDURA, A. (1992). Self-efficacy mechanism in psychobiologic functioning. In R. Schwarzer (Ed.), *Self-*

efficacy: Thought control of action, (pp. 335–394). Washington, DC: Hemisphere.

BANDURA, A. (1997). *Self-efficacy: The exercise of control*. New York: Freeman.

BANDURA, A. (1999). Social cognitive theory of personality. In L. A. Pervin & O. P. John (Eds.), *Handbook of personality: Theory and research* (pp. 154–196). New York: Guilford.

BANDURA, A. (2001). Social cognitive theory: An agentic perspective. *Annual Review of Psychology, 52*, 1-26.

BANDURA, A. (2002). Environmental sustainability by sociocognitive deceleration of population growth. In P. Schmuch & W. Schultz (Eds.), *The psychology of sustainable development* (pp. 209–238). Dordrecht, The Netherlands: Kluwer.

BANDURA, A., & ADAMS, N. E. (1977). Analysis of self-efficacy theory of behavioral change. *Cognitive Therapy and Research, 1*, 287–310.

BANDURA, A., ADAMS, N. E., & BEYER, J. (1977). Cognitive processes mediating behavioral change. *Journal of Personality and Social Psychology, 35*, 125–139.

BANDURA, A., & CERVONE, D. (1983). Self-evaluative and self-efficacy mechanisms governing the motivational effect of goal systems. *Journal of Personality and Social Psychology, 45*, 1017–1028.

BANDURA, A., GRUSEC, J. E., & MENLOVE, F. L. (1967). Some social determinants of self-monitoring reinforcement systems. *Journal of Personality and Social Psychology, 5*, 449–455.

BANDURA, A., & KUPERS, C. J. (1964). Transmission of patterns of self-reinforcement through modeling. *Journal of Abnormal and Social Psychology, 69*, 1–9.

BANDURA, A., & LOCKE, E. A., (2003). Negative self-efficacy and goal effects revisited. *Journal of Applied Psychology, 88*, 87–99.

BANDURA, A., & MISCHEL, W. (1965). Modification of self-imposed delay of reward through exposure to live and symbolic models. *Journal of Personality and Social Psychology, 2*, 698–705.

BANDURA, A., PASTORELLI, C., BARBARANELLI, C., & CAPRARA, G. V. (1999). Self-efficacy pathways to childhood depression. *Journal of Personality and Social Psychology, 76*, 258-269.

BANDURA, A., REESE, L., & ADAMS, N. E. (1982). Microanalysis of action and fear arousal as a function of differential levels of perceived self-efficacy. *Journal of Personality and Social Psychology, 43*, 5–21.

BANDURA, A., & ROSENTHAL, T. L. (1966). Vicarious classical conditioning as a function of arousal level. *Journal of Personality and Social Psychology, 3*, 54–62.

BANDURA, A., ROSS, D., & ROSS, S. (1963). Imitation of film-mediated aggressive models. *Journal of Abnormal and Social Psychology, 66*, 3–11.

BANDURA, A., & SCHUNK, D. H. (1981). Cultivating competence, self-efficacy, and intrinsic interest. *Journal of Personality and Social Psychology, 41*, 586–598.

BANDURA, A., & WALTERS, R. H. (1959). *Adolescent aggression*. New York: Ronald.

BANDURA, A., & WALTERS, R. H. (1963). *Social learning and personality development*. New York: Holt, Rinehart, & Winston.

BARGH, J. A. (1997). The automaticity of everyday life. In R. S. Wyer, Jr. (Ed.), *Advances in social cognition* (Vol. 10, pp. 1-61). Mahwah, NJ: Erlbaum.

BARGH, J. A., & BARNDOLLAR, K. (1996). Automaticity in action: The unconscious as a repository of chronic goals and motives. In P. M. Gollwitzer & J. A. Bargh (Eds.), *The psychology of action* (pp. 457–481). New York: Guilford.

BARGH, J. A., & FERGUSON, M. J. (2000). Beyond behaviorism: On the automaticity of higher mental processes. *Psychological Bulletin, 126*, 925–945.

BARGH, J. A., & GOLLWITZER, P. M. (1994). Environmental control of goal-directed action: Automatic and strategic contingencies between situations and behavior. In W. D. Spaulding (Ed.), *Nebraska symposium on motivation: Vol. 41. Integrative views of motivation, cognition, and emotion* (pp. 71–124). Lincoln, NE: University of Nebraska Press.

BARGH, J. A., & TOTA, M. E. (1988). Context-dependent automatic processing in depression: Accessibility of negative constructs with regard to self but not others. *Journal of Personality and Social Psychology, 54*, 925–939.

BARLOW, D. H. (1991). Disorders of emotion. *Psychological Inquiry, 2*, 58–71.

BARON, R. A. (1987). Outlines of a grand theory. *Contemporary Psychology, 32*, 413–415.

BARONDES, S. H. (1998). Mood genes: Hunting for the origins of mania and depression. New York: W. H. Freeman.

BARTHOLOMEW, K., & HOROWITZ, L. K. (1991). Attachment styles among young adults: A test of a four-category model. *Journal of Personality and Social Psychology, 61*, 226–244.

BASEN-ENGQUIST, K. (1994). Evaluation of theory-based HIV prevention intervention in college students. *AIDS Education and Prevention, 6*, 412–424.

BAUMEISTER, R. F. (Ed.) (1991). *Escaping the self.* New York: Basic Books.

BAUMEISTER, R. F. (1999). On the interface between personality and social psychology. In L. A. Pervin & O. P. John (Eds.), *Handbook of personality: Theory and research* (pp. 367–377). New York: Guilford.

BAUMEISTER, R. F., CAMPBELL, J. D., KRUEGER, J. I., &

VOHS, K. D. (2003). Does high self-esteem cause better performance, interpersonal success, happiness, or healthier lifestyles? *Psychological Science in the Public Interest*, 4, Whole Issue (Supplement to Psychological Science).

BAUMRIND, D. (1993). The average expectable environment is not good enough: A response to Scarr. *Child Development, 64*, 1299–1317.

BECHARA, A., DAMASIO, H., & DAMASIO, A. R. (2000). Emotion, decision making and the orbitofrontal cortex. *Cerebral Cortex, 10*, 295–307.

BECK, A. T. (1987). Cognitive models of depression. *Journal of Cognitive Psychotherapy, 1*, 2–27.

BECK, A. T. (1988). *Love is never enough.* New York: Harper & Row.

BECK, A. T. (1993). Cognitive therapy: Past, present, and future. *Journal of Consulting and Clinical Psychology, 61*, 194–198.

BECK, A. T., FREEMAN, A., & ASSOCIATES. (1990). *Cognitive therapy of personality disorders.* New York: Guilford Press.

BECK, A. T., WRIGHT, F. D., NEWMAN, C. D., & LIESE, B. S. (1993). *Cognitive therapy of drug abuse.* New York: Guilford Press.

BENET, V., & WALLER, N. G. (1995). The Big Seven factor model of personality description: Evidence for its cross-cultural generality in a Spanish sample. *Journal of Personality and Social Psychology, 69*, 701–718.

BENET-MARTINEZ, V., & JOHN, O. P. (1998). Los Cinco Grandes across cultures and ethnic groups: Multitrait multimethod analyses of the Big Five in Spanish and English. *Journal of Personality and Social Psychology, 75*, 729–750.

BENJAMIN, J., LIN, L., PATTERSON, C., GREENBERG, B. D., MURPHY, D. L., & HAMER, D. H. (1996). Population and familial association between the D4 dopamine receptor gene and measures of novelty seeking. *Nature Genetics, 12*, 81–84.

BERGMAN, L. R., MAGNUSSON, D., & EL-KHOURI, B.M. (2003). *Studying individual development in an interindividual context: A process-oriented approach.* Mahwah, NJ: Erlbaum.

BERKOWITZ, L., & DONNERSTEIN, E. (1982). External validity is more than skin deep. *American Psychologist, 37*, 245–257.

BERNDT, T. J. (2002). Friendship quality and social development. *Current Directions in Psychological Science, 11*, 7–10.

BERNTSON, G. G., & CACIOPPO, J. T. (2000). Psychobiology and social psychology: Past, present, and future. *Personality and Social Psychology Review, 4*, 3–15.

BIERI, J. (1955). Cognitive complexity-simplicity and predictive behavior. *Journal of Abnormal and Social Psychology, 51*, 263-268.

BIERI, J. (1986). Beyond the grid principle. *Contemporary Psychology, 31*, 672–673.

BIERI, J., ATKINS, A., BRIAR, S., LEAMAN, R. L., MILLER, H., & TRIPOLDI, T. (1966). *Clinical and social judgment.* New York: Wiley.

BLOCK, J. (1971). *Lives through time.* Berkeley, CA: Bancroft Books.

BLOCK, J. (1977). Advancing the psychology of personality: Paradigmatic shift or improving the quality of research? In D. Magnusson & N. Endler (Eds.), *Personality at the crossroads* (pp. 37–64). Hillsdale, NJ: Erlbaum.

BLOCK, J. (1993). Studying personality the long way. In D. C. Funder, R. D. Parke, C. Tomlinson-Keasey, & K. Widaman (Eds.), *Studying lives through time*, (pp. 9–41). Washington, DC: American Psychological Association.

BLOCK, J. (1995). A contrarian view of the five-factor approach to personality description. *Psychological Bulletin, 117*, 187–215.

BLOCK, J. & ROBINS, R. W. (1993). A longitudinal study of consistency and change in self-esteem from early adolescence to early adulthood. *Child Development, 64*, 909–923.

BOLDERO, J., & FRANCIS, J. (2002). Goals, standards, and the self: Reference values serving different functions. *Personality & Social Psychology Review, 6*, 232-241.

BOLGER, N., DAVIS, A., & RAFAELI, E. (2003). Diary methods: Capturing life as it is lived. *Annual Review of Psychology, 54*, 579–616.

BORKENAU, P., & OSTENDORF, F. (1998). The big five as states: How useful is the five-factor model to describe intraindividual variations over time? *Journal of Research in Personality, 32*, 202–221.

BORNSTEIN, R. F., & MASLING, J. M. (1998). *Empirical perspectives on the psychoanalytic unconscious.* Washington, DC: American Psychological Association.

BORSBOOM, D., MELLENBERGH, G. J., & VAN HEERDEN, J. (2003). The theoretical status of latent variables. *Psychological Review, 110*, 203–219.

BOUCHARD, T. J., JR., LYKKEN, D. T., MCGUE, M., SEGAL, N. L., & TELLEGEN, A. (1990). Sources of human psychological differences: The Minnesota study of twins reared apart. *Science, 250*, 223–228.

BOUTON, M. E. (1994). Context, ambiguity, and classical conditioning. *Current Directions in Psychological Science, 3*, 49–53.

BRADLEY, R. H., & CORWYN, R. F. (2002). Socioeconomic status and child development. *Annual Review of Psychology, 53*, 371–399.

BRAMEL, D., & FRIEND, R. (1981). Hawthorne, the myth of the docile worker, and the class bias in psychology. *American Psychologist, 36*, 867–878.

BRÄNDTSTADTER, J., & WENTURA, D. (1995). Adjustment to shifting possibility frontiers in later life: Complementary adaptive modes. In R. A. Dixon & L. Bäckman (Eds.), *Compensating for psychological deficits and declines: Managing losses and promoting gains.* Mahwah, NJ: Erlbaum.

BRAUDEL, F. (1981). *The structures of everyday life: Civilization and capitalism, 15th–18th century* (Vol. 1). New York: Harper & Row.

BRESSLER, S. L. (2002). Understanding cognition through large-scale cortical networks. *Current Directions in Psychological Science, 11,* 58–61.

BRETHERTON, I. (1992). The origins of attachment theory: John Bowlby and Mary Ainsworth. *Developmental Psychology, 28,* 759–775.

BREWIN, C. R. (1996). Theoretical foundations of cognitive-behavior therapy for anxiety and depression. *Annual Review of Psychology, 47,* 33–57.

BRIGGS, S. R. (1989). The optimal level of measurement for personality constructs. In D. M. Buss & N. Cantor (Eds.), *Personality psychology: Recent trends and emerging directions* (pp. 246–260). New York: Springer-Verlag.

BRODY, N. (1988). *Personality: In search of individuality.* New York: Academic Press.

BROWN, I. B., JR., & INOUYE, D. K. (1978). Learned helplessness through modeling: The role of perceived similarity in competence. *Journal of Personality and Social Psychology, 36,* 900–908.

BROWN, J. D. (1998). *The self.* New York: McGraw-Hill.

BROWN, N. O. (1959). *Life against death.* New York: Random House.

BRUNER, J. S. (1956). You are your constructs. *Contemporary Psychology, 1,* 355–356.

BURGER, J. M., & COOPER, H. M. (1979). The desirability of control. *Motivation and Emotion, 3,* 381–387.

BUSHMAN, B. J., & ANDERSON, C. A. (2002). Violent video games and hostile expectations: A test of the general aggression model. *Personality & Social Psychology Bulletin, 28,* 1679–1686.

BUSS, A. H. (1988). *Personality: Evolutionary heritage and human distinctiveness.* Hillsdale, NJ: Erlbaum.

BUSS, A. H. (1989). Personality as traits. *American Psychologist, 44,* 1378–1388.

BUSS, A. H. (1997). Evolutionary perspectives on personality traits. In R. Hogan, J. Johnson, & S. Briggs (Eds.), *Handbook of personality psychology* (pp. 345–366). New York: Academic Press.

BUSS, A. H., & PLOMIN, R. (1975). *A temperament theory of personality development.* New York: Wiley Interscience.

BUSS, A. H., & PLOMIN, R. (1984). *Temperament: Early-developing personality traits.* Hillsdale, NJ: Erlbaun,

BUSS, D. M. (1989). Sex differences in human mate preferences : Evolutionary hypotheses tested in 37 cultures. *Behavioral and Brain Sciences, 12,* 1-14 .

BUSS, D. M. (1991). Evolutionary personality psychology. *Annual Review of Psychology, 42,* 459–492.

BUSS, D. M. (1995). Evolutionary psychology: A new paradigm for psychological science. *Psychological Inquiry, 6,* 1–30.

BUSS, D. M. (1999). Human nature and individual differences: The evolution of human personality. In L. A. Pervin & O. P. John (Eds.), *Handbook of personality: Theory and Research* (pp. 31–56). New York: Guilford.

BUSS, D. M. (2000). The evolution of happiness. *American Psychologist, 55,* 15–23.

BUSS, D. M., & CRAIK, K. H. (1983). The act frequency approach to personality. *Psychological Review, 90,* 105–126.

BUSS, D. M., & KENRICK, D. T. (1998). Evolutionary social psychology. In D. T. Gilbert, S. T. Fiske, & Lindzey, G. (EDS.), *The handbook of social psychology* (4th ed.) (pp. 982–1026). New York: McGraw-Hill.

BUSS, D. M., LARSEN, R., WESTEN, D., & SEMMELROTH, J. (1992). Sex differences in jealousy: Evolution, physiology and psychology. *Psychological Science, 3,* 251-255.

BUSSEY, K., & BANDURA, A. (1999). Social cognitive theory of gender development and differentiation. *Psychological Bulletin, 106,* 676–713.

CACIOPPO, J. T. (1999). The case for social psychology in the era of molecular biology. Keynote address at the Society for Personality and Social Psychology Preconference, June 3, 1999, Denver, CO.

CACIOPPO, J. T., & BERNTSON, G. G. (1992). Social psychological contributions to the decade of the brain: Doctrine of multilevel analysis. *American Psychologist, 47,* 1019–1028.

CAMPBELL, J. B., & HAWLEY, C. W. (1982). Study habits and Eysenck's theory of extroversion-introversion. *Journal of Research in Personality, 16,* 139–146.

CAMPBELL, J. D., & LAVALLEE, L. F. (1993). Who am I? The role of self-concept confusion in understanding the behavior of people with low self-esteem. In R. F. Baumeister (Ed.), *Self-esteem: The puzzle of low self-regard* (pp. 3–20). New York: Plenum.

CAMPBELL, W. K. (1999). Narcissism and romantic attraction. *Journal of Personality and Social Psychology, 77,* 1254–1270.

CANTOR, N. (1990). From thought to behavior: "Having" and "doing" in the study of personality and cognition. *American Psychologist, 45,* 735–750.

CANTOR, N. & KIHLSTROM, J. F. (1987). *Personality and social intelligence.* Englewood Cliffs, NJ: Prentice Hall.

CANTOR, N., NOREM, J. K., NEIDENTHAL, P. M., LANGSTON, C. A., & BROWER, A. M. (1987). Life tasks, self-concept ideals, and cognitive strategies in a life transition. *Journal of Personality and Social Psychology, 53,* 1178–1191.

CAPOREAL, L. R. (2001). Evolutionary psychology: Toward a unifying theory and a hybrid science. *Annual Review of Psychology, 52,* 706–628.

CAPRARA, G. V., & CERVONE, D. (2000). *Personality: Determinants, dynamics, and potentials.* New York: Cambridge University Press.

CAPRARA, G. V., & CERVONE, D. (2003). A conception of personality for a psychology of human strengths: Personality as an agentic, self-regulating system. In L. G. Aspinwall and U. M. Staudinger (Eds.), *A psychology of human strengths: Perspectives on an emerging field* (pp. 61–74). Washington, DC: American Psychological Association.

CAPRARA, G. V., & PERUGINI, M. (1994). Personality described by adjective: The generalizability of the Big Five to the Italian lexical context. *European Journal of Personality, 8,* 351–369.

CARNELLEY, K. B., PIETROMONACO, P. R., & JAFFE, K. (1994). Depression, working models of others, and relationships functioning. *Journal of Personality and Social Psychology, 66,* 127–140.

CARSTENSEN, L. L. (1995). Evidence for a life-span theory of socioemotional selectivity. *Current Directions in Psychological Science, 4,* 151–156.

CARSTENSEN, L. L. (1998). A life-span approach to social motivation. In J. Heckhausen & C. Dweck (Eds.), *Motivation and self-regulation across the life span* (pp. 341–364). New York: Cambridge University Press.

CARSTENSEN, L. L., & CHARLES, S. T. (2003). Human aging: Why is even good news taken as bad? In L. G. Aspinwall & U. M. Staudinger (Eds.), *A psychology of human strengths: Perspectives on an emerging field* (pp. 75–86). Washington, DC: American Psychological Association.

CARSTENSEN, L. L., & FREDRICKSON, B. L. (1998). Influence of HIV status and age on cognitive representations of others. *Health Psychology 17,* 494–503.

CARSTENSEN, L. L., ISAACOWITZ, D. M., & CHARLES, S. T. (1999). Taking time seriously: A theory of socioemotional selectivity. *American Psychologist, 54,* 165–181.

CARTWRIGHT, D. S. (1956). Self-consistency as a factor affecting immediate recall. *Journal of Abnormal and Social Psychology, 52,* 212–218.

CARVER, C. S., & BAIRD, E. (1998). The American dream revisited: Is it what or why you want it that matters? *Psychological Science, 9,* 289–292.

CARVER, C. S., & SCHEIER, M. F. (1998). *On the self-regulation of behavior.* New York: Cambridge University Press.

CASPI, A. (2000). The child is father of the man: Personality correlates from childhood to adulthood. *Journal of Personality and Social Psychology, 78,* 158–172.

CASPI, A. (2002). Social selection, social causation, and developmental pathways: Empirical strategies for better understanding how individuals and environments are linked across the life course. In L. Pulkkinen and A. Caspi (Eds.), *Paths to successful development; Personality in the life course* (pp. 281–301). Cambridge, UK: Cambridge University Press.

CASPI, A., & BEM, D. J. (1990). Personality continuity and change across the life course. In L. A. Pervin (Ed.), *Handbook of personality: Theory and research* (pp. 549–575). New York: Guilford Press.

CASPI, A., BEM, D. J., & ELDER, G. H. (1989). Continuities and consequences of interactional styles across the life course. *Journal of Personality, 57,* 375–406.

CASPI, A., & ROBERTS, B. (1999). Personality continuity and change across the life course. In L. A. Pervin & O. P. John (Eds.), *Handbook of personality: Theory and research* (pp. 300–326). New York: Guilford.

CASPI, A., SUGDEN, K., MOFFITT, T. E., TAYLOR, A., CRAIG, I. W., HARRINGTON, H., McCLAY, J., MILL, J., MARTIN, J., BRAITHWAITE, A., & POULTON, R. (2003). Influence of life stress on depression: Moderation by a polymorphism in the 5-HTT gene. *Science, 301,* 386-389.

CASSIDY, J., & SHAVER, P. R. (Eds.) (1999). *Handbook of attachment theory and research.* New York: Guilford.

CATTELL, R. B. (1965). *The scientific analysis of personality.* Baltimore: Penguin.

CATTELL, R. B. (1979). *Personality and learning theory.* New York: Springer.

CATTELL, R. B. (1990). Advances in Cattellian personality theory. In L. A. Pervin (Ed.), *Handbook of personality: Theory and research* (pp. 101–110). New York: Guilford Press.

CAVALLI-SFORZA, L. L., & CAVALLI-SFORZA, F. (1995). *The great human diasporas: The history of diversity and evolution.* Reading, MA: Addison-Wesley 1995

CERVONE, D. (1991). The two disciplines of personality psychology. *Psychological Science, 6,* 371–377.

CERVONE, D. (1997). Social-cognitive mechanisms and personality coherence: Self-knowledge, situational beliefs, and cross-situational coherence in perceived self-efficacy. *Psychological Science, 8,* 43–50.

CERVONE, D. (1999). Bottom-up explanation in personality psychology: The case of cross-situational coherence. In D. Cervone & Y. Shoda (Eds.), *The coherence of personality: Social-cognitive bases of personality consistency, variability, and organization* (pp. 303–341). New York: Guilford Press.

CERVONE, D. (2000a). Evolutionary psychology and explanation in personality psychology: How do we know which module to invoke? Special issue on Evolutionary Psychology (J. Heckhausen & P. Boyer, Eds.), *American Behavioral Scientist, 6,* 1001-1014.

CERVONE, D. (2004). The architecture of personality. *Psychological Review, 111.*

CERVONE, D., & CAPRARA, G. V. (2001). Personality assessment. In N. J. Smelser & P. B. Baltes (Eds.), *International encyclopedia of the social and behavioral sciences* (pp. 11281–11287). Oxford, UK: Elsevier.

CERVONE, D., KOPP, D. A., SCHAUMANN, L., & SCOTT, W. D. (1994). Mood, self-efficacy, and performance standards: Lower moods induce higher standards for performance. *Journal of Personality and Social Psychology, 67,* 499–512.

CERVONE, D., & MISCHEL, W. (2002). Personality science. In D. Cervone & W. Mischel (Eds.), *Advances in personality science* (pp. 1–26). New York: Guilford.

CERVONE, D., & PEAKE, P. K. (1986). Anchoring, efficacy, and action: The influence of judgmental heuristics on self-efficacy judgments and behavior. *Journal of Personality and Social Psychology, 50,* 492–501.

CERVONE, D., & SCOTT, W. D. (1995). Self-efficacy theory of behavioral change: Foundations, conceptual issues, and therapeutic implications. In W. O'Donohue & L. Krasner (Eds.), *Theories in behavior therapy.* Washington, DC: American Psychological Association.

CERVONE, D., & SHADEL, W. G. (2003). Idiographic methods. In R. Ferdandez-Ballasteros (Ed.), *Encyclopedia of psychological assessment* (pp. 456-461). London: Sage.

CERVONE, D., SHADEL, W. G., & JENCIUS, S. (2001). Social-cognitive theory of personality assessment. *Personality and Social Psychology Review, 5,* 33–51.

CERVONE, D., & SHODA, Y. (1999a). Beyond traits in the study of personality coherence. *Current Directions in Psychological Science, 8,* 27–32.

CERVONE, D., & WILLIAMS, S. L. (1992). Social cognitive theory and personality. In G. Caprara & G. L. Van Heck (Eds.), *Modern personality psychology* (pp. 200–252). New York: Harvester Wheatsheaf.

CHAPLIN, W. F., JOHN, O. P. & GOLDBERG, L. R. (1988). Conceptions of states and traits: Dimensional attributes with ideals as prototypes. *Journal of Personality and Social Psychology, 54,* 541–557.

CHEN, M., & BARGH, J. A. (1999). Consequences of automatic evaluation: Immediate behavioral predispositions to approach or avoid the stimulus. *Personality and Social Psychology Bulletin, 25,* 215–224.

CHEN, S., & ANDERSEN, S. M. (1999). Relationships from the past in the present: Significant-other representations and transference in interpersonal life. In M. P. Zanna (Ed.), *Advances in experimental social psychology* (pp. 123–190). San Diego, CA: Academic Press.

CHEUNG, F. M., LEUNG, K., FAN, R. M., SONG, W. Z.,

ZHANG, J. X., & ZHANG, J. P. (1996). Development of the Chinese Personality Assessment Inventory. *Journal of Cross-Cultural Psychology, 27,* 181–199.

CHIU, C. HONG, Y., MISCHEL, W., & SHODA, Y. (1995). Discriminative facility in social competence: conditional versus dispositional encoding and monitoring-blunting of information. *Social Cognition, 13,* 49–70.

CHODORKOFF, B. (1954). Self perception, perceptual defense, and adjustment. *Journal of Abnormal and Social Psychology, 49, 508–512.*

CHODRON, T. (1990). *Open heart, clear mind.* Ithaca, NY: Snow Lion.

CHOI, I., NISBETT, R. E., & NORENZAYAN, A. (1999). Causal attribution across cultures: Variation and universality. *Psychological Bulletin, 125,* 47–63.

CHOMSKY, N. (1987). Psychology and ideology. In J. Peck (Ed.), *The Chomsky reader* (pp. 157-182). New York: Pantheon Books.

CHURCH, A. T., KATIGBAK, M. S., & REYES, J. A. (1996). Towards a taxonomy of trait adjectives in Filipino: Comparing personality lexicons across cultures. *European Journal of Personality, 10,* 3–24.

CHURCHLAND, P. S. (2002). *Brain-wise: Studies in neurophilosophy.* Cambridge, MA: MIT Press.

CLARK, D. A., BECK, A. T., & BROWN, G. (1989). Cognitive mediation in general psychiatric outpatients: A test of the content-specificity hypothesis. *Journal of Personality and Social Psychology, 56,* 958–964.

CLARK, L. A., & WATSON, D. (1999). Temperament: A new paradigm for trait psychology. In L. A. Pervin & O. P. John (Eds.), *Handbook of personality: Theory and research* (pp. 399–423). New York: Guilford.

CLONINGER, C. R., SVRAKIC, D. M., & PRZBECK, T. R. (1993). A psychobiological model of temperament and character. *Archives of General Psychiatry, 50,* 975–990.

COHEN, S. (1996). Psychological stress, immunity, and upper respiratory infections. *Current Directions in Psychological Science, 5,* 86–90.

COLLINS, W. A., MACCOBY, E. E., STEINBERG, L., HETHERINGTON, E. M., & BORNSTEIN, M. H. (2000). Contempory research on parenting: The case for nature and nurture. *American Psychologist, 55,* 218–232.

COLVIN, C. R. (1993). "Judgable" people: Personality, behavior, and competing explanations. *Journal of Personality and Social Psychology, 64,* 861–873.

COLVIN, C. R., & BLOCK, J. (1994). Do positive illusions foster mental health? An examination of the Taylor and Brown formulation. *Psychological Bulletin, 116,* 3–20.

COLVIN, C. R., BLOCK, J., & FUNDER, D. C. (1995). Overly positive self-evaluations and personality: Negative implications for mental health. *Journal of Personality and Social Psychology, 68,* 1152–1162.

CONLEY, J. J. (1985). Longitudinal stability of personality traits: A multitrait-multimethod-multioccasion analysis. *Journal of Personality and Social Psychology, 49*, 1266–1282.

CONTRADA, R. J., CZARNECKI, E. M., & PAN, R. L. (1997). Health-damaging personality traits and verbal-autonomic dissociation: The role of self-control and environmental control. *Health Psychology, 16*, 451–457.

CONTRADA, R. J., LEVENTHAL, H., & O'LEARY, A. (1990). Personality and health. In L. A. Pervin (Ed.), *Handbook of personality: Theory and research* (pp. 638–669). New York: Guilford Press.

CONWAY, M. A., & PLEYDELL-PEARCE, C. W. (2000). The construction of autobiographical memories in the self-memory system. *Psychological Review, 107*, 261–288.

COOPER, M. L. (2002). Personality and close relationships: Embedding people in important social contexts. *Journal of Personality, 70*, 757–782.

COOPER, R. M., & ZUBEK, J. P. (1958). Effects of enriched and restricted early environments on the learning ability of bright and dull rats. Canadian *Journal of Psychology, 12*, 159–164.

COOPERSMITH, S. (1967). *The antecedents of self-esteem.* San Francisco: Freeman.

COSMIDES, L. (1989). The logic of social exchange: Has natural selection shaped how humans reason? Studies with the Wason selection task. *Cognition, 31*, 187–276.

COSTA, P. T., JR., & MCCRAE, R. R. (1985). *The NEO Personality Inventory manual.* Odessa, FL: Psychological Assessment Resources.

COSTA, P. T., JR., & MCCRAE, R. R. (1989). *The NEO-PI/NEO-FFI manual supplement.* Odessa, FL: Psychological Assessment Resources.

COSTA, P. T., JR., & MCCRAE, R. R. (1992). *NEO-PI-R: Professional manual.* Odessa, FL: Psychological Assessment Resources.

COSTA, P. T., JR., & MCCRAE, R. R. (1994b). Stability and change in personality from adolescence through adulthood. In C. F. Halverson, Jr., G. A. Kohnstamm, & Roy P. Martin (Eds.), *The developing structure of temperament and personality from infancy to adulthood* (pp. 139–155). Hillsdale, NJ: Erlbaum.

COSTA, P. T., JR., & MCCRAE, R. R. (1995). Primary traits of Eysenck's PEN system: Three- and five-factor solutions. *Journal of Personality and Social Psychology, 69*, 308–317.

COSTA, P. T., JR., & MCCRAE, R. R., (1998). TRAIT THEORIES OF PERSONALITY. IN BARONE, D. F., HERSEN, M., & VAN HASSELT, V. B. (Eds.), *Advanced Personality* (pp. 103–121). New York: Plenum.

COSTA, P. T., JR., & MCCRAE, R. R. (2001). A theoretical context for adult temperament. In T. D. Wachs & G. A. Kohnstamm (Eds.), *Temperament in context* (pp. 1–22). Mahwah, NJ: Erlbaum.

COSTA, P. T. JR., & MCCRAE, R. R. (2002). Looking backward: Changes in the mean levels of personality traits from 80 to 12. In D, Cervone & W. Mischel (Eds.), *Advances in personality science* (pp. 219–237). New York: Guilford Press.

COSTA, P. T., & WIDIGER, T.A. (Eds.) (1994). *Personality disorders and the five factor model of personality.* Washington, DC: American Psychological Association.

COSTA, P. T. JR., & WIDIGER, T. A. (2001). *Personality disorders and the five-factor model of personality* (2nd ed.). Washington, DC: American Psychological Association.

COX, T., & MACKAY, C. (1982). Psychosocial factors and psychophysiological mechanisms in the etiology and development of cancer. *Social Science and Medicine, 16*, 381–396.

COYNE, J. C. (1994). Self-reported distress: Analog or ersatz depression? *Psychological Bulletin, 116*, 29–45.

COZZARELLI, C. (1993). Personality and self-efficacy as predictors of coping with abortion. *Journal of Personality and Social Psychology, 65*, 1224–1236.

CRAIGHEAD, W. E., CRAIGHEAD, L. W., & ILARDI, S. S. (1995). Behavior therapies in historical perspective. In B. Bongar & L. E. Bentler (Eds.), *Comprehensive textbook of psychotherapy* (pp. 64–83). New York: Oxford University Press.

CRAMER, P. (1991a). *The development of defense mechanisms: Theory, research and assessment.* New York: Springer-Verlag.

CRAMER, P. (1996). *Storytelling, narrative, and the Thematic Apperception Test.* New York: Guilford.

CRAMER, P. (2003). Personality change in later adulthood is predicted by defense mechanism use in early adulthood. *Journal of Research in Personality, 37*, 76–104.

CRAMER, P., & BLOCK, J. (1998). Preschool antecedents of defense mechanism use in young adults: A longitudinal study. *Journal of Personality and Social Psychology, 74*, 159–169.

CREWS, F. (1993). The unknown Freud. *The New York Review of Books*, November 18, 55–66.

CROCKER, J., SOMMERS, S. R., & LUHTANEN, R. K. (2002). Hopes dashed and dreams fulfilled: Contingencies of self-worth and graduate school admissions. *Personality & Social Psychology Bulletin, 28*, 1275–1286.

CROCKER, J., & WOLFE, C. T. (2001). Contingencies of self-worth. *Psychological Review, 108*, 593–623.

CROCKETT, W. H. (1982). The organization of construct systems: The organization corollary. In J. C. Mancuso & J. R. Adams-Webber (Eds.), *The construing person* (pp. 62–95). New York: Praeger.

CRONBACH, L. J., & MEEHL, P. E. (1955). Construct validity in psychological tests. *Psychological Bulletin, 52*, 281–302.

CROSS, H. J. (1966). The relationship of parental training conditions to conceptual level in adolescent boys. *Journal of Personality, 34,* 348–365.

CROSS, S. E., & MARKUS, H. R. (1990). The willful self. *Personality and Social Psychology Bulletin, 16,* 726–742.

CROSS, S. E., & MARKUS, H. R. (1999). The cultural constitution of personality. In L. A. Pervin & O. P. John (Eds.), *Handbook of personality: Theory and research* (2nd ed., pp. 378–396). New York: Guilford Press.

CSIKSZENTMIHALYI, M. (1990). *Flow: The psychology of optimal experience.* New York: Harper & Row.

CSIKSZENTMIHALYI, M. (1997). *Finding flow: The psychology of engagement with everyday life.* New York: Basic Books.

CSIKSZENTMIHALYI, M. (1999). If we are so rich, why aren't we happy? *American Psychologist, 54,* 821–827.

CURTIS, R. C., & MILLER, K. (1986). Believing another likes or dislikes you: Behaviors making the beliefs come true. *Journal of Personality and Social Psychology, 51,* 284–290.

CYRANOWSKI, J. M., & ANDERSEN, B. L. (1998). Schemas, sexuality, and romantic attachment. *Journal of Personality and Social Psychology, 74,* 1364-1379.

DABBS, J. M., JR. (2000). *Heroes, rogues and lovers: Outcroppings of testosterone.* New York: McGraw-Hill.

DAMASIO, A. R. (1994). *Descartes' error.* New York: Avon.

DANNER, D. D., SNOWDON, D. A., & FRIESEN, W. V. (2001). Positive emotions in early life and longevity: Findings from the nun study. *Journal of Personality & Social Psychology, 80,* 804–813.

DARLEY, J. M., & FAZIO, R. (1980). Expectancy confirmation processes arising in the social interaction sequence. *American Psychologist, 35,* 867–881.

DARWIN, C. (1859). *The origin of the species.* London: Murray.

DARWIN, C. (1872). *The expression of the emotions in man and animals.* London: Murray.

DAVIDSON, R. J. (1994). Asymmetric brain function, affective style, and psychopathology. *Development and Psychopathology, 66,* 486–498.

DAVIDSON, R. J. (1995). Cerebral asymmetry, emotion, and affective style. In R. J. Davidson & K. Hugdahl (Eds.), *Brain asymmetry* (pp. 361–387). Cambridge, MA: Massachusetts Institute of Technology.

DAVIDSON, R. J. (1998). Affective style and affective disorders: Perspectives from affective neuroscience. *Cognition and Emotion, 12,* 307–330.

DAVIDSON, R. J., & FOX, N. A. (1989). Frontal brain asymmetry predicts infants' response to maternal separation. *Journal of Abnormal Psychology, 98,* 127-131.

DAVIS, P. J., & SCHWARTZ, G. E. (1987). Repression and the inaccessibility of affective memories. *Journal of Personality and Social Psychology, 52,* 155–162.

DAWES, R. M. (1994). *House of cards: Psychology and psychotherapy built on myth.* New York: The Free Press.

DEAUX, K. (1976). *The behavior of women and men.* Monterey, CA: Brooks/Cole.

DECI, E. L., KOESTNER, R., & RYAN, R. M. (1999). A meta-analytic review of experiments examining the effects of extrinsic rewards on intrinsic motivation. *Psychological Bulletin, 125,* 627–668.

DECI, E. L., & RYAN, R. M. (1985). *Intrinsic motivation and self determination in human behavior.* New York: Plenum.

DECI, E. L., & RYAN, R. M. (1991). A motivational approach to self: Integration in personality. *Nebraska Symposium on Motivation, 38,* 237–288.

DE FRUYT, F., & SALGADO, J. F. (Eds.) (2003). Personality and industrial, work and organizational applications. *European Journal of Personality, 17* (whole issue).

DEGLER, C. (1991). *In search of human nature.* New York: Oxford University Press.

DE LA RONDE, C., & SWANN, W. B., JR. (1998). Partner verification: Restoring shattered images of our intimates. *Journal of Personality and Social Psychology, 75,* 374–382.

DENES-RAJ, V. & EPSTEIN, S. (1994). Conflict between intuitive and rational processing: When people behave against their better judgment. *Journal of Personality and Social Psychology, 66,* 819–829.

DENNETT, D. C. (1984). *Elbow room: The varieties of free will worth wanting.* Cambridge, MA: MIT Press.

DENNETT, D. C. (2003). *Freedom evolves.* New York: Viking.

DEPUE, R. A. (1995). Neurobiological factors in personality and depression. *European Journal of Personality, 9,* 413–439.

DEPUE, R. A. (1996). A neurobiological framework for the structure of personality and emotion: Implications for personality disorders. In J. Clarkin & M. Lenzenweger (Eds.), *Major theories of personality disorders* (pp. 347–390). New York: Guilford.

DEPUE, R. A., & COLLINS, P. F. (1999). Neurobiology of the structure of personality: Dopamine, facilitation of incentive motivation, and extraversion. *Behavioral and Brain Sciences, 22,* 491–517.

DE RAAD, B., PERUGINI, M., HREBICKOVA, M., & SZAROTA, P. (1998). Lingua franca of personality: Taxonomies and structures based on the psycholexical approach. *Journal of Cross-Cultural Psychology, 29,* 212–232.

DERAKSHAN, N., & EYSENCK, M. W. (1997). Interpretive biases for one's own behavior and physiology in high-trait-anxious individuals and repressors.

Journal of Personality and Social Psychology, 73, 816–825.

DeSteno, D., Bartlett, M. Y., Braverman, J., & Salovey, P. (2002). Sex differences in jealousy: Evolutionary mechanism or artifact of measurement? *Journal of Personality and Social Psychology, 83,* 1103–1116.

Dewsbury, D. A. (1997). In celebration of the centennial of Ivan P. Pavlov's (1897/1902) *The Work of the Digestive Glands. American Psychologist, 52,* 933–935.

Di Blas, L., & Forzi, M. (1999). Refining a descriptive structure of personality attributes in the Italian language: The abridged big three circumplex structure. *Journal of Personality and Social Psychology, 76,* 451–481.

Dobson, K. S., & Shaw, B. F. (1995). Cognitive therapies in practice. In B. Bongar & L. E. Bentler (Eds.), *Comprehensive textbook of psychotherapy* (pp. 159–172). New York: Oxford University Press.

Dolnick, E. (1998). *Madness on the couch: Blaming the victim in the heyday of psychoanalysis.* New York: Simon & Schuster.

Donahue, E. M. (1994). Do children use the Big Five, too? Content and structural form in personality descriptions. *Journal of Personality, 62,* 45–66.

Donahue, E. M., Robins, R. W., Roberts, B., & John, O. P. (1993). The divided self: Concurrent and longitudinal effects of psychological adjustment and self-concept differentiation. *Journal of Personality and Social Psychology, 64,* 834–846.

Downey, G., & Feldman, S. I. (1996). Implications of rejection sensitivity for intimate relationships. *Journal of Personality and Social Psychology, 70,* 1327–1343.

Downey, G., Freitas, A. L., Michaelis, B., & Khouri, H. (1998). The self-fulfilling prophecy in close relationships: Rejection sensitivity and rejection by romantic partners. *Journal of Personality and Social Psychology, 75,* 545–560.

Duck, S. (1982). Two individuals in search of agreement: The commonality corollary. In J. C. Mancuso & J. R. Adams-Webber (Eds.), *The construing person* (pp. 222–234). New York: Praeger.

Dudycha, G. J. (1936). An objective study of punctuality in relation to personality and achievement. *Archives of Psychology, 29,* 1–53.

Dunn, J., & Plomin, R. (1990). *Separate lives: Why siblings are so different.* New York: Basic Books.

Dutton, K. A., & Brown, J. D. (1997). Global self-esteem and specific self-views as determinants of people's reactions to success and failure. *Journal of Personality and Social Psychology, 73,* 139–148.

Dweck, C. S. (1991). Self-theories and goals: Their role in motivation, personality, and development. In R. D. Dienstbier (Ed.), *Nebraska Symposium on Motivation* (pp. 199–235). Lincoln, NE: University of Nebraska Press.

Dweck, C. S. (1999). *Self-theories: Their role in motivation, personality, and development.* Philadelphia: Psychology Press/Taylor & Francis.

Dweck, C. S., Chiu, C., & Hong, Y. (1995). Implicit theories and their role in judgments and reactions: A world from two perspectives. *Psychological Inquiry, 6,* 267–285.

Dweck, C., & Leggett, E. (1988). A social-cognitive approach to motivation in personality. *Psychological Review, 95,* 256–273.

Dykman, B. M. (1998). Integrating cognitive and motivational factors in depression: Initial tests of a goal-orientation approach. *Journal of Personality and Social Psychology, 74,* 139–158.

Dykman, B. M., & Johll, M. (1998). Dysfunctional attitudes and vulnerability to depressive symptoms: A 14-week longitudinal study. *Cognitive Therapy and Research, 22,* 337–352.

Eagle, M., Wolitzky, D. L., & Klein, G. S. (1966). Imagery: Effect of a concealed figure in a stimulus. *Science, 18,* 837–839.

Eagly, A. H., & Wood, W. (1999). The origins of sex differences in human behavior. *American Psychologist, 54,* 408–423.

Ebstein, R. P. Novick, O. Umansky, R., Priel, B., Osher, Y., Blaine, D., Bennett, E., Newmanov, L., Katz, M., & Belmaker, R. (1996). Dopamine D4 receptor (D4DR) exon III polymorphism associated with the human personality trait of novelty seeking. *Nature Genetics, 12,* 78–80.

Edelman, G. M., & Tononi, G. (2000). *A universe of consciousness: How matter becomes imagination.* New York: Basic Books.

Edelson, M. (1984). *Hypothesis and evidence in psychoanalysis.* Chicago: University of Chicago Press.

Ehrlich, P. R. (2000). *Human natures: Genes, cultures, and the human prospect.* Washington, DC: Island Press.

Eisenberg, N., Fabes, R. A., Guthrie, I. K., & Reiser, M. (2000). Dispositional emotionality and regulation: Their role in predicting quality of social functioning. *Journal of Personality and Social Psychology, 78,* 136–157.

Eisenberger, R., Pierce, W. D., & Cameron, J. (1999). Effects of reward on intrinsic motivation—negative, neutral, and positive: Comment on Deci, Koestner, and Ryan. *Psychological Bulletin, 125,* 677–691.

Ekman, P. (1992). An argument for basic emotions. *Cognition and Emotion, 6,* 169–200.

Ekman, P. (1993). Facial expression and emotion. *American Psychologist, 48,* 384–392.

Ekman, P. (1994). Strong evidence for universals in

facial expressions: A reply to Russell's mistaken critique. *Psychological Bulletin, 115*, 268–287.

ELFENBEIN, H. A., & AMBADY, N. (2002). On the universality and cultural specificity of emotion recognition: A meta-analysis. *Psychological Bulletin,128*, 203–235.

ELIASZ, A., & KLONOWICZ, T. (2001). Top-down and bottom-up approaches to personality and their application to temperament. In A. Eliasz & A. Angleitner (Eds.), *Advances in research on temperament* (pp. 14–42). Lengerich, Germany: Pabst Science Publishers.

ELLIOTT, A. J., & DWECK, C. S. (1988). Goals: An approach to motivation and achievement. *Journal of Personality and Social Psychology, 54*, 5–12.

ELLIOT, A. J., & SHELDON, K. M. (1998). Avoidance personal goals and the personality-illness relationship. *Journal of Personality and Social Psychology, 75*, 1282–1299.

ELLIOT, A. J., SHELDON, K. M., & CHURCH, M. A. (1997). Avoidance personal goals and subjective well-being. *Personality and Social Psychology Bulletin, 9*, 915–927.

ELLIS, A. (1962). *Reason and emotion in psychotherapy.* Secaucus, NJ: Lyle Stuart.

ELLIS, A. (1987). The impossibility of achieving consistently good mental health. *American Psychologist, 42*, 364–375.

ELLIS, A., & HARPER, R. A. (1975). *A new guide to rational living.* North Hollywood, CA: Wilshire.

EMMONS, R. A. (1987). Narcissism: Theory and measurement. *Journal of Personality and Social Psychology, 52*, 11–17.

EMMONS, R. A. (1989). The personal striving approach to personality. In L. A. Pervin (Ed.), *Goal constructs in personality and social psychology* (pp. 87-126). Hillsdale, NJ: Erlbaum.

EMMONS, R. .A., & KAISER, H. A. (1996). Goal orientation and emotional well-being: Linking goals and affect through the self. In L. Martin & A. Tesser (Eds.), *Striving and feeling: Interactions among goals, affect, and self-regulation* (pp. 79-98). Mahwah, NJ: Erlbaum.

EPSTEIN, N., & BAUCOM, N. (1988). *Cognitive-behavioral marital therapy.* New York: Springer.

EPSTEIN, S. (1977). Traits are alive and well. In D. Magnusson, D. & N. S. Endler (Eds.), *Personality at the crossroads: Current issues in interactional psychology* (pp. 83-98). Hillsdale, NJ: Erlbaum.

EPSTEIN, S. (1979). The stability of behavior: I. On predicting most of the people much of the time. *Journal of Personality and Social Psychology, 37*, 1092–1126.

EPSTEIN, S. (1983). A research paradigm for the study of personality and emotions. In M. M. Page (Ed.), *Personality: Current theory and research* (pp. 91–154). Lincoln, NE: University of Nebraska Press.

EPSTEIN, S. (1992). The cognitive self, the psychoanalytic self, and the forgotten selves. *Psychological Inquiry, 3*, 34–37.

EPSTEIN, S. (1994). Integration of the cognitive and the psychodynamic unconscious. *American Psychologist, 49*, 709–724.

ERDELYI, M. (1984). *Psychoanalysis: Freud's cognitive psychology.* New York: Freeman.

ERDLEY, C. A., LOOMIS, C. C., CAIN, K. M., & DUMAS-HINES, F. (1997). Relations among children's social goals, implicit personality theories, and responses to social failure. *Developmental Psychology, 33*, 263–272.

ERICSSON, K. A., & SIMON, H. A. (1993). *Protocol analysis: Verbal reports as data.* Cambridge, MA: MIT Press.

ERIKSON, E. (1950). *Childhood and society.* New York: Norton.

ERIKSON, E. H. (1982). *The life cycle completed: A review.* New York: Norton.

ESTERSON, A. (1993). *Seductive mirage: An exploration of the work of Sigmund Freud.* New York: Open Court.

EVANS, R. I. (1976). *The making of psychology.* New York: Knopf.

EWART, C. K. (1992). The role of physical self-efficacy in recovery from heart attack. In R. Schwarzer (Ed.), *Self-efficacy: Thought control of action* (pp. 287–304). Washington, DC: Hemisphere.

EXNER, J. E. (1986). The Rorschach: A comprehensive system: Basic foundations (Volume 1, 2nd ed.). New York: Wiley.

EYSENCK, H. J. (1953). *Uses and abuses of psychology.* London: Penguin.

EYSENCK, H. J. (1970). *The structure of personality.* (3rd edition). London: Methuen

EYSENCK, H. J. (1979). The conditioning model of neurosis. *Behavioral and Brain Sciences, 2*, 155–199.

EYSENCK, H. J. (1982). *Personality genetics and behavior.* New York: Praeger.

EYSENCK, H. J. (1990). Biological dimensions of personality. In L. A. Pervin (Ed.), *Handbook of personality: Theory and research* (pp. 244–276). New York: Guilford Press.

EYSENCK, H. J., & BEECH, H. R. (1971). Counter conditioning and related methods. In A. E. Bergin & S. Garfield (Eds.), *Handbook of psychotherapy and behavior change* (pp. 543–611). New York: Wiley.

EYSENCK, S. B. G., & LONG, F. Y. (1986). A cross-cultural comparison of personality in adults and children: Singapore and England. *Journal of Personality and Social Psychology, 50*, 124–130.

FARBER, I. E. (1964). A framework for the study of personality as a behavioral science. In P. Worchel & D. Byrne (Eds.), *Personality change* (pp. 3–37). New York: Wiley.

Fazio, R. H., & Olson, M. A. (2003). Implicit measures in social cognition research: Their meaning and use. *Annual Review of Psychology, 54*, 297–327.

Feeney, J. A., & Noller, P. (1990). Attachment style as a predictor of adult romantic relationships. *Journal of Personality and Social Psychology, 58*, 281–291.

Ferster, C. B. (1973). A functional analysis of depression. *American Psychologist, 28*, 857- 870.

Fisher, S., & Fisher, R. L. (1981). *Pretend the world is funny and forever: A psychological analysis of comedians, clowns, and actors.* Hillsdale, NJ: Erlbaum.

Fiske, A. P., Kitayama, S., Markus, H. R., & Nisbett, R. E. (1998). The cultural matrix of social psychology. In D. T. Gilbert, S. T. Fiske, & G. Lindzey (Eds.) (1998). *The handbook of social psychology* (4th ed.) (pp. 915–981). New York: McGraw-Hill.

Fiske, S. T., & Taylor, S. E. (1991). *Social Cognition.* New York: McGraw-Hill.

Flavell, J. H. (1999). Cognitive development: Children's knowledge about the mind. *Annual Review of Psychology, 50*, 21–45.

Fleeson, W (2001). Toward a Structure- and Process-Integrated View of Personality: Traits as Density Distributions of States *Journal of Personality and Social Psychology, 80*, 1011–1027.

Fodor, J. A. (1983). *The modularity of mind: An essay on faculty psychology.* Cambridge, MA: MIT Press.

Folkman, S., Lazarus, R. S., Gruen, R. J., & DeLongis, A. (1986). Appraisal, coping, health status, and psychological symptoms. *Journal of Personality and Social Psychology, 50*, 571–579.

Fraley, R. C. (1999). *Attachment continuity from infancy to adulthood: Meta-analysis and dynamic modeling of developmental mechanisms.* Unpublished manuscript, University of California, Davis.

Fraley, R. C. (2002). Attachment stability from infancy to adulthood: Meta-analysis and dynamic modeling of developmental mechanisms. *Personality and Social Psychology Review, 6*, 123–151.

Fraley, R. C., & Shaver, P. R. (1998). Airport separations: A naturalistic study of adult attachment dynamics in separating couples. *Journal of Personality and Social Psychology, 75*, 1198–1212.

Fraley, R. C., & Spieker, S. J. (2003). Are infant attachment patterns continuously or categorically distributed? A taxometric analysis of strange situation behavior.*Developmental Psychology.*

Frankl, V. E. (1955). *The doctor and the soul.* New York: Knopf.

Frankl, V. E. (1958). On logotherapy and existential analysis. *American Journal of Psychoanalysis, 18*, 28–37.

Freud, A. (1936). *The ego and the mechanisms of defense.* New York: International Universities Press.

Freud, S. (1933). *New introductory lectures on psychoanalysis.* New York: Norton.

Freud, S. (1949). *Civilization and its discontents.* London: Hogarth Press. (Original edition, 1930.)

Freud, S. (1953). *A general introduction to psychoanalysis.* New York: Permabooks. (Boni & Liveright edition, 1924.)

Freud, S. (1953). The interpretation of dreams. In *Standard edition*, Vols. 4 & 5. London: Hogarth Press. (First German edition, 1900.)

Freud, S. (1953). *Three essays on sexuality.* London: Hogarth Press. (Original edition, 1905.)

Freud, S. (1959). Analysis of a phobia in a five-year-old boy. In *Standard edition*, Vol. 10. London: Hogarth Press. (First German edition, 1909.)

Freund, A. M., & Baltes, P. B. (1998). Selection, optimization, and compensation as strategies of life management: Correlations with subjective indicators of successful aging. *Psychology and Aging, 13*, 531–543.

Friedman, H. S., Tucker, J. S., Schwartz, J. E., Martin, L. R., Tomlinson-Keasy, C., Wingard, D. L., & Criqui, M. H. (1995b). Childhood conscientiousness and longevity: Health behaviors and cause of death. *Journal of Personality and Social Psychology, 68*, 696–703.

Friedman, H. S., Tucker, J. S., Schwartz, J. E., Tomlinson-Keasy, C., Martin, L. R., Wingard, D. L., & Criqui, M. H. (1995a). Psychosocial and behavioral predictors of longevity: The aging and death of the "Termites." *American Psychologist, 50*, 69–78.

Friman, P. C., Allen, K. D., Kerwin, M. L. E., & Larzelere, R. (1993). Changes in modern psychology: A citation analysis of the Kuhnian displacement thesis. *American Psychologist, 48*, 658–664.

Fromm, E. (1959). *Sigmund Freud's mission.* New York: Harper.

Funder, D. C. (1989). Accuracy in personality judgment and the dancing bear. In D. M. Buss & N. Cantor (Eds.), *Personality psychology: Recent trends and emerging directions* (pp. 210–223). New York: Springer-Verlag.

Funder, D. C. (1993). Judgments of personality and personality itself. In K. H. Craik, R. Hogan, & R. N. Wolfe (Eds.), *Fifty years of personality psychology* (pp. 207–214). New York: Plenum.

Funder, D. C. (1995). On the accuracy of personality judgment: A realistic approach. *Psychological Review, 102*, 652–670.

Funder, D. C., Kolar, D. C., & Blackman, M. C. (1995). Agreement among judges of personality: Interpersonal relations, similarity, and acquaintanceship. *Journal of Personality and Social Psychology, 69*, 656–672.

Funder, D. C., & Ozer, D. J. (1983). Behavior as a function of the situation. *Journal of Personality and Social Psychology, 44*, 107–112.

GABLE, S. L., REIS, H. T., & DOWNEY, G. (2003). He said, she said: A quasi-signal detection analysis of daily interactions between close relationship partners. *Psychological Science, 14,* 100–105.

GAENSBAUER, T. J. (1982). The differentiation of discrete affects. *Psychoanalytic Study of the Child, 37,* 29–66.

GAY, P. (1998). *Freud: A life for our time.* New York: Norton.

GEEN, R. G. (1984). Preferred stimulation levels in introverts and extroverts: Effects on arousal and performance. *Journal of Personality and Social Psychology, 46,* 1303–1312.

GEEN, R. G. (1997). Psychophysiological approaches to personality. In R. Hogan, J. A. Johnson, & S. R. Briggs (Eds.), *Handbook of Personality Psychology* (pp. 387–414). San Diego: Academic Press.

GEERTZ, C. (1973). *The interpretation of cultures.* New York: Basic Books.

GEERTZ, C. (2000). *Available light: Anthropological reflections on philosophical topics.* Princeton, NJ: Princeton University Press.

GEISLER, C. (1986). The use of subliminal psychodynamic activation in the study of repression. *Journal of Personality and Social Psychology, 51,* 844–851.

GERARD, H. B., KUPPER, D. A., & NGUYEN, L. (1993). The causal link between depression and bulimia. In J. M. Masling & R. F. Bornstein (Eds.), *Psychoanalytic perspectives in psychopathology* (pp. 225–252). Washington, DC: American Psychological Association.

GERGEN, K. J. (1971). *The concept of self.* New York: Holt.

GERGEN, K. J. (2001). Psychological science in a postmodern context. *American Psychologist, 56,* 803–813.

GIERE, R. N. (1999). *Science without laws.* Chicago: University of Chicago Press.

GIESLER, R. B., JOSEPHS, R. A., & SWANN, W. B., JR. (1996). Self-verification in clinical depression: The desire for negative evaluation. *Journal of Abnormal Psychology, 105,* 358–368.

GLADUE, B. A., BOECHLER, M., & McCAUL, D. D. (1989). Hormonal response to competition in human males. *Aggressive Behavior, 15,* 409–422.

GOBLE, F. (1970). *The third force: The psychology of Abraham Maslow.* New York: Grossman.

GOLDBERG, L. R. (1981). Language and individual differences: The search for universals in personality lexicons. In L. Wheeler (Ed.), *Review of personality and social psychology* (pp. 141–165). Beverly Hills, CA: Sage.

GOLDBERG, L. R. (1990). An alternative "description of personality": The Big-Five factor structure. *Journal of Personality and Social Psychology, 59,* 1216–1229.

GOLDBERG, L. (1992). The development of markers for the Big-Five factor structure. *Psychological Assessment, 4,* 26–42.

GOLDBERG, L. R. (1993). The structure of phenotypic personality traits. *American Psychologist, 48,* 26–34.

GOLDBERG, L. R., & ROSOLACK, T. K. (1994). The Big Five factor structure as an integrative framework: An empirical comparison with Eysenck's P-E-N model. In C. F. Halverson, Jr., G. A. Kohnstamm, & R. P. Martin (Eds.), *The developing structure of temperament and personality from infancy to adulthood* (pp. 7–35). New York: Erlbaum.

GOLDSMITH, H. H., & CAMPOS, J. J. (1982). Toward a theory of infant temperament: In R. M. Emde and R. J. Harmon (Eds.), *The development of attachment and affiliative systems* (pp. 161–193). New York: Plenum.

GOLDSMITH, T. H. (1991). *The biological roots of human nature.* Oxford, UK: Oxford University Press.

GOLDSTEIN, K. (1939). *The organism.* New York: American Book.

GOSLING, S. D., & JOHN, O. P. (1998, May). Personality dimensions in dogs, cats, and hyenas. Paper presented at the annual meeting of the American Psychological Society, Washington, DC.

GOSLING, S. D., & JOHN, O. P. (1999). Personality dimensions in nonhuman animals: A cross-species review. *Contemporary Directions in Psychological Science, 8,* 69–75.

GOSLING, S. D., JOHN, O. P., CRAIK, K. H., & ROBINS, R. W. (1998). Do people know how they behave? Self-reported act frequencies compared with on-line codings by observers. *Journal of Personality and Social Psychology, 74,* 1337–1349.

GOTTLIEB, G. (1998). Normally occurring environmental and behavioral influences on gene activity: From central dogma to probabilistic epigenesis. *Psychological Review, 105,* 792–802.

GOULD, E., REEVES, A. J., GRAZIANO, M. S. A., & GROSS, C. G. (1999). Neurogenesis in the neocortex of adult primates. *Science, 286,* 548–552.

GOULD, S. J. (1981). *The mismeasure of man.* New York: Norton.

GRANT, H., & DWECK, C. (1999). A goal analysis of personality and personality coherence. In D. Cervone & Y. Shoda (Eds.), *The coherence of personality: Social-cognitive bases of consistency, variability, and organization* (pp. 345–371). New York: Guilford Press.

GRAY, J. A. (1987). *The psychology of fear and stress.* Cambridge, UK: Cambridge University Press.

GRAY, J. A. (1990). A critique of Eysenck's theory of personality. In H. J. Eysenck (Ed.), *A model for personality,* (2nd ed.) Berlin: Springer-Verlag.

GRAY, J. A. (1991). Neural systems, emotion and personality. In J. Madden IV (Ed.), *Neurobiology of learning, emotion and affect.* New York: Raven Press.

GREENBERG, J. R., & MITCHELL, S. A. (1983). *Object*

relations in psychoanalytic theory. Cambridge, MA: Harvard University Press.

GREENE, J. D., SOMMERVILLE, R. B., NYSTROM, L. E., DARLEY, J. M., & COHEN, J. D. (2001). An fMRI investigation of emotional engagement in moral judgment. *Science, 293,* 2105–2108.

GREENSPOON, J. (1962). Verbal conditioning and clinical psychology. In A. J. Bachrach (Ed.), *Experimental foundations of clinical psychology.* New York: Basic Books.

GREENWALD, A. G., & BANAJI, M. R. (1995). Implicit social cognition: Attitudes, self-esteem, and stereotypes. *Psychological Review, 102,* 4–27.

GREENWALD, A. G., BANAJI, M. R., RUDMAN, L. A., FARNHAM, S. D., NOSEK, B. A., & MELLOT, D. S. (2002). A unified theory of implicit attitutudes, stereotypes, self-esteem, and self-concept. *Psychological Review, 109,* 3–25.

GRICE, J. W. (in press). Bridging the idiographic-nomothetic divide in ratings of self and others on the big five. *Journal of Personality.*

GRIFFIN, D., & BARTHOLOMEW, K. (1994). Models of the self and other: Fundamental dimensions underlying measures of adult attachment. *Journal of Personality and Social Psychology, 67,* 430–445.

GRIGORENKO, E. L. (2002). In search of the genetic engram of personality. In D. Cervone & W. Mischel (Eds.), *Advances in personality science* (pp. 29–82). New York: Guilford Press.

GRODDECK, G. (1961). *The book of the it.* New York: Vintage. (ORIGINAL EDITION, 1923.)

GROSS, J. L. (1999). Emotion and emotion regulation. In L. A. Pervin & O. P. John (Eds.), *Handbook of personality: Theory and research* (pp. 525–552). New York: Guilford.

GRUNBAUM, A. (1984). *Foundations of psychoanalysis: A philosophical critique.* Berkeley: University of California Press.

GRUNBAUM, A. (1993). *Validation in the clinical theory of psychoanalysis: A study in the philosophy of psychoanalysis.* Madison, CT: International Universities Press.

GRUSEC, J. E. (1992). Social learning theory and developmental psychology: The legacies of Robert Sears and Albert Bandura. *Developmental Psychology, 28,* 776–786.

HAGGBLOOM, S. J., WARNICK, R., WARNICK, J. E., JONES, V. K., YARBROUGH, G. L., RUSSELL, T. M., BORECKY, C. M., McGAHHEY, R., POWELL, J. L. III, BEAVERS, J., & MONTE, E. (2002). The 100 most eminent psychologists of the 20th century. *Review of General Psychology, 6,* 139–152.

HALL, C. S. (1954). *A primer of Freudian psychology.* New York: Mentor.

HALL, C. S., & LINDZEY, G. (1957). *Theories of personality.* New York: Wiley.

HALPERN, J. (1977). Projection: A test of the psychoanalytic hypothesis. *Journal of Abnormal Psychology, 86,* 536–542.

HALVERSON, C. F., KOHNSTAMM, G. A., & MARTIN, R P. (Eds.) (1994). *The developing structure of temperament and personality from infancy to adulthood.* Hillsdale, NJ: Erlbaum.

HALVERSON, C. F., JR., & WAMPLER, K. S. (1997). Family influences on personality development. In R. Hogan, J. Johnson, & S. Briggs (Eds.), *Handbook of personality psychology* (pp. 241–267). New York: Academic Press.

HAMER, D. (1997). The search for personality genes: Adventures of a molecular biologist. *Current Directions in Psychological Science, 6,* 111–114.

HAMER, D., & COPELAND, P. (1998). *Living with our genes.* New York: Doubleday.

HARARY, K., & DONOHUE, E. (1994). *Who do you think you are?* San Francisco: Harper.

HARKNESS, A. R., & LILIENFELD, S. O. (1997). Individual differences science for treatment planning: Personality traits. *Psychological Assessment, 9,* 349–360.

HARRÉ, R. (1998). *The singular self: An introduction to the psychology of personhood.* London: Sage.

HARRÉ, R., & SECORD, P. F. (1972). *The explanation of social behaviour.* Oxford, UK: Blackwell.

HARRINGTON, D. M., BLOCK, J. H., & BLOCK, J. (1987). Testing aspects of Carl Rogers's theory of creative environments: Child-rearing antecedents of creative potential in young adolescents. *Journal of Personality and Social Psychology, 52,* 851–856.

HARRIS, B. (1979). Whatever happened to Little Albert? *American Psychologist, 34,* 151–160.

HARRIS, C. R. (2000). Psychophysiological responses to imagined infidelity: The specific innate modular view of jealousy reconsidered. *Journal of Personality and Social Psychology, 78,* 1082–1091.

HARRIS, C. R. (2002). Sexual and romantic jealousy in heterosexual and homosexual adults. *Psychological Science, 13,* 7–12.

HARRIS, J. R. (1995). Where is the child's environment? A group socialization theory of development. *Psychological Review, 102,* 458–489.

HARRIS, J. R. (1998). *The nurture assumption: Why children turn out the way they do.* New York: Free Press.

HARRIS, J. R. (2000). Context-specific learning, personality, and birth order. *Current Directions in Psychological Science, 9,* 174–177.

HARTSHORN, H., & MAY, M. A. (1928). *Studies in the nature of character. Vol.1: Studies in deceit.* New York: Macmillen.

HAWKINS, R. P., PETERSON, R. F., SCHWEID, E., & BIJOU, S. W. (1966). Behavior therapy in the home:

Amelioration of problem parent-child relations with the parent in a therapeutic role. *Journal of Experimental Child Psychology, 4,* 99–107.

HAYDEN, B. C. (1982). Experience—A case for possible change: The modulation corollary. In J. C. Mancuso & J. R. Adams-Webber (Eds.), *The construing person* (pp. 170–197). New York: Praeger.

HAZAN, C., & SHAVER, P. (1987). Romantic love conceptualized as an attachment process. *Journal of Personality and Social Psychology, 52,* 511–524.

HAZAN, C., & SHAVER, P. (1990). Love and work: An attachment-theoretical perspective. *Journal of Personality and Social Psychology, 59,* 270–280.

HEILBRONER, R. L. (1986). *The wordly philosophers: The lives, times and ideas of the great economic thinkers.* New York: Simon and Schuster.

HEIMPEL, S. A., WOOD, J. V., MARSHALL, M. A., & BROWN, J. D. (2002). Do people with low self-esteem really want to feel better? Self-esteem differences in motivation to repair negative moods. *Journal of Personality & Social Psychology, 82,* 128–147.

HEINE, S. J., LEHMAN, D. R., MARKUS, H. R., & KITAYAMA, S. (1999). Is there a universal need for positive self-regard? *Psychological Review, 106,* 766–794.

HELSON, R., & KWAN, V. S. Y. (2000). Personality change in adulthood: The broad picture and processes in one longitudinal study. In S. Hampson (Ed.), *Advances in personality psychology* (Vol. 1), (pp. 77–106). East Sussex, UK: Psychology Press, Ltd.

HELSON, R., KWAN, V. S. Y., JOHN, O. P., & JONES, C. (2002). The growth of evidence for personality change in adulthood: Findings from research with personality inventories. *Journal of Research in Personality, 36,* 287–306.

HERMANS, H. J. M. (2001). The construction of a personal position repertoire: Method and practice. *Culture and Psychology, 7,* 323-365.

HESSE, H. (1951). *Siddhartha.* New York: New Directions.

HIGGINS, E. T. (1987). Self-discrepancy: A theory relating self and affect. *Psychological Review, 94,* 319–340.

HIGGINS, E. T. (1989). Continuities and discontinuities in self-regulatory self-evaluative processes: A developmental theory relating self and affect. *Journal of Personality, 57,* 407–444.

HIGGINS, E. T. (1990). Personality, social psychology, and person-situation relations: Standards and knowledge activation as a common language. In L. A. Pervin (Ed.), *Handbook of Personality: Theory and Research* (pp. 301-338). New York: Guilford.

HIGGINS, E. T. (1996). Knowledge activation: Accessibility, applicability, and salience. In E. T. Higgins & A. W. Kruglanski (Eds.), *Social psychology: Handbook of basic principles* (pp. 133–168). New York: Guilford.

HIGGINS, E. T. (1997). Beyond pleasure and pain. *American Psychologist, 52,* 1280–1300.

HIGGINS, E. T. (1999). Persons and situations: Unique explanatory principles or variability in general principles? In D. Cervone & Y. Shoda (Eds.), *The coherence of personality* (pp. 61–93). New York: Guilford.

HIGGINS, E. T., BOND, R. N., KLEIN, R., & STRAUMAN, T. (1986). Self-discrepancies and emotional vulnerability: How magnitude, accessibility, and type of discrepancy influence affect. *Journal of Personality and Social Psychology, 51,* 5–15.

HIGGINS, E. T., & KING, G. (1981). Accessibility of social constructs: Information processing consequences of individual and contextual variability. In N. Cantor & J. F. Kihlstrom (Eds.), *Personality, cognition, and social interaction* (pp. 69-121). Hillsdale, NJ: Erlbaum.

HIGGINS, E. T., KING, G. A., & MAVIN, G. H. (1982). Individual construct accessibility and subjective impressions and recall. *Journal of Personality and Social Psychology, 43,* 35–47.

HOFSTEE, W. K. B. (1994). Who should own the definition of personality? *European Journal of Personality, 8,* 149–162.

HOFSTEE, W. K. B., KIERS, H. A., DERAAD, B., GOLDBERG, L. R., & OSTENDORF, F. (1997). A comparison of Big Five structures of personality traits in Dutch, English, and German. *European Journal of Personality, 11,* 15–31.

HOGAN, J, & ONES, D. S. (1997). Conscientiousness and integrity at work. In R. Hogan, J. Johnson & S. Briggs (Eds.), *Handbook of personality psychology* (pp. 849–870). San Diego, CA: Academic Press.

HOLENDER, D. (1986). Semantic activation without conscious identification in dichotic listening, parafoveal vision, and visual masking: A survey and appraisal. *Behavioral and Brain Sciences, 9,* 1–66.

HOLLAND, J. L. (1985). *Making vocational choices: A theory of vocational personality and work environments.* Englewood Cliffs, NJ: Prentice-Hall.

HOLLON, S. D., DE RUBEIS, R. J., & EVANS, M. D. (1987). Causal mediation of change in treatment for depression: Discriminating between nonspecificity and noncausality. *Psychological Bulletin, 102,* 139–149.

HOLLON, S. D., & KENDALL, P. C. (1980). Cognitive self-statements in depression: Development of an Automatic Thoughts Questionnaire. *Cognitive Therapy and Research, 4,* 383–395.

HOLLON, S. D., SHELTON, R. C., & DAVIS, D. D. (1993). Cognitive therapy for depression: Conceptual issues and clinical efficacy. *Journal of Consulting and Clinical Psychology, 61,* 270–275.

HOLMES, D. S. (1981). Existence of classical projection and the stress-reducing function of attributive projection: A reply to Sherwood. *Psychological Bulletin, 90,* 460-466.

HOLT, R. R. (1978). *Methods in clinical psychology*. New York: Plenum.

HONG, Y., MORRIS, M. W., CHIU, C., & MARTINEZ, V. (2000). Multicultural minds: A dynamic constructivist approach to culture and cognition. *American Psychologist, 55*, 709–720.

HORNEY, K. (1937). *The neurotic personality of our time*. New York: Norton.

HORNEY, K. (1945). *Our inner conflicts*. New York: Norton.

HORNEY, K. (1973). *Feminine psychology*. New York: Norton.

HOUGH, L. M., & OSWALD, F. L. (2000). Personal selection: Looking toward the future—Remembering the past. *Annual Review of Psychology, 51*, 631–664.

HUESMANN, L. R., MOISE-TITUS, J., PODOLSKI, C., & ERON, L. D. (2003). Longitudinal relations between children's exposure to TV violence and their aggressive and violent behavior in young adulthood: 1977–1992. *Developmental Psychology, 39*, 201–221.

HULL, J. G., YOUNG, R. D., & JOURILES, E. (1986). Applications of the self-awareness model of alcohol consumption: Predicting patterns of use and abuse. *Journal of Personality and Social Psychology, 51*, 790–796.

HYMAN, S. (1999). Susceptibility and "second hits." In R. Conlan (Ed.), *States of mind* (pp. 24–28). New York: Wiley.

INGRAM, R. E., MIRANDA, J., & SEGAL, Z. V. (1998). *Cognitive vulnerability to depression*. New York: Guilford.

IYENGAR, S. S., & LEPPER, M. R. (1999). Rethinking the value of choice: A cultural perspective on intrinsic motivation. *Journal of Personality and Social Psychology, 76*, 349–366.

IZARD, C. E. (1991). *The psychology of emotion*. New York: Plenum.

IZARD, C. E. (1994). Innate and universal facial expressions: Evidence from developmental and cross-cultural research. *Psychological Bulletin, 115*, 288–299.

JACKSON, D. N., & PAUNONEN, S. V. (1985). Construct validity and the predictability of behavior. *Journal of Personality and Social Psychology, 49*, 554-570.

JACKSON, J. F. (1993). Human behavioral genetics, Scarr's theory, and her views on interventions: A critical review and commentary on their implications for African American children. *Child Development, 64*, 1318–1332.

JACOBY, L. L., LINDSAY, D. S., & TOTH, J. P. (1992). Unconscious influences revealed. *American Psychologist, 47*, 802–809.

JAMES, W. (1890). *Principles of psychology*. New York: Holt.

JANKOWICZ, A. D. (1987). Whatever became of George Kelly? *American Psychologist, 42*, 481–487.

JENSEN, M. R. (1987). Psychobiological factors predicting the course of breast cancer. *Journal of Personality, 55*, 317–342.

JOHN, O. P. (1990). The "Big Five" factor taxonomy: Dimensions of personality in the natural language and in questionnaires. In L. A. Pervin (Ed.), *Handbook of personality: Theory and research* (pp. 66–100). New York: Guilford Press.

JOHN, O. P., ANGLEITNER, A., & OSTENDORF, F. (1988). The lexical approach to personality: A historical review of trait taxonomic research. *European Journal of Personality, 2*, 171–203.

JOHN, O. P., CASPI, A., ROBINS, R. W., MOFFITT, T. E., & STOUTHAMER-LOEBER, M. (1994). The "Little Five": Exploring the nomological network of the Five-Factor model of personality in adolescent boys. *Child Development, 65*, 160–178.

JOHN, O. P., HAMPSON, S. E., & GOLDBERG, L. R. (1991). The basic level in personality-trait hierarchies: Studies of trait use and accessibility in different contexts. *Journal of Personality & Social Psychology, 60*, 348–361.

JOHN, O. P., & ROBINS, R. W. (1993). Gordon Allport: Father and critic of the Five-Factor model. In K. H. Craik, R. T. Hogan, & R. N. Wolfe (Eds.), *Fifty years of personality psychology* (pp. 215–236). New York: Plenum.

JOHN, O. P., & ROBINS, R. W. (1994a). Accuracy and bias in self-perception: Individual differences in self-enhancement and the role of narcissism. *Journal of Personality and Social Psychology, 66*, 206–219.

JOHN, O. P., & SRIVASTAVA, S. (1999). The Big Five: History, measurement, and development. In L. A. Pervin & O. P. John (Eds.), *Handbook of personality: Theory and research* (pp. 102–138). New York: Guilford.

JOLLY, A. (1999). *Lucy's legacy*. Cambridge, MA: Harvard University Press.

JONES, A., & CRANDALL, R. (1986). Validation of a short index of self-actualization. *Personality and Social Psychology Bulletin, 12*, 63–73.

JONES, M. C. (1924). A laboratory study of fear. The case of Peter. *Pedagogical Seminar, 31*, 308–315.

JOSEPHS, R. A., MARKUS, H., & TAFARODI, R. W. (1992). Gender and self-esteem. *Journal of Personality and Social Psychology, 63*, 391–402.

JOURARD, S. M., & REMY, R. M. (1955). Perceived parental attitudes, the self, and security. *Journal of Consulting Psychology, 19*, 364–366.

JUNG, C. G. (1939). *The integration of the personality*. New York: Farrar & Rinehart.

JUNG, C. G., AND COLLABORATORS (1964). *Man and his symbols*. New York: Doubleday & Company

KAGAN, J. (1994). *Galen's prophecy: Temperament in human nature*. New York: Basic Books.

KAGAN, J. (1998). *Three seductive ideas*. Cambridge, MA: Harvard University Press.

KAGAN, J. (1999). Born to be shy? In R. Conlan (Ed.), *States of mind* (pp. 29–51). New York: Wiley.

KAGAN, J. (2003). Biology, context, and developmental inquiry. *Annual Review of Psychology, 54*, 1–23.

KAGAN, J., ARCUS, D., & SNIDMAN, N. (1993). The idea of temperament: Where do we go from here? In R. Plomin & G. E. McClearn (Eds.), *Nature, nurture and psychology* (pp. 197–210). Washington, DC: American Psychological Association.

KANDEL, E. R. (2000). Autobiography. Retrieved August 28, 2002 from http://www.nobel.se/medicine/laureates/2000/kandel-autobio.html.

KANFER, F. H., & SASLOW, G. (1965). Behavioral analysis: An alternative to diagnostic classification. *Archives of General Psychiatry, 12*, 519–538.

KASSER, T., & RYAN, R. M. (1996). Further examining the American dream: Differential correlates of intrinsic and extrinsic goals. *Personality and Social Psychology Bulletin, 22*, 280–287.

KAVANAGH, D. (1992). Self-efficacy as a resource factor in stress appraisal processes. In R. Schwarzer (Ed.), *Self-efficacy: Thought control of action* (pp. 177–194). Washington, DC: Hemisphere.

KAZDIN, A. E. (1977). *The token economy: A review and evaluation*. New York: Plenum.

KAZDIN, A. E., & BOOTZIN, R. R. (1972). The token economy: An evaluative review. *Journal of Applied Behavior Analysis, 5*, 343–372.

KAZDIN, A. E., & WILSON, G. T. (1978). *Evaluation of behavior theory: Issues, evidence, and research strategies*. Cambridge, MA: Ballinger.

KELLER, H., & ZACH, U. (2002). Gender and birth order as determinants of parental behaviour. *International Journal of Behavioral Development, 26*, 177–184.

KELLEY, W. M., MACRAE, C. N., WYLAND, C. L., CAGLAR, S., INATI, S., & HEATHERTON, T. F. (2002). Finding the self? An event-related fMRI study. *Journal of Cognitive Neuroscience, 14*, 785–794.

KELLY, G. A. (1955).*The psychology of personal constructs*. New York: Norton.

KELLY, G. A. (1964). The language of hypothesis: Man's psychological instrument. *Journal of Individual Psychology, 20*, 137–152.

KELTNER, D., GRUENFELD, D. H., & ANDERSON, C. (2003). Power, approach, and inhibition. *Psychological Review, 110*, 265–284.

KENNY, D. A. (1994). *Interpersonal perception*. New York: Guilford.

KENNY, D. A., ALBRIGHT, L., MALLOY, T. E., & KASHY, D. A. (1994). Consensus in interpersonal perception: Acquaintance and the Big Five. *Psychological Bulletin, 116*, 245–258.

KENRICK, D. T. (1994). Evolutionary social psychology: From sexual selection to social cognition. *Advances in Experimental Social Psychology, 26*, 75–121.

KENRICK, D. T., & FUNDER, D. C. (1988). Profiting from controversy: Lessons from the person-situation debate. *American Psychologist, 43*, 23–34.

KENRICK, D. T., SADALLA, E. K., GROTH, G., & TROST, M. R. (1990). Evolution, traits, and the stages of human courtship: Qualifying the parental investment model. *Journal of Personality, 58*, 97–116.

KIHLSTROM, J. F. (1990). The psychological unconscious. In L. A. Pervin (Ed.), *Handbook of personality: Theory and research* (pp. 445–464). New York: Guilford Press.

KIHLSTROM, J. F. (1999). The psychological unconscious. In L. A. Pervin & O. P. John (Eds.), *Handbook of personality: Theory and research* (pp. 424–442). New York: Guilford.

KIHLSTROM, J. F., BARNHARDT, T. M., & TATARYN, D. J. (1992). The cognitive perspective. In R. F. Bornstein & T. S. Pittman (Eds.), *Perception without awareness*, (pp. 17–54). New York: Guilford Press.

KING, J. E., & FIGUEREDO, A. J. (1997). The Five-Factor Model plus dominance in chimpanzee personality. *Journal of Research in Personality, 31*, 257–271.

KIRKPATRICK, L. A. (1998). God as a substitute attachment figure: A longitudinal study of adult attachment style and religious change in college students. *Personality and Social Psychology Bulletin, 9*, 961–973.

KIRKPATRICK, L. A., & DAVIS, K. E. (1994). Attachment style, gender, and relationship stability: A longitudinal analysis. *Journal of Personality and Social Psychology, 66*, 502–512.

KIRSCHENBAUM, H. (1979). *On becoming Carl Rogers*. New York: Delacorte.

KITAYAMA, S., & MARKUS, H. R. (1999). Yin and Yang of the Japanese self: The cultural psychology of personality coherence. In D. Cervone & Y. Shoda (Eds.), *The coherence of personality: Social-cognitive bases of consistency, variability, and organization* (pp 242–302). New York: Guilford.

KITAYAMA, S., MARKUS, H. R., MATSUMOTO, H., & NORASAKKUNIT, V. (1997). Individual and collective processes of self-esteem management: Self-enhancement in the United States and self-depreciation in Japan. *Journal of Personality and Social Psychology, 72*, 1245–1267.

KITAYAMA, S., & MASUDA, T. (1997). [A cultural mediation model of social inference: Correspondence bias in Japan.] In K. Kashiwagi, S. Kitayama. & H. Azuma (Eds.), [*Cultural psychology: Theory and research*] (pp. 109–127). Tokyo: University of Tokyo Press. (IN JAPANESE; CITED IN KITAYAMA & MARKUS, 1999)

KLEIN, S. B., & KIHLSTROM, J. F. (1998). On bridging

the gap between social-personality psychology and neuropsychology. *Personality and Social Psychology Bulletin, 2*, 228–242.

KLEINMUNTZ, B. (1967). *Personality measurement.* Homewood, IL: Dorsey.

KLINGER, M. R., & GREENWALD, A. G. (1995). Unconscious priming of association judgments. *Journal of Experimental Psychology: Learning, Memory, and Cognition, 21*, 569–581.

KNUTSON, B., WOLKOWITZ, O. M., COLE, S. W., CHAN, T., MOORE, E. A., JOHNSON, R. C., TERPESTRA, J., TURNER, R. A., & REUS, V. I. (1998). Selective alteration of personality and social behavior by serotonergic intervention. *American Journal of Psychiatry, 155*, 373–378.

KOESTNER, R., LEKES, N., POWERS, T. A., & CHICOINE, E. (2002). Attaining personal goals: Concordance plus implementation intentions equals success. *Journal of Personality and Social Psychology, 83*, 231–244.

KOESTNER, R., & MCCLELLAND, D. C. (1990). Perspectives on competence motivation. In L. A. Pervin (Ed.), *Handbook of personality: Theory and research* (pp. 527–548). New York: Guilford Press.

KOHUT, H. (1984). *How does analysis cure?* Chicago: University of Chicago Press.

KRANTZ, D., S., & MANUCK, S. B. (1984). Acute psychophysiologic reactivity and risk of cardiovascular disease: A review and methodologic critique. *Psychological Bulletin, 96*, 435–464.

KRASNER, L. (1971). The operant approach in behavior therapy. In A. E. Bergin & S. L. Garfield (Eds.), *Handbook of psychotherapy and behavior change* (pp. 612–652). New York: Wiley.

KROSNICK, J. A., BETZ, A. L., JUSSIM, L. J., & LYNN, A. R. (1992). Subliminal conditioning of attitudes. *Journal of Personality and Social Psychology, 18*, 152–162.

KUNDA, Z. (1990). The case for motivated reasoning. *Psychological Bulletin, 108*, 480–498.

LANDFIELD, A. W. (1971). *Personal construct systems in psychotherapy.* Chicago: Rand McNally.

LANDFIELD, A. W. (1982). A construction of fragmentation and unity. In J. C. Mancuso & J. R. Adams-Webber (Eds.), *The construing person* (pp. 198–221). New York: Praeger.

LAU, R. R. (1982). Origins of health locus of control beliefs. *Journal of Personality and Social Psychology, 42*, 322–324.

LAZARUS, A. A. (1965). Behavior therapy, incomplete treatment and symptom substitution. *Journal of Nervous and Mental Disease, 140*, 80–86.

LAZARUS, R. S. (1990). Theory-based stress measurement. *Psychological Inquiry, 1*, 3–13.

LAZARUS, R. S. (1991). *Emotion and adaptation.* New York: Oxford University Press.

LAZARUS, R. S. (1993). From psychological stress to the emotions: A history of changing outlooks. *Annual Review of Psychology, 44*, 1–21.

LEARY, M. R., & TANGNEY, J. P. (Eds.) (2002). *Handbook of self and identity.* New York: Guilford.

LECKY, P. (1945). *Self-consistency: A theory of personality.* New York: Island.

LEDOUX, J. L. (1995). Emotion: Clues from the brain. *Annual Review of Psychology, 46*, 209-235.

LEDOUX, J. (1999). The power of emotions. In R. Conlan (Ed.), *States of mind* (pp. 123–149). New York: Wiley.

LEHMAN, D. R., & TAYLOR, S. E. (1987). Date with an earthquake: Coping with a probable, unpredictable disaster. *Personality and Social Psychology Bulletin, 13*, 546–555.

LEPPER, M. R., GREENE, D., & NISBETT, R. E. (1973). Undermining children's intrinsic interest with extrinsic rewards: A test of the "overjustification" hypothesis. *Journal of Personality and Social Psychology, 28*, 129–137.

LESTER, D., HVEZDA, J., SULLIVAN, S., & PLOURDE, R. (1983). Maslow's hierarchy of needs and psychological health. *Journal of General Psychology, 109*, 83–85.

LEVIS, D. J., & MALLOY, P. F. (1982). Research in infrahuman and human conditioning. In G. T. Wilson & C. M. Franks (Eds.), *Contemporary behavior therapy: Conceptual and empirical foundations* (pp. 65–118). New York: Guilford Press.

LEVY, S. M. (1984). The expression of affect and its biological correlates: Mediating mechanisms of behavior and disease. In C. Van Dyke, L. Temoshok, & L. S. Zegans (Eds.), *Emotions in health and illness.* New York: Grune & Stratton.

LEVY, S. (1991). Personality as a host risk factor: Enthusiasm, evidence and their interaction. *Psychological Inquiry, 2*, 254–257.

LEWIS, M. (2002). Models of development. Cervone, D. & Mischel, W. (EDS.), *Advances in personality science* (pp. 153–176). New York: Guilford Press.

LEWIS, M., & BROOKS-GUNN, J. (1979). *Social cognition and the acquisition of self.* New York: Plenum.

LEWIS, M., FEIRING, C., MCGUFFOG, C., & JASKIR, J. (1984). Predicting psychopathology in six year olds from early social relations. *Child Development, 55*, 123–136.

LEWONTIN, R. (2000). *The triple helix: Gene, organism, and environment.* Cambridge, MA: Harvard University Press.

LILIENFELD, S. O., WOOD, J. M., & GARB, H. N. (2000). The scientific status of projective techniques. *Psychological Science in the Public Interest, 1*, (whole issue).

LINVILLE, P. (1985). Self-complexity and affective extremity: Don't put all your eggs in one basket. *Social Cognition, 3*, 94-120.

LINVILLE, P. (1987). Self-complexity as a cognitive buffer against stress-related illness and depression. *Journal of Personality and Social Psychology, 52*, 663-676.

LITTLE, B. R. (1999). Personality and motivation: Personal action and the conative revolution. In L. A. Pervin & O. P. John (Eds.), *Handbook of personality: Theory and research* (pp. 501–524). New York: Guilford.

LOCKE, E. A., & LATHAM, G. P. (1990). *A theory of goal setting and task performance.* Englewood Cliffs, NJ: Prentice-Hall.

LOCKE, E. A., & LATHAM, G. P. (2002). Building a practically useful theory of goal setting and task motivation: A 35–year odyssey. *American Psychologist, 57*, 705–717.

LOEHLIN, J. C. (1982). Rhapsody in G. *Contemporary Psychology, 27*, 623.

LOEHLIN, J. C. (1992). *Genes and environment in personality development.* Newbury Park, CA: Sage.

LOEHLIN, J. C., McCRAE, R. R., COSTA, P. T., & JOHN, O. P. (1998). Heritabilities of common and measure-specific components of the Big Five personality factors. *Journal of Research in Personality, 32*, 431–453.

LOEHLIN, J. C., & NICHOLS, R. C. (1976). *Heredity, environment, and personality: A study of 850 sets of twins.* Austin, TX: University of Texas Press.

LOEVINGER, J. (1993). Measurement in personality: True or false. *Psychological Inquiry, 4*, 1–16.

LOEVINGER, J., & KNOLL, E. (1983). Personality: Stages, traits, and the self. *Annual Review of Psychology, 34*, 195–222.

LOFTUS, E. F. (1993). The reality of repressed memories. *American Psychologist, 48*, 518–537.

LONDON, P. (1972). The end of ideology in behavior modification. *American Psychologist, 27*, 913–920.

LUCAS, R. E., DIENER, E., GROB, A., SUH, E. M., & SHAO, L. (2000). Cross-cultural evidence for the fundamental features of extraversion. *Journal of Personality and Social Psychology, 79*, 452–468.

LYKKEN, D. T. (1971). Multiple factor analysis and personality research. *Journal of Experimental Research in Personality, 5*, 161–170.

LYKKEN, D. T. (1995). *The antisocial personalities.* Mahwah, NJ: Earlbaum.

LYKKEN, D. T., BOUCHARD, T. J., JR., McGUE, M., & TELLEGEN, A. (1993). Heritability of interests: A twin study. *Journal of Applied Psychology, 78*, 649–661.

LYNAM, D. R., CASPI, A., MOFFIT, T. E., WIKSTROEM, P., LOEBER, R., & NOVAK, S. (2000). The interaction between impulsivity and neighborhood context on offending: The effects of impulsivity are stronger in poorer neighborhoods. *Journal of Abnormal Psychology, 109*, 563–574.

MacCOBY, E. E. (2000). Parenting and its effects on children: On reading and misreading behavior genetics. *Annual Review of Psychology, 51*, 1–27.

MacKENZIE, K. R. (1994). Using personality measurements in clinical practice. In P. T. Costa, Jr. & T. A. Widiger (Eds.), *Personality disorders and the five-factor model of personality* (pp. 237–250). Washington, DC: American Psychological Association.

MacLEOD, R. B. (1964). Phenomenology: A challenge to experimental psychology. In T. W. Wann (Ed.), *Behaviorism and phenomenology* (pp. 47–73). Chicago: University of Chicago Press.

MADISON, P. (1961). *Freud's concept of repression and defence: Its theoretical and observational language.* Minneapolis: University of Minnesota Press.

MAGNUSSON, D. (1999). Holistic interactionism: A perspective for research on personality development. In L. A. Pervin & O. P. John (Eds.), *Handbook of personality: Theory and research* (pp. 219–247). New York: Guilford.

MAIER, S. F., WATKINS, L. R., & FLESHNER, M. (1994). Psychoneuroimmunology. *American Psychologist, 49*, 1004–1017.

MANCUSO, J. C., & ADAMS-WEBBER, J. R. (Eds.) (1982). *The construing person.* New York: Praeger.

MARCIA, J. (1994). Ego identity and object relations. In J. M. Masling & R. F. Bornstein (Eds.), *Empirical perspectives on object relations theory,* (pp. 59–104). Washington, DC: American Psychological Association.

MARKUS, H. (1977). Self-schemata and processing information about the self. *Journal of Personality and Social Psychology, 35*, 63–78.

MARKUS, H. (1983). Self-knowledge: An expanded view. *Journal of Personality, 51*, 543–565.

MARKUS, H., & CROSS, S. (1990). The interpersonal self. In L. A. Pervin (Ed.), *Handbook of personality: Theory and research* (pp. 576–608). New York: Guilford Press.

MARKUS, H., & KITAYAMA, S. (1991). Culture and the self: Implications for cognition, emotion, and motivation. *Psychological Review, 98*, 224–253.

MARKUS, H., & NURIUS, P., (1986). Possible selves. *American Psychologist, 41*, 954–969.

MARKUS, H., & RUVOLO, A. (1989). Possible selves: Personalized representations of goals. In L. A. Pervin (Ed.), *Goal concepts in personality and social psychology* (pp. 211–241). Hillsdale, NJ: Erlbaum.

MARKUS, H., & WURF, E. (1987). The dynamic self-concept: A social psychological perspective. *Annual Review of Psychology, 38*, 299–337.

MARLATT, G. A., BAER, J. S., & QUIGLEY, L. A. (1995). Self-efficacy and addictive behavior. In A. Bandura (Ed.), *Self-efficacy in changing societies* (pp. 289–315). New York: Cambridge.

MARLATT, G. A., & GORDON, J. R. (1980). Determinants

of relapse: Implications for the maintenance of behavior change. In P. O. Davidson & S. M. Davidson (Eds.), *Behavioral medicine: Changing health lifestyles.* New York: Brunner/Mazel.

Maslow, A. H. (1954). *Motivation and personality.* New York: Harper.

Maslow, A. H. (1968). *Toward a psychology of being.* Princeton, NJ: Van Nostrand.

Maslow, A. H. (1971). *The farther reaches of human nature.* New York: Viking.

Massimini, F., & Delle Fave, A. (2000). Individual development in a bio-cultural perspective. *American Psychologist, 55*, 24–33.

Matthews, G. (1997). The Big Five as a framework for personality assessment. In N. Anderson & P. Herriot (Eds.), *International handbook of selection and assessment*, (pp. 475–492). Chichester, UK: Wiley.

Mayo, C. W., & Crockett, W. H. (1964). Cognitive complexity and primacy; recency effects in impression formation. *Journal of Abnormal and Social Psychology, 68*, 335–338.

McAdams, D. P. (1992). The five-factor model in personality: A critical appraisal. *Journal of Personality, 60*, 329–361.

McAdams, D. P. (1999). Personal narratives and the life story. In L. A. Pervin & O. P. John (Eds.), *Handbook of personality: Theory and research* (pp. 478–500). New York: Guilford.

McCaul, K. D., Gladue, B. A., & Joppe, M. (1992). Winning, losing, mood, and testosterone. *Hormones and Behavior, 26*, 486–504.

McClelland, D., Koestner, R., & Weinberger, J. (1989). How do self-attributed and implicit motives differ? *Psychological Review, 96*, 690-702.

McCoy, M. M. (1981). Positive and negative emotion: A personal construct theory interpretation. In H. Bonarius, R. Holland, & S. Rosenberg (Eds.), *Personal construct psychology: Recent advances in theory and practice* (pp. 96–104). London: Macmillan.

McCrae, R. R. (1996). Social consequences of experiential openness. *Psychological Bulletin, 120*, 323–337.

McCrae, R. (2002). The maturation of personality psychology: Adult personality development and psychological well-being. *Journal of Research in Personality, 36*, 307–317.

McCrae, R. R., & Costa, P. T. (1987). Validation of the five-factor model of personality across instruments and observers. *Journal of Personality and Social Psychology, 52*, 81–90.

McCrae, R. R., & Costa, P. T., Jr. (1990). *Personality in adulthood.* New York: Guilford Press.

McCrae, R. R., & Costa, P. T., Jr. (1994). The stability of personality: Observations and evaluations. *Current Directions in Psychological Science, 3*, 173–175.

McCrae, R. R., & Costa, P. T. (1996). Toward a new generation of personality theories: theoretical contexts for the five-factor model. In J.S. Wiggins (Ed.), *The five-factor model of personality. Theoretical perspectives* (pp. 51-87). New York: Guilford.

McCrae, R.R., & Costa, P. T. (1997). Personality trait structure as a human universal. *American Psychologist, 52*, 509–516.

McCrae, R. R., & Costa, P. T., Jr., (1999). A Five-factor Theory of Personality. In L. A. Pervin & O. P. John (Eds.), *Handbook of Personality: Theory and Research* (pp. 139–153). New York: Guilford.

McCrae, R. R., & Costa, P. T. Jr. (2003). *Personality in adulthood: A five-factor theory perspective* (2nd edition). New York; Guilford.

McCrae, R. R., Costa, P. T., Ostendorf, F., Angleitner, A., Hrebickova, M., Avia, M. D., Sanz, J., Sanchez-Bernardos, M. L., Kusdil, M. E., Woodfield, R., Saunders, P. R., & Smith, P. B. (2000). Nature over nurture: Temperament, personality, and lifespan development. *Journal of Personality and Social Psychology, 78*, 173–186.

McCrae, R. R., & John, O. P. (1992). An introduction to the five-factor model and its applications. *Journal of Personality, 60*, 175–215.

McCrae, R. R., Yik, S. M., Trapbell, P. D., Bond, M. H., & Paulus, D. L. (1998). Interpreting personality profiles across cultures: Bilingual, acculturation, and peer rating studies of Chinese undergraduates. *Journal of Personality and Social Psychology, 74*, 1041–1055.

McGregor, I., & Little, B. R. (1998). Personal projects, happiness, and meaning: On doing well and being yourself. *Journal of Personality and Social Psychology, 74*, 494–512.

McGinnies, E. (1949). Emotionality and perceptual defense. *Psychological Review, 56*, 244–251.

Medinnus, G. R., & Curtis, F. J. (1963). The relation between maternal self-acceptance and child acceptance. *Journal of Consulting Psychology, 27*, 542–544.

Meehl, P. (1992). Factors and taxa, traits and types, differences of degree and differences in kind. *Journal of Personality, 60*, 117–174.

Meichenbaum, D. (1995). Cognitive-behavioral therapy in historical perspective. In B. Bongar & L. E. Bentler (Eds.), *Comprehensive textbook of psychotherapy.* (pp. 140–158). New York: Oxford University Press.

Menand, L. (Nov. 25, 2002). What comes naturally: Does evolution explain who we are? *The New Yorker.*

Mendel, G. (1865/1966). Experiments on plant hybrids. In C. Stern & E. R. Sherwood (Eds.), *The origin of genetics: A Mendel source book.* San Francisco: Freeman.

Metcalfe, J., & Mischel, W. (1999). A hot/cool-system

analysis of delay of gratification: Dynamics of willpower. *Psychological Review, 106,* 3–19.

MILGRAM, S. (1965). Some conditions of obedience and disobedience to authority. *Human Relations, 18,* 57–76.

MILLER, J. G. (1984). Culture and the development of everyday social explanation. *Journal of Personality and Social Psychology, 46,* 961–978.

MILLER, L. C., PUTCHA-BHAGAVATULA, A., & PEDERSEN, W. C. (2002). Men's and women's mating preferences: Distinct evolutionary mechanisms? *Current Directions in Psychological Science, 11,* 88–93.

MILLER, S. M., & MANGAN, C. E. (1983). Interacting effects of information and coping style in adapting to gynecologic stress: Should the doctor tell all? *Journal of Personality and Social Psychology, 45,* 223–236.

MILLER, S. M., SHODA, Y., & HURLEY, K. (1996). Applying cognitive-social theory to health-protective behavior: Breast self-examination in cancer screening. *Psychological Bulletin, 119,* 70–94.

MILLER, T. R. (1991). Personality: A clinician's experience. *Journal of Personality Assessment, 57,* 415–433.

MINEKA, S., DAVIDSON, M., COOK, M., & KLEIR, R. (1984). Observational conditioning of snake fear in rhesus monkeys. *Journal of Abnormal Psychology, 93,* 355–372.

MISCHEL, W. (1968). *Personality and assessment.* New York: Wiley.

MISCHEL, W. (1971). *Introduction to personality.* New York: Holt, Rinehart & Winston.

MISCHEL, W. (1973). Toward a cognitive social learning reconceptualization of personality. *Psychological Review, 80,* 252–283.

MISCHEL, W. (1974). Processes in delay of gratification. In L. Berkowitz (Ed.), *Advances in experimental social psychology* (Vol. 7, pp. 249-292). San Diego, CA: Academic Press.

MISCHEL, W. (1976). *Introduction to personality.* New York: Holt, Rinehart & Winston.

MISCHEL, W. (1990). Personality dispositions revisited and revised: A view after three decades. In L. A. Pervin (Ed.), *Handbook of personality: Theory and research* (pp. 111–134). New York: Guilford Press.

MISCHEL, W. (1999). Personality coherence and dispositions in a cognitive-affective processing system (CAPS) approach. In D. Cervone and Y. Shoda (Eds.), *The coherence of personality: Social-cognitive bases of consistency, variability, and organization* (pp. 37-60). New York: Guilford Press.

MISCHEL, W. (1999b). Personality coherence and dispositions in a cognitive-affective personality system (CAPS) approach. In D. Cervone & Y. Shoda (Eds.), *The coherence of personality* (pp. 37–60). New York: Guilford.

MISCHEL, W., & BAKER, N. (1975). Cognitive transfor-

mations of reward objects through instructions. *Journal of Personality and Social Psychology, 31,* 254-261.

MISCHEL, W., & EBBESEN, E. B. (1970). Attention in delay of gratification. *Journal of Personality and Social Psychology, 16,* 239-337.

MISCHEL, W., & LIEBERT, R. M. (1966). Effects of discrepancies between observed and imposed reward criteria on their acquisition and transmission. *Journal of Personality and Social Psychology, 3,* 45–53.

MISCHEL, W., & MOORE, B. (1973). Effects of attention to symbolically-presented rewards on self-control. *Journal of Personality and Social Psychology, 28,* 172-197.

MISCHEL, W., & MORF, C. (2002). The self as a psycho-social dynamic processing system: a meta-perspective on a century of the self in psychology. In M. R. Leary & J. P. Tangney (Eds.), *Handbook of self and identity* (pp. 15–43). New York: Guilford.

MISCHEL, W., & PEAKE, P. K. (1982). Beyond déjà vu in the search for cross-situational consistency. *Psychological Review, 89,* 730–755.

MISCHEL, W., & PEAKE, P. K. (1983). Analyzing the construction of consistency in personality. In M. M. Page (Ed.), *Personality: Current theory and research* (pp. 233–262). Lincoln, NE: University of Nebraska Press.

MISCHEL, W., & SHODA, Y. (1995). A cognitive-affective system theory of personality: Reconceptualizing the invariances in personality and the role of situations. *Psychological Review, 102,* 246–286.

MISCHEL, W., & SHODA, Y. (1998). Reconciling processing dynamics and personality dispositions. *Annual Review of Psychology, 49,* 229–258.

MISCHEL, W., & SHODA, Y. (1999). Integrating dispositions and processing dynamics within a unified theory of personality: The cognitive-affective personality system. In L. A. Pervin, & O. P. John (Eds.), *Handbook of personality: Theory and research* (pp. 197–218). New York: Guilford.

MOHAMMED, S. (2001). Personal communication networks and the effects of an entertainment-education radio soap opera in Tanzania. *Journal of Health Communication, 6,* 137–154.

MONSON, T. C., HESLEY, J. W., & CHERNICK, L. (1982). Specifying when personality traits can and cannot predict behavior: An alternative to abandoning the attempt to predict single-act criteria. *Journal of Personality and Social Psychology, 43,* 385–399.

MOORE, B., MISCHEL, W., & ZEISS, A. R. (1976). Comparative effects of the reward stimulus and its cognitive representation in voluntary delay. *Journal of Personality and Social Psychology, 34,* 419-424.

MOORE, M. K., & NEIMEYER, R. A. (1991). A confirmatory factor analysis of the threat index. *Journal of Personality and Social Psychology, 60,* 122–129.

MORF, C. C., & RHODEWALT, F. (2001). Unraveling the paradoxes of narcissism: A dynamic self-regulatory processing model. *Psychological Inquiry, 12,* 177–196.

MORGAN, M. (1985). Self-monitoring of attained subgoals in private study. *Journal of Educational Psychology, 77,* 623–630.

MOROKOFF, P. J. (1985). Effects of sex, guilt, repression, sexual "arousability," and sexual experience on female sexual arousal during erotica and fantasy. *Journal of Personality and Social Psychology, 49,* 177–187.

MORRIS, M. W., & PENG, K. (1994). Culture and cause: American and Chinese attributions for social and physical events. *Journal of Personality and Social Psychology, 67,* 949–971.

MORRISON, J. K., & COMETA, M. C. (1982). Variations in developing construct systems: The experience corollary. In J. C. Mancusco & J. R. Adams-Webber (Eds.), The construing person (pp. 152–169). New York: Praeger.

MOSS, P. D., & McEVEDY, C. P. (1966). An epidemic of over-breathing among school-girls. *British Medical Journal, 2,* 1295–1300.

MOWRER, O. H., & MOWRER, W. A. (1928). Enuresis: A method for its study and treatment. American *Journal of Orthopsychiatry, 8,* 436–447.

MURRAY, H. A. (1938). *Explorations in personality.* New York: Oxford University Press.

NASH, M. (1999). The psychological unconscious. In V. J. Derlega. B. A. Winstead, & W. H. Jones, (Eds.), *Personality: Contemporary theory and research* (pp. 197–228). Chicago: Nelson-Hall.

NATHAN, P. E. (1985). Aversion therapy in the treatment of alcoholism: Success and failure. *Annals of the New York Academy of Sciences, 443,* 357–364.

NEIMEYER, G. J. (1992). Back to the future with the psychology of personal constructs. *Contemporary Psychology, 37,* 994–997.

NEIMEYER, R. A. (1994). *Death anxiety handbook: Research, instrumentation, and application.* Washington, DC: Taylor & Francis.

NEIMEYER, R. A., & NEIMEYER, G. J. (Eds.) (1992). *Advances in personal construct psychology* (Vol. 2). Greenwich, CT: JAI Press.

NESSELROADE, J. R., & DELHEES, K. H. (1966). Methods and findings in experimentally based personality theory. In R. B. Cattell (Ed.), *Handbook of multivariate experimental psychology* (pp. 563–610). Chicago: Rand McNally.

NICHOLSON, I. A. M. (2002). *Inventing personality: Gordon Allport and the science of selfhood.* Washington, D C: American Psychological Society.

NISBETT, R. (2003). *The geography of thought: How Asians and Westerners think differently.* New York: Free Press.

NISBETT, R. E., PENG, K., CHOI, I., & NORENZAYAN, A. (2001). Culture and systems of thought: Holistic versus analytic cognition. *Psychological Review, 108,* 291–310.

NISBETT, R., & ROSS, L. (1980). *Human inference: Strategies and shortcomings of social judgment.* Englewood Cliffs, NJ: Prentice Hall.

NISBETT, R. E., & WILSON, T. D. (1977). Telling more than we know: Verbal reports on mental processes. Psychological Review, 84, 231–279.

NOREM, J. K. (2001). *The positive power of negative thinking: Using defensive pessimism to manage anxiety and perform at your peak.* New York: Basic Books.

NORMAN, W. T. (1963). Toward an adequate taxonomy of personality attributes. *Journal of Abnormal and Social Psychology, 66,* 574–583.

NOWAK, A., VALLACHER, R. R., & ZOCHOWSKI, M. (2002). The emergence of personality: Personality stability through interpersonal synchronization. In D. Cervone & W. Mischel (eds.), *Advances in personality science* (pp. 292-331). New York: Guilford.

NOZICK, R. (1981). *Philosophical explanations.* Cambridge, MA: Belknap Press of Harvard University Press.

OGILVIE, D. M. (1987). The undesired self: A neglected variable in personality research. *Journal of Personality and Social Psychology, 52,* 379–385.

OHMAN, A., & SOARES, J. F. (1993). On the automaticity of phobic fear: Conditional skin conductance responses to masked phobic stimuli. *Journal of Abnormal Psychology, 102,* 121–132.

O'LEARY, A. (1990). Stress, emotion, and human immune function. *Psychological Bulletin, 108,* 363–382.

O'LEARY, A. (1992). Self-efficacy and health: Behavioral and stress-physiological mediation. *Cognitive Therapy and Research, 16,* 229–245.

O'LEARY, K. D. (1972). The assessment of psychopathology in children. In H. C. Quay & J. S. Werry (Eds.), *Psychopathological disorders of childhood* (pp. 234–272). New York: Wiley.

ORNE, M. T. (1962). On the social psychology of the psychological experiment: With particular reference to demand characteristics and their implications. *American Psychologist, 17,* 776–783.

ORR, H. A. (Feb. 27, 2003). Darwinian storytelling. *The New York Review of Books, 50,* 17–20.

OSGOOD, C. E., & LURIA, Z. (1954). A blind analysis of a case of multiple personality using the semantic differential. *Journal of Abnormal and Social Psychology, 49,* 579–591.

OSGOOD, C. E., SUCI, G. J., & TANNENBAUM, P. H. (1957). *The measurement of meaning.* Urbana, IL: University of Illinois Press.

OZER, D. J. (1999). Four principles for personality

assessment. In L. A. Pervin & O. P. John (Eds.), *Handbook of personality: Theory and research* (pp. 671–686). New York: Guilford.

OZER, E., & BANDURA, A. (1990). Mechanisms governing empowerment effects: A self-efficacy analysis. *Journal of Personality and Social Psychology, 58,* 472–486.

PATTON, C. J. (1992). Fear of abandonment and binge eating. *Journal of Nervous and Mental Disease, 180,* 484–490.

PAULHUS, D. L. (1990). Measurement and control of response bias. In J. P. Robinson, P. R. Shaver, & L. Wrightsman (Eds.), *Measures of personality and social-psychological attitudes* (pp. 17–59). San Diego, CA: Academic Press.

PAULHUS, D. L., FRIDHANDLER, B., & HAYES, S. (1997). Psychological defense: Contemporary theory and research (pp. 544–579). In R. Hogan, J. Johnson., & S. Briggs (Eds.), *Handbook of personality psychology* (pp. 543–579). San Diego, CA: Academic Press.

PAULHUS, D. L., TRAPNELL, P. D., & CHEN, D. (1999). Birth order effects on personality and achievement within families. *Psychological Science, 10,* 482–488.

PAVLOV, I. P. (1927). *Conditioned reflexes.* London: Oxford University Press.

PAVOT, W., FUJITA, F., & DIENER, E. (1997). The relation between self-aspect congruence, personality and subjective well-being. *Personality & Individual Differences, 22,* 183-191.

PENNEBAKER, J. W. (1985). Traumatic experience and psychosomatic disease: Exploring the roles of behavioral inhibition, obsession, and confiding. *Canadian Psychology, 26,* 82–95.

PENNEBAKER, J. W. (1990). *Opening up: The healing powers of confiding in others.* New York: Morrow.

PERVIN, L. A. (1960b). Existentialism, psychotherapy, and psychology. *American Psychologist, 15,* 305–309.

PERVIN, L. A. (1964). Predictive strategies and the need to confirm them: Some notes on pathological types of decisions. *Psychological Reports, 15,* 99–105.

PERVIN, L. A. (1967a). A twenty-college study of student/college interaction using TAPE (Transactional Analysis of Personality and Environment): Rationale, reliability, and validity. *Journal of Educational Psychology, 58,* 290–302.

PERVIN, L. A. (1967b). Satisfaction and perceived self-environment similarity: A semantic differential study of student-college interaction. *Journal of Personality, 35,* 623–634.

PERVIN, L. A. (1983). Idiographic approaches to personality. In J. McV. Hunt & N. Endler (Eds.), *Personality and the behavior disorders* (pp. 261–282). New York: Wiley.

PERVIN, L. A. (1984). *Current controversies and issues in personality.* New York: Wiley.

PERVIN, L. A. (1985). Personality: Current controversies, issues, and directions. *Annual Review of Psychology, 36,* 83–114.

PERVIN, L. A. (1988). Affect and addiction. *International Journal of Addictive Behaviors, 13,* 83–86.

PERVIN, L. A. (1994a). A critical analysis of current trait theory. *Psychological Inquiry, 5,* 103-113.

PERVIN, L. A. (1999). Epilogue: Constancy and change in personality theory and research. In L. A. Pervin & O. P. John (Eds.), *Handbook of personality: Theory and research* (pp. 689–704). New York: Guilford.

PERVIN, L. A. (2003). *The science of personality* (2nd ed.). London: Oxford University Press.

PETRIE, K. J., BOOTH, R. J., & PENNEBAKER, J. W. (1998). The immunological effects of thought suppression. *Journal of Personality and Social Psychology, 75,* 1264–1272.

PFUNGST, O. (1911). *Clever Hans: A contribution to experimental, animal, and human psychology.* New York: Holt, Rinehart & Winston.

PICKERING, A. D., & GRAY, J. A. (1999). The neuroscience of personality. In L. A. Pervin & O. P. John (Eds.), *Handbook of personality: Theory and research* (pp. 277–299). New York: Guilford.

PINKER, S. (1997). *How the mind works.* New York: Norton.

PINKER, S. (1999). *Words and rules: The ingredients of language.* New York: Basic Books.

PINKER, S. (2002). *The blank slate: The modern denial of human nature.* New York: Viking.

PLAUT, V. C., MARKUS, H. R., & LACHMAN, M. E. (2002). Place matters: Consensual features and regional variation in American well-being and self. *Journal of Personality and Social Psychology, 83,* 160–184.

PLOMIN, R. (1990). *Nature and nurture.* Pacific Grove, CA: Brooks/Cole.

PLOMIN, R. (1994). *Genetics and experience: The interplay between nature and nurture.* Newbury Park, CA: Sage.

PLOMIN, R., & CASPI, A. (1998). DNA and personality. *European Journal of Personality, 12,* 387–407.

PLOMIN, R., & CASPI, A. (1999). Behavioral genetics and personality. In L. A. Pervin & O. P. John (Eds.), *Handbook of personality: Theory and research* (pp. 251–276). New York: Guilford.

PLOMIN, R., CHIPUER, H. M., & LOEHLIN, J.C. (1990). Behavioral genetics and personality. In L.A. Pervin (Ed.), *Handbook of personality: Theory and research* (pp. 225–243). New York: Guilford Press.

PLOMIN, R., & DANIELS, D. (1987). Why are children in the same family so different from each other? *Behavioral and Brain Sciences, 10,* 1–16.

PLOMIN, R., & NEIDERHISER, J. M. (1992). Genetics and experience. *Current Directions in Psychological Science, 1,* 160–163.

POLKINGHORNE, D. (1988). *Narrative knowing and the human sciences*. Albany, NY: State University of New York Press.

PONOMAREV, I., & CRABBE, J. C. (1999). Genetic association between chronic ethanol withdrawal severity and acoustic startle parameters in WSP and WSR mice. *Alcoholism: Clinical & Experimental Research, 23*, 1730–1735.

POWELL, R. A., & BOER, D. P. (1994). Did Freud mislead patients to confabulate memories of abuse? *Psychological Reports, 74*, 1283–1298.

PROCTOR, R. W., & CAPALDI E. J. (2001). Empirical evaluation and justification of methodologies in psychological science. *Psychological Bulletin, 127*, 759–772.

PULKKINEN, L., & CASPI, A. (Eds.) (2002). *Paths to successful development: Personality in the life course.* New York: Cambridge University Press.

RAFAELI-MOR, E., & STEINBERG, J. (2002). Self-complexity and well-being: A Review and Research Synthesis. *Personality and Social Psychology Review, 6*, 31–58.

RÄIKKÖNON, K., MATTHEWS, K. A., & SALOMON, K. (2003). Hostility predicts metabolic syndrome risk factors in children and adolescents. *Health Psychology, 22*, 279–286.

RALEIGH, M. J., & MCGUIRE, M. T. (1991). Bidirectional relationships between typtophan and social behavior in vervet monkeys. *Advances in Experimental Medicine and Biology, 294*, 289–298.

RASKIN, R., & HALL, C. S. (1979). A narcissistic personality inventory. *Psychological Reports, 45*, 590.

RASKIN, R., & HALL, C. S. (1981). The Narcissistic Personality Inventory: Alternate form reliability and further evidence of construct validity. *Journal of Personality Assessment, 45*, 159–162.

RASKIN, R., & SHAW, R. (1987). *Narcissism and the use of personal pronouns*. Unpublished manuscript.

RASKIN, R., & TERRY, H. (1987). *A factor-analytic study of the Narcissistic Personality Inventory and further evidence of its construct validity*. Unpublished manuscript.

RAZRAN, G. (1939). A quantitative study of meaning by a conditioned salivary technique. *Science, 90*, 89–91.

REISS, D. (1997). Mechanisms linking genetic and social influences in adolescent development: Beginning a collaborative search. *Current Directions in Psychological Science, 6*, 100–105.

REISS, D., NEIDERHISER, J., HETHERINGTON, E. M., & PLOMIN, R. (1999). *The relationship code: Deciphering genetic and social patterns in adolescent development.* Cambridge, MA: Harvard University Press.

REYNOLDS, G. S. (1968). *A primer of operant conditioning*. Glenview, IL: Scott, Foresman.

RHODEWALT, F., & MORF, C. C. (1995). Self and interpersonal correlates of the Narcissistic Personality Inventory: A review and new findings. *Journal of Research in Personality, 29*, 1–23.

RHODEWALT, F., & MORF, C. C. (1998). On self-aggrandizement and anger: A temporal analysis of narcissism and affective reactions to success and failure. *Journal of Personality and Social Psychology, 74*, 672–685.

RHODEWALT, F., & SORROW, D. L. (2002). Interpersonal self-regulation: Lessons from the study of narcissism. In M. R. Leary & J. P. Tangney (Eds.), *Handbook of self and identity* (pp. 519–535). New York: Guilford.

RIDLEY, M. (2003). *Nature via nurture: Genes, experience, and what makes us human.* New York: Harper Collins.

RIEMANN, R., ANGLEITNER, A., & STRELAU, J. (1997). Genetic and environmental influences on personality: A study of twins reared together using the self- and peer report NEO-FFI scales. *Journal of Personality, 65*, 449–476.

ROBERTS, B. W. (1997). Plaster or plasticity: Are adult work experiences associated with personality change in women? *Journal of Personality, 65*, 205–232.

ROBERTS, B. W., & CHAPMAN, C. N. (2000). Change in dispositional well-being and its relation to role quality: A 30–year longitudinal study. *Journal of Research in Personality, 34*, 26–41.

ROBERTS, B. W., & DEL VECCHIO, W. F. (2000). The rank-order consistency of personality traits from childhood to old age: A quantitative review of longitudinal studies. *Psychological Bulletin, 126*, 3–25.

ROBERTS, B. W., & DELVECCHIO, W. F. (2002). The rank-order consistency of personality traits from childhood to old age: A quantitative review of longitudinal studies. *Psychological Bulletin, 126*, 3-25.

ROBERTS, B. W., & HOGAN, R. (Eds.) (2001). *Personality in the workplace.* Washington, DC: American Psychological Association.

ROBERTS, J. A., GOTLIB, I. H., & KASSEL, I. D. (1996). Adult attachment security and symptoms of depression: The mediating roles of dysfunctional attitudes and low self-esteem. *Journal of Personality and Social Psychology, 70*, 310–320.

ROBINS, C. J., & HAYES, A. M. (1993). An appraisal of cognitive therapy. *Journal of Consulting and Clinical Psychology, 61*, 205–214.

ROBINS, R. W., GOSLING, S. D., & CRAIK, K. H. (1999). An empirical analysis of trends in psychology. *American Psychologist, 54*, 117–128.

ROBINS, R. W., & JOHN, O. P. (1996). The quest for self-insight: Theory and research on the accuracy of self-perception. In R. Hogan, J. Johnson, & S. Briggs (Eds.), *Handbook of personality psychology* (pp. 647–679). New York: Academic Press.

ROBINS, R. W., & JOHN, O. P. (1997). Self-perception, visual perspective, and narcissism: Is seeing believing? *Psychological Science, 8*, 37–42.

ROBINS, R. W., NOREM, J. K., & CHEEK, J. M. (1999).

Naturalizing the self. In L. A. Pervin & O. P. John (Eds.), *Handbook of personality: Theory and research* (pp. 443–477). New York: Guilford.

ROBINSON, R. G., & DOWNHILL, J. E. (1995). Lateralization of psychopathology in response to focal brain injury. In R. J. Davidson & K. Hugdahl (Eds.), *Brain asymmetry* (pp. 693–711). Cambridge, MA: MIT Press.

ROCCAS, S., & BREWER, M. (2002). Social identity complexity. *Personality & Social Psychology Review, 6,* 88–106.

ROGERS, C. R. (1942). *Counseling and psychotherapy.* Boston: Houghton Mifflin.

ROGERS, C. R. (1947). Some observations on the organization of personality. *American Psychologist, 2,* 358–368.

ROGERS, C. R. (1951). *Client-centered therapy.* Boston: Houghton Mifflin.

ROGERS, C. R. (1954). The case of Mrs. Oak: A research analysis. In C. R. Rogers & R. F. Dymond (Eds.), *Psychotherapy and personality change* (pp. 259–348). Chicago: University of Chicago Press.

ROGERS, C. R. (1956). Some issues concerning the control of human behavior. *Science, 124,* 1057–1066.

ROGERS, C. R. (1959). A theory of therapy, personality, and interpersonal relationships as developed in the client-centered framework. In S. Koch (Ed.), *Psychology: A study of science* (pp. 184–256). New York: McGraw-Hill.

ROGERS, C. R. (1963). The actualizing tendency in relation to "motives" and to consciousness. In M. R. Jones (Ed.), *Nebraska symposium on motivation* (pp. 1–24). Lincoln, NE: University of Nebraska Press.

ROGERS, C. R. (1964). Toward a science of the person. In T. W. Wann (Ed.), *Behaviorism and phenomenology* (pp. 109–133). Chicago: University of Chicago Press.

ROGERS, C. R. (1966). Client-centered therapy. In S. Arieti (Ed.), *American handbook of psychiatry* (pp. 183–200). New York: Basic Books.

ROGERS, C. R. (Ed.) (1967). *The therapeutic relationship and its impact: A study of psychotherapy with schizophrenics.* Madison: University of Wisconsin Press.

ROGERS, C. R. (1970). *On encounter groups.* New York: Harper.

ROGERS, C. R. (1977). *Carl Rogers on personal power.* New York: Delacorte Press.

ROGERS, C. R. (1980). A *way of being.* Boston: Houghton Mifflin.

ROGERS, T. B., KUIPER, N. A., & KIRKER, W. S. (1977). Self-reference and the encoding of personal information. *Journal of Personality and Social Psychology, 35,* 677–688.

RORER, L. G. (1990). Personality assessment: A conceptual survey. In L. A. Pervin (Ed.), *Handbook of Personality: Theory and Research* (pp. 693-720). New York: Guilford.

ROSENBERG, S. (1980). A theory in search of its zeitgeist. *Contemporary Psychology, 25,* 898–900.

ROSENTHAL, R. (1994). Interpersonal expectancy effects: A 30–year perspective. *Current Directions in Psychological Science, 3,* 176–179.

ROSENTHAL, R., & RUBIN, D. (1978). Interpersonal expectancy effects: The first 345 studies. *Behavioral and Brain Sciences, 3,* 377–415.

ROSENTHAL, T., & BANDURA, A. (1978). Psychological modeling: Theory and practice. In S. L. Garfield & A. E. Bergin (Eds.), *Handbook of psychotherapy and behavior change* (pp. 621–658). New York: Wiley.

ROSENZWEIG, S. (1941). Need-persistive and ego-defensive reactions to frustration as demonstrated by an experiment on repression. *Psychological Review, 48,* 347–349.

ROSS, L. (1977). The intuitive psychologist and his shortcomings: distortions in the attribution process. In L. Berkowitz (Ed.), *Advances in experimental social psychology.* (Vol.10). (pp. 174–220). New York : Academic Press.

ROTHBARD, J. C. & SHAVER, P. R. (1994). Continuity of attachment across the life-span. In M. B, Sperling & W. H. Berman (Eds.), *Attachment in adults: Clinical and developmental perspectives* (pp. 31–71). New York: Guilford Press.

ROTHBART, M. K., AHADI, S. A., & EVANS, D.E. (2000). Temperament and personality: Origins and outcomes. *Journal of Personality and Social Psychology, 78,* 122–135.

ROTHBART, M. K., & BATES, J. E. (1998). Temperament. In W. Damon (Ed.), *Handbook of child psychology: Vol. 3. Social, emotional, and personality development* (5th ed.). (pp. 105–176). New York: Wiley.

ROWE, D. C. (1999). Heredity. In V. J. Derlega, B. A. Winstead, & Jones, W. H. (EDS.), *Personality: Contemporary theory and research* (pp. 66–100). Chicago: Nelson-Hall.

ROZIN, P., & ZELLNER, D. (1985). The role of Pavlovian conditioning in the acquisition of food likes and dislikes. *Annals of the New York Academy of Sciences, 443,* 189–202.

RUGGIERO, K. M., & MARX, D. M. (2001). "Less pain and more to gain: Why high-status group members blame their failure on discrimination": Retraction. *Journal of Personality & Social Psychology, 81,* 178.

RYAN, R. M. (1993). Agency and organization: Intrinsic motivation, autonomy, and the self in psychological development. In J. Jacobs (Ed.), *Nebraska symposium on motivation.* (Vol. 40). (pp. 1–56). Lincoln, NE: University of Nebraska Press.

RYAN, R. M., & DECI, E. L. (2000). Self-determination theory and the facilitation of intrinsic motivation, social development, and well-being. *American Psychologist, 55*, 68–78.

RYFF, C. D. (1995). Psychological well-being in adult life. *Current Directions in Psychological Science, 4*, 99–104.

RYFF, C. D., & SINGER, B. (1998). The contours of positive human health. *Psychological Inquiry, 9*, 1–28.

RYFF, C. D., & SINGER, B. (2000). Interpersonal flourishing: A positive health agenda for the new millennium. *Personality and Social Psychology Review, 4*, 30–44.

SANDERSON, C., & CLARKIN, J. F. (1994). Use of the NEO-PI personality dimensions in differential treatment planning. In P. T. Costa, Jr. & T. A. Widiger (Eds.), *Personality disorders and the five-factor model of personality* (pp. 219–236). Washington, DC: American Psychological Association.

SANDERSON, C. A., & CANTOR, N. (1999). A life task perspective on personality coherence: Stability versus change in tasks, goals, strategies, and outcomes. In D. Cervone & Y. Shoda (Eds.), *The coherence of personality: Social-cognitive bases of consistency, variability, and organization* (pp. 372–392). New York: Guilford Press.

SAPOLSKY, R. M. (1994). *Why zebras don't get ulcers.* New York: W.H. Freeman.

SANFREY, A. G., RILLING, J. K., ARONSON, J. A., NYSTROM, L. E., & COHEN, J. D. (2003). The neural basis of economic decision-making in the Ultimatum game. *Science, 300*, 1755–1758.

SAUCIER, G. (1997). Effects of variable selection on the factor structure of person descriptors. *Journal of Personality & Social Psychology, 73*, 1296-1312.

SAUCIER, G., & GOLDBERG, L. R. (1996). Evidence for the Big Five in analyses of familiar English personality adjectives. *European Journal of Personality, 10*, 61–77.

SAUCIER, G., & GOLDBERG, L. R. (2001). Lexical studies of undigenous personality factors: Premises, products, and prospects. *Journal of Personality, 69*, 847–880.

SAUCIER, G., HAMPSON, S. E., & GOLDBERG, L. R. (2000). Cross-language studies of lexical personality factors. In S. E. Hampson (Ed.), *Advances in personality psychology* (Vol. 1, p. 1–36). East Sussex, UK: Psychology Press, Ltd.

SAUDINO, K. (1997). Moving beyond the heritability question: New directions in behavioral genetic studies of personality. *Current Directions in Psychological Science, 6*, 86–90.

SCARR, S. (1992). Developmental theories for the 1990s: Development and individual differences. *Child Development, 63*, 1–19.

SCARR, S. (1993). Biological and cultural diversity: The legacy of Darwin for development. *Child Development, 64*, 1333–1353.

SCHAFER, R. (1954). *Psychoanalytic interpretation in Rorschach testing.* New York: Grune & Stratton.

SCHAFER, R. (1984). The pursuit of failure and the idealization of unhappiness. *American Psychologist, 39*, 398–405.

SCHEIER, M. F., & CARVER, C. S. (1985). Optimism, coping, and health: Assessment and implications of generalized outcome expectancies. *Health Psychology, 4*, 219–247.

SCHMIDT, L. A., & FOX, N. A. (2002). Individual differences in childhood shyness: Origins, malleability, and developmental course. In D. Cervone & W. Mischel (Eds.), *Advances in personality science* (pp. 83–105). New York: Guilford Press.

SCHNEIDER, D. J. (1982). Personal construct psychology: An international menu. *Contemporary Psychology, 27*, 712–713.

SCHNEIDER, J. A., O'LEARY, A., & AGRAS, W. S. (1987). The role of perceived self-efficacy in recovery from bulimia: A preliminary examination. *Behavior Research and Therapy, 25*, 429–432.

SCHUNK, D. H., & COX, P. D. (1986). Strategy training and attributional feedback with learning disabled students. *Journal of Educational Psychology, 1986*, 78, 201–209.

SCHWARTZ, C. E., WRIGHT, C. I., SHIN, L. M., KAGAN, J., & RAUCH, S. L. (2003). Inhibited and uninhibited children "grown up": Amygdalar response to novelty. *Science, 300*, 1952–1953.

SCHWARZ, N. (1999). Self-reports: How the questions shape the answers. *American Psychologist, 54*, 93-105.

SCHWARZER, R. (Ed.) (1992). *Self-efficacy: Thought control of action.* Washington, DC: Hemisphere.

SCOTT, J. P., & FULLER, J. L. (1965). *Genetics and the social behavior of the dog.* Chicago: University of Chicago Press.

SCOTT, W. D., & CERVONE, D. (2002). The impact of negative affect on performance standards: Evidence for an affect-as-information mechanism. *Cognitive Therapy and Research, 26*, 19–37.

SECHREST, L. (1963). The psychology of personal constructs. In J. M. Wepman & R. W. Heine (Eds.), *Concepts of personality* (pp. 206–233). Chicago: Aldine.

SECHREST, L., & JACKSON, D. N. (1961). Social intelligence and accuracy of interpersonal predictions. *Journal of Personality, 29*, 167–182.

SEGAL, Z. V., & DOBSON, K. S. (1992). Cognitive models of depression: Report from a consensus development conference. *Psychological Inquiry, 3*, 219–224.

SELIGMAN, M. E. P., & CSIKSZENTMIHALYI, M. (2000). Positive psychology. *American Psychologist, 55*, 5–14.

SHAH, J., & HIGGINS, E. T. (1997). Expectancy x value effects: Regulatory focus as a determinant of magnitude and direction. *Journal of Personality and Social Psychology, 73*, 447-458.

SHEDLER, J., MAYMAN, M., & MANIS, M. (1993). The illusion of mental health. *American Psychologist, 48*, 1117–1131.

SHELDON, K. M., & ELLIOT, A. J. (1999). Goal striving, need satisfaction, and longitudinal well-being: The self-concordance model. *Journal of Personality and Social Psychology, 76*, 482–497.

SHELDON, K. M., RYAN, R. M., RAWSTHORNE, L. J., & ILARDI, B. (1997). Trait self and true self: Cross-role variation in the Big-Five personality traits and its relations with psychological authenticity and subjective well-being. *Journal of Personality and Social Psychology, 73*, 1380–1393.

SHELDON, W. H. (1940). *The varieties of human physique.* New York: Harper.

SHELDON, W. H. (1942). *Varieties of temperament.* New York: Harper.

SHINER, R. L. (1998). How shall we speak of children's personalities in middle childhood? A preliminary taxonomy. *Psychological Review, 124*, 308–332.

SHODA, Y. (1999). Behavioral expressions of a personality system: Generation and perception of behavioral signatures. In D. Cervone & Y. Shoda (Eds.), *The coherence of personality: Social-cognitive bases of consistency, variability, and organization* (pp. 155–181). New York: Guilford Press.

SHODA, Y., MISCHEL, W., & PEAKE, P. K. (1990). Predicting adolescent cognitive and self-regulatory competencies from preschool delay of gratification: Identifying diagnostic conditions. *Developmental Psychology, 26*, 978–986.

SHODA, Y., MISCHEL, W., & WRIGHT, J. C. (1994). Intraindividual stability in the organization and patterning of behavior: Incorporating psychological situations into the idiographic analysis of personality. *Journal of Personality and Social Psychology, 67*, 674–687.

SHOWERS, C. J. (2002). Integration and compartmentalization: A model of self-structure and self-change. In D. Cervone & W. Mischel (Eds.), *Advances in personality science* (pp. 271–291). New York: Guilford Press.

SHWEDER, R. A & SULLIVAN, M. A. (1990). The semiotic subject of cultural psychology. In L. Pervin (Ed.) *Handbook of Personality* (pp. 399–416). New York: Guilford.

SHWEDER, R. A., & SULLIVAN, M. A. (1993). Cultural psychology: Who needs it? *Annual Review of Psychology.44* 1993, 497–523.

SIEGEL, S. (1984). Pavlovian conditioning and heroin overdose: Reports by overdose victims. *Bulletin of the Psychonomic Society, 22*, 428–430.

SIEGEL, S., HINSON, R. E., KRANK, M. D., & McCULY, J. (1982). Heroin "overdose" death: Contribution of drug-associated environmental cues. *Science, 216*, 436–437.

SIGEL, I. E. (1981). Social experience in the development of representational thought: Distancing theory. In I. E. Sigel, D. Brodzinsky, & R. Golinkoff (Eds.), *New directions in Piagetian theory and practice* (pp. 203–217). Hillsdale, NJ: Erlbaum.

SILVERMAN, L. H. (1976). Psychoanalytic theory: The reports of its death are greatly exaggerated. *American Psychologist, 31*, 621–637.

SILVERMAN, L. H. (1982). A comment on two subliminal psychodynamic activation studies. *Journal of Abnormal Psychology, 91*, 126–130.

SILVERMAN, L. H., ROSS, D. L., ADLER, J. M., & LUSTIG, D. A. (1978). Simple research paradigm for demonstrating subliminal psychodynamic activation: Effects of oedipal stimuli on dart-throwing accuracy in college men. *Journal of Abnormal Psychology, 87*, 341–357.

SIMPSON, J. A., & RHOLES, W. S. (1998). (Eds.), (1998). *Attachment theory and close relationships.* New York: Guilford.

SKINNER, B. F. (1948). *Walden two.* New York: Macmillan.

SKINNER, B. F. (1953). *Science and human behavior.* New York: Macmillan.

SKINNER, B. F. (1956). A case history in the scientific method. *American Psychologist, 11*, 221–233.

SKINNER, B. F. (1959). *Cumulative record.* New York: Appleton-Century-Crofts.

SKINNER, B. F. (1967). Autobiography. In E. G. Boring & G. Lindzey (Eds.), *A history of psychology in autobiography* (pp. 385–414).

SKINNER, B. F. (1971). *Beyond freedom and dignity.* New York: Knopf.

SKINNER, B. F. (1990). Can psychology be a science of mind? *American Psychologist, 45*, 1206–1210.

SMITH, D. (October, 2002). The theory heard 'round the world: Albert Bandura's social cognitive theory is the foundation of television and radio shows that have changed the lives of millions. APA *Monitor on Psychology, 33*.

SMITH, D. (November, 2002). Dissolving myths about human nature. *Monitor on Psychology, 33*, 42–43.

SMITH, D. (January, 2003). Five principles for research ethics: Cover your bases with these ethical strategies. *Monitor on Psychology, 34*, 56.

SMITH, E. R. (1998). Mental representations and memory. In D. T. Gilbert, S. T. Fiske, & G. Lindzey (Eds.), *The handbook of social psychology* (4th ed.), (Vol. 1), (pp. 391–445). Boston: McGraw-Hill.

SMITH, R. E. (1989). Effects of coping skills training on generalized self-efficacy and locus of control. *Journal of Personality and Social Psychology, 56*, 228–233.

SOLOMON, R. C., & HIGGINS, K. M. (1996). *A short history of philosophy.* New York: Oxford university Press.

SOMER, O., & GOLDBERG, L. R. (1999). The structure of Turkish trait-descriptive adjectives. *Journal of Personality and Social Psychology, 76,* 431–450.

SPENCER, S, J., STEELE, C. M., & QUINN, D. M. (1999). Stereotype threat and women's math performance. *Journal of Experimental Social Psychology, 35,* 4–28.

SPERLING, M. B., & BERMAN, W. H. (Eds.) (1994). *Attachment in adults: Clinical and developmental perspectives.* New York: Guilford Press.

SRIVASTAVA, S., JOHN, O. P., GOSLING, S. D., & POTTER, J. (2003). Development of personality in early and middle adulthood: Set like plaster or persistent change? *Journal of Personality and Social Psychology, 84,* 1041–1053.

SROUFE, L. A., CARLSON, E., & SHULMAN, S. (1993). Individuals in relationships: Development from infancy. In D. C. Funder, R. D. Parke, C. Tomlinson-Keasey, & K. Widaman (Eds.), *Studying lives through time* (pp. 315–342). Washington, DC: American Psychological Association.

STAATS, A. Q., & BURNS, G. L. (1982). Emotional personality repertoire as cause of behavior: Specification of personality and interaction principles. *Journal of Personality and Social Psychology, 1982,* 43, 873–886.

STAJKOVIC, A. D., & LUTHANS, F. (1998). Self-efficacy and work-related performance: A meta-analysis. *Psychological Bulletin, 124,* 240–261.

STEELE, C. M. (1997). A threat in the air: How stereotypes shape intellectual identity and performance. *American Psychologist, 52,* 613–629.

STEINER. J. F. (1966). *Treblinka.* New York: Simon & Schuster.

STEPHENSON, W. (1953). *The study of behavior.* Chicago: University of Chicago Press.

STEWART, V., & STEWART, A. (1982). *Business applications of repertory grid.* London: McGraw-Hill.

STOCK, J., & CERVONE, D. (1990). Proximal goal-setting and self-regulatory processes. *Cognitive Therapy and Research, 14,* 483–498.

STONE, V. E., COSMIDES, L., TOOBY, J., KROLL, N., & KNIGHT, R. T. (2002). Selective impairment of reasoning about social exchange in a patient with bilateral limbic system damage. *Processing of the National Academy of Sciences, 99,* 11531–11536.

STOOLMILLER, M. (1999). Implications of the restricted range of family environments for estimates of heritability and nonshared environment in behavior-genetic adoption studies. *Psychological Bulletin, 125,* 392–409.

STRAUMAN, T. J. (1989). Self-discrepancies in clinical depression and social phobia: Cognitive structures that underlie emotional disorders? *Journal of Abnormal Psychology, 98,* 14-22.

STRAUMAN, T. J. (1990). Self-guides and emotionally significant childhood memories: A study of retrieval efficiency and incidental negative emotional content. *Journal of Personality and Social Psychology, 59,* 869–880.

STRAUMAN, T. J., KOLDEN, G. G., STROMQUIST, V., DAVIS, N., KWAPIL, L., HEEREY, E., & SCHNEIDER, K. (2001). The effects of treatments for depression on perceived failure in self-regulation. *Cognitive Therapy and Research, 25,* 693–712.

STRAUMAN, T. J., LEMIEUX, A. M., & COE, C. L. (1993). Self-discrepancy and natural killer cell activity: Immunological consequences of negative self-evaluation. *Journal of Personality and Social Psychology, 64,* 1042–1052.

STRELAU, J. (1997). The contribution of Pavlov's typology of CNS properties to personality research. *European Psychologist, 2,* 125–138.

STRELAU, J. (1998). *Temperament: A psychological perspective.* New York: Plenum Press.

STRUBE, M. J. (1990). In search of self: Balancing the good and the true. *Personality and Social Psychology Bulletin, 16,* 699–704.

SUEDFELD, P., & TETLOCK, P. E. (Eds.) (1991). *Psychology and social policy.* New York: Hemisphere.

SUGIYAMA, L. S., TOOBY, J., & COSMIDES, L. (2002). Cross-cultural evidence of cognitive adaptations for social exchange among the Shiwiar of Ecuadorian Amazonia. *Processing of the National Academy of Sciences, 99,* 11537–11542.

SUH, E., DIENER, E., OISHI, S., & TRIANDIS, H. C. (1998). The shifting basis of life satisfaction judgments across cultures: Emotions versus norms. *Journal of Personality and Social Psychology, 74,* 482-493.

SUINN, R. M., OSBORNE, D., & WINFREE, P. (1962). The self concept and accuracy of recall of inconsistent self-related information. *Journal of Clinical Psychology, 18,* 473–474.

SULLIVAN, H. S. (1953). *The interpersonal theory of psychiatry.* New York: Norton.

SULLOWAY, F. J. (1979). *Freud: Biologist of the mind.* New York: Basic Books.

SULLOWAY, F. J. (1991). Reassessing Freud's case histories. ISIS, 82, 245–275.

SULLOWAY, F. J. (1996). *Born to rebel: Birth order, family dynamics, and creative lives.* New York: Pantheon.

SUOMI, S. (1999, June). Jumpy monkeys. Address presented at the annual meeting of the American Psychological Association, Denver, CO.

SWANN, W. B., JR. (1991). To be adored or to be known? The interplay of self-enhancement and self-verification. In E. T. Higgins & R. M. Sorrentino (Eds.),

Handbook of motivation and cognition (pp. 408–450). New York: Guilford Press.

SWANN, W. B., JR. (1992). Seeking "truth," finding despair: Some unhappy consequences of a negative self-concept. *Current Directions in Psychological Science, 1*, 15–18.

SWANN, W. B., JR. (1997). The trouble with change: Self-verification and allegiance to the self. *Psychological Science, 8*, 177–180.

SWANN, W. B. JR., DE LA RONDE, C., & HIXON, J. G. (1994). Authenticity and positivity strivings in marriage and courtship. *Journal of Personality and Social Psychology, 66*, 857–869.

SWANN, W. B., JR., GRIFFIN, J. J., JR., PREDMORE, S. C., & GAINES, B. (1987). The cognitive-affective crossfire: When self-consistency confronts self-enhancement. *Journal of Personality and Social Psychology, 52*, 881–889.

SWANN, W. B., JR., PELHAM, B. W., & KRULL, D. S. (1989). Agreeable fancy or disagreeable truth? Reconciling self-enhancement and self-verification. *Journal of Personality and Social Psychology, 57*, 782–791.

TANG, T. Z., & DE RUBEIS, R. J. (1999a). Reconsidering rapid early response in cognitive behavioral therapy for depression. *Clinical Psychology: Science and Practice, 6*, 283–288.

TANG, T. Z., & DE RUBEIS, R. J. (1999b). Sudden gains and critical sessions in cognitive-behavioral therapy for depression. *Journal of Consulting and Clinical Psychology, 67*, 894–904.

TAYLOR, M. C. (2001). *The moment of complexity: Emerging network culture.* Chicago: University of Chicago Press.

TAYLOR, S. E. (1989). *Positive illusions: Creative self-deception and the healthy mind.* New York: Basic Books.

TAYLOR, S. E., & ARMOR, D.A. (1996). Positive illusions and coping with adversity. *Journal of Personality, 64*, 874–898.

TAYLOR, S. E., & BROWN, J. D. (1988). Illusion and well-being: Where two roads meet. *Psychological Bulletin, 103*, 193–210.

TAYLOR, S. E., & BROWN, J. D. (1994). Positive illusions and well-being revisited: Separating fact from fiction. *Psychological Bulletin, 116*, 21–27.

TAYLOR, S. E., KEMENY, M. E., REED, G. M., BOWER, J. E., & GRUENEWALD, T. L. (2000). Psychological resources, positive illusions, and health. *American Psychologist, 55*, 99–109.

TELLEGEN, A. (1985). Structures of mood and personality and their relevance to assessing anxiety, with an emphasis on self-report. In A. H. Tuma & J. D. Maser (Eds.), *Anxiety and the anxiety disorders* (pp. 681–706). Mahwah, NJ: Erlbaum.

TEMOSHOK, L. (1985). The relationship of psychosocial factors to prognostic indicators in cutaneous malignant melanoma. *Journal of Psychosomatic Research, 29*, 139–153.

TEMOSHOK, L. (1991). Assessing the assessment of psychosocial factors. *Psychological Inquiry, 2*, 276–280.

TESSER, A., PILKINGTON, C. J., & MCINTOSH, W. D. (1989). Self-evaluation maintenance and the mediational role of emotion: The perception of friends and strangers. *Journal of Personality and Social Psychology, 57*, 442–456.

TETLOCK, P. E., PETERSON, R. S., & BERRY, J. M. (1993). Flattering and unflattering personality portraits of integratively simple and complex managers. *Journal of Personality & Social Psychology, 64*, 500-511.

THOMAS, A., & CHESS, S. (1977). *Temperament and development.* New York: Brunner/Mazel.

THOMPSON, R. A. (1998). Early socialization and personality development. In N. Eisenberg (Ed.), *Handbook of child psychology* (5th ed.), (Vol. 3), (pp. 25–104). New York: Wiley.

TILLEMA, J., CERVONE, D., & SCOTT, W. D. (2001). Dysphoric mood, perceived self-efficacy, and personal standards for performance: The effects of attributional cues on self-defeating patterns of cognition. *Cognitive Therapy and Research, 25*, 535–549.

TOBACYK, J. J., & DOWNS, A. (1986). Personal construct threat and irrational beliefs as cognitive predictors of increases in musical performance anxiety. *Journal of Personality and Social Psychology, 51*, 779–782.

TOMKINS, S. S. (1962). Commentary. The ideology of research strategies. In S. Messick & J. Ross (Eds.), *Measurement in personality and cognition* (pp. 285–294). New York: Wiley.

TONINI, G., & EDELMAN, G. M. (1998). Consciousness and complexity. *Science, 282*, 1846-1851.

TOOBY, J., & COSMIDES, L. (1992). The psychological foundations of culture. In J. H. Barkow, L. Cosmides, & J. Tooby (Eds.), *The adapted mind: Evolutionary psychology and the generation of culture.* New York: Oxford University Press.

TRIANDIS, H. (1995). *Individualism and collectivism.* Boulder, CO: Westview Press.

TRIVERS, R. (1972). Parental investment and sexual selection. In B. Campbell (Ed.), *Sexual selection and the descent of man: 1871–1971* (pp. 136–179). Chicago: Aldine.

TRIVERS, R. (1976). Foreword. R. Dawkins, *The selfish gene.* New York: Oxford University Press.

TVERSKY, A., & KAHNEMAN, D. (1974). Judgment under uncertainty: Heuristics and biases. *Science, 185*, 1124–1131.

TWENGE, J. (2002). Birth cohort, social change, and personality: The interplay of dysphoria and individualism in the 20th century. D. Cervone & W. Mischel

(Eds.), *Advances in personality science* (pp. 196–218). New York: Guilford.

UNITED NATIONS POPULATION FUND (2002). *State of World Population 2002: People, Poverty, and Possibilities.* New York: United Nations.

VAN KAAM, A. (1966). *Existential foundations of psychology.* Pittsburgh: Duquesne University Press.

VAN LIESHOUT, C. F., & HASELAGER, G. J. (1994). The Big Five personality factors in Q-sort descriptions of children and adolescents. In C. F. Halverson, G. A. Kohnstamm, & R. P. Martin (Eds.), *The developing structure of temperament and personality from infancy to childhood,* (pp. 293–318). Hillsdale, NJ: Erlbaum.

VAUGHN, P. W., ROGERS, E. M., SINGHAL, A., & SWALEHE, R. M. (2000). Entertainment-education and HIV/AIDS prevention: A field study in Tanzania. *Journal of Health Communication, 5* (Supplement), 81–200.

VERNON, P. E. (1963). *Personality assessment.* New York: Wiley.

WALLER, N. G. (1999). Evaluating the structure of personality. In C. R. Cloninger (Ed.), *Personality and psychopathology* (pp. 155–197). Washington, DC: American Psychiatric Press.

WALLER, N. G., & SHAVER, P. R. (1994). The importance of nongenetic influences on romantic love styles. *Psychological Science, 5,* 268–274.

WALTERS, R. H., & PARKE, R. D. (1964). Influence of the response consequences to a social model on resistance to deviation. *Journal of Experimental Child Psychology, 1,* 269–280.

WARE, A. P., & JOHN, O. P. (1995). Punctuality revisited: Personality, situations, and consistency. Poster presented at the 103rd Annual Meetings of the American Psychological Association, New York, August 11–15, 1995.

WATSON, D. (2000). *Mood and temperament.* New York: Guilford.

WATSON, D., & CLARK, L.A. (1997). Extraversion and its positive emotional core. In R. Hogan, J. Johnson, & S. Briggs (Eds.), *Handbook of personality psychology* (pp. 681–710). San Diego, CA: Academic Press.

WATSON, D., & TELLEGEN, A. (1999). Issues in the dimensional structure of affect-effects of descriptors, measurement error, and response formats: Comment on Russell and Carroll. *Psychological Bulletin, 125,* 601–610.

WATSON, D., WIESE, D., VAIDYA, J., & TELLEGEN, A. (1999). The two general activation systems of affect: Structural findings, evolutionary considerations, and psychobiological evidence. *Journal of Personality and Social Psychology, 76,* 820–838.

WATSON, J. B. (1919). *Psychology from the standpoint of a behaviorist.* Philadelphia: Lippincott.

WATSON, J. B. (1924). *Behaviorism.* New York: People's Institute Publishing.

WATSON, J. B. (1936). Autobiography. In C. Murchison (Ed.), *A history of psychology in autobiography* (pp. 271–282). Worcester, MA: Clark University Press.

WATSON, J. B., & RAYNER, R. (1920). Conditioned emotional reactions. *Journal of Experimental Psychology, 3,* 1–14.

WATSON, M. W., & GETZ, K. (1990). The relationship between Oedipal behaviors and children's family role concepts. *Merrill-Palmer Quarterly, 36,* 487–506.

WATSON, R. I. (1963). *The great psychologists: From Aristotle to Freud.* Philadelphia: Lippincott.

WEBER, S. J., & COOK, T. D. (1972). Subject effects in laboratory research: An examination of subject roles, demand characteristics, and valid inference. *Psychological Bulletin, 77,* 273–295.

WEGNER, D. M. (1992). You can't always think what you want: Problems in the suppression of unwanted thoughts. *Advances in Experimental Social Psychology, 25,* 193–225.

WEGNER, D. M. (1994). Ironic processes of mental control. *Psychological Review, 101,* 34–52.

WEGNER, D. (2003). The mind's best trick: How we experience conscious will. *Trends in Cognitive Science, 7,* 65–69.

WEGNER, D. M., SHORTT, G. W., BLAKE, A. W., & PAGE, M. S. (1990). The suppression of exciting thoughts. *Journal of Personality and Social Psychology, 58,* 409–418.

WEINBERG, R. S., GOULD, D., & JACKSON, A. (1979). Expectations and performance: An empirical test of Bandura's self-efficacy theory. *Journal of Sport Psychology, 1,* 320–331.

WEINBERGER, D. A. (1990). The construct reality of the repressive coping style. In J. L. Singer (Ed.), *Repression and dissociation: Implications for personality, psychopathology, and health,* (pp. 337–386). Chicago: University of Chicago Press.

WEINBERGER, D. A., & DAVIDSON, M. N. (1994). Styles of inhibiting emotional expression: Distinguishing repressive coping from impression management. *Journal of Personality, 62,* 587–595.

WEINBERGER, D. A., SCHWARTZ, G., & DAVISON, R. J. (1979). Low-anxious, high-anxious, and repressive coping styles: Psychometric patterns and behavioral and psychological responses to stress. *Journal of Abnormal Psychology, 88,* 369–380.

WEINBERGER, J. (1992). Validating and demystifying subliminal psychodynamic activation. In R. F. Bornstein & T. S. Pittman (Eds.), *Perception without awareness* (pp. 170–188). New York: Guilford Press.

WEINER, B. (1979). A theory of motivation for some classroom experiences. *Journal of Educational Psychology, 71,* 3–25.

WEINER, B. (1990). Attribution in personality psychology. In L. A. Pervin (Ed.), *Handbook of personality: Theory and research* (pp. 465–485). New York: Guilford Press.

WEINER, B. (1993). On sin versus sickness: A theory of perceived responsibility and social motivation. *American Psychologist, 48*, 957–965.

WEINER, B. (1996). Searching for order in social motivation. *Psychological Inquiry, 7*, 1–24.

WEINER, B., & GRAHAM, S. (1999). Attribution in personality psychology. In L. A. Pervin & O. P. John (Eds.), *Handbook of personality: Theory and research* (pp. 605–628). New York: Guilford.

WEITLAUF, J., CERVONE, D., & SMITH, R. E. (2001). Assessing generalization in perceived self- efficacy: Multidomain and global assessments of the effects of self-defense training for women. *Personality and Social Psychology Bulletin, 27*, 1683-1691.

WENZLAFF, R. M., & BATES, D. E. (1998). Unmasking a cognitive vulnerability to depression: How lapses in mental control reveal depressive thinking. *Journal of Personality and Social Psychology, 75*, 1559–1571.

WEST, S. G., & FINCH, J. F. (1997). Personality measurement: Reliability and validity issues. In R. Hogan, J. Johnson, & S. Briggs (Eds.), *Handbook of personality psychology* (pp. 143–165). San Diego, CA: Academic Press.

WESTEN, D. (1991). Clinical assessment of object relations using the TAT. *Journal of Personality Assessment, 56*, 56-74.

WESTEN, D. (1998). The scientific legacy of Sigmund Freud: Toward a psychodynamically informed psychological science. *Psychological Bulletin, 124*, 333–371.

WESTEN, D., & GABBARD, G. O. (1999). Psychoanalytic approaches to personality. In L. A. Pervin & O. P. John (Eds.), *Handbook of personality: Theory and research* (pp. 57–101). New York: Guilford.

WESTEN, D., LOHR, N., SILK, K. R., GOLD, L., & KERBER, K. (1990). Object relations and social cognition in borderlines, major depressives, and normals: A Thematic Apperception Test analysis. *Psychological Assessment, 2*, 355-364.

WHITE, P. (1980). Limitations of verbal reports of internal events: A refutation of Nisbett and Wilson and of Bem. *Psychological Review, 87*, 105–112.

WHITE, R. W. (1959). Motivation reconsidered: The concept of competence. *Psychological Review, 66*, 297–333.

WIDIGER, T. A. (1993). The DSM-III-R categorical personality disorder diagnoses: A critique and an alternative. *Psychological Inquiry, 4*, 75–90.

WIDIGER, T. A., VERHEUL, R., & VAN DEN BRINK, W. (1999). Personality and psychopathology. In L. A. Pervin & O. P. John (Eds.), *Handbook of personality: Theory and research* (pp. 347–366). New York: Guilford.

WIEDENFELD, S. A., BANDURA, A., LEVINE, S., O'LEARY, A., BROWN, S., & RASKA, K. (1990). Impact of perceived self-efficacy in coping with stressors in components of the immune system. *Journal of Personality and Social Psychology, 59*, 1082–1094.

WIERSON, M. & FOREHAND, R. (1994). Parent behavioral training for child noncompliance: Rationale, concepts and effectiveness. *Current Directions in Psychological Science, 3*, 146–150.

WIGGINS, J. S. (1984). Cattell's system from the perspective of mainstream personality theory. *Multivariate Behavioral Research, 19*, 176–190.

WIGGINS, J. S. (1997). In defense of traits. In R. Hogan, J. Johnson, & S. Briggs (Eds.), *Handbook of personality psychology* (pp. 97–115). New York: Academic Press.

WIGGINS, J. S., PHILLIPS, N., & TRAPNELL, P. (1989). Circular reasoning about interpersonal behavior: Evidence concerning some untested assumptions underlying diagnostic classification. *Journal of Personality and Social Psychology, 56*, 296–305.

WIGGINS, J. S., & PINCUS, A. L. (1994). Personality structure and the structure of personality disorders. In P. T. Costa, Jr., & T. A. Widiger (Eds.), *Personality disorders and the five-factor model of personality* (pp. 73–94). Washington, DC: American Psychological Association.

WILLIAMS, L. (1994). Recall of childhood trauma: A prospective study of women's memories of child sexual abuse. *Journal of Consulting and Clinical Psychology, 62*, 1167–1176.

WILLIAMS, S. L. (1992). Perceived self-efficacy and phobic disability. In R. Schwarzer (Ed.), *Self-efficacy: Thought control of action* (pp. 149–176). Washington, DC: Hemisphere.

WILSON, T. D. (1994). The proper protocol: Validity and completeness of verbal reports. *Psychological Science, 5*, 249–252.

WILSON, T. D., HULL, J. G., & JOHNSON, J. (1981). Awareness and self-perception: Verbal reports on internal states. *Journal of Personality and Social Psychology, 40*, 53–71.

WILSON, T. D., & LINVILLE, P. W. (1985). Improving the performance of college freshmen with attributional techniques. *Journal of Personality and Social Psychology, 49*, 287–293.

WINTER, D. G. (1992). Content analysis of archival productions, personal documents, and everyday verbal productions. In C. P. Smith (Ed.), *Motivation and personality: Handbook of thematic content analysis* (pp. 110–125). Cambridge, UK: Cambridge University Press.

WINTER, D. G., JOHN, O. P., STEWART, A. J., KLOHNEN, E. C., & DUNCAN, L. E. (1998). Traits and motives:

Toward an integration of two traditions in personality research. *Psychological Review, 105,* 230-250.

WINTER, D. G., & STEWART, A. J. (1995). Commentary: Tending the garden of personality. *Journal of Personality, 63,* 711–727.

WISE, R. A. (1996). Addictive drugs and brain stimulation reward. *Annual Review of Neuroscience, 19,* 319–340.

WITTGENSTEIN, L. (1953). *Philosophical investigations* (G. E. M. Anscombe, Trans.). Oxford, UK: Blackwell.

WOIKE, B. A. (1995). Most-memorable experiences: Evidence for a link between implicit and explicit motives and social cognitive processes in everyday life. *Journal of Personality and Social Psychology, 68,* 1081–1091.

WOIKE, B. A., GERSHKOVICH, I., PIORKOWSKI, R, & POLO, M. (1999). The role of motives in the content and structure of autobiographical memory. *Journal of Personality and Social Psychology, 76,* 600–612.

WOIKE, B., & POLO, M. (2001). Motive-related memories: Content, structure, and affect. *Journal of Personality, 69,* 391–415.

WOLF, S. (1977). "Irrationality" in a psychoanalytic psychology of the self. In T. Mischel (Ed.), *The self: Psychological and philosophical issues* (pp. 203–223). Totowa, NJ: Rowman & Littlefield.

WOLPE, J. (1961). The systematic desensitization treatment of neuroses. *Journal of Nervous and Mental Disorders, 132,* 189–203.

WOLPE, J., & RACHMAN, S. (1960). Psychoanalytic "evidence." A critique based on Freud's case of Little Hans. *Journal of Nervous and Mental Disease, 130,* 135–148.

WOOD, J. V. (1989). Theory and research concerning social comparison of personal attributes. *Psychological Bulletin, 106,* 231–248.

WOOD, J. V., SALTZBERG, J. A., & GOLDSAMT, L. A. (1990). Does affect induce self-focused attention? *Journal of Personality and Social Psychology, 58,* 899–908.

WOOD, W., & EAGLY, A. H. (2002). A cross-cultural analysis of the behavior of women and men: Implications for the origins of sex differences. *Psychological Bulletin, 128,* 699–727.

WOODWARD, S. A., LENZENWEGER, M. F., KAGAN, J., SNIDMAN, N., & ARCUS, D. (2000). Taxonic structure of infant reactivity: Evidence from a taxometric perspective. *Psychological Science. 11,* 296–301.

WYLIE, R. C. (1974). *The self-concept,* (Rev. ed.) Lincoln, NE: University of Nebraska Press.

YANG, K., & BOND, M. H. (1990). Exploring implicit personality theories with indigenous or important constructs: The Chinese case. *Journal of Personality and Social Psychology, 58,* 1087–1095.

ZIMBARDO, P. G. (1973). On the ethics of intervention in human psychological research: With special reference to the Stanford prison experiment. *Cognition, 2,* 243–256.

ZUCKERMAN, M. (1990). The psychophysiology of sensation seeking. *Journal of Personality, 58,* 313–345.

ZUCKERMAN, M. (1991). *Psychobiology of personality.* New York: Cambridge University Press.

ZUCKERMAN, M. (1995). Good and bad humors: Biochemical bases of personality and its disorders. *Psychological Science, 6,* 325–332.

ZUCKERMAN, M. (1996). The psychobiological model for impulsive unsocialized sensation seeking: A comparative approach. *Neuropsychobiology, 34,* 125–129.

ZUCKERMAN, M. (1998). Psychobiological theories of personality. In D. F. Barone, M. Hersen, & V. B. Van Hasselt (Eds.), *Advanced personality* (pp. 123–154). New York: Plenum.

PHOTO CREDITS

CHAPTER 1

Page 10: Drawing by Gary Larson; ©1990 FarWorks, Inc./Dist. by Universal Press Syndicate. Page 12: David Madison/Stone/Getty Images Inc. Page 15: Ellen Senisi/The Image Works. Page 22 (left): Mike Stewart/Corbis Sygma. Page 22 (right): AFP/Corbis Images. Page 23: Elizabeth Crews/The Image Works. Page 25: Charles Gupton/Corbis Stock Market.

CHAPTER 2

Page 47 (top): David Buffington/Getty Images. Page 47 (bottom left): David Young Wolff/PhotoEdit. Page 47 (bottom right): David Young Wolff/PhotoEdit. Page 50: Hazel Hankin/Stock Boston. Page 52: Jerry Gay/Archive Photos/Getty Images. Page 56: Laura Dwight/PhotoEdit. Page 57: Mark Richard/PhotoEdit.

CHAPTER 3

Page 72: ©Bettmann/CORBIS. Page 79: Illustration by Patrick McDonnell; ©1987 Psychology Today Magazine (Sussex Publishers Inc.). Page 80: Drawing by Stan Hunt; ©1980 The New Yorker Magazine from cartoonbank.com. All Rights Reserved. Page 86: Drawing by Handelsman; ©1972 The New Yorker Magazine from cartoonbank.com. All Rights Reserved. Page 90: CALVIN AND HOBBES ©Watterson. Dist. by UNIVERSAL PRESS SYNDI-CATE. Reprinted with permission. All rights reserved. Page 92 (left): The New York Times, July 30, 1983. Page 92 (right): The New York Times, April 4, 1987. Page 94: Charles Gupton/Stone/Getty Images. Page 96: Charles HarbuttActuality. Page 105 (top): Sara KrulwichNew York Times Pictures. Page 105 (bottom): Courtesy Jon Erikson. Page 107: Nita Winter/The Image Works.

CHAPTER 4

Page 116 (top): Courtesy Dr. Henri Ellenberger. Page 116 (bottom): Drawing by Ross; ©1974 The New Yorker Magazine, Inc. from cartoonbank.com. All Rights Reserved. Page 117: Hermann Rorschach, Rorschach ®Test. ©Verlag Hans Huber AG, Bern, Switzerland, 1921, 1948, 1994. Page 118: Reprinted by permission of Hans Huber, Publishers. Page 119: Reprinted by permission of the publisher from Henry A. Murray, THEMATIC APPERCEPTION TEST, Cambridge, MA: Harvard University Press; ©1943 by the President & Fellows of Harvard College, ©1971 by Henry A. Murray. Page 127: ©1985 American Psychological Association. Reprinted by permission from Psychology Today. Page 129: Edwin Engleman. Page 138: Courtesy Alfred Adler Consultation Center. Page 139: Courtesy NASA. Page 140: Yousuf KarshWoodfin Camp & Associates. Page 142 (left): Alen MacWeeney/Corbis Images. Page 142 (right): Penfield Gallery of Indian Arts. Page 143: Courtesy Karen Horney Clinic, Inc., NYC. Page 144: Courtesy William Alanson, White Psychiatric Foundation. Page 145: Mary Kate Denny/Stone/Getty Images.

CHAPTER 5

Page 164: Antony di Gesu. Page 168: Bruce Ayres/Stone/Getty Images. Page 169: Reprinted with permission of King Features Syndicate. Page 174: Dean Abramson/Stock, Boston. Page 177: Drawing by H. Martin; ©1971 The New Yorker Magazine from cartoonbank.com. All Rights Reserved. Page 180: Charles Thatcher/Stone/Getty Images. Page 181: Andy Sacks/Stone/Getty Images.

CHAPTER 6

Page 194: Stewart Cohen/Stone/Getty Images. Page 206 (left): Daisuke Morita/Getty Images. Page 206 (right): Digital Vision. Page 210 (top): Courtesy Kurt Goldstein. Page 210 (bottom): Courtesy Brandeis University.

CHAPTER 7

Page 225: Courtesy Harvard University News Office. Page 227: Elizabeth Crews/Stock, Boston. Page 230: Courtesy Hans Eysenck. Page 234: Penny Tweedie/Stone/Getty Images. Page 241: Courtesy University of Illinois. Page 247: UPI/Corbis-Bettmann.

CHAPTER 8

Page 253: Drawing by Bill Amend; ©1993 Universal Press Syndicate. Page 254: Courtesy L.R. Goldberg. Page 264 (top): Paul T. Costa, Jr. Page 264 (bottom): Robert McCrae. Page 269: AP/Wide World Photos. Page 273: Marc Romanelli/Getty Images. Page 285: GEECH reprinted by permission of United Feature Syndicate, Inc.

NAME INDEX

Abramson, L. Y., 481, 567
Adams, N. E., 487, 488, 569
Adams-Webber, J. R., 392, 396, 402, 408, 412, 567, 581, 584, 585
Ader, R., 361, 567
Adler, A., 138–140
Adler, J. M., 103, 593
Adolphs, R., 331, 567
Agras, W. S., 485, 592
Ahadi, S. A., 296, 591
Ainsworth, A., 150, 567
Ainsworth, M. D. S., 148, 567, 571
Albright, L., 40, 583
Alexander, F., 130, 567
Allen, J. J., 332, 567
Allen, K. D., 542, 578
Allen, W., 261
Alloy, L., 481, 567
Allport, F. H., 226, 567
Allport, G., 24
Allport, G. W., 6, 40, 225–229, 248, 291, 567
Ambady, N., 15, 577
Andersen, B. L., 462, 567, 575
Andersen, S. M., 129, 417, 511, 512, 567, 573
Anderson, C., 140, 442–443, 567, 571, 583
Anderson, N., 272, 567, 586
Angleitner, A., 254, 264, 268, 322, 323, 328, 577, 582, 586, 590
Antonuccio, D. O., 482, 567
Arbisi, P., 332, 567
Arcus, D., 302, 583, 598
Armor, D. A., 91, 94, 595
Aronson, E., 178, 567
Aronson, J. A., 340, 592
Asendorpf, J. B., 9, 216, 271, 568
Ashton, M. C., 231, 568
Aspinwall, L. G., 212, 568, 572
Atkins, A., 395, 570
Avia, M. D., 264, 268, 586
Ayduk, O., 506, 509, 510, 568
Ayllon, T., 372, 568
Azrin, H. H., 372, 568
Azuma, H., 583

Bachrach, A. J., 580
Bäckman, L., 571
Baer, J. S., 475, 585

Baird, E., 205, 572
Baker, N., 452, 587
Bakermans-Kranenburg, M. J., 9, 568
Balay, J., 82, 568
Baldwin, A., 393, 568
Baldwin, A. L., 181, 568
Baldwin, M. W., 154, 409, 410, 568
Baltes, M. M., 523, 568
Baltes, P. B., 108, 522, 523, 568, 573, 578
Banaji, M., 462, 463, 568
Banaji, M. R., 39, 216, 580
Bandura, A., 11, 25, 273, 377, 416–419, 421, 422, 423, 425–428, 431, 432, 434, 435, 440, 443–449, 459, 482–486, 488, 489, 495, 498, 499, 500, 516, 534, 535, 540, 553, 568, 569, 571, 585, 589, 591, 597
Banse, R., 216, 568
Barbaranelli, C., 483, 569
Bargh, J. A., 83, 345, 481, 569, 573
Barkow, J. H., 595
Barlow, D. H., 483, 569
Barndollar, K., 83, 569
Barnhardt, T. M., 84, 583
Baron, R. A., 499, 569
Barondes, S. H., 298, 569
Barone, D. F., 574
Bartholomew, K., 153, 154, 569, 580
Bartlett, M. Y., 312, 576
Basen-Enquist, K., 431, 569
Bates, D. E., 481, 597
Bates, J. E., 299, 591
Baucom, N., 482, 577
Baumeister, R. F., 23, 204, 205, 427, 569, 570, 571
Baumrind, D., 340, 570
Beavers, J., 229, 240, 421, 580
Bechara, A., 340, 570
Beck, A. T., 480, 481, 482, 570, 573
Beech, H. R., 377, 577
Belmaker, R., 324, 576
Bem, D. J., 286, 518, 572
Benet-Martinez, V., 262, 570
Benjamin, J., 324, 570
Bennett, E., 324, 576

Bentler, L. E., 574, 586
Bergin, A. E., 584, 591
Bergman, L. R., 351, 570
Berkowitz, L., 62, 570, 591
Berman, W. H., 154, 591, 594
Berndt, T. J., 19, 570
Berntson, G. G., 554, 570, 571
Berry, J. M., 396, 595
Betz, A. L., 361, 584
Beyer, J., 487, 488, 569
Bibring, G., 158
Bieri, J., 395, 405, 570
Bijou, S. W., 369, 370, 580
Blackman, M. C., 40, 578
Blaine, D., 324, 576
Blake, A. W., 596
Bleher, M., 150, 567
Block, J. H., 38, 91, 118, 170, 183, 204, 282, 286, 289, 570, 573, 574, 580
Boechler, M., 337, 579
Boer, D. P., 156, 590
Boesky, I., 171
Boldero, J., 470, 570
Bolger, N., 39, 570
Bonarius, H., 586
Bond, M. H., 288, 531, 586, 598
Bond, R. N., 191, 472, 581
Bongar, B., 574, 586
Booth, R. J., 76, 127, 589
Bootzin, R. R., 377, 583
Borecky, C. M., 229, 240, 421, 580
Boring, E. G., 567, 593
Borkenau, P., 266, 570
Bornstein, M. H., 18, 573
Bornstein, R. F., 84, 570, 579, 583, 585, 596
Borsboom, D., 266, 267, 289, 570
Bouchard, T. J., Jr., 319, 321, 322, 323, 570, 585
Bouton, M. E., 361, 570
Bower, J. E., 91, 595
Bowlby, J., 148, 567, 571
Boyer, P., 572
Bradley, R. H., 18, 570
Braithwaite, A., 325, 572
Bramel, D., 46, 570
Brändtstadter, J., 523, 571
Braudel, F., 522, 571
Braverman, J., 312, 576

Bressler, S. L., 297, 571
Bretherton, I., 148, 571
Breuer, J., 72
Brewer, M., 396, 591
Brewin, C. R., 481, 571
Briar, S., 395, 570
Briggs, S. R., 289, 571, 579, 580, 581, 589, 590, 596, 597
Brody, N., 288, 291, 571
Brodzinsky, D., 593
Brooks-Gunn, J., 109, 168, 584
Brower, A. M., 512, 513, 514, 571
Brown, G., 482, 573
Brown, I. B., Jr., 571
Brown, J. D., 91, 179, 183, 202, 208, 481, 571, 576, 581, 595
Brown, N. O., 71, 571
Brown, S., 273, 485, 486, 597
Brücke, E., 72, 74
Bruner, J. S., 411, 571
Burger, J. M., 493, 571
Burns, G. L., 361, 594
Burt, J., 105
Burt, Sir C., 45
Bush, G., 261
Bush, G. W., 338, 397
Bushman, B. J., 442–443, 567, 571
Buss, A. H., 289, 290, 291, 299, 313, 315, 571
Buss, D. M., 14, 286, 304, 305, 308, 309, 310, 312, 571, 578
Bussey, K., 417, 571
Byrne, D., 577

Cacioppo, J. T., 361, 554, 570, 571
Cage, N., 269
Caglar, S., 338, 339, 340, 583
Cain, K. M., 470, 577
Camacho, H., 171
Cameron, J., 184, 576
Campbell, B., 595
Campbell, J. B., 236, 571
Campbell, J. D., 204, 205, 216, 427, 569, 570, 571
Campbell, W. K., 148, 571
Campos, J. J., 299, 579
Cantor, N., 316, 424, 463, 512, 513, 514, 571, 578, 581, 592

Capaldi, E. J., 31, 385, 590
Caporeal, L. R., 304, 572
Caprara, G. V., 39, 258, 259, 418, 483, 498, 569, 572, 573
Carlson, E., 154, 594
Carnelley, K. B., 154, 572
Carroll, L., 261
Carstensen, L. L., 523, 524, 525, 572
Cartwright, D. S., 177, 178, 572
Carver, C. S., 11, 20, 205, 470, 492, 572, 592
Caspi, A., 9, 13, 14, 19, 108, 238, 267, 271, 282, 286, 288, 291, 321–325, 327, 328, 329, 341, 518–521, 551, 568, 572, 585, 589, 590
Cassidy, J., 154, 572
Cattell, R. B., 65, 240–248, 253, 289, 345, 572
Cavalli-Sforza, F., 15, 572
Cavalli-Sforza, L. L., 15, 572
Cervone, D., 23, 39, 41, 65, 286, 287, 316, 418, 425, 429, 430, 432, 436, 446, 447, 470, 484, 488, 490, 492, 496, 498, 499, 515, 516, 517, 568, 569, 572, 573, 574, 579, 580, 583, 584, 587, 588, 592–595, 597
Chan, T., 203, 584
Chaplin, W. F., 226, 257, 573
Chapman, C. N., 184, 185, 590
Charcot, J., 73
Charles, S. T., 523, 572
Cheek, J. M., 23, 168, 202, 216, 590
Chen, D., 18, 588
Chen, M., 573
Chen, S., 129, 417, 511, 512, 567, 573
Chernick, L., 286, 587
Chess, S., 299, 595
Cheung, F. M., 259, 573
Chicoine, E., 584
Chipuer, H. M., 13, 341, 589
Chiu, C., 469, 474, 532, 573, 576, 582
Chodorkoff, B., 177, 573
Chodron, T., 526, 573
Choi, I., 17, 304, 573, 588
Chomsky, N., 374, 573
Church, A. T., 573
Church, M. A., 203, 577
Churchland, P. S., 339, 573
Clark, D. A., 482, 573
Clark, L. A., 236, 237, 262, 288, 333, 335, 573, 596

Clarkin, J., 575
Clarkin, J. F., 274, 592
Cleckley, H., 171
Clinton, B., 90, 261
Cloninger, C. R., 333, 573, 596
Coe, C. L., 473, 594
Cohen, J. D., 340, 580, 592
Cohen, N., 361, 567
Cohen, S., 304, 573
Cole, S. W., 203, 512, 567, 584
Collins, P. F., 333, 335, 336, 575
Collins, W. A., 18, 573
Colvin, C. R., 40, 91, 204, 573
Cometa, M. C., 402, 588
Conley, J. J., 282, 574
Contrada, R. J., 98, 484, 574
Conway, M. A., 23, 574
Cook, M., 444, 587
Cook, T. D., 62, 596
Cooper, H. M., 493, 571
Cooper, M. L., 506, 574
Cooper, R. M., 325, 574
Coopersmith, S., 181, 182, 216, 574
Copeland, P., 295, 303, 318, 334, 337, 580
Corwyn, R. F., 18, 570
Cosmides, L., 305–307, 315, 574, 594, 595
Costa, P. T., Jr., 60, 255, 260, 264–267, 273, 274, 300, 327, 521, 574, 585, 592, 597
Cox, P. D., 446, 592
Cox, T., 98, 574
Coyne, J. C., 40, 574
Cozzarelli, J. C., 448, 574
Crabbe, J. C., 318, 590
Craig, I. W., 325, 572
Craighead, L. W., 482, 574
Craighead, W. E., 482, 574
Craik, K. H., 236, 286, 542–544, 571, 578, 579, 582, 590
Cramer, P., 118, 121, 270, 574
Crandall, R., 173, 582
Crews, F., 156, 574
Criqui, M. H., 272, 273, 578
Critelli, J. W., 393, 568
Crocker, J., 200, 201, 574
Crockett, W. H., 396, 402, 408, 411, 574, 586
Cronbach, L. J., 44, 574
Cross, H. J., 402, 575
Cross, S. E., 18, 216, 466, 528, 575, 585
Csikszentmihalyi, M., 575
Curtis, F. J., 181, 586

Curtis, R. C., 178, 575
Cyranowski, J. M., 462, 567, 575
Czarnecki, E. M., 98, 574

Dabbs, J. M., Jr., 337, 575
Damasio, A. R., 294–295, 336, 340, 436, 570, 575
Damasio, H., 340, 570
Damon, W., 591
Daniels, D., 19, 288, 327, 589
Danner, D. D., 50–53, 575
Danton, W. G., 482, 567
Darley, J. M., 178, 340, 575, 580
Darwin, C., 16, 575
Davidson, M. N., 444, 587, 596
Davidson, P. O., 586
Davidson, R. J., 332, 335, 575
Davidson, S. M., 586
Davis, A., 39, 570
Davis, D. D., 482, 581
Davis, K. E., 154, 583
Davis, N., 473, 594
Davis, P. J., 98, 99, 575
Davison, R. J., 97, 98, 596
Dawes, R. M., 121, 575
De Fruyt, F., 272, 575
De La Ronde, C., 101, 465, 466, 575, 595
De Raad, B., 259, 575
De Rubeis, R. J., 482, 581, 595
Deaux, K., 476, 575
Deci, E. L., 184, 203, 575, 591
Degler, C., 340, 575
Del Vecchio, W. F., 22, 267, 271, 590
Delhees, K. H., 246, 588
Delle Fave, A., 586
DeLongis, A., 477, 494, 578
Denes-Raj, V., 575
Dennett, D. C., 374, 575
Depue, R. A., 332, 333, 335, 336, 567, 575
DeRaad, B., 258, 581
Derakhshan, N., 98, 575
Derlega, V. J., 591
DeSteno, D., 312, 576
Deutsch, H., 158
Dewsbury, D. A., 351, 576
Di Blas, L., 258, 259, 576
Diener, E., 231, 473, 531, 585, 588, 594
Dixon, R. A., 571
Dobson, K. S., 480, 482, 576, 592
Dollard, J., 362, 419

Dolnick, E., 158, 576
Donahue, E. M., 176, 177, 216, 394, 402, 576
Donnerstein, E., 62, 570
Donohue, E., 177, 190, 580
Downey, G., 506–510, 568, 576, 579
Downhill, J. E., 332, 591
Downs, A., 400, 595
Duck, S., 408, 411, 576
Dudycha, G. J., 284, 285, 576
Dumas-Hines, F., 470, 577
Duncan, L. E., 290, 597
Dunn, J., 323, 576
Dutton, K. A., 183, 202, 576
Dweck, C. S., 432, 467, 469, 470, 474, 572, 576, 577, 579
Dykman, B. M., 203, 481, 576
Dylan, B., 90
Dymond, R. F., 591

Eagle, M., 81, 576
Eagly, A. H., 311, 312, 316, 576, 598
Ebbesen, E. B., 452, 587
Ebstein, R. P., 324, 576
Edelman, G. M., 23, 297, 316, 436, 576, 595
Edelson, M., 156, 576
Ehrlich, P. R., 316, 576
Eisenberg, N., 296, 576
Eisenberger, R., 184, 576
Ekman, P., 15, 314, 315, 576
El-Khouri, B. M., 351, 570
Elder, G. H., 518, 572
Elfenbein, H. A., 15, 577
Eliasz, A., 497, 577
Elliott, A. J., 203, 467, 470, 577, 593
Ellis, A., 479, 480, 577
Emde, R. M., 579
Emmons, R. A., 147, 470, 577
Epstein, N., 482, 577
Epstein, S., 60, 84, 102, 283, 288, 481, 545, 575, 577
Erdelyi, M., 81, 577
Erdley, C. A., 470, 577
Ericsson, K. A., 64, 577
Erikson, E. H., 105–108, 138, 577
Eron, L. D., 441, 582
Esterson, A., 156, 577
Evans, D. E., 296, 591
Evans, M. D., 482, 581
Evans, R. I., 419, 577
Ewart, C. K., 484, 577
Exner, J. E., 121, 577
Eysenck, H. J., 65, 224, 225, 229–240, 242, 248, 288, 289, 333, 345, 377, 577, 579

Eysenck, M. W., 98, 575

Fabes, R. A., 296, 576
Fan, R. M., 259, 573
Farber, I. E., 347, 577
Farnham, S. D., 39, 216, 580
Faulkner, W., 209
Fazio, R. H., 39, 178, 575, 578
Feeney, J. A., 152, 578
Feiring, C., 145, 584
Feldman, S. I., 506–509, 576
Ferdandez-Ballasteros, R., 573
Ferguson, M. J., 345, 569
Ferster, C. B., 368, 578
Figueredo, A. J., 314, 315, 583
Finch, J. F., 43, 44, 63, 597
Fisher, R. L., 119, 578
Fisher, S., 119, 578
Fiske, A. P., 18, 578
Fiske, S. T., 60, 571, 578, 593
Flavell, J. H., 522, 578
Fleeson, W., 286, 578
Fleshner, M., 304, 585
Fodor, J. A., 306, 578
Folkman, S., 477, 494, 578
Forehand, R., 597
Forzi, M., 258, 259, 576
Fox, N. A., 14, 302, 332, 575, 592
Fraley, R. C., 22, 152, 153, 154, 578
Francis, E. L., 481, 567
Francis, J., 470, 570
Frank, L. K., 115
Frankl, V. E., 213, 578
Fredrickson, B. L., 524, 525, 572
Freitas, A. L., 509, 576
French, T. M., 130, 567
Freud, A., 95, 145, 158, 578
Freud, S., 21, 29, 70, 71–80, 83, 84, 86–89, 95, 96, 99, 104, 110, 122, 123, 126, 128, 130–134, 137, 146, 155–158, 162, 163, 173, 217, 225, 226, 228, 421, 550, 552, 578
Freund, A. M., 523, 578
Fridhandler, B., 40, 589
Friedman, H. S., 272, 273, 578
Friend, R., 46, 570
Friesen, W. V., 50–53, 575
Friman, P. C., 542, 578
Fromm, E., 73, 138, 143, 578
Fromm-Reichman, F., 158
Fujita, F., 473, 588

Fuller, J. L., 318, 592
Funder, D. C., 40, 204, 288, 537, 570, 573, 578, 583, 594

Gable, S. L., 506, 579
Gaensbauer, T. J., 108, 579
Gage, P., 294–295
Galen, 232, 296
Gall, F. J., 296–297
Galton, F., 297
Garb, H. N., 120, 121, 122, 584
Garfield, S. L., 584, 591
Gay, P., 72, 74, 140, 579
Geen, R. G., 236, 237, 579
Geertz, C., 26, 34, 229, 259, 260, 505, 525–528, 541, 579
Geisler, C., 82, 579
Gerard, H. B., 82, 579
Gergen, K. J., 176, 532, 579
Gershkovich, I., 121, 598
Getz, K., 104, 596
Giere, R. N., 533, 579
Giesler, R. B., 465, 579
Gilbert, D. T., 571, 578, 593
Gladue, B. A., 337, 579, 586
Glassman, N. S., 512, 567
Goble, F., 210, 579
Goettel, D., 352
Gold, L., 597
Goldberg, L. R., 11, 226, 254, 256–260, 262, 290, 313, 526, 573, 579, 581, 582, 592, 594
Goldsamt, L. A., 481, 598
Goldsmith, H. H., 299, 579
Goldsmith, T. H., 304, 579
Goldstein, K., 210, 579
Golinkoff, R., 593
Gollwitzer, P. M., 345, 569
Gooden, D., 92
Gordon, J. R., 475, 585
Gosling, S. D., 236, 269, 270, 315, 422, 542–544, 579, 590, 594
Gotlib, I. H., 154, 590
Gottlieb, G., 13, 579
Gould, D., 447, 596
Gould, E., 336, 579
Gould, S. J., 43, 579
Graf, P., 523, 568
Graham, S., 597
Grant, H., 432, 467, 470, 579
Gray, J. A., 240, 288, 299, 333, 579, 589
Graziano, M. S. A., 336, 579
Greenberg, B. D., 324, 570
Greenberg, J. R., 146, 579
Greene, D., 184, 584
Greene, J. D., 340, 580
Greenspoon, J., 215, 580

Greenwald, A. G., 39, 84, 216, 580, 584
Grice, J. W., 395, 580
Griffin, D., 153, 154, 580
Griffin, J. J., Jr., 466, 595
Grigorenko, E. L., 13, 14, 321, 324, 580
Grob, A., 231, 585
Groddeck, G., 78, 580
Gross, C. G., 336, 579
Gross, J. L., 237, 580
Groth, G., 313, 583
Gruen, R. J., 477, 494, 578
Gruenewald, T. L., 91, 595
Gruenfeld, D. H., 140, 583
Grunbaum, A., 156, 580
Grusec, J. E., 449, 498, 569, 580
Guthrie, I. K., 296, 576

Haggbloom, S. J., 229, 240, 421, 580
Hall, C. S., 28, 29, 74, 147, 580, 590
Halpern, J., 92, 580
Halverson, C. F., Jr., 18, 270, 574, 579, 580, 596
Hamer, D. H., 295, 303, 317, 318, 324, 333, 334, 337, 570, 580
Hampson, S. E., 11, 259, 290, 582, 592
Harary, K., 177, 190, 580
Harkness, A. R., 274, 580
Harmon, R. J., 579
Harper, R. A., 479, 577
Harré, R., 23, 26, 377, 422, 580
Harrington, D. M., 183, 580
Harrington, H., 325, 572
Harris, B., 354, 580
Harris, C. R., 19, 312, 580
Harris, J. R., 19, 326, 580
Hartshorn, H., 282, 286, 580
Haselager, G. J., 270, 596
Hawkins, R. P., 369, 370, 580
Hawley, C. W., 236, 571
Hayden, B. C., 402, 581
Hayes, A. M., 482, 590
Hayes, S., 40, 589
Hazan, C., 150, 151, 152, 581
Heatherton, T. F., 338, 339, 340, 583
Heckhausen, J., 572
Heilbroner, R. L., 17, 581
Heimpel, S. A., 179, 581
Heine, R. W., 592
Heine, S. J., 206, 207, 208, 216, 259, 531, 581
Helson, R., 268, 269, 581

Herbey, E., 473, 594
Hermans, H. J. M., 47, 48, 581
Herriot, P., 586
Hersen, M., 574
Hesley, J. W., 286, 587
Hesse, H., 219, 581
Hetherington, E. M., 18, 328, 573, 590
Higgins, E. T., 41, 93, 191, 192, 463, 471, 472, 511, 581, 592, 594
Higgins, K. M., 212, 594
Higgins, T., 408, 470
Hinson, R. E., 353, 593
Hippocrates, 232, 296
Hixon, J. G., 465, 466, 595
Hofstee, W. K. B., 9, 258, 568, 581
Hogan, J., 272, 288, 581
Hogan, R. T., 272, 571, 578, 579, 580, 582, 589, 590, 596, 597
Holender, D., 82, 581
Holland, J. L., 247, 581
Holland, R., 586
Hollon, S. D., 482, 493, 581
Holmes, D. S., 92, 581
Holt, R. R., 118, 582
Hong, Y., 469, 474, 532, 573, 576, 582
Horney, K., 9, 143–144, 157, 582
Horowitz, L. K., 153, 154, 569
Hough, L. M., 272, 582
Hrebickova, M., 259, 264, 268, 575, 586
Huesmann, L. R., 441, 582
Hugdahl, K., 575
Hull, C., 362, 419
Hull, J. G., 63, 194, 582, 597
Hulme, E., 440
Hunt, S., 80
Hurley, K., 484, 485, 587
Hvezda, J., 211, 584
Hyman, S., 329, 333, 582

Iacono, W. G., 332, 567
Ilardi, B., 202, 593
Ilardi, S. S., 482, 574
Inati, S., 338, 339, 340, 583
Ingram, R. E., 481, 582
Inouye, D. K., 571
Isaacowitz, D. M., 523, 572
Iyengar, S. S., 205, 531, 582
Izard, C. E., 15, 582

Jackson, A., 447, 596
Jackson, D. N., 285, 402, 582, 592
Jackson, J. F., 340, 582

Jacobs, J., 591
Jacoby, L. L., 83, 582
Jaffe, K., 154, 572
James, W., 16, 17, 582
Jankowicz, A. D., 412, 582
Jaskir, J., 145, 584
Jensen, M. R., 127, 582
Johll, M., 481, 576
John, O. P., 11, 40, 94, 147, 176, 177, 216, 223, 226, 228, 236, 253, 254, 257, 262, 269–271, 284, 285, 288–290, 290, 315, 327, 422, 569–573, 575, 576, 579–583, 585–587, 589, 590, 591, 594, 596, 597
Johnson, J., 63, 571, 580, 589, 590, 596–597
Johnson, J. A., 579
Johnson, R. C., 203, 584
Jolly, A., 554, 582
Jones, A., 173, 582
Jones, C., 269, 581
Jones, E., 73
Jones, M. C., 355, 356, 582
Jones, M. R., 591
Jones, V. K., 229, 240, 421, 580
Jones, W. H., 591
Joppe, M., 337, 586
Joriles, E., 194, 582
Josephs, R. A., 464, 465, 579, 582
Jourard, S. M., 181, 582
Jung, C. G., 140–143, 167
Jussim, L. J., 361, 584

Kagan, J., 14, 40, 108, 296, 300–303, 324, 332, 336, 582, 583, 592, 598
Kahneman, D., 429, 595
Kaiser, H. A., 470, 577
Kandel, E. R., 362, 583
Kanfer, F. H., 369, 583
Kant, I., 296–297, 460
Kashiwagi, K., 583
Kashy, D., 40, 583
Kassel, I. D., 154, 590
Kasser, T., 184, 203, 205, 583
Katigbak, M. S., 573
Katz, M., 324, 576
Kavanagh, D., 483, 583
Kazdin, A. E., 372, 377, 583
Keller, H., 18, 583
Kelley, W. M., 338, 339, 340, 583
Kelly, G. A., 11, 40, 383, 384–389, 392, 398, 400, 401, 403–408, 410–412, 547, 550, 551, 553, 583

Keltner, D., 140, 583
Kemeny, M. E., 91, 595
Kendall, P. C., 493, 581
Kenny, D. A., 40, 263, 583
Kenrick, D. T., 14, 288, 313, 315, 571, 583
Kerber, K., 597
Kernberg, O., 146
Kerwin, M. L. E., 542, 578
Khouri, H., 509, 576
Kierkegaard, Søren, 212
Kiers, H. A., 258, 581
Kihlstrom, J. F., 24, 83, 84, 424, 463, 512, 513, 555, 571, 581, 583
King, G., 93, 581
King, G. A., 41, 581
King, J. E., 314, 315, 583
Kirker, W. S., 193, 459, 591
Kirkpatrick, L. A., 154, 583
Kirschenbaum, H., 213, 583
Kitayama, S., 18, 206–208, 216, 259, 527–531, 578, 581, 583, 585
Klein, G. S., 81, 576
Klein, M., 145
Klein, R., 191, 472, 581
Klein, S. B., 555, 583
Kleinmuntz, B., 411, 584
Kleir, R., 444, 587
Klinger, M. R., 84, 584
Klohnen, E. C., 290, 597
Klonowicz, T., 497, 577
Knoll, E., 286, 402, 585
Knutson, B., 203, 584
Koch, S., 591
Koestner, R., 121, 184, 575, 584, 586
Kohnstamm, G. A., 270, 574, 579, 580, 596
Kohut, H., 146, 157, 584
Kolar, D. C., 40, 578
Kolden, G. G., 473, 594
Kopp, D. A., 484, 573
Kraepelin, E., 298
Krank, M. D., 353, 593
Krantz, D., 50, 584
Krasner, L., 371, 573, 584
Kretschmer, E., 298
Krosnick, J. A., 361, 584
Krueger, J. I., 204, 205, 427, 569, 570
Kruglanski, A. W., 581
Krull, D. S., 595
Kuiper, N. A., 193, 459, 591
Kunda, Z., 463, 584
Kupers, C. J., 449, 569
Kupper, D. A., 82, 579
Kusdil, M. E., 264, 268, 586

Kwan, V. S. Y., 268, 269, 581
Kwapil, L., 473, 594

Lachman, M. E., 208, 209, 589
Landfield, A. W., 392, 408, 412, 584
Langston, C. A., 512, 513, 514, 571
Larsen, R., 309, 310, 312, 571
Larzelere, R., 542, 578
Latham, G. P., 432, 585
Lau, R. R., 475, 584
Lavallee, L. F., 216, 571
Lazarus, A. A., 359, 584
Lazarus, R. S., 94, 459, 477, 494, 515, 578, 584
Leaman, R. L., 395, 570
Leary, M. R., 202, 584, 587
Lecky, P., 175, 584
LeDoux, J. L., 331, 332, 336, 584
Lee, K., 231, 568
Leggett, E., 432, 467, 469, 576
Lehman, D. R., 91, 206, 207, 208, 216, 259, 531, 581, 584
Lekes, N., 584
Lemieux, A. M., 473, 594
Lenzenweger, M. F., 302, 575, 598
Lepper, M. R., 184, 205, 531, 582, 584
Lester, D., 211, 584
Leung, K., 259, 573
Leventhal, H., 484, 574
Levine, S., 273, 485, 486, 597
Levis, D. J., 584
Levy, S. M., 98, 127, 584
Lewis, M., 22, 108, 109, 145, 168, 282, 584
Lewontin, R., 13, 316, 584
Liebert, R. M., 449, 587
Lilienfeld, S. O., 120, 121, 122, 274, 580, 584
Lin, L., 324, 570
Lindenberger, U., 108, 568
Lindsay, D. S., 83, 582
Lindzey, G., 28, 29, 567, 571, 578, 580, 593
Linville, P. W., 396, 474, 584, 585, 597
Little, B. R., 174, 585, 586
Locke, E. A., 428, 432, 569, 585
Loeber, R., 519, 585
Loehlin, J. C., 13, 238, 240, 323, 327, 341, 585, 589
Loevinger, J., 286, 402, 585
Loftus, E. F., 585

Lohr, N., 597
London, P., 377, 585
Long, F. Y., 234, 577
Loomis, C. C., 470, 577
Lucas, R. E., 231, 585
Luhtanen, R. K., 200, 201, 574
Luria, Z., 171, 172, 588
Lustig, D. A., 103, 593
Luthans, F., 428, 448, 594
Lykken, D. T., 289, 319, 322, 323, 330, 570, 585
Lynam, D. R., 519, 585
Lynn, A. R., 361, 584

MacCoby, E. E., 18, 573, 585
MacKay, C., 98, 574
MacKenzie, K. R., 274, 585
MacLeod, R. B., 214, 218, 585
MaCrae, C. N., 338, 339, 340, 583
Madden, J., IV, 579
Madison, P., 87, 585
Magnusson, D., 5, 351, 541, 570, 585
Mahler, M., 158
Maier, S. F., 304, 585
Malloy, P. F., 584
Malloy, T. E., 40, 583
Mancuso, J. C., 402, 408, 412, 567, 581, 584, 585
Mangan, C. E., 94, 587
Manis, M., 60, 61, 91, 593
Manuck, S. B., 50, 584
Manzella, L. M., 512, 567
Marcia, J., 106, 107, 585
Markus, H. R., 18, 41, 178, 206–209, 216, 259, 460–466, 527, 528–531, 575, 578, 581, 582, 583, 585, 589
Marlatt, G. A., 475, 585
Marshall, M. A., 179, 581
Martin, H., 177
Martin, J., 325, 572
Martin, L. R., 272, 273, 578
Martin, R. P., 270, 574, 579, 580, 596
Martinez, V., 532, 582
Marx, D. M., 45, 591
Marx, G., 465
Maser, J. D., 595
Masling, J. M., 84, 570, 579, 585
Maslow, A. H., 210–212, 586
Massimini, F., 586
Masuda, T., 531, 583
Matsumoto, H., 208, 527, 530, 531, 583
Matthews, G., 272, 586

Matthews, K. A., 54, 55, 590
Mavin, G. H., 41, 581
May, M. A., 282, 286, 580
Mayer, K. U., 522, 568
Mayman, M., 60, 61, 91, 593
Mayo, C. W., 396, 586
McAdams, D. P., 12, 287, 291, 586
McCaul, D. D., 337, 579
McCaul, K. D., 337, 586
McClay, J., 325, 572
McClearn, G. E., 583
McClelland, D. C., 121, 184, 584, 586
McCoy, M. M., 411, 586
McCrae, R. R., 21, 39, 40, 44, 60, 253, 254, 255, 257, 258, 260–268, 273, 274, 282, 288–291, 300, 315, 327, 496, 521, 526, 531, 541, 574, 585, 586
McCuly, J., 353, 593
McDonnell, P., 79
McDougall, W., 241
McEvedy, C. P., 236, 588
McGahhey, R., 229, 240, 421, 580
McGinnies, E., 81, 586
McGregor, I., 174, 586
McGue, M., 319, 321–323, 570, 585
McGuffog, C., 145, 584
McGuire, M. T., 336, 590
Mcintosh, W. D., 323, 465, 595
Medinnus, G. R., 181, 586
Meehl, P. E., 44, 153, 574, 586
Meese, E., 90
Meichenbaum, D., 478, 480, 586
Mellenbergh, G. J., 266, 267, 289, 570
Mellot, D. S., 39, 216, 580
Menand, L., 16, 17, 586
Mendel, G., 586
Mendeleyev, D., 241
Menlove, F. L., 449, 569
Messick, S., 595
Metcalfe, J., 423, 450, 452, 586
Mettee, D. R., 178, 567
Michaelis, B., 509, 576
Milgram, S., 45, 587
Mill, J., 325, 572
Miller, H., 395, 570
Miller, J. G., 531, 587
Miller, K., 178, 575
Miller, L. C., 312, 587
Miller, N., 362, 419

Miller, S. M., 94, 484, 485, 587
Miller, T. R., 274, 587
Mineka, S., 444, 587
Miranda, J., 481, 582
Mischel, T., 598
Mischel, W., 9, 21, 23, 38, 281, 282, 283, 285, 286, 371, 408, 411, 416–424, 426, 436, 437, 439, 449–453, 498, 506, 509, 510, 545, 568, 569, 573, 574, 580, 584, 586–588, 592, 593, 595
Mitchell, S. A., 146, 579
Moffitt, T. E., 270, 271, 325, 519, 572, 582, 585
Mohammed, S., 535, 536, 587
Moise-Trrus, J., 441, 582
Monson, T. C., 286, 587
Monte, E., 229, 240, 421, 580
Moore, B., 452, 587
Moore, E. A., 203, 584
Moore, M. K., 401, 587
Morf, C. C., 147, 148, 498, 587, 588, 590
Morgan, C., 118
Morgan, M., 446, 588
Morokoff, P. J., 97, 588
Morris, M. W., 531, 532, 582, 588
Morrison, J. K., 402, 588
Moss, P. D., 236, 588
Mowrer, O. H., 356, 588
Mowrer, W. A., 356, 588
Mücke, D., 216, 568
Murchison, C., 596
Murphy, D. L., 324, 570
Murray, H. A., 59, 63, 115, 118, 147, 290, 588

Nash, M., 84, 588
Nathan, P. E., 356, 588
Neidenthal, P. M., 512, 513, 514, 571
Neiderhiser, J. M., 322, 328, 329, 589, 590
Neimeyer, G. J., 383, 384, 588
Neimeyer, R. A., 38, 383, 384, 401, 408, 587, 588
Nesselroade, J. R., 246, 588
Newcombe, D., 92
Newmanov, L., 324, 576
Newton, I., 287, 377
Nguyen, L., 82, 579
Nicholson, I. A. M., 229, 588
Nisbett, R. E., 17, 18, 63, 184, 231, 304, 573, 578, 584, 588
Nixon, R., 261
Noller, P., 152, 578
Norasakkunit, V., 208, 527, 530, 531, 583

Norem, J. K., 23, 53, 168, 202, 216, 512, 513, 514, 571, 588, 590
Norenzayan, A., 17, 304, 573, 588
Norman, W. T., 254, 588
Nosek, B. A., 39, 216, 580
Novak, S., 519, 585
Novick, O., 324, 576
Nowak, A., 23, 588
Nozick, R., 230, 588
Nurius, P., 216, 466, 585
Nystrom, L. E., 340, 580, 592

Odbert, H. S., 226, 567
O'Donohue, W., 573
Ogilvie, D. M., 191, 588
Ohman, A., 361, 588
Oishi, S., 531, 594
O'Leary, A., 273, 369, 484–486, 574, 588, 592, 597
O'Leary, K. D., 588
Olson, M. A., 39, 578
Ones, D. S., 272, 288, 567, 581
Orne, M. T., 62, 588
Orr, H. A., 17, 588
Osborne, D., 178, 594
Osgood, C. E., 170, 171, 172, 588
Osher, Y., 324, 576
Ostendorf, F., 254, 264, 266, 268, 570, 582, 586
Oswald, F. L., 272, 582
Ozer, D. J., 38, 44, 537, 578, 588
Ozer, E., 488, 589

Page, M. M., 577, 587
Page, M. S., 596
Pan, R. L., 98, 574
Parke, R. D., 450, 570, 594, 596
Pastorelli, C., 483, 569
Patterson, C., 324, 570
Patton, C. J., 82, 589
Paulhus, D. L., 18, 40, 216, 531, 586, 588, 589
Paunonen, S. V., 231, 285, 568, 582
Pavlov, I. P., 298, 350–351, 353–354, 588
Pavot, W., 473, 588
Peake, P. K., 38, 282, 283, 285, 429, 430, 437, 439, 453, 573, 587, 593
Peck, J., 573
Pedersen, W. C., 312, 587
Pelham, B. W., 595
Peng, K., 17, 304, 531, 588

Pennebaker, J. W., 76, 127, 588, 589
Perugini, M., 258, 259, 572, 575
Pervin, L. A., 11, 20, 24, 39, 40, 45, 83, 171, 194, 202, 213, 223, 263, 290, 340, 361, 399, 490, 545, 568, 569, 571, 572, 573, 575, 577, 580–587, 589, 591, 593, 597
Peterson, R. F., 369, 370, 580
Peterson, R. S., 396, 595
Petrie, K. J., 76, 127, 589
Pfungst, O., 62, 589
Phillips, N., 288, 597
Piaget, J., 421
Pickering, A. D., 288, 333, 589
Pierce, W. D., 184, 576
Pietromonaco, P. R., 154, 572
Pilkington, C. J., 323, 465, 595
Pincus, A. L., 288, 597
Pinker, S., 16, 17, 23, 305, 306, 341, 589
Piorkowski, R., 121, 598
Pittman, T. S., 583, 596
Plaut, V. C., 208, 209, 589
Pleydell-Pearce, C. W., 23, 574
Plomin, R., 13, 14, 19, 238, 288, 299, 322–324, 326–329, 341, 571, 576, 583, 589, 590
Plourde, R., 211, 584
Podolski, C., 441, 582
Podres, J., 92
Polkinghorne, D., 26, 590
Polo, M., 41, 121, 598
Ponomarev, I., 318, 590
Potter, J., 269, 270, 594
Poulton, R., 325, 572
Powell, J. L., III, 229, 240, 421, 580
Powell, R. A., 156, 590
Powers, T. A., 584
Predmore, S. C., 466, 595
Prentice, D. A., 462, 463, 568
Priel, B., 324, 576
Proctor, R. W., 31, 385, 590
Przbeck, T. R., 333, 573
Pulkkinen, L., 551, 572, 590
Putcha-Bhagavatula, A., 312, 587

Quay, H. C., 588
Quigley, L. A., 475, 585
Quinn, D. M., 58, 594

Rachman, S., 359, 598
Rafaeli, E., 39, 570

Rafaeli-Mor, E., 396, 590
Räikkönon, K., 54, 55, 590
Raleigh, M. J., 336, 590
Raska, K., 273, 485, 486, 597
Raskin, R., 147, 590
Rauch, S. L., 302, 303, 592
Rawsthorne, L. J., 202, 593
Rayner, R., 350, 354, 355, 596
Razran, G., 360, 590
Reagan, R., 261
Reed, G. M., 91, 595
Reese, L., 488, 569
Reeves, A. J., 336, 579
Reis, H. T., 506, 579
Reiser, M., 296, 576
Reiss, D., 328, 590
Remy, R. M., 181, 582
Reus, V. I., 203, 584
Reyes, J. A., 573
Reynolds, G. S., 365, 590
Reznik, I., 512, 567
Rhodewalt, F., 147, 148, 588, 590
Rholes, W. S., 154, 593
Ride, S., 247
Ridley, M., 13, 331, 590
Riemann, R., 322, 323, 328, 590
Rilling, J. K., 340, 592
Roberts, B., 176, 177, 216, 267, 291, 572, 576
Roberts, B. W., 22, 184, 185, 267, 271, 272, 590
Roberts, J. A., 154, 590
Robins, C. J., 482, 590
Robins, R. W., 23, 40, 94, 147, 168, 176, 177, 202, 216, 228, 236, 270, 271, 542–544, 570, 576, 579, 582, 590
Robinson, J. P., 589
Robinson, R. G., 332, 591
Roccas, S., 396, 591
Rogers, C. R., 162–168, 170, 172–176, 179, 180, 182, 183, 184, 189, 191, 192, 193, 195, 199, 200, 204, 205, 206, 208, 213–218, 373, 547, 550, 551, 552, 591
Rogers, E. M., 535, 536, 596
Rogers, T. B., 193, 459, 591
Roosevelt, T., 124
Rorer, L. G., 121, 266, 591
Rorschach, H., 116
Rosenberg, S., 412, 586, 591
Rosenthal, R., 62, 591
Rosenthal, T. L., 444, 489, 569, 591
Rosenzweig, S., 96, 591
Rosolack, T. K., 262, 579

Ross, D. L., 103, 443, 569, 593
Ross, J., 595
Ross, L., 231, 531, 588, 591
Ross, S., 443, 569
Rothbard, J. C., 148, 591
Rothbart, M. K., 296, 299, 591
Rowe, D. C., 14, 591
Rozin, P., 357, 591
Rubin, D., 62, 591
Rudman, L. A., 39, 216, 580
Ruggiero, K. M., 45, 591
Russell, B., 363
Russell, J. A., 331, 567
Russell, S., 393, 568
Russell, T. M., 229, 240, 421, 580
Ruvolo, A., 466, 585
Ryan, R. M., 184, 202, 203, 205, 575, 583, 591, 593
Ryff, C. D., 174, 592

Sabido, M., 534, 535
Sadalla, E. K., 313, 583
Salgado, J. F., 272, 575
Salomon, K., 54, 55, 590
Salovey, P., 312, 576
Saltzberg, J. A., 481, 598
Sanchez-Bernardos, M. L., 264, 268, 586
Sanderson, C. A., 274, 512, 592
Sanfrey, A. G., 340, 592
Sanz, J., 264, 268, 586
Sartre, J.-P., 213
Saslow, G., 369, 583
Saucier, G., 258, 259, 290, 526, 592
Saudino, K., 299, 592
Saunders, P. R., 264, 268, 586
Scarr, S., 286, 340, 592
Schafer, R., 80, 117, 592
Schaumann, L., 484, 573
Scheider, K., 473, 594
Scheier, M. F., 11, 20, 470, 492, 572, 592
Schindlovsky, D., 337
Schmidt, L. A., 14, 302, 592
Schmuch, P., 569
Schneider, D. J., 412, 592
Schneider, J. A., 485, 592
Schultz, W., 569
Schunk, D. H., 432, 446, 569, 592
Schwartz, C. E., 302, 303, 592
Schwartz, G., 97, 98, 596
Schwartz, J. E., 272, 273, 578
Schwarz, N., 40, 592

Schwarzer, R., 447, 484, 568, 583, 592, 597
Schweid, E., 369, 370, 580
Scott, J. P., 318, 592
Scott, W. D., 484, 490, 573, 592, 595
Sechrest, L., 384, 389, 402, 412, 592
Secord, P. F., 377, 422, 580
Segal, N. L., 319, 322, 323, 570
Segal, Z. V., 480, 481, 582, 592
Seligman, M. E. P., 212, 592
Shadel, W. G., 41, 492, 573
Shah, J., 592
Shao, L., 231, 585
Shaver, P. R., 148, 150, 151, 152, 154, 572, 578, 581, 589, 591, 596
Shaw, B. F., 480, 482, 576
Shaw, G. B., 85
Shaw, R., 147, 590
Shedler, J., 60, 61, 91, 593
Sheldon, K. M., 202, 203, 470, 577, 593
Sheldon, W., 298
Shelton, R. C., 482, 581
Sherwood, E. R., 586
Shevrin, H., 82, 568
Shin, L. M., 302, 303, 592
Shiner, R. L., 299, 593
Shoda, Y., 21, 23, 38, 286, 287, 416, 417, 418, 421, 424, 436, 437, 439, 453, 484, 485, 496, 498, 568, 572, 573, 579, 583, 587, 592, 593
Shortt, G. W., 596
Showers, C. J., 409, 410, 593
Shulman, S., 154, 594
Shweder, R. A., 527, 537, 593
Siegel, S., 352, 353, 593
Sigel, I. E., 402, 593
Silverman, L. H., 81, 103, 593
Simon, H. A., 64, 577
Simpson, J. A., 154, 593
Singer, B., 174, 592
Singer, J. L., 596
Singhal, A., 535, 536, 596
Skinner, B. F., 21, 347, 362–368, 369, 372, 373, 374, 421, 551, 593
Smelser, N. J., 573
Smith, C. P., 597
Smith, D., 17, 533, 534, 593
Smith, E. R., 460, 593
Smith, P. B., 264, 268, 586
Smith, R. E., 488, 593, 597

Snidman, N., 302, 583, 598
Snowdon, D. A., 50–53, 575
Soares, J. F., 361, 588
Solomon, R. C., 212, 594
Somer, O., 259, 594
Sommers, S. R., 200, 201, 574
Sommerville, R. B., 340, 580
Song, W. Z., 259, 573
Sorrentino, R. M., 594
Sorrow, D. L., 147, 590
Spaulding, W. D., 569
Spence, K., 419
Spencer, S. J., 58, 594
Sperling, M. B., 154, 591, 594
Spieker, S. J., 152, 578
Srivastava, R. W., 253, 262, 582
Srivastava, S., 269, 270, 594
Sroufe, L. A., 154, 594
Staats, A. Q., 361, 594
Stajkovic, A. D., 428, 448, 594
Staudinger, U. M., 108, 212, 523, 568, 572
Steele, C. M., 56, 57, 58, 594
Steinberg, J., 396, 590
Steinberg, L., 18, 573
Steiner, J. F., 91, 594
Stephenson, W., 169, 594
Stern, C., 586
Stevens, L. C., 393, 568
Stewart, A. J., 290, 393, 594, 597, 598
Stewart, V., 393, 594
Stock, J., 432, 594
Stone, V. E., 307, 594
Stoolmiller, M., 594
Stouthamer-Loeber, M., 270, 271, 582
Strauman, T. J., 191, 472, 473, 481, 581, 594
Strelau, J., 14, 296, 298, 299, 322, 323, 328, 351, 590, 594
Stromouist, V., 473, 594
Strube, M. J., 466, 594
Suci, G. J., 170, 588
Suedfeld, P., 397, 594
Sugden, K., 325, 572
Sugiyama, L. S., 307, 594
Suh, E. M., 231, 531, 585, 594
Suinn, R. M., 178, 594
Suler, J., 171
Sullivan, H. S., 144–145, 594
Sullivan, M. A., 527, 537, 593
Sullivan, S., 211, 584
Sulloway, F. J., 72, 76, 88, 139, 140, 594
Suomi, S., 271, 594

Svrakic, D. M., 333, 573
Swalehe, R. M., 535, 536, 596
Swann, W. B., Jr., 12, 101, 178, 465, 466, 575, 579, 594, 595
Szarota, P., 259, 575

Tafarodi, R. W., 464, 465, 582
Tang, T. Z., 482, 595
Tangney, J. P., 202, 584, 587
Tannenbaum, P. H., 170, 588
Tataryn, D. J., 84, 583
Taylor, A., 325, 572
Taylor, M. C., 595
Taylor, S. E., 26, 60, 91, 94, 481, 578, 584, 595
Tellegen, A., 289, 319, 322–323, 333, 334, 570, 585, 595, 596
Temoshok, L., 91, 98, 127, 584, 595
Terpestra, J., 203, 584
Terry, H., 590
Tesser, A., 323, 465, 595
Tetlock, P. E., 396, 397, 594, 595
Thigpen, C., 171
Thomas, A., 299, 595
Thomas, M., 482, 567
Thompson, C., 158
Thompson, R. A., 154, 595
Tillema, J., 484, 595
Tobacyk, J. J., 400, 595
Tomkins, S. S., 289, 595
Tomlinson-Keasey, C., 272, 273, 570, 578, 594
Tononi, G., 23, 297, 316, 436, 576, 595
Tooby, J., 305, 307, 315, 594, 595
Tota, M. E., 481, 569
Toth, J. P., 83, 582
Tranel, D., 331, 567
Trapnell, P. D., 18, 288, 531, 586, 588, 597

Triandis, H. C., 529, 531, 594, 595
Tripoldi, T., 395, 570
Trivers, R., 304, 308, 309, 595
Trost, M., 313, 583
Tucker, J. S., 272, 273, 578
Tuma, A. H., 595
Turner, R. A., 203, 584
Tversky, A., 429, 595
Twenge, J., 265, 266, 595

Umansky, R., 324, 576

Vaidya, J., 334, 596
Vallacher, R. R., 23, 588
van Aken, M. A. G., 9, 568
van den Brink, W., 597
Van Dyke, L., 584
Van Hasselt, V. B., 574
Van Heck, G. L., 573
van Heerden, J., 266, 267, 289, 570
Van Izendoorn, M., 9, 568
Van Kaam, A., 213, 596
Van Lieshout, C. F., 270, 596
Vaughn, P. W., 535, 536, 596
Vernon, P. E., 596
Vohs, K. D., 204, 205, 427, 569, 570

Wachs, T. D., 574
Wall, S., 150, 567
Waller, N. G., 154, 289, 596
Walters, R. H., 419, 450, 498, 569, 596
Wampler, K. S., 18, 580
Wann, T. W., 585, 591
Ware, A. P., 284, 285, 596
Warnick, J. E., 229, 240, 421, 580
Warnick, R., 229, 240, 421, 580
Waters, E., 150, 567
Watkins, L. R., 304, 585
Watson, D., 236, 237, 262, 288, 333, 334, 335, 573, 596

Watson, J. B., 65, 349–350, 350, 354, 355, 460, 596
Watson, M. W., 104, 596
Weber, M., 530
Weber, S. J., 62, 596
Wegner, D., 76
Wegner, D. M., 98, 345, 373, 596
Weinberg, R. S., 447, 596
Weinberger, D. A., 97, 98, 596
Weinberger, J., 121, 586
Weiner, B., 473, 476, 596, 597
Weitlauf, J., 488, 597
Wentura, D., 523, 571
Wenzlaff, R. M., 481, 597
Wepman, J. M., 592
Werheul, R., 597
Werry, J. S., 588
West, S. G., 43, 44, 63, 597
Westen, D., 24, 84, 121, 146, 158, 309, 310, 312, 571, 597
Wheeler, L., 579
White, P., 64, 597
White, R. W., 12, 597
Widaman, K., 570, 594
Widiger, T. A., 273, 274, 574, 585, 592, 597
Wiedenfeld, S. A., 273, 485, 486, 597
Wierson, M., 597
Wiese, D., 334, 596
Wiggins, J. S., 223, 248, 288, 586, 597
Wikstroem, P., 519, 585
Williams, L., 488, 490, 597
Williams, S. L., 445, 573
Wilson, G. T., 583
Wilson, T. D., 63, 101, 474, 588, 597
Winfree, P., 178, 594
Wingard, D. L., 272, 273, 578
Winstead, B. A., 591
Winter, D. G., 290, 383, 412, 597, 598
Wise, R. A., 333, 598

Wittgenstein, L., 6, 598
Wohlers, M., 427
Woike, B. A., 41, 121, 598
Wolf, S., 146, 598
Wolfe, C. T., 200, 574
Wolfe, R. N., 578, 582
Wolfe, T., 247
Wolitzky, D. L., 81, 576
Wolkowitz, O. M., 203, 584
Wolpe, J., 358, 359, 598
Wood, J. M., 120, 121, 122, 584
Wood, J. V., 179, 465, 481, 581, 598
Wood, W., 311, 312, 316, 576, 598
Woodfield, R., 264, 268, 586
Woodward, S. A., 302, 598
Worchel, P., 577
Wright, C. I., 302, 303, 592
Wright, J. C., 38, 437, 439, 593
Wrightsman, L., 589
Wurf, E., 462, 463, 585
Wyer, R. S., Jr., 569
Wyland, C. L., 338, 339, 340, 583
Wylie, R. C., 216, 598

Yang, K., 288, 598
Yarbrough, G. L., 229, 240, 421, 580
Yik, S. M., 531, 586
Young, R. D., 194, 582

Zach, U., 18, 583
Zanna, M. P., 573
Zegans, L. S., 584
Zeiss, A. R., 452, 587
Zellner, D., 357, 591
Zhang, J. P., 573
Zhang, J. X., 573
Zimbardo, P. G., 45, 598
Zochowski, M., 23, 588
Zubek, J. P., 325, 574
Zuckerman, M., 288, 289, 323, 333, 336, 554, 598

SUBJECT INDEX

A

A, *see* Agreeableness
ABA research design (own-control design), 371
ABC assessment, 369–371
Ability traits, 243
ABS (attachment behavioral system), 149
Achievement, need for, 83
Acquiescence, 60, 61
Acquisition, performance vs., 441, 443–444
Activity dimension (of temperament), 299
Activity level, 313
Actual standards, 471–472
Adam and Eve, story of, 75
Addiction, 92, 475
Adjective checklist, 170–171
Adlerian psychology, 138–140
Adolescence:
　impulsivity and social development, 518–519
　and personality, 271
Adolescent Aggression (Bandura & Walters), 419
Adoption studies, 320
Adulthood, attachment styles in, 150–152
Affiliation, need for, 83
Age differences, 267–270
Aggression/aggressive behavior, 313, 324, 441–440
　Freud's early views on, 73
　and testosterone, 335, 337
Aging, *see* Later life
Agreeableness (A), 255, 256, 259
　in animals, 314
　and shared environment, 327–328
AIDS, *see* HIV/AIDS
Alcohol abuse/alcoholism:
　and awareness of painful negative experiences, 194
　classical conditioning for treatment of, 356
　and reduced serotonin functioning, 335
　selective breeding studies on, 318
Allport's trait theory, 225–229, 248
　functional autonomy in, 227–228
　and idiographic research, 228
　limitations of, 229
　traits in, 226, 227
Altruism, 15

American culture:
　regional variations in well-being in, 208–209
　self-esteem in, 206–208
American Psychological Association, 165, 364, 419, 421
American Psychologist, 542
Amygdala, 303, 307, 331, 332, 334, 336
Anal personality, 124
Anal stage, 102
Anal triad, 124
Analytical Psychology, 140–143
Anchoring, 429–430
Anima (archetype), 141
Animals:
　neurotransmitters in, 335
　traits in, 314
Animus (archetype), 141
Anna O, 72
ANS (autonomic nervous system), 51
Anticipating events, 398–399
Anxiety:
　castration, 103, 124
　and conflict, 125–126
　and goals, 203
　measures of, 97, 98
　and personal construct theory, 399–401, 403
　in psychoanalytic theory, 89–90
　in Rogerian psychology, 216–217
　self-efficacy in, 483
　Sullivan's view of, 144
Anxiety hierarchies, 358
Anxious-ambivalent attachment style, 150–152
Appraisal, 515
Appraisal, knowledge vs., 515–516
Archetypes, 141, 142
Architecture, personality, 515–518
Architecture (of mental systems), 306
Asian cultures, 205–208, 259–260, 527–532
Assessment of personality, 42
Association for Research in Personality, 421
Asthenic body type, 298
Astronauts, 139
Athletic body type, 298
Attachment behavior, 109–110
Attachment behavioral system (ABS), 149
Attachment styles, 150–154
Attachment theory, 148–155
Attentional focus, hot vs. cool, 508–509

Attributions, 473–476
Attributional Style Questionnaire, 493
Authenticity, 202–203, 205
Automatic Thoughts Questionnaire, 493
Autonomic nervous system (ANS), 51
Autonomy, functional, 227–228
Autonomy vs. Shame and Doubt, 106
Aversive conditioning, 356–357
Avoidant attachment style, 150–152
Awareness:
　perception without, 79, 81
　states of, 24–25, 546–547

B

"Baby box," 364
Bad me, 144
Bali, 527–528
Balinese culture, 259–260
Bandwidth (of a theory), 28–29
Baseline period, 370
Basic anxiety, 143, 144
Basic instinct, 87
Basic Trust vs. Mistrust, 106
BAT, *see* Behavioral Avoidance Test
Bedwetting, 356
Behavior(s):
　Cattell's views of, 246
　influence of past, present, and future on, 548
　internal vs. external determinants of, 21, 544–545
　situational specificity of, 347
　superstitious, 368–369
　target, 369
　unity of, 545–546
Behavioral assessment, 369–372
Behavioral Avoidance Test (BAT), 487, 488
Behavioral genetics, 318–325
　adoption studies, 320
　definition of, 318
　heritability coefficient in, 320–322
　and heritability of personality, 322–324
　molecular genetic paradigms in, 324–325
　selective breeding studies, 318
　twin studies, 318–320
Behavioral signatures, 438
Behavior change:
　Eysenckian theory of, 238–239
　in psychoanalytic theory, 126, 128–134

Behaviorism, 27, 32, 345–374
  basic assumptions of, 345
  classical conditioning, 350–362
  criticisms of, 377–378
  personality as viewed by, 345–349
  scientific research as defining feature of, 348–349
  and Skinnerian theory, 362–374
  social-cognitive theory vs., 417, 430–431, 439–440
  Watson's, 349–350
Behaviorism (Watson), 350
Behavior (Watson), 350
Beliefs:
  person-situation, 409
  in social-cognitive theory, 425–431, 459–473
Bias:
  in case studies and clinical research, 59
  in correlational research and questionnaires, 60, 61
  in experimental research, 61–62
Bible, 75
Big Five trait factors, *see* Five-factor model of personality
Biological foundations of personality, 32, 294–295, 553–555. *See also* Evolutionary psychology(-ies); Genetics
  and brain plasticity, 336–337
  in Eysenckian theory, 237–238
  in five-factor theory, 264, 265
  and temperament, 295–304
  and trait theory, 288
Bipolar disorder, 298
Birth order, 18
Bivariate research, 241, 242
The Blank Slate (Pinker), 16
Bodily fluids, ancient beliefs about, 296
Body types, 298
The Book of It (Groddeck), 78
Brain, 331–333
  amygdala, 331, 332
  Freud's study of, 72
  injuries to, 210, 294–295
  left/right hemispheric dominance in, 332–334
  and moral judgment, 339–340
  neurotransmitters in, 14, 324, 333–336
  and phrenology, 296–297
  plasticity of, 336–337
  and social exchange, 307
  and temperament, 14, 302–303, 336
  and unity of experience, 23
Buddhism, 526

C

C, *see* Conscientiousness
CAPS model, *see* Cognitive-affective processing system model

Cardinal traits, 226
Carrot theories, 11
Case study(-ies), 46–49. *See also* Clinical research
  advantages of, 58, 59
  example of, 47–48
  limitations of, 48–49, 59
Castration anxiety, 103, 124
Catharsis, 72
Cathartic hypnosis, 126, 128
Causal analysis, 265
Causal attributions, 473–476
Causality, locus of, 474
Causes:
  effects vs., 519–521
  ultimate vs. proximate, 304
Center for the Studies of the Person, 164–165
Central traits, 226, 227
Cerebrum, 331
C factor, 314
Change, *see* Behavior change; Personality change
Cheating, social exchange and detection of, 306–307
Chemotherapy, 361
Child Behavior Profile, 109
Children. *See also* Development; Infants; Parent-child relations
  birth order of, 18
  inhibited vs. uninhibited, 300–302
  personality of, 270–271
  preadolescent relationships among, 144–145
  Rep test for, 394
Chimpanzees, self-recognition in, 168
Chinese culture, 531–532
"Chinese tradition" factor, 259
Chromosomes, 317
Civilization, 75, 76
Classical conditioning, 350–362
  and case of Little Hans, 359–360
  and emotional reactions, 354–356
  principles of, 351, 353
  and psychopathology, 353–354
  research on, 360–362
  and systematic desensitization, 357–359
Cleanliness, 124
Clever Hans, 62
Client-centered therapy, 192–193, 195, 214–215
Clinical psychology, five-factor model applied to, 273–274
Clinical research:
  advantages of, 58, 59
  Cattell's view of, 242
  Kelly's view of, 386
  limitations of, 59
Clowns, projective tests on, 119–120

Cocaine, 333
Cognitive-affective processing system (CAPS) model, 436–439
Cognitive complexity, 395–397, 402–403
Cognitive theory of personality, 383
Cognitive therapy, 480–482
Cognitive triad, 480
Cognitive unconscious, 83–84
Collective unconscious, 140–141
Comedians, projective tests on, 119–120
Compartmentalized constructs, 409–410
Compensatory strivings, 138
Competence motivation, 12
Competencies, 424–425
Comprehensiveness (of a theory), 28–29
Compulsions, 126
Compulsive behavior, 475
Computers, 306
Conditioned emotional reactions, 354–356
Conditioned Reflexes (Pavlov), 363
Conditioned response (CR), 351
Conditioned stimulus (CS), 351
Conditioning:
  classical, *see* Classical conditioning
  direct, 355–356
  operant, 364–367
Conditions of worth, 179
Condom use, 431
Conflict, and defense, 125–126
Congruence, 175, 177–179
Conscientiousness (C), 255, 256, 259, 314
  cross-cultural comparisons of, 268, 284–286
  genetic basis for, 324
  and longevity, 272–273
  and shared environment, 327–328
Conscious (in psychoanalytic theory), 77–78
Consequences, vicarious experiencing of, 454
Conservation of energy, 74
Constitution, 298
Constructive alternativism, 385, 387
Constructs:
  core/peripheral, 391
  definition of, 388
  interpersonal consequences of, 389
  superordinate/subordinate, 391
  types of, 389–392
  verbal/preverbal, 389–391
Construct validity, 44
Contexts:
  interpersonal relationships, 506–512
  of personality, 504–505
  socioeconomic, 518–522

Context specificity, 424–425
Contextual personality variable, 508
Contingencies of self-worth, 200
Contrast pole, 388
Controlled emotional reactions, 354–356
Conversion symptoms, 552
Cool attentional focus, 508–509
Coping, and social-cognitive theory, 477–479
Coping strategies, 512
Coping style, repressive, 97, 99
Core constructs, 391
Corpus callosum, 331
Corrective emotional experience, 130
Correlational research, 50–53, 58
    advantages of, 59–60
    example of, 51–52
    limitations of, 52–53, 60
    as term, 50–51
Correlation coefficient, 50–51
Cortisol, 333, 334
CR (conditioned response), 351
Creativity, 183
Criminal behavior, 330
Cross-cultural research, 257–260
Cross-situational stability, 282–286
CS (conditioned stimulus), 351
Cultural productivity, 75
Culture (*See also* Asian cultures):
    as determinant of personality, 17–18
    in Horney's theories, 143–144
    and personality, 525–532
    and the self, 205–209

D

Data, 37–42. *See also* Observation(s)
    fixed vs. flexible measures of, 41–42
    fraudulent, 45
    LOTS categories of, 38–39
    relationship of sources of, 39–41
Death, and personal construct theory, 399–401
Death instinct, 88
Decontextual personality variables, 508
Defense mechanism(s), 89–90
    and conflict, 125–126
    denial as, 90–92, 94
    isolation as, 93
    projection as, 92–93
    rationalization as, 95
    reaction formation as, 95
    repression as, 95–97, 99, 100
    in Rogerian psychology, 216–217
    sublimation as, 95
    undoing as, 95
Defensive pessimism, 512–515
Delay of gratification, 449–453
Demand characteristics, 61–62

Denial:
    in psychoanalytic theory, 90–92, 94
    in Rogerian theory, 175
Depression, 480–484
Desirability of Control Scale, 493
Development, 13–19, 551–552
    age factors in, 267–270
    childhood factors in, 270–271
    environmental determinants in, 15, 17–19
    Erikson's psychosocial stages of, 105–108
    in five-factor model, 267–271
    genetic determinants in, 14–15
    in personal construct theory, 401–403
    in psychoanalytic theory, 102–105, 108–110
    in Rogerian theory, 180–185
    Skinnerian view of, 367–368
    in social-cognitive theory, 453–454
    in socioeconomic context, 518–522
    stability/change in, 271
Diary methods, 39
Differences, individual, 15
Direct conditioning, 355–356
Direct external consequences, 454
Discriminant validity, 44
Discrimination (classical conditioning), 351, 353
Disgust response, 357
Disinhibition versus Constraint (DvC), 334–335
Dismissing attachment style, 153, 154
Dispositions, 226–227
Distortion, 175
Dizygotic (fraternal) twins, 318–319, 321–323
DNA, 317
Domain-specific mechanisms, 305
Dominance, 313
Dopamine, 333–335
Dreams, 128
Drive, 11
Dunedin study, 520
DvC (Disinhibition versus Constraint), 334–335
Dynamic traits, 243
Dysfunctional expectancies, 480, 482
Dysfunctional self-evaluations, 483

E

E, *see* Extraversion
Early life events (in psychoanalytic theory), 108–110
Earthquakes, denial of, 91
EASI, 299
Eating disorders, 82
Ectomorphy, 298
Ego, 85, 86, 89, 125, 126, 128

Emotionality dimension (of temperament), 299
Emotional reactions, 354–356
Emotional suppression, 127
Emotions, Darwin's writings on, 297
Emotion-focused coping, 477
Empathic understanding, 193
Empirical translation (of a theory), 29
Encounter groups, 199
Endomorphy, 298
Energy system:
    in Goldstein's theory, 210
    in psychoanalytic theory, 74, 89
Environmental determinants of personality, 15, 17–19, 325–331
Environments, shared vs. nonshared, 326–329
Erogenous zones, 102
Error of measurement, 283
Ethics of research and public policy, 44–46
Ethology, 148, 149
Evaluative standards (in social-cognitive theory), 433–434, 470–473
Eve, "three faces" of, 171, 172
Evolutionary psychology(-ies), 14–17, 27, 304–317. *See also* Genetics
    and Big Five personality dimensions, 313, 315
    and sex differences, 308–313
    social-cognitive theory vs., 417
    and social exchange, 306–307
    trait theory vs., 305–306, 313–315
Evolved psychological mechanisms, 304–306
Exciting thoughts, suppression of, 76
Exhibitionism, 124
Existentialism, 212–214
Expectancies, 425–426, 432–433, 482
Experiential thinking, 101–102
Experimental neuroses, 353
Experimental research, 38, 53, 55–58, 61–63
Experimenter expectancy effects, 62
Experiments on Plant Hybrids (Mendel), 297
The Expression of Emotions in Man and Animals (Darwin), 297, 314
External criteria, 44
Extinction (classical conditioning), 353
Extraversion (E), 235, 255, 256, 259, 262
    in animals, 314
    biological bases of, 237–238
    research on, 236–237
    and shared environment, 327–328
Extrinsic motivation, 203
Eysenckian theory, *see* Three-factor trait theory
Eysenck Personality Inventory, 235

Eysenck Personality Questionnaire, 235

F
Facets, 260–262
Factor analysis, 230–232
Factor-analytic trait theory (Cattell), 240–248
    behavior stability/variability in, 246
    Big Five integration of, 262
    classification of traits in, 242–243
    influences on development of, 240–241
    limitations of, 248, 289–290
    science of personality as viewed in, 241–242
    sources traits in, 243–246
Failure:
    pursuit of, 80
    of tolerance, 352–353
"False memories," 100–101
Family, as determinant of personality, 18
Fantasy, 189
Faulty reasoning, 479
Fear/fearfulness, 313, 332, 355–356, 399, 401, 403. *See also* Phobia(s)
Feedback, 446–447, 465–466
Feminine Psychology (Horney), 144
Feminism, and psychoanalytic theory, 157
Fidelity (of a theory), 28–29
First-born children, 18
Five-factor model of personality, 254–287
    diagnosis/treatment applications of, 273–274
    and evolutionary theory, 313–315
    growth and development in, 267–271
    health applications of, 272–273
    and "Jim" case study, 274–281
    limitations of, 265–267, 274, 289, 290, 521
    and non-Western cultures, 526
    and person-situation controversy, 281–287
    proposed, 263–267
    research on, 254–263
    and shared environments, 326–329
    and temperament, 299–300
    vocational applications of, 271–272
Fixations, 123
Fixed measures, 41
Fixed-role therapy, 404–405
Flexible measures, 41–42
Flow (optimal experience), 212
fMRI, *see* Functional magnetic resonance imaging
Focus of convenience, 386, 391
"Frame switching," 532
Fraternal (dizygotic) twins, 318–319, 321–323

Fraudulent data, 45
Free association, 73, 128
Free will, behaviorist view of, 372–374
Freudian psychology, 70–76. *See also* Psychoanalysis
    contributions of, 155
    early challenges to, 138–143
    and Freud the person, 71–74
    views of, 74–76
Frontal cortex, 295, 307
Functional analysis, 369
Functional autonomy, 227–228
Functional magnetic resonance imaging (fMRI), 303, 338–340
Fundamental lexical hypothesis, 257, 288, 313

G
Gender differences, *see* Sex differences
Generalizability, 526
Generalization (classical conditioning), 351
Generalized reinforcers, 366
General principles approach (Higgins), 473
General systems theory, 149
Generativity vs. Stagnation, 106
Genes, 317
Genetics, 317–331. *See also* Evolutionary psychology(-ies)
    behavioral, 318–325
    and development of personality, 14–15
    and environment, 325–331
    Mendel as founder of modern, 297
    molecular, 324–325
Genital stage, 105
Goals:
    and authenticity, 203, 205
    hierarchy of, 9–10
    learning vs. performance, 466–470
    in social-cognitive theory, 431–433
Goal systems, 432
Good me, 144
"Grand Auto Theft" (video game), 442
Gratification:
    delay of, 449–453
    and fixations, 123
Greeks, ancient, 232, 233, 296, 300
Growth and development, *see* Development of personality
Guided mastery, 486–487, 490
Guilt, 80
    and goals, 203
    and superego, 85

H
"Hardwired" psychological tendencies, 304
Head Start, 46

Health:
    emotional suppression and, 127
    five-factor model applied to, 272–273
    personality and, 54–55
    and self-efficacy, 484–486
Health-related responses, 361
Hemispheric lateralization, 332–334
Heritability coefficient, 320–322
Heroin overdose, death by, 352–353
Hierarchical point of view, 224, 225
Hierarchical structure:
    of constructs, 391
    of neuroticism, 232, 233
    of psychoticism, 234
Hierarchy, 10–11
Hierarchy of needs, 210–212
Hippocampus, 331
HIV/AIDS, 431, 525, 533, 535–537
Holocaust, 91
Hostility, control of, 509–510
Hot attentional focus, 508–509
Human nature, 20
Human potential movement, 209–212
    and Goldstein's theory, 210
    and Maslow's hierarchy of needs, 210–212
Human strengths movement, 212
Humors, 296
Hypertension, and emotional suppression, 127
Hypnosis:
    cathartic, 126, 128
    in psychoanalytic theory, 78–79
Hypothalamus, 331, 337
Hysterical personality, 124–125

I
Id, 85, 89
Ideal self, 167, 170
Identical (monozygotic) twins, 318–323
Identification:
    modeling vs., 441
    in psychoanalytic theory, 104
Identity formation, 106–107
Identity vs. Role Diffusion, 106, 107
Idiographic measures, 42, 46
Idiographic research, 228, 229
Ill-temperedness, 521–522
Imitation, 440, 441
Immune system, 485–486
Implicit measures, 39
Implicit theories, 468–470
Impulsiveness, 313, 518–519
Impulsivity dimension (of temperament), 299
Incentive models, 11
Incongruence, 175, 177–179
Index of Self-Actualization, 173
Individual Psychology, 138–140

Industry vs. Inferiority, 106
Infants:
    attachment behavioral system in, 149
    internal working models in, 149–150
    prefrontal activation in, 332–333
    self-recognition in, 168
    temperament of, 299
Infatuation, 226
Inferiority feelings, 138
Information processing, 306
Inhibited temperament, 300–303
Initiative vs. Guilt, 106
Inkblot test, see Rorschach Inkblot Test
Instincts, 88–89
Integrity vs. Despair, 106
Intellectualization, 93
Intelligence (Eysenck), 230
Internal working models, 149–150
International Psychoanalytic Association, 140
Internet, 172
Internet survey, 269–270
Interpersonal relationships, 506–512
    and rejection sensitivity, 506–510
    in Sullivan's theories, 144–145
    transference in, 510–512
Interpersonal Theory of Psychiatry, 144–145
Interpretation, of partner's behavior, 506
The Interpretation of Dreams (Freud), 73
Intimacy vs. Isolation, 106
Intrinsic motivation, 184, 203, 205
Introspection, 64
Introversion, 235
    biological bases of, 237–238
    research on, 236–237
Introversion-extraversion dimension, 232, 234–237, 255, 256
IQ tests/scores, 153, 320–323
Irrational beliefs, 479
Isolation (defense mechanism), 93
Italian (language), 258, 259

J
Japanese culture (*See also* Asian culture), 206–208, 531 Jealousy, 305, 310, 312–313
Jim (hypothetical case study), 66, 555–557
    biographical sketch, 66–67
    and five-factor model, 274–281
    NEO-PI, 279–281
    Role Construct Rep test with, 406–408
    Rorschach and Thematic Apperception tests with, 134–137
    semantic differential with, 197–199
    16 P.F. Questionnaire with, 274–276
    and social-cognitive theory, 490–494

stability of personality in, 274–276
Jungian psychology, 140–143

K
Karma, 526
Knowledge, appraisal vs., 515–516
Knowledge-and-appraisal personality architecture (KAPA) model, 516

L
Laboratory studies, 53, 58, 61. *See also* Experimental research
Language, *see* Fundamental lexical hypothesis
Latency stage, 105
Later life:
    emotional life in, 523–525
    psychological resilience in, 522–523
    self-actualization in, 183–185
L-data, *see* Life record data
Leadership:
    and cognitive complexity, 397
    traits associated with, 247
Learning, observational, 439–445
Learning approaches to personality, 344–345, 544. *See also* Behaviorism
    limitations of, 376–378
    strengths of, 375–376
    uniqueness of, 374–375
Learning goals, performance goals vs., 466–470
Learning theory, social-cognitive theory vs., 496
Left cerebral hemisphere, 332–333, 335
Lemon drop test, 235
Libido (life instinct), 88, 140
Life Orientation Test, 492
Life record data (L-data), 38, 243–245
Limbic system, 331, 334
Literacy, 534
Little Albert, 354–355
Little Hans, 130–134, 359–360
Locus of causality, 474
Logotherapy, 214
Loneliness, 213
Longevity, 272–273
Longitudinal stability, 282, 283, 286
LOTS categories of data, 38–39

M
Madonna-whore complex, 93
Magnetic resonance imaging (MRI), 339
Maladaptive attention, 480
Maladaptive attributions, 480
Maladaptive responses, 368–369
Mandalas, 141–142
Manic-depressive illness, 298
Manifest motives, 225

Maslow's hierarchy of needs, 210–212
Mate preferences, 308–312
Maudsley Personality Inventory, 235
Measurement, error of, 283
Mechanism (mechanist movement), 72
Mechanisms, psychological, *see* Psychological mechanisms
Media modeling, 533–537
Media violence, 441
Memories, "false," 100–101
Memory distortions, 480
Mental modules, 306
Mesomorphy, 298
Meta-analysis, 203
Metabolic syndrome, 54–55
Mexico, 534
Microanalytic research strategy, 428
Mirrors, self-recognition in, 168
Modeling, 440–444, 486–490
Modules, mental, 306
Molecular genetics, 324–325
Mona Lisa (Leonardo da Vinci), 26
Monozygotic (identical) twins, 318–323
Moral judgment, 339–340
Mother archetype, 141
Motivated unconscious, 78, 80, 88
Motivation, 11–13
    competence, 12
    and dopamine, 335
    and hierarchy of needs, 211–212
    intrinsic, 184
    in personal construct theory, 398, 411–412
    in psychoanalytic theory, 78, 88
    and self-schemas, 463, 465–466
    in social-cognitive theory, 446–448
    in trait theory, 227–228
MRI (magnetic resonance imaging), 339
Mrs. Oak, 195–197, 215
Multivariate research, 241, 242

N
N, *see* Neuroticism
Narcissism (narcissistic personality), 123, 146–149
Narcissistic Personality Inventory (NPI), 147, 148
Natural selection, theory of, 27
Nature and Nurture (Plomin), 326
Nature-nurture interactions, 329
"Nature versus nurture," 13, 298, 340
Nausea, anticipatory, 361
Nazi Germany, 91, 340
Need for positive regard, 179–180
Negative Emotionality (NE), 334–335
Negative self-views, 480
Negative tests, 29
NE (Negative Emotionality), 334–335
NEO Five-Factor Inventory, 322

Neo-Freudians, 143–145
NEO-Personality Inventory (NEO-PI), 279–281, 284
NEO-Personality Inventory Revised (NEO-PI-R), 260–263, 271, 273
Nervous system, 298, 316
Neurobiological functioning, plasticity in, 336–337
Neurosis(-es):
    and defense, 125, 126
    Horney's theory of, 143–144
Neuroticism (N), 232, 255, 256, 262
    in animals, 314
    biological bases of, 238
    and shared environment, 327–328
Neurotransmitters, 14, 324, 333–336
Neutral stimuli, 350
New York Longitudinal Study (NYLS), 299
Nomothetic measures, 41–42
Nonshared environments, 326–329
Norm-orientation, 269
Not me, 144
NPI, *see* Narcissistic Personality Inventory
"Nun study," 51–52
Nurturance, 313
NYLS (New York Longitudinal Study), 299

O

O, *see* Openness
Objective-test data (OT-data), 243–245
Objectivity, 45–46
Object relations theory, 146–148
Observation(s), 4, 42–44
    in behaviorist theory, 348–349
    by Freud, 75
    O-data from, 38
    reliability of, 43
    validity of, 43–44
Observational learning, 439–445
    acquisition vs. performance in, 441, 443–444
    vicarious conditioning in, 444–445
Obsessions, 126
Obstinacy, 124
OCEAN (Big Five factors), 255
O-data, 38, 40
Oedipus conflict/complex, 22, 103–105, 124, 133
On Becoming a Person (Rogers), 163
On Encounter Groups (Rogers), 199
Openness (O), 255, 256, 258, 262, 327–328
Operants, 365
Operant conditioning, 364–367
Optimal experience (flow), 212
Optimism, 504, 512–515
Oral personality, 123, 124

Oral stage, 102
Orderliness, 124
Organ inferiorities, 138
The Origin of Species (Darwin), 297, 314
OT-data, *see* Objective-test data
"Ought" standards, 471–472
Outcome expectations, self-efficacy expectations vs., 428
Own-control design (ABA research design), 371

P

Paralysis, psychological, 126
Parental investment theory, 308–309
Parent-child relations, 9
    in Rogerian psychology, 181–183
    and temperament, 299
Parenthood probability, 309
Parsimony (of a theory), 29
Parsimony (personality trait), 124
Peers, as determinant of personality, 18–19
Penis envy, 104, 157
PEN (Psychoticism Extraversion Neuroticism), 234
PE (Positive Emotionality), 334–335
Perceived self-efficacy, 426–431
Perception without awareness (subliminal perception), 79, 81
Perceptual defense, 81
Performance:
    acquisition vs., 441, 443–444
    and feedback, 446–447
    and self-efficacy, 428–431
Performance goals, 466–470
Peripheral constructs, 391
Permissiveness, 182
Person, the:
    Kelly's view of, 387–388
    philosophical view of, 20–21, 541, 544
    in psychoanalytic theory, 157–158
    Rogers's view of, 165–166
    in social-cognitive theory, 422–423, 498
Persona (archetype), 141
Personal construct theory (Kelly), 383–413
    and compartmentalization, 409–410
    growth and development in, 401–403
    and "Jim" case study, 406–408
    and Kelly the person, 384
    the person in, 387–388
    and person-situation beliefs, 409
    process aspect of, 398–401
    psychopathology in, 403–406
    recent developments in, 408–411
    science of personality as viewed in, 385–386

social-cognitive theory vs., 417–418, 495–496
    strengths/limitations of, 411–413
    structural aspect of, 388–397
Personal Growth Scale, 174
Personality. *See also specific headings*
    basic dimensions of, 232–238
    behaviorist view of, 345–349
    consistency of, 21–23
    contexts of, 504–505
    creating a science of, 26
    and culture, 525–532
    definition of, 6–7
    and health, 54–55
    reasons for studying, 5–6
    as research field, 6
    and social change, 532–537
    socioeconomic context of, 518–522
Personality: A Psychological Interpretation (Allport), 228
Personality and Assessment (Mischel), 281, 420
Personality and Individual Differences, 230
Personality architecture, 515–518
Personality change:
    in five-factor model, 271
    and heritability, 324
    in personal construct theory, 404–406
    in Rogerian psychology, 192–193, 195
Personality construct theory, 32–33
Personality questionnaires, *see* Questionnaires, personality
Personality science, *see* Science of personality
Personality structure, 8–11, 548, 550
Personality tests, *see* Tests/testing
Personality theory(-ies). *See also specific headings*
    as answer to what, how, and why, 7–8, 548
    and assessment, 42
    biological foundations of, 553–555
    change in, 553
    comprehensiveness of, 28–29
    and concept of self, 23–24
    and consistency over time and place, 21–23
    and determinants of behavior, 21
    differences among, 33–34, 541–549
    difficulty of constructing a, 30–31
    evaluation of, 27–30
    functions of a, 27
    growth and development in, 13–19, 551–552
    and influence of past, present, and future, 25
    main issues in, 20–27

parsimony of, 29
and personality research, 64–65
and philosophical view of the person, 20–21
process aspects of, 550–551
process in, 11–13
psychopathology in, 18–19, 552
relevancy of, 19
research relevance of, 29–30
as science, 26
similarities and differences between, 541–549
and states of awareness, 24–25
structural aspects of, 8–11, 548, 550
theory, assessment, and research in, 555
and unity of experience, 23
Personality traits, *see* Trait(s)
Personality types, *see* Types
Personality variables, contextual vs. decontextual, 508
Personal standards, 433–434
"Person-as-scientist" metaphor, 387
Person-situation beliefs, 409
Person-situation controversy, 281–287, 420
Pessimism, defensive, 504, 512–515
P factor (Eysenck), 324
Phallic character, 124–125
Phallic stage, 103
Phenomenal field, 166
Phenomenological theories, 32, 166, 214–215, 417–418, 495. *See also* Rogerian psychology
Phenomenology, 166, 199, 214–215
Phobia(s):
    in Little Hans, 130–134, 359–360
    and self-efficacy, 485–490
    snake, 485–487
Phrenology, 296–297
Physique, 298
Physique and Character (Kretschmer), 298
"Pitchfork" models of motivation, 11
Plasticity, 336–337
Play therapy, 146
Pleasure principle, 75, 85
Positive Emotionality (PE), 334–335
Positive psychology, 212
Positive regard, need for, 179–180
Positive self-regard, as human universal, 206–208
Possible selves, 466
Preadolescence, 144–145
Preconscious (in psychoanalytic theory), 77
Prefrontal cortex, 338–339
Preoccupied attachment style, 154
Preverbal constructs, 389–391

Primary appraisal, 477
Primary process thinking, 99, 101
Primates, personality traits in, 313–315
Principles of Behavior Modification (Bandura), 419
Principles of Psychology (William James), 16
Problem-focused coping, 477
Process, 11–13, 550–551
Projection, 92–93
Projective tests, 114, 115–122
    research use of, 119–120
    Rorschach Inkblot Test, 116–118
    Thematic Apperception Test (TAT), 118–119
    validity of, 120–122
Proximate causes, 304
Psychoanalytic Society, 73
Psychoanalytic theory, 25, 74–110, 544. *See also* Freudian psychology; Psychodynamic theory
    anxiety in, 89–90
    behavior change in, 126, 128–134
    clinical applications of, 114–122
    cognitive theory vs., 83–84
    conceptualizations of pheonemena in, 87
    and current evidence of unconscious, 82–83
    death instinct in, 88
    defense mechanisms in, 89–99
    denial in, 90
    dynamics of functioning in, 88–89
    ego in, 85, 86
    Eysenck's criticism of, 239
    five-factor model vs., 265–267
    growth and development in, 99, 101–110
    id in, 85
    influence of, 70
    instinct development in, 102–110
    levels of consciousness in, 77–78
    libido in, 87–88
    limitations of, 155–158
    motivated unconscious in, 78, 88
    origins of, 71
    personality development in, 99, 101–110
    the person in, 157–158
    processes in, 87–100
    psychopathology in, 122–126
    and research, 78–79, 81–82
    Rogerian theory vs., 166, 167
    scientific status of, 156–157
    social-cognitive theory vs., 494–495
    structural units in, 76–87
    superego in, 85
    symbolization in, 77–78
    therapeutic process in, 128–134

thinking development in, 99, 101–102
three-factor trait theory vs., 230
trait theory vs., 224
unconscious in, 77–78
Psychodynamic theory, 27, 31, 71
    Adler's theory, 138–140
    attachment theory, 148–155
    interpersonal functioning (Sullivan), 144–145
    Jung's psychology, 140–143
    neurotic functioning (Horney), 143–144
    object relations theory, 146–148
    recent developments in, 145–146
Psychological mechanisms, 14–15
    domain-specific, 305
    evolved, 304–306
Psychological Review, 350, 421, 542
Psychology from the Standpoint of a Behaviorist (Watson), 350
Psychopathology, 18–19, 552
    in behaviorist theory, 347
    and classical conditioning, 353–354
    in Eysenckian theory, 238–239
    in personal construct theory, 403–406
    in psychoanalytic theory, 122–126
    in Rogerian theory, 189, 191–192, 216–217
    Skinnerian view of, 368–369
    in social-cognitive theory, 479–486
Psychopathology of Everyday Life (Freud), 73
Psychosexual development stages (Freud), 102–105
Psychosocial development stages (Erikson), 105–108
Psychosocial stages of development, 105–108
Psychoticism, 232, 234
    and Big Five, 262
    biological bases of, 238
Psychoticism Extraversion Neuroticism (PEN), 234
Puberty, and genital stage, 105
Publications, psychology, 542–543
Public policy, 46
Pull theories, 11
Punctuality, 284–285
Punishment:
    in parent-child relationship, 182
    and superego, 85
Push theories, 11
Pyknic body type, 298

Q

Q-data, *see* Questionnaire data
Q-sort technique, 169–171
Questionnaire data (Q-data), 243–245

Questionnaires, personality, 40, 50–51, 58
  advantages of, 61
  Big Five in, 260–262
  introversion-extraversion, 235
  limitations of, 60–61

R

Rabbit, "unconditioning" the fear of a, 355–356
Range of convenience, 386, 391
Rational emotive therapy (RET), 479–480
Rationalization, 95
Rational thinking, 101–102
Reaction formation, 95
Reaction-time measures, 461–463
Reality principle, 85
Reciprocal determinism, 435–436
Reciprocal interactions, 33
Recovered memories, 100–101
Reflected appraisal, 144, 182
Regression, 123
Reinforcement, schedule of, 366
Reinforcers, 365–367
Rejection sensitivity, 506–510
Rejection Sensitivity Questionnaire (RSQ), 507–509
Relationship schemas, 409
Relaxation, in systematic desensitization, 358
Reliability (of data), 43
Religion, Rogers's view of, 165
Reports, verbal, 63–64
Repression, 95–97, 99, 100
Repressive coping style, 97, 99
Rep test, *see* Role Construct Repertory Test
Research, 64–65. *See also* Correlational research; Experimental research
  behaviorist approach to, 348–349
  on classical conditioning, 360–362
  ethical issues in, 44–45
  five-factor model, 254–263
  on parent-child relationships, 181–183
  projective tests in, 119–120
  psychoanalytic, 78–79, 81–82
  on self-consistency and congruence, 177–179
  social-cognitive, 497–498
  "theory-free," 37
  trait theory, 288
Research methods, comparison of strengths and weaknesses of, 58
Research relevance (of a theory), 29–30
Resilience, 522–523
Response styles, 60
RET, *see* Rational-emotive therapy
Reward, and self-esteem, 182
Right cerebral hemisphere, 332–333

Rogerian psychology, 162–185
  authenticity in, 202–203, 205
  client-centered therapy in, 192–193, 195, 214–215
  cognitive approaches to, 202
  congruence and incongruence in, 175, 177–179
  contingencies of self-worth in, 200
  and cross-cultural differences, 205–209
  denial in, 175
  distortion in, 175
  and existentialism, 209–214
  fluctuations of self-esteem in, 200–202
  growth and development in, 180–185
  and human potential movement, 209–212
  loneliness in, 213
  measures of self-concept in, 168–172
  need for positive regard in, 179–180
  and parent-child relationships, 181–183
  personality change in, 192–193, 195
  phenomenological approach in, 166
  processes in, 173–180
  psychoanalytic theory vs., 166, 167
  psychopathology in, 189, 191–192, 216–217
  research in, 199–200
  and Rogers the person, 163–165
  self-actualization in, 173–174, 180–181
  self-consistency in, 174–179
  self-esteem and objective outcomes in, 204–205
  self-experience discrepancy in, 189, 191
  the self in, 167, 215–216
  subception in, 175
  view of the person in, 165–166
  and well-being in later life, 183–185
Role Construct Repertory Test (Rep test), 392–396, 408, 409, 411, 492
  for children, 394
  of cognitive complexity, 395–396
  unique information revealed by, 393–395
Role (of behavior), 246
Romantic relationships, rejection sensitivity in, 506–509
Rorschach Inkblot Test, 114, 116–118, 121–122, 134–137

S

Safe-sex behaviors, 431
Sample approach, 372
Schedule of reinforcement, 366
Schemas, 409, 460–466
Schizophrenia, 298, 333

Schools of psychology, rise and fall of, 542–544
Scientific observation, *see* Observation(s)
Scientific theories, 4
S-data, 38–40
Secondary appraisal, 477
Secondary dispositions, 227
Secondary factor analysis, 231–232
Secondary process thinking, 99, 101
Secure attachment style, 150–152, 154
Selective breeding studies, 318
Selective serotonin reuptake inhibitors (SSRIs), 333
Self:
  cross-cultural research on the, 205–209
  ideal, 167, 170
Self, concept of, 23–24, 546
  and the brain, 338–339
  within cultural context, 528–532
  fluctuations in, 200–202
  in Jungian psychology, 141–142
  and narcissism, 146–148
  Rogers's view of, 167, 176, 215–216
  Sullivan's view of, 144
Self-actualization, 173–174
  in Goldstein's theory, 210
  and healthy psychological development, 180–181
  in Maslow's theory, 211
Self-analysis, 72–73
Self-complexity, 396
Self-concept:
  cultural influences on, 528–532
  Rogers's view of, 167–172, 215–216
  working, 462–463
Self-confidence, sex differences in, 170
Self-consistency, 174–179
Self-control, 449–453
Self-criticism, 208, 531
Self-deception, 91
Self-defeating strategies, 480
Self-determination theory, 203
Self-discrepancies, 471–473
Self-efficacy, 426–431
  appraisals of, 516–517
  and performance, 428–431, 446–448
  and phobias, 485–490
Self-enhancement, 463, 465–466
Self-esteem:
  and age, 523
  and congruence, 177–179
  cultural differences in, 206–208
  fluctuations in, 200–202
  and life outcomes, 204–205
  perceived self-efficacy vs., 427
  in Rogerian theory, 178–183, 200–202, 204, 216
Self Esteem Inventory, 181–182

Self-evaluations, dysfunctional, 483
Self-evaluative reactions, 433
Self-experience discrepancy, 189, 191
Self-processes, 419
Self-produced consequences, 454
Self-recognition, 168
Self-regulation, 33, 445–449
Self-report measures, 38–39, 263
Self-report questionnaires, 40
Self-schemas, 460–466
    and motivation, 463, 465–466
    and reaction-time methods, 461–463
Self-standards, 471–473
Self-verification, 463, 465–466
Semantic differential, 171, 197–199
Sensory construct system, 390
Septal area, 331
Serotonin, 333, 334
Sex differences, 18, 464–465
    evolutionary origins of, 308–313
    ill-temperedness, 521–522
    in self-confidence, 170
    societal factors in, 311
Sex Rep test, 393
Sexual abuse, "false memories" of,
    100–101
Sexual infidelity, reactions to, 312–313
Sexuality, Freud's early views on, 73,
    74–75
Sexual Self-Schema Scale, 462
Shaping (successive approximation),
    366–367
Shared environments, 326–328
Sign approach, 371–372
Similarity pole, 388
Situational specificity, 347
Sixteen Personality Factor (16 P.F.)
    Questionnaire, 243–245, 274–276
Skinnerian theory:
    behavioral assessment in, 369–374
    growth and development in,
        367–368
    operant conditioning as process in,
        365–367
    psychopathology in, 368–369
    response as structural unit in,
        362–364
    and Skinner the person, 362–364
Slips of the tongue, 70, 79
SMEP (Society for Multivariate
    Experimental Research), 246
Snake phobias, 485–487
Sociability, 313
Sociability dimension (of tempera-
    ment), 299
Social change, personality processes
    and, 532–537
Social class, as determinant of person-
    ality, 18, 518–522
Social-cognitive theory, 25, 416–454, 545

attributions in, 473–476
Bandura's role in, 418–419, 421–423
beliefs in, 425–431, 459–473
CAPS model in, 436–439
and case of Jim, 490–494
clinical applications of, 476–482
competencies in, 424–425
delay of gratification in, 449–453
distinguishing features of, 416–418
evaluative standards in, 425,
    433–434
expectancies in, 425–426
goals in, 425, 431–433
growth and development in, 453–454
limitations of, 499–501
Mischel's role in, 419–423
observational learning in, 439–445
perceived self-efficacy in, 426–431
the person in, 422–423, 498
processes in, 434–441, 443–453
psychopathology in, 479–486
reciprocal determinism in, 435–436
science of personality as viewed in,
    423–424
self-regulation in, 445–449
standards of evaluation in, 470–473
strengths of, 497–499
structural aspects of, 424–434
and therapeutic change, 479–482,
    486–490
unique features of, 494–497
Social concern, 499
Social desirability, 60
Social engineering, by behaviorists, 372
Social exchange, and detection of
    cheating, 306–307
*Social Foundations of Thought and
    Action* (Bandura), 419
Social identity complexity, 396
Social intelligence, 513
*Social Learning and Personality
    Development* (Bandura & Walters),
    419, 498
Society. *See also* Culture
    as corrupting influence, 75
    and sex differences, 311
Society for Multivariate Experimental
    Research (SMEP), 246
Socio-cognitive theory, 33
Socioeconomic context, 518–522
Socioemotional selectivity theory,
    523–524
Source traits, 243
Spontaneous skin resistance, 98
Spouse-report measures, 263
SSRIs (selective serotonin reuptake
    inhibitors), 333
Stability of personality, 271, 276–279,
    288
    cross-situational, 282–286

longitudinal, 282
Standards, evaluative, 433–434,
    470–473
State (of behavior), 246
Stereotypes, 56–58, 475
Stinginess, 124
Strange Situation procedure, 150
Strategies:
    coping, 512
    self-defeating, 480
Stress:
    and cortisol, 333
    and regression, 123
    and social-cognitive theory, 477–479
Stress inoculation training, 478–479
Structure, *see* Personality structure
Studies in Hysteria (Breuer and Freud),
    72
Stutters, 138
Subception, 175
Sublimation, 95
Subliminal perception, 79, 81
Subliminal psychodynamic activation,
    81–82
Submerged constructs, 390–391
Subordinate constructs, 391
Success, traits associated with, 247
Successive approximation (shaping),
    366–367
Suicide, 88
Superego, 85, 89
Superfactors, 232
Superordinate constructs, 391
Superstitious behavior, 368–369
Suppression, of exciting thoughts, 76
Surface traits, 243
Symbolization, 77–78, 141–143
Symptoms, 126
Systems, 9–10
Systematic desensitization, 357–359

T

Tachistoscope, 79, 81
Tanzania, 535–537
Target behaviors, 369
Target behaviors (target responses),
    369
TAT, *see* Thematic Apperception Test
T cells, 485–486
T-data, 38, 40
Television, 441
Television violence, 46
Temperament:
    and brain, 14, 295–304
    definition of, 295–296
    dimensions of, 333–336
    early views of, 296–298
    Kagan's research on inhibited vs.
        uninhibited, 300–303
    longitudinal studies of, 298–300

Temperament traits, 243
Tests/testing, 50
  fixed vs. flexible, 42
  projective, 114, 115–122
  reliability of, 43
  validity of, 43–44
Testosterone, 334, 335, 337
Thalamus, 331
Thematic Apperception Test (TAT),
    114, 118–119, 121, 122, 134–137
Theories, 4, 28–30
"Theory-free" research, 37
Therapy/therapeutic process:
  in behaviorist theory, 347–348
  in Rogerian theory, 192–193, 195
  transference and, 128–130
Thinking:
  experiential vs. rational, 101–102
  in narcissistic individuals, 147, 148
  primary process vs. secondary
    process, 99, 101
  in psychoanalytic theory, 99,
    101–102
"Those Wrecked by Success" (Freud),
    80
Threat:
  and personal construct theory, 403
Threat, and personal construct theory,
    399–401
Threat Index, 400–401
Three-dimensional temperament
    model, 336
Three Essays on the Theory of Sexuality
    (Freud), 73
"The three faces of Eve," 171, 172
Three-factor trait theory (Eysenck),
    229–240, 248
  basic dimensions of personality in,
    232–238
  Big Five integration of, 262
  factor analysis in, 230–232
  limitations of, 240

psychopathology and behavior
    change in, 238–239
Tics, 126
Token economies, 372
Tolerance, failure of, 352–353
Trait(s), 8–9
  ability, 243
  Allport's classifications of, 226, 227
  cardinal, 226
  Cattell's concept of, 242–243
  central, 226, 227
  definition of, 223
  dynamic, 243
  hierarchy of, 11
  problems with concept of, 290–291
  secondary, 227
  source, 243
  surface, 243
  temperament, 243
Trait approaches to personality, 32,
    544–545
Trait theory(-ies), 222–248
  Allport's, 225–229
  basic assumptions of, 223–225
  Cattell's, 240–249
  differences between, 248
  evaluation of, 287–291
  evolutionary psychology vs.,
    305–306, 313–315
  Eysenck's, 229–240
  limitations of, 289–291
  social-cognitive theory vs., 417,
    496–497
  strengths of, 288
Transference, 128–130, 510–512
Twin studies, 13, 318–320
Types, 9, 123–125

U

Ultimate causes, 304
"Unbridled gratification," 75, 76
Unconditional positive regard, 193

Unconditioned response (UR), 351
Unconditioned stimulus (US), 351
"Unconditioning," 355–356
Unconscious, 24–25, 77, 546–547
  collective, 140–141
  current status of concept of, 82–83
  motivated, 78, 80, 88
  psychoanalytic vs. cognitive views
    of, 83–84
Undoing, 95
Unhappiness, idealization of, 80
Uninhibited temperament, 300–303
Units of analysis, 8
Unity of experience, 23
Universals, human, 15
UR (unconditioned response), 351
Usefulness, 385
US (unconditioned stimulus), 351

V

Validity, 43–44
  construct, 44
  discriminant, 44
Verbal constructs, 389–391
Verbal reports, 63–64
Verbal slips, 70, 79
Vicarious conditioning, 444–445
Vicarious experiencing of conse-
    quences, 454
Video games, 442–443
Violence, 441–443
Vocational interests, 271–272

W

Waking suggestion, 128
Walden Two (Skinner), 364
Ways of Coping Scale, 477, 494
Well-being, regional variations in,
    208–209
Will to power, 139
Working self-concept, 462–463